up 69.00

INDUSTRIAL ORGANIZATION AND PUBLIC POLICY

Third Edition

Douglas F. Greer
San Jose State University

MACMILLAN PUBLISHING COMPANY
New York

MAXWELL MACMILLAN CANADA
Toronto

MAXWELL MACMILLAN INTERNATIONAL
New York   Oxford   Singapore   Sydney

To ROBERT E. SMITH and ALFRED E. KAHN

Macmillan Publishing Company
866 Third Avenue, New York, New York 10022

Macmillan Publishing Company is part of the
Maxwell Communication Group of Companies.

Maxwell Macmillan Canada, Inc.
1200 Eglinton Avenue East
Suite 200
Don Mills, Ontario M3C 3N1

Library of Congress Cataloging-in-Publication Data

Greer, Douglas F.
    Industrial organization and public policy / Douglas F. Greer. —
3rd ed.
        p.   cm.
    Includes index.
    ISBN 0-02-347140-9
    1. Industrial organization (Economic theory)   2. Industry and
state.   I. Title.
HD2326.G73   1992
658 — dc20   91-2259
                                                        CIP

Printing: 1 2 3 4 5 6 7 8   Year: 2 3 4 5 6 7 8 9 0 1

Preface

This third edition of *Industrial Organization and Public Policy* represents a major revision. Much has happened since the second edition was published in 1984 to warrant significant changes in the content of this book. Theories have matured regarding strategic behavior, the firm, and many other topics. Empirical studies have proceeded apace on subjects like mergers, innovation, pricing, entry, and advertising. Public policies have come and gone with the rise and fall of politicians.

Still, well over half of the second edition's text reappears here. Likewise, the basic format and philosophy of earlier editions remain untouched. Users of previous editions should experience some of the comfort of familiarity, as well as some refreshing novelty, in these pages.

The following changes are among the most notable:

- A lengthy discussion of the theory of the firm has been added. This discussion is joined with material on profit maximization (which previously appeared late in the book) to form a new Chapter 3.

- Chapter 5, which covers product differentiation in depth, has been completely rewritten. The scholarly literature here is a hodgepodge of theories and empiricism. I have tried to develop a new synthesis that clarifies the nature of product differentiation and its sources.

- The massive merger movement of the 1980s receives serious analysis. The question of whether or not, on balance, mergers reflect efficiency comprises much of this discussion.

- A comprehensive introduction to conduct comprises Chapter 11. Immense effort went into an attempt to organize material that, on its face, may seem diffuse and unrelated, e.g., game theory, dominance, strategic behavior, switching costs, tacit collusion, and price leadership. Even the basic notion of "market power" deserves greater clarification than has been achieved in other texts, so this new chapter tackles that task too.

- Long-run pricing strategies gain fresh treatment. In addition, theories and evidence concerning "raising rivals' costs" are now covered together with strategies that "reduce rivals' revenue."

- Vertical restrictions receive expanded treatment. This has been a "hot" topic, so I surrender to fashion here.

- The continuing debate over the interpretation of the profit–concentration relationship has been updated. Special attention has been given to the relationships linking unionism, concentration, profits, and high wages.

- Two chapters devoted to macroeconomics in the second edition have been eliminated. Inflation, incomes policies and the like have drifted too far from current public focus to warrant continued inclusion.

- Lastly, the book has been updated throughout. New data fill the tables. New examples illustrate the theories. New policies pepper the applications chapters. New empirical findings have been inserted whenever possible and appropriate.

Contributing to the final form of this new edition have been a number of reviewers whose comments proved helpful: Sanford Berg, Daniel O. Fletcher, David Brownstone, Wade L. Thomas, Albert M. Link, Don E. Waldman, Jon P. Nelson, and Catherine C. Eckel. I am most grateful to these scholars for their work and deeply appreciate their fine contributions. A team of typists also deserves great thanks: Lill Greer, Janiece Fister, and Linda Garcia. Finally, I am indebted to Dora Rizzuto of Macmillan for her skill in handling the production of this edition, as well as an earlier edition that Macmillan published.

D. F. G.

Contents

Part I

INTRODUCTION

1

Introduction and Overview

Because we live in a market-run society, we are apt to take for granted the puzzling — indeed almost paradoxical — nature of the market solution to the economic problem.
—ROBERT HEILBRONER and LESTER THUROW[1]

Markets comprise the central nervous system of our economy. We rely on them for most of what life is all about — food, entertainment, fuel, transport, shelter, and so forth. Still, markets are neither widely understood nor greatly appreciated. Most people seem to think of markets as places where fish, produce, or shares of equity stock are bought and sold. They fail to recognize the economist's broader use of the term, which encompasses an enormous variety of markets, including those for stereos, apparel, autos, steel, gasoline, soap, beer, motion pictures, and air travel.

The purpose of this book is to give the reader a broad understanding of markets and their regulation. In particular, we shall attempt (1) to bring some *order* to this diversity by developing a systematic way of looking at markets, (2) to *analyze* how markets function, (3) to *evaluate* how well markets function in light of society's desires, and (4) to *explain* and *assess* many of the policies governing markets. Among the numerous issues that will be addressed along the way, the following may be of greatest interest to the reader: Why are markets so important to the

[1] Robert Heilbroner and Lester Thurow, *The Economic Problem*, 4th ed. (Englewood Cliffs, N.J.: Prentice-Hall, Inc.), p. 12.

3

economy? What factors determine price and output? Why do just a few firms dominate some of our key markets, such as those for computers, autos, and beer? What are the effects of such dominance on profits, wages, innovation, and efficiency? Why are soaps, cereals, and cosmetics heavily advertised, whereas sugar, cement, and coal go largely unpromoted? Does advertising foster market power? What do policymakers hope to accomplish with measures like grade rating and product standardization? Should the government take action to break up big corporations or subsidize small ones? What has the government done about mergers, price fixing, and false advertising? Are there such things as "natural monopolies"? If there are, can they be regulated effectively? In a nutshell, under what conditions do our markets best serve the public interest?

First, a few words need to be defined, including the word "market." Second, we shall briefly explore the place markets occupy in the scheme of things. Third, because evaluation is one of our objectives, a discussion of certain values held by our society is needed for later use in evaluating various types of markets and regulations. Fourth, to facilitate understanding and analysis, we need to devise a systematic way of looking at markets. Finally, we shall explain our particular methods and indicate the organization of remaining chapters.

I. SETTING THE SCENE

Simply put, a **market** is an organized process by which buyers and sellers exchange goods and services for money, the medium of exchange. Notice that every market has two sides to it—a demand side (made up of buyers) and a supply side (made up of sellers). Notice also that markets can be local, regional, national, or international in scope. When the exchange alternatives of either buyers or sellers are geographically limited—as is true of barbering and grocery retailing, for example—then exchange and competition are correspondingly limited in geographic scope. Strictly speaking, the word "industry" denotes a much broader concept than market because an industry can include numerous local or regional markets. When we speak of the construction industry or the banking industry, we usually refer to something more than local business. In practice, however, "market" and "industry" are often used synonymously, without careful distinction, a practice we too will follow when precision is not required. Indeed, economists commonly use the term "industrial organization" rather than "market organization" to describe the areas of study we cover.

The crucial importance of markets can be fully appreciated only after it is recognized that the "market" is the basic economic *institution* upholding our private free-enterprise capitalist system. An **institution** may be defined as selected elements of a scheme of values mobilized and coordinated to accomplish a particular purpose or function.[2] This definition implies that "markets" have two principal aspects—a *value* aspect and a *functional* aspect.

A. The Functional Aspect

With respect to function, we rely on markets to cope with the fundamental problem of scarcity, which is what economics is all about. Scarcity would be no problem if desires were severely curtailed. Scarcity would be no problem if our productive capabilities knew no bounds. But, alas, neither of these conditions holds for our society. We have neither limited desires nor unlimited resources. Quite the contrary, Americans are among the most prosperous people who have ever lived; yet we still want more goods and services—more than our limited resources of land, capital, labor, energy, and time can produce. Proof of this statement is easy: Markets, prices, wages, and all the other trappings of our economy would not exist in the absence of scarcity.

To be more specific about the *function* of markets, scarcity rudely forces us to make certain decisions:

1. *What goods and services shall we produce and in what amounts?* At first glance the answer may seem obvious. We need such basics as food, clothing, and shelter. But even in this context our limitations impose tradeoffs. Shall it be more Twinkies and less Granola; more apartments and fewer single-family dwellings; more sweaters and fewer jackets? Similarly, if we commit more of our resources to autos, trains, and planes, sacrifices will have to be made elsewhere. What combination of goods is most desirable?

2. *How are goods and services to be produced?* Many different methods of production are possible for most goods. Cigars, for instance, can be made by humans as well as by machine. What mixture of the two will it be? Should coal be mined by strip or underground methods? In short, what combination of resource commitments is most efficient?

3. *Who shall get and consume the goods and services we produce?* There are two aspects to this question. One aspect relates to income distribution—what share of our total national income should each household receive? At present, some enjoy riches and others suffer poverty, while most of us hold down the middle. The other aspect relates to rationing of specific goods. Not enough gasoline can be produced for all people to get as much as they would like. Hence some form of rationing is required.

[2] Talcott Parsons and Neil Smelser, *Economy and Society* (New York: The Free Press, 1965), p. 102.

4. *What's new?* No condition of scarcity is unchanging. Advances in technology and better educational attainments continually expand our productive capabilities. Consumer tastes also alter. Thus we are confronted with questions of change. Shall we convert to solar power and alcohol-burning autos? Decisions affecting change must be made continually.

Although every human society has had to answer these fundamental questions, only three basic institutional devices (or answer machines) have evolved to handle them — tradition, command, and the market. **Tradition** is typical of most primitive societies, wherein each generation merely emulates its ancestor's pattern of life support. **Command** involves centralized decision making, usually by government authorities (as in Communist China) but also by high priests, warlords, and the like. Elements of tradition and command can of course be found in our own economy. But, by and large, we entrust these decisions to the *market*, to millions of consumers, workers, employers, land owners, investors, and proprietors, each pursuing self-interest in the market place. *Thus, the function of markets is to coordinate and control this decentralized decision-making process, which answers these four crucial questions of what, how, who, and what's new.* It should also be noted that private property and contract assist markets in this task. *Private property* provides material incentives for individual actions and enables decentralized decision making. *Contract* allows individuals to determine their own terms of exchange and permits stabilizing, long-run commitments.

B. The Value Aspect

As far as its values are concerned, our society generally believes that markets tend to perform the function of coordination and control very nicely. That is to say, the market system accords well with many of our society's values by (1) typically providing fairly good answers to the four questions and (2) arriving at these answers in a particularly appealing way. Exactly what these answers are and exactly how the market system goes about arriving at them will be discussed in subsequent chapters. Right now we need to explain which values we refer to and thereby specify what is meant here by "good" and "appealing."

In the present context, **values** are simply generalized concepts of the desirable. They are objectives or aims that guide our attitudes and actions. Among the most generalized concepts of the desirable are such notions as "welfare and happiness," "freedom," "justice," and "equality." These may be called **ultimate** values because they reign supreme in the minds of most of us. Indeed, they even justify occasional bloodshed.

Although these are undeniably noble aims, they are too vague and too illdefined to provide a basis for specific institutional arrangements and policy decisions. So, for purposes of actual application, they can be translated into more specific concepts — like "full employment" and "allocation efficiency" — which may be called **proximate** values. Table 1–1 presents a summary list of proximate values that are relevant here, together with the ultimate values from which they are derived. Allocation efficiency, full employment, clean environment, and health and safety, for example, are several proximate values that convey the spirit of "welfare and happiness." The list is intended to be more illustrative than exhaustive, so only a brief discussion of it is warranted.

1. Freedom. Proximate values reflecting freedom include such notions as "free choice in consumption and occupation" and "free entry and investment." They imply active, unhampered participation in the economic decision-making process by all of us. The market furthers these objectives because, unlike tradition or command, the market affords free expression to individual choice in answering the key economic questions outlined earlier — what, how, who, and what's new? Unfet-

TABLE 1–1. Some Proximate Values and the Ultimate Values from Which They Derive

Ultimate Values	Proximate Values
Freedom	Free choice in consumption and occupation Free entry and investment Limited government intervention Free political parties National security
Equality	Diffusion of economic and political power Equal bargaining power for buyers/sellers Equal opportunity Limited income inequality
Justice and fairness	Prohibition of unfair practices Fair labor standards Honesty Full disclosure
Welfare and happiness	Allocation and production efficiency Full employment Price stability Health and safety Clean environment
Progress	Rising real income Technological advancement

tered individual choice is possible *only* under favorable circumstances, however. For if markets are burdened with barriers to entry, monopoly power, price fixing, or similar restraints of trade—imposed *either* by government *or* by private groups—then this freedom is sharply curtailed. Although the government has often imposed these and other restraints (usually under the influence and for the benefit of special interest groups), most people in our society favor "limited government intervention" and "free political parties," both of which tend to inhibit centralized command and coercion. Thus, to the extent government intervention is properly called for, most would probably agree that it should be for purposes of *preventing* private restraints of trade rather than for *imposing* official restraints.

2. Equality. When one person's freedom encroaches upon another person's freedom, some criterion is needed to resolve the conflict. In our society the ideal criterion is "equality" or "equity."[3] This usually means that everybody's preferences and aspirations are weighed equally, as in the political cliché: one man, one vote. In economics, the notion that each individual's dollar counts the same as anyone else's dollar reflects a similar sentiment. Among the more important proximate values stemming from equality are "a wide diffusion of economic and political power," "equal bargaining power on both sides of an exchange transaction," "equal opportunity, regardless of race, religion, or sex," and "*limited in*equality in the distribution of income." Under favorable conditions, the market system can further these objectives.

3. Justice and Fairness. The market is often given high marks for justice and fairness because, under ideal circumstances, it generates answers to the key economic questions that are not arbitrary, imperious, or despotic. Answering a series of pollsters' questions about the fairness of the American free-enterprise system, very large majorities of sampled respondents have said that the system is "fair and wise" (82%) and "gives everyone a fair chance" (65%), and that it is a "fair and efficient system" (63%).[4] Unfortunately, real-world circumstances often fall short of the ideal, so that free pursuit of profits in the marketplace may not always yield fair or just results. As Vernon Mund has written, "Profit can be made not only by producing more and better goods but also by using inferior materials, by artificially restricting supply to secure monopoly profits, by misleading and deceiving consumers, and by exploiting labor."[5] Thus, to account for these sad possibilities and to introduce several forms of market regulation that will be discussed later, we have

3 Robert A. Dahl and Charles E. Lindblom, *Politics, Economics, and Welfare* (New York: Harper & Row, 1963), p. 41.

4 Herbert McClosky and John Zaller, *The American Ethos: Public Attitudes Toward Capitalism and Democracy* (Cambridge, Mass: Harvard University Press, 1985), Chapter 5.

5 Vernon A. Mund, *Government and Business*, 4th ed. (New York: Harper & Row, 1965), p. 24.

listed "full disclosure," "honesty," and "prohibition of unfair practices" among the proximate values of Table 1–1.

4. Welfare, Happiness, and Progress. The foregoing discussion of freedom, equality, justice, and fairness helps to explain our earlier statement that the market system arrives at answers to the key economic questions in a *particularly appealing way*, but it remains to be demonstrated that the answers themselves are *fairly good answers*. In other words, as far as markets are concerned, the foregoing values relate more to the decision-making process than to the decisions made — to *means* rather than to *ends*. So, what about ends? Fortunately for us, the answers provided by the market system (again under favorable circumstances) comport fairly well with our society's concepts of welfare, happiness, and progress. As already indicated, a thorough exploration of these answers is deferred until later chapters, especially Chapter 2, when we can elaborate on the meaning of the phrases "favorable circumstances" and "ideal conditions" that have echoed interchangeably across these pages. Nevertheless, for a prelude, we can note briefly that the market system is generally efficient and flexible. Thus, markets answer the question "what will be produced" by allocating labor and material resources to the production of goods and services yielding the greatest social satisfaction. And, with respect to the question of how goods are produced, markets encourage the use of low-cost production techniques that consume the least amount of scarce resources possible for a given bundle of output. Finally, flexibility: the market is generally receptive to good new ideas and new resource capabilities so that, with each passing year, we can produce more and better goods with less and less time, effort, and waste; all of which implies progress.

Although these ultimate and proximate values are widely shared and vigorously advocated by most people in our society, they are also sources of conflict, frustration, and disappointment simply because they are not always consistent with each other. Among the more obvious examples of inconsistency are the following:

1. "Health and safety" may be furthered by requiring seat belts and air bags in every auto, but this requirement would inevitably interfere with "free choice in consumption."
2. Measures designed to procure a "clean environment," such as banning the use of sulfur laden coal, may seriously diminish what we can achieve in the way of "rising real income."
3. Enforcement of "honesty" and the "prohibition of unfair practices" in the marketing of products may conflict with many people's concepts of "limited government intervention."

Lest the picture painted by these examples look too bleak, we hasten to add that in many instances there may not be inconsistencies among values, and in other instances the inconsistencies may be so mild that they are readily amenable to compromise. Still, inconsistencies do exist and are often sharp, which helps to explain several important facts of political-economic life.

First, for various reasons (including material self-interest, educational background, and emotional empathy) each individual gives differing *weights* and *definitions* to these values. It is the particular weight and definition that guides each person's judgment of conflicts among values, precluding unanimous agreement on almost anything. (For a brief contrast of American and Japanese values see the appendix to this chapter.)

Second, several "economic philosophies" or "schools of thought" have evolved that differ primarily in terms of the weights they apply to these values and the definitions they give to them. Thus, for example, "conservatives" generally believe that "freedom" is superior to "equality" and "fairness." They prefer less government intervention. In contrast, "liberals" often stress "equality" and "fairness" over "freedom," and their list of preferences is consequently quite different from that of "conservatives."

Third, people's definitions and weights are by no means static or immutable. They change with time and events. Indeed, economic policy formulation has been described as "a trial and error process of self-correcting value judgments."[6] *Knowledge* and *policy* have within them and between them certain irreconcilable inconsistencies. They are both undergoing continuous review and revision, and opinions about both are strongly influenced by values. For these several reasons, we shall frequently return to this matter of value judgments.[7]

II. A SYSTEM FOR ANALYSIS

Having examined the place markets occupy in our economy and having described the basic ideals that will be applied in our evaluation of markets, we are ready to develop a systematic way of looking at markets. Such a system is necessary if any headway is to be made in analyzing market operations or evaluating how well various markets perform their function. In essence, all that is required is (1) a workable categorization of the principal attributes of markets and (2) a theoretical scheme tying these attributes together. The process is analogous to analyzing the op-

---

6. H. H. Liebhafsky's entire book *American Government and Business* (New York: John Wiley, 1971) is devoted to this theme, but see especially Chapters 1, 2, 6, and 18.

7 For more extensive discussions of values and their importance see *Ibid;* Donald Watson, *Economic Policy* (Boston: Houghton Mifflin, 1960), Chapters 2–6; Duncan MacRae, Jr., *The Social Function of Social Science* (New Haven, Conn: Yale University Press, 1976); Scott Gordon, *Welfare, Justice, and Freedom* (New York: Columbia University Press, 1980); Marc R. Tool, *Essays in Social Value Theory* (Armonk, N.Y.: Sharpe, 1986); and Amitai Etzioni, *The Moral Dimension* (New York: The Free Press, 1988).

eration of an automobile—the categorization of attributes (or parts) would distinguish between the electrical system, fuel supply system, and so on, and the theoretical scheme would relate each of these attributes to the others to explain how a car works. This "modeling" of the problem not only helps us organize our thoughts, it also helps us formulate testable hypotheses about how markets work. For example, one obvious and familiar hypothesis is that an unregulated monopoly sets higher prices than would prevail under competitive conditions.

The traditional model of markets is outlined in Figure 1–1.[8] As indicated there, the principal components of market analysis are the basic conditions, structure, conduct, and performance. The **basic conditions** may be thought of as characteristics that are either inherent to the product (as is largely true of price elasticity of demand, purchase method, and product durability) or relatively impervious to easy manipulation by policy (as is largely true of technology and historical background). The elements of market **structure** also tend to be stable over time, but they can be affected by either private or government policy. Among the more important variables of structure are the number of sellers and their size (both of which can be altered by antitrust divestiture and dissolution), product differentiation (determined chiefly by private advertising and promotion), and the condition of entry (which is affected by patents, licensing, and product differentiation, among other things). The word **conduct** denotes behavior and strategy on the part of firms in the market, so the several items listed under conduct in Figure 1–1 reflect action, not static condition. Finally, **performance** relates to achievements or end results as determined by such variables as efficiency and technological advances. In short, structure and conduct relate to *how* the market functions within the limits of its basic conditions, whereas performance relates to *how well* the market functions.

The solid arrows of Figure 1–1 indicate possible relationships among these attributes. In particular, traditional theory assumes a causal flow running from the basic conditions and structure to conduct and performance. Technology and growth, for instance, could greatly influence the number and size distribution of firms in the market. In turn, the structural characteristics of number and size distribution might determine price and production strategies (conduct) that cause good or bad allocation and production efficiency (performance). The broken lines of Figure 1–1 represent causal flows running in the opposite direction from those of the traditional model. As recent research has increasingly turned its attention to these latter possibilities, they too will attract our attention.

---

[8] Basic sources include Edward Mason, "Price and Production of Large-Scale Enterprise," *American Economic Review*, Supplement (March, 1939), pp. 61–74; Joe Bain, *Industrial Organization* (New York: John Wiley, 1959); J. M. Clark, *Competition as a Dynamic Process* (Washington, D.C.: Brookings Institution, 1961); and F. M. Scherer, *Industrial Market Structure and Economic Performance* (Chicago: Rand McNally, 1970).

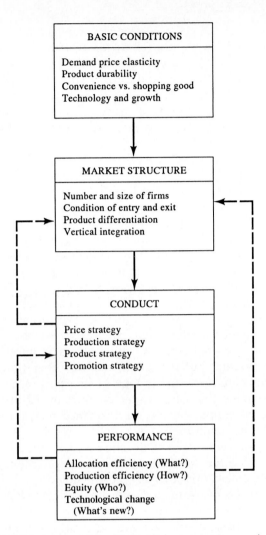

FIGURE 1–1. A model of industrial organization analysis.

Sticking with the traditional model for now, a more explicit por-trayal of structure-conduct-performance relationships is contained in Table 1–2. Four traditional market types are summarized there — **perfect com-petition, monopolistic competition, oligopoly,** and **monopoly.** Among the more obvious theoretical relationships depicted is that between the number of firms and price strategy. Notice first that under perfect com-petition the large number of firms prevents any one firm from being large enough to influence price. These many firms thus have no price strategy. They take prices as given by the market and independently determine their production with an eye to maximizing profits. Under

TABLE 1–2. Basic Market Types

Market Type	Structure			Conduct			Performance		
	Number of Firms	Entry Condition	Product Type	Price Strategy	Production Strategy	Promotion Strategy*	Profits (What?, Who?)	Production Efficiency	Progressiveness
Perfect Competition	Very large number	Easy	Standardized	None	Independent	b	Normal	Good	Poor perhaps
Monopolistic Competition	Large number	Easy	Differentiated	Unrecognized interdependence		a	Normal	Moderately good	Fair
Oligopoly	Few	Impeded	Standardized or differentiated	Recognized interdependence		a,b,c	Somewhat excessive	Poor perhaps	Good
Monopoly	One	Blocked	Perfectly differentiated	Independent		a = b c	Excessive	Poor perhaps	Poor perhaps

*Key: a = promotion of firm's brand product; b = industry- or marketwide advertising and promotion; c = institutional or political advertising.

oligopoly, however, with just a few sellers, each firm knows that its price and output actions are likely to affect its rivals' behavior. Hence "recognized interdependence" is said to prevail in oligopoly. Only the monopolist enjoys full independence in *both* price and production because he is the sole supplier in his market.

Another simple example of causal flow concerns the relationship between product type and promotion strategy. Intensive brand name advertising is likely to arise only for products that are differentiable, that is, products that people *believe* can have significant brand differences, whether or not the differences are real. Examples include drugs, cosmetics, soft drinks, and autos—each of which is vigorously advertised by brand. In contrast, standardized products—like milk, eggs, and potatoes—might be promoted on an industrywide basis or by large segments of the industry (for example, Idaho peddles potatoes), but the perfect substitutability of various suppliers' offerings of these products makes brand advertising and promotion by individual producers unprofitable. Table 1–2 also acknowledges the possibility of institutional or political advertising, which is generally practiced by firms self-conscious about their public image, as seems especially true of large oligopolists and monopolists.

The relationship between condition of entry and profits also deserves mention. According to the traditional model, industry profits (averaging all member firms) can be excessively high in the long run only if the entry of new firms into the industry is at least partially impeded. Otherwise, such high profits would attract newcomers seeking a piece of the profitable action. The new competition would in turn expand production, lower prices, and reduce profits. Thus, Table 1–2 specifies a positive, direct relationship between the height of barriers to entry (structure) and the likely level of industry profits (performance).

On the whole, then, it may seem that perfect competition provides the "ideal circumstances" and "favorable conditions" alluded to earlier. To some extent it does, but, as we shall explain in the next chapter, this is only partly true.

Table 1–2 also illustrates the two principal methods employed by industrial organization economists to analyze structure-conduct-performance relationships and test their significance—the "case study" approach and the "cross-section" approach. Under the former approach, the researcher narrows his focus to one industry for his "case study"; at the same time he usually considers almost all important aspects of the industry's structure, conduct, and performance. This approach is like viewing Table 1–2 *horizontally*, concentrating on only one row (for example, oligopoly) and moving from left to right across all the columns. In contrast, the cross-section approach is more inclusive of industries covered but less comprehensive in its study of attributes or variables. With this approach one can usually focus on only a few items of structure, conduct, or performance (for example, the number of firms and profits). Thus the cross-section approach is like viewing Table 1–2 *vertically*, concentrating on relatively few columns, but including as many industries as the available data permit.

The two approaches have different advantages and disadvantages, so their contributions to our fund of knowledge are complementary. In particular, each industry is in some ways unique in its basic conditions, structure, or regulation. The case study approach can take these unique characteristics into account and assess their impact on conduct and performance. The main shortcoming of case studies, however, is that generalizations cannot reliably be drawn from them — that is, their conclusions may not be applicable to industries other than those under study. By contrast, the cross-section approach cannot include all the unique attributes of all the industries under its purview (because of data limitations and measurement problems), but with this approach the researcher can test the *general* validity of certain hypotheses by estimating statistically the relationships between the variables of structure, conduct, and performance. For example, cross-section evidence indicates that industry profits are generally associated positively with the height of barriers to entry. However, certain unique features of a particular industry may have been left out of the cross-section analysis, thus precluding a direct and accurate application of this generalization to its specific case. Public pressure, weak demand, or some other factor that could only be accounted for by a thorough case study might cause low profits in a certain industry despite the presence of quite formidable barriers to entry. In sum, then, neither approach by itself is foolproof.

The case study and cross-section approaches differ not only in their substantive strengths and weaknesses. They also offer alternative ways to learn about the field of industrial organization, each of which has its pedagogical advantages and disadvantages. To most students' eyes, case studies appear concrete and lifelike, but the abstract overall view tends to be obscured by the wealth of detail they contain. On the other hand, cross-section evidence has opposite qualities — it provides an overall view but lacks the concrete and often engrossing details one finds in case studies. Although this book is based primarily on the cross-section approach, it includes large doses of case study material. To blend approaches, we treat each major attribute of markets outlined in Figure 1–1 and Table 1–2 with a *pair* of chapters rather than just one chapter. As a glance at the table of contents will show, the first chapter of each pair presents "abstract" theories and cross-section evidence, whereas the second presents "concrete" case study illustrations and relevant policy provisions. Each pair of chapters is classified under the broad heading to which it corresponds, beginning with structure and ending with performance.

III. AN OVERVIEW OF POLICIES

Government policies concerning markets can also be classified within the structure-conduct-performance framework because, generally speaking, the focus or impact of such policies is limited to just one or a few of the market attributes outlined in Figure 1–1 and Table 1–2. Indeed, a chief reason for organizing this book into a sequence on structure, conduct, and performance was the integrated treatment of policies and economics that could be achieved by such an organization. Most of the major policies that will be reviewed are outlined in Table 1–3, according to where they fit in this three-part scheme. Each policy has also been cross-classified in terms of how the policy relates to one important attribute of markets — *competition*. Thus, the left hand side of Table 1–3 shows three designations concerning competition: (1) maintenance of competition, (2) setting the plane of competition, and (3) reliance on a "public utility" type of regulation instead of competition. It must be stressed that the resulting alignment of policies and market attributes is only a very loose representation of reality. Moreover, space limitations prevent the mention of numerous other policies. Nevertheless, the table serves as a lofty perch from which to catch a panoramic view.

Setting details aside until later, we may illustrate these points by highlighting some of the contents of Table 1–3. Mergers between firms in the same market, for example, are prohibited by the Clayton Act (as amended by the Celler-Kefauver Act of 1950) if their effect "may be substantially to lessen competition." The courts, when judging whether a given case produces this effect, examine the number of firms in the market, the trend in numbers over time, and the market shares of the merging firms, all of which obviously relate to two attributes of market structure, namely, the number and size distribution of firms. Thus, Table 1–3 lists "merger laws" under the column headed "Structure." And, since prosecutions of monopolization under the Sherman Act are grounded on similar types of evidence, particularly size of market share, monopoly law joins merger law under "Structure" in Table 1–3. Without further reference to judicial considerations, it should be fairly clear that the remaining policies listed under structure belong there, for they relate primarily to product differentiation.

Under the column headed "Conduct" are laws governing price-fixing (collusion), price discrimination, exclusive dealing, tying, and false advertising. There can be no question that, among these, price fixing and false advertising policies should be classified under conduct. Price fixing's per se illegality (regardless of the extent of market power behind it or its effect on performance) illustrates the reasons for this. On the other hand, as will be shown later, simply designating price discrimination, tying, and exclusive dealing policies under "Conduct" may be

TABLE 1-3. Basic Government Policies Concerning Markets

Policy Type	Structure	Conduct	Performance
Maintenance of competition	1. Monopoly law 2. Merger laws	1. Price fixing law 2. Price discrimination law 3. Exclusive dealing law 4. Tying law	
Setting the plane of competition	1. Disclosure of information, truth-in-lending 2. Grading and standardization agricultural products, general weights and measures 3. Trademark and copyright protection	1. False advertising 2. Deceptive practices	1. Health and safety disclosures 2. Health and safety regulation in products, transportation, etc. 3. Pollution limitations
"Public utility" regulation		1. Price regulation in railroads, telephone, electricity and gas, banking and insurance 2. Abandonment of service	1. Profit regulation 2. Service requirements 3. Safety 4. Innovation regulation

somewhat misleading. Standards of illegality in these cases require that structural circumstances be taken into account before violation can be determined.

"Performance" is the third classification. It will be recalled that allocation efficiency, production efficiency, economic equity, and technological progress are attributes of major concern here. Performance measured by these attributes lies largely outside the purview of policies designed to maintain competition. Hence, the first cell of the "Performance" column in Table 1–3 has been left blank. The remaining performance policies are divided into two categories: (1) those policies that apply to almost all industries, regardless of competitive structure (since structure may have no effect on these particular forms of performance), and (2) those policies that apply to specific industries regulated by government commissions rather than by competition.

The first category includes such policies as pollution control, minimum safety requirements, and standards of purity for food and drugs (undeniably important matters of performance not hitherto mentioned because their connection to the traditional variables of structure and conduct is tenuous). The second category includes similar policies to some extent, but its main contents are profit regulation, service requirements, investment control, and supervision of innovation and technological change, for these policies typically lie within the jurisdiction of numerous independent commissions that regulate these aspects of specific industries — for example the Interstate Commerce Commission and the Federal Communications Commission. Instances of such direct performance regulation are usually rationalized on the ground that competitive structure cannot be attained or, if attainable, cannot be relied upon to provide desirable performance. For this reason the last structural policy cell of Table 1–3, corresponding to public utility–type regulation, has been left blank even though these industries are subject to certain forms of structural supervision.

IV. VALUES, ATTRIBUTES, AND POLICIES TOGETHER

This chapter cannot be concluded without an explicit acknowledgment of the links between all three of its major components — value judgments, market attributes, and public policies. The ties connecting the latter two have just been dealt with, so all that remains is a brief exploration of whatever correspondence they may have to value judgments. To state the obvious: All public policies have some *purpose* or *objective*, usually (or hopefully) the furtherance of one or more social values. And, broadly speaking, the purpose of most policies governing markets is to further one or more of the ultimate and proximate values listed earlier in Table 1–1. This observation may be comforting but it is not really very illuminating. We need to know a few specifics. In particular, which policies are designed to further which objectives? And which objectives are associated with which market attributes?

To best understand the answers to these questions, the reader must use his or her mind's eye to divide Table 1–1 into three main groups of ultimate values—(1) freedom and equality, (2) justice and fairness, and (3) welfare, happiness, and progress—retaining within each group the appropriate proximate values listed under each broad heading. Now (without straining your mind's eye too much), align the resulting three groups of values next to the three categories of market attributes outlined in Figure 1–1 that are, in principle, readily amenable to policy change—that is, (1) market structure, (2) conduct, and (3) performance. By this procedure it is possible to gain a loose appreciation for the fact that, generally speaking, (1) policies dealing primarily with market structure have as their main purpose the furtherance of "freedom and equality," (2) policies dealing primarily with market conduct are typically designed to enhance "justice and fairness," and (3) policies dealing chiefly with performance usually have as their objective the enrichment of "welfare and happiness" or the encouragement of "progress." Finally, if tilted properly, the policy outline of Table 1–3 could join this rough conceptual alignment of values and market attributes to complete an overall pattern of correspondence among values, market attributes, and policies, as indicated in Table 1–4. This summary alignment is of course only a very crude representation of reality, for numerous overlaps and inconsistencies could easily be pointed out. Still, for introductory purposes, it has the benefit of brevity.

The interrelationships between values, policies, and market characteristics, together with some qualifications, may be illustrated with special reference to the antitrust laws, which have been labeled "Maintenance of competition" policies in Table 1–3 and which may be the most important of all policies considered in this book because they constitute the "general rule" applying to most industries. Regarding values, antitrust policy could serve one or more of a wide variety of possible aims, nearly all of which may be grouped in the following three classes:[9]

1. *Maintenance of competition and limited business power.* This broad objective would draw its justification from the desirability of having (a) free entry and investment; (b) a large number of alternatives for exercising free choice in consumption and investment; (c) limited business power, or a diffusion of economic power; and (d) equal bargaining power on both sides of the market. These aims embody

[9] For a more thorough treatment of antitrust objectives see Carl Kaysen and Donald Turner, *Antitrust Policy* (Cambridge, Mass.: Harvard University Press, 1965), pp. 11–22; and Joel B. Dirlam and Alfred E. Kahn, *Fair Competition* (Ithaca, N.Y.: Cornell University Press, 1954).

TABLE 1–4. Overall Correspondence Among Values, Policies, and Market Attributes

Values	Policies	Market Attributes
Freedom and equality	Maintenance of competitive opportunity	Structure and (to a lesser extent) conduct
Justice and fairness	Rules regarding pricing, promotion, tying, etc.	Conduct
Welfare, happiness, and progress	Direct regulation of performance	Performance

certain desirable *economic* traits or conditions descriptive of *markets,* but antitrust could help to achieve certain *political* or *social* aims as well for political and social power are often grounded on economic power.[10] Many if not most of us believe that furtherance of these several aims tends to foster "freedom" and "equality" as defined earlier.

2. *Fair conduct.* The foregoing relates primarily to the *mere possession* of power, not to its *exercise.* In contrast, aims of "fair conduct" relate more to the way business power is used rather than its mere presence. Should large buyers be charged less than small buyers? Should a seller be allowed to tie the sale of two products together, like computers and software, one of which is monopolistically controlled by patents? Also, what about group boycotts and aggregated rebates? Antitrust could attempt to lay down standards of fair business conduct that would curtail these kinds of practices without attacking the economic power that makes them onerous.

3. *Desirable economic performance.* Because market structure and conduct greatly affect market performance, antitrust policy could be concerned with structure and conduct *only* in so far as they might produce poor performance, while overlooking any concentrations of power or unfair practices that had no discernible effect on performance or promised potential improvements therein. Indeed, despite ample evidence to the contrary, a few economists believe that bigness brings about efficiency, equity, and progress; that cartels are relatively harmless; and that "restrictive practices" are not really restrictive at all. Hence they emphatically favor having performance as the only goal, arguing that "the *process* of choice itself must not be a value,"[11] and that our policy objectives should be confined to

---

[10] Robert Pitofsky, "The Political Content of Antitrust," *University of Pennsylvania Law Review* (April, 1979), pp. 1051–1075.

[11] C. E. Ferguson, *A Macroeconomic Theory of Workable Competition* (Durham: University of North Carolina Press, 1964), p. 56 (emphasis added).

"maximizing economic benefits, *whatever* the number of firms may turn out to be."[12]

Which of these three broad aims actually predominates? This is a much debated question. However, notwithstanding the views of the performance minded minority, the general consensus among economists, legislators, and jurists seems to be that our antitrust policy should be aimed primarily at the maintenance of competition as an end in itself and secondarily at the enforcement of fair conduct. To quote a few authorities:

> The greatest common denominator in antitrust decisions is a commitment to smallness and decentralization as ways of discouraging the concentration of discretionary authority. — Donald Dewey[13]

> The grounds for the policy include not only dislike of restriction of output and of one-sided bargaining power but also desire to prevent excessive concentration of wealth and power, desire to keep open the channels of opportunity, and concern lest monopolistic controls of business lead to political oligarchy. — Corwin Edwards[14]

> Throughout the history of these [antitrust] statutes it has been constantly assumed that one of their purposes was to perpetuate and preserve, for its own sake and in spite of possible cost, an organization of industry in small units which can effectively compete with each other. — Judge Learned Hand[15]

As for the views of laypersons, the reader need merely ask: Would most people like to see each and every industry turned over to the control of two or three firms, and the economy as a whole (including mining, manufacturing, transportation, finance, and wholesale and retail trade) subjected to the overwhelming dominance of only 50 corporations, assuming for the sake of illustration that economists believed this massive restructuring would eventually yield 5% greater efficiency, 3% less cyclical instability, and slightly faster growth in GNP? In all probability, the answer is no (or NO!). Moreover, the same answer would most likely greet a similar question regarding unfair or restrictive business practices. Thus our major antitrust policies have been assigned to the "Structure" and "Conduct" sections of Table 1–3, and it is not inappropriate to draw an association between these policies and certain classes of values addressed at the outset — freedom, equality, justice, and

---

[12] John McGee, *In Defense of Industrial Concentration* (New York: Praeger, 1971) p. 21 (emphasis added).

[13] Donald Dewey, "The New Learning: One Man's View," in *Industrial Concentration: The New Learning,* edited by H. J. Goldschmid, H. M. Mann, and J. F. Weston (Boston: Little, Brown, 1974) p. 13.

[14] Corwin Edwards, *Maintaining Competition* (New York: McGraw-Hill, 1949), p. 9

[15] *United States* v. *Aluminum Company of America,* 148 F.2d 416 (1945). For more recent views see E.M. Fox, "The Modernization of Antitrust," *Cornell Law Review* (1981), pp. 1140–1182; and F. M. Scherer, "Antitrust, Efficiency, and Progress," *New York University Law Review* (November, 1987), pp. 998–1019.

fairness. If, for one reason or another, the antitrust approach fails to satisfy these objectives in a specific industry, or if the approach is irrelevant to certain performance objectives (like clean air), or if the approach is considered *too* costly in terms of poor performance in an industry, then direct regulation of performance often ensues. But this step is usually taken only with great reluctance and often in response to crisis.

SUMMARY

A few steps toward an understanding of markets have now been taken. In a nutshell, the market system should be looked upon not only as the organized process by which buyers and sellers exchange goods and services but as an *institution*—the key institution upholding our private free-enterprise capitalistic economy. Because markets are institutional by nature, they embody certain social values, they perform an essential economic function, and they are the target of many governmental policies. In function, markets coordinate and control the largely decentralized decision-making process that provides answers to the four fundamental questions scarcity forces upon us: (1) What should be produced? (2) How should goods and services be produced? (3) Who shall get the benefits of our productive efforts? (4) How can we maintain flexibility for changes over time? Given their assigned task, markets may be analyzed and evaluated by both the specific *answers provided* and the *process by which the answers are obtained*. If the decision process seems "bad" but the answers themselves are considered "good," society might want to reject the system despite its considerable "goodness." Indeed, the way decisions are made may be important enough to people to make them willing to suffer an occasional bad answer in order to maintain a system or process to their liking. Ideally, of course, both the process of choice and the answers produced should conform to society's concepts of the desirable—that is, society's values.

Translating "process" and "answers" into a model of markets, we come up with a four-part categorization of market attributes—the basic conditions, structure, conduct, and performance. The last three command special attention because structure and conduct constitute the market's decision-making process, whereas performance consists of the achievements, outcomes, or answers provided by the process. In other words, structure refers to such factors as the number and size distribution of the decision makers (buyers and sellers), the condition of entry, and product differentiation. Conduct includes, among other things, price strategy, production strategy, promotion activity, and coercive tactics. Last, the principal attributes of performance are allocation and production efficiency, economic equity, and progress.

Returning to goodness and badness, value judgments furnish standards for assessing market structure, conduct, and performance. Moreover, value judgments guide policy formulation and enforcement. Antitrust policy illustrates this junction of market attributes, value judgments, and public policies: (1) antitrust focuses most intently on structure and conduct; (2) among its several possible purposes a principal purpose is the maintenance of competition as an end in itself; and (3) maintenance of competition is, in essence, a shorthand way of saying freedom, equality, fairness, and justice, together with most of the relevant proximate values they represent.

APPENDIX TO CHAPTER 1: VALUES IN JAPAN AND AMERICA

The values of Table 1–1, especially as they pertain to economic matters, may vary from one country to another because they are culturally determined. For example, after extensive study of Japanese ways, James Fallows concluded that some fundamental differences in economic value judgments distinguish Japan from America:

> The starting point of western economics, especially in America, is that the world is full of "economic men," who go through life making rational cost-benefit decisions. This picture rests on an even more basic assumption about the purpose of life—at least the economic part of it. Efficient production and foreign trade are good because they lead to lower prices, and lower prices are good because they let people have more: more food, more clothes, more leisure, more variety, more of everything that money can buy. This is the principal justification for the turmoil of capitalism.
>
> For most of its history, the United States has behaved more or less in accordance with the pro-consumer capitalist model. Japan has not. The welfare of its consumers has consistently taken second place to a different goal: preserving every person's place in the productive system. The primary reward of working hard in Japan is to continue to be able to work. Japan has consistently protected its producers—farmers, unions, small shops, big corporations—at the expense of Japanese consumers, who must pay exorbitant prices for everything they buy.
>
> Food is the classic illustration of the bias in favor of production and effort. Rice grown on tiny plots—which together, take up about half the non-mountainous land in the country—costs at least six times as much as American-grown rice.[16]

[16] James Fallows, "For Those Who Have a Yen for the Japanese Way: Think Twice," *Washington Post*, National Weekly Edition, February 20–26, 1989, p. 23.

2

Competition Versus Monopoly: Variations

Competition may be the spice of life, but in economics it has been more nearly the main dish.

— GEORGE STIGLER

Chapter 1 described, in general, the linkage between market structure, conduct, and performance. We now move from the general to the particular. The first part of this chapter surveys traditional theories of structure, conduct, and performance as they relate to perfect competition and pure monopoly. These traditional theories introduce market *analysis*. That is to say, they demonstrate how sellers make market decisions under certain conditions. Moreover, these traditional theories offer an opportunity to review some basic concepts that will be useful later, concepts like elasticity of demand, marginal cost, and marginal revenue. Finally, these traditional theories open the door to market *evaluation* because they generate definitions of "allocation efficiency" and "equity."

Though instructive, these traditional theories of perfect competition and pure monopoly are limited. In particular, they are *static* theories that more or less misrepresent the competitive and monopolistic behavior that occurs in the real world. Hence this chapter goes on to outline what may be called *dynamic* competition and monopoly. Technological change plays a major role in this dynamic view.

Finally, the chapter offers a standard for evaluating markets that draws upon both static and dynamic theories, namely, the standard of *workable competition*. It is workable competition that provides the best guide for public policy.

I. PERFECT COMPETITION VERSUS PURE MONOPOLY

A. The Perfectly Competitive Model

Economic theory's conventional ideal is perfect competition. In this section we (1) specify the structural conditions that must be met to obtain perfect competition, (2) show how these structural conditions affect market conduct, and (3) elaborate on the performance produced by this combination of structure and conduct. Emerging from this exercise is an understanding of a market's two essences—demand and supply.

1. Perfect Competition: Structure and Demand. Perfect competition is defined by four main structural conditions. First, perfect competition requires a very large number of small buyers and sellers. Indeed, each buyer and each seller must be so small relative to the total market that none of them *individually* can affect product price by altering their volume of purchases, if they are buyers, or their level of output, if they are sellers.

Second, the product of any one seller must be a perfect substitute for the product of any other seller. In economists' jargon, the product is homogeneous or standardized.

Third, perfect competition requires that productive resources be freely mobile into and out of markets. Of course any such movement will take time, and in the short run some factors like land and capital are said to be "fixed" because of their short-run immobility once they are committed to production. However, in the long run, all factors are variable and perfectly mobile. This means an absence of barriers to new firm entry—that is, an absence of patents, economies of scale, and the like.

Finally, perfect competition requires that all market participants have full knowledge of the economic and technical data relevant to their decision making. Buyers must be aware of the price and product offerings of sellers. Sellers must know product prices, wage rates, materials costs, and so on.

Under these several conditions the demand curve facing each individual firm will be infinitely elastic with respect to price. This is a supremely important statement, yet its specific content is meaningless without an understanding of two of its key terms: "demand" and "elasticity." In the very broad sense, **demand** refers to the quantity of product that would be purchased at various possible prices during some given period of time, holding all determinants of demand other than product price constant. Specifically, demand can refer (1) to the demand *of an individual buyer*, (2) to the demand *of all buyers* in the market taken together, or (3) to the demand *facing an individual seller* in the market. Generally speaking, structural conditions do not influence demand in the first two respects. That is to say, the purchases of a single buyer are only a function of product price, income, tastes, prices of substitute goods (for example, coffee for tea or vice versa), prices of complements (for example, coffee and donuts), and expectations. Individual demand is *not* a function of the number of sellers in the market or the condition of new firm entry. Similarly, since total market demand is simply the summation of all the demands of the individual buyers in the market, total market demand is a function of the same variables that determine individual demand (price, incomes, tastes, prices of related goods, and expectations), plus one additional factor — the number of buyers in the market. Now the number of buyers was mentioned as a structural element. But the number is typically large, so in all but a few instances we are safe in saying that *market structure does not directly affect marketwide demand.*

Figure 2–1 illustrates several **marketwide** demand curves. According to the conventional "law" of demand each demand curve must have a negative slope because price and quantity are inversely related. Thus, on curve D_1D_1, an increase in the price of the product from P_1 to P_2 causes quantity demanded to drop from Q_1 to Q_2, resulting in a movement along the demand curve from point K to J. Such movements along the demand curve, under the impetus of price changes, should not be confused with *shifts* of demand, which are caused by changes in variables *other* than the product's price. An increase in income, for instance, is likely to shift demand outward from D_1D_1 to D_2D_2. Conversely, a reduction of income is likely to shift demand down from D_1D_1 to D_3D_3, resulting in fewer purchases than before at each possible price.

Later, it will be important to know just *how responsive* demand is to variations in price. To measure such responsiveness, economists rely on the **elasticity** of demand in relation to price, which is defined as follows:

$$\text{price elasticity of demand} = \frac{\text{percentage change in quantity demanded}}{\text{percentage change in price}}$$

Strictly speaking, the negative slope of demand always yields a negative elasticity, but the negative sign is usually suppressed for simplification. When the percentage change in quantity demanded exceeds the percentage change in price for some given price change, quantity demand is

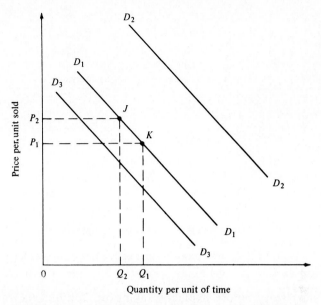

FIGURE 2–1. Examples of marketwide product demand.

highly responsive to price and the elasticity ratio will be greater than 1, or *elastic*. Conversely, if the percentage change in quantity demanded is less than the percentage change in price, demand is relatively *unresponsive* to price variations and the elasticity will be less than 1, or *inelastic*.

Marketwide demand cannot be the same view of demand held by the typical *individual firm* selling in the market, unless, of course, there is only one firm in the market (a monopolist). In the case of perfect competition the number of sellers is very large, and each seller is so small relative to the total market that it views its demand as in Figure 2–2, a horizontal line running parallel to the quantity axis and intersecting the vertical axis at the going market price. This demand is infinitely elastic.

Thus, market structure is a *crucial determinant* of demand as viewed by the typical firm in the market, even though structure generally does *not* influence the marketwide demand curve. It is precisely through this influence on the firm's view of demand that structure subsequently influences firm conduct and, thereby, market conduct as well. How does the firm's view of demand influence firm conduct? By influencing the way firms in the market go about maximizing their profits—assuming that firms want to maximize profits. In summary,

structure⟶ firm's view of demand⟶ firm conduct

profit maximization

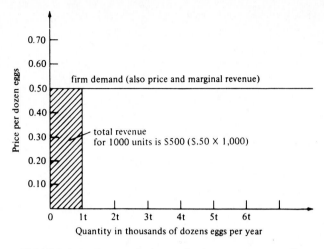

FIGURE 2–2. Demand of a perfectly competitive seller.

The next step, before explicitly taking up conduct, is to extract the element of demand particularly relevant to the firm's profit-maximizing calculation.

There are numerous profit-maximizing rules of thumb (for example, "never give a sucker an even break"). The formal economic principle is, in essence, *equalize marginal revenue and marginal cost*. Because demand determines marginal revenue, we shall discuss the revenue portion of the formula first, postponing consideration of marginal cost until the next section. **Marginal revenue** *is the change in total revenue attributable to the sale of one more unit of output.* Indeed, "incremental revenue" might be a better name for it. As price and quantity are always the two basic components of demand and as total revenue is always price *times* quantity sold, there is a very intimate relationship between demand and marginal revenue. In the purely competitive case, the firm's total revenue will rise directly with quantity sold at a constant rate of increase because, according to the firm's demand curve, price is constant over the firm's range of product sales. In other words, the additional sale of one unit of output always adds to total revenue an amount that *just equals the price.* Hence, price and marginal revenue are equal when, as shown in Figure 2–2, the demand curve of the firm is infinitely elastic. Using that figure's data, an additional sale of 1 dozen eggs adds 50 cents to the firm's total revenue regardless of whether it is the first dozen sold or the 3000th dozen sold. Hence, marginal revenue is 50 cents.

2. Perfect Competition: Supply and Conduct. **Marginal cost,** the second portion of the profit-maximizing rule of thumb, may be defined as *the addition to total costs due to the additional production of one unit of* *output.* What are "total costs"? In the short run, total costs are made up of two components—total fixed costs and total variable costs. The short run is a time period short enough for certain factors of production—such as land, buildings, and equipment—to be immobile. Those immobile factors generate **total fixed costs**—such as rent, debt repayments, and property taxes—that *in terms of total costs* do not vary with output. In terms of *cost per unit* of output or "average fixed cost," however, these costs actually decline with greater output because average fixed cost is total fixed cost (a constant) divided by the number of units produced. Thus as output rises these fixed costs are "spread" over a larger and larger number of units.

Total variable costs, on the other hand, are those costs associated with variable factors of production such as labor, raw materials, and purchased parts. In terms of *total costs* these costs *always* rise with greater amounts of output, but in terms of *per unit* or "average costs" these may fall, remain unchanged, or rise, depending on the prices and productivity of these variable factors as they are variously applied to the fixed factors. Average, or per-unit, variable cost is the total variable cost at some given level of output, divided by the number of units in that quantity of output. Thus, functionally speaking, if total variable cost rises less rapidly than quantity, per unit variable cost will fall; if total variable cost rises one for one with quantity at a constant rate, per unit variable cost will be constant; and if the total rises more rapidly than the quantity, per unit variable cost will rise.

Figure 2–3 depicts this family of cost curves on a per unit or average basis, according to conventional forms. ATC indicates short-run average total cost, and AVC indicates short-run average variable cost. Average fixed cost, AFC, constitutes the difference between ATC and AVC. When ATC is falling, marginal cost, MC, will be below ATC. Once ATC begins to rise, however, MC exceeds ATC. If the P = MR (price equals marginal revenue) line represents the individual firm's demand curve for a prevailing price of *0A*, profit maximization is achieved by producing *0H* units of output because, at that level of output, marginal cost just equals marginal revenue at point *K*. Bearing in mind that total profits are simply total revenue less total cost, the profit-maximizing firm will add to its output so long as the added revenue thereby obtained, MR, exceeds the added cost thereby incurred, MC. This is true of all output levels up to *0H*. However, once the added cost of added output, MC, exceeds the added revenue obtained, MR, total profits will begin to fall. Hence, the astute firm will not produce an output greater than *0H*. At output *0H* total economic profit is the shaded rectangle *BAKD*, which is the economic profit per unit, *KD*, times the number of units produced *AK*. This is called **economic profit** or **excess profit** because the average total costs *includes* a "normal" profit for the investors that is just sufficiently large, say, 8% per year, to pay the cost of capital. Provision of

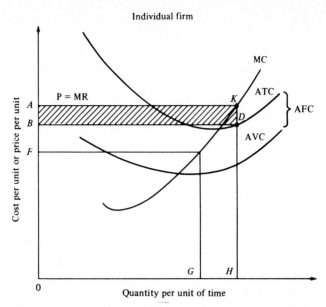

FIGURE 2–3. Short-run cost curves of the firm together with perfectly competitive demand.

this normal profit rate discourages the investors from withdrawing their capital in the long run and investing it elsewhere.

At price *0F* there would be neither excess profit nor normal profit; there would be a loss. Still, in the short run, the firm would continue to produce an amount *0G*, which would again equate marginal revenue (now *0F*) with marginal cost. The firm will thus minimize its losses. Only if price were to drop so low that the firm could not recover its variable cost AVC on each unit would it minimize loss by closing down. The firm should *never* lose in total dollars more than its total fixed cost. If it cannot even cover its variable cost on each unit, then its continued operation will result in losses exceeding total fixed cost.

Two major conclusions emerge from this analysis. First, since price equals marginal revenue for the perfectly competitive firm, the MR = MC profit rule of thumb causes price to equal marginal cost and fulfills the optimal welfare requirement to be explained shortly. Second, the supply curve for the firm is identical to its marginal cost curve above the AVC curve. Over the range of possible prices, the quantity offered for sale by the firm may be read from the MC curve. It follows, then, that market-wide short-run supply is determined by simply adding up the short-run supplies of all individual firms in the market at each possible price, as is illustrated in Figure 2–4.

The ties between the typical firm and the market may now be seen in Figure 2–5. Figure 2–5(a) shows the major short-run cost curves of a

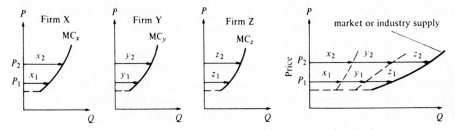

FIGURE 2–4. Horizontal summation of firm supply curves for industry supply.

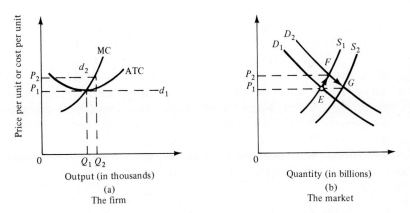

FIGURE 2–5. Long-run adjustment and equilibrium for the firm and market.

typical firm; Figure 2–5(b) depicts marketwide supply and demand curves. The first thing to note is that price in the market is determined by the interaction of supply and demand. Thus, given demand D_1 and supply S_1, the market will generate a price of P_1. As viewed by the individual firm in Figure 2–5(a), price P_1 establishes the demand curve P_1d_1, which is infinitely elastic. Short-run profit maximization leads to an output of Q_1.

Of course, changes in tastes, income, and other factors will cause demand to shift. If demand shifts from D_1 to D_2, point E will no longer represent equilibrium. In the short run, the enhanced demand will boost prices to P_2, inducing existing firms to move up along their short-run marginal cost curves (MC) to an output level Q_2. This translates into a movement *along* the short-run industry supply curve S_1 from E to F when viewed in the marketwide perspective of Figure 2–5(b). With price greater than short-run average total cost, ATC, economic or excess profits mount up. New firms will enter the market and shift the supply curve to the right to S_2. Entry continues until price falls low enough to wipe out the prospect of excess profits for new entrants. In Figure 2–5 it is assumed that price returns to P_1, a movement that implies that, in the long run, industry supply has increased from E to G without any long-run change of price.

3. Demand, Supply, and Performance. Figure 2–6 completes the perfect competition story. Note that the intersection of demand and supply, E, is an equilibrium position because price at that point, P_1, will not be budged up or down by discrepancies between demand and supply. A price higher than P_1, such as P_2, could not last because a glut of quantity supplied (Q_2) over quantity demanded (Q_0), measured by distance AB, would with competition press price down until demand matched supply. Conversely, a price below P_1, would tend to rise as the excess of demand over supply bid price up until equilibrium was reached. That is, price is determined by the mating of demand and supply.

In the short run, price P_1 might mean excess profits for firms in the market, due, perhaps, to a recent boom in demand. Losses are also possible in the short run, due for instance to depressed demand. In the long run, however, entry would wipe out excess profits and exit would tend to erase any losses. Entry implies expanding supply and downward price adjustment, while exit contracts supply and bolsters price. In the long run, after all adjustments are completed, equilibrium implies only "normal" profit, with average total costs and marginal costs equaling price. Thus entry and exit are essential to competitive control.

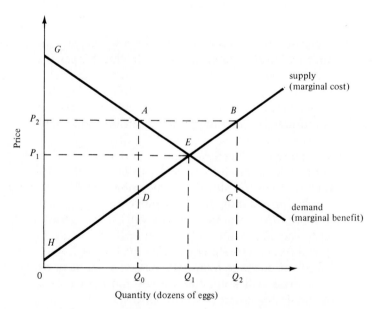

FIGURE 2–6. Demand, supply, and market equilibrium.

To assess *how well* this market performs we must evaluate its answers to the basic questions raised by scarcity—namely, what, how, who, and what's new. The questions of "what" and "how" receive answers—namely, allocation efficiency and production efficiency—that are highly desirable. These are desirable answers because they give society as much economic well being as possible within the bounds imposed by scarcity.

Allocation Efficiency (re: What?): The nice answer to "What should be produced in what amounts?" is seen through an appreciation of the fact that Q_1 in Figure 2–6 is just the right amount—not too much, not too little. The demand curve indicates the **benefit** society gains from the production of this good, say eggs, both at the margin and overall. For example, distance Q_1E, which is the same as price $0P_1$, indicates the benefit of the last dozen eggs at Q_1, so-called *marginal benefit*, because that is the amount people *are willing to pay* for that *last dozen* at Q_1. Area $0GEQ_1$ indicates the benefit of all dozens over the range of $0Q_1$, or *total benefit*, because that is the amount people *would be willing to pay* for the *entire* quantity $0Q_1$. Given a price of $0P_1$, they actually pay only amount $0P_1EQ_1$, which is price times quantity. The difference between what they are willing to pay, $0GEQ_1$, and what they actually pay, $0P_1EQ_1$, is triangular area P_1GE, which is like a gift and which accordingly is called *consumers' surplus*.

For its part, the supply curve in Figure 2–6 represents society's cost of producing eggs—that is, the cost of land, labor, and other scarce resources, both at the margin and overall. At output $0Q_1$, distance Q_1E depicts the *marginal cost*, and the area under supply curve, $0HEQ_1$, depicts the *total cost* of producing output $0Q_1$.

Hence, amount $0Q_1$ is just the right amount because any marginal unit of output associated with a lesser amount, such as Q_0, yields a marginal social benefit, A, that exceeds the marginal social cost of producing that unit, D. So long as a unit's benefit exceeds its cost in this way, additional units of output should be produced, which holds true up to Q_1. Output should not exceed Q_1, however, because any marginal unit associated with a greater amount, such as Q_2, carries a social cost, B, that exceeds social benefit, C. Thus, if the ideal output is one that maximizes "total benefit—total cost," as guided by society's preferences, Q_1 is that output, where "marginal social benefit = marginal social cost," or MSB=MSC. Net *pluses* occur up to Q_1, as added benefits exceed added costs. Net *minuses* arise thereafter.

Another way of appreciating this result, one that stresses the problem of producing an optimal *mix* of goods when constrained by scarcity, focuses on the P=MC, or price equals marginal cost, condition. Price, as read off the demand curve, indicates the value of the output of productive resources when they are used *here* to provide this commodity, say, eggs. Marginal cost, as read off the supply curve, indicates the value of the resources if they were used *elsewhere* to produce other things like wheat, books, records, whatever. After all, the producers of eggs must pay enough for labor, land, energy, and capital to attract them away from those alternative activities. In short, then:

$$\text{price} = \text{value of resources here}$$
$$\text{marginal cost} = \text{value of resources elsewhere}$$

Ideally, *value here should equal value elsewhere*, which is attained when $P = MC$.

Assume otherwise as a test. If value here exceeded value elsewhere, as *A* exceeds *D* in Figure 2–6 at Q_0, then resources are more valuable here and should therefore be transferred from elsewhere to here, expanding output to Q_1. Competitive markets spur such transfers as profits would be greater here than elsewhere. Conversely, if value elsewhere exceeded value here, as *B* exceeds *C* in Figure 2–6, then resources are worth more elsewhere than here, and output here should be reduced to Q_1 from Q_2, freeing resources for more worthy application elsewhere. Competitive markets foster such transfers by offering greater profit elsewhere than here in such cases. Table 2–1 puts all this in a nutshell.

Production Efficiency (re: How?): The nice answer to "How are goods produced?" is more easily understood because we know that firms in this kind of market will be forced by competition to adopt the most efficient, lowest cost technologies available, and firms will also be compelled to operate at the low point on their long-run average cost curves. Otherwise, their costs would exceed price and they could not long survive.

Taken together, production efficiency and allocative efficiency achieve what is called **Pareto optimality,** after its formulator Vilfredo Pareto. This ideal is *a situation where no one can be made better off without making someone else worse off.* Stated otherwise, we are *not* at Pareto optimality if Smith's lot can be improved at no loss to anyone else—Jones, Adams, whoever. Ideal markets move society toward Pareto optimality because they entail *exchange.* Whenever *free* and *voluntary* exchange occurs with no adverse third-party effects, at least one person is made better

TABLE 2–1. Various Resource Allocation Conditions

	Optimal Allocation	Under Allocation	Over Allocation
Market result	$P = MC$	$P > MC$	$P < MC$
General requirement	$MSB = MSC$	$MSB > MSC$	$MSB < MSC$
English translation	value here = value elsewhere	value here > value elsewhere	value here < value elsewhere

off and no one is made worse off. Usually, of course, *both* parties to an exchange benefit. Your trade of $500 for a stereo set makes you *and* the retailer better off. Exchange or market processes can therefore move society from inefficiency toward efficiency.

Equity (re: Who?): The foregoing achievements of the perfectly competitive model are indeed marvelous. Strictly speaking, however, the model cannot claim perfection on the ethical criteria of equity — that is, the question of "who gets the goods and services?" The term "equity" does not have nearly the clarity of "efficiency," but it generally means some "equitable" distribution of income or "equal opportunity." Equity and efficiency *are separable* in the theoretical sense that efficiency can be achieved regardless of whether or not the income distribution is "equitable" or "just." Equity and efficiency *are related* in the sense that the prevailing distribution will substantially influence the kinds of goods included in an efficient mix. Thus a lopsided, unequal distribution of income could yield an efficient mix that includes more Rolls Royces and more caviar than a distribution that is relatively equal. Although theory cannot heighten the attraction of perfect competition by lights of equity, intuition tells us that its absence of excess long-run profits could further ideals of equity.

Technological Change (re: What's New?): Theoretically, the perfectly competitive model is less than ideal when it comes to the question of "What's new?" The model is perfectly static, fixed in time, and by definition progressive performance in new products and new processes requires *dynamic* developments.

We shall elaborate on this point shortly when we take up the topic of dynamic competition in earnest. Meanwhile, we shall develop a deeper appreciation for the efficiency and equity achievements of perfect competition if we take a theoretical glimpse at pure monopoly.

B. The Pure Monopoly Model

1. Pure Monopoly Structure and Conduct. The structural conditions for pure monopoly are just the opposite of those for perfect competition. Instead of a large number of relatively small sellers, there is just one. Instead of a standardized product, identical across all sellers, the product may be said to be perfectly differentiated because the monopolist's offering has no close substitutes. Instead of easy entry for newcomers, entry is blocked in the case of pure monopoly (even though the monopolist may be earning massive excess profits).

Under these conditions, the demand facing the individual seller and the marketwide demand are one and the same. With conventional cost curves, the resulting profit-maximizing price and quantity for a monopolist are shown in Figure 2–7.

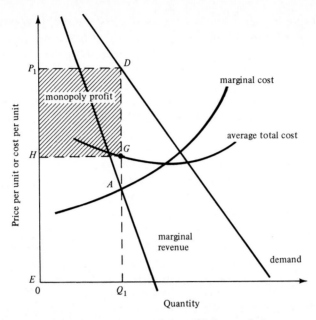

FIGURE 2–7. Monopoly equilibrium solution.

As before, the rule of thumb for maximizing profit is marginal cost equals marginal revenue, which occurs at point A with output $0Q_1$ and price $0P_1$. Although the MC=MR rule applies here as under perfect competition, the result is markedly different in this case because the downward-sloping demand of the monopolist generates a downward-sloping marginal revenue curve that lies below the demand curve. Recalling that marginal revenue is the addition to total revenue due to the additional sale of one more unit of output, we may illustrate the relationship between price, quantity, total revenue, and marginal revenue in the simplified schedule of Table 2–2.

Each extra unit sold *adds* to total revenue an amount equal to the

TABLE 2–2. Marginal Revenue and Price

P($)	Q(units)	TR(P x Q) ($)	Marginal Revenue ($)
11	0	0	—
10	1	10	10
9	2	18	8
8	3	24	6
7	4	28	4
6	5	30	2
5	6	30	0
4	7	28	-2

price of that unit, but from this the monopolist must *subtract* the price reductions necessary to sustain the sale of all preceding units. Thus in Table 2–2 the marginal revenue of producing the third unit is $6 even though price at that point is $8, because three units generate a total revenue of $24 ($8 × 3), whereas two units generate a total revenue of $18 ($9 × 2), and 24 − 18 = 6. Marginal revenue is lower than price. And, as price declines, marginal revenue declines faster. Thus, once again, we have seen how structure, via its influence on the firm's view of demand, affects conduct.

Economic or excess profit *per unit* in Figure 2–7 is indicated by the distance *DG*. Total dollar excess profit is consequently the area *DGHP*₁. (This assumes once again that ATC includes a normal profit.) Some monopolists may not be able to earn excess profits. Their costs may be high relative to their demand, or their demand may be low relative to their costs. If there were only one movie theater in Ottertail, Minnesota, for instance, it would probably be only a weak monopoly earning only a normal profit. Still, the classic case is one involving excess profit.

2. Pure Monopoly Performance. In traditional theory, monopoly causes poor performance in two main ways, both of which derive from the foregoing profit story. These are illustrated in Figure 2–8, which simplifies matters by assuming constant cost per unit (thereby causing average total cost to match marginal cost). Under perfect competition, price would be P_c, which equals cost and therefore yields no excess profit.

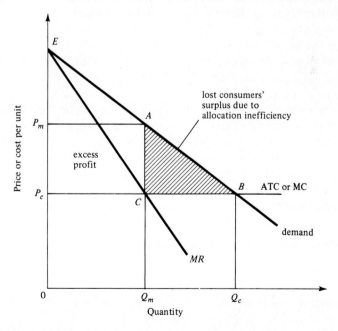

FIGURE 2–8. Monopoly's adverse impact on allocation efficiency and equity.

The quantity corresponding to P_c is Q_c, which is optimal by previously shown standards, namely, $P_c = MC$. In contrast, the monopolist's price is higher at P_m and corresponding quantity is lower at Q_m.

Consumers' surplus under perfect competition would amount to area EBP_c, because the amount consumers would be willing to pay, which is the area under the demand curve, $0EBQ_c$, exceeds the amount they actually pay, $0P_cBQ_c$, by a value represented by EBP_c. Under pure monopoly, consumers' surplus shrinks to triangle EAP_m. Hence monopoly causes consumers to lose an amount equivalent to P_cP_mAB.

This lost consumers' surplus, P_cP_mAB, may be divided into two kinds of loss. The first part, area ABC, is due to the misallocation of resources that occurs when output falls from Q_c to Q_m. This value, ABC, disappears from the economy completely; it is lost by consumers and not gained by the monopolist. It is the same kind of loss that would occur if earthquakes obliterated our coal reserves, but it is a welfare loss due to *inefficiency*.

The second part, area P_cP_mAC, is the excess profit earned by the monopolist at the expense of consumers. This is a *transfer* from consumers to the monopoly's owners, a transfer that may result in undesirable *inequity*. How markedly the excess profit contributes to an unequal distribution of income depends on the relative financial condition of (1) those who pay the higher price and thereby lose the surplus and (2) those who earn the excess profit and thereby gain the surplus. If those who pay are generally poorer than those who receive, as typically seems to be true, then income distribution is made more unequal by monopoly.

As regards production efficiency and technological change (the performance questions of How? and What's new?), the theoretical case against monopoly is less clear cut. For reasons we shall explore extensively later, a monopolist's production efficiency might be good because of economies of scale, which lower average and marginal cost as size grows. On the other hand, a monopolist's production efficiency might suffer from slack and sloth—so-called X-inefficiency. Theories concerning a monopolist's progressiveness are equally ambiguous. Invention and innovation can be said to thrive or die under monopoly depending on one's theoretical assumptions. Once again difficulties naturally arise when conclusions concerning dynamics are wrongly extracted from the static, conventional theory of monopoly surveyed to this point.

C. Problems with the Traditional Models

These theories of perfect competition and pure monopoly suggest a simple rule of thumb for public policy—namely, stamp out monopoly and create perfect competition. However, this rule is foolish for several reasons.

First, there are countless instances where, in the real world, it would be impossible or imprudent to achieve all or even most of the conditions required for perfect competition—that is, a large number of sellers, easy entry, standardized product, and perfect knowledge. For example, physical laws of nature make it impossible to have a very large number of New York seaports or National Football League teams. Similarly, substantial economies of scale mean that up to a point, bigness is better (i.e., technically more efficient) for the production of refrigerators, electricity, and many other goods. In these instances enforcement of perfect competition would be imprudent even if it was physically possible because the resulting costs of production would be much higher than necessary. Producing these goods is not the same as producing home-grown tomatoes.

Second, traditional theory suffers from what is called the **second-best theorem**. As originally formulated by R. Lipsey and K. Lancaster,[1] the second-best theorem holds that there are no reliable "second-best" policies that can be justified by the theory of perfect competition. The favorable result of price = marginal cost ($P = MC$), which perfect competition provides, must be achieved in *every* market of the economy if Pareto optimal results are to be achieved. In other words, the theory of perfect competition can justify an "all-or-nothing" policy, whereby price equals marginal cost in every market. But the second-best theorem says that overall welfare will not necessarily improve if we strive to impose perfect competition in some markets (say, wheat and corn) while at the same time we allow monopoly, or even oligopoly, in other markets (such as those for electricity, autos, and breakfast cereal). We have no *general* basis for believing that selective, partial achievement of perfect competition will improve resource allocation. Such second-best attempts might improve allocation efficiency. Then again, they might not. There is no way of knowing for sure.

And if, as we just noted in the first point, perfect competition is impossible for many markets, then theory provides no solid reason for enforcing perfect competition in any market. (Similarly, *all* of the conditions for perfect competition must be met in *all* markets in order to achieve Pareto optimality. Having competition without full information, for instance, would not, in general, be Pareto efficient.[2])

Third, these theories of competition and monopoly are severely limited by their *static* nature. In these models business managers easily maximize their short-run profits by producing a certain level of output with full knowledge of their *given* demand and cost constraints. They do not change their demand or cost conditions through innovation. They cannot affect the demands of their rivals by advertising. They do not

[1] R. Lipsey and K. Lancaster, "The General Theory of Second Best," *Review of Economic Studies*, Vol. 24 (1956–1957), pp. 11–32.

[2] Bruce Greenwald and Joseph E. Stiglitz, "Pareto Inefficiency of Market Economies," *American Economic Review* (May 1988), pp. 351–355.

invent new products or production processes. Business managers in these theories act as if they are shooting tin cans off fences with rifles. In fact, the real world is quite different. *Dynamics* intrude importantly, even overwhelmingly. As Lee Iacocca says, good managers must act as if they are duck hunting. They have to take into account the uncertain movement of their target by using a shotgun and aiming ahead of its flight path.[3] Indeed, this matter of dynamics is so important that it warrants extensive discussion.

II. DYNAMIC COMPETITION VERSUS MONOPOLY

Dynamic theories of competition and monopoly are much less refined than traditional theories. They are like scattershot as compared to a bullet. One reason for this is that dynamic theories are newer and less fully developed. Another reason is that they attempt to incorporate more realism, as the conditions for either perfect competition or pure monopoly very rarely actually occur. Finally, and perhaps most important, dynamic theories introduce a time dimension foreign to traditional theories. This introduces the vagaries of indeterminance, a variety of historical circumstances, and the vibrations of changing tastes and technologies, all of which complicate matters immensely. We consider "dynamic competition" first, then "dynamic monopoly."

A. Dynamic Competition

What is happening when ARCO drops credit cards and cuts the price of gasoline? What is happening when Apple Computer introduces a "friendly" new model called Macintosh for people who know nothing about computers? These are acts of vigorous competition, yet they spring from contexts that are not perfectly competitive at all. While perusing the description of dynamic competition following, notice that such competition does not require masses of firms, standardized products, or any of the other conditions of "perfect" competition.

    1. Dynamic Competition: Structure. Structurally, theories of dynamic competition often stress two features—industry life cycle and market imperfections. The **industry's life cycle,** as shown in Figures 2–9 and 2–10, divides into four distinct phases.[4]

---

[3] Lee Iacocca, *Iacocca: An Autobiography* (New York: Bantam Books, 1984), p. 56.
[4] For elaboration see Michael E. Porter, *Competitive Strategy* (New York: The Free Press, 1980), pp. 156–188.

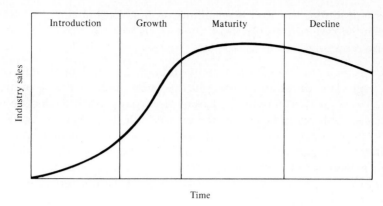

FIGURE 2–9. Industry life cycle over time.

Phase	Introduction	Growth	Maturity	Decline
Market growth rate	Rapid	Rapid	Slow-level	Negative
Market size	Small	Medium-expanding	Large	Contracting
Competition	Dominance by innovator, few firms	Entry, many competitors, shifting shares	Solidified shares, product stability	Exits, price competition
Profits	Variable, risky, high to low or negative	High and rising profits	Moderate to low profits	Low and falling profits

FIGURE 2–10. Industry life cycle and competition.

- *Introduction*, during which the product is just getting off the ground. The innovator, such as Atari in video games, may enjoy a period of dominance merely by virtue of its great innovative stride. But it faces substantial risk and profits may even be negative.

- *Growth*, during which time the market expands rapidly. Competition takes the form of new entry, new innovations, and new promotions. Market shares are fluid. Profits are typically high.

- *Maturity*, during which time growth subsides as the market reaches relatively large dimensions. Market shares and firm rankings solidify during this phase, and profits may settle at normal levels.

- *Decline*, during which time the market contracts and perhaps even disappears. Competition may center on price level and costs. Exits are prompted by low and falling profits. Decline in one industry may be caused by growth of another, as iceboxes gave way to electric refrigerators.

Of course this pattern fits many industries only loosely and others not at all. The duration of the phases varies widely. Some industries skip a phase or two, moving, for example, from growth to decline without pause. Still, as indicated in the appendix to this chapter, the theory yields several broad generalities that cannot be found in traditional, static theory. In particular, the dynamics of the cycle reveal situations where a fewness of firms need not indicate a lack of competition (the "introduction" phase) and where high profits may not reflect monopoly power (the "growth" phase). The kind of competition that emerges from "the new commodity, the new technology, the new source of supply, the new type of organization" is according to Joseph Schumpeter, a "process of creative destruction."[5]

As regards **structural imperfections,** the business rivalry that results from dynamic competition is itself a symptom of the absence of perfect competition.[6] For example, whereas the perfectly competitive firm is almost invisibly small, the theory of dynamic competition posits firms large enough to have noteworthy identities and to influence price. For another example, perfect competition assumes that buyers and sellers have perfect information while dynamic competition assumes imperfect information:

> In fact, the entrepreneur's role in society is to discover things which seem to meet such an obvious need that people will think the discoveries were invented by themselves. Or to put the point another way, entrepreneurs act as marriage brokers between that which is possible from a scientific and technological point of view and that which is desirable from an economic point of view.[7]

In the end, the theory of dynamic competition downplays the importance of structure altogether. Its main focus is conduct.

2. Dynamic Competition: Conduct. Dynamic competition could also be called *rivalrous competition*, for it assumes that firms vie with each other in ways not appreciated by the theory of perfect competition. According to J. M. Clark, for instance, dynamic competition "includes initiatory action by a firm, responses by those with whom it deals, and responses to these responses by rival firms, to which one could add the

---

5 Joseph A. Schumpeter, *Capitalism, Socialism, and Democracy* (New York: Harper Torchbooks, 1962), p. 84.

6 George W. Stocking and Willard F. Mueller, "The Cellophane Case and the New Competition," *American Economic Review* (March 1955), pp. 29–31.

7 Burton H. Klein, "Dynamic Competition and Economic Stability," in *Economics and Human Welfare*, edited by M. T. Boskin (New York: Academic Press, 1979), p. 300.

subsequent rejoinders of the initiators."[8] Moreover, these rivalrous actions may involve the entire range of business decision variables — selling prices, advertising promotions, product design, distribution channels, production processes, the lot. Thus a list of conduct characteristics would include the following:

- Dynamic competition is first and foremost an *activity* of sellers.
- Dynamic competition arises out of conscious attempts by firms to devise an *overall product offering* that will be perceived by buyers as more attractive.
- Dynamic competition entails an *independent* striving for patronage whereby firms employ various strategies and counterstrategies in efforts to outmaneuver one another over time.
- As the competitive process unfolds over the long term, active rivalry will result in firms both *creating* and *responding* to new market forces, market trends, and customer tastes and preferences.[9]

3. Dynamic Competition: Performance. The theory of dynamic competition does not offer highly refined definitions of allocation efficiency and production efficiency such as those derived from static theory. Still, a conceptual definition of dynamic efficiency is possible. As a first step recall than an industry's *static* efficiency would minimize net benefit in a given year. Hence in Figure 2–6 the static efficient output that maximizes the difference between total benefit (area under the demand) and total cost (area under the supply) is Q_1. In brief, $0GEQ_1 - 0HEQ_1 = HGE$ is the maximum net benefit in that static context. **Dynamic efficiency** would generalize static efficiency over time. It would maximize the *present value* of the *flow* of net benefits to be received from all possible ways of allocating our scarce resources over time. "Present value" is stressed because future values of net benefits must be discounted into present value form. Despite such discounting, it should be clear that sacrificing some present net benefits in order to invest in the creation of future innovations can pay off handsomely by generating large future net benefits. Twenty-first-century autos will get 100 miles per gallon of gas, for instance.

Similarly, some notion of **dynamic equity** could be imagined in principle. The general idea would be that you and I and other present-generation people should not "rip off" future generations. We should not take actions (like destruction of atmospheric ozone) that push the

---

[8] J. M. Clark, "Competition: Static Models and Dynamic Aspects," in *Readings in Industrial Organization and Public Policy*, edited by Heflebower and Stocking (Homewood, Ill.: Richard D. Irwin, 1958), p. 251.

[9] Adapted from Arthur A. Thompson, Jr., "Competition as a Strategic Process," *Antitrust Bulletin* (Winter 1980), pp. 789–790.

well-being of future generations down below our own well-being (their future net benefits being made comparable to our own by again discounting).

Unfortunately such *theoretical* notions of dynamic efficiency and dynamic equity are too vague to be of any real *practical* use. For instance, how can future values be accurately discounted into present values when we do not know the appropriate interest rate to be used in the discounting?[10] How can future values even be calculated given the radical and uncertain changes in tastes and technologies that routinely occur over time?[11] Hence, one cannot say where the steel industry, or any other industry, has been or will be in comparison to these dynamic ideals. One cannot say with certainty what structural changes or policy initiatives might "improve" the dynamic performance of the oil companies, or any other collection of enterprises.

Although dynamic ideals for performance thus lack details and specifics, they clearly point out the serious limitations of purely static ideals. We know, for instance, if only as a rough approximation of dynamic efficiency, that brisk technological change is better than static stagnation. Similarly, an appreciation of dynamic equity, vague though that concept might be, gives us some appreciation for the interests of future generations.

Dynamic competition is often said to perform well in these respects (1) when new products and services are developed to better meet the needs of buyers, (2) when new production processes emerge to lower costs and prices while at the same time maintaining or improving quality, and (3) when these new products and new processes spread rapidly into wide usage to promote a better standard of living in general. Reduced to a few words, good performance here implies brisk progress through improved varieties, qualities, and prices in response to changing circumstances and conditions.

Petrochemicals illustrate these points nicely. Dynamic competition has generated dozens of new and better petrochemical products. Once placed on the market, their product life cycles typically foster substantial reductions in real prices, as illustrated in Figure 2–11 for cyclohexane, methanol, and phenol. Prices decline for two reasons—the profit margins of producers are compressed, and the costs of production fall. R. B. Stobaugh and P. L. Townsend have studied the causes of compressed profit margins and falling production costs for 82 petrochemicals and their conclusions are summarized in Figure 2–12. There it may be seen that, first, the profit margin on a typical petrochemical product declines after its introduction because of increasing numbers of competing

10 R. C. Lind et al., *Discounting for Time and Risk in Energy Policy* (Washington, D.C.: Resources for the Future, 1982).

11 R. R. Nelson and S. G. Winter, *An Evolutionary Theory of Economic Change* (Cambridge, Mass.: Harvard University Press, 1982), pp. 355–356.

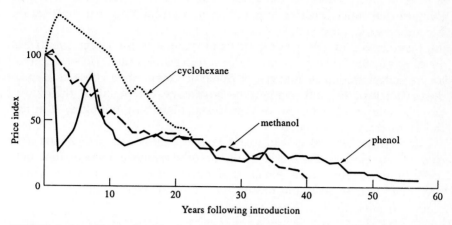

FIGURE 2–11. Price index trends in constant dollars for three petrochemical products from year of first availability through 1972. Source: Robert B. Stobaugh, *Innovation and Competition* (Boston, Mass.: Harvard Business School Press, 1988), p. 70.

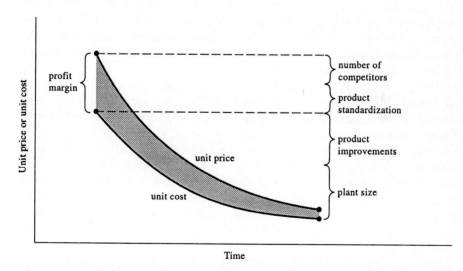

FIGURE 2–12. Causes of petrochemical price declines (summary for 82 products). Source: Robert B. Stobaugh and Phillip L. Townsend, "Price Forecasting and Strategic Planning: The Case of Petrochemicals," *Journal of Marketing Research* (February 1975), p. 20.

suppliers and greater product standardization. These are dynamic changes that reflect greater competition in a traditional, structural sense. Second, the per unit cost of production falls mainly because of process improvements and ever greater scales of plant size (the larger plant sizes yielding greater efficiencies through economies of scale). These developments reflect the consequences of dynamic competitive conduct as producers attempt to gain competitive advantages or maintain their positions by taking steps to reduce their costs (something not allowed in the theory of static competition).

In light of what was said just a few sentences ago, we cannot conclude from Figures 2–11 and 2–12, or other such evidence, that petrochemical markets have achieved dynamic efficiency or equity. Still, such evidence suggests the presence of dynamic competition.

B. Monopoly in a Dynamic Context

Perhaps the main conclusion to be drawn from the theory of dynamic competition is that, in the real world, we do not need to achieve the fairyland structural conditions of perfect competition to achieve *effective* competition and many economic benefits. Indeed, some "imperfections" or monopoly power may, after all, be desirable. A few economists press this conclusion to an extreme form, arguing that monopoly power *cannot* be attained or maintained except by firms who win the dynamic competitive race with superior efficiency, outstanding innovativeness, and other forms of good behavior and performance.[12] In this light, monopoly is not a problem. It may even be a solution.

Defenders of dominance notwithstanding, the introduction of dynamics does not do away with the problem of monopoly power. In a dynamic world monopoly power can be attained and maintained by artificial, restrictive means just as readily as by efficient, innovative means. Moreover, such monopoly power may adversely affect performance — stifling technological change, for instance, or fostering inefficiency. Indeed, many experts on market dynamics argue against monopoly in favor of numerous varied firms. In their view, good dynamic performance, innovation especially, requires that firms respond well to uncertain changes (for example, Iacocca's flying duck). And the best way for the market to respond well to uncertain changes is to have a variety of firms pursuing a variety of approaches to those changing conditions.[13]

The theories of monopoly in a dynamic context are much more complicated than the static theory outlined earlier. But five main points can be made.

---

12 Yale Brozen, *Concentration, Mergers, and Public Policy* (New York: Macmillan, 1982).

13 Burton H. Klein, *Dynamic Economics* (Cambridge, Mass.: Harvard University Press, 1977); Richard R. Nelson, *Understanding Technological Change as an Evolutionary Process* (New York: Elsevier Science, 1987); and A. Jacquemin, *The New Industrial Organization: Market Forces and Strategic Behavior* (Oxford: Clarendon Press, 1987).

First, a monopolist can often behave strategically, planning and acting to achieve long-run, anticompetitive aims.[14] For example, an established monopolist might build greater production capacity than is needed to meet immediate demand. This excess capacity would then deter the entry of new competitors. Such preemptive capacity would be costly to the established monopolist (and an inefficient use of scarce resources from society's point of view), but the strategy could prove to be highly profitable to the monopolist in the long run, more profitable than allowing competitive entry.[15] (As will be shown in later chapters, anticompetitive strategic behavior can occur because (1) large established firms typically have advantages over small rivals or potential entrants and (2) history is important because "first movers," like Xerox in the copy machine business, have advantages over "late movers."[16])

Second, the variables that can be used strategically to attain and maintain monopoly power artificially are for the most part the same variables that are used in the course of socially desirable dynamic competition. That is, a monopolist can use a number of "weapons" to gain strategic advantages over its rivals or potential entrants. These arms include predatory pricing, preemptive research and development, brand proliferation, product proliferation, and escalated advertising.[17] Each of these create short-run costs but generate long-run gains. Moreover, this list points out the fact that a firm's actions — such as price cutting or advertising — can be either *procompetitive* (as under the theory of dynamic competition) or *anticompetitive* (as under the theory of dynamic monopoly). The reader is thus duly warned that simple analyses and sweeping generalizations are rare in industrial organization economics.

Third, the main motive assumed for static theory is *short-run* profit maximization whereas the main motive assumed for dynamic theories is *long-run* profit maximization. This is true most obviously of monopolistic strategic behavior, as when for instance, a large predatory firm intentionally loses money in the short run in order to drive out rivals and thereby increase future profit.

[14] Steven C. Salop, "Strategic Entry Deterrence," *American Economic Review* (May 1979), pp. 335–338; and S. C. Salop and D. T. Scheffman, "Raising Rival's Costs," *American Economic Review* (May 1983), pp. 267–271.

[15] A. Michael Spence, "Entry, Capacity, Investment and Oligopolistic Pricing," *Bell Journal of Economics* (Autumn 1977), pp. 534–544.

[16] See, for example, W. J. Lane, "Product Differentiation in a Market with Endogenous Sequential Entry," *Bell Journal of Economics* (Spring 1980), pp. 237–260; or more generally, D. Encaoua, P. Geroski, and A. Jacquemin, "Strategic Competition and the Persistence of Dominant Firms," in *New Developments in the Analysis of Market Structure*, edited by J. E. Stiglitz and G. F. Mathewson (Cambridge, Mass.: MIT Press, 1986), pp. 55–86.

[17] See the papers by Steven Salop, Michael Spence, Richard Craswell, Richard Gilbert, Janusz Ordover, and Robert Willig in *Strategy, Predation, and Antitrust Analysis* (Washington, D.C.: Bureau of Economics, Federal Trade Commission, 1981). See also Richard Schmalensee "Entry Deterrence in the Ready-to-Eat Breakfast Cereal Industry," *Bell Journal of Economics* (Autumn 1978), pp. 305–327; Marius Schwartz and Earl Thompson, "Entry Patterns Under Decreasing Cost Conditions," Economic Policy Office Discussion Paper, Department of Justice (1983); and Oliver Williamson, "Predatory Pricing: A Strategic and Welfare Analysis," *Yale Law Journal* (December 1977), pp. 284–340.

Fourth, strategic practices that have monopolistic consequences tend to reverse the causal flows found in the traditional structure-conduct-performance model. In the traditional, static model, market structure causes certain kinds of conduct. Now we see that, conversely, strategic conduct can influence structure, as when monopoly is created by predatory conduct. In truth, *simultaneous* causal flows may often be at work in the real world — moving from structure to conduct and from conduct to structure simultaneously. For example, a fewness of sellers may cause intensive advertising while at the same time the intensive advertising may hold down the number of sellers. This obviously complicates analysis and evaluation.

Fifth, dynamics do not necessarily assure good economic performance, especially not in the presence of monopolistic motives and achievements.[18] The emphasis on product differentiation might lead to inefficient wastes — such as too much advertising, too much style change, and too many product varieties. (On the serious side, ask your ophthalmologist about the value of eye drops. On the lighter side, watch the new product horizon for bulletproof paper towels.) As regards worthwhile technological change, *some* market power may produce favorable results while *too much* might be undesirable.

III. WORKABLE COMPETITION

Where does all this leave us? We have explored the model of perfect competition, discovering some attractive properties that might be useful in evaluating real world industries. In particular, perfect competition yields allocative efficiency, something that cannot be said of monopoly. Production efficiency and equity are also apparently served by perfect competition, but less certainly so. Should we then adopt perfect competition as our ideal, pressing public policies to achieve that end? No. We have also learned that the perfectly competitive model is too remote from reality to provide proper guidance and, moreover, it may be downright undesirable. Notions of dynamic competition, which allow for some "imperfections" like product differentiation and which appreciate the importance of technological change, make up for these failings of the perfectly competitive model. Elements of dynamic competition should thus enter any final standard we adopt to evaluate industries. We cannot go so far as to say, however, that dynamics allow a standard so loose as to permit monopoly power that is artificially attained or maintained. Monopolists can use dynamics in their own interest against the public interest.

---

[18] Robin Marris and Dennis Mueller, "The Corporation, Competition, and the Invisible Hand," *Journal of Economic Literature* (March 1980), pp. 32–63.

What finally emerges, then, is the concept of **workable competition,** a set of *operational* norms or standards by which markets may be evaluated. In many ways, workable competition is a first cousin to perfect competition, if not a sibling. Factual *experience*, rather than theory, has shown that, even though the "perfection" of theory is not possible and probably undesirable, vigorous competition in the marketplace is generally better than no competition — better for political and social ends as well as for economic ends. Thus, borrowing heavily from F. M. Scherer, we conclude this chapter with an outline of some of the criteria of "workability" that have evolved in the literature:"[19]

Structural Norms

1. The number of traders should be at least as large as scale economies and industry life cycle permit.
2. There should be no artificial inhibitions on mobility and entry.
3. Where appropriate, there should be moderate and price-sensitive quality differentials in the products offered.
4. Buyers should be well informed about prices, quality, and other relevant data.

Conduct Criteria

5. Some uncertainty should exist in the minds of rivals as to whether price initiatives will be followed.
6. Firms should strive to achieve their goals independently, without collusion.
7. There should be no unfair, exclusionary, predatory, or coercive tactics.
8. Inefficient suppliers and customers should not be shielded permanently.
9. Sales promotion should not be misleading.
10. Persistent, harmful price discrimination should be absent.

Performance Criteria

11. Firms' production operations should be efficient.
12. Promotional expenses should not be excessive.
13. Profits should be at levels just sufficient to reward investment, efficiency, and innovation.

[19] F. M. Scherer, *Industrial Market Structure and Economic Performance* (Chicago: Rand McNally, 1970), p. 37. For other reviews of workable competition, see S. Sosnick, "A Critique of Concepts of Workable Competition," *Quarterly Journal of Economics* (August 1958), pp. 380–423; and H. H. Liebhafsky, *American Government and Business* (New York: John Wiley, 1971), pp. 236–262.

14. Output levels and the range of qualities should be responsive to consumer demands.
15. Opportunities for introducing technically superior new products and processes should be exploited.
16. Success should accrue to sellers who best serve consumer wants.

It should be obvious that this approach is basically pragmatic, somewhat rough and ready, largely judgmental, certainly "unscientific," and rather imprecise. As H. H. Liebhafsky says, "Such an approach is not satisfactory to anyone who either believes that it is possible to achieve absolute certainty or who is driven into an attempt to achieve it as a matter of his personal emotional makeup."[20] Moreover, value judgments unavoidably enter any application of these criteria. Scherer correctly points out, for instance, that on many of the variables a line must be drawn separating "enough" from "not enough" or "too much." How much uncertainty should exist in the minds of rivals as to whether their price initiatives will be followed? How moderate should quality differentials be? What constitutes misleading sales promotion? How long must price discrimination persist before it becomes persistent? And so on.[21] Moreover, these various criteria need not be given equal weight. And when some criteria are satisfied but not others, how is one to determine workability? If performance is fairly good but structure is irregular, what then?

Some of the values that may influence our judgments on these issues were discussed earlier in Chapter 1. In subsequent chapters we shall discover what specific judgments have been made in the past. We shall also develop a body of information from which you the reader may fashion your own informed judgments. In any case, you should recognize that workable competition is, despite its many flaws, the best standard available.[22]

SUMMARY

Table 2–3 outlines the main theoretical models we have covered — static and dynamic. The traditional static model defines perfect competition in structural terms — that is, a large number of small sellers producing a standardized product which could easily be produced by new entrants (if high profits attracted them). With price given by marketwide forces of demand and supply, perfectly competitive firms maximize short-run

---

[20] Liebhafsky, *American Government and Business.* p. 261.
[21] Scherer, *Industrial Market Structure and Economic Performance*, p. 37.
[22] Indeed, "the very fact that it does not offer cut and dried solutions makes a welcome contrast to the spurious precision of marginalist theory." See D. Swann, D. P. O'Brien, W. P. J. Maunder and W. Stewart Howe, *Competition in British Industry* (London: Allen & Unwin, 1974), p. 109.

TABLE 2–3. Outline of Main Theories of Competition and Monopoly

Feature	Static Theory	Dynamic Theory
Definition of competition	Atomistic structure with standardized product and easy entry	Centered on rivalrous conduct concerning price, promotion, and product innovation
Main motive assumed	Short-run profit maximization	Long-run profit maximization
Direction of causal flow	From structure to conduct to performance	Both ways, including conduct causing structural change
Competition's benefits	Allocation and production efficiency plus equity	Technological progress plus some differentiation
Source of monopoly power	Structural conditions	Strategic behavior as well as structural conditions
Monopoly's main drawbacks	Allocation inefficiency and income inequity	Slow technological change and inefficiencies

profits by producing where price and marginal revenue equal marginal cost. The resulting overall performance is ideal in terms of allocation and production efficiency. Given no more than "normal" profits, it is likely to be good in terms of equity as well.

The traditional static model of monopoly posits structural conditions of an opposite sort—namely, a solitary firm unworried by threats of entry producing a product with no close substitutes. The MC = MR profit rule holds again, but the downward-sloping demand curve facing the monopolist causes price to exceed marginal revenue and therefore also to exceed marginal cost. With price greater than marginal cost, allocation inefficiency results. Moreover, the associated excess profits can create inequities.

Dynamic theory introduces some realism, mainly by introducing a time dimension that allows significant volatility and change. Dynamic competition centers on rivalrous conduct, motivated by long-run profit maximization and concerning such diverse variables as price, product quality, promotion, and innovation. Technological progress is the main benefit claimed for such rivalry. Some product differentiation might also be deemed desirable under certain circumstances. Unfortunately, monopolistic evils lurk in a dynamic world as well as a static world. They can take the form of strategic behavior that bolsters monopoly and hinders entry. Poor innovative performance is another possibility.

When trying to devise a reasonable set of standards to depict desirable structure, conduct, and performance, elements of both theories can be blended into what may be called workable competition. This standard assumes that vigorous competition is good, but shies away from insisting on "perfect" competition. This standard has its vaguenesses and is therefore imperfect. But it also has the attraction of being practical. The characteristics of workable competition are outlined on the pages immediately preceding.

APPENDIX TO CHAPTER 2: EVIDENCE ON PRODUCT LIFE CYCLES

The year 1988 marked the 50th birthday of Teflon®, Du Pont's nonstick coating. Its old age might suggest that Teflon® was stuck in a rut, with sales stagnating or even falling as the twenty-first century approached. However, according to *The Wall Street Journal*, that 50th birthday found Du Pont diligently trying to avoid the doldrums of a "mature product."

> Du Pont's search for new products [using Teflon] is accelerating and advertising budgets and sales forces are being strengthened. . . . This spring, for example, the . . . chemicals giant will introduce Teflon in a spray can. The company envisions customers coating neckties with it to repel food stains and spraying wall and light switches to protect against dirty fingers.[23]

This indicates that product life cycles vary across products and may be manipulated by producers. Still, regularities are sufficiently strong to be important.

Both the varieties and the regularities are illustrated in the research of Michael Gort and Steven Klepper.[24] They define five stages according to the number of firms in the market, as follows:

1. *Introduction:* The first producer (innovator) and a few early imitators in the market.
2. *Growth:* A sharp increase in the number of firms due to many new entries.
3. *Maturity:* The number of entrants is balanced by the number of exits, so firm numbers level off at a peak.
4. *Decline:* Exits exceed entries in a "shake out" causing the number of firms to fall.
5. *Stability:* A second period of zero net entry, that may continue for some time before eventual decline and demise.

---

23 *The Wall Street Journal*, April 7, 1988, p. 1.
24 Michael Gort and Steven Klepper, "Time Paths in the Diffusion of Product Innovations," *Economic Journal* (September 1982), pp. 630–653.

TABLE 2–4. Changing Conditions over Product Life Cycle, Average Data for 46 Products

Variable	Stage of Life Cycle				
	I	II	III	IV	V
Annual net entry rate (new firms per year)	0.5	5.7	0.1	-4.8	-0.5
Number of years in stage indicated	14.4	9.7	7.5	5.4	—
Change in output during stage (annual percentage)*	56.6	35.1	12.3	8.1	1.0
Change in price during stage (annual percentage)*	-13.6	-13.0	-7.2	-9.0	-5.2
Number of important innovations per year*	0.24	0.29	0.28	0.24	0.26

*Data for these variables were unavailable for all 46 products, so the averages are based on observations for 23 to 25 products.

Source: Michael Gort and Steven Klepper, "Time Paths in the Diffusion of Product Innovations," *Economic Journal* (September 1982), pp. 630–653.

Next they analyzed data on 46 products. Regarding varieties, the number of years spanned by stage I varied from 50 for artificial Christmas trees and 41 for gyroscopes, down to zero (a matter of just months) for penicillin and fluorescent lamps. The regularities may be seen in Table 2–4. During stage I introduction the entry of new firms into the market starts out very slowly (1 every 2 years on average, or 0.5 per year). Thereafter entry jumps to a rate of 5.7 firms per year, levels off in stage III (when exits roughly match entries), turns negative when exits exceed entries during "shakeouts," and then finally approaches renewed stability. Data in the second row show the average duration of the stages falling over time. Similarly, the greatest percentage increases in output and reductions in prices occur in the early stages, followed by more modest changes in the later stages. As regards the intensity of innovative activity in the market, that too varies over the life cycle. The data in the bottom row show innovation reaching a peak during the "growth" of stage II.

3

■ The Firm and Its Motives

Nobody at Chrysler seemed to understand that interaction among the different functions in a company is absolutely critical. People in engineering and manufacturing almost have to be sleeping together. These guys weren't even flirting!
—LEE IACOCCA (explaining why Chrysler Corporation was on the brink of collapse when he took over as CEO)

Markets dominate this book's story. The key economic decisions of What? How? Who? and What's new? are made primarily in markets. **Firms** play secondary roles. Yet they are also immensely important because many key decisions are made entirely inside firms. Moreover, firms participate in market decision making. Hence this chapter is devoted to firms.

That firms are quite different from markets is suggested by Lee Iacocca. Effective operation of a firm typically requires close and continuous relations among its employees, who more or less pull together for some common purpose. In contrast, your market participation as a car buyer or coffee drinker entails no such intimacy, either with sellers or with other buyers. That firms differ from markets is further suggested by the questions tackled in this chapter.

1. What is the "firm"?
2. Why do firms exist to the extent they do?
   a. What are the benefits of having firms (as opposed to just having markets)?

     b. What are the costs of having firms (as opposed to just having markets)?

     c. How can the firm's benefits be maximized relative to its costs?

3. Do firms maximize profits, as traditional theory assumes?

4. Is the profit maximizing of traditional theory feasible?

5. What is the "managerialism" critique of traditional theory?

6. What is the "behaviorist" critique of traditional theory?

We take each issue in turn.

I. THE FIRM: DEFINITION AND IDENTIFICATION

A. Definition

Defining the "firm" might *seem* an easy task. Prominent examples abound—Chrysler Corporation, IBM, and General Electric, to name three. Yet defining the "firm" is actually complicated. Your family dentist runs a firm, but it has little in common with Exxon or General Motors. Moreover, every scholar who studies the firm in the abstract seems to arrive at a different definition.

In traditional neoclassical theory a firm is a profit-maximizing entity that operates very mechanically. All members of the neoclassical firm work in perfect harmony, with full information, and always to the utmost of their ability. More recently, several contrary schools of commentary about the firm have sprouted, including the "transaction-cost," "X-efficiency," "principal-agent," and "sociological" approaches.[1]

These modern theories all agree that the traditional neoclassical firm does not exist (except in outdated textbooks). They agree that the neoclassical firm is much too simplistic to be realistic. Beyond this common ground, however, the new theories diverge. In the "transaction-cost" view, firms grow in internal organization and size in order to minimize transaction costs (which will be defined later). In this view corporate growth is always good because it reflects added efficiency. On the other hand, the "X-efficiency" view holds that large firms grow *despite* the serious *in*efficiencies associated with their huge size.

We shall not attempt to compare and contrast all the various theoretical viewpoints. Instead, we shall try to summarize some of the strongest voices in the literature, stressing areas of agreement among them.

---

[1] For surveys, see Beth V. Yarbrough and Robert M. Yarbrough, "The Transactional Structure of the Firm," *Journal of Economic Behavior and Organization*, Vol. 10 (1988), pp. 1–28; Paul Milgrom and John Roberts, "Economic Theories of the Firm: Past, Present, and Future," *Canadian Journal of Economics* (August 1988), pp. 444–458; and Roger Clarke and Tony McGuinness (eds.), *The Economics of the Firm* (Oxford: Basil Blackwell, 1987).

In defining the "firm," three main characteristics deserve emphasis: (1) *collectivity* of people in an organization, (2) action by superior-subordinate *direction*, and (3) *continuity* over time due to incomplete contracts among those in the organization. Each of these characteristics contrasts with some major characteristic of the market.

First, the **collectivity characteristic** of the firm implies a group of people working together in some way. The group may be small—as is true of the receptionist, dental hygienist, and DDS in a dentist's firm. Or the group may include several hundreds of thousands of employees, as is true of General Motors. The idea that all these people are supposed to be on the same team is conveyed by our opening quote from Lee Iacocca. In contrast, those in the "market" typically act *individually*. Buyers in a market, for instance, usually extend no effort at coordination.

Second, the firm is characterized by some degree of hierarchy, in which superiors with authority give **direction** to subordinates. This point needs qualification. It cannot be said that *all* firm decisions are hierarchical. Many of them are reached by democratic procedures and individual employee discretion. Still, direction is a distinguishing feature of the firm.[2] The market operates on free and voluntary *exchange* instead of direction.

Third, there is **continuity** to a firm that arises from the incomplete "contracts" that hold the firm's members together. In the market, contracts are usually completed, ending with the market transaction itself. The result is some degree of discontinuity in the market. When you attend a major league baseball game, for instance, you pay your money, watch the game, and then depart the ballpark. That's it. On the other hand, those who work for the teams (firms) in the game—the ball players, managers, and coaches—have continuing relationships with their firms. This is so because their contracts are "incomplete." The contracts say, in essence, "play, manage, and coach as well as you can, exercising your best judgment in the process." A firm's workers must thus work to complete their contracts. They exercise considerable discretion, day to day, in the process.

---

[2] This is illustrated by Lee Iacocca's story of why Henry Ford II (CEO of Ford) fired Bunkie Knudsen (president of Ford) in 1969:

> I wish I could say that Bunkie got fired because he ruined the Mustang or because his ideas were all wrong. But the actual reason for the firing was nothing like that. Bunkie Knudsen was fired because he used to walk into Henry's office without knocking. That's right—without knocking! . . .
>
> Of course, this minor transgression was merely the last straw in a relationship that had never been very good to begin with. Henry was a king who could tolerate no equals, a point Bunkie never seemed to grasp. He tried to get palsy-walsy with Henry, and that was a big mistake.

See Lee Iacocca, *Iacocca: An Autobiography* (New York: Bantam Books, 1984), pp. 95–96.

In light of these several characteristics, here is a short definition of the **firm:**[3]

[A] coalition among owners of separately owned resources [including labor] whose value as a team exceeds the sum of the market values each could get separately.[4]

B. Identification: The Corporation

Of all the "firms" in our economy, those of greatest significance are corporations — which are distinct from proprietorships and partnerships. A **corporation** is a firm created by government charter. The law grants certain powers, privileges, and liabilities to the corporation, as if it were an entity separate from the stockholder-owners. Although the population of corporations comprises only about 20% of all business firms in simple numbers, the corporate form is paramount because it accounts for over 90% of all private business activity in the U.S. economy measured by sales revenues. Table 3–1, which reports basic data on some of America's largest corporations, hints as much.

Figure 3–1 sketches the hierarchy embodied by a simple corporate structure. Figure 3–1 also identifies some of the members of the "coalition" constituting the typical "firm" as defined previously. They are stockholder-owners, members of the board of directors, managers (including vice presidents, heads of departments, and most critically the chief executive officer), and the regular employees. In *theory*, the hierarchy is as depicted, with stockholder-owners in command. The stockholders elect a board of directors to represent their views. The board meets only infrequently, and it does not make daily decisions. However, the board supposedly hires and fires managing officers according to how well they serve the owners' interests. Their power corresponds to placement.

In *practice*, the managers, not the stockholder-owners, control most major corporations. Only stockholders or *proxyholders* who attend the annual meeting of owners can cast votes in the election of directors. The emphasis here is on proxyholders because the stockholders of most major corporations are too numerous, too apathetic, too timid, and too far-flung geographically to attend the annual meetings. Hence the usual election procedure is for *management* to nominate a slate of candidates and then ask the stockholders for proxies, that is, permission to use the stockholders' votes on behalf of this slate of candidates. Ninety-nine percent of the time a majority of stockholders sign over their proxies to management. In short, the managers select and control the board. In-

---

[3] For a long definition see Felix R. FitzRoy and Dennis C. Mueller, "Cooperation and Conflict in Contractual Organizations," *Quarterly Review of Economics and Business* (Winter 1984), pp. 24–49.

[4] Armen A. Alchian and Susan Woodward, "The Firm Is Dead; Long Live the Firm," *Journal of Economic Literature* (March 1988), pp. 65–79.

TABLE 3–1.   Some of America's Largest Industrial Firms, 1989

Rank	Company	Main Line of Business	Sales (billions)
1	General Motors	Motor vehicles	$127.0
2	Ford Motor	Motor vehicles	96.9
3	Exxon	Oil and gasoline	86.7
4	IBM	Computers	63.4
5	General Electric	Electronics and TV	55.3
6	Mobil	Oil and gasoline	51.0
7	Philip Morris	Tobacco, beer, food	39.1
8	Chrysler	Motor vehicles	36.2
9	Du Pont	Chemicals	35.2
10	Texaco	Oil and gasoline	32.4
11	Chevron	Oil and gasoline	29.4
14	Procter & Gamble	Detergents, paper	21.7
15	Boeing	Aircraft	20.3
18	Eastman Kodak	Photo supplies	18.4
21	Xerox	Copy machines	17.6
23	Pepsico	Food and drinks	15.4
37	Alcoa	Aluminum	11.1

Source: *Fortune*, April 23, 1990, p. 346.

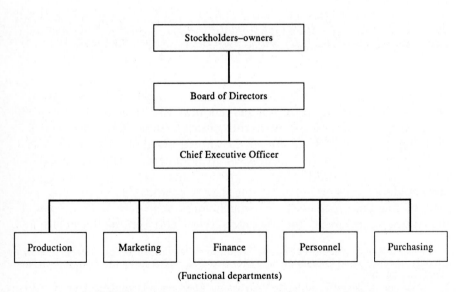

(Functional departments)

FIGURE 3–1. Corporation structure: U-form organization.

TABLE 3–2.   Summary According to Type of Ultimate Control of the 200 Largest Nonfinancial U.S. Corporations, 1974 and 1929

Type of Control	Number of Corporations		Proportion of Companies	
	1929	1974	1929	1974
Management control	81	165	40.5%	82.5%
Minority control	65	29	32.5	14.5
Private or majority ownership	19	3	9.5	1.5
Other (e.g., legal device)	35	3	17.5	1.5
Total	200	200	100%	100%

Source: Edward S. Herman, *Corporate Control, Corporate Power* (Cambridge: Cambridge University Press, 1981), pp. 58–64.

deed, managers *themselves* hold a majority of seats on the boards of many major corporations. "The board of directors becomes, in effect, a rubberstamping body routinely approving the decisions and recommendations of management rather than an independent watchdog with a vigilant eye to the interests and desires of the corporation's owners."[5]

The extend and trend of management control over corporations in the United States is illustrated in Table 3–2. The data refer to the top 200 corporations in 1929 and 1974. It is easy to see that among these firms management control predominates and is on the rise. In 1929, 40.5% of the top 200 qualified for the management-control category, more than any other group. By 1974 this percentage reached 82.5%. The only remaining bastion of stockholder control is so-called "minority control," in which no single owner or close-knit group of owners holds more than a majority of outstanding shares, but a big chunk of the voting stock is in the hands of an influential individual, family, or group of business associates.

Of course, owners retain the option of buying and selling stock, no matter how diverse or detached they may be. Furthermore, such buying and selling conceivably offers a means of rewarding and punishing management. If it does, stockholders are not irredeemably "poor cousins in the corporate family, ignored by a management which, if not feathering its own nest with bonuses and stock options, is yielding to the greater pressure of unions, customers, and government."[6] Rather, stockholders

[5] Robert Larner, *Management Control and the Large Corporation* (New York: Dunellen, 1970), p. 3.

[6] Shorey Peterson, "Corporate Control and Capitalism," *Quarterly Journal of Economics* (February 1965), pp. 3, 20–21.

are catered to and pampered as a source of capital, even though most capital is raised from other sources. Economists who hold this view argue that the equity investor is not so unlikely a source of capital as to suffer anyone to treat him highhandedly. Unfortunately, this argument is often exaggerated. Such indirect stock market control cannot be stringent. At best, share trading is a long leash. After analyzing this form of control in some detail, Oliver Williamson concluded that "individually and collectively, capital market controls experience weaknesses sufficient to warrant much of the expressed concern over the separation of ownership from control in the large corporation."[7]

The threat of a "takeover" is today the main way in which the capital market could urge managers to act in the owners' interests. A **takeover** occurs when an acquiring firm buys enough stock to gain ownership control of a target firm and then replaces the old directors and management staff with new blood. The idea here is that, if the target firm's stock market value could be increased with new and better management, then the acquiring firm would be acting rationally to buy the outstanding shares of stock from current stockholders, even paying a premium price for the stock. The acquiring firm could then remove the bad management, improve decision making, and thereby increase the earnings of the target firm to make money from the takeover. TWA, Phillips Petroleum, and Irving Bank are among the many major companies that have been the targets of actual or threatened takeover in recent years.

The takeover threat is *not* a fully effective means of controlling management, however.[8] This is true for several reasons. First, there are *information problems*. A firm may be doing poorly not because of bad management but because of extraneous setbacks, such as bad luck in oil exploration. In this case successful takeovers offer no rewards to acquiring firms, something that generally discourages takeovers motivated by prospective management improvements. Second, rewards to acquiring firms are severely limited by *competition among acquirers*. The poorly managed target firm may become a small "gold mine" with prospectors vying for ownership rights and bidding up the price of those rights in the process. If forced to pay high prices in this way, acquiring firms will be discouraged because their efforts will go unrewarded and they may even experience losses. Indeed, evidence indicates that acquisition activ-

---

[7] Oliver Williamson, *Corporate Control and Business Behavior* (Englewood Cliffs, NJ.: Prentice-Hall, 1970), p. 104. Empirical support for this position is provided by B. Hindley, "Separation of Ownership and Control in the Modern Corporation," *Journal of Law and Economics* (April 1970), pp. 185–210.

[8] Dieter Helm, "Mergers, Take-overs, and the Enforcement of Profit Maximization," in *Mergers and Merger Policy*, edited by J. A. Fairburn and J. A. Kay (Oxford: Oxford University Press, 1989), pp. 133–147.

ity is a losing proposition on average.[9] Third, managers of prospective target firms can engage in *defensive* tactics to protect themselves against takeover threats. These tactics include:

1. The staggered board, in which directors' terms are altered to prevent expiration at the same time.
2. The supermajority, which changes corporate bylaws to require that buyouts be approved by a very large percentage of shareholders, often 80%.
3. The scorched earth, in which a firm sells valuable proprieties or proposes a financing program that makes it unattractive to suitors.

Finally, some firms may enjoy *natural immunities*. For example, everything else being equal, a firm's susceptibility to takeover is inversely related to its size; the larger the firm the less likely it will become a target (because huge size reduces the number of prospective acquirers and typically complicates the financing of the takeover). Indeed, some poor managers may try to build immunity by enlarging the size of their firms through the acquisition of others. If so, takeovers then become a means of protecting poor managers rather than a means of ousting or disciplining them.[10] In summary, then, takeover threats may keep managers from deviating too far from the stockholders' desired direction, but managers typically sit in the drivers' seat, enjoying very substantial "control."

II. WHY DO FIRMS EXIST TO THE EXTENT THEY DO?

The market economies of the United States, Japan, and the European Economic Community have been spectacularly successful in comparison to the nonmarket economies of the communist countries. Apparently, the market is a fantastic decision-making institution. Why, then, do firms exist at all? And why is it that firms account for an enormous share of all economic decisions, a share that over the long run appears to be expanding with the disproportionate growth of gigantic firms? If, as Milgrom and Roberts put it, "market-mediated transactions work so well, why don't firms hire more inputs—both products and services— from independent suppliers in the market?"

---

[9] D. J. Ravenscraft and F. M. Scherer, *Mergers, Sell-offs, and Economic Efficiency* (Washington, D.C.: Brookings Institution, 1987); and Alan Hughes, "The Impact of Merger: A Survey of the Evidence for the UK," in Fairburn and Kay (eds.) *Mergers and Merger Policy*, pp. 30–98.

[10] D. F. Greer, "Acquiring in Order to Avoid Acquisition," *Antitrust Bulletin* (Spring 1986), pp. 155–186. More generally, see R. A. Walkling and M. S. Long, "Agency Theory, Managerial Welfare, and Takeover Bid Resistance," *Rand Journal of Economics*, Vol. 15 (1984), pp. 54–68.

Why do [firms] so often distribute and sell their own products? Mine their own raw materials? Provide their own personnel, accounting, computer, and other services?[11]

The answer is that firms have certain advantages over markets as decision making institutions. The resources comprising the firm are therefore worth more in coalition than separately. The advantages, or "benefits," are discussed in Section A. Despite its considerable advantages, the firm also has certain institutional shortcomings, or "costs," which limit the firm as an alternative to the market. Section B covers these. Finally, Section C discusses some devices that managerial science has developed to maximize the firm's benefits while minimizing its costs.

A. The Firm's Benefits

Different theorists stress different benefits. We shall briefly review four: (1) specialization in teams, (2) transaction-cost economizing, (3) enlarged capital formation, and (4) morale boosting.

1. Specialization in Teams: Figure 3-1 identifies production, marketing, finance, and several other special activities that go into a firm's operation. The idea that specialization increases productivity and efficiency is an ancient one. Adam Smith illustrated the point by referring to a pin factory in *The Wealth of Nations* (1776). Although specialization is readily observed in firms, it alone cannot be credited as a benefit of the firm. After all, specialization also lies behind the exchange process of the market, where "specialists" in effect exchange their outputs. Therefore it is resource specialization plus teamwork that distinguishes the firm, allowing the collective value of the resources to exceed their separate values. As Alchian and Woodward remark,

> We observe that in most cooperative production (teamwork), people show up for work at the same place every day. . . . Team members are more productive working together than working separately, and this differential at least partly depends on knowledge of one another's personal talents.[12]

2. Transaction-Cost Savings: In 1937 Ronald Coase advanced the theory that the firm has significant advantages in being able to carry out some transactions more cheaply than the market.[13] To appreciate this view, note that buying a $180,000 house is a transaction that entails costs other than the $180,000 passing directly between the buyer and seller. There are "transaction costs" arising from shopping time, termite

---

11 Milgrom and Roberts, "Economic Theories of the Firm," p. 445.
12 Alchian and Woodward, "The Firm Is Dead; Long Live the Firm," p. 70.
13 R. M. Coase, "The Nature of the Firm," *Economica* Vol. 4 (1937), pp. 386–405.

inspection, realtor services, title insurance, mortgage application, escrow, and so on. Coase identified the costs of negotiating agreements and determining appropriate prices as the chief costs of market-mediated transactions.

More recently, Oliver Williamson has argued "that the modern corporation is mainly to be understood as the product of a series of organizational innovations that have the purpose and effect of economizing transactions costs."[14] Moreover, Williamson has taken pains to specify what "transaction costs" he has in mind. He stresses three dimensions along which transactions may vary: asset specificity, uncertainty, and frequency. By "asset specificity," Williamson refers to the fact that some assets are of value only or mainly to a specific firm, while other assets are not "specific" to the firm because they have value elsewhere as well. (Candlestick Park is asset specific to the San Francisco 49ers, but Jerry Rice is not because he could play for any other NFL team if traded.) By "uncertainty," Williamson is recognizing that circumstances continually change, precluding certainty about the future. An organization that is adaptive is therefore needed. (If Jerry Rice gets injured, a backup receiver to catch Joe Montana's passes would be required.) By "frequency," Williamson means the extent to which transactions are often repeated or consolidated into long-term contracts. Retaining the services of a worker or machine could be renegotiated daily or weekly, but the transaction costs of that high frequency would be burdensome. To summarize, then, the firm saves on transaction costs (compared to the market) because it curbs the protracted bargaining that arises from asset specificity, it facilitates the adaptability necessary to cope with uncertainty, and it reduces the frequency of transactions.

The contribution of the firm is easy to see for uncertainty and frequency. The contribution of the firm is more difficult to see regarding asset specificity, but the basic idea is this. The firm's coalition of assets creates a "surplus value" or "rents," as we'll see. Who gets the surplus? That is decided in the terms and conditions of the transactions, as negotiated by bargaining. Williamson argues that the transactions involving specific assets become very costly if the negotiations break down into intense bargaining, with bluffs, impasses, and so on. Such is particularly possible when each negotiator must protect himself against any "opportunistic behavior" by another, as those with specific assets might be exploited by those with more mobile assets. For example, if an electric power plant locates close to a coal mine on the expectation of cheap fuel, it must guard against the coal company taking the "opportunity" to raise its price of coal after the electricity plant is built, perhaps by

[14] Oliver E. Williamson, *The Economic Institutions of Capitalism* (New York: The Free Press, 1985).

owning the coal company.[15] By internalizing transactions involving specific assets, the firm can minimize bargaining costs because all gains and losses at stake will then likewise be internalized to the firm. With the stakes internalized, there is, in a sense, nothing more at stake to cause wasteful bargaining.

Some empirical support for Williamson's theory comes from studies of vertical integration, whereby a single firm spans several stages of the production process. Observed instances of vertical integration are often associated with reduced transaction costs.[16]

3. Corporate Capital Formation: Frank Knight recognized in 1921 that financial resources for short-term investments (like employee training and inventories) and long-term investments (like R&D and manufacturing plants) constitute the blood supply and bone structure of an ongoing enterprise. Easy access to abundant financial capital would therefore be favorable to firm formation and growth. Here the corporate form of organization has advantages over all others.[17] Unlike proprietorships or partnerships, corporations can sell shares of company ownership in the form of common stock or preferred stock. Moreover, "limited liability" protects these shareholders. The upshot of all this is that corporate firms can undertake hugely expensive and risky projects well beyond the means of the typical individual market transactor — projects like building 747 aircraft and $1 billion steel plants — that are immensely beneficial to the economy.

4. Morale. A final benefit of the firm is a sense of belonging, a spirit of communal worth for the people in it. This is similar to the proud feelings people gain from association with a particular university, or a fraternity, or from merely living in the same city that is home to a championship football team. Of course this matter of good morale is not necessarily part of all firms. But it is fairly clear that individual participation in impersonal markets cannot provide a similar benefit.[18]

---

[15] This example of opportunism is called "holdup." Another form of opportunisim is "moral hazard," which arises when one person relies on the behavior of another (as you might rely on an agent to find you movie roles if you were an actor) and information about that behavior is costly to come by (as you might have difficulty checking on the diligence of your agent).

[16] Richard E. Caves and Ralph M. Bradburd, "The Empirical Determinants of Vertical Integration," *Journal of Economic Behavior and Organization*, Vol. 9 (1988), pp. 265–279; and Jean-Francois Hennart, "Upstream Vertical Integration in the Aluminum and Tin Industries," *Journal of Economic Behavior and Organization*, Vol. 9 (1988), pp. 281–299.

[17] Frank Knight, *Risk, Uncertainty, and Profit* (Chicago: University of Chicago Press, 1971).

[18] This could be labeled the "sociological view." See, for example, Yarbrough and Yarbrough, The Traditional Structure of the Firm, p. 8.

B. The Firm's Costs

If the firm's characteristics of collectivity, direction, and continuity were associated with nothing but benefits, then firms would completely supplant markets. If that were the case, the entire economy might best be run by a single enormous firm. However, the firm incurs costs.[19] These limit the incidence and scope of firms. The costs include (1) shirking in pursuit of leisure, (2) agent misdirection, and (3) rent seeking.

1. Shirking: Because the firm is a team of people, the contributions of individual team members are sometimes difficult or impossible to measure. This gives workers opportunities for on-the-job leisure, or shirking, in a narrow sense of the word. Such shirking can be costly because of its inherent inefficiency. Efforts to reduce shirking through intensified employee monitoring may reduce the costs of shirking by reducing its incidence, but those monitoring efforts themselves entail costs, so the problem is inherent to the firm.[20]

2. Agent Misdirection. Because of its hierarchy, the firm embodies several "principal-agent" relationships. A "principal" delegates an "agent" to take some actions on the principal's behalf. The agent is often an expert, as is the real estate agent you would hire to sell your house. Thus, in the typical corporate firm, owners are principals who hire managers as their agents. Problems (and costs) arise when these agents pursue goals that are not in the interests of their principals. For example, managers may not be lazy shirkers, but they may diminish the owner's profit by spending lavishly on their office furnishings, private jets, and other perks.[21] For another example, a top scientist employed by the firm may strive more to win the Nobel Prize than to invent a commercially viable product. Whatever the nature of the agent's misdirection, the behavior imposes costs on the firm.

3. Rent Seeking. The "surplus" or "rents" associated with the firm stimulate efforts by those in the firm to capture the rents. This creates costs. As Milgrom and Roberts explain,

> [The] mere willingness of the center [management] to consider seriously a decision with large redistributional consequences will cause other economic agents to waste significant resources in attempts to influence or block it or to delay its implementation. . . . In bureaucracies—private as well as pub-

[19] Harvey Leibenstein, *Inside the Firm: The Inefficiencies of Hierarchy* (Cambridge, Mass.: Harvard University Press, 1987).
[20] A. A. Alchian and H. Demsetz, "Production Information Costs and Economic Organization," *American Economic Review*, Vol. 62 (1972), pp. 777–795.
[21] In 1989 the stockholders of Occidental Petroleum filed a class-action suit to prevent Armand Hammer, the company's CEO, from spending $86 million in corporate money on a museum to house his private art collection. *The Wall Street Journal*, May 12, 1989, p. A3B.

lic—individuals angle for promotions and projects, and advocate rule changes that enhance their power or status.[22]

In short, the pulling and tugging that is prompted by the surplus, as people try to get their hands on it, raises costs.

C. Managing the Firm

The firm is thus an institution generating benefits *and* costs. Management methods may therefore be conceived, very roughly, as efforts to maximize the net difference between the two—that is, benefits *minus* costs. Here we have space to mention a few basic ideas along these lines.

1. Monitor and Punish. Perhaps the most obvious way to discourage shirking or misdirection is to monitor and punish such behavior. On-site supervision and time clocks are examples of this. Early in this century "scientific management" became synonymous with efforts of this sort. Jobs, especially factory jobs, were broken down into very simple tasks that could be repeated over and over again. Through "time-and-motion" studies, task specification could be further refined in hopes of boosting productivity. These approaches facilitated monitoring and punishment efforts, but they also created worker hostility (which itself can be costly).

2. Prevention by Reward Structures. A more positive approach is to design reward schemes that *prevent* shirking or misdirection of effort. "Incentive" is the key idea here. Paying managers with stock options as well as with fixed salaries is an example of this. For blue-collar workers there are piece-rate wage schemes and collective bonus schemes. Certainly one of the most interesting developments along these lines is the recent spread of employee stock-ownership plans (or ESOPs). With an ESOP all employees gain an ownership interest, which can be quite substantial if not a controlling interest. Company profits then supplement their regular salary, resulting, it is presumed, in some added incentive to work hard. Over 10 million employees in over 10,000 firms are now covered by ESOPs, including the employees of Avis, Procter & Gamble, Texaco, and Polaroid. Whether or not these schemes usually boost efficiency is debatable. But they certainly seem to in certain cases. For example, Brunswick Corporation's ESOP, set up in 1983, is credited with contributing to a 50% increase in sales per employee by 1988.[23]

---

[22] Milgrom and Roberts, "Economic Theories of the Firm," p. 448. For a good example see Gary Jacobson and John Hillkirk, *Xerox: American Samurai* (New York: Macmillan, 1986), pp. 180–181.

[23] Business Week, May 15, 1989, pp. 116–123. See also Alan S. Blinder (ed.), *Paying for Productivity* (Washington, D.C.: Brookings Institution, 1990).

3. Team Spirit.   Feelings of team spirit or loyalty may provide incentives for high productivity apart from monetary rewards or threats of punishment. Japanese management systems take extensive advantage of this possibility. Team spirit may be fostered by workers advising management through quality circles, by uniforms and company songs, by cafeterias that serve all workers (abolishing the executive dining room), and by minimizing explicit monitoring.[24]

4. M-Form Organization.   As firms have grown in size and complexity, new approaches to their organization have evolved. Replacement of the old unitary form, or *U-form* organization, by the more recent *multidivision form*, or *M-form* organization is perhaps the most significant such change.

The U-form organization was illustrated earlier in Figure 3–1. Centralization is its main characteristic. The chief executive officer has responsibility for both day-to-day operations and long-run strategic planning. Given the limits of the CEO's mental capacity, the daily efforts of directing and coordinating all the diverse functions (production, finance, marketing, and so on) tend to dominate, resulting in neglect for longer-run concerns. Shortly after World War I the limitations of the U-form led to crisis conditions in four major companies — Du Pont; General Motors; Sears, Roebuck; and Standard Oil of New Jersey (now Exxon). Their huge size contributed to their inability to use the U-form.

Reorganization of these companies led to the M-form, as illustrated in Figure 3–2. Decentralization is the hallmark of this multidivision structure. Division managers are responsible for supervising day-to-day operations, leaving the management free for long-term strategic planning. Note from Figure 3–2, for instance, that each division has its own personnel office for hiring workers, scheduling vacations, registering employees into health plans, and so on. As early as the 1920s General Motors decentralized itself into five main independent divisions — one each for Chevrolet, Pontiac, Oldsmobile, Buick, and Cadillac. The M-form proved so successful for GM and the other big firms that it spread widely. Now most major corporations follow the M-form. Indeed, it is more significant today than ever before because the M-form can accommodate the vast diversification common to conglomeracy and mul-

---

[24] Here is Harvey Leibenstein's report on the last point:

Recently I spent six months in Japan and visited some large firms. In all cases I inquired about the way in which employees were monitored. The managers were extremely sensitive to the idea and convinced me . . . that no monitoring by superiors was attempted. Promotions, by and large, were a consequence of age and duration of employment. Here we have examples of some highly [efficient] firms who did everything possible to avoid monitoring. See Harvey Leibenstein, "Property Rights and X-efficiency: Comment," *American Economic Review*, Vol. 73 (1983), pp. 831–842.

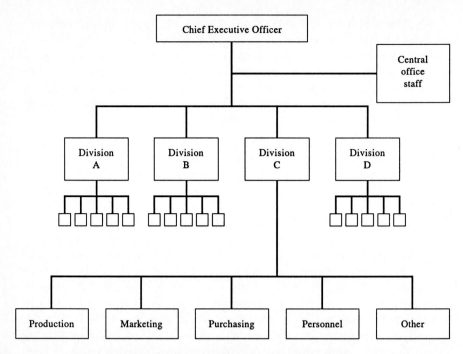

FIGURE 3–2. Multidivision, M-form organization.

tinationalism (which we explore in Chapter 18.).[25] Some of today's firms do not look like a firm at all, but rather like a collection of individual firms tied together by a holding company.

D. Summary

The collectivity, direction, and continuity that characterize firms generate certain advantages, especially in corporations—advantages we have identified as specialization in teams, transaction-cost savings, ease of capital formation, and spirited morale. On the other hand, there are inherent problems or costs, especially in large corporations experiencing separation between ownership and control. These are costs resulting from shirking, misdirection, and rent seeking. Monitoring methods, pay schemes, organizational structures, and the like have been invented to exploit the firm's advantages while coping with its disadvantages, but these efforts have proved successful only up to a point. The disadvantages of the firm's hierarchy seem especially costly once the firm surpasses a certain size. That size may be gargantuan, but there are apparently limits.

[25] For details on the M-form, see O.E. Williamson, *Corporate Control and Business Behavior* (Englewood Cliffs, N. J.: Prentice-Hall, 1970); and A. D. Chandler, Jr., *Strategy and Stucture: Chapters in the History of Industrial Enterprise* (Cambridge, Mass.: MIT Press, 1962).

During the 1970s and 1980s there was a massive amount of growth by merger in the American economy. During the late 1980s this trend reversed itself to some degree. Downsizing became popular. As *Fortune* reported in February 1988, "company after company, including over half of the *Fortune* 500, [has] restructured—shedding businesses, laying off employees, cutting costs."[26] Disadvantages of corporate size were said to have become particularly pronounced because of recent developments in "global competition, deregulation, accelerating technological change, and the threat of takeover." Whatever its causes, the restructuring could be illustrative of our discussion thus far.

III. PROFIT MAXIMIZATION: TRADITIONAL THEORY

A. Introduction

Now we must ask what motivates firms. Do they aim to maximize profit, as traditional theory assumes?

This matter of motivation is important to our later study of firm conduct—that is, price strategies, promotion efforts, and so on. Market structure alone does not determine conduct. The *combination* of structural conditions and firm motivation determines conduct. According to traditional theory, profit maximization motivates all firms in *all* market settings. It is the diversity of structures that produces diverse conduct from this universal motivation. For example, if a monopolist charges a higher price than a group of purely competitive firms would, it is not because the monopolist is a profit maximizer and the competitive firms are philanthropists.

If, contrary to conventional theory, firm motivation varied as much as structure varies, conduct would be less predictable. Economists would have to step aside in favor of psychologists (or other motivation experts). Unfortunately for economists, variance in structure itself probably promotes some variances in motivation. Owners of purely competitive firms are *compelled* to toe the profit maximizing line lest they go bankrupt. On the other hand, monopolistic and oligopolistic firms may have sufficient market power that their owners and managers need not scratch for every penny of possible profit. Such firms have the option of enjoying the "easy life," of coasting along with only "satisfactory" or "reasonable" earnings. As an executive of U.S. Steel once claimed, "U.S. Steel has never tried to price to maximum profit. . . . "[27]

This relation between structural and motivational variances, as well

[26] Walter Kiechel III, "Corporate Strategy for the 1990s," *Fortune*, February 29, 1988, p. 34.

[27] A. D. H. Kaplan, J. B. Dirlam, and R. F. Lanzillotti, *Pricing in Big Business* (Washington, D.C.: Brookings Institution, 1958), p. 23.

as related factors, has sparked controversy. Like a ravenous bookworm the controversy has consumed thousands of pages of scholarly journals and dozens of books. Some economists stick to conventional theory. Some advocate alternative possible motivations, such as sales maximization or growth maximization. Some argue that firms are not motivated to maximize anything. They say that firms are merely "satisficers." This brief catalog of positions on firm motivation provides an outline for what follows.

B. Traditional Theory's Assumptions

The hypothesis of firm profit maximization rests on three assumptions concerning the people who own and operate "the firm": (1) single-minded purpose, (2) rational or forced choice of objective, and (3) the adherence to operational rules of optimality.

1. Single-Minded Purpose. The first of these assumptions infers that no matter how big and diverse the firm happens to be, all its owners and employees work as one to achieve its objective. Warehousemen may have the hoarding instincts of squirrels. Salespeople may simply want to sell, sell, sell, even at giveaway prices. However, traditional theory holds that while on the job these dedicated souls either set aside their personal obsessions or bend them to benefit the enterprise.

2. Rationality. What objectives do the efforts of these single-minded individuals further? Since in theory, control of a capitalistic firm rests with its owners, and since the owners are rewarded by profits, the traditional assumption of rationality implies a goal of profit maximization.

3. Operational Rules. "Profit maximization" is meaningless unless it can be translated into an operational objective. Left in vague form, the objective does not specifically indicate precisely what businesspeople must do in their daily affairs to achieve it. Many operational rules are possible (such as "no one ever went broke underestimating the taste of the American public"). However, as outlined in Chapter 2, traditional economic theory offers a rather technical rule: *Expand production and promotion as long as added revenues exceed added costs; cut back whenever the resulting reductions in costs exceed the reductions in revenues.* In short, operate where marginal revenue equals marginal cost or, symbolically, MR = MC. This rule stems from the standard definition of total profit, which is the difference between total revenue and total cost, that is, TP = TR − TC.

C. Criticism of Traditional Theory

If traditional theory is vulnerable to criticism, it must be vulnerable in one or more of these three underlying assumptions. In fact, virtually all criticism may be gathered under three broad labels designating focuses of attack: (1) realism in process, (2) managerialism, and (3) behaviorialism. These classifications of criticism are outlined in Table 3–3 according to the degree in which each school of criticism accepts (yes) or rejects (no) the three basic assumptions of traditional theory itemized on the left-hand side.

"Realism in process" thus identifies a form of criticism that generally accepts the assumptions of single-mindedness and rational choice but rejects the notion that MR=MC is an adequate operational objective for businesspeople. Conversely, "managerialism" identifies the position of analysts who are not much bothered by the problem of operational feasibility. However, they seriously doubt that the typical firm is run for the single-minded pursuit of the owners' interests. They argue that in most large corporations the owners and managers are *not* the same people and they are *not* driven by the same objectives. Since *managers* are allegedly the ones in control, they can pursue objectives in *their* self-interest rather than the owners'. This split obliterates the assumption of single-mindedness (or redirects it) and opens the door to goals other than profit maximization. Finally, there is a third group of critics called the "behavioralists." They deny that profit maximization is typical of American business for reasons that blend realism in process and managerialism. They stress the complexity of business organizations. They note a diversity of motives among salespeople, production workers, warehouse operators, and others in the firm besides those of owners and managers. As for goals, they believe that humans engage in "satisficing" rather than maximizing behavior and that human rules of daily operation reflect this.

The remainder of this chapter is divided into three parts, one for each class of criticism. One important thread of thought to which we

TABLE 3–3. Outline of Three Main Schools of Criticism According to Their Acceptance (YES) or Rejection (NO) of Traditional Theory's Key Assumptions

Traditional Theory's Assumption	Classification of Criticism		
	Realism in Process	Managerialism	Behavioralism
Single-mindedness	Yes	No	No
Rational profit maximization	Yes	No	No
Operational feasibility	No	Yes	No
Overall acceptance of profit maximization?	No	No	No

shall return repeatedly in this: Pricing policy and cost experience are two largely *separable* issues in this question of profit maximizing. On the whole, a firm is more likely to *price* its wares in conformity with profit-maximizing precepts than to manage its *costs* in the miserly, tightfisted fashion that profit maximization implies.

The reason for this asymmetry is simple. The main burden of most price policy adjustments would be carried by persons *outside* the firm — by customers if it is a price increase or by competitors if it is a price decrease. Hence sound price adjustments are likely to have been made *already by the firm.* The main burden of any cost adjustments, on the other hand, would be borne by persons *inside* the firm — by folks who would lose their jobs or would have to work harder. Hence, profitable adjustments in this area are *not* likely to have already been made. It is here we would probably find flab.[28]

IV. REALISM IN PROCESS

The basic thrust of the realism in process criticism is that the simple rule MR = MC is *non*operational. Businesspeople cannot maximize profits by this rule alone, even if they wanted to. Among the many pertinent questions left unanswered by this rule are the following:

1. *What costs and revenues are supposed to be included in this calculation over what time period?* An accountant's view of "costs" differs from an economist's view, as is illustrated by their differing treatments of "depreciation" and "normal profit." Moreover, the economist's "short run" and "long run" do not correspond to the accountant's "calendar quarter" and "fiscal year." Their decisions on the content of calculations will differ. On top of all this, many decisions are nonmarginal from anyone's viewpoint (for example, acquiring a large subsidiary or bribing a senator). The MR = MC rule allegedly collapses under the weight of these big decisions.

   In defense of traditional theory, it ought to be acknowledged that experts in managerial economics have unraveled many of these knotty problems.[29] They have shown that wide application of marginal concepts is by no means impossible.

2. *How can risk be properly accounted for?* Even assuming the business-person knows the probabilities associated with the various possible outcomes of his or her decisions, there is no universally acceptable way of identifying the profit-maximizing course of action whenever

[28] D. C. Hague stresses this point in *Pricing in Business* (London: Allen & Unwin, 1971), pp. 83–84.

[29] See, for example, Ralph Turvey, "Marginal Cost," *Economic Journal* (June 1969), pp. 282–298; and E. F. Brigham and J. L. Pappas, *Managerial Economics* (Hinsdale, Ill.: Dryden Press, 1976).

substantial risk is involved. Scherer explains the situation with the aid of a problem:

> Imagine a decision-maker weighing two alternative policies, one offering a best-guess profit expectation of $1 million with a 10 percent chance of bankrupting the firm (whose net worth is currently $4 million), the other an expected profit of $2 million with a 30 percent chance of disaster. Which is the rational choice?[30]

Application of sophisticated expected-value criteria cannot yield the "right" answer. The answer requires extensive information on the attitudes of the firm's owners toward increases in wealth versus total loss of their equity, *plus* some technique for properly aggregating these attitudes. Achieving world peace would be easier.

3. *What is the profit-maximizing course of action when uncertainty prevails?* In the preceding problem it was assumed that the 10% and 30% probabilities for bankruptcy were *known* to be the true probabilities. Hence, it was purely a case of "risk." As with the toss of a coin, the ultimate outcome was unknown, but the probabilities were certain. When the decision maker knows *neither* the ultimate outcome *nor* the probabilities of the possible outcomes, he knows about as much as a blind man in a dark room looking for a black cat that may not be there. Economists have devised a number of techniques to assist decision making in this situation (including "maximax," "maximin," and "regret hedging").[31] But none of these really qualifies as profit maximizing.

Defenders of orthodoxy argue that full knowledge is not necessary, that an earnest effort and an "intuitive understanding" are all that are required. Fritz Machlup, for example, uses the analogy of one driver passing another on a two-lane country road, which motorists do all the time without the aid of sophisticated physics. He summarizes his argument by stressing the uses of *subjective* knowledge:

> It should hardly be necessary to mention that all the relevant magnitudes involved — costs, revenue, profit — are subjective — that is, perceived or fancied by the men whose decisions or actions are to be explained rather than "objective". . . . Marginal analysis of the firm should not be understood to imply anything but subjective estimates, guesses and hunches.[32]

The critics remain unmoved by this analysis, however. They claim that Machlup's argument rests on a tautology — that "maximization" becomes

[30] F. M. Scherer, *Industrial Market Structure and Economic Performance* (Chicago: Rand McNally, 1970), p. 28.

[31] For a popular account see Shlomo Maital, *Minds, Markets, and Money* (New York: Basic Books, 1982). On the technical side G. Loomes and R. Sugden, "Regret Theory," *Economic Journal* (December 1982), 805–824.

[32] Fritz Machlup, "Marginal Analysis and Empirical Research," *American Economic Review* (September 1946), pp. 521–522.

meaningless if it is allowed that anything businesspeople happen to do is considered maximizing. Even if Machlup's theory is interpreted to mean that businesspeople merely try to—rather than actually do—maximize profits, uncertainty critics would reply that this has little value as a description, prescription, or prediction of business behavior.[33]

V. MANAGERIALISM (OR REALISM IN MOTIVATION)

A. Introduction

As we have seen (Section IB), managers, not owners, tend to sit in the driver's seat. Do manager's turn the steering wheel in directions of fostering profit maximization? The answer is "yes," "no," and "sometimes," depending on whom you consult. Those who say "yes" argue that (1) managerial rewards are atuned to profit performance and (2) managers respond accordingly. Those who say "no" argue that (1) managers lack the incentive to steer toward profit because their incomes are not directly linked to profit levels or (2) if there is close linkage, managers are moved by *non*monetary motives. This skepticism of traditional theory may be called *managerialism*. Of course, the best answer of all might be "sometimes," because it is difficult to generalize one way or the other. Some firms may profit maximize while others follow a managerialist course. With this caveat in mind, we shall survey several theories of managerialism and then summarize the available evidence.

B. Theories of Managerialism

1. Managerial Utility. Oliver Williamson's theories of managerial utility assume that for tax and other reasons managers are interested in executive jets, liberal expense accounts, and other emoluments or perquisites as well as personal income and company profits.[34] Let the horizontal axis of Figure 3–3 indicate the monetary value of "perks" and the vertical axis indicate profits. Each curve, I_1, I_2, and I_3, represents a given level of manager satisfaction realized from various combinations of perks and profits. I_1 is the lowest level of satisfaction depicted, and I_3 is the highest. Managers are *indifferent* as between any two points on a given *I* curve, such as A and B on I_3; that is, all points on I_3 yield the same degree of reward. Accordingly, these are called indifference curves.

Managers would obviously like the very generous volumes of perks and profits that lie in the region northeast of I_3, but they are restrained

[33] Joseph McGuire, *Theories of Business Behavior* (Englewood Cliffs, N.J.: Prentice-Hall, 1964), p. 83.

[34] O.E. Williamson, *The Economics of Discretionary Behavior: Managerial Objectives in a Theory of the Firm* (Chicago: Markham, 1967).

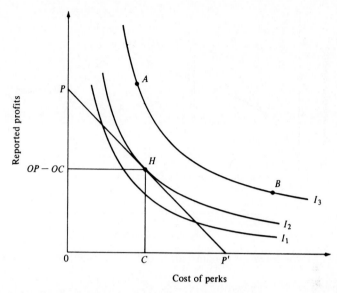

FIGURE 3–3. Managerial trade-off between company profits and executive perks.

by realities. Point P on the vertical axis represents the *maximum* level of profits the company can earn. Perks at that point are zero, but it defines the extent to which perks are possible. Since $1 worth of increased perks must reduce profits by $1, movement to the right from P reduces profits along the line PP', which as a negative slope of 1. At point H on PP' the value of perks is $0C$. Hence the corresponding level for profit is $0P$ minus $0C$, or $0P - 0C$, as indicated on the vertical axis. In other words, line PP' is a perks/profits possibilities curve. Any point *in*side the triangle $P0P'$ is possible. Any point *out*side is not. Managers maximize their satisfaction by choosing that combination of possible perks and profits landing them on their highest indifference curve. In this case it is I_2 at point H.

Notice that, according to this model, managers select the *same* price and output policies as a simple profit maximizer. If they did not, the PP' line would be closer to the origin, meaning reduced overall managerial satisfaction on an indifference curve such as I_1. However, internal costs will be higher in this model than in the simple profit-maximizing model because perks don't grow on trees.

2. Sales Maximization. Figure 3–4 presents the basic sales revenue maximization model developed by W. J. Baumol.[35] The horizontal axis measures output and quantity sold. The vertical axis depicts total dollar

[35] W. J. Baumol, *Business Behavior, Value and Growth* (New York: Macmillan, 1959).

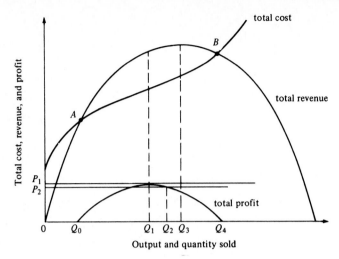

FIGURE 3–4. Sales revenue maximization, subject to minimum profit constraint.

cost, revenue, and profit. Assuming the firm faces a linear negatively
sloped demand curve (such as that facing the monopolist on page 36),
total revenue will look like a McDonald's golden arch. Subtracting total
cost from total revenue yields total profit, which is zero at two quantities
(Q_0 and Q_4), corresponding to the intersection of total cost and total
revenue at points A and B. Profit-maximizing output would be $0Q_1$ with
profit equal to $0P_1$. Sales revenue maximization would require greater
output at Q_3. Note that profits are lower at Q_3 than Q_1. Moreover, although it is not shown here, Q_3 implies a lower product price than the
profit maximizing solution Q_1.

If managers were operating under a minimum profit constraint that
was *above* the profit level associated with absolute revenue maximization,
they would be forced to raise price, reduce output, and move in the
direction of profit maximization. One such profit floor might be $0P_2$ in
Figure 3–4, in which case quantity would be Q_2 instead of Q_3. Why a
minimum profit constraint? One is probably necessary to satisfy the neglected but not totally forgotten stockholders. Although these are the
most often cited conclusions for this model it should be noted that the
assumption of monopoly limits its generality. It has been argued that
under oligopoly there is no substantial behavioral difference between
profit and sales maximization.[36]

[36] W. G. Shepherd, "On Sales Maximizing and Oligopoly Behavior," *Economica*
(November 1962), pp. 420–424; and B. D. Mabry, "Sales Maximization vs. Profit Maximization: Are They Inconsistent?" *Western Economic Journal* (March 1968), pp. 154–160. Moreover, risk lowers Q below the standard result, so revenue maximization in the face of risk

3. Maximizing Growth or Present Value of Revenue.[37] Growth motivations may propel mergers. Here we shall focus on simple theories of "internal" growth maximization, which follow from the preceding analysis. We begin by announcing two important principles:

1. Growth of sales requires expansions of capacity and, consequently, adequate capital to finance expansion. Maximum profits can supply the needed funds either directly through retained earnings or indirectly by attracting the capital of additional equity investors and bond buyers. In theory, growth rate maximization often corresponds exactly to profit maximization; in fact, numerous statistical studies demonstrate a close positive association between growth rate and profit.[38]

2. Growth *rate* is only one possible measure of growth. Another is the *present value of the firm's future stream of sales revenues.* This is the sum of each future years' expected sales revenue, discounted by an appropriate percentage rate to account for the fact that each dollar obtained five or ten years from now is worth less than each dollar obtained in the current year. In other words, an added dollar's worth of sales in the current period is actually "worth" more to the firm in terms of present value than is an added dollar's worth of sales in any subsequent period. This principle may be seen in Figure 3–5. Each curve, V_1, V_2, and V_3, indicates a *given present* value of sales revenue, with V_1 being the lowest and V_3 the highest present values explicitly depicted. Any two points on a single curve, such as G and H on V_3, represent the *same* present value. The negative slope of these curves indicates that a given present value can be achieved by high current sales revenues and low growth (low future revenues), *or* by low current sales revenues and high growth, *or* by some combination in between. To appreciate this, note that the horizontal axis is *current sales* revenue and the vertical axis is the *growth rate* of sales. These V curves may be called **given-present-value** lines.

Figure 3–6 compares these possibilities. Because growth rate is closely linked to profit, it will rise and fall in an arc as current sales rise from zero, just as total profit in Figure 3–4 rises and falls in an arc as quantity rises. Maximum growth rate then corresponds to the peak in the arc and to profit maximization. In contrast, an objective of maximizing present value will lead to greater current sales revenue and a slower

---

could yield a Q that matches the Q of orthodox theory. See Stephen M. Miller and Anthony A. Romeo, "Alternative Goals and Uncertainty in the Theory of the Firm," *Southern Economic Journal* (July 1979), pp. 189–205.

[37] On growth maximization, see Robin Marris, *The Economic Theory of Managerial Capitalism* (New York: The Free Press, 1964); John Williamson, "Profit, Growth, and Sales Maximization," *Economica* (February 1966), pp. 1–16; for a simpler treatment, K. Heidensohn and N. Robinson, *Business Behavior* (New York: John Wiley, 1974), Chapter 8.

[38] J. L. Eatwell, "Growth Profitability and Size: The Empirical Evidence," in *The Corporate Economy*, edited R. Marris and A. Wood (Cambridge, Mass.: Harvard University Press, 1971), pp. 409–418. See also William E. Fruhan, Jr., "How Fast Should Your Company Grow?" *Harvard Business Review* (January 1984), pp. 84–93.

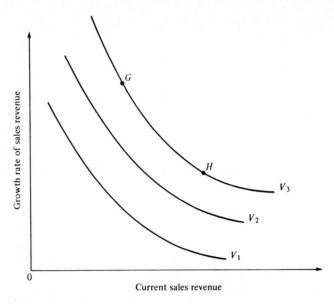

FIGURE 3–5. Relationship between the present value of future sales (Vs), growth rate of sales, and current sales.

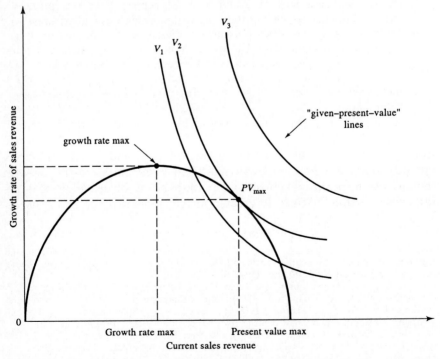

FIGURE 3–6. Growth maximization and present value maximization compared.

growth rate. This latter result is like the sales maximization objective of Figure 3–4. It yields the highest "given-present-value" possible (V_2) subject to the constraint of growth limitations.

As in the simple sales maximization model, these theories ignore the problem of oligopolistic interdependence. This is undoubtedly their greatest weakness because oligopoly is typical of American industry.

Avoidance of Risk and Uncertainty. Avoidance of risk and uncertainty should not be regarded as a goal in itself. Nevertheless, recent theoretical and empirical work has established that many firms, especially managerially controlled firms, strive to avoid risk and uncertainty.[39] Hence avoidance of risk could be considered an important secondary or supplementary objective to those already discussed. Introduction of this element increases the complexity of the theorizing and alters the conclusions reached by simpler models.

C. Empirical Findings on Manager's Motives

Empirical tests of managerial motivation are difficult to devise. The simplest approach, for instance, might be to question managers directly about their motives. But how could we be sure that managers would be fully candid? They might hold back, fearful that an admission of determined profit maximization might make them appear particularly greedy, something inconsistent with good public relations. Even if they were candid in their answers, those answers could be confusing.

For example, a questionnaire survey of British firms found a close correspondence between profit and growth maximization. The two responses outweighing all others in "importance" as long-run company objectives were

- "maximizing growth in total profits"
- "maximizing rate of return on capital"

Moreover, when asked *why* their company was interested in a "high level of profitability," the managers said mainly "to provide finance for expansion." And when asked *why* they were interested in pursuing a "high rate of growth in size," they mainly replied, "to secure or increase future profits."[40] Now growth and high profits can be consistent objec-

---

[39] J. K. Galbraith, *The New Industrial State* (Boston: Houghton Mifflin, 1967), Chapters 3 and 7; R. E. Caves, "Uncertainty, Market Structure and Performance: Galbraith as Conventional Wisdom," in *Industrial Organization and Economic Development*, edited by J. W. Markham and G. F. Papanek (Boston: Houghton Mifflin, 1970); R. Schramm and R. Sherman, "Profit Risk Management and the Theory of the Firm," *Southern Economic Journal* (January 1974), pp. 353–363; and K. J. Boudreaux, "Managerialism and Risk-Return Performance," *Southern Economic Journal* (January 1973), pp. 366–372.

[40] Arthur Francis, "Company Objectives, Managerial Motivations, and the Behavior of Large Firms," *Cambridge Journal of Economics* (December 1980), pp. 349–361.

tives, as our theorizing has just revealed. Hence, in themselves these responses show no inconsistency. However, the same survey rated the stockholder's interests very poorly. Profitability was pursued *not* to "pay dividends" or to "increase the price of a company's shares," but rather to finance "expansion." This suggests that, in the end, these managers might be pursuing sales, or growth in sales, more vigorously than the owners might wish, something inconsistent with profit maximization.

Apart from questionnaire surveys, researchers have attempted statistical tests. For example, data from 300 firms might show a strong positive correlation between firm profits and managers' salaries, suggesting that managers have a strong incentive to maximize profits and actually do so. However, there are serious problems with this approach also. These include (1) poor data, (2) an enormous number of variables affecting the outcomes in question, and (3) the fact that much observed behavior can be explained by more than one theory. Nevertheless, a few testable hypotheses emerge from the theories, and economists have attempted to test them.

Are managers' incomes more closely associated with profits, sales, or growth? Snap judgment might lead you to conclude that most managers steer in the direction of sales maximization. Everyone knows that the presidents of IBM and GM make more money than the president of your local pizza parlor, even when all three firms earn 20% on investment. In this sense raw size does determine executive remuneration, suggesting perhaps that size guides executive action. Even so, an accurate test of the relation between managers' incomes and profit, sales, or growth would require an explanation of what happens to the manager's income *within* a given firm (or what kind of performance would *cause* the manager's interfirm promotion). The best of the appropriate studies have reached the following conclusion: Managers' monetary rewards are more closely and more positively associated with *profit* performance than either sales volume or growth rate, although these latter factors do have an effect.[41] As profits go up, measured in terms of absolute dollars or percentage return on capital invested, so do executives' salaries, bonuses, stock options, and the price of their ownership shares. These

41 Robert Masson, "Executive Motivations, Earnings, and Consequent Equity Performance," *Journal of Political Economy* (November 1971), pp. 1278–1292; Larner, *Management Control and the Large Corporation*, pp. 33–61; W. G. Lewellen and B. Huntsman, "Managerial Pay and Corporate Performance," *American Economic Review* (September 1970), pp. 710–720; G. K. Yarrow, "Executive Compensation and the Objectives of the Firm," in *Market Structure and Corporate Behavior*, edited by K. Cowling (London: Gray-Mills, 1972), pp. 149–173; Samuel Baker, "Executive Incomes, Profits and Revenues: A Comment," *Southern Economic Journal* (April 1969), pp. 379–383; G. Meeks and G. Whittington, "Directors Pay, Growth, and Profitability," *Journal of Industrial Economics* (Sept. 1975), pp. 1–14; and Daryl N. Winn and John D. Shoenhair, "Compensation Based (Dis)incentives for Revenue-Maximizing Behavior," *Review of Economics and Statistics* (February 1988), pp. 154–158.

particular studies do not show that managers actually maximize profits.[42] Reaping and sowing are two different things. Still, the research does tend to bolster traditional theory.

Are managers moved by nonmonetary rewards? Human nature tells us that they are and so does some empirical evidence. Williamson finds that executive compensation is positively associated with "staff" personnel and other emolument expenditures. He has also assembled a number of case studies showing "excessive" emoluments.[43] Corroborating these results, several statistical studies of the banking industry show that managerial control boosts occupancy, equipment, furniture, and personnel expenses, especially when such management control is accompanied by market power.[44] (Of course business lore's most famous executive hedonist is Hugh Hefner, whose flamboyant life-style at the expense of Playboy Enterprises, Inc. once caused company auditors to bill him $796,413 on behalf of stockholders.[45])

More comprehensively, R. A. Gordon offers evidence and argument that managers are moved by "the urge for power, the desire for prestige and the related impulse of emulation, the creative urge, the propensity to identify oneself with a group and the related feeling of group loyalty, the desire for security, the urge for adventure and for 'playing the game' for its own sake, and the desire to serve others."[46] These findings are not necessarily inconsistent with profit maximizing on the price side, but they do suggest cost-side conduct that is less than frugal.

Can anything be concluded from direct observation of price and output behavior? In a broad sense we shall be exploring empirical evidence of this sort throughout most of the remainder of this book. We shall observe many earmarks of extensive profit maximization, including price discrimination, positive associations between price level and concentration, and positive associations between profits and market power. However, this evidence does not explicitly refute sales or growth maximizing because these latter theories include allowance for profit constraints. If these profit constraints varied in accordance with market structure, the

[42] Moreover, some managers are grossly overpaid. *After retiring* as chairman of ITT, Harold Geneen won a $1.7 million "consulting agreement" with ITT, plus "supplementary" pension payments of $112,384 annually, plus his regular pension of $130,713, plus office space, staff, security, and transportation "assistance." *The Wall Street Journal*, April 3, 1980, p. 26.

[43] Williamson, *The Economics of Discretionary Behavior* (1967), pp. 85–135.

[44] Cynthia Glassman and Stephen A. Rhoades, "Owner vs. Manager Control Effects on Bank Performance," *Review of Economics and Statistics* (May 1980), pp. 263–270; T. H. Hannan and F. Mavinga, "Expense Preference and Managerial Control: The Case of the Banking Firm," *Bell Journal of Economics* (Autumn 1980), pp. 671–682; and James A. Verbrugge and John S. Jahera, Jr., "Expense-Preference Behavior in the Savings and Loan Industry," *Journal of Money, Credit, and Banking* (November 1981), pp. 465–476.

[45] *The Wall Street Journal*, April 4, 1980, p. 4.

[46] R. A. Gordon, *Business Leadership in the Large Corporation* (Berkeley: University of California Press, 1966), pp. 305–316.

broad empirical findings just mentioned could emerge despite the adoption of sales or growth maximization objectives. Thus, several economists have attempted specific tests of these theories, particularly sales revenue maximization. Virtually all of those testing the sales objective have concluded that it is not the goal adopted by most firms. Rather, firms seem to favor some form of profit or growth maximization.[47]

When manager-controlled firms and owner-controlled firms are placed side by side and compared, do any differences appear? The "box scores" for tests of this question are presented in Table 3–4, which classifies the names of researchers in this area according to their findings. One's immediate impression is that their findings vary widely. The results vary because each researcher uses his or her own blend of sample, time period, and statistical technique. Still, a few tentative conclusions are possible. First, the "profit rate" column shows that *no* empirical study has found manager controlled firms earning higher average rates of profit than owner-controlled firms, whereas 11 have found managerial rates to be generally lower (as usually predicted by "managerial" theories), and 8 have found no significant difference. Among those finding "no difference" are several that do find managerial profits somewhat lower on average than owner-controlled profits, but not "significantly" so. It appears, on balance, that owner-controlled firms probably have an edge in profit performance, but nothing outstanding.

This broad summary conceals a noteworthy refinement. One would expect very little difference in profit rates among firms facing intense competition. Profit maximizing for them is a matter of survival, not of type of control. Conversely, greater differences are likely among firms with substantial market power. For them, managerial discretion comes into play. In other words, managerial discretion ought to depend on the presence of monopoly power. Palmer explored this possibility and found very little difference in profit rates where monopoly power was "low": 9.98% for manager control versus 10.59% for owner control. On the other hand, where monopoly power was "high," he found a significant difference: 11.41% for manager control versus 14.77% for owner control.[48]

Under growth rate, variance in profit (risk), and the rate at which

---

[47] M. Hall, "Sales Revenue Maximization: An Empirical Examination," *Journal of Industrial Economics* (April 1967), pp. 143–156; B. D. Mabry and D. L. Siders, "An Empirical Test of the Sales Maximization Hypothesis," *Southern Economic Journal* (January 1967), pp. 367–377; Samuel Baker, "An Empirical Test of the Sales Maximization Hypothesis," *Industrial Organization Review*, Vol. 1, no. 1 (1973), pp. 56–66; J. W. Elliot, "A Comparison of Models of Marketing Investment in the Firm," *Quarterly Review of Economics and Business* (Spring 1971), pp. 53–70. An interesting exception is C. L. Lackman and J. L. Craycroft, "Sales Maximization and Oligopoly: A Case Study," *Journal of Industrial Economics* (December 1974), pp. 81–95.

[48] See also Y. Amihud and J. Kamin, "Revenue vs. Profit Maximization: Differences in Behavior by the Type of Control and by Market Power," *Southern Economic Journal* (January 1979), pp. 838–846.

TABLE 3–4. Summary of Tests for Differences in Firm Performance by Type of Control

Direction of Managerial Divergence	Performance Measure			
	Profit Rate	Growth Rate	Variance in Profit	Retention Rate
Higher	—	—	Palmer, Stano	Williamson
Lower	Monsen et al., Palmer, Radice, Larner, Shelton, Boudreaux, Bothwell, Stano, McEachern, Steer, Glassman	Radice, Steer	Boudreaux, McEachern, Herman	Kamerschen, Herman
No difference	Qualls, Hindley, Sorenson, Holl, Kamerschen, Kania, Thonet, Herman	Sorenson, Holl, Kania, Thonet, Herman	Larner, Holl, Kania, Thonet	Sorenson, Holl, Kania

Sources: Boudreaux, *Southern Economic Journal* (1973), pp. 366–372; Hindley, *Journal of Law and Economics* (1970), pp. 185–221; Holl, *Journal of Industrial Economics* (1975), pp. 257–271; Kamerschen, *American Economic Review* (1968), pp. 432–447; Kamerschen, *Quarterly Journal of Economics* (1970), pp. 668–673; Larner, *Management Control and the Large Corporation* (New York: Dunnellen, 1970), pp. 25–32; Monsen et al., *Quarterly Journal of Economics* (1968), pp. 435–451; Palmer, *Bell Journal of Economics* (1973), pp. 293–303; Palmer, *Western Economic Journal* (1973), pp. 228–231 (see also March 1975 issue); Qualls, *Essays on Industrial Organization* (1976), pp. 89–104; Radice, *Economics Journal* (1971), pp. 547–562; Shelton, *American Economic Review* (1967), pp. 1252–1258; Sorenson, *Southern Economic Journal* (1974), pp. 145–148; Williamson, *Economics of Discretionary Behavior*, (Chicago: Markham, 1967), pp. 135–138; Kania and McKean, *Kyklos* (1976), pp. 272–290; Mario Stano, *Bell Journal of Economics* (1976), pp. 672–679; Steer and Cable, *Journal of Industrial Economics* (1978), pp. 13–30; Bothwell, *Journal of Industrial Economics* (1980), pp. 303–311; Thonet and Poensgen, *Journal of Industrial Economics* (1979), pp. 23–37; McEachern, *Managerial Control and Performance* (Lexington, Mass.: D. C. Heath, 1975); Herman, *Corporate Control, Corporate Power* (Cambridge: Cambridge University Press, 1981); Glassman and Rhoades, *Review of Economics and Statistics* (1980), pp. 263–270.

profit earnings are retained (rather than paid-out), Table 3–4 discloses fewer studies and an even greater spread of results, rendering conclusions for these measures all the more tentative. Still, this writer tends to side with those who find *no* significant difference between manager- and owner-controlled firms in these three categories. Once again, the two types of control seem so similar that we need not be greatly concerned with the influence "managerialism" may have on motivation.

Are the empirical answers to all the foregoing questions consistent? Broadly speaking, "yes." The fact that managers' compensation is generally tied to profits leads one to expect that profit performance will not vary markedly by type of control, which is the case. On the other hand, the discoveries concerning perks and emoluments touch a responsive chord in anyone who can imagine himself in the expensive shoes of a senior executive fairly free from the reins of influential owners. For this and other reasons, we should expect some indication that profits of managerially-controlled firms are less than those of owner-controlled firms, which is also the case, especially where monopoly power is present. By the same token, there are indications that monopoly power and management control permit an attitude toward costs more lackadaisical than otherwise. Finally, these several inferences are consistent with conclusions emerging from direct tests of the sales revenue maximization hypothesis. These tests reveal that, as a general policy, most firms do not strive after short-term sales, heedless of the consequences for profits.

VI. BEHAVIORALISM AND "SATISFICING"

A. The Behavioralist View

Although the empirical studies just reviewed typically give primacy to profits (or profitable price behavior), they do not prove conclusively that profit maximization is in fact the sole objective of most businesses. General Motors' executives might shoot for and attain profits equaling 20% of stockholders' equity. This is well above the average for all manufacturers, and the executives might be generously rewarded for the achievement. However, might they be capable of attaining 30% if they *really* tried? No one really knows for sure, but it is this kind of possibility that leaves room for those holding "behavioralist" views. Behavioralists attack all three basic assumptions of the traditional position — single-mindedness, maximizing rationality, and operational rules of thumb.[49]

Against single-mindedness, behavioralists argue that "the firm" cannot have goals. Only individuals have goals. And, although a few executives at the top may be rewarded for the firm's profit performance, their benefits may not encourage the tens of thousands of other workers scattered throughout the typical large corporation. Buried in the organization's countless nooks and crannies are specialists in production scheduling, sales, repair service, transportation, engineering, materials procurement, personnel, safety, insurance, tax, finance, accounting, payroll, research and development, environmental protection, and so on ad infinitum. To believe that all segments of all echelons can march in lock-step fashion after profits strains credulity. We are not talking about

---

[49] R. M. Cyert and J. G. March, *A Behavioral Theory of the Firm* (Englewood Cliffs, N.J.: Prentice-Hall, 1963); and Herbert A. Simon, "Rational Decision Making in Business Organizations," *American Economic Review* (September 1979), pp. 493–513.

the cells of a cheetah's body; we are talking about imperfect and willful human beings. Assembly-line supervisors may find make-work jobs for surplus workers in order to be "one of the boys." Environmental engineers may be more dedicated to preserving the foliage than to preserving the discounted present value of the firm.[50]

In place of maximizing rationality the behavioralists postulate "organizational slack" and "satisficing." Slack takes many forms they say:

> prices are set lower than necessary to maintain adequate income from customers; wages in excess of those required to maintain labor are paid; executives are provided with services and personal luxuries in excess of those required to keep them; subunits are permitted to grow without real concern for the relation between additional payments and additional revenues; public services are provided in excess of those required.[51]

Satisficing is a corollary. Whereas a "maximizer" tries to find the course of action that brings him as close as possible to some objective (often a lofty objective), a "satisficer" does not. He sets *minimum* levels of performance in several variables below which he does not want to fall. To explain the matter by analogy, suppose the proverbial haystack has more than one needle hidden in it. Whereas the maximizer would search until he believed he had found the sharpest needle in the haystack, the satisficer would stop when he found one "sharp enough" for his immediate purpose.[52] Once such a minimum aspiration level is achieved, the satisficer coasts.

As far as operational rules of thumb are concerned, the behavioralists reject the notion of MR = MC and put a wide variety of rules in its place: (1) standard percentage markups above cost for pricing, (2) maintenance of some minimum inventory as a percentage of sales, (3) percentage market share goals and salesmen's quotas, and (4) minimum profit measured in an absolute dollar amount or percentage return on investment. Specific examples of these goals might be a 40% markup for pricing, a market share of 20%, and a 10% return on investment. Whenever one of these minimum aspiration levels is not achieved, behavioralists assume that nonroutine problem-solving activities will find a "satisfactory" solution. There may be inconsistencies among the objectives, and various efforts at problem solving may proceed in isolation from each other; but complete consistency and coordination are beyond the capability of human beings (acting individually or as a group).

Behavioralists advance these thoughts largely on the basis of realism. They do not believe that business action can be deduced from theoretical postulates of firm maximization of any variable. They em-

---

[50] K. J. Cohen and R. M. Cyert, *Theory of the Firm* (Englewood Cliffs, N.J.: Prentice-Hall, 1965), p. 331.

[51] Ibid., p. 333.

[52] J. C. March and H. A. Simon, *Organizations* (New York: John Wiley, 1958), p. 141.

phasize observation of how businesspeople act every day, hoping that perhaps such observation may eventually, through induction, yield some generalizations.

B. Problems and Evidence

As you should by now expect, traditionalists espousing profit maximization and managerialists do not agree with these tenets of behavioralism. Traditionalists and managerialists criticize behavioralism on several grounds, three of which may be taken up here.[53]

In the first place, behavioralism is said to suffer from the "fallacy of misplaced concreteness" or "hyperfactualism." A theory is supposed to be like a road map of New York State. It is a simplified, condensed, somewhat inaccurate view of reality. Nevertheless the map shows the best route from Ithaca to Buffalo without detailing every pothole and traffic light.

A second line of criticism questions the status of behavioralism as a theory, claiming that to a great extent behavioralism is more "framework" than "theory":

> Frameworks outline the components of a set of phenomena that must be taken into account when efforts to explain the phenomena are undertaken. In themselves, however, they are not explanatory. . . .[54]

Thus, behavioralists may list a number of possible goals, a variety of actors and several colorful experiences. But without hypotheses, which are subject to disproof, their list is just a list (like a grocery list). Behavioralists might even observe that a 40% markup is the basic price policy in the lingerie department of a department store, and thereby predict the *exact* retail price of 99% of all garments sold, knowing only the garments' wholesale cost. Yet this is not the application of a theory. It does not explain why the action occurs or what might cause the markup to increase or fall substantially. Behavioralism merely predicts that a firm will behave in a certain fashion because past experience of what firms do indicates that a certain course of action is probable. "Such predictions are often *ad hoc* in nature and applicable only to a given situation."[55]

---

[53] F. Machlup, "Theories of the Firm: Marginalist, Behavioral Managerial," *American Economic Review* (March 1967), pp. 1–33; R. Marris, *The Economic Theory of Managerial Capitalism*; pp. 266–277; W. J. Baumol and Maco Stewart, "On the Behavioral Theory of the Firm," in *The Corporate Economy*, edited by R. Marris and A. Wood (Cambridge, Mass.: Harvard University Press, 1971), pp. 118–143.

[54] N. A. McDonald and J. N. Rasenau, "Political Theory as an Academic Field and Intellectual Activity," in *Political Science: Advance of the Discipline*, edited by M. D. Irish (Englewood Cliffs, N. J.: Prentice-Hall, 1968), p. 44.

[55] J. V. Koch, *Industrial Organization and Prices* (Englewood Cliffs, N. J.: Prentice-Hall, 1974), p. 43.

Finally, and perhaps most important, the minimum "aspiration levels" that guide behavioralist managers may actually be "maximizing levels." If the managers of GM state that their profit goal is "no less" than 20% return on invested capital, their phrase "no less" seems to suggest that they are satisficers. On the other hand, 20% might be the best they can do, in which case they would actually be maximizers.

Despite these criticisms, evidence of behavioralism may be found in statistical studies which show firms sacrificing profits to seek out the "easy life" when monopoly power permits them to.[56] Also, in-depth corporate histories and business autobiographies provide countless examples of behavioralism in action. "Pettiness, jealousy, arrogance, narrow ambition, bloody-mindedness, stupidity, spite: these were motives which played a significant part in initiating and shaping policy." [57] Thus behavioralism cannot be dismissed.

At the same time, behavioralism cannot supplant profit maximizing completely. In-depth studies of firm motivation reveal that many firms attempt to profit maximize even as many others seem to profit satisfice.[58] Moreover, among the profit satisficers there are many firms whose *prices* conform to profit-maximizing principles even if their costs do not. A study stoutly backing behavioralism concluded that "firms that are satisficers when taking decisions about production, inventories, employment, etc., may become maximizers when they set prices" because they "are forcing those outside the firm to bear the burden of change."[59] What is more, pricing frequently remains the responsibility of top-drawer executives, many of whom have a monetary stake in policies that improve profits.[60] Thus, even in hostile settings, maximizing is at least partially applicable. Later we shall encounter much evidence of profit-maximizing pricing as well as much evidence of cost-side inefficiency.

SUMMARY

A good understanding of markets rests partly on a good understanding of the "firm." Firms supplant the market to some degree and otherwise participate prominently.

[56] Franklin Edwards and Arnold Heggestad, "Uncertainty Market Structure and Performance," *Quarterly Journal of Economics* (August 1973), pp. 455–473; and Jeffrey A. Clark, "Market Structure, Risk, and Profitability: The Quiet Life Hypothesis Revisited," *Quarterly Review of Economics and Business* (Spring 1986), pp. 45–56.

[57] From B. W. E. Alford's review of *Courtaulds: An Economic and Social History*, Vol. III, by D. C. Colman (Oxford: Oxford University Press, 1980), appearing in *The Economic Journal* (June 1981), p. 569. More generally, see Peter E. Earl, *The Corporate Imagination: How Big Companies Make Mistakes* (Brighton, England: Wheatsheaf, 1984).

[58] Hague, *Pricing in Business.*

[59] Ibid. p. 83. The best research on managerialism suggests much the same thing. See Glassman and Rhoades, "Owner vs. Manager Control Effects on Bank Performance," pp. 263–270, where lower managerial profits appear to be caused by higher costs.

[60] Hague presents evidence on this point (pp. 200–243). See also D. Tuson, "Pricing:

The firm is characterized by collectivity (as opposed to the individuality of the market), by direction (as opposed to exchange), and by continuity (as opposed to discontinuity). Hence the *firm* may be defined as a coalition of investors, workers, and other resource owners, bound by ongoing implicit agreement to act as a team, collectively creating a surplus.

Among types of firms, corporations dominate the economy. Among large corporations, ownership (which typically rests with diverse stockholders) tends to be separate from management (which rests with the chief executive officer, division directors, etc.). The interests of management correspond to those of the owners to some degree, partly because of capital market controls. Poor management performance can be reflected in poor stock market performance for the ownership shares. This may set the scene for a takeover and purge by outsiders. The takeover threat is an imperfect control device, however, because of information problems that obscure realities, competition among acquirers (which limits the rewards of acquiring firms), defensive tactics by target-firm management, and because of natural immunities that tend to free some firms from this threat, especially those too large to be easy takeover targets.

The firm exists by being better than the market in several respects — (1) specialization in teams, (2) transaction-cost economizing, (3) enlarged capital formation, and (4) morale boosting. On the other hand, the firm encounters costs from (1) shirking, (2) agent misdirection, and (3) rent seeking. Methods of management have attempted to exploit the firm's benefits while curbing costs. Efforts at monitoring and punishment have with time and experience given way to innovative reward structures (like employee stock ownership plans), efforts to build team spirits, and decentralized M-form organizations.

The postulate of profit maximization rests on three basic assumptions: single-mindedness, rational maximizing, and operational feasibility. The first of these postulates holds that, despite much diversity, all people associated with "the firm" work together toward a single objective. The second assumption specifies that this objective is profit maximization. Profit is the owner's reward, and, because owners control the traditional firm, profit maximization is both natural and rational. The third assumption rules out any real-world difficulties in following the simple MR = MC recipe.

Attacks on traditional theory have chewed away at the validity of these assumptions. Early on, the critics were most bothered by the *non*operational nature of the MR = MC calculus. Perhaps their most en-

---

Whose Responsibility?" in *Creative Pricing*, edited by E. Marting, (New York: American Management Association, 1968), pp. 39–48.

during blow in this respect was to point out that rigorous profit maximization is either meaningless or impossible in the face of risk and uncertainty. A second school of criticism, managerialism, has attacked the notion of a single-minded firm and displaced profit as the firm's sole object. Arguing that managers control the largest modern corporations, managerialists have devised such theories as managerial utility, sales maximization subject to minimum profit constraint, growth rate maximization, and maximization of the discounted present value of sales revenues. However, empirical tests of the observable implications of these managerial theories have done no more than tarnish the traditional theory except on the cost side, and then primarily under conditions of market power. Where competition does not keep costs in check, profit maximization has been rather bruised and battered by the tests.

Finally, the behavioralists attack every one of traditional theory's assumptions. They argue that "the firm" can only be multiminded in light of its complexity and internal diversity. They claim that satisficing makes more sense and is more frequently observed than maximizing. They also deny that profit maximization can be an operational objective. Although common sense and a rudimentary knowledge of the modern bureaucratic corporation tell us that these claims carry much truth, it is difficult to test the extent of this truth empirically. Satisficing behavior is often similar to profit maximizing, especially in price policy.

In the end, then, profits remain a major concern of the modern firm. There is enough truth in managerialism and behavioralism, however, that pure profit maximizing, as assumed by traditional neoclassical theory, is in reality rather rare.

Part II

STRUCTURE

4

Introduction to Structure

The emergence of Big Business . . . as a social reality during the past fifty years is the most important event in the recent social history of the western world.
—PETER F. DRUCKER (1946)

Once we look beyond the perfectly competitive firms and markets of neoclassical theory, the world becomes more interesting. It also becomes more complex. To cope with the complexity we shall focus our attention on power—economic power in general and market power in particular—as follows:

1. What is economic power?
2. What is market power?
3. How can market power be measured?
4. What are the sources and causes of market power?
5. How can these sources and causes be measured?
6. What policies can be devised to control the distribution of power?

The purpose of this chapter is to provide the introductory answers to the first four questions. It serves to preface the more detailed answers to all the questions that follow in the next six chapters covering "structure."

I. WHAT IS ECONOMIC POWER?

Forbes recently reported on the economic power of General Electric Corp. During the first six years of the 1980s, GE changed dramatically, reshuffling its "corporate portfolio like a riverboat gambler, acquiring 338 business and product lines for $11.1 billion."

> Nothing like this has been seen in corporate America since the conglomerator days of LTV's Jimmy Ling and Gulf & Western's Charles Bluhdorn. With GE, it's a case of enormous financial might, coupled with the readiness to acquire — or to dump. Says one former GE official, "This company is prepared to buy or sell any business, depending on how it fits into its overall strategy."[1]

Thus GE has an enormous capacity to influence events. This suggests that **economic power** *is the ability of some persons or firms to produce intended effects on others.*[2]

This definition is limited in that it implies omnipotence when economic power is actually a matter of degree. Power almost always has its confines. The *Forbes* article on GE, for instance, points out that GE has been *selling* businesses as well as buying them. During the period it bought 338 businesses and product lines for $11.1 billion, the company sold 232 others for $5.9 billion, and many of these divestitures were GE failures. Hence an alternative definition that conveys "capacity to influence" yet acknowledges the limitations faced by even the most powerful of firms may be credited to Robert E. Smith. He says that **economic power** *is a constrained set of conduct options.*[3] Fewer and weaker constraints grant greater discretion and therefore more economic power.

The "conduct options" referred to in this definition include acquisitions, product innovations, public relations advertising, plant expansions, intensive government lobbying, joint venturing, and the manipulation of many other variables.

Both definitions assume the existence of "power sources" and "power targets." *Power sources* give the firm its "capacity to influence," its "conduct options." Firm size is, in general, a major power source. And that size can occur in a single-market context or multimarket context. A firm's rank or share in a specific market indicates single market size. For example, GE enjoys first place ranking and huge market shares in each of the following U.S. markets — aircraft engines, electric motors, lighting, turbine generators, and railroad locomotives. According to Jack

---

[1] Edwin A. Finn, Jr., "General Eclectic," *Forbes*, March 23, 1987, p. 75.

[2] Derived from Dennis H. Wrong, *Power: Its Forms, Bases, and Uses* (New York: Harper & Row, 1979), p.2.

[3] Robert E. Smith, "Economic and Political Characteristics of Cartel and Cartel-like Practices," in *Competition in International Business*, edited by O. Schachter and R. Hellawell (New York: Columbia University Press, 1981), p. 182.

Welch, GE's chairman, single-market position is a key source of GE's power:

> To prosper in this world, Welch believes GE must achieve competitive advantages that allow it to rank first or second in every market it serves. So often is this simple concept repeated around GE that people express it as a single, seven-syllable word: 'number-one-an'-number-two.'[4]

In contrast, multimarket size can refer to overall corporate size, as illustrated again by *Forbes*, which reports that overall size is a major source of GE's power and that still greater overall size is apparently one of its main objectives:

> Clearly, GE has the stomach to swallow huge companies with barely a burp. The next takeover could be the size of Corning Glass, Honeywell, or Merrill Lynch. Outlandish? Not at all. . . . Only last December, in a rare and closed-door meeting with analysts in New York, GE Chairman Jack Welch, 51, noted that, in just six years since he took over as chief executive, the company had moved from tenth largest company in the U.S. as measured by stock market capitalization, to third largest. Then, astonishingly, he went on to suggest he would like GE to be the nation's largest company.[5]

Power targets are those who are influenced, those affected, when the firm exercises its conduct options. They include consumers, workers, raw materials suppliers, competing firms, other businesses generally, government regulators, voters, and so on.

Table 4–1 presents an eight-part matrix that results from crossing two possible *sources* of economic power with four classes of power *targets*. As indicated by the column headings, the sources are single-market size and multiple-market size. The targets are distributed by rows. A brief description of each cell's contents will help.

1. *Single-market power with the customers and suppliers of the firm as targets.* This is the traditional case in neoclassical theory, where a pure monopolist raises selling price to customers (and a pure monopsonist lowers the purchase price paid to suppliers).
2. *Single-market power with actual and potential rivals as targets.* Dynamic monopolization fits here (see pages 46–48 of Chapter 2). A powerful firm may injure rivals or potential entrants with predatory tactics.
3. *Single-market power vis-à-vis business enterprises in general.* Power in one market (like jet engines) may help fund acquisitions in other markets (like TV broadcasting).
4. *Single-market power influencing society in general.* There is evidence

---

4 Stratford P. Sherman, "The Mind of Jack Welch," *Fortune*, March 27, 1989, p. 40.
5 Finn, "General Eclectic," pp. 75–76.

TABLE 4–1.   Sources of the "Capacity" and Targets of the "Influence" That Constitute Economic Power

Targets of the Influence	Source of Power	
	Size in Single Market	Size in Multiple Markets
Customers and suppliers	1	5
Market rivals (actual and potential)	2	6
Businesses at large	3	7
Society in general	4	8

that political activity is associated with single-market power.[6] Moreover, such power can affect the "market" for ideas when present in TV broadcasting, newspapers, and other media.

5. *Multimarket power: customers and suppliers.*   Prominent positioning in several markets can bestow power to influence a firm's customers or suppliers in a single market. An example is price discrimination achieved by tying — as when IBM tied punch cards to its data processing equipment.[7]

6. *Multimarket power: actual and potential rivals.*   Dynamic monopolization reappears here, as multimarket power may give a firm exclusionary advantages vis-à-vis actual or potential rivals. For example, Kodak exploited its multimarket powers in photography to curb the competition of rivals who originally developed miniature cameras and cartridge-loading film formats.[8]

7. *Multimarket power: business at large.*   The key issue here is the firm's power in acquiring other firms or in blocking its own acquisition by others. Immense overall size, as may derive from multimarket expanse, is helpful in this respect.

8. *Multimarket power: society in general.*   The political implications of large multimarket size are fairly easy to imagine. As Kenneth Elzinga observes, "small enterprises, located in but one congressional district and without a potent trade association, cannot marshal the

[6] Russell Pittman, "Market Structure and Campaign Contributions," *Public Choice* (Fall 1977), pp. 37–52; and John S. Heywood, "The Structural Determinants of Corporate Campaign Activity," *Quarterly Review of Economics and Business* (Spring 1988), pp. 39–45.

[7] M. L. Burstein, "A Theory of Full-Line Forcing," *Northwestern University Law Review* (March–April 1960), pp. 62–95.

[8] James W. Brock, "Structural Monopoly, Technological Performance, and Predatory Innovation," *American Business Law Journal* (Fall 1983), pp. 291–306.

forces of a large, diversified firm with facilities in over a hundred districts."[9]

Although the scope of *economic* power thus extends to all eight cells of Table 4–1, the scope of *market* power extends only to the subset indicated by cells 1, 2, 5, and 6. These four cases are what this book is about. Hence market power now takes center stage.

II. WHAT IS MARKET POWER?

Market power *is the ability to influence market price and/or subdue rivals.* A firm's ability to subdue rivals (cells 2 and 6 of Table 4–1) will be discussed in Chapter 11, which introduces market "conduct." Here, to introduce market structure further, we concentrate on the firm's ability to influence market price (cells 1 and 5 of Table 4–1).

The key word here is "ability." A buyer or seller may have the ability to influence price but may not actually use that ability. Still, power would be present, just as a boxer's power is always present, outside and inside the ring. Stress on ability is important because pricing behavior is not, in and of itself, a feature of market structure. Structure does, however, determine ability.

As already indicated in Chapter 2, variations in the features of market structure cause variations in the ways individual sellers view their demand and individual buyers view their supply. Figure 4–1 summarizes individual seller views of demand according to variations in market structure. Figure 4–1(a) depicts the horizontal demand curve of a perfectly competitive seller who has no power to influence price. At the other extreme, 4–1(b) shows a monopolist's demand curve, which is labeled DD because, by definition, this is the marketwide demand curve as well. The monopolist's power is reflected in the wide range of price options offered by this demand curve.

Between these two extreme cases is an intermediate situation of "rivalry" among a limited number of sellers. Here the firm confronts two demand curves with downward slope, neither of which is the marketwide demand curve. The firm might perceive either one or both (or portions of both) of these demand curves, depending on what assumptions it makes concerning its rivals' behavior. If the firm assumes that its

---

[9] Kenneth G. Elzinga, "The Goals of Antitrust: Other than competition and Efficiency, What Else Counts?" *University of Pennsylvania Law Review* (June 1977), p. 1197. In 1987 Farley Industries, Inc., launched a campaign promoting the company's CEO, William Farley, for purposes of building his public image "should he decide to run for political office" as well as for boosting the corporation's public image. *The Wall Street Journal*, April 9, 1987, p.31. For a report on corporate image campaigns by Waste Management, Inc., W. R. Grace & Co., Coors Co., and others, see Anne B. Fisher, "Spiffing Up the Corporate Image," *Fortune*, July 21, 1986, pp. 68–72.

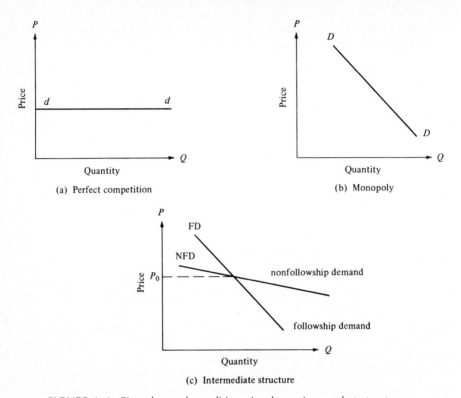

FIGURE 4–1. Firm demand conditions in alternative market structures.

rivals will follow any price change it makes up or down from P_o, which is the going price, then it will consider the "followship demand" FD curve the applicable demand curve. With rivals matching its every price move, the particular firm cannot gain or lose market share because it will neither take sales away from nor give sales to its rivals through any price change it makes. The downward slope derives entirely from sales variations at the marketwide level, with the individual firm always getting its constant share of marketwide sales. Thus this FD curve could also be called a "constant share" demand curve, and it is a close reflection of the marketwide demand curve.

In contrast, the "nonfollowship demand" NFD curve of Figure 4–1(c) is based on the assumption that rivals in the market do *not* follow the price changes of the firm depicted but instead leave their prices unchanged at P_o. The elasticity of this NFD curve is much greater than the elasticity of the followship curve because, without followship, the firm will win customers away from its rivals when it cuts price below P_o, or lose customers to its rivals when it raises price above P_o. With customers moving among firms as well as into and out of the market, the firm's market share will rise with a price cut and fall with a price hike. The NFD curve could therefore also be called a "changing market share curve." A firm confronting this set of demand curves has *some* power over price, but not as much as a monopolist.

III. HOW CAN MARKET POWER BE MEASURED?

The **Rothschild index** is a *theoretical* measure of market power based on a comparison of the slopes of the followship and nonfollowship demand curves.[10] Redrawing these curves in Figure 4–2 and labeling certain points for purposes of computation, we may summarize the Rothschild index as follows:

$$\text{Rothschild index} = \frac{\text{slope of NFD}}{\text{slope of FD}} = \frac{JK/JM}{JL/JM} = \frac{JK}{JL}$$

Under perfect competition the nonfollowship curve would be perfectly horizontal, yielding a ratio of JK/JL equal to zero. On the other hand, a monopolist would observe no difference between the followship and nonfollowship curves. Because the monopolist does not share the market with any rivals, there is no question whether they will or won't follow his price initiatives. When FD and NFD coalesce, the ratio JK/JL

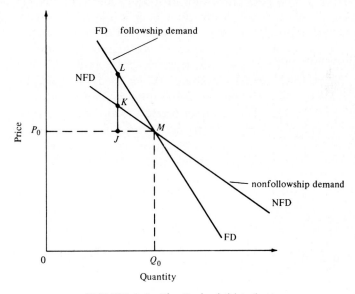

FIGURE 4–2. The Rothschild index.

[10] K. W. Rothschild, "The Degree of Monopoly," *Economica* (February 1942), pp. 24–40.

equals one. From these two extreme observations it should be clear that intermediate cases range between zero and one, varying directly with market power. In short, the Rothschild index provides one answer to this question: "How can market power be measured?" Other, more practical, measures derive from the sources of market power.

IV. WHAT ARE THE SOURCES OF MARKET POWER?

Moving beyond size alone, the following chapters focus on three structural characteristics that contribute to market power:

1. *Product differentiation:* The greater the degree of product differentiation, the steeper the nonfollowship demand curve and the greater the JK/JL ratio. With differentiation, many buyers prefer particular brands for *non*-price reasons, such as style and advertising image. Product differentiation thus produces less price-induced brand switching and more stable market shares in the face of price differentials than would be observed with standardized products.

2. *Market share:* The larger the firm's market share, the closer NFD approaches FD and, consequently, the higher the JK/JL ratio. To see this relationship, consider a price cut by a firm with 1% of the market and compare its effect to that of a price cut by a firm with 90% of the market. The small firm will have a highly elastic NFD curve because it can easily double or triple its sales and market share by cutting price. On the other hand, the monster with the 90% share already has so much of the market that, even if it takes the remaining 10% away from its rivals, it won't achieve much of a gain in sales or market share. When measuring the power of a *group* of firms, their market shares may be combined.

3. *Barriers to entry:* The effect of barriers is not directly observable in Figure 4–2 as it stands. Entry is a long-run matter, whereas these curves relate to the short run. However, let FD depict short-run demand and NFD depict long-run demand (allowing sufficient time for entry to occur); then high barriers to entry will cause NFD to coincide more closely with FD above price P_o, and the JK/JL ratio will be greater the more formidable the barriers. In other words, we could look upon new entrants as nonfollowers who eventually come into the market charging price P_o, in the event the established firm boosts price above P_o. Accordingly, the long-run NFD curve will be more elastic under conditions of easy entry than it would be with difficult entry.

There are numerous other elements of structure that might influence market power—including growth, vertical integration, and diversification. Unfortunately, we have only enough space to touch on these other elements in various spots later[11]. By concentrating on differentiation, market shares, and entry, we follow in the footsteps of Joe Bain, Richard Caves, and Willard Mueller.[12] It should also be stressed that the Rothschild index provides only one answer to the question, "How can market power be measured?" And it is not necessarily the best answer.[13] Its greatest shortcoming is its purely theoretical nature. In practice, it is not possible to estimate the index accurately, so measures of differentiation, market share, and entry barriers are used instead.

V. PERFORMANCE MEASURES OF MARKET POWER

Because market power can influence economic performance, economists have devised several measures of market power that refer explicitly to performance. We shall note two such measures—one devised by Abba Lerner, the other by Joe Bain.

The **Lerner index** measures the divergence between price and marginal cost that may result from the exercise of market power.[14]

$$\text{Lerner index} = \frac{\text{price} - \text{marginal cost}}{\text{price}}$$

Under perfect competition there is no divergence between price and marginal cost, in which case the Lerner index is zero. With monopoly, however, the divergence can be substantial. Looking back to the monopoly result in Figure 2–7 on page 36, we can see that the Lerner index in that case would be DA/DQ_1. In Figure 2–8 on page 37 the index would be AC/AQ_m. It will be noted that in no case could the index exceed a value of one, so its theoretical range is from zero to one.

Table 4–2 reports Lerner indexes for American auto producers, estimated from data during 1973–1982. General Motors has the highest degree of market power with an index of .329, followed by Ford at .252, and then Chrysler and AMC at the bottom. Table 4–2 also reports on

---

[11] Still others we must ignore altogether. See, for example, Sanford V. Berg and Philip Friedman, "Impacts of Domestic Joint Ventures" *Review of Economics and Statistics* (May 1981), pp. 293–298.

[12] Joe Bain, *Industrial Organization* (New York: John Wiley & Sons, 1959); R. Caves, *American Industry: Structure, Conduct and Performance* (Englewood Cliffs, N.J.: Prentice-Hall, 1964): and W. F. Mueller, *A Primer on Monopoly and Competition* (New York: Random House, 1970).

[13] Other authors of such measures include A. G. Papandreou, "Market Structure and Monopoly Power," *American Economic Review* (September 1949), pp. 883–897; and R. Triffin, *Monopolistic Competition and General Equilibrium Theory* (Cambridge, Mass.: Harvard University Press, 1940).

[14] A. P. Lerner, "The Concept of Monopoly and the Measurement of Monopoly Power," *Review of Economic Studies* (June 1934), pp. 157–175.

TABLE 4–2. Estimates of Lerner Indexes (Price-Cost Margins) and Market Shares for U.S. Automobile Companies (1973–1982)

Company	Lerner Index	Market Share
General Motors	.329	39.5%
Ford Motor	.252	25.9
Chrysler Corporation	.149	9.7
AMC	.165	1.9

Source: Stephen Martin, "The Measurement of Profitability and the Diagnosis of Market Power," *International Journal of Industrial Organization* (September 1988), pp. 301–321.

market shares, showing GM at 39.5%, Ford at 25.9%, and so on down to AMC at 1.9%. Hence there is considerable correlation between the Lerner index and market share in these data, as one would expect.[15]

One problem with the Lerner index is that marginal costs usually cannot be estimated. This severely limits its practical application. Another problem rests in the fact that the Lerner index is a measure of actual conduct—a measure of the *exercise* of power rather than its mere existence. A value of zero, though indicating pure competition, would be observed if a monopolist for some reason chose to keep price low, close to marginal cost, rather than to raise price and maximize profit.

This problem of exercise versus existence also bedevils the **Bain index**, which focuses directly on excess profit.[16] The idea is that competition produces zero excess profit. Hence monopoly power would be revealed by a persistence of positive excess profit—the higher the more the monopoly power.

Estimation of such excess profits, though more practical than estimation of the Lerner index, requires a modification of accounting profit plus an assumption. Accounting profit in total dollars, which may be found in a firm's annual income statement, is

$$\pi_a = R - C - D$$

[15] It is also interesting that the Lerner indexes rose with the imposition of quotas on Japanese imports. For example, GM's index was .342 pre-quota and .424 post-quota. The protection from Japanese competition thus gave the U.S. firms added market power. Stephen Martin, "The Measurement of Profitability and the Diagnosis of Market Power," *International Journal of Industrial Organization* (September 1988), pp. 301–321. For more on Lerner-type measures, see Timothy F. Bresnahan, "Empirical Studies of Industries with Market Power," in *Handbook of Industrial Organization*, edited by R. Schmalensee and R. Willig (Amsterdam: North-Holland, 1989), chapter 17.

[16] Joe S. Bain, "The Profit Rate as a Measure of Monopoly Power," *Quarterly Journal of Economics*, (February 1941), pp. 271–293.

where R = total revenues
$\quad\quad C$ = total current costs
$\quad\quad D$ = depreciation

To obtain excess profit, Bain deducts from accounting profit an assumed (or estimated) "cost" of investors capital, that is

$$\pi_e = R - C - D - iV$$

where i = the rate of return that could be earned on alternative (normal profit) investments
$\quad\quad V$ = the total value of the owners' investment

If converted to a percentage rate, the Bain index would be π_e/V.

This discussion does not exhaust the possibilities. However, we must postpone further discussion of performance measures until after we have studied structure in detail.

SUMMARY

The structural discussions of the next six chapters have now been introduced by considering economic and market power. Variations in structure correspond to variations in power.

What is economic power? It is the ability to produce intended effects—a constrained set of conduct options. With economic power, a firm can easily buy other firms, or comfortably raise price above cost when selling its product, or behave fairly freely in other ways. Power sources (such as single-market and multimarket size) bestow this ability while power targets (such as customers or society in general) are those affected by the firm's power. (See Table 4–1).

Market power is the subset of economic power that applies to customers, suppliers, and rivals (cells 1,2,5, and 6 of Table 4–1). It is the ability to influence market price and/or subdue rivals. Here we focus on power over price.

Because price is always determined by prevailing supply and demand conditions, at least some control of supply or demand or both is required before such power can be said to exist. Even when the government wants to influence price it must resort to one of these controls, as is illustrated by the government's reliance on rationing tickets to "control" demand when it sets a legal price ceiling below the free-market equilibrium level.

Where do the elements of market structure fit into the picture? They are the means, the elements, or the indices of demand and supply control, the chief sources of market power. Product differentiation may be looked upon as a form of demand control. Similarly, a firm with a 70% market share may be said to control 70% of market supply. Also, high barriers to entry give existing firms some degree of control over long-run supply.

Given structure's potential effects on performance, market power may be measured by performance as well as by structure. For the next six chapters, however, we focus on structure.

5

Product Differentiation: Theory and Cross-section Evidence

What's a good product image worth? Philip Morris'
Marlboro man could be worth as much as $10 billion.
— *Forbes*, February 9, 1987

Once upon a time, there was a colorless, odorless, and tasteless beverage that was produced by an essentially simple, easily imitated process. The producers of brand "S" couldn't make their brand any more colorless, odorless, or tasteless than other brands of this beverage. But, by advertising heavily and by pricing brand S above the others, they convinced many drinkers that S was the best. In particular, S's advertising stressed the gaiety and modernity of brand S because this theme would appeal to young, affluent adults. As for pricing, the producers of S were so confident that consumers believed price was an index of quality that at one point they actually *raised* the price of S in response to a competitor's price *cut*. The sales of brand S soared.

This sounds like a fairy tale, but it's not. It's the true story of Smirnoff vodka.[1] Indeed, Smirnoff was so successful with this marketing strategy that during the 1970s it became the number one brand of vodka. Why do we tell the story here? Because it illustrates product differentiation, which gives a firm some power over price.

This chapter has four objectives:

1. To define "product differentiation" and a related phenomenon, "market segmentation"
2. To show how differentiation and segmentation affect a firm's demand
3. To review the main sources of product differentiation, namely,
   a. product attributes
   b. imperfect information
   c. subjective (nonrational) preferences
4. To relate this chapter's findings to some later topics

The scholarly literature on these subjects is immense. But we must be content with a summary.

I. WHAT IS PRODUCT DIFFERENTIATION?

A. Definition

Stated simply, product differentiation occurs when buyers perceive differences among the brands of a product. Table 5–1, for instance, reports on alternatives for chicken and potatoes, as seen in Chicago food stores in 1985, together with the different prices per pound paid by consumers. The range of prices is huge in each case, $0.79 to $4.92 and $0.40 to $2.88, respectively. Of course the main differences in these alternatives is convenience. The higher-priced versions take less time and effort to prepare. Because many consumers willingly pay dearly for convenience,[2] this example illustrates a further feature of product differentiation. There is a certain degree of buyer loyalty or attachment to certain brands. Buyers do not make choices randomly. They do so more or less purposefully, as indicated by their willingness to pay more for some brands than others (thereby sustaining the existence of those favored brands).

Big differences also appear for other products. Perfumes selling for $100 to $300 an ounce contain ingredients costing as little as $2.50 an ounce, leading to imitations. Giorgio brand perfume sells for $135 an

---

[1] R. D. Buzzell, R. E. M. Nourse, J. B. Matthews, Jr., and T. Levitt, *Marketing: A Contemporary Analysis* (New York: McGraw-Hill, 1972), pp. 10–11.

[2] According to industry estimates, only about 30% of all meals are the old-fashioned, home-cooked kind for the whole family, the balance being frozen meals, takeout food, and so on. *The Wall Street Journal*, July 25, 1985, p. 21.

TABLE 5–1. Different Chicken and Potato Products and Their Price to Consumers

Chicken Product	Price per Pound	Potato Product	Price per Pound
Whole fryer	$0.79	5 lb potatoes	$0.40
Swanson fried chicken entree with whipped potatoes	2.58	Ore-Ida frozen cottage fries	0.85
Swift Chicken Cordon Bleu (filled with cheese, Canadian bacon)	3.99	Frozen Green Giant stuffed potatoes	2.13
Tyson frozen breaded breast fillets	4.92	Betty Crocker au gratin potatoes (mix)	2.88

Source: Betsy Morris, "How Much Will People Pay to Save a Few Minutes of Cooking? Plenty," *The Wall Street Journal*, July 25, 1985, p. 21.

ounce while at the same time imitators like Primo and Georgy Girl sell for only $7.50.[3]

The differences between brands can thus range widely — image, convenience, flavor, quality, service, store location (if retailing), and price. In sum, **product differentiation** *occurs when consumers perceive that a product differs from its competition on any physical or nonphysical characteristic, including price.*[4]

Product differentiation may be illustrated using a two-dimensional attribute space, such as that depicted for grocery stores in Figure 5–1. One axis represents variations in price-service combinations. The other represents variations in assortments offered, with broad assortments yielding opportunities for one-stop shopping. Convenience stores, like 7–11 and Circle K, are thus quite different from conventional supermarkets, like most Safeway and Winn Dixie stores, and even more different than superwarehouse stores.

Figure 5–1 also illustrates market segmentation, which is related to product differentiation but distinct. Notice that the substantial supply-side variations in type of store (differentiation) would not occur unless

---

[3] *Business Week*, June 1, 1987, p. 97; *The Wall Street Journal*, December 10, 1987.

[4] Peter R. Dickson and James L. Ginter, "Market Segmentation, Product Differentiation, and Marketing Strategy," *Journal of Marketing* (April 1987), p. 4. See also Jacob Jacoby and Robert W. Chestnut, *Brand Loyalty Measurement and Management* (New York: John Wiley, 1978), pp. 80–81.

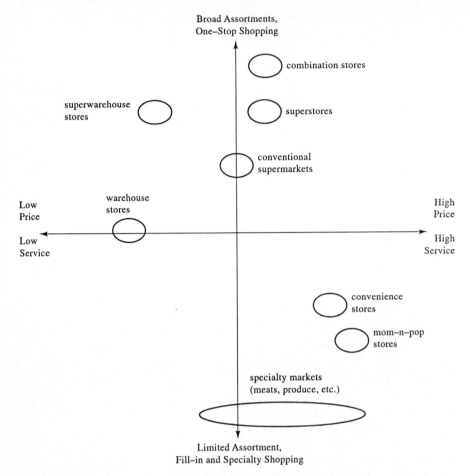

FIGURE 5–1. Grocery store formats on two dimensions. Source: Bruce W. Marion, "Entry Barriers: Theory, Empirical Evidence, and the Food Industries" in R. L. Wills, J. A. Caswell and J. D. Culbertson (eds.) *Issues After a Century of Federal Competition Policy* (Lexington, Mass.: Lexington Books, 1987), p. 196.

there were demand-side variations among shoppers (market segmentation), with some shoppers occasionally preferring convenience stores and mom and pop stores over warehouse stores despite the substantial differences in price levels. Hence **market segmentation** may be defined as *heterogeneity in demand functions such that marketwide demand can be divided into segments or clusters of fairly distinct demands.*[5] Examples of such segmentation include the automobile market (sports cars, family sedans,

[5] Dickson and Ginter, "Market Segmentation, Differentiation, and Marketing Strategy," p. 4.

vans, etc.), beer (superpremiums, premiums, lights, etc.), and grocery stores (as indicated in Figure 5–1).

Figures 5–2 and 5–3 clarify these concepts. The two-dimensional attribute space, YY' on the one hand and XX' on the other, may represent any two attributes (such as fiber content and the degree of sweetness in breakfast cereals). Each dot indicates the ideal combination of these attributes for each individual consumer (like Jack and Sue). In Figure 5–2, which illustrates product differentiation in the absence of market segmentation, the dots are evenly distributed throughout the attribute space. Hence a wide diversity of demand side preferences is assumed for Figure 5–2. This rules out market segmentation. However, the diversity does allow, it even encourages, product differentiation. This is shown for brand A. Assume that, gathered in the center, brands A, B, and C are perceived as identical by buyers, each brand getting one-third of total sales. After A differentiates to location A*, taking on

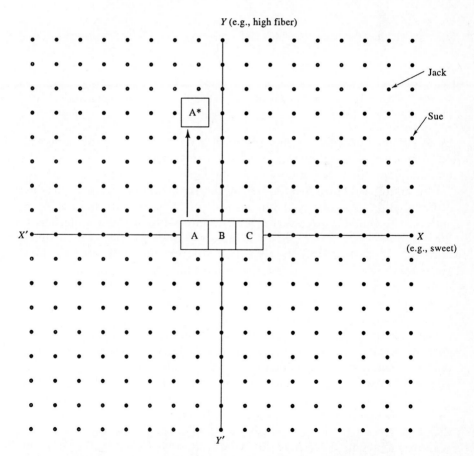

FIGURE 5–2. Product differentiation with no market segmentation.

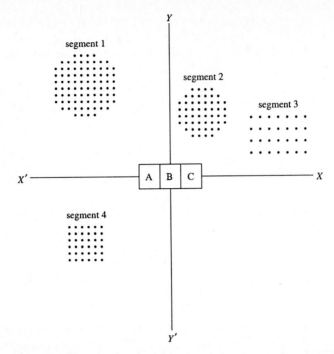

FIGURE 5–3. Market segmentation without product differentiation.

greater Y attribute (e.g., higher fiber), it gains market share by appealing more closely to the preferences of those favoring the Y attribute. The market shares then become, say, $A^* = 46\%$, $B = 27\%$, and $C = 27\%$.

In contrast, Figure 5–3 shows market segmentation without product differentiation. Assume that buyers see no differences in brands A, B, and C. The brands are gathered indistinguishably at the intersection of the attribute axes. As regards the buyers, however, they are clustered into four separate segments according to concentrations of their ideal preferences. The largest market segment, for instance, is segment 1. People in that segment like a YX' combination of attributes. Segments 2 and 3 represent clusters of preferences for YX combinations, while segment 4 lies in the $Y'X'$ quadrant.

As Figure 5–3 stands, none of the brands exactly matches the preferences of any of the segments. It is easy to imagine, however, that brand A could be changed to move in the direction of segment 1 by taking on greater amounts of Y and X' attributes. Brand A's incentive to differentiate in this way would be the greater market share it would gain. Of course, brands B and C could play the same game. Imagine that B differentiates toward segment 4 and C moves to segment 2 once A moves to segment 1. The result would then be a combination of product differentiation (with brands A, B, and C differentiated) and market segmentation (with 1, 2, 3, and 4 separated). Indeed, it is easy to imagine a fourth brand being created, say, D, such that each segment of the market in Figure 5–3 would then have a brand with attributes closely corresponding to those of the segment.

To this point we have assumed that buyer preferences are given. Product differentiation has tailored brands to fit those preferences more closely than otherwise, but preferences haven't changed. In Figure 5–2, A became A*, which more closely matched some preferences for the Y attribute. In Figure 5–3, we imagined alterations in A, B, and C plus the introduction of D to cater to the distinct preferences of the four segments. These product changes will change the firm's perception of its demand, even though the buyers' demands and preferences have not changed. For example, until the late 1920s Ford's "Model T" and "Model A" cars—which were cheap, simple, and black—dominated the auto market. During the 1920s and 1930s General Motors took business away from Ford and expanded GM sales tremendously by differentiating its offering into a "full line" of cars, from the inexpensive, plain Chevrolet to the pricy, luxurious Cadillac, with intermediate preferences filled by Oldsmobile and Buick. Recent experience in the ice cream industry has been similar. Traditionally, most ice cream has been "economy" or "regular" ice cream with about 10% butter fat and priced at $2 to $3 a half gallon. Now, since 1980, "superpremium" ice creams, like Häagen Dazs and Frusen Gladje, have come on the scene with butter fats exceeding 14% and prices soaring to $8 to $10 a half gallon. Their huge success, approaching $1 billion in total sales in 1989, suggests the presence of a previously unmet demand among ice cream lovers.[6]

Instead of more closely meeting some preexisting consumer demand by varying product features, a firm may also be able to *change buyer preferences* to correspond more closely with those being offered. As shown later in this chapter, this may be achieved by persuasive advertising. For mysterious reasons many people are now convinced, for example, that, contrary to nature, calcium ought to be in orange juice (Citrus Hill), that bloodshot eyes are disgraceful (Visine), and that dogs should be fed gourmet food (Select Pedigree Dinners).

Figure 5–4 shows a before and after comparison illustrating a shift of buyer preferences toward brand A. Segmentation and differentiation are present both before and after. The change occurs when the promoters of brand A coax the circular segment out of the X'Y quadrant into the YX quadrant. This could be called a "differentiation demand change."

In contrast, Figure 5–5 illustrates a "segmentation demand change." Before, in panel (a), there is no market segmentation. After, in panel (b) of Figure 5–5, a new segment has been created around brand A. Miller's

---

[6] *The Wall Street Journal*, December 21, 1988, p. B1.

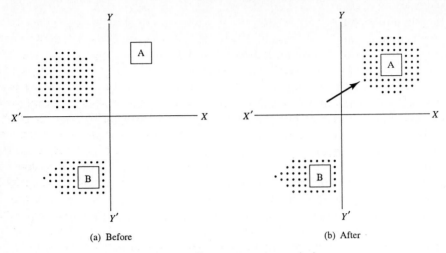

(a) Before   (b) After

FIGURE 5–4. Differentiation demand change.

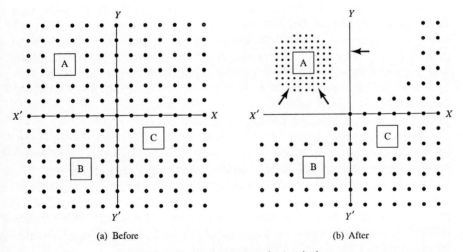

(a) Before   (b) After

FIGURE 5–5. Segmentation demand change.

Lite beer probably qualifies as an example of this. Miller was not the first brewing company to market a light beer (it was Rheingold with Gablinger's in 1968). However, Miller was the first to promote its Lite among beer drinkers generally, spending enormous sums on an especially successful advertising campaign that had ex-athletes arguing over the beer's taste and tummy volume. Miller can therefore be credited with creating the light beer segment which now has Bud Light, Coors

Light, and many other brands, all differentiated from Miller's Lite by brand name if not by taste.

Four concepts have now been identified: product differentiation, market segmentation, differentiation demand change, and segmentation demand change. Though strictly speaking each is distinct, we shall often use the term "product differentiation" as a catchall term to cover them all. This will simplify matters considerably because it is often difficult to know exactly where real-world events fit among the specifics. Super-premium ice cream, for instance, was said to be a case of "product differentiation." In fact, it also has many characteristics of "differentiation demand change" and "segmentation demand change." The example of Miller Lite was said to be a "segmentation demand change," but the incident started out as a simple case of "product differentiation." The overlaps and ambiguities further arise when assessing the impact these several phenomena have on the firm's view of demand. Although we have four concepts, there are essentially only two consequences for the firm's demand curve. We consider those next as effects of "product differentiation" with the understanding that they may also be due to market segmentation, differentiation demand change, or segmentation demand change.

B. Impact on Firm Demand

Successful differentiation can either shift the individual seller's demand curve outward, enabling her to sell a larger quantity at a given price, or tilt her demand curve to a steeper slope, and therefore lower elasticity, enabling her to raise her price without losing many customers. *In short, differentiation gives sellers some power over price.*[7]

Figure 5–6 illustrates the first of these effects. A successful exhortative advertising campaign for brand G shifts the demand curve for G from d_{g1} to d_{g2}, resulting in a greater volume of sales, Q_{g2}, as compared with original sales, Q_{g1}. At constant price P_g, total revenues (price times quantity) rise from $0P_gAQ_{g1}$ to $0P_gBQ_{g2}$, suggesting increased profits, provided the additional costs of producing and marketing G are less than the added revenue. Alternatively, price could rise *while quantity is constant.* Assuming brand F and brand G are to some degree substitutes, this favorable shift of tastes to brand G will shift the demand curve of brand F to the left, lowering brand F revenues. Of course, sellers of brand F might try to retaliate by changing their promotional pitch or boosting their advertising outlays, but we shall ignore such gamesmanship until later.

Figure 5–7 illustrates the second possible effect of successful product differentiation. Let curve d_1 depict demand under conditions of little

---

[7] E. H. Chamerlin, *The Theory of Monopolistic Competition* (Cambridge, Mass.: Harvard University Press, 1933).

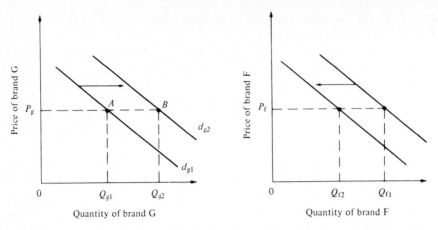

FIGURE 5–6. A shift of sales to brand G by means of advertising or differentiation.

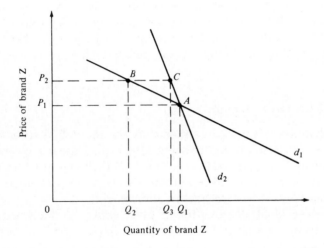

FIGURE 5–7. Reducing elasticity of demand by means of product differentiation.

product differentiation. Then let d_2 depict demand after the introduction of a new advertising theme, which proclaims incessantly that "brand Z folks would rather fight than switch." If the price of brand Z had been raised prior to the new campaign from P_1 to P_2, sales would have fallen from Q_1 to Q_2, and total revenues would have dropped from area $0P_1AQ_1$ to area $0P_2BQ_2$. But, once most brand Z buyers are convinced that they would rather fight than switch, the same increase in price would trim sales only slightly, from Q_1 to Q_3, and total sales receipts would actually rise to an amount represented by area $0P_2CQ_3$. In brief, product differentiation can reduce the price elasticity of demand as well as shift a brand's demand curve outward.

Empirical evidence of shifting firm demand is abundantly available in many of the examples already cited — for example, GM's full line of cars, Häagen-Dazs ice cream, and Miller Lite. Empirical evidence of low price elasticity is more difficult to obtain for technical reasons, but it too is readily available. W. D. Hoyer found from interview evidence that consumers who are not "brand loyal" are more likely to choose their detergent on the basis of price than those who are "brand loyal."[8] Econometric studies of gasoline and breakfast cereal reveal reduced price elasticities of demand for the "major" brands because of product differentiation.[9] The lower elasticities of demand for the major brands of gasoline are particularly interesting because chemically gasoline is essentially identical across brands. Finally, lower price elasticities of demand have been associated with higher levels of advertising expenditure among U.S. food and tobacco products at marketwide levels. The estimated price elasticities of breakfast cereals and soft drinks are more than 11 times lower than those of meat-packing plants and fresh or frozen packed fish, and the former products are much more heavily advertised.[10]

C. Sources of Product Differentiation

We have established that brand differences (and market segmentation) give sellers some power over price. The next question is this: What are the *sources* of this differentiation (and segmentation)? Stated differently, why, exactly, does someone always eat at McDonald's and shun Burger King (or vice versa)? How can high-priced Michelob beer outsell low-priced Schlitz by tens of millions of cases per year when blind taste tests prove that most people cannot taste any difference between them?

As the rest of this chapter explains in detail, all the important sources of product differentiation fall into three categories:

1. *Product attributes.* These are objective variations in products — such as the durability of light bulbs, the size of automobiles, the flavor of soft drinks, the energy efficiency of refrigerators, or the packaging of fruit juices. Different buyers have different preferences which cause them to favor certain brands over others for these objective reasons. They are willing to pay accordingly.

2. *Imperfect information.* Many consumers may not know that cheap brand J orange juice is just as good in every way as the more

---

[8] Wayne D. Hoyer, "An Examination of Consumer Decision Making for a Common Repeat Purchase Product," *Journal of Consumer Research* (December 1984), pp. 822–829.

[9] Margaret E. Slade, "Conjectures, Firm Characteristics and Market Structure: An Empirical Assessment," *International Journal of Industrial Organization* (December 1986), pp. 347–370; J. Nellie Lang, "An Empirical Conjectural Variation Model of Oligopoly," FTC Working Paper No. 151, February 1987.

[10] Emilio Pagoulatos and Robert Sorensen, "What Determines the Elasticity of Industry Demand?" *International Journal of Industrial Organization* (September 1986), pp. 237–250.

expensive Minute Maid brand. Hence they may pay more for Minute Maid simply out of ignorance. This source of differentiation is also "objective" to the extent that improved information would erase the buyers' loyalty to the more expensive brand.

3. *Subjective desires*. Humans are not always or even usually rational (or objective). Hence they may succumb to persuasive advertising, brand image, and other nonrational prompters when spending their money.

Most economic literature on product differentiation centers on the first two sources.[11] Their objective nature, when coupled with assumptions of profit maximization for sellers and utility maximization for buyers, allows theorists to devise elaborate formal models about them. The "subjective" nature of the last source discourages formal economic theorizing and grants a great deal of authority on the topic to non-economists—especially applied psychologists and marketing experts. The rationality governing modern economic theory on the first two sources (product attributes and imperfect information) includes these assumptions:

- People can express preferences among all commodities.
- They have relatively stable preferences.
- They have transitive preferences (i.e., *a* is greater than *b* and *b* is greater than *c* means *a* is greater than *c*).
- They always choose that set of available goods which maximizes their preferences, subject to the constraints of their resources.

However appealing these assumptions may be to economic theorists, there is a mountain of evidence that, in reality, consumers do not fit this description very well. On the contrary, consumers might best be described as being "nonrational," strongly moved by subjective and even subconscious desires.[12] Hence the third category of sources is as impor-

---

11 Richard E. Caves and Peter J. Williamson, "What Is Product Differentiation, Really?" *Journal of Industrial Economics* (December 1985), pp. 113–132; Norman Ireland, *Product Differentiation and Nonprice Competition* (Oxford: Basil Blackwell, 1987); and Michael Waterson, "Models of Product Differentiation," *Bulletin of Economic Research* (January 1989), pp. 1–28.

12 H. A. Simon, "A Behavioral Model of Rational Choice," *Quarterly Journal of Economics*, Vol. 69 (1955), pp. 99–118; James G. March, "Bounded Rationality, Ambiguity, and the Engineering of Choice," *Bell Journal of Economics* (Autumn 1978), pp. 587–608; Barry Schwartz, *The Battle for Human Nature* (New York: W. W. Norton, 1986), pp. 152–181; Jon Elster, *Sour Grapes: Studies in the Subversion of Rationality* (Cambridge: Cambridge University Press, 1983); Amitai Etzioni, *The Moral Dimension* (New York: The Free Press, 1988), pp. 89–180; Richard Thaler, "The Psychology of Choice and the Assumptions of Economics," in *Laboratory Experimentation in Economics*, edited by Alvin E. Roth (Cambridge: Cambridge University Press, 1987) pp. 99–130; and the articles in the June 1989 issue of the *American Economic Review* by John Conlisk (pp. 392–407) and James C. Cox and Seth Epstein (pp. 408–426).

tant as the first two, and in many ways perhaps even more important. To a large extent, advertising succeeds by flattering people's fantasies about themselves or by stimulating false fears and hopes, not by revealing a product's genuine attributes or by informing consumers of their best buys.[13] As Laurel Cutler, Chrysler's marketing vice president, puts it, "very often, the difference between one product and another is the advertising, the brand personality."[14]

II. PRODUCT ATTRIBUTES

Assuming for the moment that buyers *are* fully informed and act rationally, variations in real product attributes may be a source of product differentiation. The basic idea underlying this proposition, an idea stressed by Kevin Lancaster,[15] is that people buy a product or a brand not because of some sweeping subjective image of it, but rather because of the bundle of specific attributes possessed by the product or brand. Lancaster defines "attributes" as "those properties or characteristics of a product which are intrinsic to it, and are concrete, observable, objectively measurable, and relevant to choice among alternatives." The relevant attributes of autos, for instance, would include size, fuel efficiency, horsepower, reliability, and so on. Product differentiation based on variations in such product attributes comes in two forms—*horizontal* differentiation and *vertical* differentiation.

A. Horizontal Differentiation

Horizontal differentiation occurs when one brand contains more of some attributes but less of some other attributes in comparison to another brand. When brands have differing strong and weak points in this manner, consumers having different tastes will select different brands given identical prices. Indeed, each consumer would be willing to pay some extra premium to obtain his or her favored brand.

For example, compare Pizza Hut, Domino's, Godfather's, and your local independent pizza parlor (say, "Angelo's"). Some feature fast delivery. Others stress video games, convivial atmosphere, or menu diversity. Assuming an identical price of $10 for a large pepperoni pizza from any of these alternatives, it is easy to imagine that some people will favor fast delivery, others quality ingredients, still others a diverse menu (something for the whole family), and so on. Hence those sellers featur-

13 S. H. Britt, *Psychological Principles of Marketing and Consumer Behavior* (Lexington, Mass.: Lexington Books, 1978); and Eric Clark, *The Want Makers* (New York: Viking, 1988).

14 *Business Week*, June 12, 1989, p. 80.

15 Kevin Lancaster, *Consumer Demand: A New Approach* (New York: Columbia University Press, 1971).

ing fast delivery may be able to raise their price a little to $11 without losing all their customers to rivals. Other sellers may be able to gain price premiums from their differentiation as well. (And it might be, then, that Angelo's has the best tasting pizza at the lowest prices.)

Some of the earliest theorizing about horizontal differentiation concerned retail store locations. The central idea is that people generally prefer nearby store locations to more distant ones (just as they prefer products with attributes closer to their preferences). Imagine an ice cream stand located in the middle of a long beach, for instance. If the ice cream stand could vary its price level according to the distance sunbathers had to walk for refreshment, a higher price could be charged to nearby sunbathers than to more distant sunbathers.

When generalizing this matter of retail location one must take into account the kinds of goods being retailed. In particular, there is an important difference between convenience goods and shopping goods. The distinction is based primarily on frequency of purchase and product price because **convenience goods** are relatively inexpensive items that people buy regularly, such as food, cigarettes, beverages, drugs, and gasoline. **Shopping goods,** on the other hand, are more costly and more intermittently purchased — appliances, stereos, autos, and furniture, for example. Locating close to consumers has obvious advantages for convenience goods retailers, since consumers value their time and transportation expenses. Convenience may be so important that some retailers (the back road neighborhood gas station, and the 7 — 11 store around the corner) may *specialize* in convenience, extracting a price premium from those consumers who particularly favor ease of access.[16]

Thus, food stores, gas stations, and drugstores dot the landscape here and there. However, shopping goods retailers tend to be clustered closer together in the heart of town, along major thoroughfares, or in large shopping centers. Such clustering enables people who are "in the market" for a new car, washing machine, or suit of clothes to shop around before they buy, comparing prices, terms, styles, service facilities, and so forth.[17]

B. Vertical Differentiation

In 1988 and 1989 some of the major pizza chains expanded their menus to include inexpensive "economy" pizzas and more pricy "gourmet" pizzas. Godfather's, for example, introduced a less expensive, thin-crusted

---

[16] L. W. Weiss, *Economics and American Industry* (New York: John Wiley, 1961), pp. 392–394.

[17] Frederick E. May, "Buying Behavior: Some Research Findings," *Journal of Business* (October 1965), p. 391, and the references therein. See also J. W. Newman and R. Staelin, "Prepurchase Information Seeking for New Cars and Major Household Appliances," *Journal of Marketing Research* (August 1972), pp. 249–257.

pie to be used in its 2-for-1 specials (prompted by the 2-for-1 success of Little Caesars). Asked why Godfather's didn't simply cut price on its regular pizza, Charles Henderson, marketing vice president, said: "We didn't want to cannibalize our premium-product sales." Moreover, he added, "There's a high end and a low end, and we don't want to get caught in the middle."[18]

Vertical differentiation occurs when brands vary in quality, or are at least perceived to do so, such that *all* buyers would prefer a high-quality option to a low-quality option if they had identical prices. Hence, everyone would pick a gourmet pizza over an economy pizza if both were priced at $9. In terms of attributes, two brands are vertically differentiated when the first contains more of all desired characteristics than the second, so that fully informed rational buyers would always choose the first if the price of each happened to be the same. Of course, the prices of different brands *do* vary, as do human preferences. So with low prices on "economy" models and high prices on "premium" versions, some people select the former and some the latter (without deviating from our current assumptions of full information and rationality).

Table 5–2 illustrates this for Xerox copiers. For purposes of pricing strategy, product design, and other key decisions, Xerox sees three main segments in the market, based primarily on the number of copies the machine can make per minute. Low-volume, low-speed machines are priced under $4,000. High-volume, high-speed machines go for $80,000 to $130,000. The middle range lies between.

Firms quite often like to be strongly positioned in the premium levels of a market because that can be especially profitable. The higher price of the higher-quality product is often *disproportionately* high compared to the cost of the higher quality, yielding exceptionally high profit margins to the high quality producers. In copy machines, for example, profit margins tend to be relatively thin at the low end of the market, partly because of vigorous Japanese competition. However, "In the high-

---

TABLE 5–2.   Xerox Market Segments Illustrating Vertical Differentiation

Segment Description	Copies per Minute	Price Range
Low volume	Less than 25	Under $4,000
Mid volume	25–90	$4,000–60,000
High volume	90 plus	$80,000–130,000

Source: Gary Jacobson and John Hillkirk, *Xerox: American Samurai* (New York: Macmillan, 1986), p.17.

---

18 *The Wall Street Journal*, January 12, 1988, p. 31.

volume end of the business, the last thing either Xerox or Kodak wants is a price war."[19] Of course this observation should be qualified by recognizing that *quantities* of sales are important to overall total dollar profit. Hence a low-price strategy (by Ricoh in copiers or Little Caesar's in pizza) can pay off well if it generates an appreciable volume of business.

III. IMPERFECT INFORMATION

A. Introduction

There is a certain clarity to horizontal and vertical differentiation because, at their best, they are grounded on variations in objective product attributes. They arise even when buyers are fully informed and rational. Once imperfect information intrudes, however, as it often does, there is an additional basis for differentiation, one which is the concern of this section. (Still, we continue to assume "rationality" until the next section.)

For example, in 1987 IBM introduced a "new and improved" personal computer called the PS/2. IBM was hoping to regain market share that it had lost to imitating "clones" of equal quality and also to support a 10% to 20% premium in its prices over most rivals. The "new and improved" feature of the PS/2 was what IBM called "Micro Channel," something which caused Chase Manhattan Bank to buy 40 of the computers. But as explained by *The Wall Street Journal* a year after Micro Channel's introduction, this was a case of imperfect information rather than vertical product differentiation:

> Funny thing about this Micro Channel. . . . Even now, many people still aren't sure what it does. Like Robert Schwartz, the computer specialist who selected the IBMs for Chase. "I don't know a lot about it, quite frankly," he confesses. "It facilitates communications, if I'm not mistaken. You tell me."
>
> What some would tell Mr. Schwartz is that Micro Channel isn't mere technology. It is IBM's mystery ingredient: an electronic version of "MFP" in Colgate toothpaste . . . intended to give IBM's PC extra zing in a crowd of look-alikes. . . .
>
> Nobody suggests the Micro Channel . . . is a fake . . . . But as much as anything, its mission is to create a premium image, and preferably command a premium price, that will rebuild IBM's prowess and profit margins in a business that is starting to resemble the hawking of the lowliest of commodities.

[19] Gary Jacobson and John Hillkirk, *Xerox: American Samurai* (New York: Macmillan, 1986), p. 16. For intriguing examples of how vertical differentiation can give firms control of their prices during business recessions, see Naomi R. Lamoreaux, *The Great Merger Movement in American Business, 1895–1904* (Cambridge: Cambridge University Press, 1985), pp. 16–21.

> Promoting Micro Channel, admits one IBM strategist, is like "telling you that the engine in your car has aluminum double-skirted pistons . . . . There is a benefit, but it's a techno-weenie."[20]

An even better example of differentiation based on poor information, one completely free of horizontal or vertical differentiation and also free of subjective manipulation by persuasion, derives from an experiment by a professor of marketing, W. T. Tucker. He arranged to have a large sample of Texas housewives choose a loaf of bread from several alternative "brands" delivered fresh to their door on 12 occasions over several weeks. The "brands" were distinguished only by a neutral letter from the middle of the alphabet—M, P, L, or H. Unknown to the consumers, the loaves were otherwise perfectly identical in every way— same batch, same wrap, same size, etcetera. However, Tucker found brand loyalty developing among these consumers within a few weeks, where "brand loyalty" was defined as three successive selections of the same "brand." Moreover, the strength of the brand loyalty was such that a majority of loyal housewives continued to choose "their" brand even after monetary rewards were offered for switching to other brands. One persistently brand-loyal woman said, in effect, "I know why you put money on those other brands; they're lousy."[21] It thus appears that consumers frequently do not know much about product attributes or which brand best satisfies their needs. As a consequence, imperfect information creates conditions for product differentiation.

Information deficiencies divide neatly into two types: those concerning *prices* and those concerning *qualities*. Deficiencies in price information relate primarily to the retail level. For instance, once you decide you want to buy an IBM PS/2, you have a problem discovering where to buy it most cheaply. Deficiencies in quality information relate more to the manufacturer's level: What really is the benefit of Micro Channel? Which brand of bread tastes best and is most nutritious? We tackle price information deficiencies first, then quality problems.

B. Price Information Imperfections

Lack of information about price is a simpler problem to analyze than is that about quality. In a 1961 article that remains influential today, George Stigler argued that buyers benefit by having good information about prices, but their information falls considerably short of perfection

---

[20] Michael W. Miller, "Mystery Machine," *The Wall Street Journal*, March 22, 1988, p. 1. The article goes on to quote another IBM marketing strategist: "In a world that wants to make these things into commodities, you'd like to have exclusive features," he says. "Nobody wants to get into a price war" (p. 27).

[21] W. T. Tucker, "The Development of Brand Loyalty," *Journal of Marketing Research* (August 1964), pp. 32–35.

because such information can be costly to obtain. To find out about retail prices on an IBM PS/2, for instance, or a Ford Mustang, one would have to spend considerable time, effort, shoe leather, and gasoline comparative shopping among the retail alternatives. Stigler theorized that buyers inform themselves about prices in the marketplace *only up to a point*, the point where the marginal cost of gathering more information equals or exceeds the marginal expected benefits of continued search. How does this create opportunities for product differentiation, which in this case would be indicated by a persistence of different retail prices for what is essentially the same item (e.g., an IBM PS/2)? Stigler had a good answer. Because different buyers perceive different costs and benefits from search activities, some buyers will become more fully informed about available prices than other buyers. The existence of less informed buyers allows some sellers to charge higher prices than other sellers and still remain in business. This creates a dispersion of prices and a higher average level of prices than otherwise, thereby fostering differentiation.[22]

Empirical research of various kinds has produced much evidence that broadly agrees with this theory or more modern versions of it.[23] Of particular interest are changes that improve buyer information by substantially lowering the cost of search. This, in turn, reduces price dispersion among sellers or lowers average price levels. For example, posting gasoline prices on signs big enough to be visible to passing motorists has a significant tendency to reduce gasoline prices below what they would otherwise be. A 1970 comparison of New York City, where there was no price posting, and Los Angeles, where price posting was widespread, illustrates the point. Prices in New York would have been 0.73 cents per gallon lower for regular gas and 1.50 cents per gallon lower for premium gas (yielding a total saving of $25.4 million) if price posting in New York had been as extensive as it was in Los Angeles.[24]

Other evidence supporting the theory derives from the differences between convenience goods and shopping goods we noted earlier. The expected benefits of price searching for low-priced convenience goods tend to be low because of the low prices. (Why worry about 5 cents?) In contrast, the expected benefits of price searches for autos, refrigerators,

---

[22] George J. Stigler, "The Economics of Information," *Journal of Political Economy* (June 1961), pp. 213–225.

[23] Joel E. Urbany, "An Experimental Examination of the Economics of Information," *Journal of Consumer Research* (September 1986), pp. 257–265.

[24] Alex Maurizi and Thom Kelly, *Prices and Consumer Information* (Washington, D.C.: American Enterprise Institute, 1978), p. 40. For additional examples, see D. Grant Devine and Bruce W. Marion, "The Influence of Consumer Price Information on Retail Pricing and Consumer Behavior," *American Journal of Agricultural Economics* (May 1979), pp. 228–237; and Vicki A. McCracken, Robert D. Boynton, and Brian F. Blake, "The Impact of Comparative Food Price Information on Consumers and Grocery Retailers," *Journal of Consumer Affairs* (Winter 1982), pp. 224–240.

and other shopping goods can be quite large because of the inherently high price levels involved. For example, a study of 166 Illinois couples who had recently purchased one of nine durable goods found that their search efforts were greater for the most expensive durables (e.g., auto or refrigerator) than for the least expensive durables (e.g., black and white television).[25] Other studies show that consumers typically seek very little information about grocery prices.[26]

Although consumers may variously become more or less informed about prices depending on their perceived benefits and costs of search, the theory informs us that *no* consumer will become fully informed, and indeed *most* may be rather poorly informed. These results are exploited by retailers in ways that neatly illustrate interesting instances of differentiation arising from the price information problem. In brief, retailers have devised simple *cues* that lead consumers to believe that they are getting a "good deal" on price when in fact they often are not. For example, retailer print advertisements of "featuring" and special in-store displays are often poor predictors of price, contrary to consumer beliefs that these are signals of price cuts.[27] For another example, retailers (like Wards and Sears) often attempt to convince consumers of their allegedly low prices by promising to match the lowest advertised price a shopper can find. This could be called "price insurance." And it may cause consumers to relax their vigilance. As *The Wall Street Journal* reports:

> When a store pledges to match a competitor's advertised prices, it isn't promising that all its prices are the lowest in town. What's more, such stores expect only a small percentage of shoppers to try to collect on price-matching promises . . . .
>
> Ivan Png, a pricing specialist at the Graduate School of Management at [UCLA], says price-matching policies actually give merchants "a way to keep prices a little higher for the loyal customers while giving a lower price" to new customers the store is trying to attract. "It's a way to make more money," he adds.[28]

The problem of information about *quality* is much more complicated than the problem of price information. Still, much of the theory and empirical work regarding quality information likewise centers on cues.

---

[25] Linda K. Zimmerman and Loren V. Geistfield, "Economic Factors Which Influence Consumer Search for Price Information," *Journal of Consumer Affairs* (Summer 1984), pp. 119–130.

[26] Wayne D. Hoyer, "An Examination of Consumer Decision Making for a Common Repeat Purchase Product," *Journal of Consumer Research* (December 1984), pp. 822–829.

[27] Michael L. Katz and Carl Shapiro, "Consumer Shopping Behavior in the Retail Coffee Market," in *Empirical Approaches to Consumer Protection Economics*, edited by P. M. Ippolito and D. T. Scheffman (Washington, D.C.: Federal Trade Commission, 1984), pp. 415–435.

[28] Francine Schwadel, "Who Wins with Price-Matching Plans," *The Wall Street Journal*, March 16, 1989, p. B1.

We next consider two broad classes of quality cues: the seller's market position and advertising.

C. Quality Information Imperfections: Seller's Market Position

As a consumer you have undoubtedly heard sellers claiming to be "The First in the Business." Another ploy is to shout "We're Number One." What is happening here is obvious. Sellers are suggesting that they have superb quality to buyers who are less than perfectly informed about quality. (Here "quality" covers a variety of nonprice features, including for instance, durability, added gadgetry, reliability, taste, service, and so on.)

If it is difficult for buyers to assess the quality of goods sold, sellers of low-quality goods may try to pass their goods off as high-quality goods, charging a profitably high price in the process. Aware of this possibility, buyers will try to obtain quality information. But like price information, quality information is costly to obtain, often more costly than price information. A habitual reading of *Consumer Reports*, a diligent sample purchasing of products — these and the other tasks involved indicate a heavy burden for the careful consumer. Hence easy sources of quality information are attractive to consumers, and one such source is the market position of the seller as reflected in the seller's historic origins and relative size. The uninformed buyer may assume (or hope) that most other buyers are well informed about quality. Quick deduction leads the uninformed buyer to conclude that those other buyers have acted on their presumed knowledge, thereby (1) bestowing longevity and large market shares on those sellers who offer good quality for the money and (2) penalizing sellers of inferior-quality goods by giving them brief life spans and small market shares. In a word, market position reflects *reputation*. (Note the ignorant consumer's key assumption, however, that others are well informed. What if those others are also poorly informed and making the same assumption?)

Another factor here emerged from Tucker's experiment with bread in Texas. Lacking knowledge of quality, consumers tend to stick with their initial choices if they find those choices satisfactory. They tend to "satisfice" rather than "maximize."[29] They often perceive risk in the uncertainty of the unknown brand. Consequently, they display inertia, repeatedly purchasing what they purchased previously unless given some very strong reason for switching.

Numerous empirical studies show that pioneer brands, like Coke in cola-flavored soft drinks and Tide in home laundry detergents, have

---

[29] Stephen H. Hoch and John Deighton, "Managing What Consumers Learn from Experience," *Journal of Marketing* (April 1989), pp. 1–20; Hoyer, "An Examination of Consumer Decision Making".

larger market shares than follow-on brands. Moreover, pioneer brands hang on to their inflated market shares for very long periods, even when priced considerably higher than imitative brands of equal or better quality.[30] Pioneer brands are said to possess *"first-mover" advantages*. That those advantages relate at least partially to quality information problems is indicated by two kinds of further evidence. First, eliminating interbrand quality differences, as has been achieved in some instances by prescription drug regulation, tends to reduce the first-mover advantages substantially.[31] Second, experimental studies suggest that first-mover advantages often stem from consumer biases that develop in the process of gaining quality information. When qualities are ambiguous, the consumer's

> trial of the pioneer has an important role in the formation of preferences for *all* brands. All are compared to the pioneer, the ideal is perceived as close to it, and the pioneer is perceived as prototypical — representative yet competitively distinct. In this situation the pioneer occupies a favorable perceptual position that is difficult to imitate and costly to compete against, yielding a powerful competitive advantage.[32]

Apart from historical ordering, another consistent finding of empirical research is that *market share* confers market power. This shall be explored in greater detail later. Suffice it to say here that "inherent product differentiation" has been cited to explain this phenomenon,[33] and larger market shares are associated with lower price elasticities of demand for firms.[34]

D. Quality Information Imperfections: Advertising

Much information theory is devoted to the notion that sellers try to signal buyers about the quality of their products through their advertising. A *signal* is any bit of information (e.g., the existence of a warranty) that can improve the predictability of a second item of information (e.g.,

---

[30] Ronald Bond and David Lean, *Sales, Promotion, and Product Differentiation in Two Prescription Drug Markets* (Washington, D.C.: Federal Trade Commission, 1977); and Glen Urban et al., "Market Share Rewards to Pioneering Brands: An Empirical Analysis and Strategic Implications," *Management Science* (June 1986), pp. 645–659.

[31] Paul K. Gorecki, "The Importance of Being First: The Case of Prescription Drugs in Canada," *International Journal of Industrial Organization* (December 1986), pp. 371–395. But standardization doesn't necessarily eliminate the advantage. Producers of generic drugs battle to be first among the generics. *The Wall Street Journal*, June 9, 1989, p. 1A.

[32] Gregory S. Carpenter and Kent Nakamoto, "Consumer Preference Formation and Pioneering Advantage," *Journal of Marketing Research* (August 1989), pp. 285-298.

[33] Stephen A. Rhoades, "Market Share as a Source of Market Power: Implications and Some Evidence," *Journal of Economics and Business*, Vol. 37 (1985), pp. 343–363.

[34] Margaret E. Slade, "Conjectures, Firm Characteristics, and Market Structure: An Empirical Assessment," *International Journal of Industrial Organization* (December 1986), pp. 347–370.

product quality). How could advertising predict anything about quality, given that biased advertisers could easily exaggerate? Pauline Ippolito explains:

> In an economic setting, this predictability is derived from economic forces: for an activity to serve as an economic signal of quality, it must be *less* costly (or *more* productive) for high quality sellers to undertake the activity than for low quality sellers to do so.[35]

Hence, the hypothesis is that sellers of *higher*-quality products have a *greater* incentive to advertise heavily than do sellers of low-quality products. It's a matter of market forces. *Assuming consumers cannot be fooled*, they might buy a heavily advertised product of poor quality once on trial, but they won't repeat their purchase, thereby penalizing in the long run the seller whose advertising expenditures do not have a positive correspondence to quality. Advertising is, in this view, an investment in durable brand name recognition.

Although theories of this sort abound, they rely heavily on the assumptions that (1) consumers cannot be fooled (i.e., that they gain *complete* information about quality from simple consumption experience) and (2) producers attempt to signal quality in this way.[36] These assumptions can be seriously questioned. In particular, buyer knowledge and capacity for learning vary with varying circumstances. So advertising's effect likewise varies. Our sequence discussing these circumstances covers (1) professional buyers versus consumers, (2) search goods versus experience goods, and (3) convenience goods versus shopping goods.

1. Professional Buyers Versus Consumers.   Among buyers, business buyers come about as close to being highly knowledgeable and fully informed as one could normally expect. Indeed, professional purchasing agents of large firms often specialize in buying such broad categories of goods and services as raw materials, transportation, heavy machinery, and office supplies. Moreover, they often have the assistance of engineers, scientists, financial wizards, and other experts who conduct tests, arrange credit terms, and the like—all with an eye to maximizing profits. The most important reason for this expertise is the ability of professional buyers to spread the costs of obtaining the expertise over a large volume of purchases. Thus, their total dollar costs of purchasing may be huge, but on a *per unit* basis these costs will be small.

---

[35] Pauline M. Ippolito, "Consumer Protection Economics: A Selective Survey," in Ippolito and Scheffman (eds.), *Empirical Approaches to Consumer Protection Economics*, p. 8 (emphasis added).

[36] I. Ehrlich and L. Fisher, "The Derived Demand for Advertising," *American Economic Review* (June 1982), pp. 366–388; R. E. Kihlstrom and M. H. Riordan, "Advertising as a Signal," *Journal of Political Economy* (June 1984), pp. 427–450; and Paul Milgrom and John Roberts, "Price and Advertising Signals of Product Quality," *Journal of Political Economy* (August 1986), pp. 796–821.

On the other hand, we have the typical American consumer, who by comparison is an intellectual weakling. Although not a moron, he or she runs a very small-scale operation. Moreover, many if not most of the thousands of decisions consumers make each year are terribly complex, precluding the cultivation of genuine, low-cost per unit expertise. As we have seen, their ignorance forces them to rely on an array of homely little cues, many of which may not be accurate indicators of product value or quality at all. To the extent advertising is informative, then, advertising could be more helpful to consumers than professional buyers. (On the other hand, as we soon see, consumer ignorance makes them susceptible to subjective, persuasive advertising as well. For this reason, too, advertising directed at consumers could be more voluminous than that directed at professional buyers.)

Another important element distinguishing professional buyers and consumers is sheer numbers. Typically, there are millions more consumer buyers for any given consumer product than professional buyers for a producer product. A hundred million families buy bread, but only a few hundred steel companies buy iron ore. This means that sellers will likely try to reach consumers by media advertising and professional buyers by other means, such as salespeople in the field.

2. Search Goods Versus Experience Goods.   Lest we overstate the ignorance and gullibility of the typical consumer, we hasten to add that product type will also determine the degree to which the purchase decision is made knowledgeably. The goods *least* prone to quality information problems may be called **search goods**. In the case of search goods — like fresh fruits and vegetables, raw meat, apparel, jewelry, and maybe furniture as well — the consumer can judge on the basis of fairly simple inspection *prior* to actual purchase whether a given article is wholesome, handsomely styled, and reasonably priced for the level of quality it represents. In these instances, then, consumers may act in a relatively well-informed manner. They are in less need of informative advertising. And (to anticipate later pages) they are less open to the blandishments of subjective, persuasive advertising.

In contrast, there are **experience goods**. The utility of these can be fully assessed only *after* purchase. To evaluate brands of bottled beer accurately, for example, the consumer would obviously have to buy alternative brands in order to experience their taste. The same is true of canned foods, soaps, personal computers, appliances, and related products. Ideally, advertising could convey abundant information about these goods to aid consumers. Hence advertising outlays for experience goods might be expected to exceed substantially those for search goods. Realistically, the same expectation could be based on the observation that the hidden qualities of these experience goods make them liable to subjective persuasive advertising as well as objective informative advertising.[37] (Remember IBM's Micro Channel?)

Goods and services bought by commercial enterprises may also be divided into experience and search categories. The distinguishing characteristic of items in the latter classification is, again, the ability of the buyer to evaluate quality accurately before purchase. Thus, search goods bought by professional buyers include raw materials, basic office supplies (such as pencils and paper), and many semifinished articles. Although the high-powered capabilities of these buyers may seem to rule out the existence of producers' experience goods, it seems reasonable to place in this category such items as computers, aircraft, complex machinery, and financial services.

Table 5–3 summarizes these several categorizations. Our division of buyers into two groups — producers and consumers — and our division of all products into two groups — search and experience goods — define four broad market categories. The first division is made vertically, the second division horizontally, yielding a matrix of four cells in Table 5–3. Brief notations within each cell summarize the advertising intensives predicted by information theory.[38] Buyers of producer search goods are very well informed (and relatively few in number) leading to an expectation of *low* advertising outlay. At the other extreme, buyers of consumer experience goods will be quite poorly informed (and relatively numerous), generating an expectation of *high* advertising outlay.

Evidence that advertising may reflect variations in quality signaling according to information deficiencies is given in Table 5–4. Advertising/ sales ratios (in percentages) are shown for 24 broadly defined industries, each of which fits fairly neatly into one of the four classes outlined in Table 5–3. Advertising intensity is indeed lowest for the producer search goods of Table 5–4, followed next by producer experience goods. The overall average for all listed producers' goods in 0.8% of sales revenue. In contrast, the overall average for all listed consumers' goods is over five times greater, at 4.1%. Most of this difference is attributable to the consumer experience category, which obviously contains the highest ratios in the table. Comparing all search goods with all experience goods, the averages are 1.4% and 3.5%, respectively. These data do not prove the theories of advertising as an informative quality signal, but they are supportive.[39]

---

[37] For elaborations on search and experience goods, see R. H. Holton, "Consumer Behavior, Market Imperfections and Public Policy," in *Industrial Organization and Economic Development* edited by J. W. Markham and G. F. Papanek (Boston: Houghton Mifflin, 1970), pp. 102–115; and Phillip Nelson, "Information and Consumer Behavior," *Journal of Political Economy* (March/April 1970), pp. 311–329.

[38] For more sophisticated theorizing than we can engage in here, see Steven N. Wiggins and W. J. Lane, "Quality Uncertainty, Search, and Advertising," *American Economic Review* (December 1983), pp. 881–894.

[39] Other data support the relatively low advertising for producer goods. Sellers of

TABLE 5–3. Advertising by Broad Market Categories According to Quality Information Theory

Type of Buyer	Type of Product	
	1. Search	2. Experience
1. Producer	Buyer: *Well Informed* Advertising level: *Low*	Buyer: *Moderately Informed* Advertising level: *Medium*
2. Consumer	Buyer: *Moderately Informed* Advertising level: *Medium*	Buyer: *Poorly Informed* Advertising level: *High*

TABLE 5–4. Advertising Outlays as a Percentage of Sales by Broad Market Categories, 1985

Producer search goods		*Producer experience goods*	
Crude petroleum	0.2%	Biological products	1.8%
Wet corn milling	0.2	Engines and turbines	1.6
Lumber and wood products	0.3	Farm machinery	0.6
Manifold business forms	0.5	Industrial controls	1.4
Flat glass	0.2	Data processing services	0.9
Rolled nonferrous metals	0.2	Commercial testing labs	2.3
Average: 0.2%		Average: 1.4%	
Consumer search goods		*Consumer experience goods*	
Meat products	1.7%	Canned fruits and vegetables	5.3%
Apparel	2.3	Beer	8.4
Greeting cards	3.7	Books, publishing	4.0
Footwear	4.5	Soap and detergents	7.9
Household furniture	2.6	Household appliances	4.3
Retail food stores	1.4	Hotels and motels	3.5
Average: 2.7%		Average: 5.6%	

Source: *Advertising Age*, September 15, 1986, p. 60.

---

producer goods rely much more on sales personnel, sampling, and other promotions than on media advertising, 6.1% versus 0.6%, respectively, by one estimate. The "other" versus "media" figures for consumer goods are 9.8% and 3.6%, respectively. Although consumer goods are relatively heavily advertised, the "media" and "other" outlays are positively correlated, indicating complementarity. See L. W. Weiss, George Pascoe, and Stephen Martin, "The Size of Selling Costs," *Review of Economics and Statistics* (November 1983), pp. 668–672.

3. Convenience Goods Versus Shopping Goods. Theories of advertising as information predict different advertising levels for convenience goods and shopping goods. Prepurchase information requirements for *convenience goods* would seem to be slight. They are low-priced, frequently purchased goods like soda pop and frozen corn. Consumers can easily learn about them through low-cost sampling. Mistakes could be taken in stride. In contrast, extensive prepurchase information concerning *shopping goods* would seem to be imperative. These high-priced, infrequently purchased goods, like autos and carpeting, could be the focus for some rather enormous purchasing mistakes. The implication is that advertising for shopping goods would be comparatively greater than advertising for convenience goods, because consumer demand for information about shopping goods is typically greater. "In a comparative sense," says David Laband, "consumers will make greater use of signals present in advertising of high-priced, infrequently purchased goods than of low-priced, repeat purchase items."[40]

Laband finds support for this expectation in the Yellow Pages of telephone directories. Retailers of convenience goods (e.g., service stations, pharmacies, bakeries, and liquor stores) rely very *little* on advertising in the Yellow Pages. In contrast, vendors of shopping goods (e.g., travel agents, carpet stores, and plumbers) rely *heavily* on the Yellow Pages, using large display ads to report on their experience in business and certification achievements.[41]

This may seem like resounding proof that advertising informs us about quality. But there is strong conflicting evidence. Examining the advertising expenditures of *manufacturers*, Michael Porter found their average outlay as a percentage of sales to be 4.7% for 19 convenience goods industries and 2.1% for 23 shopping goods industries.[42] Contrary to information theory, low-priced, frequently purchased items get *more than twice* the advertising that others do, although those are presumably the goods about which consumers are most well informed.

The conflict creates a puzzle, one having a two-part solution. The first part stress the difference between retailers and manufacturers. The retailer's contribution to the differentiation of specific brands is much greater for shopping goods than convenience goods. Retailers of *shopping goods* offer sales assistance, demonstrations, credit, repair services, installation service, delivery, and so on—each of which greatly affects brand differentiation. Consumers tend to seek information from *retailers* in this case, relative to their reliance on manufacturers. Hence it is not surprising that retailers of shopping goods advertise vigorously in the

---

[40] David N. Laband, "Advertising as Information: An Empirical Note," *Review of Economics and Statistics* (August 1986), pp. 517–521.

[41] Ibid.

[42] Michael E. Porter "Consumer Behavior Retailer Power and Market Performance in Consumer Good Industries," *Review of Economics and Statistics* (November 1974), pp. 419–436.

Yellow Pages, in keeping with the major role for shopping goods. Manufacturers step aside.

Retailers of *convenience goods*, on the other hand, make relatively little contribution. They typically offer little or no sales assistance, repair service, or other help. Moreover, the low price and frequent purchase of these goods make "in-store" information search by consumers rather costly relative to the potential benefits. Buyers therefore enter convenience stores "presold," and the retailer's contribution to specific brand differentiation or information is slight. This places the major burden of building brand image and preselling on the manufacturer. Manufacturers are therefore the big advertisers for groceries, gas, and headache remedies.

The second part of the solution comes from a comparison of the information one finds in the typical Yellow Pages ad of an appliance dealer versus the information one finds in a TV ad for Coca-Cola. Advertising intensities for convenience and shopping goods conform to the expectations of information theory *only to the extent advertising is actually informative* (as in the Yellow Pages). When blatantly persuasive, advertising will be most intense where its persuasive powers are greatest, not where information is most needed. Hence, there is much truth to the information theory of advertising.[43] But we must now recognize that much advertising differentiates by *persuasion* rather than by information.

IV. SUBJECTIVE IMPULSES

We have seen that product differentiation can be based on product attributes (assuming informed and rational buyers). We have also seen it with uninformed buyers (assuming identical product attributes and rational buyers). Is differentiation possible when product attributes are essentially identical and buyers are fully informed? Yes, because buyers are *not* wholly rational. This provides a third basis for differentiation.

A. Inadequacies of Previous Explanations

What would happen if buyers of Smirnoff vodka were informed that Smirnoff could not be distinguished from cheaper brands in blind taste tests, perhaps even participating in the taste tests themselves? Would they continue to buy Smirnoff? What would happen if buyers of Tide detergent were informed that much cheaper brands of essentially identical chemical composition cleaned clothes just as well as Tide? Would

---

[43] For still more evidence, see Richard E. Caves, "Information Structures and Product Markets," *Economic Inquiry* (April 1986), pp. 195–212.

they continue to pay premium prices for Tide? Studies of situations like these show that a surprisingly large number of people willingly pay high prices for favored brands *even after being fully informed about attribute uniformity.*[44] Hence, people often behave as if there is vertical or horizontal differentiation in attributes when in fact no such objective differentiation exists.

Equally perplexing is the finding that vertical differentiation may be genuine, with some products of higher quality than others, yet buyers pay prices that do not correspond to the vertical quality variations and even *run counter to them.* All too often people pay *more* for brands that are *inferior* to cheaper alternatives in every attribute. A study of 127 commodities by Hjorth-Anderson found such perverse purchasing behavior 54% of the time. He concluded that such "inefficient variants appear to be the rule rather than the exception."[45] More generally, the correlation between price level and brand quality is extremely low according to numerous assessments of price-quality relationships. For different models and brands of a given product low quality should sell only at a low price, whereas high quality should justifiably bring a high price (with a maximum positive correlation of $+1.0$). In fact, the average correlation for wide varieties of consumer products tends to be in the range of only $+0.10$ to $+0.20$, closer to zero than to $+1.0$. And the correlation for many products have been *negative* — for example, household detergents (-0.28), vacuum cleaners (-0.66), and frozen pizza (-0.44).[46] Attribute theories of product differentiation are further refuted by findings

[44] See, for example, G. Scherhorn and K. Wieken, "On the Effect of Counter-Information on Consumers," in *Human Behavior in Economic Analysis,* edited by B. Strumpel, J. Morgan, and E. Zahn (San Francisco: Jossey-Bass, 1972), pp. 421–431. Despite the fact that all heavy-duty laundry detergents are pretty much the same, Scherhorn and Wieken found that seven-eighths of a large sample of West German housewives bought expensive detergents because of "preferences resulting from misinformation about quality." Only one-eighth had "no preferences for certain brands . . . or brand name detergents in general." Having thus identified the true believers, Scherhorn and Wieken then sent them a large amount of authoritative but readable "counterinformation," which explained why most detergents were alike and why they were wasting money on expensive brands. Follow-up interviews disclosed that only 55% of the housewives were "generally convinced by the counterinformation that all detergents tend to meet the same standards of quality," and only "⅓ of the buyers interviewed were ready to buy the detergent which was actually the cheapest."

[45] Christian Hjorth-Anderson, "Lancaster's Principle of Efficient Choice," *International Journal of Industrial Organization* (September 1983), pp. 287–295.

[46] Alfred R. Oxenfeldt, "Consumer Knowledge: Its Measurement and Extent," *Review of Economics and Statistics* (October 1950), pp. 300–316; R. T. Morris and C. S. Bronson, "The Chaos of Competition Indicated by Consumer Reports," *Journal of Marketing* (July 1969), pp. 26–34; Peter Riesz, "Price-Quality Correlations for Packaged Food Products," *Journal of Consumer Affairs* (Winter 1979), pp. 236–247; George B. Sproles, "New Evidence on Price and Quality," *Journal of Consumer Affairs,* Vol. 11 (1977), pp. 63–77; and Y. Yamada and N. Ackerman, "Price-Quality Correlations in the Japanese Market," *Journal of Consumer Affairs* (Winter 1984), pp. 251–265.

that consumers tend to respond more to subjective images than to objective attributes.[47]

Evidence also shows information theories to be seriously incomplete. According to information theory "the consumer's own past experience is a reliable source of information" about "inexpensive, frequently purchased goods"[48]—that is, convenience goods. Yet some of the very lowest price-quality correlations, *negative ones*, have been found for exactly these kinds of products.[49] Also according to information theory advertising is a good signal of product quality. Yet formal tests of this fail.[50] Thus the rational "robot" model of consumer behavior assumed by information theory does not apply. *Consumers do not learn to buy what they like* after random sampling. It seems more accurate to say that consumers quite often *learn to like what they buy*, without random sampling, especially in the case of experience goods (as opposed to search goods). Consumers often learn to like what they choose simply because they have made the choice. This is due partially to what is called "cognitive dissonance" and often works even when consumers carefully weigh their options before purchase. For example, if Smith thinks brands X, Y, and Z are about equally attractive before purchase, her judgment of Y, if selected, will rise after purchase merely because of its selection.[51]

Theories of product differentiation based on product attributes and information imperfections are incomplete because they assume buyer "rationality" in the traditional economic sense. They focus on the functional needs of buyers to the neglect of more subjective symbolic needs and experiential needs:

Functional needs are those that motivate problem-solving product selections, based on objective attributes such as fuel economy, nutrition requirements, and convenience.

---

[47] T. W. Wu, R. L. Day, and D. B. MacKay, "Consumer Benefits Versus Product Attributes: An Experimental Test," *Quarterly Journal of Business and Economics* (Summer 1988), pp. 88–113.

[48] Rachel Dardis, *The Economics of Consumer Product Information* (Washington, D.C.: National Bureau of Standards, 1980), p. iv.

[49] Mayonnaise (−.13), biscuit mixes (−.46), and so on. See Oxenfeldt *op. cit.* and Riesz, *op. cit.*

[50] John R. Lott, Jr., "Brand Names, Ignorance, and Quality Guaranteeing Premiums," *Applied Economics* (February 1988), pp. 165–176.

[51] G. D. Bell, "The Automobile Buyer After Purchase," *Journal of Marketing* (July 1967) pp. 12–16; L. A. Losciuto and R. Perloff, "Influence of Product Preference on Dissonance Reduction," *Journal of Marketing Research* (August 1967) pp. 286–290; R. Mittelstaedt, "A Dissonance Approach to Repeat Purchasing Behavior," *Journal of Marketing Research* (November 1969), pp. 444–446; J. Jacoby and D. B. Kyner, "Brand Loyalty vs. Repeat Purchasing Behavior," *Journal of Marketing Research* (February 1973), pp. 1–9; J. B. Cohen and M. J. Houston, "Cognitive Consequences of Brand Loyalty," *Journal of Marketing Research* (February 1972), pp. 97–99; F. W. Winter, "The Effect of Purchase Characteristics on Post Decision Product Reevaluation," *Journal of Marketing Research* (May 1974), pp. 164–171; and J. L. Ginter, "An Experimental Investigation of Attitude Change and Choice of a New Brand," *Journal of Marketing Research* (February 1974), pp. 30–40.

Symbolic needs are desires for products that fulfill internally generated needs of self-enhancement, role position, prestige, group membership, or ego identification.

Experiential needs are desires for products that provide sensory pleasure, variety, or cognitive stimulation.[52]

Perhaps the easiest way to contrast the symbolic needs with the functional needs is to compare certain brands of a given product, for example, Carlton (functional) versus Marlboro (symbolic), Toyota Corolla (functional) versus Cadillac (symbolic). As regards experiential need, contemplate gourmet ice cream, snakeskin shoes, and bumper stickers that proclaim hedonic philosophies — "I shop, therefore I am" and "born to shop."[53]

B. Advertising As Persuasion

Differentiation based on subjective impulse is most clearly seen in "persuasive" advertising, as distinct from "informative" advertising. How much advertising is "informative" and how much "persuasive"? There is no clear cut answer, but much of it is informative, providing facts on prices, locations, and availabilities (e.g., newspaper classified ads and mail-order house catalogs), much of it is purely persuasive (e.g., see the appendix on Marlboro's cowboy), and much of it is a blend of both (e.g., the magazine car ad that gives you EPA miles per gallon, an itemization of standard equipment, and a pretty woman sitting in the passenger's seat).

In one of the most extensive opinion surveys ever taken, conducted by R. A. Bauer and S. A. Greyser, a large sample of people were asked, first to press the button on a counter "every time you see or hear an ad," and, second, to fill out a card for each of these tallied ads that "you consider especially annoying, enjoyable, informative, or offensive." The results indicate that, of the hundreds of ads the average person is ex-

---

[52] C. W. Park, B. J. Jaworski, and D. J. MacInnis, "Strategic Brand Concept-Image Management," *Journal of Marketing* (October 1986), pp. 135–145.

[53] According to *The Wall Street Journal:*
Increasingly, purchases are linked less and less closely to [functional] need. "We're not talking ironing boards that have worn out," says Isaac Lagnado, the director of research for Associated Merchandising Corp., a merchandising consulting firm. "You're talking replacement just for the sake of change. People are buying new sheets not because old ones have worn out but because they're stimulated by a new set of plaid ones." Long true of apparel, the trend is rapidly spreading to other areas. Six years ago, all but one quarter to one-third of all houseware purchases were to replace items that had worn out. Today, less than half are replacements.
A tremendous amount of buying is done on impulse. About 53% of groceries and 47% of hardware-store buys are spur of the moment, studies say. When Stillerman Jones & Co., a marketing-research firm, asked 34,300 mall shoppers across the country the primary reason for their visit, only 25% had come in pursuit of a specific item. See Betsy Morris, "Big Spenders," *The Wall Street Journal* July 30, 1987, pp. 1–16.

posed to every day, he or she is conscious of only about 76 per day. Of these 76, only 6 of them, or 16%, are sufficiently moving to warrant the completion of a report card. Reactions to the rest were, "So what?" Of the 16% most noteworthy, only 36% (or 5.8% of all tallied ads) were considered "informative" by the respondents.[54]

Of course, the purpose of advertising is not to inform buyers—not in a purely cognitive, unbiased sense anyway. The idea is to sell goods by *influencing* buyers. It will therefore come as no surprise to learn that, when the same survey asked whether "advertising often persuades people to buy things they shouldn't buy," 73% of the respondents agreed. This response corresponds fairly well to earlier polls, taken in 1940 and 1950, that found 80% of those surveyed agreeing that "advertising leads people to buy things they don't need or can't afford."[55]

Although the information quotient for all major media was 36%, the ratings for individual media were quite diverse. The print media, as everyday experience indicates, seem to contain the highest proportions of informative ads, with 59% of especially noteworthy newspaper ads winning this designation in the survey. Magazines were a distant second with 48%, followed by radio with 40% and TV with 31%.[56] Thus, a fuller impression of information content can be gained by considering the distribution of all advertising outlays across the media. These data for 1985 are shown in Table 5–5. The total amount spent during that year came to over $90 billion, or about 2% of the gross national product. Of this grand total, 34.8% went to newspapers, magazines, and farm and business publications, which entails more information than one who is used to watching TV might suppose. Much direct-mail advertising is also fairly rich in information (despite its rude intrusiveness). F. M. Scherer may be on target when he says, "If a horseback generalization must be hazarded, it would be that half of all advertising expenditures cover messages of a primarily informative character, while the other half serve largely to persuade."[57]

[54] R. A. Bauer and Stephen A. Greyser, *Advertising in America: The Consumer View* (Boston: Division of Research Graduate School of Business Administration, Harvard University, 1968), pp. 175–183.

[55] Ibid., p. 71. See also Helmut Becker, "Advertising Image and Impact," *Journal of Contemporary Business*, Vol. 7, no. 4 (1979), p. 84.

[56] Again, however, these are a very small minority of all counted ads. For an econometric test indicating very little, if any, information content in magazine ads, see L. L. Duetsch, "Some Evidence Concerning the Information Content of Advertising," *American Economist* (Spring 1974), pp. 48–53. On the lack of information in TV advertising see A. Resnik and Bruce Stern, "An Analysis of Information Content in Television Advertising," *Journal of Marketing* (January 1977), pp. 50–53; also see R. W. Pollay, J. Zaichkowsky, and C. Fryer, "Regulation Hasn't Changed TV Ads Much!," *Journalism Quarterly* (Autumn 1980), pp. 438–446.

[57] F. M. Scherer, *Industrial Market Structure and Economic Performance* (Chicago: Rand McNally, 1970), p. 326. Interestingly, it is possible to pinpoint the origins of persuasive advertising in the history of the messages advertisers have used. See Daniel Pope, *The Making of Modern Advertising* (New York: Basic Books, 1983), pp. 238–250.

TABLE 5–5.   United States Advertising in 1985 by Media

Medium	Amount (billions of dollars)		As a % of Total	
Newspaper total	$25.2		26.6%	
National		3.4		3.5
Local		21.8		23.1
Magazines	5.2		5.5	
Farm publications	0.2		0.2	
Television total	20.8		21.9	
Network		8.3		8.7
Spot		6.0		6.3
Local		5.7		6.0
Cable		0.8		0.8
Radio	6.5		6.8	
Direct mail	15.5		16.3	
Business publications	2.4		2.5	
Outdoor	0.9		0.9	
Miscellaneous	18.2		19.2	
Grand total	$94.9		100.0%	

Source: Reprinted with permission from *Advertising Age*, May 12, 1986, p. 76. Copyright 1986 by Crain Communications, Inc.

Still another way of judging this issue is by product and buyer type. Anyone who has leafed through *Mining Magazine* or *Electrical Review* will conclude that advertising directed toward professional buyers is largely informative.[58] This obviously does not hold for most advertising aimed at consumers, but there does seem to be substantial variance across consumer products.

Drawing again from the Bauer–Greyser survey of consumer opinion, the variance across products may be seen in Table 5–6 which includes some data on producers' goods as well as consumers' goods because a number of the consumers surveyed were also producers (that is, businesspeople). This table shows, for individual product groups, the distribution of especially noteworthy ads (as explained) across the four categories of noteworthiness. It is easy to see that respondents were most often impressed by the informative nature of producer goods ads and, to a slightly lesser extent, consumer search goods ads. Moreover, in only a relatively few instances were these ads considered annoying or offensive. By stark contrast, ads promoting most consumer experience goods were apparently not very informative. They often gained

[58] C. D. Edwards, "Advertising and Competition," *Business Horizons* (February 1968), p. 60.

TABLE 5–6. Percent of Especially Noteworthy
Advertisements Categorized as Being Informative, Enjoyable,
Annoying, and Offensive

Industry Classification	Categorization			
	Informative	Enjoyable	Annoying	Offensive
Producer goods				
Agriculture and farming	84	11	5	0
Industrial materials	75	16	9	0
Freight, industrial development	82	18	0	0
Building materials and equipment	64	16	14	6
Consumer search goods				
Apparel, footwear, accessories	52	25	17	6
Household furnishings	65	23	12	0
Retail and direct by mail	62	19	19	0
Horticulture	72	28	0	0
Consumer experience goods				
Food and food products	31	54	14	1
Toilet goods and toiletries	31	35	31	3
Soaps, cleansers, polishes	28	24	45	3
Smoking materials	8	38	36	18
Confectionery and soft drinks	12	69	17	2
Beer, wine, liquor	5	50	22	23
Automobiles and accessories	48	31	20	1
Drugs and remedies	41	18	36	5

Source: R. A. Bauer and S. A. Greyser, *Advertising in America: The Consumer View* (Cambridge, Mass: Harvard University Press, 1968), pp. 296–297.

noteworthy status on other counts, but these other counts seem more clearly associated with persuasive appeals—that is, enjoyable (attention grabbing) and annoying (repetitious).

A plausible explanation for this large difference between search goods and experience goods advertising rests on the prepurchase evaluation that can be made of search goods. If the advertised properties of search goods stray too far from their actual properties, consumers are readily able to detect the discrepancies and penalize the promoters with refusals to buy. Advertisers of these products, therefore, feel constrained to use a more informative approach. They have relatively little use for exaggeration, humor, sex, jingles, plays on insecurity, and cajolery, all of which may be found in the tool boxes of experience goods advertisers. Recalling the advertising expenditures data of Table 5–4, we can postulate a rather interesting conclusion: Advertising intensity and information content are *inversely* related. Generally speaking, the greater the dollar outlay relative to product sales, the lower is the information content of the advertising messages.[59] Furthermore, in terms of adequate amounts and efficient applications of buyer knowledge, it seems that advertising is *least* informative where the need for information is greatest (consumer experience goods), whereas it is *most* informative where the need for information is least (producer search goods).[60] This paradox makes it clear that the purpose of advertising is *not* to inform buyers; it is to gain sales by influencing buyers.

Economists have no theories of how persuasion works, but many social psychologists and marketing experts earn their living by conjuring up such theories and testing them. Since this is an economics book, we can do little more than touch on the subject and refer readers who have an interest in pursuing it further to a few surveys of this vast literature.[61]

First, we should clarify our use of the word "persuasion" by mentioning several well-established exhortative advertising techniques that are now commonly used to promote most consumer goods:[62]

- There will be more opinion change in the desired direction if the communicator has high credibility than if he or she has low credibility, where credibility is expertise and trustworthiness. Thus, regarding expertise, race drivers sell oil, singers sell Memorex tape, a washer repairman sells Maytag, and so on.

- Present one side of the argument when the audience is generally friendly, but present both sides or present comparisons when the audience starts out disagreeing with you. Thus, number one selling

[59] Alfred Arterburn and John Woodbury, "Advertising, Price Competition and Market Structure," *Southern Economic Journal* (January 1981), pp. 763–775. The information content of television advertising is lowest for beer, soft drinks, candy, and other convenience goods with high advertising as a percentage of sales while information content is highest for home furnishings, appliances, and other shopping goods with low advertising/sales ratios. M. G. Weinberger and H. E. Spotts, "A Situational View of Information Content in TV Advertising in the U.S. and U.K.," *Journal of Marketing* (January 1989), pp. 89–94.

[60] See T. Scitovsky, *Welfare and Competition* (Homewood, Ill,: Richard D. Irwin, 1951), Chapter XVIII, for an elaboration of this point.

[61] P. Zimbardo and E. B. Ebbesen, *Influencing Attitudes and Changing Behavior* (Reading, Mass.: Addison-Wesley, 1969); H. C. Triandis, *Attitude and Attitude Change* (New York: John Wiley, 1971); M. Fishbein and I. Aizen, *Belief, Attitude, Intention and Behavior: An Introduction to Theory and Research* (Reading, Mass.: Addison-Wesley, 1975); R. L. Applbaum and K. W. E. Anatol, *Strategies for Persuasive Communication* (Columbus, Ohio: Chas. E. Merrill, 1974); G. R. Miller and M. Burgoon, *New Techniques of Persuasion* (New York: Harper & Row, 1973); and S. H. Britt, *Psychological Principles of Marketing and Consumer Behavior* (Lexington, Mass.: Lexington Books, 1978).

[62] This list borrows heavily from Zimbardo and Ebbesen, *Influencing Attitudes and Changing Behavior*, p. 20–23. See also G. E. Belch, M. A. Belch, and A. Villarreal, "Effects of Advertising Communications: Review of Research," in J. N. Sheth (e.d.), *Research in Marketing*, Vol. 9 (New York: JAI Press, 1987), pp. 59–117.

brands very rarely mention competing products, but Avis is No. 2 to Hertz, so it tries harder; B. F. Goodrich touts its lack of a blimp; and so on.

- Repeating a communication tends to prolong its influence and slight variations of the repetition are advantageous. Thus, how many ways has Miller "Lite" said "It's less filling"?

Second, the persuasive effect of advertising is especially powerful when there is an interaction between the advertising and the consumer's experience. Message and evidence interact to affect behavior. Hence the persuasive process often works in two steps:[63]

1. Advertising first arouses an expectation (e.g., Bud Light is fun), which is weak because consumers skeptically recognize that the source is biased.
2. The consumer then tends to confirm the expectation upon exposure to more objective information such as product experience (e.g., Bud Light was served at a fun party).

For example, during the 1980s Ford's advertising stressed product quality with such messages as "Quality Is Job One" and "The Best-Built American Cars." John Deighton tested the impact of this advertising in an experimental setting by asking a sample of consumers to rate the reliability of six auto manufacturers (Chrysler, Ford, GM, Volkswagen, Datsun, and Toyota) after exposure to quality advertising and actual evidence of reliability in one of the four following combinations:

1. No advertising, no evidence
2. No advertising, objective evidence
3. Advertising, no evidence
4. Advertising, objective evidence

The evidence shown to groups 2 and 4 was the "frequency-of-repair records" from *Consumer Reports* for 16 models of cars. Ford's repair record was in fact mediocre (ranked eighth by a summary index well behind Mazda and Honda, among others). Figure 5–8 shows the amazing results. Without any actual evidence of Ford's reliability, advertising had very little effect on Ford's reliability rating among respondents, but it raised it slightly (see the dashed line). On the other hand, the quality advertising was very persuasive among those who saw the evidence, *even though the evidence did not agree with the advertising*. Ratings among those seeing only evidence were lowest ($-.2$). Adding advertising lifted the ratings immensely (past $+.6$). The ability of advertising to *reverse completely* the impact of the evidence attests to its persuasive power in

[63] John Deighton, "The Interaction of Advertising and Evidence," *Journal of Consumer Research* (December 1984), pp. 763–770.

FIGURE 5–8. Consumers' ratings of Ford's reliability depending on advertising and evidence. Source: John Deighton, "The Interaction of Advertising and Evidence," *Journal of Consumer Research* (December 1984), pp. 768.

this case.[64] Confirmation of this effect shows that ambiguous evidence has the greatest positive impact on the persuasive power of advertising.[65]

The psychology of what is happening here is rather complex and diverse. One factor, for instance, is "confirmation bias." Consumers spend more energy looking for evidence consistent with their expectations than inconsistent evidence. Another factor is "cognitive conservatism," in which case consumers rate evidence supportive of their expectations as quite convincing while discounting contrary evidence.[66] Oversimplifying, *people tend to like what they buy (once primed by advertising) rather than buy what they like (after objective search).*

[64] Ford's Taurus had an exceptionally bad record of reliability during its first two years on the market, yet Ford found it to be very popular with customers. *Business Week,* June 27, 1988, p. 55.

[65] Stephen J. Hoch and Young-Won Ha, "Consumer Learning: Advertising and the Ambiguity of Product Experience," *Journal of Consumer Research* (September 1986), pp. 221–232.

[66] Stephen J. Hoch and John Deighton, "Managing What Consumers Learn from Experience," *Journal of Marketing* (April 1989), pp. 1–20.

C. Product and Firm Conditions

The persuasive impact of advertising varies from product to product and firm to firm. For later purposes (when we study barriers to entry and conduct) we shall outline here the conditions where persuasive advertising seems most potent:[67]

1. In the presence of powerful emotional buying motives, like health, romance, and safety
2. For low-price convenience goods (as opposed to shopping goods)
3. For new products (as opposed to old)
4. For top-dog brands (as opposed to underdog brands)

1. Emotional Connotations.   Some products naturally lend themselves to strong emotional appeals like health (drugs, vitamins, and food, for example), sex and romance (perfumes, cosmetics, mouthwash), and safety (smoke detectors, tires, shock absorbers). The implications of having the opportunity to exploit these appeals should be obvious to the reader, for they make the job of persuasion easier. What is probably not so obvious is the subtlety and sophistication with which these opportunities can be exploited.[68] The persuasive power of sex, for instance, does not work equally well across all products.[69]

2. Convenience Goods.   Consumers seem to be more susceptible to persuasive advertising for low-priced convenience goods like prepared foods, detergent, soda pop, beer, candy, soup, and cigarettes than for high-priced shopping goods like autos, refrigerators, and carpeting. The low price of convenience goods apparently causes consumers to relax their vigilance, to decide in the easiest possible manner, and to be guided more by symbolic and experiential needs than purely functional ones.[70] Also, the high frequency of purchase common to convenience goods leads people to believe that they have greater knowledge of the product than they actually do.

3. New Products.   Rapidly growing product sales usually stem from a relatively quick accumulation of new users of the product or new uses for the product or both. Thus, rapid growth in the early stages of a product's life cycle provides a fertile field for advertising because ad-

---

[67] One of the earliest such listings is that of Neil Borden, *The Economic Effects of Advertising* (Chicago: Richard D. Irwin, 1942), pp. 424–428.

[68] On the use of fear see B. Sternthal and C. S. Craig, "Fear Appeals: Revisited and Revised," *Journal of Consumer Research* (December 1974), pp. 22–34. On the use of sex see Meyers and Reynolds, pp. 91–93, and Zimbardo and Ebbesen, *Influencing Attitudes and Changing Behavior*, pp. 34–38.

[69] R. N. Kanungo and S. Pang, "Effects of Human Models on Perceived Product Quality," *Journal of Applied Psychology* (April 1973), pp. 172–178; *The Wall Street Journal*, November 18, 1980, pp. 1, 19.

[70] Adrian Furnham and Alan Lewis, *The Economic Mind* (New York: St. Martins, 1986), pp. 208–209.

vertising may effectively "spread the news," encouraging these conversions and new applications.[71]

4. Leading Firms and Brands.   Leading firms and brands have opportunities to use especially powerful advertising messages or themes. Tactics used by top dogs include the following:[72]

> *Block consumer exposure to evidence* of the smaller rival's product ("Why change if it works?"; "You get what you pay for").
>
> *Reinforce the agenda* by limiting or guiding the consumer's evoked set of brands or attributes ("The King of Beers"; Budweiser is "beechwood aged," and irrelevant attribute).
>
> *Explain the experience* on consuming the product in such a way as to be favorable to the leading brands ("This Bud's for you" after a long day's work; "If you've got the time, we've got the beer" — Miller).

These methods are especially effective when, as in the case of beer, cola-flavored soft drinks, cigarettes, and laundry detergents, the taste or performance spectrum across brands is narrow. Then the advertising can literally affect people's perceptions.[73] Hoch and Deighton argue that "consumers are active if not infallible partners in their own persuasion."[74]

D. Advertising Data by Company

Taken together, the several factors discussed in the preceding section help to explain why some firms advertise more heavily than others. Table 5–7 shows total dollar outlay and advertising as a percentage of sales for some of the top advertisers in the United States. By both measures of intensity, most of the leaders are manufacturers of foods, soaps and cleansers, soft drinks, beer, tobacco, drugs and cosmetics, and liquor — all convenience goods, (many susceptible to emotional or symbolic appeals). Auto firms rank high in total expenditures but relatively low

[71] David I. Rosenbaum, "Advertising and Entry: The Case of Light Beer," in *Issues After A Century of Federal Competition Policy*, edited by R. L. Wills, J. A. Caswell, and J. D. Culbertson (Lexington, Mass.: Lexington Books, 1987), pp. 223–234. See also Mark A. Hurwitz and Richard E. Caves, "Persuasion or Information? Promotion and Shares of Brand Name and Generic Pharmaceuticals," *Journal of Law and Economics* (October 1988), pp. 299–320.

[72] S. J. Hoch and J. Deighton, "Managing What Consumers Learn from Experience," *Journal of Marketing* (April 1989), pp. 1–20.

[73] An experimental study of Jacoby, Olsen, and Haddock illustrates this point for beer. Their subjects tasted beers without labels (blind) and with labels. Adding the brand label to the "ultrapremium" beer *raised* its mean quality rating 24%, while brand identification of the "regional inexpensive" beer *lowered* its mean rating 30%. J. Jacoby, J. C. Olsen, and R. A. Haddock, "Price, Brand Name, and Product Composition Characteristics as Determinants of Perceived Quality," *Journal of Applied Psychology* (December 1971), pp. 570–579.

[74] Hoch and Deighton, "Managing What Consumers Learn from Experience" p. 16.

TABLE 5–7.   Advertising Outlay of Selected Firms, 1987

Rank in Terms of Dollars Spent	Firm	Main Product Area	Dollars Spent (millions)	Advertising as a % of Sales
1	Philip Morris	Tobacco, beer food	$1558	6.7%
2	Procter & Gamble	Soaps, paper, food	1387	5.3
3	General Motors	Autos	1025	3.5
4	Sears, Roebuck	Retailing	886	3.4
5	RJR Nabisco	Tobacco, food	840	7.7
6	Pepsico	Soft drinks, snacks	704	5.2
7	Kodak	Photo supplies	658	8.9
8	McDonald's	Fast food	650	3.8
9	Ford Motors	Autos	639	6.5
10	Anheuser-Busch	Beer	635	6.8
12	Unilever	Detergents	580	3.1
13	General Mills	Food	572	5.1
15	Warner-Lambert	Toiletries, cosmetics	558	8.5
17	Kellogg	Cereals	525	10.4
20	Johnson & Johnson	Pharmaceuticals	459	10.4
23	American Home Products	Pharmaceuticals	390	16.8
25	Coca-Cola	Soft drinks	365	12.0
26	Bristol-Myers	Pharmaceuticals	359	13.1
27	Quaker Oats	Foods	344	4.8

Source: Reprinted with permission from *Advertising Age*, September 28, 1988, pp. 1, 152. Copyright 1988 by Crain Communications, Inc.

in costs as a percentage of sales. Since the latter measure is economically the more meaningful, autos may be considered moderately advertised, perhaps because of their high-price, high-risk character.

Product differentiation is thus grounded on nonrational subjective impulses as well as objective product attributes and information imperfections. Persuasive advertising is the single most important signal of the presence of these impulses. And a comparison of Table 5–6 (which shows the highly persuasive nature of advertising for food products, toiletries, tobacco, beer, and soft drinks) and Table 5–7 (which shows these same products to be the ones hawked by the nation's leading advertisers) reveals the substantial significance of subjective impulses.

V. MARKET SEGMENTATION, STRATEGIC GROUPS, AND PRODUCT PROLIFERATION

The market segmentation that goes hand in hand with product differentiation fosters several phenomena that are interesting in themselves and relevant to an understanding of other features of structure and conduct. Two concepts that arise later are "strategic groups" and "product proliferation."

Recall that market segmentation arises when the market is made up of a number of rather distinct segments, each of which has within it brand offerings that are quite similar. For example, minivans, sport cars, and luxury sedans constitute different segments of the auto market.

A *strategic group* is a group of firms pursuing a similar strategy in terms of such things as advertising intensity, product quality, price policy, vertical integration, geographic scope, and breadth of product line. This covers a lot of ground. But it should be clear that strategic groups are very commonly centered on different possible segments of the same overall market. In detergents, for example, Procter & Gamble, Colgate, and Lever Brothers follow a high-price, intensive advertising, consumer-oriented strategy. Less well-known firms sell under the private labels of retail chains and accordingly follow a low-price, no advertising strategy. Still other firms specialize in bulk, industrial detergents.

A common strategy for relatively small firms to follow is niche specialization. A "niche" is a narrow segment of the market. Following the distinction between horizontal and vertical differentiation in attributes, there can be horizontal and vertical niches. Examples of horizontal niches include root beer–flavored soft drinks, malt liquors, meusli cereals, and sugarless gum. Examples of vertical niches include gourmet dog foods, low-budget motels, and ultraluxury automobiles. Thus, small sellers that focus on a single niche might constitute one strategic group, while others focusing on mainstream segments would comprise a different strategic group. There are dozens of small microbreweries, for instance, specializing in brewing small batches of beer to be sold locally at restaurants and brewpubs. On the other hand, there are Anheuser-Busch, Miller, and Coors.

Product proliferation occurs when firms market numerous different brands of products in an attempt to cover most or almost all of the possible segments a market might have. In beer, for example, Anheuser-Busch offers a premium beer (Budweiser), two superpremiums (Michelob and Michelob Classic Dark), a "popular" priced beer (Busch), three lights at different price levels (Bud Light, Michelob Light, and Natural Light), a malt liquor (King Cobra), a low-alcohol beer (LA), two "dry" beers (Michelob Dry and Bud Dry), plus several import-style brands. Achieving this spread was not cheap. In the first three years of their introduction Anheuser-Busch spent millions for advertising alone—

Natural Light $92.3 million, Bud Light $129.8 million, LA $57.7 million, and Michelob Light $78.4 million.[75] Why would Anheuser-Busch behave this way? The answer takes us into topics beyond the reach of this chapter, so textbook segmentation requires that we postpone the explanation.

SUMMARY

Product differentiation occurs when a firm's product offering differs from its competition in the eyes of buyers because of physical or nonphysical characteristics. Just the image of a brand name may be enough. Market segmentation, a related phenomenon, arises when marketwide demand may be divided into segments or clusters of fairly distinct demands. Efforts at differentiation by sellers may foster segmentation. And, conversely, segmentation may encourage differentiation. The two therefore commonly occur together, but they should not be confused. Differentiation, for instance, can occur within a given segment, as Miller Lite, Bud Light, and Coors Light are differentiated light beers.

Differentiation and segmentation alter a firm's demand, shifting it outward and/or lowering its elasticity. This gives the firm some power over price (and provides the revenue to cover the cost of the effort).

Three main sources of differentiation deserve special attention. The first is variation in the *objective attributes* of products, such as size, shape, color, packaging, durability, and location (if retail trade). Objective attributes provide a basis for differentiation even for buyers who are fully informed and rational. Horizontal and vertical differentiation constitute two subcategories of this kind of differentiation. The former occurs when different buyers prefer different brands that are priced identically because of different mixes of product attributes and buyer preferences. Vertical differentiation would have all buyers buying the higher-quality product if priced the same as the lower-quality alternative, as everyone would choose a Mercedes over a Yugo if priced the same.

The second source of differentiation is *imperfect information*, which may concern either price or quality or both. You may buy an IBM PS/2 out of ignorance as to its true quality, and you may pay $300 more for it than necessary because of ignorance of different retailers' prices for it. Regarding price information, theory predicts search behavior up to the point where the expected benefits of added search fall below the added costs. Variations of perceived benefits and costs among buyers allow price dispersions. Regarding quality information, consumers often rely on cues or signals, such as a brand's duration on the market (first-mover

---

[75] These are actually underestimates because they represent measured media alone, for example, network television, and they exclude point of sales display and other non-measured media.

pioneering), market share (bigger implying better), and advertising intensity (assuming buyers cannot be fooled and producers actually attempt to signal quality in this way). Important factors explaining variations in knowledge of quality include buyer type (professional versus consumer) and product type (search goods versus experience goods). The difference between convenience goods (low priced, frequently purchased) and shopping goods (high priced, infrequently purchased) is also important. Informative advertising is highest for shopping goods, especially at retail level. Persuasive advertising is especially intense for convenience goods at manufacturers' level.

This last finding overflows into the third source of differentiation — *subjective impulses*. Evidence indicates that attribute and information theories of differentiation cannot explain all differentiation. For example, the correlation between price and quality is surprisingly low, so attributes cannot be credited. Furthermore, differentiation is commonly based on nonrational, nonfunction needs — symbolic and experiential needs, in particular. Persuasive advertising exploits these needs, and roughly half of all advertising could probably be considered persuasive instead of informative. Indeed, the inadequacies of the information theory of differentiation are highlighted by the observation that advertising intensity and information content are *inversely* related. Also it is interesting that advertising can be most persuasive when some information, even contrary information, is present (product experience especially).

Persuasive advertising seems most profitable and potent (1) in the presence of powerful emotional buying motives, (2) for low-priced convenience goods, (3) for new products, and (4) for top-dog brands. Observations on ad spending support these impressions.

Finally, strategic groups and product proliferation spring from the concepts covered in this chapter. A strategic group is comprised of firms following a similar strategy, such as those that may specialize in one market segment. Product proliferation results when a firm blankets the market with numerous brands or products, filling the segments. This may reflect an attempt to discourage new entry into the market because it closes each open product space that a newcomer could use as a launching pad for entry.

APPENDIX: MARLBORO'S SEX CHANGE

A smoker's brand makes a statement to peers. Its image is symbolic. Marlboro, with its cowboy, symbolizes masculinity, adventure, and freedom. Market researcher Srully Blotnick questioned 1546 cigarette smokers to learn why they preferred Marlboro. He concluded, "They use the cigarette as part of their wardrobe, the way some use costume jewelry or a watch."[76] Interestingly, the cigarette previously had a feminine image. Here, from *The Wall Street Journal*, is the story of how the cowboy came about.

> Perhaps more than any other consumer brand, Marlboro's advertising and promotions help keep it smoking. The ubiquitous cowboy is used throughout the world to plug Marlboro . . . . As for promotions Philip Morris sticks with the macho image, sponsoring auto races, skiing competitions and country music concerts . . . .
>
> But Marlboro wasn't always such a hit. In fact, it underwent a sex change of sorts. This most macho of cigarettes was once a women's brand. That's right, it was the Virginia Slims of the Roaring '20s. Marlboro was marketed with a rose tip so that the red imprint of women's lipstick wouldn't show. Its advertising slogan: "Mild as May."
>
> But Marlboro never achieved great success as a feminine brand, partly because women didn't smoke as much in those days. "It wasn't ladylike to smoke in public," recalls Joseph Cullman, chairman emeritus of Philip Morris.
>
> Unlike most brands, Marlboro got a second shot at fame. With filtered cigarettes coming on strong in the 1950s, Philip Morris deliberately needed to come up with its own filter-tip brand. Rather than start with a new name the company decided to gamble on repositioning lackluster Marlboro. Working with legendary ad man Leo Burnett, Philip Morris developed the trademark red and white box and the cowboy image.[77]

---

[76] *Forbes*, February 9, 1987, p. 109.
[77] Ronald Alsop, "Enduring Brands Hold Their Allure," *The Wall Street Journal*, Centennial Edition, 1989, p. B4.

6

Product Differentiation: Practice and Policy

Ironically, standards have not been completely standardized.

—DAVID HEMENWAY

Two case studies concerning beer and computers occupy the first third of this chapter. The main message they convey is simply this: *Trademarks may serve merely to identify the "origin" of goods, but consumers often go further by relying on trademarks to identify a given level of product quality. This reliance often grants sellers some power over price.*

The balance of this chapter reviews policies that affect product differentiation. These policies are related to the case studies and our previous evidence by the following hypothesis: *If quality identifications could be made independent of trademarks, the market power generated by trademarks would weaken.* To achieve this independent identification, policies would have to make consumers behave more like professional buyers, or make experience goods more like search goods. In short, buyers must be well informed, or readily informed. And, indeed, these are the broad objectives of the information disclosure policies discussed in this chapter.

148

I. CASE STUDIES

A. Beer

Legend has it that cockroaches are attracted to beer. Indeed, they will even drown in it if given the chance. The author is a believer. He has built ramps to bowls of brew to give roaches the chance, and they took it. Legend also holds that cockroaches favor certain brands of beer, but the author's experiments do not confirm this. Many folks are like cockroaches in that they, too, are attracted to beer. But they, unlike cockroaches, reveal a substantial degree of brand loyalty.

What makes this loyalty rather interesting — perhaps even astounding — is the fact that most beer drinkers cannot taste any difference between all but a few brands of American beer. This lack of any "genuine" difference among beers has been demonstrated by numerous researchers in a variety of ways, but all of them rely on one basic approach — the "blind" taste test. One of these studies was conducted by R. I. Allison and K. P. Uhl.[1] Their test went through two rounds using five well-known national or regional brands of beer on a sample of 326 who drank beer at least three times a week. Round 1 was designed to answer these questions:

1. Could beer drinkers, in general, distinguish among various beers in a blind test?
2. Could beer drinkers identify "their" brands in a blind test?

For this purpose each participant tested and evaluated (at their leisure) a six-pack of various unlabeled bottled beers, identified only by lettered tags — AB, CD, EF, GH, and IJ.

Possible scoring ranged from 0, which would be "very poor," to 100, which would be "excellent." On average, *all* beers scored within 1 point of 64, and there was no significant difference between brands. Thus the first answer is clearly "no." Drinkers cannot, in general, distinguish among brands.

The answer to the second question is found in Table 6–1. There the drinkers are segregated into five groups, depending on which of the five brands they claimed was their usual brand, as shown by the left-hand column. The blind ratings of the beers are presented in the body of the table. Thus, for example, drinkers who claimed EF was "their" brand rated EF at 65.0, but gave CD a rating of 74.5. And those who favored

---

[1] R. I. Allison and K. P. Uhl, "Influence of Beer Brand, Identification on Taste Perception," *Journal of Marketing Research* (August 1964), pp. 36–39. Another example of this genre is S. H. Rewoldt, J. D. Scott, and M. R. Warshaw, *Introduction to Marketing Management* (Homewood, Ill.: Richard D. Irwin, 1973), Case 2–1, "Falstaff Brewing Corporation," pp. 177–190.

TABLE 6–1. Drinkers' Loyalty to "Their" Brand in Blind Test
(Own Brand Rating on the Diagonal)

Brand Drunk Most Often	Taste Test Ratings by Brand Rated					Own Brand Rates Significantly Higher Than All Others?
	AB	CD	EF	GH	IJ	
AB	67.0	62.4*	57.7*	65.0	65.8	No
CD	64.9	65.6	65.4	63.2	63.9	No
EF	68.8	74.5*	65.0	62.5	61.4	No
GH	55.4	59.2	68.7	60.0	71.4*	No
IJ	68.4	60.5*	69.2	62.0	65.6	No

* Brand significantly different from user's own brand.

Source: R. I. Allison and K. P. Uhl, "Influence of Beer Brand Identification on Taste Perception," *Journal of Marketing Research* (August 1964), p. 38. Reprinted by permission of The American Marketing Association.

a fully dressed GH gave the nude GH a lowly 60.0 rating, which compared unfavorably to their rating of the nude IJ. As indicated by the right-hand column of Table 6–1, the answer to question 2 was negative in every case.

Round 2 was designed to answer one further question:

3. If the labels were left on, how would they influence the evaluations of various brands?

For this purpose Allison and Uhl picked up the unlabeled empties and gave each drinker a six-pack of labeled beer to taste and rate in the same fashion as in round one. Table 6–2 reveals these results. The first thing to note is that, generally speaking, the labels seemed to have improved the taste of all five beers to all drinkers because the numbers in Table 6–2 usually exceed their corresponding numbers in Table 6–1 by a substantial margin. Note next that this "improvement" is especially evident in the way the drinkers rated their "own" brands, as revealed by a comparison of the diagonal entries of Tables 6–1 and 6–2. Thus AB devotees boosted their rating of AB by 10.3 points once it was labeled, and the other increments were CD, 18.0 points; EF, 17.3; GH, 20.0; and IJ, 7.9. It is not unreasonable to conclude that drinkers generally rated "their" brand above the others when brand image could prompt their taste buds. Statistically significant divergences in this brand name "improvement" direction are indicated in the right-hand column of Table 6–2.[2]

---

[2] See also J. D. McConnell: "The Price-Quality Relationship in an Experimental Setting," *Journal of Marketing Research* (August 1968), pp. 300–303.

TABLE 6–2. Drinkers' Loyalty to "Their" Brand in Label Test (Own Brand Rating on the Diagonal)

Brand Drunk Most Often	Taste Test Ratings by Brand Rated					Own Brand Rates Significantly Higher?
	AB	CD	EF	GH	IJ	
AB	77.3	61.1	62.8	73.4	63.1	Yes
CD	66.3	83.6	67.4	78.3	63.1	Yes
EF	67.3	71.5	82.3	71.9	71.5	Yes
GH	73.1	72.5	77.5	80.0	67.5	Only over IJ
IJ	70.3	69.3	67.2	76.7	73.5	Only over EF

Source: R. I. Allison and K. P. Uhl, "Influence of Beer Brand Identification on Taste Perception," *Journal of Marketing Research* (August 1964), p. 38.

This is not to say that *all* brands of beer are identical or that cheap beer is always the best buy. Still, the evidence indicates that brand image is of utmost importance.[3]

B. Computer Systems

Although product differentiation for most consumer goods seems to be based on advertising, differentiation in the main frame computer industry is based primarily on close customer-manufacturer contacts. As Gerald Brock has written, "The user is not purchasing just a machine but a relationship with a manufacturer."[4] This observation is particularly apropos of the heart of main frame computer installations—the central processing unit, or CPU. These units are complex, costly, delicate—and IBM's special claim to fame. Indeed, IBM's dominance of this aspect of the business led one industry expert to remark that "IBM doesn't have to sell equipment at the same price-performance ratio as its competitors . . . . Most customers won't take the risk of leaving IBM for less than 30% improvement."[5]

The peripheral equipment of computer systems—such as tape drives and disk memories—may be considered much less differentiable. The choice between IBM and competitive "plug-compatible" peripheral equipment is straightforward because rivals have successfully copied IBM's specifications and because no substitution of the complete com-

[3] For a brief review of other tests (covering cola drinks and cigarettes as well as beer), the interested reader should consult J. H. Meyers and W. H. Reynolds, *Consumer Behavior and Marketing Management* (Boston: Houghton Mifflin, 1967), pp. 16–19.

[4] Gerald W. Brock, *The U.S. Computer Industry: A Study of Market Power* (Cambridge, Mass.: Ballinger, 1975), p. 46.

[5] "Itel's Powerful New Computer," *Business Week*, October 25, 1976, p. 74.

TABLE 6–3. IBM Disk Customer Loyalty in the Face of
Competitor's Discounts

Competitive Discount (%)	IBM Customers Remaining with IBM		
	Overall (%)	2319A Users (%)	3330 Users (%)
1–5%	97	99	94
6–10	92	95	88
11–15	70	58	64
16–20	46	37	36
Over 20	31	23	22

Source: G.W. Brock, *The U.S. Computer Industry: A Study of Market Power* (Cambridge, Mass.: Ballinger, 1975), p. 48. Reprinted by permission.

puter system is involved. Still, even in this simplified situation, IBM enjoys an impressive amount of brand loyalty. To measure the intensity of this loyalty, IBM conducted a questionnaire survey of its disk customers in the early 1970s, asking them how much lower competitive disk equipment would have to be priced in order for these customers to switch from IBM to a competitor. As may be seen in Table 6–3, IBM would apparently retain 92% of its customers despite competitive discounts of 10%. Furthermore, almost half of IBM's customers were willing to pass up competitive equipment that was priced as much as 20% below IBM's equipment. It seems, then, that IBM's customers and Budweiser's two-legged clientele share at least two things in common — they are human and they tend to be loyal to their chosen brand.

C. A Bit of Theory

It may seem to the reader that these two groups also have in common a good deal of irrationality, but this is not necessarily so. They may merely be uninformed. We may therefore conclude these case studies and preface our discussion of public policy with a brief explanation of the monetary benefits of correct information.[6] In essence, benefits arise from *error avoidance*. And there are two types of errors to be avoided — errors of commission and omission.

[6] This section draws heavily from S. Peltzman, "An Evaluation of Consumer Protection Legislation: The 1962 Drug Amendments," *Journal of Political Economy* (September/October 1973), pp 1049–1091; T. McGuire, R. Nelson, and T. Spavins, "Comment on the Peltzman Paper," *Journal of Political Economy* (June 1975), pp. 655–661; M. R. Darby and E. Karni, "Free Competition and the Optimal Amount of Fraud," *Journal of Law and Economics* (April 1973), pp. 67–88; George Akerlof, "The Market for 'Lemons': Quality Uncertainty and the Market Mechanism," *Quarterly Journal of Economics* (August 1970), pp. 488–500; and R. H. Nelson, "The Economics of Honest Trade Practices," *Journal of Industrial Economics* (June 1976), pp. 281–293.

An **error of commission** occurs when the buyer makes a purchase on the basis of an excessively favorable prepurchase assessment of the acquired good. In other words, the buyer gets not what he or she thinks he or she is getting but something less. The monetary loss of making such an error (or the gain from avoiding same) is illustrated in Figure 6–1 as the shaded area ABC. The demand curve $DACD$ refers to what demand would be like if the good were correctly evaluated, whereas $D'BD'$ depicts an erroneously optimistic level of demand. The latter lies to the right of the former since the uninformed buyer wants to buy more at each possible price then he or she would if he or she were fully informed. Thus, given a fixed price equal to $0P_0$ (or constant marginal costs of supply indicated by P_0AB), the consumer buys an excess equal to the difference between Q_1 and Q_2, that is $Q_1 - Q_2$. The amount he or she pays for this excess is the area Q_2ABQ_1, price times the excess quantity. However, the *true value* of the extra units amounts only to Q_2ACQ_1, or the trapezoid below A and C. Thus, the difference between dollar outlay Q_2ABQ_1 and true value Q_2ACQ_1 is ABC, the net loss.

Errors of omission are the opposite. They occur when the buyer buys *less* than she would with full knowledge. The monetary loss from making such an error is illustrated in Figure 6–2 by the area GHE. In this case the demand curve $D'GED'$ depicts what the demand would be like if the commodity were correctly evaluated, whereas DHD represents

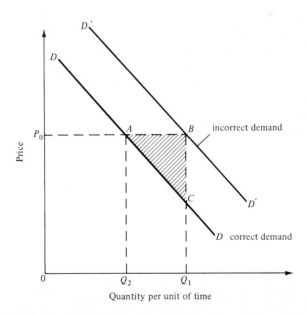

FIGURE 6–1. The monetary loss from an error of commission.

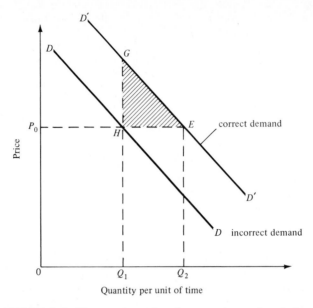

FIGURE 6–2. The monetary loss from an error of omission.

the erroneously pessimistic demand of buyers who underestimate the value of the product. Given a constant price P_0, a corrective movement from the poorly chosen amount Q_1 to the proper amount Q_2 requires an additional cash outlay equal to area Q_1HEQ_2. But the move yields a greater addition to total benefit, indicated by Q_1GEQ_2. Subtracting the added cost from this added benefit yields a *net* benefit of *HGE*, which in technical jargon is the amount of "consumer's surplus" the consumer misses out on when she errs in the direction of omission. It may now be seen that errors of omission lead to *under*allocations of resources to the particular products or brands, whereas errors of commission lead to *over*allocations to the chosen products or brands. Both forms of error are *mis*allocations, and they often represent opposite sides of the same coin. When someone overspends on sugary snacks, for instance, she probably also underspends on nutritious meals.[7]

The next question is: What policies assist buyers in avoiding these errors? Incredible though it may seem in light of what has been said to this point, one such policy is the issuance and enforcement of

---

[7] For concrete evidence, see Tyzoon T. Tyebjee, "Affirmative Disclosure of Nutrition Information and Consumers' Food Preferences: A Review," *Journal of Consumer Affairs* (Winter 1979), pp. 206–223; G. J. Gorn and M. E. Goldberg, "Behavioral Evidence of the Effects of Televised Food Messages on Children," *Journal of Consumer Research* (September 1982), pp. 200–205; and Bruce W. Marion, *The Organization and Performance of the U.S. Food System* (Lexington, Mass: Lexington Books, 1986), p. 275.

trademarks. To see this clearly, the reader might imagine what the world would be like in the absence of trademarks. Without them how could *Consumer Reports* tell us that Panasonic microwave ovens were better than the Sunbeam brand? Or how could a friend advise us that Levi's trousers are a good buy? How could we be sure that, having been wholly satisfied with an Arrow shirt, we could ever get another one from the same manufacturer? How could we sue the Coca-Cola Company for damages if we found a dead mouse in one of its soda bottles? In other words, it can be argued that, to the extent consumers do learn from experience and to the extent they do learn to buy what they like (rather than like what they buy), trademarks can minimize *repeated* errors merely by identifying good, bad, and mediocre goods and services. Similarly, trademarks are necessary to spreading an individual's or a testing agency's specific knowledge to others. And, finally, in extreme cases of error, individual producers may be held legally as well as economically accountable for their share in any disaster. As Richard Caves and William Murphy put it, "By offering the seller's good name as hostage, the trademark provides the buyer with cheap information and assurance about product quality."[8]

Despite these considerable social benefits, the trademark laws also involve *social costs*. Trademark policies are based on the assumption that trademarks serve primarily to identify the *origin* of goods, and that the purposes of such identification are twofold:[9]

1. Protection is furnished the seller from "unfair" competition through the infringement of his mark by an imitator or poacher.
2. Protection is furnished buyers who might be deceived into purchasing the goods of one seller in the belief that the goods are another's.

Unfortunately, this emphasis on origin adds substantially to the social costs of the trademark system without contributing to its social benefits. Benefits derive from the *identification of a given level of quality*, not from the identification of a given origin. Identification of origin on an exclusive, perpetual, and carefully protected basis, as is now practiced, may serve *indirectly* to identify a given level of quality. But it also facilitates the creation of substantial market power, power that translates into social costs, power achieved by exhortative advertising and other means of questionable social worth.[10] As we shall see later, the available evidence

---

[8] R. E. Caves and W. F. Murphy II, "Franchising: Firms, Markets, and Intangible Assets," *Southern Economic Journal* (April 1976), pp. 572–586.

[9] E. W. Kintner and J. L. Lahr, *An Intellectual Property Law Primer* (New York: Macmillan, 1975), p. 250.

[10] Robert Feinberg, "Trademarks, Market Power, and Information," *Review of Industrial Organization*, Vol. 2, no. 4 (1986), pp. 376–385.

indicates that, when quality guarantees or quality identifications are established independently of trademarks (by professional buyers themselves, by government grade rating and standardization, by consumers search shopping for easily analyzable goods, and so on), monopoly power cannot be based on trademark differentiation and advertising, and burdensome social costs are avoided. The effects of the trademark system are therefore negative when (1) trademarks (and the persuasive advertising promoting them) provide the sole or major source of quality identification for the product *and* (2) grants of exclusive trademark use protect the goodwill (or monopoly) profits that attach to trademarks under such circumstances. Corrective policies should therefore be focused on one or both of the following objectives:

1. Permit trademarks to identify or guarantee quality but remove the rights of exclusivity currently awarded them.
2. Establish quality identifications and guarantees that are *independent* of the trademark system.

With respect to the first, nonexclusive trademark use, we could have a policy that would permit imitation as long as quality was maintained.[11] Such a policy would focus the law on identifying quality instead of origin. But this policy is radical, and its adoption is unlikely. With respect to the second possible focus of policy, quality identifications and guarantees that are independent of the trademark system, regulations abound. They merit the sections that follow.

II. STANDARDIZATION AND DISCLOSURE

As suggested by the heading "Standardization and Disclosure," information or identification policies other than trademarks may be divided into two categories.[12] And, as suggested by the items listed for each category, the ultimate purpose of these policies is to assist consumers in avoiding errors. *They make consumers more like professional buyers and make experience goods more like search goods.*

A. Standardization for easier price comparisons
   1. Simplified quantity labeling
   2. Uniform sizes
   3. Price standardization, for example, "unit" pricing
   4. Warranty standards

---

[11] Edward H. Chamberlin, *The Theory of Monopolistic Competition*, 8th ed. (Cambridge, Mass.: Harvard University Press, 1962), p. 273; see also W. J. Lane, "Compulsory Trademark Licensing," *Southern Economic Journal* (January 1988), pp. 643–654.

[12] This division and much else in this section owe their origin to David Hemenway, *Industrywide Voluntary Product Standards* (Cambridge, Mass.: Ballinger, 1975).

B. Quality disclosures
   1. Ingredient disclosure
   2. Open dating of perishables
   3. Specific performance disclosures
   4. Grade rating

Standardization policies typically promote simplification or uniformity or both. The distinction between simplification and uniformity may be seen by an example. Suppose ten brick manufacturers were each making the same 50 kinds of brick. Since each producer offered a full range of 50 kinds, each firm's bricks would match those of the others and there would be perfect **uniformity** among sellers. With 50 varieties, however, the situation would not be simple. **Simplification** would be achieved if these firms agreed to cut down the number of their offerings to, say, 12 common types. This would yield a combination of simplification and uniformity — ten firms, each producing the same 12 kinds of brick. Alternatively, simplification could be achieved at the expense of uniformity. If each of the ten brick makers cut back their offerings to four *unique* items, with no one producing the same item, uniformity would disappear. The total, industrywide variety, however, would have been simplified from 50 down to 40. As far as buyer errors are concerned, uniformity facilitates the comparison of different seller's offerings, whereas simplification may help to keep buyers' minds from boggling.

Quality disclosures are quite different. They sharpen the buyer's awareness of "better" or "worse." For example, all mattress manufacturers may uniformly adhere to a few simple sizes — twin, double, queen, and king. But this says nothing about the range of quality (and some mattresses may feel as if they were made from 50 kinds of brick). Disclosure of ingredients might be helpful in this case, and grade rating would be even more helpful. Policies revealing ingredients and grades may thus be considered quality disclosures.

Although buyer-side behavior is the primary focus of these policies, it must be recognized that they frequently change seller behavior for the better as well. Evidence concerning food and drug products indicates that standardization and disclosure policies cause sellers to reduce the intensity of their overall advertising, shift from persuasive to informative advertising, and market more private-label and generic brands.[13]

---

[13] Rhys Jenkins, "Transnational Corporations and Third World Consumption: Implications of Competitive Strategies," *World Development* (November 1988), p. 1366; P. K. Gorecki, "The Importance of Being First," *International Journal of Industrial Organization* (December 1986), pp. 371–395; and James A. Zellner, "Industrial Organization: Some Applications for Managerial Decisions," *American Journal of Agricultural Economics* (May 1988). More subtle benefits of policy emerge from an important article by Stephen Hoch and John Deighton — "Managing What Consumers Learn from Experience," *Journal of Marketing* (April 1989), pp. 1–20. These policies make postpurchase experiences more meaningful by

Before we take a detailed look at specific policies, one more preliminary point needs attention: Why must we rely on the *government* to elevate consumer knowledge and information? What is wrong with relying on free *private* enterprise? If information is a desirable "good," ought not profit opportunities abound for anyone who wants to supply information? The answer to all these questions is, in a word, *imperfections.* The nature of the commodity in question—information—is such that imperfections stand in the way of its optimal provision by private enterprise.

Among the many problems that discourage optimal private provision, two seem paramount. First, sellers of information may face the same problem as the little boy who climbs and shakes the apple tree but gets few of the fallen apples because his buddies on the ground run off with the loot before he can get down. This is "inappropriability," and it often applies to information because information may be spread by means outside the control of the information's original producer—for example, piracy by word of mouth. When private producers of information are not rewarded in proportion to the social value of their effort, they extend less effort than is socially optimal. A second problem arises because buyers of information cannot be truly *well informed* about the information they want to buy. If they were, they would not need to buy the information.[14] In other words, the seller of information cannot let potential buyers meticulously examine his product prior to sale lest he thereby give it away free. Buyers of information therefore do not know the value of the product they seek (information) until after they buy it. They are consequently vulnerable to errors of commission and omission. Only with objective, nonmarket assistance can they overcome this handicap.

A. Standardization for Easy Price Comparisons

1. Simplified Quantity Labeling.   Try this little test on yourself. Which box of detergent is the best buy—25 "jumbo" ounces for 53 cents; 1 1/2 pounds for 49 cents; or 27 1/2 "full" ounces for 55 cents? Prior to the Fair Packaging and Labeling Act of 1966 (FPLA), grocery shoppers took, and failed, real-life tests like this more often than they probably care to remember. In 1965, for instance, a selected sample of 33 married women who were students or wives of students at Eastern Michigan University were asked to pick the most economical package for each of 20 supermarket products. Despite their above–average intelligence and

---

plain product differences. The latter limits the extent to which top-dog sellers can disrupt the buyer's agenda.

[14] Kenneth Arrow, "Economic Welfare and the Allocation of Resources for Invention," in *The Rate of Direction of Inventive Activity: Economic and Social Factors* (New York: National Bureau of Economic Research, 1962).

their stimulated attention, these women typically spent 9.14% more on these groceries than they should have.[15] Small wonder they erred, what with the commingling of weight and fluid volumes for the same products; the use of meaningless adjectives, such as "jumbo" and "full"; the frequent appearance of fractional quantity units; and the designation of servings as "small," "medium," and "large," without any common standard of reference.

The Fair Packaging and Labeling Act tidied things up by stipulating

1. The net quantity be stated in a uniform and prominent location on the package
2. The net quantity be clearly expressed in a unit of measure appropriate to the product
3. The net quantity of a "serving" must be stated if servings are mentioned

This may not seem like much, but the FPLA was vigorously opposed by business interests. Some opponents claimed that it was "a power grab based on the fallacious concepts that the consumer is Casper Milquetoast, business is Al Capone, and government is Superman."[16] Their opposition was based on what they apparently thought was a more accurate concept—the housewife as Superwoman. "We suggest," argued the editor of *Food Field Reporter*, "that the housewife . . . should be expected to take the time to divide fractionalized weights into fractionalized prices in order to determine the 'best buy.' "[17] Still others worried about what would happen to the Barbie doll: "Will the package have to say, in compliance with the act's rules, 'One doll, net,' on quantity and then, on size, '34–21–34'?"[18] Despite such criticism, the FPLA seems to have worked fairly well. The Federal Trade Commission and Food and Drug Administration have encountered problems while enforcing the act, but nothing insuperable. The problem of what to do with Barbie, for instance, was solved when the Federal Trade Commission declared that she was among the many commodities that were not covered by the act—toys, chinaware, books, souvenirs, and mouse traps, to name a few.

2. Uniform Package Sizes. As already suggested, it would be easier for consumers to compare the price per unit of various brands and volumes if sellers adhered to a few common sizes of packages. Several *nonmandatory* standards emerged from the voluntary sections of FPLA.

---

[15] M. P. Friedman, "Consumer Confusion in the Selection of Supermarket Products," *Journal of Applied Psychology* (December 1966), pp. 529–534.

[16] Michigan Chamber of Commerce, as quoted by R. L. Birmingham, "The Consumer as King: The Economics of Precarious Sovereignty," in *Consumerism*, edited by D. A. Aaker and G. S. Day (New York: The Free Press, 1974), p. 186.

[17] A. Q. Mowbray, *The Thumb on the Scale* (New York: J. B. Lippincott, 1967), p. 72.

[18] *The New York Times*, June 8, 1969.

Dry cereals, for example, are supposed to be packaged in whole ounces only. Jellies and preserves are now supposed to come in sizes of 10, 12, 16, 18, 20, 24, 28, 32, 48, or 64 ounces. However, these voluntary standards do not seem to be very helpful. For more stringent action we must look to state and foreign laws. In the United States, several states have standardized the packaging of bread, butter, margarine, flour, corn meal, and milk. Among foreign countries, Germany, France, England, and Canada have rather extensive mandatory standardization.[19]

3. Price Standardization.   Price standardization is more helpful to consumers than are package uniformity and simplification. It may be found in two major forms—unit pricing and truth-in-lending. **Unit pricing** translates all package prices into a price per standard weight or measure, such as 25.3 cents per pound, or 71.4 cents per hundred count. Representing price in this way helps consumers compare prices without superhuman computations. Studies have shown that unit pricing greatly reduces price comparison errors. One such study found that with unit pricing people could pick the least cost item 25% more often than without, and at the same time cut down their shopping time considerably.[20] Extensive national regulations of this type exist only in Germany and Switzerland. In the United States, eleven states have adopted unit-pricing regulations, led by Massachusetts in 1971.[21] Although U.S. laws thus have restricted application, many grocery stores have voluntarily adopted unit pricing. As a result, it appears that roughly half of all chain-operated supermarkets in the United States and one-fourth of all independent supermarkets use unit pricing of some kind.

Truth-in-lending (TIL) is one form of price standardization that since 1969 has been provided by U.S. government regulations.[22] However, the scope of these regulations is limited to consumer credit. Before adoption of TIL, studies indicated that only a few people knew how much they actually paid for credit. Two such studies in the 1950s, for instance, indicated that 66–70% of consumers did not have even a vague idea of the annual *percentage rate*, let alone the dollar value, of interest they were paying on their *recent* installment purchases. They almost certainly did not know the interest rates charged by other credit suppliers,

[19] Committee on Consumer Policy, *Package Standardization, Unit Pricing, Deceptive Packaging* (Paris: Organization for Economic Co-operation and Development, 1975).

[20] For a summary of this and other studies see General Accounting Office, *Report to the Congress on Food Labeling: Goals, Shortcomings, and Proposed Changes* (#MWD–75–19), January 1975. This is the main source for this section.

[21] *State Consumer Action: Summary '74*, Office of Consumer Affairs, Department of Health, Education, and Welfare [Pub. No. (OS) 75–116], pp. ix–x.

[22] Material for this topic may be found in *Consumer Credit in the United States*, Report of the National Commission on Consumer Finance (Washington, D.C.: U.S. Government Printing Office, 1972), Chapter 10; and *Technical Studies, Vol. I*, of the same commission, which includes papers by R. P. Shay, M. W. Schober, G. S. Day, and W. K. Brandt.

information that is necessary to comparative shopping. Why this vast ignorance? To make a long story short, there was no price standardization in the credit industry. Depending on the method, the price for the same amount of credit might be quoted as being 1%, 7%, 12.83%, or 16%. Indeed, some lenders would not quote *any* rate of charge. They would merely state the number and amount of the monthly payments required.

The purpose of the truth-in-lending law is to let consumers know exactly what the price of credit is and to let them compare the prices of various lenders. As argued by the late Senator Paul Douglas: "The benefits of effective competition cannot be realized if the buyers (borrowers) do not have adequate knowledge of the alternatives which are available to them." To achieve these ends the law requires disclosure of two aspects of credit prices:

1. The *finance charge*, which is the amount of money paid to obtain the credit.
2. The *annual percentage rate*, or APR, which provides a simple way of comparing credit prices regardless of the dollar amount charged or the length of time over which payments are made.

From the consumer's viewpoint, things are simpler now. Several studies of credit-cost awareness subsequent to TIL have discovered improvements in debtor knowledge.

4. Warranty Standardization. The 1975 Magnuson–Moss Warranty–FTC Improvement Act contains standards for written product warranties. For products priced above $15 manufacturers must now specify whether their warranty is "full" or "limited," where

1. A *full warranty* means that charges for repair or replacement during the warranty period are either minimal or nil.
2. A *limited warranty* limits the seller's obligations, placing more financial responsibility on the consumer.

Moreover, the law holds that the terms and conditions of a written warranty must be stated "in simple and readily understood language." This was in response to consumer complaints that only sober Philadelphia lawyers could understand the language of most product warranties.

Early studies of the impact of this law indicate that its benefits may be rather limited. Apparently, only about 28% of all consumers read warranties before making their purchases, so warranty standardization would assist only a minority of consumers in comparative shopping.[23] Moreover, warranties are still very difficult to understand despite the law. Measuring language lucidity by the education level necessary to

---

[23] Federal Trade Commission, *Warranties Rules Consumer Baseline Study* (March 2, 1979), p. 129.

achieve understanding, one recent study of 125 warranties found that 34% of them were at "college graduate" level and 44% more were at "some college" level. Automobile warranties were found to be especially difficult, generating an average grade level score of 20.2.[24]

It should be noted, however, that the purposes of the Magnuson–Moss Act go well beyond warranty simplification. And in these other respects the Act seems to have been more successful. For instance, there appears to have been some shift from "limited" to "full" warranties, and warranty coverage in terms of duration, scope, and remedies seems to have improved.[25] Moreover, the Magnuson–Moss Act requires manufacturers to provide the protection they promise in their warranties, and there is evidence that warranties have consequently become much better signals of quality. For example, a five-year auto warranty signals a more reliable car than does a two-year warranty. Firms entering the market for television sets since 1976 have used their warranties as a means of supporting their reliability claims. On the whole, then, the policy may be judged a success.[26]

B. Quality Disclosures[27]

Critics of the policies mentioned heretofore correctly point out that they simply make price comparisons easier; they do not take into account differences in the *quality* of competing brands or products. The general purpose of the following policies is to help buyers identify quality.

1. Simple Disclosure of Ingredients. The Wool Products Labeling Act of 1939, the Fur Products Labeling Act of 1951, and the Textile Fiber Products Identification Act of 1958 call for the disclosure of ingredients in fur and fiber products. All are enforced by the Federal Trade Commission. Under the first of these, almost all wool products must bear labels showing the percentage of total fiber weight of "virgin" wool, reprocessed wool, and reused wool. Inclusion of any other fiber must also be identified by generic name (as opposed to trade name) if it exceeds 5% of the total. Similarly, the fur act requires fur product labels that disclose the true English name of the animal that grew the fur; the animal's home country if the fur is imported; whether the fur is bleached, dyed, or otherwise artificially colored; and whether it is composed of paws,

[24] F. Kelley Shuptrine and Ellen M. Moore, "Even After the Magnuson–Moss Act of 1975, Warranties Are Not Easy to Understand," *Journal of Consumer Affairs* (Winter 1980), pp. 394–404.

[25] T. Schmitt, L. Kauter, and R. Miller, *Impact Report on the Magnuson–Moss Warranty Act* (Washington, D.C.: Federal Trade Commission, 1980).

[26] Joshua Lyle Wiener, "An Evaluation of the Magnuson–Moss Warranty and Federal Trade Commission Improvement Act of 1975," *Journal of Public Policy and Marketing*, Vol. 7 (1988), pp. 65–82.

[27] For another survey, see John A. Miller, "Product Labeling and Government Regulation," *Journal of Contemporary Business*, Vol. 7, no. 4 (1979), pp. 105–121.

bellies, scraps, or waste fur. Thus, rabbit cannot be passed off as "Baltic Lion," and sheared muskrat cannot be called "Hudson Seal"—not as long as the FTC's agents stay awake on the job.

Finally, the main purpose of the textile act is to reduce confusion that might be caused by the proliferation of chemical fibers and their many trade names. The law requires labels revealing the *generic* names and percentages of all fibers that go into a fabric, except those that constitute less than 5% of the fabric. Thus Dacron®, which is a trade name, must be identified as "polyester," its generic name. Over 700 other trade names must be identified as belonging to one of 17 generic families specified by the FTC. To the extent consumers know the properties of these generic fibers in terms of washing, pressing, dying, and wearing them, the law helps. To the extent consumers do not know, it does not help.

Ingredient labeling regulations for food products has a shorter but more complicated history.[28] Since about 1972 the Food and Drug Administration (FDA) has vigorously expanded its activity in labeling so that detailed disclosures of composition are now required on the labels of processed food products that make claims of nutritional value. The disclosures include

1. Nutrition information, such as vitamins, minerals, caloric content, carbohydrate content, and protein.
2. Special information on foods intended for infants, nursing mothers, diabetics, the allergic, and the obese.
3. Defining natural and artificial flavors, spices, and colorings.

Steps to improve the system were initiated by the Food and Drug Administration in 1989. Words such as "natural," "light," and "organic" were being used so loosely as to become meaningless. The expression "low fat" came to mean anything lower than something higher. Indeed, labeling was especially deficient on this matter of fat. Doctors and health experts warn us to cut back on eating fat, especially saturated fat, so labels should provide information enabling us to do so.[29]

2. Open Dating.   Freshness is obviously an important aspect of the quality of perishable food products. For many years food manufacturers dated their products for inventory control and retailer rotation. Until recently, however, these dates were disguised by codes not known to the public (and often not even known to grocery store managers or clerks). Thus open dating is simply uncoded dating. Federal law does not require open dating, but 21 states have some form of mandatory

---

[28] L. E. Hicks, *Product Labeling and the Law* (New York: AMACOM, Division of American Management Association, 1974).

[29] *Washington Post*, National Weekly Edition, July 31–August 6, 1989, p. 31. See also *Business Week*, October 9, 1989, p. 133.

open dating with dairy products being the prime target.[30] In addition, many grocery chains have voluntarily adopted it. One problem that remains to be resolved is standardization. "Sell-by" dating is customary, but a confusing variety of dating methods are also used — "packing date," "expiration date," and so on.

Another form of open dating relates to autos. As of 1975, 37 states had entered the snake pit of used-car sales by prohibiting odometer tampering. Thereafter, the federal government also stepped in with passage of the Motor Vehicle Information and Cost Savings Act. This law requires a written, true-mileage disclosure statement at the time of sale for all self-propelled vehicles except those that are over 24 years old or exceed 16,000 pounds. Moreover, the law prohibits disconnecting or resetting the odometer with intent to change the mileage reading or knowingly falsifying the written odometer statement.[31]

3. Specific Performance Disclosures. Beginning with the 1977 models, all new cars sold in the United States have had labels disclosing the estimated number of miles they get per gallon of gas and an estimate of what yearly fuel cost would be if 15,000 miles were traveled per year. Thus, for example, the 1977 Volkswagon Rabbit Diesel, with a 90-cubic-inch engine, was reported to travel 44 miles per gallon and costs $188 in annual fuel expense. By contrast, the 1977 Dodge Royal Monaco with a 440-cubic-inch engine brandished a sticker saying that a standard year's travel in one of them would cost $886, since it averaged only 11 miles per gallon. The Federal Energy Act of 1975 requires these disclosures on the theory that they assist efficiency comparisons and in the hope that car buyers will react to these revelations by shying away from gas guzzlers.

The Federal Energy Act also requires that efficiency ratings appear on major home appliances like refrigerators, freezers, and dishwashers. Administered by the Federal Trade Commission through its rule-making procedures, this program is more complex than is suggested by the simple energy labels adopted (see Figure 6–3 for a sample).[32] One particularly helpful feature of the label is that it places the appliance on a relative scale, so the shopper need not strain to make comparisons of

---

[30] Congress of the United States, Office of Technology Assessment, *Open Shelf-Life Dating of Food* (Washington, D.C.: OTA, August 1979). A study prompting Minnesota's law found that 44% of the baby formula being sold was overage and that since 64% of the store managers could not read a coded date, they could not rotate the stock.

[31] In 1987 Chrysler Corporation pleaded no contest to criminal charges that it had been selling cars as "new" that had been driven by company executives with disconnected odometers for as much as 400 miles. At least 32,750 cars were involved over a three-year period. The company agreed to pay fines of $16.4 million. *The Wall Street Journal*, December 15, 1987, p. 22.

[32] Federal Trade Commission, *Labeling and Advertising of Consumer Appliances* (Washington, D.C.: FTC, February 1979).

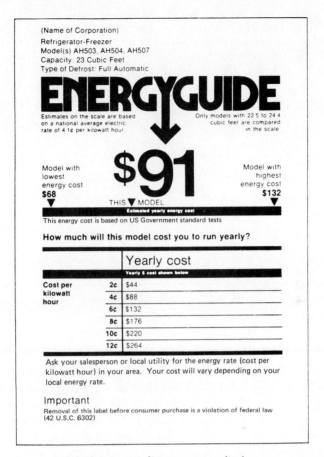

FIGURE 6–3. Appliance energy disclosure.

energy efficiency. Preliminary study of consumer response to this program indicates its favorable promise. Of particular interest is the finding that consumers now give greater weight to energy efficiency, as indicated in Table 6–4. Table 6–4 also shows that as energy efficiency has risen in importance, brand names have fallen in importance.

Another illustration of specific performance disclosure is gasoline octane posting, which has been with us in one form or another since 1973, but only haphazardly enforced. The Federal Trade Commission has argued that in the absence of octane posting, motorists would waste more than $300 million a year by purchasing gasoline with higher octane than they really need. Most people seem to think that higher octane produces greater power. But this is not true. Octane indicates only the anti-knock properties of gasoline. The major brand petroleum companies have persistently opposed octane posting for fear that it would lead

TABLE 6–4. Consumer Rating of Attribute Importance Before and After Energy Labeling: Refrigerators

	Percentage of Consumer Respondents Who Said the Attribute Was Very Important to Their Choice	
Attribute	Before Energy Labeling	After Energy Labeling
Size	73.1%	68.8%
Price	52.5	58.6
Appearance/color	49.5	47.7
Yearly energy cost	34.6	43.9
Brand name	32.5	23.6

Source: Robert F. Dyer and Thomas J. Maronick, "An Evaluation of Consumer Awareness and Use of Energy Labels in the Purchase of Major Appliances," *Journal of Public Policy and Marketing*, Vol. 7 (1988), p. 89.

people to recognize that all brands of gasoline of a given octane rating were pretty much alike (which they are).[33]

4. Grade Rating. Disclosures of ingredients, freshness, dimensions, specific performance, and the like may guide buyers toward ideal purchasing patterns. But how close to the ideal can these raw data take them? Several studies have demonstrated what most students already know from experience — namely, the information processing capabilities of the human mind are quite limited. Indeed, some evidence even suggests that beyond a certain point additional information may confuse and frustrate consumers. Thereafter they no longer move toward their ideal decision, but rather *away* from it.[34] Thus grade rating is often recommended as a means of simplifying complex quality information into an ABC format.[35]

[33] See *Business Week*, May 31, 1976, p. 21; and F. C. Allvine and J. M. Patterson, *Competition Limited: The Marketing of Gasoline* (Bloomington: Indiana University Press, 1972), pp. 24–25. The experience of Germany here is interesting. See Hans and Sarah Thorelli, *Consumer Information Systems and Consumer Policy* (Cambridge, Mass.: Ballinger, 1977), p. 155.

[34] J. Jacoby, D. E. Speller, and C. K. Berning, "Brand Choice Behavior as a Function of Information Load: Replication and Extension," *Journal of Consumer Research* (June 1974), pp. 33–42; N. K. Malhotra, A. K. Jain, and S. W. Lagakos, "The Information Overload Controversy: An Alternative Viewpoint," *Journal of Marketing* (Spring 1982), pp. 27–37; and N. K. Malhortra, "Information Load and Consumer Decision Making," *Journal of Consumer Research* (March 1982), pp. 419–430.

[35] J. R. Bettman, "Issues in Designing Consumer Information Environments," *Journal of Consumer Research* (December 1975), pp. 169–177.

The most active federal agency in this respect is the U. S. Department of Agriculture, whose agents grade meat, eggs, butter, poultry, grain, fruits, and vegetables. Beef, for example, is graded "prime," "choice," and "good." This grading is not compulsory. Hence, large brand name meat packers like Armour, Swift, Morrell, and Wilson are given some elbow room to resist it. They prefer to promote the sale of beef under their own brand names whenever and wherever possible. Among the statistics that reflect past resistance to grading, we find that during the 1950s only 27% of national packer beef was USDA graded, and all but one of the national brand name packers advocated an end to federal grading. In contrast, the main supporters of the system are independent packers, retail food chains, independent retailers, and consumers. During 1955, for instance, 94% of all beef sold by retail food chains was USDA graded, and 85% of all chains surveyed said they favored compulsory grading or continuation of the present system. These and related data led researchers to conclude that

1. Grade standards have tended to intensify competition.
2. Unbranded packers and wholesalers increased in number and volume of meat processed, whereas branded packers declined greatly in number.
3. The system has tended to increase the accuracy, ease, and effectiveness of prices in reflecting value differences at each stage in the marketing system for beef by assisting consumers in the expression of their preferences.[36]

The biggest problem with USDA grade rating is its lack of standardization across products. Top-rated apples, peaches, chickens, and some other foods are variously awarded grades of No. 1, Extra No. 1, Fancy, and Grade A. For still other products these grades would indicate second best.

Auto tires were the subject of an early demonstration of how grading could reduce buyers' erroneous reliance on brand names. Louis Bucklin found that, without grading, consumers tended to overestimate the value of heavily advertised national brands of tires as compared to mildly promoted distributor and local brands, but that with grade rating this bias tended to disappear.[37] Subsequent to that study, and despite

---

[36] Willard F. Williams, E. K. Bowen, and F. C. Genovese, *Economic Effects of U.S. Grades for Beef*, U.S. Department of Agriculture Marketing Research Report No. 298 (Washington, D. C.: USDA, 1959), pp. vii, 158–180. See also *Business Week*, September 27, 1982, p. 32. More generally, Zellner compares food products with and without USDA standards and finds that, *with* standards, informative (print) advertising tends to lower price-cost margins and concentration while persuasive (electronic) advertising is less likely to raise price-cost margins or foster concentration. James A. Zellner, "Persuasive and Informative Advertising of Standardized and Nonstandardized Food Products," USDA, mimeo, 1987.

[37] Louis P. Bucklin, "The Uniform Grading System for Tires: Its Effect upon Consumers and Industry Competition," *Antitrust Bulletin* (Winter 1974), pp. 783–801.

sharp objections by major tire manufacturers, a grade rating system was put into effect by the Department of Transportation in 1979 and 1980. Tires are now rated on three characteristics:

1. *Treadwear*, indicated by a numeral such as 200 or 400, with higher numerals indicating higher mileage
2. *Traction*, where A, B, and C indicate good, fair, and poor traction on wet roads, respectively
3. *Temperature*, where A indicates the coolest running tire, and B and C rank less well

Tire manufacturers do their own testing and interpretation under the program, which has led to problems. Although the tests are uniform, they yield a range of results. And some companies interpret their results more conservatively than other companies, leading to different grades for very similar test results and different grades for very similarly priced tires.[38] Even so, the system is probably a step in the right direction.

Finally, and most recently, the Food and Drug Administration has launched a rating system for suntan oil based on "sun protection factor" or SPF. Use a #2 SPF oil and you fry. Use a higher-numbered oil and you get more protection.[39]

SUMMARY

Most folks cannot taste any difference between different brands of beer, and computers are bought by expert buyers. Nevertheless, our case studies disclose substantial product differentiation in both industries. Buyers apparently rely heavily on trademarks to guide their purchasing decisions, since in a roundabout way trademarks may help buyers avoid errors of commission or omission. On the other hand, too heavy a reliance on trademarks and the advertising promoting them may *cause* errors of commission or omission, in which case the owners of prominent trademarks gain at the expense of buyers.

Corrective policies have to focus on one or both of the following objectives: (1) Permit trademarks to identify quality, but remove the rights of ownership exclusivity that presently prevail. (2) Establish quality identifications independent of the trademark system. The first objective lies outside the realm of political possibility. The second has been furthered by two broad classes of policies — standardization (which includes simplified quantity labeling, uniform sizes, and unit pricing) and quality disclosures (which include ingredient labeling, open dating, performance disclosure, and grade rating). These are outlined in Table 6–5.

[38] *The Wall Street Journal*, December 31, 1980, p. 5.
[39] *Forbes*, June 21, 1982, pp. 80–81.

TABLE 6–5. Summary of United States Standardization and Disclosure Policies

Policy	Enforcement Agencies*	Products Covered
A. Standardization		
1. Fair Packaging and Labeling Act (1966)	FTC, FDA	Grocery store items (for example, foods and detergents)
2. Size uniformity and simplification	Various state authorities	Bread, margarine, flour, dairy products
3. Unit pricing	Various state authorities	Grocery store items
4. Truth-in-Lending Act (1969)	FTC, FRB	Consumer credit
5. Warranty standards	FTC	Durables over $15 with written warranty
B. Quality Disclosures		
1. Ingredient labeling:		
Wool Products Labeling Act (1939)	FTC	Wool products
Fur Products Labeling Act (1951)	FTC	Furs
Textiles Fiber Identification Act (1958)	FTC	Textiles, apparel, etcetera
Food, Drug and Cosmetic Act	FDA	Food Products
2. Open dating of perishables	Various state authorities	Grocery perishables
3. Antitampering Odometer Law (1972)	NHTSA	Cars and trucks
4. Performance disclosures		
Fuel efficiency	FEA, FTC	Autos, appliances
Octane rating	FTC, FEA	Gasoline
Tar and nicotine	FTC	Cigarettes
On time performance	ICC	Moving van services
5. Grade rating	USDA	Meat, eggs, butter, etcetera
	NHTSA	Tires
	FDA	Suntan oil

* Key: FTC—Federal Trade Commission; FDA—Food and Drug Administration; FRB—Federal Reserve Board of Governors; NHTSA—National Highway Traffic Safety Administration; FEA—Federal Energy Administration; ICC—Interstate Commerce Commission; USDA—U.S. Department of Agriculture.

APPENDIX TO CHAPTER 6: VOLUNTARY STANDARDS

Standards often do more than help buyers become informed. They can be used to ensure physical compatibility between related products made by different manufacturers and to assist in achieving economies of scale. When used for these purposes, standards are usually voluntary (the work of producers themselves) rather than mandatory (the work of the government). There are over 30,000 voluntary product standards now in effect in the United States.

Many standards also prevail in Europe . . . too many. The problem is that each country has its own standards, so for many products there is little standardization. Take electrical equipment for instance. Philips, the large European electronics firm, "makes 29 different types of electrical outlets, 10 kinds of plugs, 12 kinds of cords, 3 kinds of television sets, 12 types of irons and 15 kinds of cake mixers." The number of "standard" European caps for lightbulbs is about 300. Such variety limits the scale of production runs and thereby prevents the full achievement of economies of scale. As the *The Wall Street Journal* reports,

> varying standards force Philips to make a wider spectrum of goods than it wants to, driving up production costs as economies of scale are lost. Wider variety necessitates higher inventories, meaning higher interest and storage costs. . . . Philips maintains that if Europe were truly a single market, appliances and customer electronics would be 7% to 10% cheaper, stimulating demand and adding to sales.[40]

The main reason European standards vary is that they protect local manufacturers. Indeed, these standards have become mandatory largely because of political pressures applied by local producers who want to be shielded from foreign rivals. Hence here we have yet another use for standards: they can be used to restrict competition.

Returning to the United States, it has been hypothesized that voluntary standards would be easier to devise in concentrated as opposed to unconcentrated industries. Greater concentration implies *fewer* firms, and fewness should aid in achieving the consensus that voluntary standards require. Moreover, greater concentration implies relatively *larger* firms, and large size would grant larger rewards from the net benefits standards provide. Recent empirical evidence supports these views. The incidence of voluntary product standards seems to be positively associated with concentration in high-technology industries.[41]

---

[40] *The Wall Street Journal*, August 7, 1985, pp. 1, 16.

[41] Albert N. Link, "Market Structure and Voluntary Product Standards," *Applied Economics*, Vol. 15 (1983) pp. 393–401. See also Sylvia Lane and Anastasios Papathanasis, "Certification and Industry Concentration Ratios," *Antitrust Bulletin* (Summer 1983), pp. 381–395.

7

Concentration: Theory and Cross-section Evidence

Seller concentration has for a long time received more attention from economists and those concerned with public policy towards industry than any other single characteristic of industrial structure.

—DOUGLAS NEEDHAM

The number and size distribution of firms are important determinants of market power, just as the height and weight of players are important to the strength of a football team. There are several statistical measures of such power. But, which one of these statistics best depicts sellers' power over price? Given an answer to this question, how do we define the relevant market to include all the firms that should be included and to exclude all the firms that should be excluded from our statistical calculations? Are Coca-Cola and Budweiser in the same market, for instance?

Turning next to the issue of what *causes* a given number and size distribution of firms, we must ask whether firms get the market shares they deserve. Do General Motors, Ford, and Chrysler, for example, deserve, by their efficiency and quality of product, to account for 70% of all cars sold in the United States? Or, did they attain their position merely by acquiring former competitors and hiding behind tariff barriers that inhibited imports? Finally, the federal government has by *policy* broken up large companies, such as Standard Oil of New Jersey (now Exxon) and prohibited numerous attempts at merger, such as Clorox with Procter & Gamble. Did these firms deserve what they got?

These questions highlight the issues taken up in this and the next three chapters. In this chapter, we first discuss various statistical measures of the number and size distribution of firms. Next we review the historic and present conditions of market concentration in the United States. We then consider the causes of those conditions. Finally, we shall move from individual markets to the economy as a whole and consider aggregate concentration.[1]

I. STATISTICAL MEASURES

Several statistical measures of structural power have been devised. Which of these is used in any given instance depends on data availabilities and the immediate purpose. A good measure is one that is easy to calculate, sensitive to major structural changes over time, and indicative of differences in structural power across diverse markets and firms. Above all, *an effective measure must provide fairly accurate predictions of market conduct and performance;* otherwise, it is useless. For this reason, considerations of conduct and performance necessarily intrude in our current discussion. References to a measure's potential weaknesses are most often couched in terms of that measure's lack of predictive force. Still, we shall not lose sight of our present focus, which is structural.

A. The Number of Firms

The most obvious structural measure of market power is the number of sellers. As outlined earlier, pure competition and monopolistic competition each require a large number of sellers. Monopoly entails just one seller. In between, oligopoly is characterized by the presence of only a "few" sellers.

In terms of ease of computation and sensitivity to changes over time, this measure has certain advantages. Moreover, the number of sellers is likely to influence behavior because numbers may influence each firms *expectations regarding the behavior of its rivals.* This influence is most clearly seen in extreme cases. By definition, a firm blessed with monopoly has no rivals, so it may operate in an isolated, independent

---

[1] Good surveys of this material are B. Curry and K. D. George, "Industrial Concentration: A Survey," *Journal of Industrial Economics* (March 1983), pp. 203–255; and Leslie Hannah and J. A. Kay, *Concentration in Modern Industry* (London: Macmillan, 1977).

fashion. At the other extreme, a purely competitive firm has so many rivals that it also acts independently.

Between these extremes, where "few" could mean anything from 2 to 52, numbers retain their relevance. However, their predictive capabilities are reduced.[2] Fractions, or market shares, probably influence behavior more directly than mere numbers, so it may be better to rely on a measure that actually involves these fractions. Indeed, markets are often comprised of a "central core" of a few very large firms and a behaviorally inconsequential "fringe" of many small firms. In these instances a raw tally of total numbers may give a false impression of competitive dispersion.

B. The Lorenz Curve and Gini Coefficient

Two measures of fractions are the Lorenz curve and its companion statistic, the Gini coefficient. The absolute number of firms is almost completely suppressed by these measures because they reflect *inequality*, or *relative concentration*, more than anything else.

This may be illustrated with a simple example.[3] Imagine four firms in a market with the following percentage shares of market sales (or some other indicator of size, such as assets or employees): firm A, 5%; firm B, 10%; firm C, 15%; and firm D, 70%. The key computations that generate the **Lorenz curve** are (1) the percentage of market sales, cumulated from the smallest-sized firm, and (2) the percentage of the number of firms, cumulated again from the smallest-sized firm to the largest. Thus, beginning with A, which is the smallest, 5% of market sales are accounted for by 25% of all firms, 15% of the sales are accounted for by 50% of the firms (A plus B), and so forth. The resulting Lorenz curve is shown in Figure 7–1 as *RWVUS*.

This Lorenz curve may be compared to the straight diagonal line, *RS*. If each of the four firms had 25% of market sales, the Lorenz curve would match this diagonal line; then 25% of the firms would have 25% of the sales; 50% would have 50%, and so on. Thus, the diagonal indicates an **equal size distribution**. And the more *un*equal the distribution of sales, the greater the divergence between the Lorenz curve and the diagonal. With extreme inequality of shares, the Lorenz curve would look more like a half-open jackknife than the quarter-moon-shaped curve of Figure 7–1.

The area between the diagonal and the Lorenz curve, which in the present example equals 2500 percentage points, is often called the **area**

[2] Douglas Needham, *Economic Analysis and Industrial Structure* (New York: Holt, Rinehart and Winston, 1969), p. 84.

[3] Eugene M. Singer, *Antitrust Economics* (Englewood Cliffs, N.J.: Prentice-Hall, 1968), p. 141.

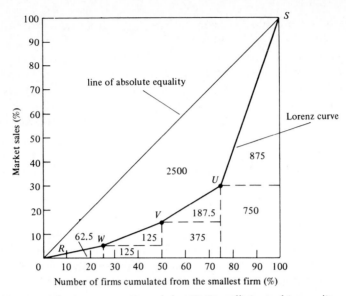

FIGURE 7–1. The Lorenz curve and the Gini coefficient of inequality.

of concentration. The **Gini coefficient** summarizes the degree of inequality, since this statistic is the ratio of the area of concentration to the total area under the diagonal. The total area under the diagonal is always 5000, because $\frac{1}{2} \times (100 \times 100) = 5000$. As for the area of concentration, one must add up the areas of the dashed lined triangles and rectangles lying beneath the Lorenz curve, and then subtract the result from 5000. In our present example this is $5000 - 2500 = 2500$. So the Gini coefficient in this case is $2500/5000 = 0.50$.

More generally, it should be clear that, as the Lorenz curve approaches the diagonal, the area of concentration shrinks and the Gini coefficient approaches 0. Conversely, as greater inequality expands the area of concentration, the Gini coefficient approaches a value of 1.

The Lorenz curve and Gini coefficient obviously emphasize the fractions that were ignored by the raw number-of-firms measure. Therefore, they have appeal. However, they also have many drawbacks. The most important of these is that they give *too much* emphasis to fractions and percentages, so much, in fact, that they neglect the absolute numbers aspect of structure to an undesirable degree.[4] For example, a Gini coefficient of 0 may give the impression of intense competition, as would be likely in the case of a market comprising 1000 firms, each with 0.1% of total market sales. Yet, a 0 would also derive from the presence of only two firms, each with 50%; or from three firms, each with 33⅓%. And,

---

[4] M. A. Adelman, "The Measurement of Industrial Concentration," *Review of Economics and Statistics* (November 1951), pp. 269–296.

in neither of these latter instances is the prospect for competition promising. These absolute numbers are so low that recognized interdependence could lead to behavior approaching that of monopoly. Similarly, a decline in the number of sellers in a market could be associated with a *decline* in the Gini coefficient, since it would leave the remaining firms more equal in size if the departing firms were all quite small.[5] The opposite could hold for increases in firm numbers. As a result, changes in structure over time would not be depicted properly.

C. The Concentration Ratio

The **concentration ratio** combines absolute numbers *and* fractions. It is the percentage of market sales (or some other measure of size, such as assets, employment, or value added) accounted for by an absolute number of the largest firms in the market—for example, the 4 or 8 or 20 largest firms. Because the concentration ratio involves both an absolute number of firms and their size distribution, and because it is also fairly easily constructed, it has become the most readily available and most widely used of all measures of structural power.

Figure 7–2 illustrates two concentration curves and the concentration ratios they generate. The vertical axis is the same as that for the

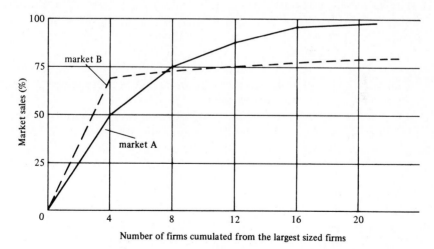

FIGURE 7–2. Concentration curves for two markets.

---

[5] J. M. Blair, "Statistical Measures of Concentration in Business: Problems of Compiling and Interpretation," *Bulletin of the Oxford University Institute of Statistics* (November 1956), p. 356.

Lorenz curve of Figure 7–1 — that is, percentage of total market sales. Its horizontal axis, however, is scaled in terms of the absolute number of firms instead of the percentage of number of firms. Another difference here is that the firms of Figure 7–2 are not cumulated from the smallest first. Instead, cumulation begins with the largest firm at the origin. Thus, the *height* of the curve above a given number of firms is the concentration ratio associated with that number. It is *the percentage of total market sales accounted for by a given number of leading firms.* Thus the four-firm concentration ratio for market A is 50. And the eight-firm concentration for market A is 75.

Among the many virtues of the concentration ratio, two deserve special mention. First, it is the combination of firm number *and* size distribution rather than one or the other alone that is most closely connected with behavior. To quote Gideon Rosenbluth, "Economic theory suggests that concentration as defined here is an important determinant of market behavior and market results."[6] Second, concentration ratios are fairly precise and easily understood indexes of market power. As we shall see in the next chapter, they appear in the courtrooms of statistically untrained judges almost as often as they appear in the writings of sophisticated scholars.

This is not to say that the concentration ratio is perfect. Nothing is. Of its many faults, the following three must be counted important:

1. Unlike the Lorenz curve, the concentration ratio describes only one slice of the market's size distribution of firms. It does not summarize conditions for all firms, only those for the top four or top eight or such. The resulting potential ambiguity is illustrated in Figure 7–2, where market B is more concentrated than market A at the four-firm level; whereas, conversely, market A is more concentrated than market B at the 12-firm level.

2. Even if we settle on one given number of firms as being the best of all possible slices, the concentration ratio provides no information about the size distribution of firms within that slice. Thus in Figure 7–2 we are ignorant of the size distribution of firms 1, 2, 3, and 4.

3. The concentration ratio does not reflect upon other aspects of structure that might be important to behavior, other aspects such as *changes* in the market shares of firms and product differentiation. Other measures have this failing, too, but this fact does not alleviate the problem. Because share changes reflect dynamic competition, an appendix to this chapter covers the subject.

6 Gideon Rosenbluth, "Measures of Concentration," in *Business Concentration and Price Policy*, edited by G. J. Stigler (Princeton, N.J.: Princeton University Press, 1955), p. 57.

D. The H Index

Many scholars have tried to invent a summary index that would solve these problems.[7] One of the best is called the **H index**, so named for its inventors Orris Herfindahl and Albert Hirschman.[8] This summary index is the sum of the squares of the sizes of firms in a market, in which sizes are expressed as a percentage of total market sales (or assets or employment). In mathematical notation:

$$\text{H index} = \sum_i (Si)^2 \quad (i = 1, 2, 3, \ldots, n)$$

where S represents the percentage share of individual firm i and n is the number of firms in the market. In terms of our earlier example of four firms with 5%, 10%, 15%, and 70% of total market sales:

$$\text{H index} = (5)^2 + (10)^2 + (15)^2 + (70)^2 = 5250$$

Under pure competition the index would equal 0. Under monopoly it would equal 10,000. These extremes are perhaps most readily seen by the fact that, if all firms in the market were of equal size, the Herfindahl–Hirschman H index with the decimal shifted left four places would equal $1/n$, which is the inverse of the total number of firms. With n equal to 1, this ratio also equals 1. As the value of n increases, this ratio collapses toward 0.

Because the H index appropriately registers the impact of absolute numbers as well as size inequality, and because the index takes account of all firms in the market simultaneously, it is held in high regard. Another property of the index attractive to some economists is the fact that it gives greater weight to the shares of especially large firms than to those of lesser firms. The squaring in the index does this as reflected in the following comparison: $60^2 = 3600$, whereas $30^2 + 30^2 = 1800$.

Does this mean the H index is superior to the concentration ratio? Not necessarily. As Curry and George conclude, "the complexity of busi-

[7] For examples see Janos Horvath, "Suggestion for a Comprehensive Measure of Concentration," *Southern Economic Journal* (April 1970), pp. 446–452; Ann Horowitz and Ira Horowitz, "Entropy, Markov Processes and Competition in the Brewing Industry," *Journal of Industrial Economics* (July 1968), pp. 196–211; Irwin Bernhardt and Kenneth D. Mackenzie, "Measuring Seller Unconcentration, Segmentation, and Product Differentiation," *Western Economic Journal* (December 1968), pp. 395–403; and Irvin M. Grossack, "The Concept and Measurement of Permanent Concentration," *Journal of Political Economy* (July 1972), pp. 745–760.

[8] A. O. Hirschman, "The Paternity of an Index," *American Economic Review* (September 1964), p. 761. For recent discussions see Richard A. Miller "The Herfindahl-Hirschman Index as a Market Structure Variable," *Antitrust Bulletin* (Fall 1982), pp. 593–618; and John E. Kwoka, Jr., "The Herfindahl Index in Theory and Practice," *Antitrust Bulletin* (Winter 1985), pp. 915–947.

ness life is such that in practice it is unlikely that there is one concentration measure which will clearly be superior in all circumstances." If, for instance, a market is dominated by four firms in a "strategic group," surrounded by an inconsequential fringe of several dozen small "niche" sellers, then the four-firm concentration ratio might be better than the H index at predicting conduct and performance. In another market setting, however, the H index might be better.

Fortunately, the choice is not one of overwhelming importance because the two measures are highly correlated. Table 7–1 reports four-firm concentration ratios and H indexes for selected industries from the 1982 Census of Manufacturers. There it may be seen that high concentration ratios are closely associated with high H indexes and low concentration ratios correspond with low H indexes. In a special tabulation, Kwoka found a correlation of +.929 between H and CR4 and a correlation of +.961 between H and CR2. Moreover, in a test of predictive performance, he found that the H index was not significantly better than the concentration ratio in explaining industry performance.[9] Likewise, there is a high correlation between two-firm and four-firm and eight-firm concentration ratios.

Much the same could be said of the choice between sales, assets, and most other units of quantity used for measuring size. Concentration ratios based on these various units of measure are highly correlated.[10] The most commonly used measure, however, is sales.

II. THE IMPORTANCE OF PROPER MARKET DEFINITION

To this point we have tossed the word "market" around offhandedly. But "market" deserves the same careful handling we would give a stink bomb. This warning applies regardless of whether one is using raw numbers, the Gini coefficient, the concentration ratio, or the H index because market definition determines the total scope of activity against which shares and numbers are computed. Indeed, the predictive accuracy of one's structural measure may depend more heavily on the proper choice of market definitions than on the proper choice of statistical index.

---

[9] Kwoka, "The Herfindahl Index in Theory and Practice," pp. 938–946.

[10] Rosenbluth, "Measures of Concentration," pp. 89–92; and John Blair, testimony, *Economic Concentration*, Part 5, Hearings before the Subcommittee on Antitrust and Monopoly of the Committee on the Judiciary, U.S. Senate (1966), pp. 1894–1902. On the other hand, Kwoka has shown that, despite high correlation, different measures can yield substantially different explanatory power. Among concentration ratios, the two-firm ratio performs best with his data. See John E. Kwoka, Jr., "Does the Choice of Concentration Measure Really Matter?" *Journal of Industrial Economics* (June 1981), pp. 445–453.

TABLE 7–1.   1982 Concentration Ratios and H Indexes of
Selected Industries

SIC Code	Name	Four-Firm Ratio	H Index
37111	Passenger cars (five digit)	99+	NA
2067	Chewing gum	95	NA
3632	Household refrigerators	94	2745
3353	Aluminum sheet, plate, and foil	74	1772
3724	Aircraft engines	72	1778
3011	Tires and inner tubes	66	1591
2062	Cane sugar refining	65	1416
2841	Soap and detergents	60	1306
3221	Glass containers	50	966
2522	Metal office furniture	45	900
2098	Macaroni and spaghetti	42	646
2211	Weaving mills, cotton	41	645
3351	Copper rolling and drawing	35	503
3171	Women's handbags	30	487
3961	Costume jewelry	27	268
2037	Frozen fruits and vegetables	27	306
2272	Tufted carpets and rugs	25	297
3645	Home lighting fixtures	19	152
2421	Sawmills and planning mills	17	113
3544	Special dies, tool, jigs	6	14

Source: U.S. Bureau of the Census, *1982 Census of Manufacturers, Concentration Rations in Manufacturing*, MC82-S-7 (Washington, D.C.: U.S. Government Printing Office, 1986).

The problem of market definition centers on the following questions:

1. Does the "market" include those firms that deserve to be in it? That is, *does it include all firms that compete with each other?*
2. Does the "market" exclude those firms that deserve to be out of it? That is, *does it exclude noncompeting firms?*

If a definition fails to include competing firms, the definition is said to be **too narrow**, and the concentration ratio will usually be biased upward. If on the other hand, it fails to exclude *non*competing firms, then it is said to be **too broad**, and the concentration ratio will tend to be biased downward. In the case of either error, the concentration ratio will not predict behavior or performance very well.

This problem of defining the market so as to include competitors while excluding noncompetitors may be further broken into two parts: product delineation and geographic scope.

Product delineation may be illustrated by taking a look at the procedures by which the U.S. Bureau of the Census computes concentration ratios in manufacturing industries. These computations are based on definitions in the federal government's Standard Industrial Classification Code, abbreviated SIC. The SIC refers to markets as industries, and it delineates market breadth with a system of numerical codes. At the broadest level are 20 separate two-digit *major industry groups*, such as "Food and kindred products" (20), "Textile mill products" (22), "Primary metal products" (34), and "Transportation equipment" (37). In turn, each of these two-digit definitions is broken down into narrower three-digit *industry groups*, which are themselves subdivided into still narrower four-digit *industries*, and so on down to the very narrow seven-digit *product*. This progressive subdivision is illustrated in Table 7–2, which displays parts of SIC major industry 20. The sales activities of each firm must be assigned to the different major industry groups, industries, products, and so on. Few firms confine their operations to just one product, or even one industry. Once sales activities are assigned, total sales are computed for each digited market. Firm shares follow. Concentration ratios are then computed, but only at the four- and five-digit level. Since there are approximately 450 four-digit industries and 1000 five-digit product classes, we can present no more than a small sample of 1982 Census concentration ratios in Table 7–1.

Most research has used ratios for SIC four-digit industries, since they seem to represent definitions of about the right amount of detail. Still, the SIC system was not designed for the computation of concentration ratios. The SIC definitions give heavy weight to similarity of production processes (or producer's substitutability) as well as to similarity of product uses (or consumer's substitutability). Although the ideal definition of a market ought to take account of substitution possibilities in *both* production and consumption, the SIC's heavy emphasis on the former yields many four-digit industries that may be considered too broad or too narrow.

Cane sugar refining, 2062, for example, is too narrow because it

---

TABLE 7–2.   Examples Taken from the SIC System

SIC Code	Number of Digits	Designation	Name
20	2	Major industry group	Food and kindred products
203	3	Industry group	Canning, preserving
2037	4	Product group or industry	Frozen fruits and vegetables
20371	5	Product class	Frozen fruits, juices, and ades
2037135	7	Product	Frozen strawberries

excludes beet sugar refining (see Table 7–1). Conversely, pharmaceutical preparations, 2834, is too broad because it includes a wide variety of drugs that are not close substitutes from the patient's point of view. In Census definition this industry has a four-firm concentration ratio of about 24%, but in narrower therapeutic groups we find four-firm ratios such as anesthetics, 69; antiarthritics, 95; cardiovascular hypotensives, 79; diabetic therapy, 93; and sulfonamides, 79.[11] This discrepancy between broad and narrow definitions in drugs arises because a few firms tend to dominate each therapeutic group but the same firms do not dominate *all* therapeutic groups. When all therapeutic groups are lumped together, the fraction of the "total" business accounted for by any one firm then shrinks.

In the end, four-digit Census industries tend to be too broadly defined. Gregory Werden demonstrates this using evidence from price-fixing conspiracies (i.e., cartels). Properly run, a cartel is supposed to stifle competition, so it will *include* all who would compete in the "market" and *exclude* those outside the "market." In this way business behavior can delineate markets. Comparing the scope of cartelized markets with four-digit SIC markets, Werden concludes the four-digit markets are typically much too broad.[12]

Another source of error is the exclusion of all imports and exports from Census computations.[13] In particular, significant imports will leave the Census ratio biased upward. The four-firm ratio for passenger cars, for instance, is said to be 99 + in Table 7–1 because there are essentially only three U. S. producers—General Motors, Ford, and Chrysler. But imports account for over 20% of all cars sold in the United States. Hence, a more accurate four-firm ratio, with Toyota ranked fourth, would be much lower, about 75%.

To illustrate the problem of **geographic scope**, we may mention the high transportation costs that prevent petroleum refiners on the East Coast from competing with those on the West Coast. Refiners do not always operate in more than one region, or all regions. Chevron, for example, accounts for 16.3% of gasoline sales in Pacific coast states, but 0% in New England and South Atlantic states. The four-firm *national* concentration ratio of 34 in 1973 thus falls below most of the more relevant four-firm *regional* ratios. Sampling a few of these, we see New England, 41.4; Mid-Atlantic, 41.6; and Pacific, 51.5.[14] Other products

---

[11] John Vernon, "Concentration, Promotion and Market Share Stability in the Pharmaceutical Industry," *Journal of Industrial Economics* (July 1971), pp. 246–266.

[12] Gregory J. Werden, "The Divergence of SIC Industries from Antitrust Markets," Department of Justice Economic Analysis Group Discussion Paper, EAG 88–9 (1988).

[13] Werner Sichel, "The Foreign Competition Omission in Census Concentration Ratios: An Empirical Evaluation," *Antitrust Bulletin* (Spring 1975), pp. 89–105.

[14] Thomas D. Duchesneau, *Competition in the U.S. Energy Industry* (Cambridge, Mass.: Ballinger, 1975), pp. 46–47.

experiencing high transportation costs or easy perishability are listed in Table 7–3. In every case the nationwide concentration ratio understates concentration as it is viewed at the more relevant regional or local level.

III. MARKET CONCENTRATION PATTERNS AND TRENDS

Lest this chapter degenerate into a parade of procedural issues, we ought now to get down to brass tacks. Just how much concentration is there anyway? And what, if anything, has been the trend over time? A generalized answer to these questions includes the following observations.

A. Manufacturing

In manufacturing, it appears that oligopoly and monopolistic competition predominate. Current concentration levels in markets in the U.S. manufacturing, as measured by the U.S. Census Bureau for 1982, are summarized in Figure 7–3. Four-firm concentration ratios for four-digit industries are shown there in two frequency distributions, one based on the percentage distribution of value of shipments (a weighted distribution) and one based simply on the percentage distribution of the 364 included industries. It may be seen that instances of very low concen-

TABLE 7–3. National Versus Regional and Local Markets

SIC Code	Name	National Four-Firm Ratio	Average Regional or Local Four-Firm Ratio
	Regional Market Products		
2095	Roasted coffee	52	71
2791	Typesetting	6	19
2911	Petroleum refining	34	52
3241	Cement, hydraulic	29	55
3446	Architectural metal work	13	37
	Local Market Products		
2024	Ice cream	37	70
2026	Fluid milk	23	57
2051	Bread and related items	23	47
2711	Newspapers	15	73
3251	Brick and structural tile	12	87
3273	Concrete	4	52

Source: David Schwartzman and Joan Bodoff, "Concentration in Regional and Local Industries," *Southern Economic Journal* (January 1971), pp. 343–348.

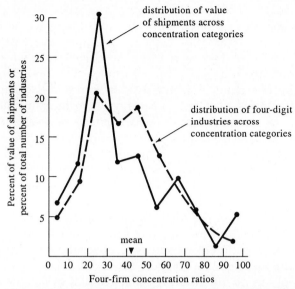

FIGURE 7–3. Concentration pattern in U.S. manufacturing, 1982 (excluding nec industries). Source: U.S. Department of Commerce, Bureau of the Census, *1982 Census of Manufacturing: Concentration Ratios in Manufacturing*, MC82–5-7 (Washington D.C.: U.S. Government Printing Office, 1986), pp. 6–50.

tration or very high concentration are relatively rare in manufacturing industries. Only about 6.6% of the total value of shipments, and about 4.9% of the number of industries, are associated with four-firm concentration ratios in the range between 0 and 10. At the opposite extreme, in the range where the top four firms have 90% to 100% of market sales, only 4.9% of the shipments and 1.9% of the industries are to be found. It is therefore in the middle ranges of concentration, where "tight" and "loose" oligopolies are depicted, that most manufacturing industries are located. The mean four-firm concentration ratio is 41.6%. On average, then, the top four firms in manufacturing markets account for 41.6% of market sales.

Adjustment of these raw data to take account of the biases surveyed above could yield a higher or lower average because judgment would have to guide the adjustments and the biases run positive and negative. William G. Shepherd's adjustment of 1966 Census data caused the average in that year to jump from 39% to 60%, but his manipulation of more recent data apparently produced an opposite shift of direction.[15]

[15] William G. Shepherd, *Market Power and Economic Welfare* (New York: Random House, 1970), pp. 106–107; and "Causes of Increased Competition in the U.S. Economy, 1939–1980," *Review of Economics and Statistics* (November 1982), p. 619.

As regards the *trend* in manufacturing markets, let's begin way back in the late 1800s, even though early data are both sketchy and unreliable. It appears that enormous increases in market concentration occurred between 1895 and 1902 as a result of a massive wave of mergers. Then between 1909 and 1947, the pattern is obscured. Some scholars believe, on the one hand, that market concentration declined or stayed the same over the first half of this century.[16] On the other hand, Alfred Chandler, Jr., determined that "The percentage of total product value produced by the oligopolists rose from 16% in 1909 to 21% in 1929, and then jumped to 28% at the end of the depression in 1939. Since World War II the figure has remained stable, being 26% in 1947, 25% in 1958, and then up to 27% in 1963."[17] "Oligopoly" in this case is defined as an industry "in which six or fewer firms contributed 50%, or twelve or fewer contributed 75% of the total product value."

Note that differences of opinion can arise from any number of causes — for example, differing sources of concentration change, such as oligopoly industries getting bigger or big industries getting more oligopolistic. In any event, whatever changes did, in fact, occur over the 1909–1947 period, they were apparently not earthshaking enough to knock you off your chair.

What has happened since 1947? Raw Census data reveal very little change, although estimates by such data are hampered by intermittent changes in the SIC system (changes that abolish some industry codes, merge others, and create new ones for new industries). For the 165 four-digit industries that stayed comparable from 1947 to 1977, average four-firm concentration inched up from 40.4 to 42.3.[18]

However, once the biases in the raw Census data are taken into account, it appears there has been a remarkable shift toward greater competition in manufacturing since the 1950s. Again, problems of definitions and judgement muddy the waters here, but the trend seems to be quite favorable. William G. Shepherd, for instance, has charted changes from 1958 to 1980 according to the following categories of competition:

1. *Pure Monopoly (PM)*. Market share of a single firm at or near 100%, plus blockaded entry, plus evidence of price control.
2. *Dominant Firms (DF)*. A market share of 50% to over 90%, with no close rival, with high entry barriers, with strong price control, and with excess profit.

---

[16] G. Warren Nutter, *The Extent of Enterprise Monopoly in the United States: 1899–1939* (Chicago: University of Chicago Press, 1951); and M. A. Adelman, "The Measurement of Industrial Concentration."

[17] Alfred D. Chandler, Jr., "The Structure of American Industry in the Twentieth Century: A Historical Overview," *Business History Review* (Autumn 1969), p. 257.

[18] Willard F. Mueller and Richard T. Rogers, "Changes in Market Concentration of Manufacturing Industries, 1974–1977," *Review of Industrial Organization* (Spring 1984), pp. 1–14.

3. *Tight Oligopoly (TO)*.   Four-firm concentration above 60%, with stable market shares; medium or high entry barriers; and a tendency toward cooperation or collusion.

4. *Workable Competition (WC)*.   Four-firm concentration below 40%, with unstable market shares and flexible pricing. Low entry barriers, little collusion, and low profit rates.[19]

His results are shown in Figure 7–4. The share of manufacturing occurring in workably competitive industries (WC) jumped from 55.9% to 69.0% between 1958 and 1980. Correspondingly, all the noncompetitive categories experienced drops.

Shepherd attributes this enormous shift in manufacturing to two primary forces. First, and most important, over a dozen major industries witnessed a flood of new import competition during the 1960s and 1970s as tariff barriers fell and Japan and Europe began flexing their industrial muscles. Imports have shaken up automobiles, steel, tires, television sets, copy machines, and cameras, to name some of the most important cases. Second, antitrust action has brought competition to numerous other manufacturing industries. Aluminum, telephone equipment, and shoe machinery provide examples.

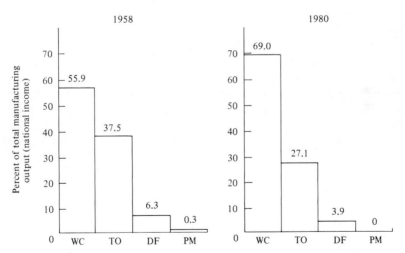

FIGURE 7–4. Trend in competition in U.S. manufacturing, 1959–1980. Source: William G. Shepherd, "Causes of Increased Competition in the U.S. Economy, 1939–1980," *Review of Economics and Statistics* (November 1982), p. 619.

[19] Shepherd, "Causes of Increased Competition in the U.S. Economy," pp. 616–617. Shepherd's term "Effective Competition" has been changed to "Workable Competition" here.

Overall, then, three phases characterize the trend in concentration in manufacturing. First, during the late 1800s and first decade of the 1900s, concentration shot upward in most major industries, propelled chiefly by mergers. Second, the sketchy record for 1909–1950 indicates relative stability or modest further increases. Finally, raw Census data reveal no change since 1950. But if Shepherd's adjustments for imports and antitrust are correct, we have recently witnessed a rise in the proportion of output coming from workably competitive industries.

Other sectors of the economy have been measured and studied less intensively than manufacturing, primarily because the Census Bureau does not publish concentration ratios for nonmanufacturing industries. Nevertheless, nonmanufacturing industries are of interest.

B. Atomistic Industries

Speaking broadly, and beginning at the competitive end of the spectrum, we may note first that, in the United States, market structures are unconcentrated and even atomistic in *agriculture, forestry, fisheries, contract construction,* and *services* (all of which together account for about 20% of gross national product). In the services sector, for instance, it has been very roughly estimated that, on average, local market four-firm concentration for hotel services is 8%; laundries, 13%; eating and drinking establishments, 8%; and automobile repair service establishments, 12%.[20]

As regards trend, agriculture, forestry, and fisheries have always been atomistic. Construction and services have less competitive traditions, but have according to Shepherd moved dramatically in that direction in the last two decades. He claims that workable competition now accounts for about 80% of the output of these sectors, up from 55% in 1958.[21]

Of course, these are just generalizations, and they mask pockets of moderately high concentration in certain localities and in certain unusual lines of product or service (such as farming, Chinese vegetables, repairing lawn mowers, or servicing cryogenic caskets). Moreover, these generalizations are somewhat misleading in their implication of vigorous rivalry. In many of these fields there is strong product differentiation (as in medical services), official government intervention inhibiting competition (as in agriculture), government ownership of substantial shares of the business or resource (as in forestry), and institutional constraints on competition of various kinds (like union organization of barbers and codes of "ethics" for dentists).

---

[20] Kenneth D. Boyer, "Informative and Goodwill Advertising," *Review of Economics and Statistics* (November 1974), p. 547. The estimates are for 1963.

[21] Shepherd, "Causes of Increased Competition in the U.S. Economy," p. 619.

C. Retail Trade

Retail trade also displays some atomistic features and favorable trends, but its oligopolistic tendencies are much more evident than in the sectors just mentioned. By relevant local market definitions, concentration in retailing varies from low to high levels. In 1972, for instance, grocery retailing concentration ranged from 26.3% for four-firms in Charleston, South Carolina, to 81.1% in Cedar Rapids, Iowa. Of the 261 cities with ratios between these bounds, a few are mentioned in Table 7–4.

Table 7–4 also contains selected estimates of local four-firm concentration — that is, multicity *averages* thereof — for grocery stores, department stores, and several other kinds of retailing. Hence, average local concentration among grocery stores was 52.4% in 1972. The other averages in the table indicate a lower level of concentration in every branch of retail trade except variety stores, which averaged 55% in 1963. One's overall impression of retailing thus hovers between monopolistic competition and loose-knit oligopoly. On top of this, there are signs that concentration in this sector is on the rise.[22]

D. Mining

Mining brings us another mixed bag. In energy mining we find only moderate levels of concentration on a national market basis, as shown in Table 7–5. The four-firm ratios for crude oil production, natural gas extraction, and coal mining were 31.0%, 24.4%, and 30.7% respectively, in 1970. The uranium ratios are twice as high. If one assumes that all these fuels are close substitutes for each other (which is doubtful[23]) then the broader product definition "energy" yields rather low ratios.

Lest these numbers lead the reader to conclude that competition runs rampant in this sector, we should also mention that (1) government intervention produces much ossification, (2) the trend in concentration has been skyward (see Table 7–5), and (3) by narrower, but perhaps more defensible geographic definitions of fuel markets, oligopolistic firms seem to be in control.[24] Furthermore, the energy sector can claim the greatest cartel in all history — the Organization of Petroleum Exporting Countries (OPEC).

Broad generalizations for other areas of mining are equally difficult. On the one hand we find substantial four-firm control in the United States for gold (79.9), copper (74.8), sulfur (72.0), iron ore (63.9), and

[22] Bruce W. Marion, *The Organization and Performance of the U.S. Food System* (Lexington, Mass.: Lexington Books, 1986), pp. 306–307.

[23] David Schwartzman, "The Cross-Elasticity of Demand and Industry Boundaries: Coal, Oil, Gas, and Uranium," *Antitrust Bulletin* (Fall 1973), pp. 483–507.

[24] See, for example, John W. Wilson, testimony in *The National Gas Industry*, Hearings before the Subcommittee on Antitrust and Monopoly, Part I, U.S. Senate (1973), pp. 456–504.

TABLE 7–4. Selected Estimates of Local Market Concentration in U.S. Retailing — 1970s

Retail Group	Four-Firm Concentration Ratio (%)
Grocery stores (SMSA average)	52.4
Albuquerque, New Mexico	66.3
Boston, Massachusetts	49.0
Chicago, Illinois	57.2
Detroit, Michigan	49.8
Houston, Texas	34.7
San Diego, California	55.2
Washington, D.C.	76.3
Department stores	34.0
Variety stores	55.0
Hardware stores	25.0
Furniture stores	25.0
Drug stores	39.0
Apparel and accessory stores	10.0

Sources: G. E. Grinnell, R. C. Parker, and L. A. Rens, *Grocery Retailing Concentration in Metropolitan Areas, Economic Census Years 1954–72* (Washington, D.C.: FTC Bureau of Economics, 1979), pp. 59–66; Kenneth D. Boyer, "Information and Goodwill Advertising," *Review of Economics and Statistics* (November 1974), p. 547.

TABLE 7–5. National U.S. Four-Firm Concentration Ratios for Major Fuels and Combined Energy Mining, 1955 and 1970

Industry	Top Four Firms		Top Eight Firms	
	1955	1970	1955	1970
Crude oil	21.2	31.0	35.9	49.1
Natural gas	18.6	24.4	30.4	39.1
Coal	17.8	30.7	25.4	41.2
Uranium	77.9	55.3	99.1	80.0
Energy ($)	16.1	23.4	27.2	37.8

Note: Natural gas production includes United States and Canada. Uranium concentration is measured in the milling stage.

Source: Joseph Mulholland and Douglas Webbink, *Economic Report on Concentration Levels and Trends in the Energy Sector of the U.S. Economy* (Washington, D.C.: Federal Trade Commission, 1974), p. 148.

lead and zinc (47.0)[25] On the other hand, there are several areas of mining that are fairly atomistic — limestone, common sand and gravel, and phosphate, for example.

E. Finance

Banking, insurance, and other forms of finance are primarily local operations, although some large corporate buyers of these services have the option of easily shifting their accounts and lines of credit across state boundaries, thereby adding an element of nationwide scope. Local concentration in commercial banking tends to be moderate or high. The following 1970 sample of *three-firm* concentration ratios is based on deposits: Atlanta, 65.6; Baltimore, 64.2; Chicago, 43.1; Columbus, Ohio, 93.4; Des Moines, 70.6; Indianapolis, 79.9; New York, 48.0; Phoenix, 92.8; Pittsburgh, 80.0; and San Francisco, 77.7.[26] Since by law banks cannot freely operate across state lines, national market three-firm concentration based on deposits is only 9.6%.

Local market concentration in life insurance, which illustrates another area of finance, is not quite as high as in banking. New Jersey is the most concentrated of all state markets, with a four-firm ratio of 56.2% in 1968.[27]

The significance of these several statistics has been shaken by extensive recent deregulation of the banking sector. This deregulation has, for instance, thrown commercial banks and savings and loan institutions into new competition with each other. According to some observers the trend is therefore favorable.[28]

F. Transportation and Public Utilities

Last are several sectors in which deregulation has had an even greater impact. Antitrust policy has also contributed. Air transport, trucking, railroading, and intercity bus services used to be oligopolistic in relevant markets and heavily regulated in cartel-like fashion, but these industries

[25] J. P. Mulholland and D. W. Webbink, *Concentration Levels and Trends in the Energy Sector of the U.S. Economy* (Washington, D.C.: Federal Trade Commission, 1974), p. 139.

[26] Federal Deposit Insurance Corporation, *Summary of Accounts and Deposits in All Commercial Banks, June 30, 1970* (Washington, D.C.: FDIC, 1970), pp. 18–20.

[27] J. D. Cummins, H. S. Denenberg, and W. C. Scheel, "Concentration in the U.S. Life Insurance Industry," *Journal of Risk and Insurance* (June 1972), pp. 177–199. Concentration in property and casualty insurance is higher and rising. Average state four-firm concentration in 1980 was 43.6% for home owners insurance and 49.8% for auto liability. See John W. Wilson and J. Robert Hunter, *Investment Income and Profitability in Property/Casualty Insurance Ratemaking* (Washington, D.C.: J. W. Wilson & Associates, 1983), p. 46.

[28] Arnold A. Heggestad and William G. Shepherd, "The Banking Industry," in *The Structure of American Industry*, edited by Walter Adams (New York: Macmillan, 1986), pp. 304–311.

are now substantially unregulated oligopolies. Parts of telephone communications, which formerly amounted to pure monopoly, have likewise become more decentralized with technological change, antitrust action, and deregulation. Local electricity and gas retain characteristics of so-called "natural monopoly" that are resistant to such changes, but they now account for only a fraction of the business conducted in these sectors. Figure 7–5 summarizes Shepherd's view of these sectors in terms of workable competition (WC), tight oligopoly (TO), dominant firm (DF), and pure monopoly (PM).

G. Conclusion

Where does this cascade of statistics leave us? Is any grand summary possible? Many observers seem to think so, but opinions differ:

> The extent of shared monopoly can modestly be called staggering.
> —Mark Green[29]

> While there are *some* markets in which the number of competitors is limited, there is not an important national market today (with the possible exception of telephone service) which lacks active competition.
> —Lee Loevinger[30]

Shepherd's view, which lies between these extremes, is reflected in Figure 7–6.

IV. THE CAUSES OF CONCENTRATION

The next question is what produces concentration? Unfortunately, the answer is complex, so much so that we cannot possibly provide a thorough reply in the remainder of this chapter. All we can do here is outline the various main parts of the answer, refer to subsequent chapters for each item in the outline that is discussed in detail later, and discuss the outline briefly, paying particular attention to those points that are not discussed extensively later on. First the outline:

A. Chance or luck.
B. Technical causes or prior conditions.
   1. Size of the market (Chapter 9, barriers to entry)
   2. Economies of scale (Chapter 9, barriers to entry)
   3. Scarce resources (Chapter 9, barriers to entry)

---

[29] *The Closed Enterprise System* (New York: Grossman, 1972), pp. 7–8. (A Nader Study Group Report.)
[30] "The Closed Mind Inquiry—Antitrust Report is Raders' Nadir," *Antitrust Bulletin* (Fall 1972), p. 758 (emphasis added).

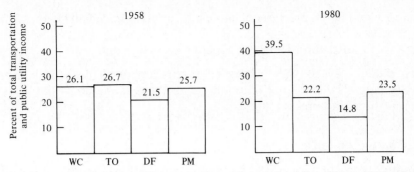

FIGURE 7–5. Trend in competition in transportation and public utilities, 1958–1980. Source: See Fig. 7–4.

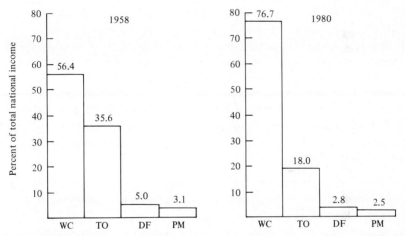

FIGURE 7–6. Trend in competition, summary of U.S. competition, 1958–1980. Source: see Fig. 7–4.

    4. Market growth rate (Chapter 9, barriers to entry)
C. Government policy.
    1. Antitrust (Chapter 8, mergers; Chapter 10, monopoly; Chapter 19, restrictive practices)
    2. Patents, licenses, tariffs, quotas (Chapter 10, monopoly; Chapter 24, patent policy)
    3. Procurement policy
    4. Miscellaneous regulations (Chapter 22, public utility regulations)
D. Business policies (within the context of the foregoing).
    1. Mergers (Chapter 8, mergers)

2. Restrictive practices (Chapter 10, monopoly; Chapters 11, 13, 14, conduct)
3. Product differentiation (Chapters 16, 17, conduct)

The outline reveals why a detailed discussion of all items is inappropriate here. The list is not only long, it contains many items that simply do not fit in the present context.

A. Chance or Luck

What do you suppose would happen if you and ten friends got together for an all-night gambling session? Assume that each of you brought $50 to fritter away, and that every game played was one of *pure* chance — bingo, perhaps — with all of you having *identical* chances of winning. What do you suppose would be the distribution of money by the break of dawn? Would everyone leave with $50? The laws of probability say "no" (and your own experience may lead you to agree). A few of you would put together a string of lucky games. A few would lose regularly. The rest would fall in between. The result is such a concentration of winnings (and losings) that two of you would end up with, say, six-elevenths or 54.5% of the total of $550 in original funds.

Several economists have argued that similar principles apply to firms in markets, that chance explains much concentration.[31] This is best seen by way of a computer simulation experiment conducted by F. M. Scherer. He simulated 16 separate histories of a single market under the following set of assumptions:

1. The market starts the first year with 50 firms, each with $100,000 in sales and a 2% market share. (The four-firm concentration ratio starts then at 8%.)
2. Each firm has *identical chances* for growth, these chances being specified by each firm annually drawing a year's growth from an identical probability distribution.
3. The probability distribution from which these annual growth rates are drawn provides for an *average* annual growth rate of 6%, but a *variance* of growth rates around this average such that the distribution is normal with a standard deviation of 16%.

Table 7–6 shows the results of the first 6 of Scherer's 16 computer runs, together with averages for all 16 simulations on the bottom line. The numbers are four-firm concentration ratios taken at 20-year intervals up to 100 years. Since Lady Luck is at work, the results are not the same

[31] P. E. Hart and S. J. Prais, "The Analysis of Business Concentration," *Journal of the Royal Statistical Society*, Series A (Part I, 1956), pp. 150–181; and Herbert A. Simon and C. P. Bonini, "The Size Distribution of Business Firms," *American Economic Review* (September 1958), pp. 607–617.

TABLE 7–6. Four-Firm Concentration Ratios Resulting from Simulation Runs of a Stochastic Growth Process

	Four-Firm Concentration Ratio at Year					
	1	20	40	60	80	100
Run 1	8.0	19.5	29.3	36.3	40.7	44.9
Run 2	8.0	20.3	21.4	28.1	37.5	41.6
Run 3	8.0	18.8	28.9	44.6	43.1	47.1
Run 4	8.0	20.9	26.7	31.8	41.9	41.0
Run 5	8.0	23.5	33.2	43.8	60.4	60.5
Run 6	8.0	21.3	26.6	29.7	35.8	51.2
Average for 16 runs	8.0	20.4	27.0	33.8	42.1	46.7

Source: Frederick M. Scherer, *Industrial Market Structure and Economic Performance* (Chicago: Rand McNally, 1970), p. 126. Reprinted by permission.

for any pair of runs, but the message is clear. Concentration rises rapidly at first, more than doubling in the first 20 years. It rises more slowly thereafter.

The key to understanding how pure chance could produce these results lies in understanding the following sequence of events: Half of the firms will enjoy better than average growth the first year. Half of that half, or one quarter, will enjoy better than average growth a second year because the same probability distribution applies anew annually to *each segment* of firms and *each firm* regardless of the prior year's experience. Half of that quarter, or one-eighth, will enjoy better than average growth in the third year, which means they enjoy three consecutive boom years. Half of that eighth, or one-sixteenth, will have better than average growth in the fourth year . . . and so on. In short, the leaders have enjoyed a run of good luck.

The assumptions of this experiment conform to what is called **Gibrat's law** of proportionate growth. Although real-world markets do not conform exactly to these assumptions, there are various forms of evidence that suggest Gibrat's law or something like it is at work.[32] One of the more prominent findings is that on *average*, the percentage growth of small firms is about the same as that of large firms.[33] This independence of size and growth was implicitly assumed for Scherer's experiment.

[32] See, for example, S. J. Prais, "A New Look at the Growth of Industrial Concentration," *Oxford Economic Papers* (July 1974), pp. 273–288.

[33] Stephen Hymer and Peter Pashigian, "Firm Size and Rate of Growth," *Journal of Political Economy* (December 1962), pp. 556–569; and M. Marcus, "A Note of the Determinants of the Growth of Firms and Gibrat's Law," *Canadian Journal of Economics* (November 1969), pp. 587–589.

Still, happenstance cannot be the whole story. It helps to explain why there is always *some* concentration in just about every market, and why the "bad guys" sometimes outstrip the "good." But the size distribution of firms in markets does not correspond closely to what the theory would predict.[34] Moreover, there is a great deal of *systematic* variation in concentration across markets, something incompatible with pure happenstance. What do we mean by systematic variation? For one thing, similar markets in diverse nations show consistent patterns in degree of concentration. If autos and cigarettes are highly concentrated in the United States, they are likely to be highly concentrated in Britain, France, and Sweden as well. Table 7–7 shows the composite ranking of 17 two-digit industries for 12 European and North American countries, as computed by Frederic Pryor. Averaged over these nations, tobacco and transportation equipment were the most highly concentrated of all manufacturing industries, whereas lumber and furniture were the least concentrated. The concordance coefficient, which indicates the *similarity* of rank orderings across all these 12 nations, was +0.51 and highly significant.[35]

Additionally, when any two nations' rank orders are compared, the correlation coefficient thereby produced is always highly positive.[36] This does *not* mean that the *average level* of market concentration for all industries taken together is the same among nations. That is a separate issue. The average height of pygmies is less than ours, even though their age-height rank ordering correlates with ours. For average market concentration in manufacturing, Pryor finds that "France, West Germany, and Italy, have weighted concentration ratios somewhat lower than the United States, while . . . Japan, the Netherlands, and the United Kingdom, have weighted concentration ratios only slightly higher than the United States. In only five nations are concentration ratios clearly higher [by about 50%], namely, Belgium, Canada, Sweden, Switzerland, and Yugoslavia."[37]

Table 7–7 also reports the rank order of two-digit industries in the United States as of 1963. These rankings may be compared with the 12-country composite rankings to support our assertion that patterns in

[34] John E. Kwoka, Jr., "Regularity and Diversity in Firm Size Distributions in U.S. Industries," *Journal of Economics and Business*, No. 4 (1982), pp. 391–395.

[35] F. L. Pryor, "An International Comparison of Concentration Ratios," *Review of Economics and Statistics* (May 1972), p. 51.

[36] Besides Pryor see K. D. George and T. S. Ward, *The Structure of Industry in the EEC* (Cambridge: Cambridge University Press, 1975), p. 16; Gideon Rosenbluth, *Concentration in Canadian Manufacturing Industries* (Princeton, N.J.: Princeton University Press, 1957); R. E. Caves and M. Uekusa, *Industrial Organization in Japan* (Washington, D.C.: Brookings Institution, 1976), pp. 19–25; and, Patricio Meller, "The Pattern of Industrial Concentration in Latin America," *Journal of Industrial Economics* (September 1978), pp. 41–47.

[37] F. L. Pryor, "An International Comparison of Concentration Ratios," p. 134. For corroboration concerning the United Kingdom, France, Germany, and Italy, see George and Ward, *The Structure of Industry in the EEC*, p. 17.

TABLE 7–7.   High to Low Concentration Rankings for Two-Digit Industries — United States and Abroad, 1929 and 1963

SIC Code	Industry	12-Country Composite Rank	United States	
			As of 1963	As of 1929
21	Tobacco products	1	1	1
37	Transportation equipment	2	3	6
35	Machinery (except electric)	3	11	9
29	Petroleum and coal products	4	2	3
28	Chemicals	5	6	7
30	Rubber products	6	8	2
36	Electrical equipment	7	5	8
32	Stone, clay, and glass	8	7	14
34	Fabricated metal products	9	13	12
33	Primary metals	10	4	4
20	Food and kindred products	11	10	5
26	Paper products	12	12	11
22	Textiles	13	9	10
31	Leather products	14	15	15
23	Apparel	15	14	13
24	Lumber and wood	16	16	16
25	Furniture and fixtures	17	17	17

Sources: Twelve countries: Frederic L. Pryor, "An International Comparison of Concentration Ratios," *Review of Economics and Statistics* (May 1972), p. 135. U.S. figures: derived from Alfred D. Chandler, Jr., "The Structure of American Industry in the Twentieth Century: A Historical Overview," *Business History Review* (Autumn 1969), pp. 258–259.

degree of concentration are consistent across nations. More important, they may be compared with the rankings of the last column, which are for the United States in 1929. This latter comparison reveals a second type of systematic pattern. That is, interindustry differences tend to be stable over long periods of time. Tobacco and transport equipment have perched high atop the list for over a quarter of a century, whereas leather, apparel, lumber, and furniture have invariably roosted on the bottom. We have thus a pattern of persistence at odds with a pattern of pure chance.

B. Technical Causes

A third form of systematic pattern could be claimed if intermarket differences in concentration were closely associated with variations in technological conditions or prior circumstances that could reasonably be expected to affect concentration. In general, such an association does seem to be borne out by research.

Consider first the relationship between market size and concentration. We have already seen how a narrow definition of the market tends to increase measured concentration, whereas a broad definition has the effect of decreasing apparent concentration. Going beyond mere definition to a more substantive association, the same inverse relationship holds between economic market size and concentration, everything else being equal.[38] Large markets, measured by volume of business or buyer population or whatever, seem to have more "room" for a larger number of sellers than small markets. Consequently, large markets have lower concentration ratios than small markets. To take just one example, Table 7–8 reproduces average *two-firm* concentration ratios for commercial banks, categorizing them in terms of four different city sizes and three different types of branching regulation. Note in particular that, for each type of branching policy taken individually, concentration is greatest in areas of smallest population, whereas it is lowest in areas of largest population. In states that permit statewide branching, for instance, the ratio falls from 69.5% to 55.0%. An even healthier drop from 68.5% to 42.7% occurs in unit banking states, where each banking firm is limited to only one office. Since branching is banned in these states, additional banking *firms* are almost a necessity for serving the additional demand that goes with additional population.

Economies of scale are another causal factor. They will be discussed at length in Chapter 9. Suffice it to say here that size of market alone is not enough. The size of *firm* required to achieve all efficiencies (and thereby attain lowest possible cost per unit) is also important. If, for example, low-cost auto production required an output of *at least* 1 million cars per year, then an auto market of 10 million sales per year could be served by ten automakers of efficient scale. If, on the other hand, efficient scale coincided with 5 million units, then there would be "room" for only two low-cost producers, a condition that would obviously aggravate concentration considerably. Stated differently, minimum efficient size and concentration should be positively correlated across markets. Without going into details now, this association has been found.[39]

[38] George and Ward, *The Structure of Industry in the EEC*, pp. 22–23; Caves and Uekusa, *Industrial Organization in Japan*, pp. 22–25; Meller, "The Pattern of Industrial Concentration in Latin America," pp. 44–45; F. M. Scherer, A. Beckenstein, E. Kaufer, and R. D. Murphy, *The Economics of Multi-Plant Operation an International Comparisons Study* (Cambridge, Mass.: Harvard University Press, 1975), pp. 221–223; M. D. Intriligator, S. I. Ornstein, R. E. Schrieves, and J. F. Weston, "Determinants of Market Structure," *Southern Economic Journal* (April 1973), pp. 612–625; and E. Pagoulatos and R. Sorensen, "A Simultaneous Equation Analysis of Advertising, Concentration, and Profitability," *Southern Economic Journal* (January 1981), pp. 728–741.

[39] R. E. Caves, J. Khalilzadeh-Shirazi, and M. E. Porter, "Scale Economies in Statistical Analyses of Market Power," *Review of Economics and Statistics* (May 1975), pp. 133–140; Caves and Uekusa, *Industrial Organization in Japan*, pp. 22–25; D. F. Greer, "Advertising

TABLE 7–8. Percentage of Total Deposits Held by the Largest Two Banking Organizations in Metropolitan Areas, 1968

Population of Standard Metropolitan Statistical Areas (SMSA)	Statewide Branching States (%)	Limited Branching States (%)	Unit Branching States (%)
50–100,000	69.5	65.4	68.5
100,000–500,000	68.5	64.4	53.5
500,000–1,000,000	69.1	57.7	47.8
1,000,000 and over	55.0	51.5	42.7

Source: "Recent Changes in the Structure of Commercial Banking," *Federal Reserve Bulletin* (March 1970), p. 207.

One of the more thoroughly researched hypotheses is that rapid growth in market demand tends to reduce concentration. It would of course be preposterous to suppose that the few leading firms of any market would consciously stand pat while the market grew up rapidly around them, permitting disproportionate expansions of their lesser rivals and a flood of entering newcomers. Still, a hypothesis that rapid growth diminishes concentration must infer some degree of such differential behavior. Accordingly, it has been theorized that leading firms tend to (1) be timid for fear of antitrust prosecution, (2) look more toward diversifying outside the market than merely keeping up within the market, or (3) suffer from the sluggishness that often accompanies large size. However true these possibilities may or may not be, there is substantial evidence indicating that *changes* in concentration *are* inversely associated with market rate of growth.[40] The association is, however, often weak statistically and of low magnitude. In particular, it has been estimated that a 100-percentage-point increase in market size would usually be necessary to trim four-firm concentration by 2 or 3 percentage points. Slim pickings, indeed.

---

and Market Concentration," *Southern Economic Journal* (July 1971), pp. 19–32; and L. W. Weiss, "Optimal Plant Size and the Extent of Suboptimal Capacity," in *Essays on Industrial Organization in Honor of Joe S. Bain*, edited by R. T. Masson and P. D. Qualls (Cambridge, Mass.: Ballinger, 1976), p. 135.

[40] Ralph L. Nelson, *Concentration in the Manufacturing Industries of the United States* (New Haven, Conn.: Yale University Press, 1963), pp. 50–56; W. G. Shepherd, "Trends of Concentration in American Manufacturing Industries, 1947–1958," *Review of Economics and Statistics* (May 1964), pp. 200–212; D. R. Kamerschen, "Market Growth and Industry Concentration," *Journal of the American Statistical Association* (March 1968), pp. 228–241; J. A. Dalton and S. A. Rhoades, "Growth and Product Differentiability as Factors Influencing Changes in Concentration," *Journal of Industrial Economics* (March 1974), pp. 235–240; and Richard E. Caves and Michael E. Porter, "The Dynamics of Changing Seller Concentration," *Journal of Industrial Economics* (September 1980), pp. 1–15.

C. Government Policies

Unlike the foregoing factors, which are largely attributable to Lady Luck or Mother Nature, government policies and business policies are obviously the work of lesser breeds, namely, government officials and businesspeople. Among government officials, we find an amazing amount of ambivalence; some would even say schizophrenia. Fritz Machlup summarized the situation when he wrote that "Governments, apparently, have never been able to make up their minds which they dislike more, competition or monopoly."[41] On the antimonopoly side, government has created and mobilized various antitrust laws to dissolve excessive concentrations of market power or to prevent such concentrations from occurring in the first place. On the other side are a host of anticompetitive government policies.[42] These include **tariffs** and **quotas**, restricting the free flow of imports; **licenses**, inhibiting the entry of finance companies, taxi cabs, liquor stores, barbers, beauticians, landscape architects, and various other professionals; **franchises**, granting rights of monopoly to bus lines, athletic stadium concessionaires, water companies, electric and gas companies, and other businesses; and **patents**, awarding 17-year monopolies over the use of new inventions and innovations. The effects of these policies on concentration should be obvious.

The effects of slightly more subtle policies governing commercial bank branching may be seen by referring again to Table 7–8. Local two-bank concentration ratios are more than ten percentage points higher in statewide branching states than in unit banking states for each size class of city, except the very smallest. Cities in the 50,000–1,000,000 population range are usually served by just a few bank offices regardless of branching regulations; hence, the effect in their cases is negligible.

Government procurement policy also has an effect. Briefly stated, the federal government's multibillion dollar purchases of tanks, planes, ships, electronic equipment, and most other durable goods are concentrated among a relatively few supplying firms. In light of the ample concentration caused by factors *unrelated* to government procurement, it is not surprising that these purchases should also be concentrated. The government, moreover, obviously has special needs—particularly in the case of complex weapon systems—needs that often force it to show some favoritism toward gargantuan suppliers. It has nonetheless been argued rather persuasively that the government's expenditures are *more* highly concentrated than these two rationalizations justify.[43] The government's ambivalence thus takes many forms.

[41] Fritz Machlup, *Political Economy of Monopoly* (Baltimore: Johns Hopkins University Press, 1952), p. 182.
[42] Walter Adams and Horace M. Gray, *Monopoly in America: The Government as Promoter* (New York: Macmillan, 1955).
[43] Ibid., Chapter V; U. S. General Accounting Office, *More Competition in Emergency Defense Procurements Found Possible*, B-171561 (Washington, D.C.: U.S. Government Printing

TABLE 7–9. Selected Major Mergers Causing High
Concentration, 1895–1904

Company (or Combine)	Number of Firms Disappearing	Rough Estimate of Market Controlled (%)
U.S. Steel	170	65
U.S. Gypsum	29	80
American Tobacco	162	90
American Smelting & Refining	12	85
DuPont de Nemours	65	85
Diamond Match	38	85
American Can	64	65–75
International Harvester	4	70
National Biscuit (Nabisco)	27	70
Otis Elevator	6	65

Source: Ralph L. Nelson, *Merger Movements in American Industry, 1895–1956* (Princeton, N.J.: Princeton University Press, 1959), pp. 161–162.

D. Business Behavior

Table 7–9 offers evidence of potential and actual effects of business mergers. It not only summarizes the merger history of the ten companies listed but also reflects the history of dozens of other modern-day mammoths that likewise rose to power through combination around the turn of the century. The ten firms of Table 7–9 accounted for the disappearance of 577 formerly independent rivals during this period. The consequences are obvious in the last column of the table, which provides rough estimates of the market shares these combinations acquired. U.S. antitrust policy currently stands in the way of further merger-built oligopoly. This is not the case in England and West Germany, however, where recent merger activity has contributed substantially to concentration in many major industries.[44]

Less measurable but no less deserving of mention are various business policies called "restrictive practices." These include group boycotts, collective rebates, predatory price discrimination, barrier pricing, and exclusive dealing. They generally have no immediate effect on concen-

---

Office, March 25, 1971), and *Opportunities for Savings by Increasing Competition in Procurement of Commercial Equipment*, B-164018 (Washington, D.C.: U.S. Government Printing Office, February 26, 1971).

[44] M. A. Utton, "The Effect of Mergers on Concentration: U.K. Manufacturing Industry, 1954–65," *Journal of Industrial Economics* (November 1971), pp. 42–58; Jürgen Müller, "The Impact of Mergers on Concentration: A Study of Eleven West German Industries," *Journal of Industrial Economics* (December 1976), pp. 113–132; and Hannah and Kay, *Concentration in Modern Industry*, pp. 64–97.

tration, but over the long haul they can cement existing market power or extend it, as will be shown later when we take up conduct in earnest.

Finally, it appears that under certain circumstances product differentiation may foster concentration. It has been found, for instance, that consumer goods industries experiencing especially high outlays on TV and radio advertising have also experienced especially high increases in concentration over the period 1947–1977.[45] Later we shall explore this area further (see Chapter 16).

V. AGGREGATE CONCENTRATION

A. Introduction

Let us now broaden our view a bit. Let us leave the lowlands of market concentration and climb into the mountains for a brief look at what is called **aggregate concentration** or **economywide concentration**. As these latter names imply, our new viewpoint involves a look at the share of *total multimarket* economic activity accounted for by some relatively small groups of enterprises. Although market and aggregate concentration are in fact related, they are quite different in principle. The many individual markets in the economy could all be highly concentrated. Yet, if the firms in each market were also highly specialized, limiting their activities to just one market, they then could be relatively small and numerous when compared to the economy as a whole. The result: relatively low aggregate concentration despite considerable market concentration. On the other hand, it is possible to have high aggregate concentration together with low market concentration.

Despite these theoretical possibilities, market and aggregate concentration are closely connected in several ways. First, firms that control large shares of the economy also hold dominant positions in major industries. Exxon and Mobil both rank among the ten largest U.S. corporations while they hold the lead positions in petroleum production. The same could be said of GM and Ford in automobiles and IBM in computers.

Second, many of the overall leaders are highly diversified. GE is into locomotives, TV broadcasting, lighting, major appliances, plastics, turbine generators, and jet engines. ITT and TRW are into so many different things that an abridged list for each would mislead you. Thus, many, if not most, of the top 100 are referred to as **conglomerates**.

Finally, aggregate dominance and diversification may augment a firm's power within specific markets. This is especially true of diversification in the form of **vertical integration**, that is, single-firm operation

---

[45] W. F. Mueller and R. T. Rogers, "Changes in Market Concentration of Manufacturing Industries, 1947–1977," *Review of Industrial Organization* (Spring 1984), pp. 1–14.

at several stages in the production and distribution of a given product. Major petroleum companies, for example, combine crude oil extraction, pipeline transportation, refining, and retail marketing.

B. Trends and Levels

Different definitions of size, different definitions of aggregate scope, and different notions of how many firms constitute a "few" obviously affect the picture. But every aggregate concentration series dating back to the first half of this century, whether it is based on assets or some other measure of economic activity, indicates rising concentration in manufacturing over the long run. Figure 7–7 shows the trend for assets and value added of the largest 200 manufacturing corporations. In addition, it shows the rising trend for assets of the largest 100 corporations in manufacturing, mining, and distributing from 1909 through 1974. (Note that the series on assets for the top 200 manufacturers changed in 1973 to exclude data on all foreign operations. The series therefore shifts down before continuing its long-term upward march.) Whether the trends and current levels are alarming or not depends on your value judgments.

Some commentators have argued that there is no cause for alarm in this trend. They claim that although the *share* of the top 100 or so may be rising, the *identity* of the top 100 is constantly changing, implying turnover and competition. There is a grain of truth to this. Our high-altitude vantage point is not Mt. Olympus, so those we see up here do not enjoy eternal life. By raw count, only 21 of the top 100 firms in 1909 remained on the list in 1976. Choice of beginning year is important, however, because 40 new firms entered the top 100 between 1909 and 1919 alone.[46] Since 1919 things have been much more stable, with 51 of that year's top 100 surviving into the 1970s.

What happened to the 49 nonsurvivors of 1919? Only 10 could be considered true failures, exiting by liquidation or suffering a decline in sales. Nine continued to grow and stayed close to the top but were replaced by faster growers. Finally, 30 of the 49 dropouts merged with other large firms, a means of exit that could not be considered "competitive."[47] Not only have truly "competitive" exits been rather rare but their frequency has apparently diminished with time.[48]

[46] Robert J. Stonebraker, "Turnover and Mobility Among the 100 Largest Firms: An Update," *American Economic Review* (December 1979), pp. 968–973.

[47] Richard C. Edwards, "Stages in Corporate Stability and the Risks of Corporate Failure," *Journal of Economic History* (June 1975), pp. 428–457.

[48] Stonebraker, *Turnover and Mobility Among the 100 Largest Firms*; N. Collins and L. Preston, "The Size Structure of the Largest Industrial Firms: 1909–1958," *American Economic Review* (December 1961), pp. 986–1011; and S. E. Boyle and J. P. McKenna, "Size Mobility of the 100 and 200 Largest U.S. Manufacturing Corporations: 1911–1964," *Antitrust Bulletin* (Fall 1970), pp. 505–519.

To end on a positive note, however, it appears that concentration in the *entire private economy* has not changed much in the last two decades.[49] This conclusion might seem odd in light of the rising concentration in manufacturing shown in Figure 7–7. But concentration in the entire private economy is influenced by the relative *size* of the main sectors as well as the trends within those sectors. A major development has been the very rapid growth of a low-concentration sector, namely, services, relative to high-concentration sectors, manufacturing in particular.[50]

SUMMARY

Measuring market concentration involves several steps and various options.

First, one or more statistical indexes ought to be selected. A good index should provide good predictions of conduct and performance. Our survey of possibilities indicates that (1) the absolute number of firms neglected fractional shares, (2) the Gini coefficient neglected absolute numbers, (3) the concentration ratio combines numbers and shares but is limited to only one slice of the size distribution of firms, and (4) the H index registers both numbers and shares in an overall summary fashion but is not necessarily superior to the concentration ratio for every industry. Fortunately, all the main indexes yield numbers that correlate well with each other.

Second, a choice must be made for size measure—sales, employment, assets, or something else. We have glossed over this problem. But for our purposes the differences between measures are not crucial.

Third, the market must be defined. Proper definition requires the inclusion of closely competitive offerings and the exclusion of noncompetitive offerings. A definition that is too narrow excludes competitive offerings. One that is too broad includes noncompetitive offerings. These criteria apply to both product breadth and geographic scope.

The data generated from taking these steps indicate a variety of conditions across the economy's many markets and several sectors. In general, four-firm concentration ratios either below 10 or above 90 are relatively rare. Observations in the 20 to 70 range are much more common.

Trends are mixed across sectors, but some interesting recent developments stand out. Manufacturing has become much more competitive since 1960 once imports and antitrust actions are taken into account. Public utilities and transportation have seen a similar transformation because of deregulation and technological change as well as antitrust.

[49] Lawrence J. White, "What Has Been Happening to Aggregate Concentration in the United States?" *Journal of Industrial Economics* (March 1981), pp. 223–230.

[50] Eli Ginzberg and George J. Vojta, "The Service Sector of the U.S. Economy," *Scientific American* (March 1981), pp. 48–55.

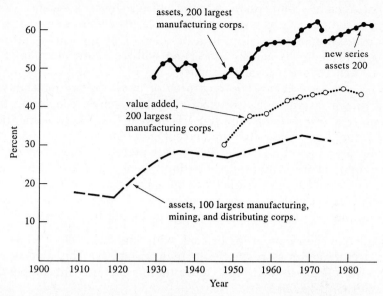

FIGURE 7–7. Long-term trend in aggregate concentration. Sources: Federal Trade Commission Staff, *Economic Report on Corporate Mergers* (1969), p. 173; Lawrence J. White, "What Has Been Happening to Aggregate Concentration in the United States?" *Journal of Industrial Economics*, (March 1981), p. 225; Bureau of the Census, *1982 Census of Manufacturers: Concentration Ratios in Manufacturing*, MC82-5-7 (Washington D.C.: U.S. Government Printing Office, 1986), p. 3; Robert J. Stonebraker, "Turnover and Mobility Among the 100 Largest Firms: An Update," *American Economic Review* (December 1979), pp. 968–973; *1986 Statistical Abstract*, p. 534.

The causes of concentration include chance (or luck), technical conditions (such as market size, growth rates, and economies of scale), government policy (such as antitrust and patents), and business behavior (such as mergers and restrictive practices).

Aggregate concentration is also of interest. Over 30% of all manufacturing, mining, and distributing corporate assets are accounted for by the 100 largest firms in these areas. Although the trend of this century's previous decades is upward, there are indications that the trend has leveled off. This leveling has occurred for the economy as a whole in part because relatively low-concentration sectors are growing more rapidly than relatively high-concentration sectors.

APPENDIX TO CHAPTER 7: MARKET SHARE INSTABILITY

Market share instability, as opposed to stability, is a measure of dynamic competition because it suggests that firms are actively vying against each other and creating turmoil. The greater the instability, the greater the apparent dynamic competition, but not always. Share instability would *not* signal competitive blessings, for example, if it were due to a rapid rise in concentration and fall in firm numbers. One indication that market share instability is usually associated with competition comes from evidence that collusion fosters stability.[51]

There are several possible measures of market share instability. A marketwide measure is the correlation of firm shares, comparing their values in one year to their values in a later year.[52] A measure specific to an individual firm would take the percentage-point change in share during some time period and then divide that percentage-point change by the beginning share. Adding up such individual changes for all firms in the market would yield a marketwide measure of instability.

What causes market share instability to be high or low? Research reveals a number of interesting findings, including the following.[53]

1. High concentration is associated with low instability, while low concentration is associated with high instability. This inverse relationship suggests that high concentration nurtures anticompetitive, collusive behavior.
2. New firm entry into a market increases market share instability, suggesting that entry is a procompetitive force. Because new entry is associated with rapid growth and the early phases of the product life cycle, it appears that rapid growth and youthful product age are also destabilizing forces.
3. Backward vertical integration tends to reduce share instability.
4. If a product is custom made rather than off the shelf, share instability seems to be higher than otherwise.
5. Product differentiation influences instability in ambiguous ways. If measured by the intensity of research and development outlays directed toward new product design and modification, product differentiation appears to destabilize shares. If measured by advertising intensity, product differentiation can be either destabilizing or stabilizing, depending on the circumstances.

[51] Jonathan D. Ogur, *Competition and Market Share Instability* (FTC Staff Report, 1976), pp. 30–48.

[52] Michael Gort, "Analysis of Stability and Change in Market Shares," *Journal of Political Economy* (February 1963), pp. 51–63.

[53] Ibid., Ogur, *Competition and Market Share*; R. McGuckin, "Entry, Concentration Change, and Stability of Market Shares," *Southern Economic Journal* (January 1972), pp. 363–370; and R. E. Caves and M. E. Porter, "Market Structure, Oligopoly, and Stability of Market Shares," *Journal of Industrial Economics* (June 1978), pp. 289–313.

8

Concentration and Oligopoly: Merger Practice and Policy

The game of picking up companies is open to everybody. All you have to do is have indefatigable drive, a desire to perpetuate yourself or your family in control of an industry, or an unabsorbed appetite for corporate power.

—MESHULAM RIKLIS (who parlayed $25,000 into a $755 million empire fittingly called Rapid-American, Inc.)

Each decade has its distinguishing characteristics. The 1980s witnessed a deluge of mergers—over 2000 occurring each year, totaling more than $50 billion annually. 1986 was a record-breaking year with 4446 mergers and acquisitions worth about $205.8 billion.[1]

Yet there is a paradox here. In 1950 Congress passed the Celler–Kefauver Act, which became one of the most stringent laws governing mergers in the world. Vigorous enforcement during the act's first 27 years resulted in 437 merger complaints, challenging 1406 acquisitions

---

[1] *Mergers and Acquisitions* (March/April 1990), p 95.

with combined assets exceeding $40 billion.[2] It seems the 1980s may have nullified these antitrust achievements of the 1960s and 1970s.

This chapter explores this paradox and related matters. We begin with a brief description of various types of mergers and proceed to a historical review of merger activity. An outline of the causes of mergers comes next, followed by a rundown of policy developments under the Celler–Kefauver Act.

I. BACKGROUND

A. Merger Types

The union of two or more direct competitors is called a **horizontal** merger. The combining companies operate in the same market, as is illustrated in Figure 8–1. Bethlehem Steel's acquisition of the Youngstown Sheet and Tube Company in 1957 is an example. A **vertical** merger links companies that operate at different stages of the production-distribution process. This too is illustrated in Figure 8–1, and Bethlehem would provide an example of this type were it to acquire Ford Motors, a big buyer of steel. Broadly speaking, **conglomerate** mergers are all those that are neither horizontal nor vertical. This conglomerate definition covers a lot of ground, however, so the category may be subdivided into three classes: (1) **product extension,** involving producers of two different but related products, such as bleach and detergent; (2) **market extension,** involving firms producing the same product but occupying different geographic markets, for example, dairies in two distant towns; and (3) **pure conglomerate,** involving firms with nothing at all in common, as would be true of a retail grocer and a furniture manufacturer.

B. Some History

A glance at Figure 8–2 reveals why it is customary to speak of four major merger movements in American history. (No single source of data spans the entire century, so "Nelson," "Thorpe," "FTC," and "M&A" designate separate sources.) The first movement occurred around the turn of the century. Over the seven-year period 1897–1903, 2,864 mergers were recorded in mining and manufacturing. Measured against our current and more recently set records, this record may not seem like much. However, measured against the economy of 1900 and the result-

---

2 Willard F. Mueller, *The Celler–Kefauver Act: The First 27 Years*, U.S. House of Representatives, Committee on the Judiciary, Subcommittee on Monopolies and Commercial Law (November 7, 1979), pp. 7–8.

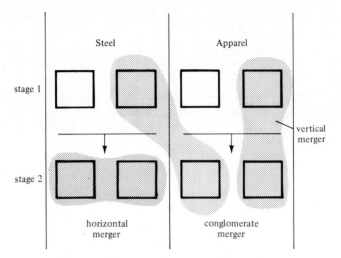

FIGURE 8–1. Types of mergers.

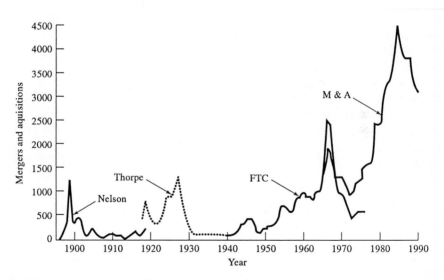

FIGURE 8–2. Annual number of mergers and acquisitions: Nelson Series, Thorpe Series, FTC "Broad" Series, and *M&A* "Domestic" Series. Source: Devra L. Golbe and Lawrence J. White, "Mergers and Acquisitions in the U.S. Economy: An Aggregate and Historical Overview," *Mergers and Acquisitions,* edited by A. J. Auerbach (Chicago: University of Chicago Press, 1988), p. 37; and *Mergers and Acquisitions* (March/April 1990), p. 95.

ing market concentration, this first great wave was awesome. The number of mergers *per dollar of real GNP* was much greater at the turn of the century than during the 1980s, almost five times greater in 1898 than 1988.[3] Horizontal mergers dominated the scene. Moreover, simultaneous *multiple* mergers, which are now very rare, were an everyday affair. Mergers involving at least five firms accounted for 75% of firm disappearances during this period.[4] This turn-of-the-century merger boom produced such giant companies as U.S. Steel, International Harvester, Du Pont, American Tobacco, Pittsburgh Plate Glass, and National Biscuit.[5]

The second major merger wave arose during the Roaring Twenties. From 1925 through 1930, 5382 mergers were recorded for manufacturing and mining. During the peak year of 1929, ownership shares moved at the feverish pace of more than four mergers per business day. This second movement exceeded the first not only in numbers tallied but also in variety of merger types. Horizontal mergers were again very popular, but vertical, market-extension, and product-extension mergers were also in vogue. It was during this second period that General Foods Corporation put together a string of product-extension acquisitions to become the first big food conglomerate. Its acquisitions included Maxwell House Coffee, Jell-O, Baker's Chocolate, Sanka, Bird's Eye, and Swan's Down Cake Flour. Unlike the first merger movement, these years also witnessed countless mergers in sectors other than manufacturing and mining. At least 2,750 utilities, 1,060 banks, and 10,520 retail stores were swallowed up by acquisition during the 1920s.[6]

After two decades of nothing more than a rather meager ripple in the late 1940s, momentum began to build once again in the mid-1950s. Thereafter, the movement swelled incredibly. From 1960 through 1970 the Federal Trade Commission recorded 25,598 mergers. Slightly more than half of these were in manufacturing and mining. The total value of manufacturing and mining assets acquired over this period exceeded $65 billion. This sector's peak year was 1968, when 2,407 firms amounting to more than $13.3 billion were acquired. Putting the matter in relative terms and using an averaging process, we can deduce that, over the period 1953–1968, approximately 21% of all manufacturing and mining assets were acquired.[7]

After a lull in the mid-1970s, the pace quickened again in the 1980s,

---

3 Devra L. Golbe and Lawrence J. White, "Mergers and Acquisitions in the U.S. Economy: An Aggregate and Historical Overview,"in *Mergers and Acquisitions,* edited by Alan J. Auerbach (Chicago: University of Chicago Press, 1988), pp. 25–47.

4 Ralph L. Nelson, *Merger Movements in American Industry, 1895–1956* (Princeton, N.J.: Princeton University Press, 1959) p. 29.

5 Jesse W. Markham, "Survey of the Evidence and Findings on Mergers," in *Business Concentration and Price Policy* (Princeton, N.J.: Princeton University Press, 1955) p. 180.

6 Ibid., pp. 168–69.

7 Federal Trade Commission, *Economic Report on Corporate Mergers* (Washington, D.C.: U.S. Government Printing Office, 1969), p. 666.

as shown in Figure 8–2. Many of the most spectacular recent acquisitions have been made by oil companies, whose financial coffers grew fat during oil shortages of the 1970s. Other interesting acquisitions include many occurring in 1988. Philip Morris' purchase of Kraft for $12.9 billion and Kodak's acquisition of Sterling Drug for $5.1 billion illustrate events.

As for merger types, these latest waves have been quite different from those of yesteryear. Horizontal mergers have become much less numerous than conglomerate mergers. Figure 8–3 shows the trend from 1948 to 1975 in percentage of *assets* acquired by merger type. As we shall see shortly, much of this trend away from horizontals and toward conglomerates, especially toward pure conglomerates, was due to public policy. The enforcement agencies cracked down on horizontal mergers whereas they generally ignored conglomerates.

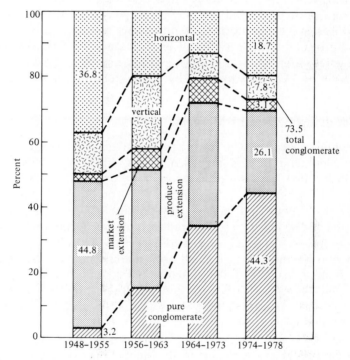

FIGURE 8–3. Distribution of total acquired assets in large manufacturing and mining mergers, by type, 1948–1978. Source: Federal Trade Commission, Bureau of Economics.

II. REASONS FOR MERGER

When counting the *reasons* for merger, one can get by with only ten fingers, but just barely. In simplest terms, corporate marriage is merely a matter of finding a price that buyers are willing to pay and sellers are willing to accept. Going beyond this truism, however, we encounter complexities. Some motives are constant in the sense that they explain a fairly steady stream of mergers year in and year out. Other motives are more cyclical, a characteristic that helps explain why merger activity heats up and cools down over time. In other words, there are two inter-related issues — underlying cause and timing.

A. Timing of Mergers

Let us consider timing first. Several researchers have found a high posi-tive correlation between the number of mergers per year and the general business cycle.[8] Merger frequency tends to rise and fall as the average level of stock market prices rises and falls.

Exactly why this correlation exists is not clear. But owners of firms expecting eventually to sell out may feel they can get the best deal when stock prices are generally high. Conversely, from the buyer's point of view, the basic problem is raising enough cash and securities to make an attractive offer. Hence, acquiring firms may find funds for acquisi-tions easier and cheaper to come by when stock prices are high.

B. Underlying Causes of Mergers

Underlying causes involve as much intuitive understanding as timing does. Sellers and buyers may see things differently while benefiting mutually.[9] *Sellers* have several reasons for wanting to seek out a buyer. First, and most obvious, is the "failing firm" problem. As every used-car owner knows, poor performance may prompt a sale. In the case of busi-ness enterprises, failure is measured in terms of declining revenues and recurring losses. Although any such aspect of failure may be an impor-tant motive for the sale of a small firm, it could be no more than a very minor motive for most sales of large firms. For example, only about 4.8% of all "large" firms bought between 1948 and 1968 were suffering losses before their acquisition, where "large" was defined as having at least $10 million in assets.[10]

A second class of seller's motives relates to individually or family-owned firms that are typically small. Merger may be the easiest means

    [8] Nelson, *op. cit.*, pp. 106–126; Golbe and White, pp. 42–44; Markham, *op. cit.*, pp. 146–154; and Willard Mueller, testimony in *Economic Concentration*, Hearings before the Senate Subcommittee on Antitrust and Monopoly, Part 2 (1965), p. 506.

    [9] For an excellent discussion of causes see Peter O. Steiner, *Mergers: Motives, Effects, Policies* (Ann Arbor: University of Michigan Press, 1975), especially Chapter 2. For a mass-ive empirical study of causes and effects, see *The Determinants and Effects of Mergers* edited by Dennis C. Mueller (Cambridge, Mass.: Oelgeschlager, Gunn & Hain, 1980).

    [10] Stanley E. Boyle, "Pre-Merger Growth and Profit Characteristics of Large Con-glomerate Mergers in the United States: 1948–1968," *St. Johns Law Review*, Special Edition,

for an aging owner-manager to "cash in" on his lifetime effort and perpetuate the business after his retirement. Again, however, this is a minor factor.

Of greater importance and keener interest are the *buyers'* motives. After all, the prices buyers pay to former owners typically exceed the book value of the purchased firms' assets and the market value of the former owners' stock holdings. This excess, or "premium," averaged around 40% in the late 1980s, which means that premiums of 50% and more were common. For example, Kodak paid $89.25 per share to acquire Sterling Drug, which just before the bidding was priced at $54.75—hence a 63% premium. Bridgestone paid a premium of 78% to acquire Firestone's stock in 1988.[11] Indeed, buyers may be so aggressive that they occasionally pull a "raid" or "takeover," in which case they succeed in buying a firm whose management opposes the acquisition. Stock owners who sell out against the management's wishes in these instances may not dislike their reluctant managers (although they frequently do); they may merely feel they have received an "offer they cannot refuse."

What about the stockholders of the acquiring companies? How do they feel about their firms paying large premiums to buy other firms? They can register their displeasure by selling on the stock market their shares in the acquiring firms when these acquisitions are announced. This would tend to depress the price of the acquirers' stock around the time of these announcements. However, numerous "event" studies of acquirers' stock prices reveal no tendency, *on average,* for those prices to fall when acquisitions are announced.[12]

Note, then, we have two important facts: (1) acquisitions always entail hefty gains for the target firms' shareholders, who receive a premium over the market value of their firm. (2) It also appears, though less certainly, that the acquiring company's shareholders break even, on average, with their share prices neither rising nor falling in response to bidding announcements. These results introduce the first of the several buyers' motives we consider next, namely, "efficiencies." The two findings suggest to some economists that mergers are generally profitable, and they are profitable because of the efficiencies they create. As Richard Caves summarizes this view, "A bundle for the target's shareholders plus zero for the bidder's still sums to a bundle, supporting the

(Spring 1970), pp. 160–161. See also Robert L. Conn, "The Failing Firm/Industry Doctrines in Conglomerate Mergers," *Journal of Industrial Economics* (March 1976), pp. 181–187.

[11] *Business Week*, April 4, 1988, pp. 28–29; May 30, 1988, pp. 82–83.

[12] For a survey of the evidence, see Michael C. Jensen and Richard S. Ruback, "The Market for Corporate Control: The Scientific Evidence," *Journal of Financial Economics* Vol. 11 (1983), pp. 5–50.

conclusion that mergers create value and accordingly are economically efficient."[13]

Some defenders of mergers thus point to this evidence as proof that acquisitions are almost always socially desirable because they generate efficiencies. The more mergers, the better, they would say. "However," as Caves critically continues, "if the *average* bidder's shareholders break even, that means they lose about half the time."[14] Hence many mergers may, on the contrary, generate substantial inefficiences and may be motivated by other aims. Indeed, mergers need not be motivated by efficiencies in order to be profitable. Monopoly power may be a profitable objective for horizontal acquisitions. Thus monopoly power and a few other items follow efficiencies in our discussion of possible merger motives.

1. Economic Efficiency.   The main argument of those who see efficiencies in mergers is that there is a "market" for corporate control, just like any other market — that for, say, apples or used cars. This merger market is said to foster efficiencies because well-managed firms will seek to acquire control of target firms in order to replace inept managements or force existing managements to maximize profits. In short, good managers oust bad managers through acquisitions.[15]

Other efficiencies (and lower costs) may stem from the larger size that the merger brings about. These efficiencies may be divided into two broad groups — pecuniary economies and technical economies. **Pecuniary economies** are monetary savings derived from buying inputs more cheaply. Pecuniary gains thus include such things as larger "volume discounts" for the bulk purchase of raw materials or advertising space, lower interest rates on borrowed capital, and greater negotiating strength vis-à-vis labor. In contrast, **technical economies** of scale are "genuine" cost savings. They imply fewer real inputs for a given level of output. Their primary sources are (1) greater specialization of equipment and operators, (2) high-speed automation, and (3) scaled-up equipment.

Although *some* acquisitions yield efficiencies, the bulk of the evidence is strongly against this as an important explanation for the vast majority. The evidence may be divided into three categories depending on its timing: (1) "event" evidence from the time of the acquisition; (2) "premerger" evidence from before the event; and (3) "postmerger" evidence from after the event.

---

13 Richard E. Caves, "Mergers, Takeovers, and Economic Efficiency," *International Journal of Industrial Organization* (March 1989), p. 153.
14 Ibid., p. 53.
15 Henry G. Manne, "Mergers and the Market for Corporate Control," *Journal of Political Economy* (April 1965), pp. 110–120; *Economic Report of the President,* 1985, Chapter 6, pp. 187–202.

The findings for share price changes during the bidding referred to previously come from *"event"* evidence. Although that evidence may seem to support the efficiencies hypothesis, it does so only very weakly. For example, the premiums paid to target-firm shareholders do not depend on prospective efficiencies because they are paid even when, as often happens, there are no intended changes in the target firm at all. Without changes, there can be no efficiencies. Since the payment of premiums does not hinge on the prospect of efficiencies, it offers no proof of efficiencies. Leveraged "management buyouts" are the clearest examples of this. In such instances, which have become very common (e.g., Dan River, Inc., and Macy's), top *existing* managers borrow heavily to buy ownership control of their firm and then take it private, preserving their jobs.[16] The premiums paid for such control match those of takeover acquisitions.

As regards the other main finding mentioned previously — of no change in share prices for stockholders of the acquiring firms, on average — the efficiency interpretation of that evidence may also be questioned. The event studies producing those finding are usually based on the "efficient stock market" hypothesis (the idea that stock prices reflect all available information at any moment in time). This hypothesis has suffered numerous setbacks, especially since the stock market crash of October 1987.[17] Moreover, any negative influences on the acquiring firm's share prices are likely to be obscured by the very large size of the typical acquirer relative to its target and by the upward trend in share price that is common for the acquirer's stock just before bidding occurs.[18] Hence, the "event" study finding of breakeven for the buyer's owners may be a mirage. Moreover, other evidence indicates they are actually losers.

The *"premerger"* evidence centers on the premerger conditions of the acquiring and target firms. If the efficiency hypothesis were correct, the superior management capabilities of the acquiring firms would presumably result in exceptionally high premerger profits for acquiring firms, while the inferior performance hypothesized for the target firms would presumably lead to poor premerger performance for the target firms.

[16] *The Wall Street Journal,* December 29, 1983, p. 1; Anne B. Fisher, "Oops! My Company," *Fortune,* July 23, 1984, p. 18. Indeed, LBOs often increase prices: *Forbes,* October 30, 1989, pp. 36–39.

[17] Douglas K. Pearce, "Challenges to the Concept of Stock Market Efficiency," *Economic Review of the Federal Reserve Bank of Kansas City* (September/October, 1987), pp. 16–33; Colin Camerar, "Bubbles and Fads in Asset Prices," *Journal of Economic Surveys,* Vol. 3, No. 1, (1989), pp. 3–41; Gary Hector, "What Makes Stock Prices Move?," *Fortune,* October 10, 1988, pp. 69–76; *Business Week,* February 22, 1988, pp. 140–142; and Robert J. Shiller, "Fashions, Fads, and Bubbles in Financial Markets," in *Knights, Raiders, and Targets,* edited by J. Coffe (New York: Oxford University Press, 1987).

[18] Dennis C. Mueller, "United States Antitrust: At the Crossroads," in *Mainstreams in Industrial Organization,* edited by H. W. de Jong and W. G. Sheperd, (Dordrecht, The Netherlands: Martinus Nijhoff, 1986), pp. 215–241.

The evidence is somewhat mixed on both points, but it generally runs against the efficiency hypothesis. Acquiring companies tend to be bigger than average, and may be growing at especially brisk paces, but in general they do not have exceptionally good managements as measured by profitability.[19] As for target companies, two massive studies of over 800 acquisitions in manufacturing and banking during the 1960s and 1970s reveal that target firms typically are *not* poor performers previous to their acquisition.[20] Indeed, those in manufacturing had especially high profits before acquisition. Hence, the bulk of the premerger evidence disrespects the theory that mergers purge the economy of bad managers and create efficiencies.

The *"postmerger"* evidence is, by its nature, most compelling. And it comes in several forms — real effects, profitability changes, market share shifts, and stock market evaluations. *Real effects* are measured by changes in productivity, in personnel staffing, and the like. Data for real effects are difficult to compile, so studies of this sort are scarce. Those available reveal some positive results and some negative results, but on the whole there appear to be no systematic efficiency gains.[21] Indeed, optimistic claims of efficiency at the time of merger have all too often proved to be embarrassing later.[22] Postmerger corporate *profitability changes* have been much more thoroughly studied. They provide very little support for the view that mergers raise relative profitability. The great weight of evidence shows a zero or negative impact on average. [23]

[19] Dennis C. Mueller, *Determinants and Effects of Mergers*; G. Meeks, *Disappointing Marriage: A Study of the Gains from Mergers* (Cambridge: Cambridge University Press, 1977); Alan Hughes, "The Impact of Merger: A Survey of Empirical Evidence for the UK," in *Mergers and Merger Policy* edited by James A. Fairburn and John A. Kay (Oxford: Oxford University Press, 1989), pp. 68–69. Australian acquirers have been exceptionally profitable premerger, but this distinction is tarnished by their exceptionally bad postmerger performance. See F. M. McDougall and David K. Round, *The Effects of Mergers & Takeovers in Australia, 1970–1981* (Melbourne: Information Australia for the Australian Institute of Management, 1986).

[20] David J. Ravenscraft and F. M. Scherer, *Mergers, Sell-offs, and Economic Efficiency* (Washington, D.C.: Brookings Institution, 1987); Stephen A. Rhoades, "The Operating Performance of Acquired Firms in Banking," in *Issues After a Century of Federal Competition Policy*, edited by R. L. Wills, J. A. Caswell, and J. D. Culbertson (Lexington, Mass: Lexington Books, 1987), pp. 280–290. See also Hughes, "The Impact of Merger," p. 66.

[21] Hughes, "The Impact of Merger," pp. 74–75. The most favorable study is Frank R. Lichtenberg and David Siegel, "Productivity Changes in Ownership of Manufacturing Plants," *Brookings Papers on Economic Activity* No. 3, (1987), pp. 643–683.

[22] For example, when RJR acquired Nabisco Brands, it claimed that Nabisco's cookie and cracker business would yield "enormous synergies" when blended with Del Monte, its fresh fruits and canned foods subsidiary. But after three years and numerous corporate reorganizations Nabisco and Del Monte were finally split apart when RJR concluded they were in very different businesses, marching at "entirely different tempos." *The Wall Street Journal*, May 12, 1980, p. 12. Even more embarrassing are cases where bankruptcy follows closely after merger (e.g., Penn-Central). For a survey, see A. A. Fisher and R. H. Lande, "Efficiency Considerations in Merger Enforcement," *California Law Review* (December 1983), pp. 1580–1696.

[23] Hughes, "The Impact of Merger;" Ravenscraft and Scherer, *op. cit.*, and Rhoades, *op. cit.*

Observed *shifts in the market shares* of acquired companies corroborate these findings on profitability. If acquired firms became more efficient as a result of merger their market shares would presumably rise as they became more competitive. On the contrary, however, evidence shows market shares to be unaffected or falling after takeover.[24] Finally, the *stock market's evaluation* of the acquiring firm typically deteriorates during the months and years following takeover, something quite different from the stock market's evaluation during the "event," when acquiring firm share prices appear to remain unaffected. Acquiring firm share prices tend to fall in the postmerger world, apparently reflecting the adverse profit and market share trends. F. M. Scherer puts the long-term share price evidence in a nutshell:

> When the time frame has been extended to one to three years after the event, acquiring firms are found to experience *negative* abnormal returns. In the seven one-year studies surveyed by Jensen and Ruback (1983), the abnormal returns averaged -5.5 percent; over the three-year post-takeover period examined by Magenheim and Mueller (1987), the abnormal returns were -16 percent by the most conservative measurement technique.[25]

Overall, the postmerger evidence is therefore not favorable to the efficiency hypothesis. The single most telling summary statistic in this regard is the fact that approximately one out of every three acquisitions of the 1960s and 1970s turned out so badly that the acquired assets were eventually sold off, as Mobil Oil Company recently divested itself of Montgomery Ward after a decade of disappointment, and Coca-Cola rid itself of Columbia Pictures after a string of box office bombs like *Ishtar*.[26]

In sum, virtually all the best evidence available stacks up against the notion that the market for corporate control breeds efficiency. It creates larger firms, but size and efficiency do not necessarily correspond. After surveying the thousands of divestitures of the late 1980s, Donald Povejsil, former executive of Westinghouse, said, "Most of the classical justifications of large size have proved to be of minimal value, or counter-productive, or fallacious."[27] Acquisitions undoubtedly yield efficiencies in certain cases, but as a general rule they do not.

Where, then, do the acquisition premiums come from? There are several explanations. They come partly from losses experienced by the bond holders of the acquiring companies. They come partly from a

---

[24] Lawrence G. Goldberg, "The Effect of Conglomerate Mergers on Competition," *Journal of Law and Economics* (April 1973), pp. 137–158; and Dennis C. Mueller, "Mergers and Market Share," *Review of Economics and Statistics* (May 1985), pp. 259–267.

[25] F. M. Scherer, "Corporate Takeovers: The Efficiency Arguments," *Journal of Economic Perspectives* (Winter 1988), p. 71.

[26] Ravenscraft and Scherer, *op. cit.*, pp. 159–191.

[27] Walter Kiechel III, "Corporate Strategy for the 1990s," *Fortune*, February 29, 1988, p. 34.

grossly mistaken optimism, or hubris, among the acquiring firms' managers.[28] Perhaps the best explanation is that of Alan Hughes, which is reproduced in the appendix to this chapter.

2. Defensive Motives.   In 1989 the press announced a huge merger between Time, Inc., and Warner Communications saying its main purpose was "To protect Time, Inc. from takeovers."[29] About the same time Maytag's Chairman Daniel Drumm announced his company's intention to acquire Chicago Pacific Corp. (maker of Hoover vacuum cleaners), saying that the deal was partly "an exercise in raider-proofing."[30] These illustrate instances where the acquiring firm is making acquisitions in an attempt to lessen its own chances of being acquired. This is therefore a "defensive" motive.

Acquisitions may insulate the acquiring firm from acquisition for a number of reasons.[31] For example, acquisitions boost the size of the acquiring firm, and statistics show that huge firms are less likely to be acquired than medium- or small-sized firms. Added size offers some protection against takeover by reducing the number of possible acquirers. Another factor here is debt. Acquiring can create a frightfully large debt obligation, something to scare off potential aquirers. Still, the most dramatic of all these possibilities is this: acquiring another company can be an especially effective defense if that other company is actively attempting to acquire the acquirer. This is the so-called "Pac-Man" defense. In 1982, for instance, Martin Marietta made a tender offer to acquire Bendix after Bendix announced its intention of buying out Martin Marietta. The strategy worked, leaving Martin Marietta independent, and the strategy has since been used by Houston Natural Gas and American Brands, Inc.[32]

If acquisitions are a means of protecting managers against job loss, one would expect more active acquiring by those managers whose job security is most shaky and less acquiring by those whose jobs are most secure. Such has been found. Managers who do not own the firms they manage feel less job security than those managers who are also owners. And the former (manager-controlled firms) engage in more acquisitions than the latter (owner-controlled firms).[33] Note that many of those managers who are trying to preserve their jobs by acquiring other firms may feel the need to do this because they are poor managers. If so, acquisi-

---

[28] Richard Roll, "The Hubris Hypothesis of Corporate Takeovers," *Journal of Business* (April 1986), pp. 197–216.

[29] *Newsweek,* June 26, 1989, p. 48; *Fortune,* November 20, 1989, p. 166.

[30] *Business Week,* January 30, 1989.

[31] D. F. Greer, "Acquiring in Order to Avoid Acquisition," *Antitrust Bulletin* (Spring 1986), pp. 155–186.

[32] *The Wall Street Journal*, February 14, 1984, p. 3; *Business Week*, February 13, 1984, p. 44: *Business Week*, February 8, 1988, p. 24.

[33] Yakov Amihud and Baruch Lev, "Risk Reduction as a Managerial Motive for Conglomerate Mergers," *Bell Journal of Economics* (Autumn 1981), pp. 605–617.

tions are a means of preserving incompetents as well as a means of purging incompetents. The market for corporate control can therefore perpetuate inefficiency as well as promote efficiency.

Although no more than a small minority of acquisitions could be called "defensive," the motive is important to recognize. And if one includes acquisitions which move the acquiring firm out of slowly growing markets into rapidly growing markets, then the defensive category would not be a trivial one. For example, the large tobacco companies have been diligently diversifying by acquisition ever since the prospects for cigarettes were damaged by the discovery that smoking causes cancer. For example, Philip Morris has acquired General Foods, Kraft Foods, and Miller Brewing Company, while RJR has taken over Del Monte and Nabisco.

3. Risk Spreading Through Diversification. Suppose you want to get two dozen eggs delivered to your grandmother. Suppose further that she lives in the woods, and the only available delivery service relies on brave but clumsy 6-year-old girls attired in red. Experience shows that stumbles over roots and stones make successful egg delivery by any one girl a 50:50 proposition (even apart from the danger of wolves). Your problem then is this: If you want at least *some* of your two dozen eggs to get through, what delivery arrangements should you make? Placing the entire shipment in the hands of one girl means a 0.5 probability that *none* will arrive. However, if you give one dozen to one girl and one dozen to another, there is only one chance in four that no eggs will be delivered because that is the probability of both girls falling down. Similarly, the split shipment offers one chance in four that all eggs will arrive safely. Two times in every four, one dozen will be broken and one dozen will get through.

This example was developed by Roger Sherman to demonstrate the power of diversification in reducing risks.[34] He also demonstrates that still further diversification yields further risk reduction: "The best thing to do is to send 24 girls, each with one egg. The chance that no egg will arrive is then infinitesimally small, and it becomes very probable that about 12 eggs will arrive safely." The obvious moral (don't put all your eggs in one basket) may motivate many vertical and conglomerate mergers.

Diversification, however, is not always favorable; nor is merger the only means of achieving diversification. The conditions required for a positive effect for an acquiring firm are more limited than this simple example suggests.[35] In particular, the variances of the components of a

[34] Roger Sherman, *The Economics of Industry* (Boston: Little, Brown, 1974), p. 105.

[35] H. Bierman, Jr., and J. L. Thomas, "A Note on Mergers and Risk," *Antitrust Bulletin* (Fall 1974), pp. 523–529. See also the discussion of Roger Clarke, *Industrial Economics* (Oxford: Basil Blackwell, 1985), pp. 209–211.

combination must be essentially independent of each other. (The independence of several delivery girls would be severely compromised if they all held hands and thereby tripped over each other.) Failure to meet the conditions necessary for risk reduction may explain why researchers have been unable to find any risk reduction among conglomerate mergers generally.[36] Indeed, there is evidence that mergers often augment risk rather than reduce it.[37]

4. Growth and Personal Aggrandizement. This survey would not be complete without mention of sheer growth and personal aggrandizement. Just how important these motives are is impossible to say. The Napoleonic aspirations of acquisitive business leaders cannot be captured by statistics, except insofar as statistics may disprove the importance of other, more publicly professed and more socially acceptable motives, such as efficiencies. You, the reader, are free to judge for yourself. You may draw upon your knowledge of human nature and your reading of whatever biographical material you may wish to look into. Two typical examples you will find are:

- Harold Geneen led ITT in the acquisition of more than 250 companies. A close colleague of his once said, "Three things should be written on Hal Geneen's tombstone—earnings per share, 15% growth per year, and size."[38]

- Charles G. Bluhdorn, who guided Gulf & Western Industries through more than 80 acquisitions in 11 years, had this to say about his company and himself: "No mountain is high enough for us, nothing is impossible. The sky is the limit. . . . I came to this country without a penny, and built a company with 100,000 employees. This is what America is all about . . . to be able to do what I've done is a matter of pride to me and to the country."[39]

5. Monopoly Power. U.S. Steel was worth more than the sum of its 170 parts. Prior to merger in 1901, the total value of the tangible

[36] R. W. Melicher and D. F. Rush, "The Performance of Conglomerate Firms: Recent Risk and Return Experience," *Journal of Finance* (May 1973), pp. 381–388.

[37] C. W. L. Hill, "Conglomerate Performance over the Business Cycle," *Journal of Industrial Economics* (December 1983), pp. 197–211; and D. H. Ciscel and R. D. Evans, "Returns to Corporate Diversification in the 1970s," *Managerial and Decision Economics*, Vol. 5, no. 2 (1984), pp. 67–71.

[38] Spoken by Richard H. Griebel, a former ITT executive and president of Lehigh Valley Industries, *Business Week*, May 9, 1970, p. 61. For more on Geneen, see Anthony Sampson, *The Sovereign State of ITT* (Greenwich, Conn.: Fawcett Crest Paperback, 1974).

[39] *Business Week*, July 5, 1969, p. 34. On Victor Posner see *The Wall Street Journal*, June 23, 1981, pp. 1, 16; on Russell Chambers see *The Wall Street Journal*, December 30, 1982, pp. 1, 12; and on the men involved in the amazing Bendix/Martin—Marietta/United Technologies battle of 1982 see *The Wall Street Journal*, September 24, 1982, pp. 1, 22. For more solid evidence favoring growth see Alan R. Beckenstein, "Merger Activity and Merger Theories: An Empirical Investigation," *Antitrust Bulletin* (Spring 1979), pp. 105–128. See also Stephen A. Rhoades, *Power, Empire Building and Mergers* (Lexington, Mass.: Lexington Books, 1983).

property of the separate firms stood at roughly $700 million. After merger, U.S. Steel estimated its value at close to $1.4 billion. Why the enormous difference? Market power. After merger, U.S. Steel produced two-thirds of all U.S. semifinished steel and similar percentages of all rails, tin plate, rods, and other products. The consequences for the price of pig iron are pictured in Figure 8–4, which shows two price trend lines, one deflated by the wholesale price index, the other not. The discontinuous price jump of about 50% in 1901 coincides with the formation of U.S. Steel. This may lead the astute reader to suspect a substantial rise in annual profit rates also, and you would be correct.

Xidex Corporation offers a more recent example. During the 1970s it acquired two competitors in microfilm. The first acquisition increased its market share from 46% to 55%; the second from 61% to 70%. As a direct result of these mergers Xidex's prices jumped first by 11% then by an additional 23%.[40]

An analysis of six airline mergers occurring during 1986–87 yields equally interesting results.[41] Those results vary depending on whether

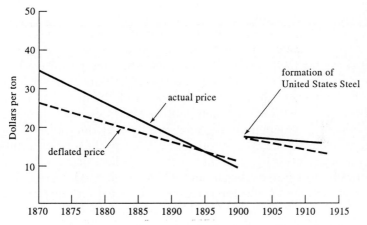

FIGURE 8–4. Pig iron price trend, before and after U.S. Steel. Source: Parsons and Ray, "The United States Steel Consolidation: The Creation of Market Control," *Journal of Law and Economics* (April 1975), p. 186.

[40] The associated gain in monopoly profit was in each case sufficient to recoup the cost of the acquisition in just two years. David M. Barton and Roger Sherman, "The Price and Profit Effects of Horizontal Merger: A Case Study," *Journal of Industrial Economics* (December 1984), pp. 165–177. Stockmarket "event" studies have not supported the market power hypothesis, but it has been demonstrated that mergers genuinely creating market power, like Xidex's acquisitions, disclose no tell-tale signs of harm to the "event" method. Hence the ability of "event" studies to detect anticompetitive mergers may be doubted. R. Preston McAfee and Michael A. Williams, "Can Event Studies Detect Anticompetitive Mergers?" *Economic Letters*, Vol. 28 (1988), pp. 199–203.

[41] Steven A. Morrison and Clifford Winston, "Enhancing the Performance of the

the reduction in competitors through merger occurred on an airline route involving a hub city or not. (Dallas is a hub for American Airlines. Chicago is one for United. An airline concentrates its flights to a given region through a hub, flying people in and then flying them out to their ultimate destination after most change planes.) In percentage terms, the price effect of losing a competitor to merger ranged "from 2 percent to 32 percent with no hub effects, and up to 55 percent when hub effects come into play."[42] These statistics speak for themselves, but corroboration is found in the words of an airline executive who explained the torrent of airline mergers during the 1980s by saying, "Carriers are trying to achieve the market dominance that will give them better control over their prices."[43]

Just how many horizontal mergers are motivated by market power is difficult to estimate, partly because U.S. law on horizontal mergers has some bite. In Britain, where the law is relatively lenient, 27% of the respondents in G. D. Newbould's interview survey of 380 firms said that achievement of "market dominance" was the single most important reason for their merger (and his sample included some nonhorizontal mergers).[44] Hence, market power is an important motive for horizontal mergers.

Whether market power could motivate *vertical* and *conglomerate* mergers as well as horizontal mergers is a much debated question. These other forms of merger produce no immediate or obvious increases in market share for the consolidated firm. Nor do they promise added *market* concentration. Hence, theories and empirical tests of possible adverse competitive effects of these mergers must attack the question indirectly.

The major potentially anticompetitive effects of vertical mergers are (1) *foreclosure,* wherein nonintegrated business at one level of the production-distribution chain are foreclosed from dealing with suppliers or buyers at other levels because those other suppliers or buyers are owned by vertically integrated rivals, and (2) strengthened *barriers to entry,* which may arise from the foreclosure of potential entrants and the en-

Deregulated Air Transportation System," *Brookings Papers on Economic Activity: Microeconomics 1989* (Washington, D.C.: Brookings Institution, 1989) pp. 81–112. Included were American Airlines and Air California plus Delta and Western Airlines.

42 *Ibid.,* p. 73. Other researchers have similar results. Gloria Hurdle and her associates found fare increases of 12–33% if two carriers merged to form a monopoly and increases of 4–12% for a merger creating duopoly. Gloria Hurdle et al., "Concentration, Potential Entry, and Performance in the Airline Industry," U.S. Department of Justice Antitrust Division Economic Analysis Discussion Paper, 1988.

43 *The Wall Street Journal,* September 17, 1986, p. 35. Another nice quote comes from *Forbes* regarding hat tycoon Irving Joel (October 17, 1988, p. 108):
[He] has bought up the brand names that account for an estimated 70% of the $75 million quality western and dress hat market in the U.S. "If you play Monopoly," says Joel of his acquisition strategy, "the idea is to own all the properties on the board."

44 Gerald D. Newbould, *Management and Merger Activity* (Liverpool: Guthstead, 1970), pp. 138–139.

larged capital cost requirements associated with multilevel entry.[45] U.S. Steel provides an example of the barrier effect because the main source of its market power was its aggressive vertical acquisition of most iron ore supplies in North America. Charles Schwab, a prominent steel executive of the day, explained the consequences of U.S. Steel's 75% ore control while testifying in 1911:

> *Mr. Schwab:* I do not believe there will be any great development in iron and steel by new companies, but rather development by the companies now in business.
> *Mr. Chairman:* Now, explain that to us.
> *Mr. Schwab:* For the reason that the possibility of a new company getting at a sufficiently large supply of raw materials would make it exceedingly difficult if not impossible.[46]

As for conglomerate mergers, we can note that the greater size and diversity they gain improves the possibility of *reciprocity*. This is a policy of "I buy from you if you buy from me," and it may tend to foreclose rivals from affected markets. Conglomerate mergers may also eliminate *potential* competitors. In either event, profits might follow from the added power implied. Substantiation or refutation of these and other possible effects is difficult in particular cases and in general. However, several researchers have found that the market shares of firms acquired by conglomerates do not usually grow inordinately after acquisition. They say this shows an absence of adverse competitive effect,[47] implying that most conglomerate mergers could not be motivated by quests for market power.

To summarize, the motives for merger are many and varied. No one explanation clearly surpasses all others. At any one time, there is a diversity of inducements; over time, trends of intention shift.

III. ANTITRUST MERGER POLICY

Antitrust law governing most mergers has a structural focus and is designed to curb market power in the early stages (to "nip it in the bud" before it fully blossoms). As stated in its preamble, the purpose of the Clayton Act of 1914 was "to arrest the creation of trusts, conspiracies

---

[45] Willard F. Mueller, "Public Policy Toward Vertical Mergers," in *Public Policy Toward Mergers*, edited by F. Weston and S. Peltzman (Pacific Palisades, Calif.: Goodyear, 1969), pp. 150–166.

[46] Donald O. Parsons and Edward J. Ray, "The United States Steel Consolidation: The Creation of Market Control," *Journal of Law and Economics* (April 1975), p. 198.

[47] L. G. Goldberg, "Conglomerate Mergers and Concentration Ratios," *Review of Economics and Statistics* (August 1974), pp. 303–309; and S. E. Boyle and P. W. Jaynes, *Economic Report on Conglomerate Merger Performance* (Washington, D.C.: Federal Trade Commission, 1972), pp. 82–83. On the other hand, see John T. Scott, "Purposive Diversification as a Motive for Merger," *International Journal of Industrial Organization* (March 1989), pp. 35–47.

and monopolies *in their incipiency and before consummation."* Section 7 of the Clayton Act prohibited potentially anticompetitive mergers—but it had enormous loopholes. These were not plugged until 1950, with passage of the Celler-Kefauver Amendment. The amended statute outlaws mergers

> where in any line of commerce in any section of the country, the effect of such acquisition may be substantially to lessen competition, or tend to create a monopoly.

The act is enforced by the Justice Department and the Federal Trade Commission. Although hundreds of cases have been decided under the act, we shall review only a few of the more important ones. Before we do, a brief outline of what to look for may be helpful:

1. The phrase "in any line of commerce" refers to product markets. Major factors affecting the courts' definition of relevant product markets include (a) the product's physical characteristics and uses, (b) unique production facilities, (c) distinct customers, (d) cross-elasticity of demand with substitutes, and (e) the absolute price level of possible substitutes.
2. The phrase "in any section of the country" refers to particular geographic markets. Major factors affecting the courts' definition of relevant geographic markets include (a) the costs of transportation, (b) legal restrictions on geographic scope, (c) the extent to which local demand is met by outside supply—for example , little in from outside, and (d) the extent to which local production is shipped to other areas—for example, little out from inside.[48]
3. The phrase "may be . . . to lessen competition" reflects the importance of *probable* adverse effect. In this regard the major factors considered by the courts differ somewhat depending on whether the merger at issue is horizontal, vertical, or conglomerate. Factors for (a) *horizontal mergers* include the market shares and ranks of the merging firms; concentration in the market; *trends* in market shares and concentration; merger history in the market; declines in the absolute number of firms; and the elimination of a strong, competitively vigorous independent firm. Factors considered for (b) *vertical mergers,* where foreclosure and entry barriers are the potentially adverse effects, include the market shares of the merging firms (each at their respective levels in the production-distribution process); and the trend toward vertical integration in the industry. Factors considered for (c) *conglomerate mergers* include the elimination of a

---

[48] K. G. Elzinga and T. F. Hogarty, "The Problem of Geographic Market Delineation in Antimerger Suits," *Antitrust Bulletin* (Spring 1973), pp. 45–81. See also Ira Horowitz, "Market Definition in Antitrust Analysis: A Regression Based Approach," *Southern Economic Journal* (July 1981), pp. 1–16.

prime potential entrant, the danger of reciprocal buying, and any severe disparity of size between the acquired firm and its competitors.

IV. HORIZONTAL MERGERS

1. The *Bethlehem-Youngstown* Case (1958).[49]   Bethlehem Steel's acquisition of Youngstown Sheet & Tube in 1957 was the first large merger challenged under the Celler-Kefauver Act. The firms ranked second and sixth nationally among steel producers. Their combined ingot capacity amounted to 20% of total industry capacity. The number one firm, U.S. Steel, had a 30% share at the time, so this merger would have boosted the share of U.S. Steel and Bethlehem taken together from 45 to 50%. In the court's opinion, "This would add substantially to concentration in an already highly concentrated industry and reduce unduly the already limited number of integrated steel companies."

Bethlehem's defense for acquiring Youngstown Sheet & Tube was that the national market was not the relevant geographic market for steel products. Its attorneys urged acceptance of three separate markets within the United States—eastern, midcontinental, and western. Since all of Youngstown's plants were located in the midcontinent area whereas all of Bethlehem's plants were either eastern or western, the defense went on to argue that the high costs of steel transportation prevented head-on competition between the merging firms. Moreover, they claimed that the acquisition would bring Bethlehem into the Chicago area, where it could then compete more effectively with U.S. Steel, the dominant force in that area.

The court rejected these arguments. It said that even though Bethlehem did not have ingot capacity in the midcontinent area, Bethlehem's annual shipments of more than 2 million tons into the area indicated direct competition with Youngstown. Furthermore, the court said that market delineation "must be made on the basis of where *potentially* they could make sales." In other words, Bethlehem was surely capable of entering the Chicago market by internal expansion instead of by acquisition. As for the argument that the combined companies could better compete with U.S. Steel, the same faulty logic could justify successive mergers until just two or three firms were left in the industry, a situation that could hardly be considered competitive. Thus the merger was enjoined. The benefits of the court's denial were realized a few years later when Bethlehem *did* build a massive steel plant 30 miles east of Chicago.

[49] *United States v. Bethlehem Steel Corp.*, 168 F. Supp. 576 (1958).

2. The *Brown Shoe* **Case (1962).**[50]   Failure to appeal the *Bethlehem* case allowed *Brown Shoe* to become the first case to reach the Supreme Court under the Celler-Kefauver Act. In 1955, the date of this merger, Brown was the fourth largest manufacturer of shoes in the United States, accounting for about 4% of total shoe production. Brown was also a big shoe retailer, owning or controlling over 1230 retail shops. The mate in Brown's merger was Kinney, which likewise engaged in shoe manufacturing and retailing. Retailing was Kinney's forte, however, as it was at the time the nation's largest "independent" retail shoe chain, with over 400 stores in more than 270 cities and about 1.2% of all retail shoe sales by dollar volume. The case thus had vertical as well as horizontal aspects. Here we take up the horizontal aspects at retail level.

The Supreme Court decided that relevant product lines could be drawn to distinguish men's, women's, and children's shoes. Defendant Brown wanted still narrower delineations such as "medium-priced" and "low-priced" shoes, but the Court did not agree. As for geographic markets at retail level, the Court decided upon "cities with a population exceeding 10,000 and their environs in which both Brown and Kinney retailed shoes." By this definition, the market shares of the merging companies were enough to arouse the Court's disapproval. For example, the combined share of Brown and Kinney sales of women's shoes exceeded 20% in 32 cities. And in children's shoes, their combined share exceeded 20% in 31 cities. In addition to raw shares, *trends* caught the Court's attention: "We cannot avoid the mandate of Congress that tendencies toward concentration in industry are to be curbed in their incipiency, particularly when those tendencies are being accelerated through giant steps striding across a hundred cities at a time. In the light of the trends in this industry we agree with the Government and the court below that this is an appropriate place at which to call a halt."

3. The Von's Case (1966).[51]   This case is to horizontal mergers what the sixth commandment is to homicide. The acquisition was denied, although neither firm involved was really very big and, by usual standards, the market was not highly concentrated. Von's ranked third among retail grocery store chains in the Los Angeles area when in 1960 it acquired Shopping Bag Food Stores, which ranked sixth. Their market shares were, respectively, 4.3 and 3.2%. Hence, their combined sales amounted to 7.5%. This would have boosted the four-firm concentration ratio in the Los Angeles market from 24.4% before merger to 28.8% after. Moreover, 8-firm and 12-firm concentration had been on the rise prior to merger.

These facts might have been moderately damning. But Justice Black

---

[50] *Brown Shoe Company* v. *United States,* 370 U.S. 294 (1962).
[51] *United States* v. *Von's Grocery Co.,* 384 U.S. 270 (1966).

chose to neglect them when writing the Supreme Court's majority opinion. He stressed other factors:

> the number of owners operating a single store in the Los Angeles retail grocery market decreased from 5,365 in 1950 to 3,818 in 1961. By 1963, three years after merger, the number of single store owners had dropped still further to 3,590.

Black thus defines concentration in terms of the *number* of independent firms. He goes on to state that "the basic purpose of the 1950 Celler-Kefauver Bill was to prevent economic concentration in the American economy by keeping a large number of small competitors in business." By this reasoning, a divestiture order was unavoidable.

However laudable these sentiments might be, we may question as a matter of economics whether the massive demise of mom-and-pop grocery stores in Los Angeles was due to mergers like the one denied. Divestiture of Shopping Bag did not resurrect them. They fell by the wayside for reasons of economies of scale, cheap automobile transportation to shopping centers, and the like. Thus the Court seems to have set a stringent legal standard while deferring to a moderate standard of economic proficiency.

4. The *General Dynamics* Case (1974).[52] With *Von's* the law reached a peak of stringency against horizontal mergers. Since then greater leniency has been shown. In grocery retailing, for instance, the enforcement agencies gave the green light to three substantial horizontal mergers by large companies—Lucky, Allied, and A&P—during 1975–1976.

The *General Dynamics* case of 1974 stands out as a turning point in this shift toward leniency. The product was coal. Through its subsidiary coal company (Materials Service Corporation), General Dynamics acquired a controlling interest in United Electric Coal. The government challenged the merger because, according to Justice Department definitions, this merger gave General Dynamics a 12.4% share of a broad midwestern coal market and a 23.2% share of a narrower Illinois submarket, shares that would easily violate the *Von's* standard.

General Dynamics successfully defended itself by arguing that rule of reason considerations should be taken into account. It claimed that the government's share figures for the acquired firm, United Electric, were biased upward by being based on current sales. The true measure of United's position, it was argued, was not current sales but rather coal *reserves* that would feed production in the near future, or better yet *uncommitted reserves* (i.e., reserves not already sold by long-term contracts). By this alternative measure, United's stature in the market shrank considerably because it was very short of reserves, especially the uncommit-

---

[52] *United States* v. *General Dynamics Corp.*, 415 (U.S.) 486 (1974).

ted kind. The Supreme Court sided with General Dynamics, finding its method of assessment more meaningful economically:

> A . . . significant indicator of a [coal] company's power effectively to compete with other companies lies in the state of a company's uncommitted reserves of recoverable coal. A company with relatively large supplies of coal which are not already under contract to a customer will have a more important influence upon competition in the contemporaneous negotiation of supply contracts than a firm with small reserves, even though the latter may presently produce a greater tonnage of coal . . .

Thus, with this case, the Court said it would not follow the rigid formulas of the 1960s.

Developments of the 1980s[53]

Horizontal mergers remain one area where the antitrust laws retain some potency. Still, the trend started by *General Dynamics* in 1974 continued through the 1980s. Among the many big horizontal mergers recently completed that probably would not pass muster under the old standards were Chevron and Gulf Oil, Texaco and Getty Oil, Jones & Laughlin Steel (a subsidiary of LTV) and Republic Steel, plus a joint venture between General Motors and Toyota. (Some of these approvals required modest divestiture or other conditions.)

The current situation is best summarized by the "Merger Guidelines" promulgated by the Department of Justice and FTC in 1982 and 1984 to alert the business world about the kinds of mergers that would likely be challenged. These guidelines relax the rules considerably. In so doing, they incorporate four new twists.

First, they measure structural impact by Herfindahl-Hirschman Indexes (or H indexes) instead of concentration ratios. The H index simply transforms market share data into a form that many economists find useful. Market shares are squared, so that, for example, a share of 10% becomes 100, a share of 2% becomes 4, and their combination of 12% becomes 144. This squaring of market shares gives especially large weight to especially large market shares, so it may be a better reflection of anticompetitive impact than market shares plain and simple. The guidelines permit horizontal mergers in markets having a postmerger H index of 1000 or less, pose a warning in the 1000–1800 range, and threaten serious trouble for any substantial merger in markets with H indexes greater than 1800. (In particular the threshold change in H is 100 in the 1000–1800 range and 50 over 1800. Very roughly, an H of 1000 corresponds to four-firm concentration ratios in the range of 45 to 55.)

---

[53] For an overview see George Hay, "Merger Policy in the US," in J. A. Fairburn and J. A. Kay (eds.), *Mergers and Merger Policy* (Oxford: Oxford University Press, 1989), pp. 231–245.

The *second* new twist in the guidelines is that they incorporate consideration of factors other than market shares and concentration when deciding whether to challenge particular mergers. That is, competition may be either less or more intense than is suggested by a given level of concentration. It may be *less* intense if, for example, barriers to entry are particularly high or if extensive joint venture activity inhibits competitive independence. Conversely, competition may be *more* intense if (1) there is *rapid technological change* to stifle collusive understandings and disrupt stodgy strategies, (2) there is *rapid industry growth*, which creates market turbulence and reduces incentives to collude, or (3) especially *easy entry* to provide potential competition. Consideration of these and related factors allows the authorities to approve mergers that look bad by H indexes alone.

Third, in defining the relevant market, the guidelines refer to traditional earmarks such as "differences between products in customary usage, design, physical composition and other technical characteristics," but they go further. They try to rely more on economic theory. The "market" is to be defined ever more broadly as long as a hypothetical 5% price hike for the product would drive a "significant percent" of buyers to purchase substitute products.

Fourth, the guidelines say that the enforcement agencies will permit otherwise illegal mergers if those mergers are likely to result in substantial *cost-reducing efficiencies*. This is a highly controversial change. Statute law grants no explicit exemptions for cost-saving mergers and Supreme Court opinions (at least its old opinions) do not permit consideration of efficiencies as a defense for otherwise illegal mergers.

The nature of the efficiency defense and the debate surrounding it may be seen in Figure 8–5. Before merger, competition prevails, with

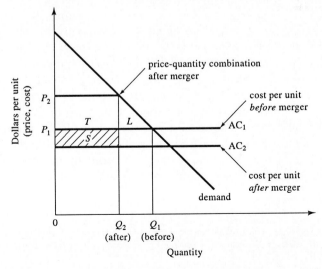

FIGURE 8–5. The cost-savings efficiency defense for horizontal mergers.

price P_1 matching average cost per unit AC_1 and output running at Q_1. After merger, two main things happen. *First*, competition is lessened, resulting in a higher price P_2 and lower output Q_2. This causes a dead-weight *loss* due to *allocation inefficiency* indicated by the triangular area L. *Second*, per unit costs of production are reduced from AC_1 to AC_2. This causes a *gain* due to enhanced *technical efficiency* represented in Figure 8–5 by the shaded area S. Those who argue for a strict efficiency standard in antitrust argue that approval of mergers should hinge solely on a comparison of any efficiency gains and losses, a computation of *net* efficiency changes. In brief, we have two possibilities:

1. If allocation inefficiency (like L) > technical efficiency (like S)
   Result: Net Loss, DENY Merger
2. If allocation inefficiency (like L) < technical efficiency (like S)
   Result: Net Gain, APPROVE Merger

In Figure 8–5 the loss of area L happens to be less than the gain of area S, so by this efficiency criterion the hypothetical merger would be approved.[54]

On the other hand, use of different criteria would cause the merger in Figure 8–5 to be denied. If, for example, the aim of antitrust is to maintain competition in a structural sense, the cost savings of area S would be irrelevant. The higher concentration caused by the merger would by itself be possible reason enough to deny the merger. Another criterion might be concern for "fairness" to consumers or "equity" in wealth distribution. Notice that in Figure 8–5 *price rises from P_1 to P_2* despite the cost savings of area S. This could be considered *"unfair"* to consumers. The reason price rises after merger is plain to see — the reduced competition allows sellers to extract an excess profit amounting to combined area T plus S. (This is the difference between the postmerger price of P_2 and postmerger cost of AC_2 times the number of units OQ_2.) Area T is a transfer of consumer surplus from buyers to sellers while S is, as we've seen, the dollar value of the cost savings. In this view, the merger could be considered *"inequitable"* because it transfers wealth from buyers to sellers. Overall, the case against "efficiency" and for "fairness" or "equity" can be summarized succinctly: "Rather than allowing price to rise to P_2 . . . a standard consistent with the intent of Congress would require price not to rise above P_1; mergers that would induce a new wealth transfer from consumers to firms should be prohibited."[55]

Resolution of the controversy rests on more than value judgments and the perceived purposes of antitrust. It also rests on empirical evi-

[54] Oliver E. Williamson, "Economies as an Antitrust Defense: The Welfare Tradeoffs," *American Economic Review* (March 1968), pp. 18–36.

[55] A. A. Fisher, F. I. Johnson, and R. H. Lande, "Mergers, Market Power, and Property Rights," Bureau of Economics Working Paper No. 130, Federal Trade Commission (1985), pp. 9–10.

dence. What are the magnitudes of areas L, T, and S in Figure 8–5, both in general and in specific cases? Unfortunately, none of these values is easily calculated, especially not in specific cases. But the sketchy evidence is instructive. By and large, estimates of area L seem rather small, barely justifying a rigorous stance against horizontal mergers and signalling relatively minor losses under lax or tolerant standards. On the other hand, however, estimates of wealth transfers like area T tend to be very large. A sample of 70 horizontal merger cases between 1954 and 1974 revealed transfer benefits averaging $12.7 million per case.[56] This suggests that a stringent policy would be quite beneficial if judged on grounds of "fairness," or "equity."

Finally, what about the cost savings represented by area S? As pointed out previously, there is very little evidence that, in general, mergers typically foster cost efficiencies. To be sure, there are undoubtedly specific cases that run counter to the general evidence by yielding substantial efficiencies, but it is debatable whether these exceptions should be allowed to hold sway. Most cases that yield efficiencies would be permitted under the guidelines even in the absence of an efficency defense because the guidelines permit horizontal mergers among those companies most likely to realize cost savings from merger, namely, those that are relatively small.[57] Moreover, it is difficult to predict whether a given merger will, in fact, produce cost savings. In sum, the present writer has doubts about an efficiency approach.[58]

V. VERTICAL MERGERS

Short of monopoly, the critical issue in vertical merger cases is "foreclosure." Before merger, numerous suppliers can compete for each independent user's purchases. After merger, supplier and user are linked by common ownership. Products then typically flow between the merged firms as far as is practicable, and the sales opportunities of other suppliers diminish. If the vertical linkage is trivial, as would be true of a farmer owning a roadside vegetable stand, competition is not affected. If, on the other hand, the foreclosure covers a wide portion of the total market, there may be anticompetitive consequences. Here, too, history shows a shift toward leniency in recent years.

---

[56] David B. Audretsch, "An Evaluation of Horizontal Merger Enforcement," *Industrial Organization, Antitrust, and Public Policy*, edited by J. V. Craven (Boston: Kluwer—Nijhoff, 1983), pp. 69–88.

[57] A. A. Fisher and R. H. Lande, "Efficiency Considerations in Merger Enforcement," *California Law Review* (December 1983), pp. 1580–1696.

[58] Unless the claimed efficiencies can be shown to increase competition. This is different than allowing claimed efficiencies to offset the effects of reduced competition, which is the efficiencies argument of Figure 8–5.

1. The *Brown Shoe* Case (1962): Vertical Aspects.[59]   Prior to Brown Shoe's acquisition of Kinney in 1955, Brown had acquired a very large number of retail shops. Thus, Kinney was just one in a series of vertical mergers by Brown. In effect, then, Brown was attempting to accumulate captive retail distributors who would buy heavily from Brown's manufacturing arm.

On these vertical aspects the Supreme Court stressed several points. First, since Kinney was the largest independent retail chain, the Court felt that, in this industry, "no merger between a manufacturer and an independent retailer could involve a larger potential market foreclosure." Second, the evidence showed that Brown would use the acquisition "to force Brown shoes into Kinney stores." Third, there was a *trend* toward vertical integration in the industry, a trend in which the acquiring manufacturers had "become increasingly important sources of supply for their acquired outlets," and the "necessary corollary of these trends is the foreclosure of independent manufacturers from markets otherwise open to them." The Court thus ordered divestiture.

2. The Cement Cases (1961–1967).   Approximately three-fourths of all cement is used to produce ready-mixed concrete (cement premixed with sand or other aggregate). Prior to 1960 there was virtually no integration between the cement and ready-mixed concrete industries. By 1966, however, after an outbreak of merger activity, at least 40 ready-mix concrete companies had been acquired by leading cement companies, and several large producers of ready-mixed concrete had begun to make cement. The Federal Trade Commission issued a series of complaints, directed its staff to make an industrywide investigation, and in January 1967 issued a policy statement challenging vertical mergers in the industry, all of which seems to have reduced acquisition activity appreciably.[60]

3. Vertical Merger Guidelines (1984).   The current status of vertical mergers is muddled by a lack of recent cases. It's clear, however, that the trend is toward greater tolerance. In their key passages the guidelines say that vertical mergers are unlikely to be challenged unless a combination of factors makes the foreclosure effect particularly odious. Among these factors are (1) very high concentration in either the upstream or downstream market, that is, an H index greater than 1800, and (2) very little capacity that is not already vertically integrated between the two markets. Thus the law here still has some bite, but very few deal makers need to fear a challenge.

---

[59] *Brown Shoe Company* v. *United States*, 370 U.S. 294 (1962).

[60] Federal Trade Commission, *Economic Report on Mergers and Vertical Integration in the Cement Industry* (Washington, D.C.: U.S. Government Printing Office, 1966); and Enforcement Policy with Respect to Vertical Mergers in the Cement Industry, January 1967, in Commerce Clearing House, 1971 *Trade Regulation Reports*, #4520.

VI. CONGLOMERATE MERGERS

The record-breaking merger statistics of the 1960s and 1980s show that the law has been inconsequential when it comes to conglomerate acquisitions. Officials are reluctant to apply curbs except where mergers clearly affect *particular markets*. And conglomerate mergers rarely have direct effects on particular markets.

Challenges to **product-extension** and **market-extension** conglomerates are usually based on arguments of *potential competition*. Absent its acquisition of the leading bleach company, for instance, a major detergent manufacturer might have entered the bleach market by itself through internal expansion *(de novo)*, or by "toehold" acquisition of a small bleach producer, thereby increasing the number of competitors in the bleach market or lessening concentration. Even in the absence of any intended *de novo* entry or toehold acquisition, potential competition might still be worth preserving. The *Proctor & Gamble* case reviewed here gives an example.

Pure conglomerates are less likely to affect specific markets. If the merging parties are truly dominant firms (IBM and GM, say), they might be vulnerable. But these instances are so rare as to leave pure conglomerates essentially untouchable.

1. The *Proctor & Gamble* Case (1967).[61] Proctor & Gamble's 1958 acquisition of Clorox Chemical Co. could be considered a product-extension merger. Among other things, Proctor was the dominant producer of soaps and detergents, accounting for 54.4% of all packaged detergent sales. Clorox, on the other hand, was the nation's leading manufacturer of household liquid bleach, with approximately 48.8% of total sales at the time. As these statistics suggest, the markets for detergents and bleach were both highly concentrated. The Supreme Court decided that the merger was illegal, but not wholly or even mainly because of these market shares.

Anticompetitive effects were found in several respects. First, Proctor was a prime prospective entrant into the bleach industry. Thus, "the merger would seriously diminish potential competition by eliminating Proctor as a potential entrant." Indeed, prior to the acquisition, "Proctor was in the course of diversifying into product lines related to its basic detergent-soap-cleanser business," and liquid bleach was a distinct possibility because it is used with detergent.

Second, the Court expressed concern that the merger would confer anticompetitive advantages in the realm of marketing. Although all liquid bleach is chemically identical (5.25% sodium hypochlorite and 94.75% water), it is nevertheless highly differentiated. Clorox spent more

---

[61] *Federal Trade Commission* v. *Proctor & Gamble Co.*, 386 U.S. 568 (1967).

than 12% of its sales revenues on advertising, and priced its bleach at a premium relative to unadvertised brands. For its part, Proctor was the nation's leading advertiser.

The Court therefore felt that Proctor would unduly strengthen Clorox against other firms in the bleach market by extending to Clorox the same volume discounts on advertising that it received from the advertising media. Moreover, "retailers might be induced to give Clorox preferred shelf space since it would be manufactured by Proctor, which also produced a number of other products marketed by retailers." In sum, "the substitution of the powerful acquiring firm for the smaller, but already dominant, firm may substantially reduce the competitive structure of the industry by raising entry barriers and dissuading the smaller firms from aggressively competing."

2. The *ITT-Grinnel* Case (1970).[62]   This case is of interest because the Justice Department tried to argue that a finding of specific anticompetitive effect in specific product and geographic markets was *not* required for illegality. It argued instead that, in the wake of a "trend among large diversified industrial firms to acquire other large corporations," it could be concluded that "anticompetitive consequences will appear in numerous though *undesignated* individual 'lines of commerce.'"

The merger at issue was ITT's acquisition of Grinnell, a very large manufacturer of automatic sprinkler devices and related products. Since ITT had been a major participant in the conglomerate merger mania, and since Grinnell was big, this was as good a case as any to test the theory that adding to *aggregate concentration* alone was offensive under the law. But the district court did not agree, and the Justice Department lost:

> The Court's short answer to this claim . . . is that the legislative history, the statute itself and the controlling decisional law all make it clear beyond a peradventure of a doubt that in a Section 7 case the alleged anticompetitive effects of a merger must be examined in the context of *specific product and geographic markets;* and the determination of such markets is a necessary predicate to a determination of whether there has been a substantial lessening of competition within an area of effective competition.

The district court opinion was not reviewed by the Supreme Court because the case was settled by consent decree prior to appeal.[63] Thus, we have bumped into the outer limit of the law. As this limit is limited, conglomerate mergers proceed apace.

The guidelines for conglomerates reflect this. They merely suggest possible challenges where main potential entrants are eliminated.

---

[62] *United States* v. *International Telephone and Telegraph Corp.,* 324 F. Supp. 19 (D. Conn. 1970).

[63] For a similar district court opinion see *United States* v. *Northwest Industries,* 301 F. Supp. 1066 (N.D.Ill. 1969) at 1096.

VII. REMEDIES AND NOTIFICATION

Judicial statements of legality tell only part of the story. *Remedies* are equally important. For if illegal mergers are allowed to stand, they might as well be declared legal. The record on this score is blemished because total divestiture to achieve premerger status is not always achieved. The data for 1951–1977 prove the point:

> Total divestiture was accomplished in 53 per cent of the completed cases brought by the antitrust agencies. The assets divested represented only 44 per cent of the total assets challenged in all complaints. On the other hand, no divestiture was achieved in 7 per cent of the completed cases . . . The remaining cases either were dismissed (13 per cent) or achieved only partial divestiture (27 per cent).[64]

One of the main reasons divestiture is reluctantly imposed is that it is difficult to unscramble the eggs once they are scrambled.[65] Less scrambling occurs when the antitrust agencies are given advance notice of mergers, for then preliminary injunctions can often be obtained preventing the merger's consummation until after completion of legal review. This, in fact, was the purpose of the premerger notification provisions of the Hart-Scott-Rodino Act of 1976. Specifically, the Antitrust Division of the Department of Justice and the Federal Trade Commission must receive thirty days notice of acquisitions where one of the parties to the transaction has sales or assets of $100 million or more and the other party has sales or assets of $10 million or more.[66]

SUMMARY

History reveals an annual stream of mergers that occasionally swells to a flood. Around the turn of the century thousands of multifirm horizontal mergers transformed many manufacturing and mining industries into tight-knit oligopolies and near monopolies. A second major movement during the late 1920s brought further horizontal couplings and introduced extensive vertical and conglomerate activity as well. During the 1960s, 25,598 mergers were recorded, involving scores of billions of dollars in assets. Most recently, the 1980s have witnessed what appears to be the most frenzied merger movement of all time.

---

[64] Willard Mueller, *The Celler-Kefauver Act, op. cit.,* p. 89. This excludes banking cases.

[65] For further discussion, see Kenneth G. Elzinga, "The Antimerger Law: Pyrrhic Victories?" *Journal of Law and Economics* (April 1969), pp. 43–78.

[66] Actually, the rules are much more complex than this. See T. W. Brunner, T. G. Krattenmaker, R. A. Skitol, and A. A. Webster, *Mergers in the New Antitrust Era* (Washington, D.C.: Bureau of National Affairs, 1985), pp. 151–170.

Generally speaking, merger frequency tends to rise and fall as the average level of stock market prices rises and falls. Thus, the timing of mergers is influenced by financial considerations. In addition, there are several basic underlying stimulants to merger, all of which have played some role in the past, none of which has clearly dominated the scene: (1) Some economists defend mergers with claims of efficiency or economies of scale. Their most sweeping assertions postulate a market for corporate control in which good managements oust bad managements through takeovers. Such claims may occasionally be valid, but the available evidence indicates rather clearly that, in general, takeovers do not yield efficiencies. (2) Managements may have their firms acquire others for defensive reasons, because acquisitions can have the effect of protecting the acquirer from acquisition or moving the acquirer out of slowly growing industries into more lively ones. (3) A desire to diversify for purposes of risk reduction may motivate many conglomerate mergers. Although some mergers may further this goal, most do not. (4) We cannot rule out growth and personal aggrandizement as significant merger motives, although these factors are difficult to quantify. (5) The pursuit of market power is most clearly associated with horizontal mergers. Examples span the twentieth century, from U.S. Steel in 1901 to many of the airline mergers of the 1980s.

As for policy, these recent surges have been possible chiefly because conglomerate mergers are almost untouchable under current law. The competitive effects of conglomerates elude structural measurement even when they are adverse, and the law bans only those mergers that may "substantially lessen competition" in some product and geographic market. Application of this standard led to a hard line against horizontal mergers during the 1960s, as illustrated by the *Brown* and *Von's* cases. *General Dynamics* relaxed matters in the 1970s. The most recent interpretations grant further relaxation. Official guidelines indicate the pattern. They (1) allow horizontal mergers when the H index is in the 1000–1800 range and thwart them only above 1800, (2) flexibly allow for other factors like barriers to entry, (3) define the market somewhat differently than before, and (4) permit otherwise illegal mergers in the event of substantial efficiencies. This last leniency has been especially controversial because of its possible burdens for consumers.[67]

Vertical merger policy has taken a similar course. Tight at first, it too has been relaxed.

---

[67] The Reagan administration's leniency in this respect may be seen by its approval of many big airline mergers of the 1980s, which, as we have seen, were anticompetitive. According to Justice Department and Transportation Department officials in 1986, the mergers "generally benefit consumers because carriers are able to pool resources, operate more efficiently and therefore offer lower fares." (*The Wall Street Journal*, May 21, 1986, p. 6.). In fact, the mergers led to higher fares.

APPENDIX: WHY TAKEOVER PREMIUMS ARE PAID WITHOUT NECESSARILY REFLECTING EFFICIENCIES[68]

The underlying methodology of the [stock market] event studies [and those who see merger efficiencies in them] assumes that demand curves for stocks are horizontal, so that normally trading investors may buy or sell any amount of stock without systematically affecting the price. The marginal price reflects average opinion; when sharp movements in price occur in association with an event (for example, a takeover), they are then interpreted as a response to the 'new information' imparted by it. Positive abnormal returns associated with bids may therefore be interpreted to suggest that the market expects improved performance to follow from merger and shareholders benefit accordingly. The distribution of these gains between the acquired and acquiring is then determined by the competitiveness of the bid market, the presence or absence of rival bids or contests, and so on.

If, however, there are, for instance, divergences of expectations and opinion over security values so that the marginal trading valuation reflects marginal opinion, then the market demand curve slopes downwards to the right and some investors will require a price above that at the margin before selling. . . . Premiums will therefore be necessary simply to effect the ownership transfer in a takeover, and they may vary with the dispersion of stockholdings and the dispersion of divergent opinion across the various blocks of shares. These premiums will therefore be highly ambiguous guides to expected efficiency gains either when taken on average or in relation to particular mergers. They tell us merely what the short-term windfall wealth effects of merger are, relative to a particular counterfactual for the small number of individuals directly involved as shareholders (or the larger number indirectly involved via changes in pensions and insurance policy premiums following financial institutions' portfolio responses to bids). There is no necessary connection between the direction and magnitude of these premiums and underlying real changes in the management and performance of the assets over which the property right embodied in the stock give control. All we can deduce is that for *some* reasons the bidders felt it worth while to offer the premiums and the sellers felt it worth while to accept. These reasons, as we saw earlier, may be as much related to the pursuit of monopoly power and empire-building as to enhanced management techniques, scale and scope economies, or other efficiency enhancing targets.

---

[68] From Alan Hughes, "The Impact of Merger: A Survey of Empirical Evidence from the UK," in *Mergers & Merger Policy*, edited by J. A. Fairburn and J. A. Kay (Oxford: Oxford University Press, 1989), pp. 94–95.

9

Barriers to Entry: Theory and Cross-section Evidence

An oligopolistic industry may not be oligopolistic for long if every Tom, Dick, and Harry can enter.
— EDWIN MANSFIELD

Eastman Kodak Company entered the $2.5 billion-a-year consumer-battery market in 1986. Attracted by the market's huge 50% profit margins, Kodak offered gold-tipped batteries, hopeful that a golden image would be golden for its bottom line. But entry was not easy. Kodak's challenge charged up the industry's dominant leaders, Duracell and Eveready, which together had over 80% of the market. Duracell aired TV commercials claiming that a toy bird powered by its products outchirped a Kodak-powered bird by 20%. Eveready answered with Jacko, a tough Australian football player. Both incumbents also put pressure on Kodak with price discounts. A key point of contention was shelf space, as retailers satisfied with Duracell and Eveready were not eager to stock another brand despite Kodak's familiar name. Duracell and Eveready were *the* brand names in batteries, and consumers couldn't easily determine which batteries actually performed best. Hence Kodak had little to show for its efforts after four years of trying.[1]

Entry is merely a shorthand way of saying that a firm *new to the market* has begun to offer a product or service that is a close *substitute* for the products or services of firms already in the market. The newcomer may be established in another market and may merely imitate the sellers already in the market entered. On the other hand, the newcomer could be a spanking new firm and might do more than merely ape existing sellers. It might offer buyers something special.

Of course entry does not occur at the drop of a hat. Attempted entry costs money, and there is no assurance that an attempt will prosper. Entry hinges on two conditions — motivation and ability. For **motivation**, the prospects of eventually earning a substantial profit must be good. In **ability**, the potential entrant must be capable of making the attempt. Any factor that reduces the motivation or ability of potential entrants despite established firms' excessively high profits may be called a **barrier to entry**. It is the purpose of this chapter to identify, explain, and measure various barriers to entry.

We are interested in barriers to entry for the same reason we were interested in product differentiation and concentration: they are a major source of market power. The concept of barriers is thus useful in explaining conduct and performance. It also helps to explain variances in observed concentration, because high barriers tend to be associated with high concentration. The concept is useful, moreover, in assessing public policy, for not all barriers are "naturally" or technologically determined. Some are artificial and due to human manipulation.

We begin by reviewing patterns of firm entry and exit in U.S. manufacturing. We follow this by identifying and classifying various structural barriers. We then review some evidence concerning their prevalence. Finally, we take a penetrating look at each main barrier.

I. PATTERNS OF ENTRY AND EXIT

How many firms enter a typical manufacturing industry during an interval of four or five years? What is the market share of these newcomers? Do firms leave industries as newcomers enter? If so, what are the numbers and market shares of those leaving?

Timothy Dunne, Mark Roberts, and Larry Samuelson recently completed a massive study of entry, growth, and exit in four-digit U.S. manufacturing industries during the Census intervals of four or five years

[1] Clare Ansberry, "Battery Makers See Surge in Competition," *The Wall Street Journal*, November 30, 1987, p. 8; and *The Wall Street Journal*, April 10, 1990, pp. B1, B5.

over the period 1963–1982.[2] Their results are interesting. They find that industries are somewhat like human bodies, in which new cells are coming alive and old cells are dying off all the time. Each industry experiences a flow of new firm entries during each four-year census interval, enough of an influx that, on average, by the end of each interval approximately 39% of the firms operating in a typical four-digit industry were not producing in that industry four years earlier. This is impressive. But the newcomers were much less important than the 39% figure suggests. Although entrants accounted for 39% of the firms in each Census year, these newcomers accounted for less than 16% of each industry's output, on average, because they were typically much smaller than the established firms in the industry. Moreover, most of these newcomers did not last long. On average, 80% of all entrants end up exiting their industry within 10 years. For example, the market share of those firms entering during the 1963–1967 interval fell from 14% in 1967 to only 5% in 1982.

Thus **exit** is as much a part of commercial life as entry. And the averages for exit are surprisingly similar to those for entry. Dunne, Roberts, and Samuelson found that, during four-year Census intervals, an average of 35% of a typical industry's firms depart. This 35% departure rate overstates exits' impact, however, because exiting firms tend to be much smaller than those remaining. Measuring exit rates by market shares reveals that departing firms accounted for only about 16% of industry output on average. And as just suggested, the exiters are comprised of a substantial number of recent entrants.

These average statistics imply there is a considerable amount of turnover among firms in a typical industry. But a key qualification softens this impression: Most of the turnover occurs on the *fringes* of industries rather than at their centers, because the turnover mainly involves smaller firms rather than larger firms. Entrants have relatively little long-run impact because of their small average size, high failure rates, and their overall decline in market share. Thus, *in industries where entry is high, exit likewise tends to be high.*

This correspondence between entry and exit is seen in Table 9–1. The market shares of entering firms and exiting firms are reported for the industries with highest entry rates and lowest entry rates. Notice from the last column that those with high entry rates also have high exit rates, and those with low entry rates also have low exit rates. The simple correlation between the average market share of entrants and the average market share of exiters in 20 industry sectors, including those of Table 9–1, is .92.

2 Timothy Dunne, Mark J. Roberts, and Larry Samuelson, "Patterns of Firm Entry and Exit in U.S. Manufacturing Industries," *Rand Journal of Economics* (Winter 1988), pp. 495–515.

TABLE 9–1. Entry and Exit Variables for Four-Digit
Industries Clustered in Selected Two-Digit Sectors,
Census Data 1963–1982

Two-Digit Sector	Market Share Accounted for by	
	Entering Firms	Exiting Firms
High-Entry Group		
Lumber	.264	.264
Apparel	.262	.291
Furniture	.239	.241
Printing	.228	.243
Low-Entry Group		
Tobacco	.021	.032
Chemicals	.086	.081
Electrical Machinery	.095	.119
Food Processing	.098	.123

Source: Timothy Dunne, Mark J. Roberts, and Larry Samuelson, "Patterns of Firm Entry and Exit in U.S. Manufacturing Industries," *Rand Journal of Economics* (Winter 1988), p. 506.

Three observations emerge from this analysis. First, successful, sustained entry of significance to an industry's competitive condition is often difficult, more difficult than it might seem from a quick glance at aggregate statistics on entrants.

Second, "mobility barriers" may be more important than "entry barriers" for many industries. **Mobility barriers** are much like entry barriers, but they make it difficult for firms to move from one strategic group to another, or from one market segment to another, within a given industry. Hence merely getting into an industry to serve some peripheral niche may be relatively easy. Producing a draft beer in a brew pub, for example, would easily qualify as entry into the beer industry. But at the same time there could be considerable mobility barriers preventing a firm from moving into the central core of an industry. Once established in the beer industry, for example, a small brew pub would find it extremely difficult to become a national producer of a full line of bottled beers in direct competition with Anheuser-Busch and Miller. There are thus mobility barriers in the beer industry.[3]

Third, the strong positive correlation between entry and exit may be explained in two ways—"displacements effects" and "common causes." *Displacement effects* occur when because of low costs or some other ad-

[3] Richard E. Caves and Michael E. Porter, "From Entry Barriers to Mobility Barriers," *Quarterly Journal of Economics* (May 1977), pp. 241–261.

vantage entering firms push out incumbents, thereby fostering exits in association with their entry. A high frequency of entry will therefore cause a high degree of exit to the extent such displacement occurs. On the other hand, *barriers to exit* may prevent displacement and thereby prevent entry. (If a fat fellow in a telephone booth cannot exit the booth because he is stuck by his obesity, then you cannot enter the booth. Turnover cannot occur because you cannot displace the booth's occupant.) Thus an exit barrier becomes an entry barrier when displacement is denied, and low frequencies of exit and entry then correspond. Overall, the highs and lows of the displacement effect seem to account for most of the correlation between entry and exit across industries.[4]

Apart from the displacement effect, in which entry causes exit and a barrier to exit is itself a barrier to entry, there may be an association between entry and exit because the factors that cause one also cause the other. Call these *common causes*. (If the door to a telephone booth jams shut regularly, with or without people inside, then this malfunction will constitute a barrier to *both* entry and exit.) A key element in this regard, one that will be referred to in following sections, is "sunk costs." An entrant invests by purchasing trucks, building a factory, advertising its product, training workers, and so on, in order to enter a market. These expenditures are *sunk costs* insofar as they cannot be recovered, or salvaged, in the event of exit. For example, if Kodak spent $10 million advertising its new batteries and then withdrew from the market after two years because its sales went dead, Kodak could not recover the $10 million. That would consequently be a sunk cost. If Kodak had also purchased some general-purpose trucks for its new battery business, it could easily sell the trucks to a trucking company or use them in its photo supply operations if need be. Kodak could therefore recover most of its investment in the trucks in the event of failure, and to that extent these costs would *not* be sunk.

Sunk costs *create barriers to entry* because they increase the riskiness of entry. That is, they cause the losses of unsuccessful entry to be much larger than they would be otherwise (everything else being equal). Sunk costs create *barriers to exit* once the firm has actually entered because the committed assets represent nonrecoverable costs that hinder divestment. If, for example, Kodak's battery factory had no other value except as a battery factory for Kodak (i.e., it was entirely "sunk"), then Kodak would tend to keep it running in battery production because it would be otherwise worthless (to Kodak or anyone else). Hence, one may reasonably expect a high correlation between entry and exit across industries for this reason as well.[5] Sunk costs could be a "common cause" explana-

4 Daniel Shapiro and R. S. Khemani "The Determinants of Entry and Exit Reconsidered,"*International Journal of Industrial Organization* (March 1987), pp. 15–26.

5 R. E. Caves and M. E. Porter, "Barriers to Exit," in *Essays on Industrial Organization*, edited by R. T. Masson and P. D. Qualls (Cambridge, Mass.: Ballinger, 1976), Chapter 3.

tion for the high correlation between entry and exit in addition to the "displacement effect."

In the course of explaining the entry-exit correlation we have thus identified two general barriers to entry—barriers to exit and sunk costs. Next we explore other more specific entry barriers. Sunk costs, for instance, are a problem only because they heighten the loss *if* entry fails. We next consider several reasons *why* entry might fail.

II. AN OVERVIEW OF BARRIERS TO ENTRY

Joe Bain, an early pioneer in research on entry barriers defined a **barrier to entry** as anything conferring advantages on "established sellers in an industry over potential entrant sellers, these advantages being reflected in the extent to which established sellers can persistently raise their prices above a competitive level without attracting new firms to enter the industry."[6] When entry is easy, the advantages of established sellers are slight. When entry is difficult, the advantages of established sellers are great, and barriers may balloon to gargantuan proportions. Following Bain, structural or "technical" barriers may be classified into four broad groups: (1) absolute unit cost differences, (2) economies of scale, (3) capital cost requirements, and (4) product differentiation.[7] (Later, we also look at behavioral or "strategic" barriers.)

A. Absolute Cost Advantage Barriers

The first category of barriers comprises absolute cost advantages of established firms. If for any given level of output, established firms can produce and market their wares at a lower cost per unit than newcomers, then any newcomer takes on the established firms with both hands tied behind its back. Take a look at Figure 9–1. Assuming unit costs go neither up nor down as a function of output, average total costs (ATC) for the entrant are indicated by the uppermost horizontal line of Figure 9–1. The lower ATC line of a typical established firm shows cost advantages at every level of output. If the potential entrant expects his demand curve to be as depicted by the solid, negatively sloped line, then there is *no* level of output where he can cover his costs with revenues. The prospect's ATC lies above his expected demand at every point. If, on the other hand, the entrant's expected demand curve were more generously located, as suggested by the dashed demand line, or if the entrant's unit costs were lower, then entry would appear profitable.

---

[6] Joe S. Bain, *Barriers to New Competition* (Cambridge, Mass.: Harvard University Press, 1956) p. 3.
[7] Ibid, pp. 15–16.

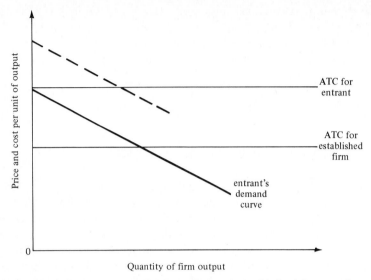

FIGURE 9–1. Absolute cost differences between established firms and potential entrants.

What is likely to raise the potential entrant's unit costs above those of established firms? The entrant may have to pay more for scarce raw materials, ship them greater distances, use inferior production technologies, or pay higher interest rates on borrowed capital.

B. Barriers Owing to Economies of Scale

Scalar economies constitute the second class of barriers. In these instances the unit cost curves confronting potential entrants and established firms are quite similar in elevation and shape. But the *shape* of the curve itself gives established firms an advantage. Figure 9–2 shows the derivation of a long-run unit cost curve for a single plant (or a single-plant firm) that reflects economies of scale. The long-run unit cost curve is best thought of as a *hypothetical* construct that carries real consequences. The potential entrant's engineers could design various possible plants of *identical* output capacity that used *different* production technologies. The resulting short-run unit cost curves might be depicted in Figure 9–2 as A, B, and C for output Q_1.

Of course it is also possible to hypothesize plants of *differing* output capacity but *identical* technological style. The resulting short-run cost curves in this case could be those labeled H, J, and C in Figure 9–2. The short-run cost curves of other plants may look like fish scales, but they illustrate the diversity of conceivable designs and capacities. Although the possibilities thus seem rich, only the *lowest*-cost plant would be chosen for any given level of projected output. For output Q_1 the choice is

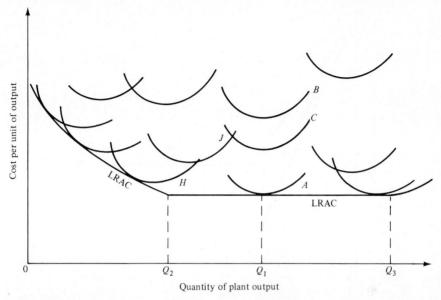

Cost per unit of output

$LRAC$

B

C

J

H

A

LRAC

0

Q_2 Q_1 Q_3

Quantity of plant output

FIGURE 9–2. Derivation of a long-run average cost (LRAC) curve with economies of scale.

A, for example. Hence, the lower boundary, or "envelope" curve, depicts the long-run average cost curve confronting potential entrants. The curve declines up to output Q_2 because added size brings added efficiency. Beyond Q_2, size confers no additional advantages. Hence Q_2 is often called the **minimum efficient scale (MES).** Beyond Q_3 it is assumed that added size yields *dis*economies, as indicated by a rise in LRAC.

How do scalar economies inhibit entry? The answer is not self-evident. We have already said that given enough money anyone—entrants and established firms alike—could easily build an MES plant. The problem is that existing firms will have *already* built efficient plants. And the added output of an entrant's efficient plant may be so large relative to industry demand that, after entry, product price will fall below the entrant's cost per unit. In other words, there may not be room in the industry for an additional seller when efficient output is large relative to existing output and demand.

For example, assume that DD' is industry demand in Figure 9–3. Assume further that LRAC is the long-run average cost confronting any firm. With two existing firms sharing total industry demand equally, each firm would view its demand as d_2, which is one half of DD' at each possible price. Since d_2 lies above LRAC over a considerable range, each of the two firms could produce and sell at a profit. However, a potential entrant would not have such a favorable view of the situation. If it is assumed that demand would be split evenly three ways in the event of

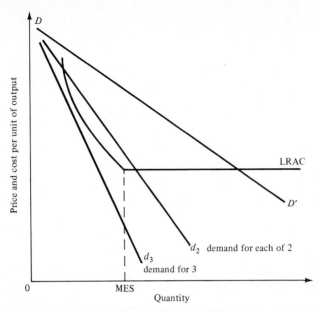

FIGURE 9–3. Economies of scale acting as a barrier to the entry of a third firm.

a third firm's entry (a very optimistic assumption for a new entrant to make), each firm's demand would then become d_3, which is one third of DD' at each possible price. But given d_3, there is *no* plant scale that yields a profit to the entrant. There is no point at which LRAC falls below d_3. The result: no third firm entry.

A shift left of LRAC, and a consequentially lower level of MES output, would permit entry. But, as it stands, Figure 9–3 looks more like a bear pit than a welcome mat to third-party prospects. Note, too, that a substantial shift outward to the right of the DD' line would make room for new entrants. Hence it is cost *relative* to demand that really counts.

Economies of scale may be of two types — pecuniary economies and technical economies. The former are merely monetary savings on the purchase of inputs derived from the greater bargaining power that often goes with greater size. Quantity and volume discounts are of this type. On the other hand, technical economies constitute "real" savings in the sense that fewer of society's scarce resources are used in the production-distribution process.

C. Capital Cost Barriers

We are now in a position to appreciate capital cost barriers to entry. Minimum efficient scale, MES as defined, will in part determine the total capital outlay required for efficient entry. Generally speaking, a large

MES necessitates a large capital cost outlay. However, since the prices of equipment and construction materials also enter the picture, MES does not always determine the cost. In any event, if the capital costs of efficient entry are appreciably more than what you and your friends can scrape together from your savings, say, $1 billion, then capital costs pose a barrier to entry.

This barrier might be classified with the other absolute cost barriers mentioned earlier, since its effect often shows up in higher costs of borrowing, namely, higher interest rates. On the other hand, there are several features of this barrier that distinguish it. For one thing, it is closely connected to scalar elements, whereas other absolute unit cost differences are not. Second, the deterrence of this barrier depends on the nature of the potential entrant as well as the nature of the industry. If the prime potential entrant is already large—a General Motors, say, or an Exxon—then even enormous capital costs pose no problem.

D. Barriers Caused by Product Differentiation

Finally, product differentiation may present a barrier to entry. A newcomer to some industry may face none of the preceding problems but nevertheless find the going tough if the industry has a highly differentiated product. Successful entry would then depend on more than passing tests in production. It would also require mastery of *marketing* problems, for the newcomer would then have to woo customers away from established firms with more than just satisfactory prices. (Remember Kodak batteries?) Marketing a differentiated product entails substantial costs—costs of advertising, packaging, style, and so on. And these marketing costs may pose problems for an entrant if they have characteristics similar to those displayed by production cost. That is, there may be absolute unit cost disadvantages, economies of scale, or high initial capital costs associated with a newcomer's differentiation effort.

Two barriers that are very similar to product differentiation (though not explored by Bain), are customer switching costs and poor access to distribution channels. *Customer switching costs* are one-time costs buyers must bear when they switch from one supplier to another (from an incumbent to an entrant, in particular). For business buyers there might be employee retraining costs, the cost of complementary equipment, and the costs of removing the old and installing the new. For example, switching from an IBM computer system to that of a new rival may cause the buyer to incur added costs for new software and employee retraining. There is *limited access to distribution channels* when normal distribution channels for a product are already filled by the established firms in the market. Kodak, for example, had some trouble securing shelf space for its new batteries because many retailers were not willing to stock a third brand of batteries in addition to Duracell and Eveready.

E. Other Barriers to Entry and a Qualification

Each of the barriers presented can be considered a structural or "technical" barrier to entry. Various behavioral or "strategic" barriers should also be acknowledged. *Behavioral barriers* are those purposely erected by incumbents to reduce the possibility of entry. Established firms, for example, may vigorously escalate their advertising outlays when an entrant appears on the horizon. Used thus, advertising poses a problem for the entrant above and beyond any advertising economies of scale or other effects just mentioned. Other behavioral possibilities include collective boycotts, collective aggregated rebates, exclusive dealing, and predatory pricing. However, these behavioral barriers will be taken up later.[8]

In addition, there are various legal barriers to entry. In the extreme, these take the form of licensing, chartering, and franchising regulations administered by local, state, or federal government authorities. Patents also constitute a legal barrier. Discussion of these legal barriers is also postponed, for they fit best in a broad review of regulation and patent policy.

Finally, dynamic factors that make entry easier instead of harder should be mentioned. Rapid growth is certainly the most important of these favorable factors, especially if such growth is associated with the early stages of an industry's life cycle, as in semiconductors the last two decades. Rapid growth tends to soften absolute cost disadvantages, counter scale economies, attract capital, and dissolve differentiation barriers.[9]

III. EVIDENCE ON THE RELATIVE IMPORTANCE OF BARRIERS IN MANUFACTURING

Before we zero in on some of these barriers and their measurements, it may be helpful to review research on the question of which barriers prove to be the most formidable. The trail blazer on this issue was again Bain, who by means of questionnaire surveys and other techniques assessed the prevalence of the four broad types of barriers previously out-

---

[8] For evidence distinguishing technical and behavioral barriers, see J. D. Gribbon and M. A. Utton, "The Treatment of Dominant Firms in the UK Competition Legislation," in *Mainstreams in Industrial Organization*, edited by H. W. de Jong and W. G. Shepherd (Dordrecht: Martinus Nijhoff, 1986), pp 259–261. Sometimes it is difficult to classify some barriers. For example, the "learning curve" could be a technical or strategic barrier. David R. Ross, "Learning to Dominate," *Journal of Industrial Economics* (June 1986), pp. 337–350.

[9] E. Ralph Biggadike, *Corporate Diversification: Entry, Strategy, and Performance* (Cambridge, Mass.: Harvard University Press, 1979); D. W. Webbink, "Entry, Price-Cost Margins and Barriers to Entry in 280 4-Digit Industries, 1967–1972," FTC Working Paper No. 19, 1979.

lined among 20 major U.S. manufacturing industries during the late 1940s and early 1950s. Bain concluded from his survey that product differentiation was most important, gaining a "very high" barrier rating in five of his sampled industries and a "substantial" rating in eight. Coming a close second was the capital cost requirements barrier, which he rated as "very high" in five industries and "substantial" in five more. Economies of scale were judged to be "very high" barriers in three industries and "substantial" in seven. Finally, absolute cost barriers seemed to be rather inconsequential except in three industries with close connections to mining — steel, copper, and gypsum.[10]

The most recent survey of business opinion was conducted by Karakaya and Stahl.[11] They obtained questionnaire responses from 137 executives in 49 major U.S. corporations. These executives were asked to assess entry opportunities in 32 hypothetical market situations. From their assessments it was possible to score various entry barriers according to the percentage of polled executives who thought they were important. Table 9-2 reports the results for the six barriers in the questionnaire:

1. Cost advantages of incumbents, including in this category absolute production costs as well as economies of scale.
2. Capital requirements associated with entry investment (if particularly large).
3. Product differentiation of incumbents due to brand allegiances.
4. Customer switching costs.
5. Limited access to distribution channels.
6. Government policy, such as licensing requirements or regulations.

The cost advantages of incumbents outrank product differentiation in importance in Table 9-2, so these results differ from Bain's. Governmental barriers rank last, especially for consumer good markets as compared to industrial goods markets. Note finally that product differentiation is a more important barrier for consumer goods than for industrial goods as one would expect.[12]

Econometrics offers another approach to detecting entry barriers. Observed variations in actual entry across industries can be matched with variations in measures of minimum efficient scale, product differentiation, and other variables that might affect entry to determine statistical significance. Table 9-3 summarizes seven such studies for the United

---

[10] Bain, *Barriers to New Competition*, Chapter 6

[11] Fahri Karakaya and Michael J. Stahl, "Barriers to Entry and Market Entry Decisions in Consumer and Industrial Goods Markets," *Journal of Marketing* (April 1989), pp. 80–91.

[12] Interestingly, a questionnaire survey of executives in Japan yielded results closer to those of Bain, with product differentiation ranking highest among barriers. See Richard E. Caves and Masu Uekusa, *Industrial Organization in Japan* (Washington, D.C.: Brookings Institution, 1976), p. 35.

TABLE 9–2. Percentage of Corporate Executive Respondents Who Considered Market Entry Barriers Important

Entry Barrier	Consumer Markets (%)	Industrial Markets (%)
1. Cost advantages of incumbents	83	83
2. Capital requirements	78	76
3. Product differentiation	70	62
4. Customer switching cost	70	69
5. Limited distribution	56	55
6. Government policy	45	55

Source: F. Karakaya and M. J. Stahl, "Barriers to Entry and Market Entry Decisions in Consumer and Industrial Goods Markets," *Journal of Marketing* (April 1989), p. 85. It should be noted that Karakaya and Stahl distinguish between early entry (e.g., first movers) and late entry. These are the results for late entry.

States, Canada, and West Germany. A "+" indicates the variable had a positive association with entry rates. A "−" shows an inverse association, such that high levels of the explanatory variable would be associated with low levels of entry. The "0" signifies no significance either way. And "NI" indicates the variable was not included in the study. Unfortunately, no study tested for absolute production costs because data for that variable do not exist. Still, the results for the rest of the factors we have reviewed support expectations. In general, entry rates tend to be low in industries with large economies of scale, high capital requirements, and strong product differentiation (usually measured by advertising as a percentage of sales). Other variables showing negative influences (but not discussed earlier) include rapid technological change (perhaps because of high risks and patents), high market concentration (which increases the likelihood of strategic barriers), and multiplant presence (which could measure the presence of economies of scale at firm level instead of plant level).[13] Finally, two positive inducements to entry show up strongly in these studies. Entry is positively associated with rapid market growth and incumbent firm profitability.

For our own detailed study of barriers we shall adopt Bain's four broad classifications — absolute costs, economies of scale, capital costs, and product differentiation. Each is treated in turn.

[13] The negative impact of concentration and its interpretation as a proxy for strategic barriers receive further support from Gribbon and Utton, "The Treatment of Dominant Firms in the UK Competition Legislation"; and Ronald W. Cotterill and Lawrence Haller, "Entry Patterns and Strategic Interaction in Food Retailing," in *Issues after a Century of Federal Competition Policy*, edited by R. L. Wills, J. A. Caswell, and J. D. Culbertson, (Lexington, Mass.: Lexington Books, 1987) pp. 203–222.

TABLE 9–3. Summary of Econometric Studies Relating Observed Rates of New Entry to Measures of Entry Barriers and Other Variables

	Authors of Major Studies						
Variable	Orr	Duetsch	Chappell et al.	Shapiro/ Khemani	Schwalbach	Yu	Austin/ Rosenbaum
Economies of Scale (MES)	NI	0	+	−	−	NI	0
Capital requirements	−	−	−	−	NI	NI	−
Product differentiation	−	0	−	−	−	−	−
Technological change	−	NI	NI	0	0	−	NI
Market concentration	−	0	−	−	NI	−	NI
Multiplant dominance	NI	−	−	−	NI	NI	NI
Growth in sales	+	+	+	+	+	+	+
Past profit rates	0	+	+	+	+	NI	+

+ = Positive association with entry rates.
− = Inverse association with entry rates.
0 = No significance either way.
NI = Not included.

Sources: Dale Orr, "The Determinants of Entry: A Study of the Canadian Manufacturing Industries, "*Review of Economics and Statistics* (February 1974), pp. 58–66; Larry L. Duetsch, "Entry and the Extent of Multiplant Operation," *Journal of Industrial Economics* (June 1984), pp. 477–487; William F. Chappell, Mwangi S. Kimenyi, and Walter J. Mayer, "A Poisson Probability Model of Entry and Market Structure," *Southern Economic Journal* (April 1990), pp. 918–927; Daniel Shapiro and R. S. Khemani, "The Determinants of Entry and Exit Reconsidered," *International Journal of Industrial Organization* (March 1987), pp. 15–26; Joachim Schwalbach, "Entry by Diversified Firms into German Industries," *International Journal of Industrial Organization* (March 1987), pp. 43–49; Shirley S. Yu, "Some Determinants of Entry into Therapeutic Drug Markets," *Review of Industrial Organization,* Vol. 1, no. 4, 1984, pp 260–275; and John S. Austin and David I. Rosenbaum, "The Determinants of Entry and Exit Rates," *Review of Industrial Organization* (Summer 1990), pp. 211–223.

IV. ABSOLUTE COST DIFFERENCES

Of all the major barriers, absolute cost differences seem to be the easiest to conceptualize but the hardest to measure systematically across industries. The sources of such differences are diverse and often subtle. The best evidence available tends to be anecdotal and limited to particular industries. Here are a few examples:

1. *Lumber milling.* Established firms owning vast timberlands have an advantage in timber costs over potential entrants. "The original cost of timber to the Weyerhaeuser Company in 1900 was estimated at 10 cents per thousand board feet, whereas the 1959–1962 average out-of-pocket cost of timber purchased from the national forests of the Douglas fir region was about 24 dollars per thousand board feet."[14]

2. *Aluminum.* "The entry barriers which are most relevant to the aluminum industry are high capital requirements, availability of high quality, easily accessible bauxite ore, and access to inexpensive sources of electric power."[15]

3. *Nickel.* International Nickel (Inco) dominated the western world's nickel industry for 75 years through control of the best ore deposits until the 1970s when Inco's share fell from 52% in 1970 to 25% in 1979 because of the entry of new producers relying on new laterite deposits.[16]

V. ECONOMIES OF SCALE

A. Sources of Economies of Scale: Plant

In contrast to absolute cost differences, *plant* economies of scale have been thoroughly studied and systematically measured. As a result there is no question that economies of scale do exist. The following lower unit production costs as scale increases.[17]

- *Specialization of labor.* As the number of workers multiplies with plant size, individual workers specialize their activities, thereby becoming more proficient and productive. As a group they can then produce more with less labor time and labor cost.

- *Specialization of machinery.* Small-scale operations often must rely on multipurpose machinery and equipment that do many different jobs but no job really well. Large-volume operations permit specialization of equipment, as in the case of iron blast furnaces and cement kilns.

---

[14] Walter J. Mead, *Competition and Oligopsony in the Douglas Fir Lumber Industry* (Berkeley: University of California Press, 1966), pp. 113, 222–223.

[15] Council on Wage and Price Stability, *Aluminum Prices 1974–75* (Washington, D.C.; The Council, 1976), p. 27.

[16] Robert D. Cairns, "Changing Structure in the World Nickel Industry," *Antitrust Bulletin* (Fall 1984), pp. 561–575. For an interesting example involving bat guano, bird guano, and cannibus, see "Birds Do It, Bats Do It," *The Wall Street Journal*, July 24, 1984, p. 1.

[17] E. A. G. Robinson, *The Structure of Competitive Industry* (Chicago: University of Chicago Press, 1958).

- *Economies of increased dimensions.* Capital equipment in the form of tanks, vessels, and pipelines generate economies because a doubling of their surface area more than doubles their volume capacity. This is often summarized by the 0.6 rule, which states that, if capacity is multiplied by a factor of x, then capital cost is multiplied by $x^{0.6}$. This rule goes a long way toward explaining the evolution of crude-oil supertankers the size of the Empire State building. On long voyages, delivering a barrel of oil in a tanker of more than 100,000 dead weight tons (dwt) capacity costs only one-fourth as much as delivery in a 25,000 ton tanker.

- *Indivisibilities.* There are many costs independent of scale, or fixed, over certain levels of output. When translated into per unit costs (dollars fixed/quantity), these fall with added output. Ball bearing production affords an example: "Setting up an automatic screw machine to cut bearing races takes about eight hours. Once ready, the machine produces from 80 to 140 parts per hour. An increase in the total number of parts produced in a batch from, say, 5,000 to 10,000, reduces unit costs by more than 10 percent due to the broader spreading of setup time and skilled labor costs."[18]

*Dis*economies of scale are obviously another possibility. In their case increased size tends to drive unit costs up rather than down. But theory and empirical evidence related to diseconomies at the plant level are not nearly as pervasive as those concerning economies. At the multiplant *firm* level there is some positive probability of stretching management too thin or of encountering some other size-related inefficiency.[19] At the individual plant level, however, the chances are slimmer.

Perhaps the only general source of plant diseconomies is outbound transportation. Plant expansion typically implies higher unit transportation costs because a large plant's output must be shipped farther afield than a small plant's output, everything else being equal. Where transportation costs bulk large relative to product value—as is the case for cement, petroleum, and steel—there is a limit to the geographic area that one plant can serve efficiently.

Of course, the effects of various sources of economies, or the lack thereof, differ from industry to industry. They may lead to a relatively

---

[18] F. M. Scherer, "Economies of Scale and Industrial Concentration," in *Industrial Concentration: The New Learning*, edited by H. Goldschmid, H. M. Mann, and J. F. Weston (Boston: Little, Brown, 1974) p. 33.

[19] Dodging diseconomies is the main motive behind the "division" structure of most large corporations. As a 3M executive recently quipped, "We are keenly aware of the disadvantages of large size. We like to say that our success in recent years amounts to multiplication by division." *The Wall Street Journal*, February 5, 1982, p. 1. For elaboration, see Oliver Williamson, *Markets and Hierarchies: Analysis and Antitrust Implications* (New York: The Free Press, 1975), Chapter 8.

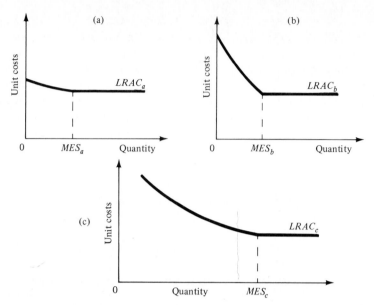

FIGURE 9–4. Alternative configurations of the long-run average cost curve.

small minimum efficient scale, as indicated by MES_a and MES_b in panels (a) and (b) of Figure 9–4. On the other hand, they may lead to a relatively large MES, such as suggested in panel (c) of Figure 9–4. The causes of economies also influence the behavior of costs below MES output. Thus in panels (a) and (b) of Figure 9–4 the two cost curves share the same level of MES. But unit costs of curve (a) rise only slightly at scales less than MES, whereas those of curve (b) rise sharply with diminished scale. By way of example, panel (a) might represent the curve confronting beer wholesalers, panel (b) electrical appliance wholesalers, and panel (c) meat and meat products wholesalers.[20]

B. Estimates of Economies

These estimates for wholesale trades are based on what is called "statistical estimation." Two other widely used techniques are the "survivor" and the "engineering" techniques. Each estimation technique has its advantages and disadvantages.[21] However, the engineering approach

---

[20] Louis P. Bucklin, *Competition and Evolution in the Distributive Trades* (Englewood Cliffs, N.J.: Prentice-Hall, 1972) pp. 253–255.

[21] A. A. Walters, "Production and Cost Functions: An Econometric Survey," *Econometrica* (January/April 1963), pp. 39–52; William G. Shepherd, "What Does the Survivor Technique Show About Economies of Scale?" *Southern Economic Journal* (July 1967), pp. 113–122.

seems to be regarded by most economists as the most reliable, especially for comprehensive multi-industry comparative studies. By this approach industrial engineers, planning experts, and other industry "insiders" actually responsible for making plant-size decisions are canvassed and questioned about how costs vary with scale and what factors generate economies or diseconomies. The work involved in any large study of this kind is immense, and for many years Joe Bain was the only researcher to undertake the task. Now his efforts have been supplemented by the work of three scholars—F. M. Scherer, C. F. Pratton, and L. W. Weiss.

Taken together, their studies contain estimates of plant economies of scale for 33 industries as of the late 1960s and early 1970s. The results for 23 of these industries are summarized in columns (1) and (2) of Table 9–4. Some industries were studied by more than one· of these researchers: in such cases the numbers reported in Table 9–4 are average or consensus figures.

To simplify interindustry comparison, the estimated MES of each industry in column (1) is expressed as a percentage of total U. S. output in 1967. In addition, the industries are arrayed from highest MES to lowest. At one extreme, efficient turbogenerator production required a plant size that would account for 23% of total U. S. output. At the other extreme, efficient shoe production could be achieved with a plant that was so small relative to total industry output as to account for only 0.2% of production.

Column (2) shows how sharply the unit cost curve rises at scales less than MES. It shows the percentage increase in unit costs that would occur by moving from a full MES plant to one just half the size (in a few cases it is one-third MES, which was Scherer's standard). It is rather interesting to note that high levels of MES, such as those observed for manmade fibers and cigarettes, are not always—or even usually—associated with high rates of cost increase at suboptimal scales. In other words, the figures of columns (1) and (2) do not correlate closely.

When the figures of column (1) are multiplied by a factor of 4, the result is column (3). This result is a rough indication of what the national four-firm concentration ratio would be like in each industry if each firm among the top four had a level of output matching MES. In other words, column (3) could be considered the degree of concentration "warranted" by economies of scale at the plant level. These figures may be compared with those of column (4), which are the actual four-firm concentration ratios of these industries in 1967. It is easy to see that columns (3) and (4) are correlated; with high values typically at the top and low values at the bottom. In a few instances actual and warranted concentration nearly coincide. Aside from these few instances, however, actual concentration is much higher than it would be if each leading firm operated one MES plant. As Scherer concludes, "nationwide oligopoly

TABLE 9–4. Minimum Efficient Scale Plants, Costs of Suboptimal Plants, and Concentration Ratios in United States Manufacturing, Circa 1967

Industry	(1) MES as a Percentage of U.S. 1967 Output	(2) Increase in Unit Cost at ½ MES (%)	(3) "Warranted" Concentration Ratio	(4) Actual Concentration Ratio 1967
Turbogenerators	23.0%	n.a.	92	100
Refrigerators	13.0	4%	52	73
Home laundry equipment	11.2	8	45	78
Manmade fiber	11.1	5	44	86
Aircraft (commercial)	10.0	20	40	69
Synthetic rubber	7.2	15	29	61
Cigarettes	6.6	2.2	26	81
Transformers	4.9	7.9	19	65
Paperboard	4.4	8	18	27
Tires and inner tubes	3.8	5	15	70
Blast furnaces and steel	2.7	10	11	48
Detergents	2.4	2.5	10	88
Storage batteries	1.9	4.6	8	61
Petroleum refining	1.8	4.0	7	33
Cement	1.7	13	7	29
Glass containers	1.5	11	6	60
Ball and roller bearings	1.4	8	6	54
Paints, varnishes	1.4	4.4	6	22
Beer	1.1	10	4	40
Flour mills	0.7	3	3	30
Machine tools	0.3	5	1	21
Cotton textiles	0.2	5	1	36
Shoes	0.2	1.5	1	26

Source: F. M. Scherer, A. Beckenstein, E. Kaufer, and R. D. Murphy, *The Economics of Multi-Plant Operation* (Cambridge, Mass.: Harvard University Press, 1975), Chapter 3; C. F. Pratton, *Economies of Scale in Manufacturing Industries* (New York: Cambridge University Press, 1971); and L. W. Weiss, "Optimal Plant Size and the Extent of Suboptimal Capacity," in *Essays on Industrial Organization in Honor of Joe S. Bain*, edited by R. T. Masson and P. D. Qualls (Cambridge, Mass.: Ballinger, 1976), pp. 123–141.

and high seller concentration cannot be viewed primarily as the inevitable consequence of production scale economies at the plant level."[22]

Now Scherer's is an *extremely* important conclusion. It indicates that policies aimed at the attainment and maintenance of competitive market structures are *not* hopelessly at odds with the cost conditions underlying most industries,[23] that most industries need *not* be dominated by only a few giants in order to be efficient.

C. Summary

The data of Table 9–4 understate levels of warranted concentration and the degree to which economies of scale might be a barrier for two reasons. First, warranted concentration would be higher for industries with narrow geographic markets, like cement. Second, warranted concentration would be higher to the extent there are multiplant efficiencies (because these figures are based on single-plant efficiencies only). Still, even after taking these factors into account, economies of scale appear to pose no more than a moderate barrier to entry for most American manufacturing industries, and they warrant no more than moderate concentration.[24] In fact, the notion that bigness is especially efficient has been increasingly questioned lately. Management consultant and popular writer Thomas J. Peters recently quipped, "The only reason Ford and GM are getting better is that pipsqueaks like Honda scared the pee out of them."[25]

This conclusion cannot be equally applicable to countries having sparse populations and lower levels of income than the United States. Minimum efficient scales would gobble up larger percentage chunks of their smaller economic markets.[26] Even abroad, however, economies of scale probably generate less concentration than many people seem to think.[27]

---

[22] F. M. Scherer, "Economies of Scale and Industrial Concentration," p. 28.

[23] C. Kaysen and D. Turner, *Antitrust Policy* (Cambridge, Mass.: Harvard University Press, 1965), p. 6.

[24] F. M. Scherer, A. Beckenstein, E. Kaufer, and R.D. Murphy, *The Economics of MultiPlant Operation* (Cambridge, Mass.: Harvard University Press, 1975), p. 339. See *Business Week*, February 26, 1979, pp. 128–132, for a very interesting story on how MetPath successfully acted on the knowledge that there were plant economies but no multiplant economies in its industry, clinical lab testing, worth $12 billion annually.

[25] "Is Your Company Too Big?" *Business Week,* March 27, 1989, p. 87. See also *Fortune*, February 29, 1989, pp. 34–58.

[26] K. S. Birks, "Economies of Scale and Concentration of the New Zealand Manufacturing Establishments," *New Zealand Economic Papers*, Vol. 15 (1981), pp. 86–110.

[27] The view that observed concentration cannot, in general, be justified by real economies is not held by all economists. John McGee claims that "the *existing* structure of industry is the *efficient* structure." ("Efficiency and Economies of Size," in *Industrial Concentration: the New Learning*, p. 93; and John McGee, *In Defense of Industrial Concentration*, New York: Praeger, 1971). There are three problems with this extreme position, however. First, it is based on the premise that firms get big *only* by virtue of their efficiency,

VI. CAPITAL COSTS

Reports from the late 1980s show:

- Sears losing $400 million in an attempt to compete with Visa and MasterCard in the credit card business.[28]

- Exxon investing $500 million in a failed attempt to enter the office equipment industry.[29]

- Du Pont spending more than $1 billion to start up a pharmaceutical business.[30]

Capital cost can thus be huge. Evidence abounds that small firms pay a higher price for their capital funds than larger firms do. The questions remaining are the following: What are the sources of this cost differential? Does it reflect real economies or just pecuniary advantages? As luck would have it, the answers are mixed because the differential is a product of at least two factors—risk and loan market imperfections.[31]

A. Risk

As regards risk, small companies seem to suffer greater fluctuations in their sales and profits than big companies. The higher risks of default that small firms present lenders and investors must be compensated by higher interest rates on loans and bonds or by a price premium on equity stock issues. In the case of bonds, for example, W. B. Hickman found that relatively small firms did default more often than large corporations. Consequently, interest rates paid were inversely related to firm size. However, Hickman also found a large "fudge" factor that worked to the disadvantage of small firms. He found that *even after adjustment* for default losses, the relation of interest rates to size was inverted. In

---

which is not true. As we have seen, efficiency may often produce bigness, but bigness is also the result of other factors, such as luck and mergers (O. E. Williamson, "Dominant Firms . . . Considerations," *Harvard Law Review*, June 1972, pp. 1512–1522). Second, McGee's argument verges on tautology. He asserts that markets are "biased toward efficiency . . ." and "market results *are* evidence of efficiency." In other words, he claims that we know big firms are better simply because they are big! On this shortcoming see Joseph Brodley, "Massive Size, Classical Economics, and the Search for Humanistic Value," *Stanford Law Review* (June 1972), pp. 1155–1178. Third, to the extent these arguments assume that efficiency evolves out of some process of natural selection from market forces they are wrong. See Alexis Jacquemin, *The New Industrial Organization* (Cambridge: MIT Press, 1987), especially Chapter 5.

[28] *The Wall Street Journal*, February 10, 1988, p. 1.

[29] *The Wall Street Journal*, September 3, 1985, p. 1.

[30] *The Wall Street Journal*, January 16, 1989, p. A1.

[31] Transaction costs are a third problem. Scherer, Beckenstein, Kaufer, and Murphy, *The Economics of MultiPlant Operation*, pp. 284–285. See also S. H. Archer and L. G. Faerber, "Firm Size and the Cost of Externally Secured Equity Capital," *Journal of Finance* (March 1966), pp. 69–83.

other words, small companies apparently pay a risk premium that exceeds the actual risk of default.[32]

To the extent the capital costs of entry are sunk, the risks associated with entry will be greater because the unrecovered costs will be greater if the attempted entry fails. This risk may take the form of a higher cost of capital to the entrant, as Stephen Martin explains:

> When a corporation borrows funds (for example, by the sale of bonds), the loan is secured by the promise that if the debt cannot be paid, lenders will be able to sell off the assets of the firm to recover a portion of their capital. The more a firm's assets are sunk in its market, the less valuable that promise is. . . . Therefore, the greater the sunk cost, the higher the rate of interest charged by lenders.[33]

B. Loan Market Imperfections

Perhaps the clearest cases of pecuniary economies in this context are those associated with market "imperfections." Suppose that competition among banks for the extension of business loans is imperfect in the following ways: Locally and regionally bank concentration is high, but nationally bank concentration is low because banks are limited in interstate branching. Suppose also that small borrowers are pretty much confined to dealing with the banks in their own local area, whereas huge borrowers such as GM, GE, and GT&E are sufficiently well known, sufficiently diverse in their operations, and sufficiently big to take their business of borrowing anywhere they fancy. Under these suppositions, you would expect banks to exploit their local market power over small firms by charging them high rates of interest. But, in the big-league nationwide market, you would expect competition to keep interest charges at a minimum.

Abundant evidence confirms these suppositions. Numerous cross-section studies have shown that business loan interest rates rise with local bank concentration, but only on loans to small businesses, not on those to big businesses.[34] One study concluded that "The level of market concentration has a statistically significant impact on rates paid by firms with assets up to at least $5 million."[35]

32 W. B. Hickman, *Corporate Bond Quality and Investor Experience* (Princeton, N.J.: Princeton University Press, 1958). See also Marc R. Reinganum and Janet K. Smith, "Investor Preference for Large Firms: New Evidence on Economies of Size," *Journal of Industrial Economics* (December 1983), pp. 221–225.

33 Stephen Martin, *Industrial Economics* (New York: Macmillan, 1988), p. 65.

34 Fine examples include F. R. Edwards, "Concentration in Banking and Its Effect on Business Loan Rates," *Review of Economics and Statistics* (August 1964), pp. 294–300; and Paul A. Meyer, "Price Discrimination, Regional Loan Rates, and the Structure of the Banking Industry," *Journal of Finance* (March 1967), pp. 37–48.

35 Donald Jacobs, *Business Loan Costs and Bank Market Structure* (New York: Columbia University Press, 1971), p. 57.

VII. PRODUCT DIFFERENTIATION (AGAIN)

A blend of barrier concepts is involved in product differentiation. We first consider advertising and then turn to other forms of differentiation.

A. Advertising

Advertising may stymie new entrants with a triple whammy: (1) it can raise the absolute costs of doing business due to "carryovers"; (2) it may entail economies of scale; and (3) it may add substantially to the capital costs of entry.[36] Economists do not argue that advertising always or inevitably has these effects. Rather, they argue that it *can* have these effects under certain circumstances. Our job now is to delineate these circumstances.

The Carryover Effect. One of the main characteristics of advertising that may give established firms an advantage over entrants is its "lagged" or "carryover" effect. January's advertising brings in September sales, and the lag may even last for years. There are several reasons for this extension of advertising effect:[37]

- Continued brand loyalty, though probably maintained by customer satisfaction, may have its origin in the persuasiveness of a single, long-forgotten ad.

- It may take a series of ads to break through the sales resistance of buyers. The last ad triggering the purchase cannot get all the credit.

- The potential customer, once persuaded, may not be "in the market" for the product until later. This is particularly true of durables, such as tires and appliances.

Thus if the annual advertising outlay of each established firm in a market is $10 million, and if all the firms enjoy an equal volume of sales, it is not enough for a new entrant to spend $10 million on advertising. It will *not* gain sales equal to the established firms during its first year in business, even if its product offering is identical to that of established firms in every other particular—price, quality, availability, and so forth. The entrant is confronted by the aggregation of entrenchment. Only *some* of the sales of the established firms during the new firm's entry

---

[36] William S. Comanor and Thomas A. Wilson, "Advertising Market Structure and Performance," *Review of Economics and Statistics* (November 1967), pp. 425–426; Comanor and Wilson, *Advertising and Market Power* (Cambridge, Mass.: Harvard University Press, 1974), Chapter 4; Comanor and Wilson, "Advertising and Competition: A Survey," *Journal of Economic Literature* (June 1979), pp. 453–476.

[37] K. S. Palda, *The Measurement of Cumulative Advertising Effects* (Englewood Cliffs N.J.: Prentice-Hall, 1964), p. 9.

year are generated by their $10 million outlay of that year. The additional sales of each are attributable to advertising outlays of *previous* years.

If the advertising outlays of established firms have a carryover effect of 0.4 (that is, an annual decay rate of 0.6), each established firm enjoys sales from its $10 million spent in the year *prior* to entry worth the equivalent of $4 million in advertising outlays the year *after* entry (0.4 × $10 million). From advertising *two* years previously each gains sales worth $1.6 million in terms of what it would cost them in current advertising dollars (0.4 × 0.4 × $10 million). Adding other prior years, this may be summarized in an equation:

$$\text{established firm's advertising value per year} = \underbrace{\$10m,}_{\text{current}} \underbrace{+ \$4m + \$1.6m + \$0.64m + \$0.256m + \cdots}_{\text{carryover}}$$

In other words, the entrant would have to spend approximately $16.67 million during its first year in the market in order to match the advertising potency of each established firm—$10 million to match their current year's outlay plus $6.67 million to make up for lost time and counter established firm carryover. Another way of looking at this phenomenon is to consider that, even if the established firms happened to spend nothing whatever on advertising during the entrant's first year, the entrant would have to spend $6.67 million on advertising just to pull even with them. Thus the entrant's advertising costs per unit of sale will, in at least the first year, exceed those of established firms at every level of possible output.

Of course this is a simplified example. The 0.4 carryover is only illustrative. Actual estimates of carryover vary, depending on the commodity and the firm in question, and the lag structure assumed is only one of a number possible. Still, the main point is adequately represented, and significant carryover effects have been found for a wide variety of products.[38] Moreover, empirical evidence has linked greater carryover with higher barriers to entry.[39]

Economies of Scale. As for economies of scale in advertising, it would be a pretty good bet that they are present whenever we observe an

[38] See Jean Jacques Lambin, *Advertising, Competition and Market Conduct in Oligopoly over Time* (Amsterdam: North-Holland Publishing Company, 1976), pp. 94–96; and Darral G. Clarke, "Econometric Measurement of the Duration of Advertising Effect on Sales," *Journal of Marketing Research* (November 1976), pp. 345–357.

[39] Randall S. Brown, "Estimating Advantages to Large Scale Advertising," *Review of Economics and Statistics* (August 1978), pp. 428–437; Sharon Oster, "Intraindustry Structure and the Ease of Strategic Change," *Review of Economics and Statistics* (August 1982), pp. 376–383; and Takeo Nakao, "Profit Rates and Market Shares of Leading Industrial Firms in Japan," *Journal of Industrial Economics* (June 1979), pp. 371–383. For theories of the effect see John M. Vernon, *Market Structure and Industrial Performance* (Boston: Allyn & Bacon, 1972), pp. 93–98; and Roger Folsom and D. F. Greer, "Advertising and Brand Loyalty as Barriers to Entry," *Symposium on Advertising and the Food System* (Madison: University of Wisconsin Press, 1983).

TABLE 9–5. Car Sales and Advertising Expense per Car Sold in the United States in 1986

Company	Car Sales	Advertising Expenditure per Car Sold
General Motors	6,285,802	$133
Ford Motor Corp.	3,462,260	188
Chrysler Corp.	2,162,669	233
Toyota	1,025,345	253
Nissan	771,026	234
Honda	693,515	296
Mazda	379,803	412
Volkswagen	277,107	636

Source: *Advertising Age*, September 28, 1988, p. 150.

inverse relationship between market share and firm advertising outlays relative to sales, while leading firms are gaining market share or holding steady. Table 9–5 illustrates this (though not perfectly). Advertising outlays *per car sold* are inversely related to sales volumes. The firms with largest sales volumes, GM and Ford, enjoy the lowest advertising costs per unit. While firms with lowest sales volumes, like Mazda and Volkswagen, experience the highest costs per car. This has been a persistent pattern for automobiles. In the past, for example, extremely high per unit advertising expenditures were not enough to save Studebaker, Packard, American Motors and other small firms from failure.[40] Another example comes from breakfast cereals. In 1964 selling and advertising expenses of the largest four firms were 14.9% of sales, for the next four 17.7%, and for all others 19.8%.[41] Despite the relatively low expenditures of the top four, their combined market share was on the rise at the time. Economies of scale here are obvious. However, they are *not* obvious for all products at all times.[42] In many instances they are either completely absent or not strong enough to make much difference.

Whether such economies arise depends on how sales respond to various levels of advertising outlay. Consider Figure 9–5, which depicts sales volume (on the vertical axis) as a function of the firm's advertising expenditures (on the horizontal axis), holding other elements such as price and rival firm advertising constant. At very low levels of advertis-

[40] L. W. Weiss, *Economics and American Industry* (New York: John Wiley, 1961). p. 342; and Charles E. Edwards, *Dynamics of the United States Automobile Industry* (Columbia: University of South Carolina Press, 1965), p. 219.

[41] National Commission on Food Marketing, *Studies of Organization and Competition in Grocery Manufacturing*, Study No. 6 (Washington, D.C.: U.S. Government Printing Office, 1966), p. 206.

[42] Kenneth D. Boyer and Kent M. Lancaster, "Are There Scale Economies in Advertising?" *Journal of Business* (July 1986), pp. 509–526.

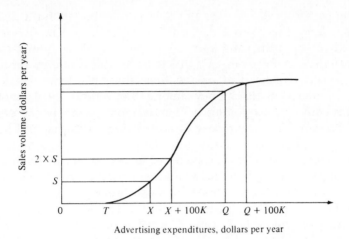

FIGURE 9–5. Sales volume as a function of advertising outlay, holding other factors constant.

ing outlay, below threshold T, advertising has little or no effect on sales. Because we are presently interested in the experience of entering firms, the $0T$ range assumes no positive sales at all. (For an established firm the entire function would have to be shifted upward to reflect the fact that even with zero current outlays there would be some positive level of sales attributable to carryover.) Explanations as to why such a threshold may be present are many and varied, depending on the product and market.[43]

- It may be impossible to buy key forms of advertising below certain minimum quantities. For instance, the smallest amount of national television advertising possible could not be bought with pocket change. The time and production costs of putting even a 10-second "spot" on the air are substantial. (A 30-second ad during the 1990 Super Bowl cost $700,000.)
- There may be a "psychological threshold" in the minds of potential buyers that may be broken only by some minimum volume of promotion.
- There may be a minimum volume of promotion needed to induce retailers and wholesalers to carry the manufacturer's product line.

Beyond threshold T, the sales response function enters a range of increasing returns. Here, increasing amounts of promotion yield *more* than proportionate increases in sales revenues. An addition of $100,000

[43] R. D. Buzzell, R. E. M. Nourse, J. B. Matthews, Jr., and T. Levitt, *Marketing: A Contemporary Analysis* (New York: McGraw-Hill, 1972) pp. 533–534.

in expenditure to outlay X does not double total outlay but it does double sales volume from S to $2 \times S$ on the vertical axis. The reasons sales may climb at an increasing rate are similar to those underlying the threshold effect. A firm can gain efficiency in this range by hiring marketing specialists (instead of having their shipping clerks dabble in ad design), by allocating its money among the various media more and more efficiently, by exploiting a "bandwagon" promotional pitch, by gaining discounts in its purchase of advertising messages; and by other means. For example, there are volume discounts for magazine advertisers,[44] and the cost of television advertising per viewer is much cheaper at the national network level (as would be used by large firms) than the local spot level (as would be used by small firms).[45]

It is the combination of threshold and increasing returns effects that is relevant to economies of scale. Over this range (roughly 0 to $X + 100K$ in Figure 9–5) advertising costs *as a percentage of sales* start out very high and then fall as absolute (total dollar) advertising outlay increases. This is not the end of the story, however. The presence of a threshold and increasing returns is commonly observed.[46] But, if these effects do not extend into very large levels of absolute outlay, then all economies could easily be exploited by rather small firms and new entrants. And beyond this small-firm range of economies, diminishing returns set in. Additional advertising outlays will eventually stimulate *less* than proportionate increases in sales revenues, as shown by Q and $Q + 100K$ in Figure 9–5. The reason for this diminishing stimulation is fairly obvious:

> Once salesmen have called on all the prospective customers with high purchase potential, they must turn to less and less promising prospects. Once advertising messages have reached the primary audiences with sufficient frequency, additional messages must be directed to audiences with lower and lower levels of response.[47]

Indeed, beyond $Q + 100K$, advertising may reach a point of complete saturation, where further promotion adds nothing at all to sales.

[44] An example of discounts is provided by the Hearst Corporation (owner of *Cosmopolitan, Good Housekeeping,* and other magazines). In 1976 it offered discounts to advertisers who bought space in any three of its magazines according to the following schedule: 12 pages, 5% off; 15 pages, 6%; 18 pages, 7%; 21 pages, 8%; 24 pages, 9%. (*The Wall Street Journal,* November 14, 1975, p. 3.) See also *Business Week,* November 24, 1980 p. 52; and *The Wall Street Journal,* July 8, 1982, p. 6.

[45] John C. Hilke and Philip B. Nelson, "An Empirical Note from Case Documents on the Economies of Network Television Advertising," *Review of Industrial Economics* (Spring 1989), pp. 131–145.

[46] Albert C. Bemmaor, "Testing Alternative Econometric Models on the Existence of Advertising Threshold Effect," *Journal of Marketing Research* (August 1984), pp. 298–308; Buzzell, et al., *Marketing,* pp. 533–534; A. G. Rao and P. B. Miller, "Advertising/Sales Response Functions," *Journal of Advertising Research* (April 1975), pp. 7–15; J. J. Lambin, *Advertising Competition and Market Conduct,* pp. 127–130; Brown, *Estimating Advantages to Large Scale Marketing;* and M. M. Metwally, "Sales Response to Advertising of Eight Australian Products," *Journal of Advertising Research* (October 1980), pp. 59–64.

[47] Buzzell et al., *Marketing,* p. 534.

In sum, economies of scale are substantial only where the threshold effect and increasing returns operate over a large range. This is reflected in the following *Business Week* quote concerning entry into the cosmetics industry:

> "The real challenge is simply gaining distribution," says market researcher Solomon Dutka . . . "to have sales volume and to be a factor in this business, you must have distribution. Yet to gain distribution, you must have sales volume or the big store groups won't bother with you. So when somebody tries to get into this business . . . they have to create volume artificially" — meaning the use of heavy and costly advertising and promotion.[48]

Unfortunately, no one can accurately estimate the range of threshold effect and increasing returns for particular industries. Moreover, experts do not agree on what causes short or long ranges. One study finds some evidence that economies of scale are most prevalent in industries with high advertising/sales ratios, but this is not wholly supported by other evidence.[49] The present author's pet theory is that economies loom largest in consumer goods industries experiencing frequent style changes (autos and cosmetics), or new titles and editions (books and records), or rapid brand multiplication (breakfast cereals and cigarettes).[50] The turbulent and continual changes endemic to these industries force successful firms to cross the threshold level of advertising outlay recurrently, not just once and for all. The expense of each crossing may be thought of as a "fixed" expense of doing business (unrelated to the level of output) because sales are not a function of advertising until after the threshold is crossed. Given high "fixed" promotional expenses in these industries, the largest firms will have the lowest advertising costs *per unit of sales* because they will be able to spread these costs over a larger volume of sales than smaller firms.

Advertising Increases Capital Cost of Entry. Finally, if economies of scale or goodwill carryovers exist in advertising, the need to obtain substantial funds for advertising will increase the capital requirements for new entry well beyond those needed for physical plant and equipment. As W. Comanor and T. Wilson point out, "this investment in market penetration will involve a particularly risky use of funds since it does not generally create tangible assets which can be resold in the event of failure."[51] In other words, advertising is a sunk cost.

---

[48] *Business Week*, November 29, 1976, p. 44.

[49] Comanor and Wilson, p. 214.

[50] D. Greer, "Some Case History Evidence on the Advertising-Concentration Relationship," *The Antitrust Bulletin* (Summer 1972), pp. 320–324. See also Richard Schmalensee, "Entry Deterence in the Ready-to-Eat Breakfast Cereal Industry," *Bell Journal of Economics* (Autumn 1978), pp. 305–327.

[51] Comanor and Wilson, p. 426.

To end on a more positive note, we should mention that advertising can *assist* entry as well as curtail it.[52] How better could a newcomer call attention to its new offering than by advertising vigorously? This procompetitive possibility is fully explored in Chapter 16. For now, no more need be said except that the procompetitive effect can easily be outweighed by the anticompetitive, barrier effects outlined previously. Empirical verification of a net procompetitive effect is limited to consumer search goods and consumer search services, such as retailing. Where retailer advertising as a percentage of sales is high, profits tend to be low, indicating intense competition.[53] Conversely, experience goods industries demonstrate just the opposite: High advertising is associated with high profits, as one would expect if advertising constituted a barrier to entry.[54] In short, it appears that advertising builds the highest barriers in consumer experience goods industries. In other industries (consumer search goods and perhaps producer goods), it may on balance be neutral or even beneficial to entry and competition.

B. Other Product Differentiation Barriers

The first thing to acknowledge with respect to other forms of differentiation is that they too may harbor economies of scale. In the medical equipment and supplies industry, where salespeople's salaries and expenses account for most promotional expenses, small firms incur selling costs per sales dollar twice as high as those of large firms.[55] Style change in the auto industry provides another example. Economists have shown that the costs of special tools and dies may decline with increasing firm size.[56]

Also, economic theory and evidence are converging on a conclusion that "pioneering" brands have an important advantage over subsequent

---

[52] This is stressed in Ioannis N. Kessides, "Advertising, Sunk Costs, and Barriers to Entry," *Review of Economics and Statistics* (February 1986), pp. 84–95. However, for a critique of Kessides, see Stephen Martin, *Industrial Economics*, p. 214.

[53] Kenneth D. Boyer, "Information and Goodwill Advertising," *Review of Economics and Statistics* (November 1974), pp. 541–548.

[54] We shall explore these studies in detail later. Three key ones, however, are M. E. Porter, "Consumer Behavior, Retailer Power and Market Performance in Consumer Goods Industries," *Review of Economics and Statistics* (November 1974), pp. 419–436; Robert J. Stonebraker, "Corporate Profits and the Risk of Entry," *Review of Economics and Statistics* (February 1976), pp. 33–39; and Emilio Pagoulatos and Robert Sorensen, "A Simultaneous Equation Analysis of Advertising, Concentration and Profitability," *Southern Economic Journal* (January 1981), pp. 728–741.

[55] R. D. Peterson and C. R. MacPhee, *Economic Organization in Medical Equipment and Supply* (Lexington, Mass.: Lexington Books, 1973), pp. 58–59.

[56] J. A. Menge, "Style Change Costs as a Market Weapon," *Quarterly Journal of Economics* (November 1962), pp. 632–647; and Lawrence White, *The Automobile Industry Since 1945* (Cambridge, Mass.: Harvard University Press, 1971), pp. 39–41.

"me too" brands. This we have called *first-mover advantage*.[57] Kellogg has held its lead in corn flakes despite the strenuous efforts of imitators. Bayer aspirin has yet to be unhorsed in aspirins. And so on. Even though an imitation brand may advertise vigorously to win converts, such information and persuasion as the advertising contains may not readily substitute for the experience consumers have with the pioneering brand:

> First entry allows a brand to exploit or shape a growing yet amorphous transition in consumer tastes. First entry also allows the brand to set product standards and levels of consumer satisfaction which consumers then come to expect as a minimum from follow-on brands.[58]

Finally, in light of Kodak's experience in batteries, we should note that entrants may have difficulty gaining access to distribution channels. This problem has characteristics we have already discussed. It is, for instance, related to first-mover advantages, since first movers (and those shortly thereafter) will typically be the ones blocking access. In another sense it could in some instances be considered a problem of sunk capital costs. In particular, most major grocery chains now charge "slotting allowances," which are fees retailers impose on manufacturers just to put new products on their shelves. According to *Business Week*, "It can easily cost $70,000 or more in fees to get a truckload's worth of a new six-item line into just one 50-store chain . . . [and] to get national distribution . . . the cost rises into the millions."[59] The reason for the fees is scarcity. The typical supermarket now carries 26,000 items, and several thousand new ones are promoted to the supermarkets every year, nine out of ten of which fail. Hence, retailers impose slotting allowances to ration their scarce shelf space and put the risk of failure onto manufacturers making new offerings. The result is a sunk capital cost to entrants.

SUMMARY

We can execute a neat exit from this chapter on entry by reiterating just a few key points:

1. Anything giving established firms substantial advantages over potential entrant firms constitutes a barrier to entry.

---

[57] Ronald S. Bond and David F. Lean, *Sales Promotion and Product Differentiation in Two Prescription Drug Markets* (Washington, D.C.: FTC Staff Report, 1977); Ira T. Whitten, *Brand Performance in the Cigarette Industry and the Advantage of Early Entry 1913–74* (Washington, D.C.: FTC Staff Report, 1979); and James J. McRae and Francis Tapon, "Some Empirical Evidence on Post-Patent Barriers to Entry in the Canadian Pharmaceutical Industry," *Journal of Health Economics* (March 1985), pp. 43–61.

[58] Whitten, *Brand Performance in the Cigarette Industry*, p. 4.

[59] *Business Week*, August 7, 1989, p. 60.

2. Because barriers are a source of market power, they are useful in explaining conduct and performance.
3. Entry into manufacturing industries is fairly frequent but usually inconsequential because entrants have small market shares that shrink substantially, leading to very frequent failure. Turnover on the fringes results.
4. Entry and exit are highly correlated because of displacement effects and common causes, sunk costs being a major example of the latter.
5. Virtually all structural barriers to entry can be classified into four factor groups: absolute unit cost differences, economies of scale, capital costs, and product differentiation. Product differentiation is a blend of the first three factors.
6. Absolute cost differences raise the entrant's costs of doing business (at every level of output) compared to the costs for established firms.
7. Economies of scale cause unit costs to fall with added size of plant or firm. If minimum efficient scale is large relative to total industry output, there will be little "room" in the industry for a large number of plants and firms, thus occasioning substantial barriers and fostering high concentration.
8. The capital costs of entry may be great, in which case new entrants will have difficulty raising funds at costs comparable to those of large established firms. To some degree this cost differential reflects real economies, for example, transaction costs. The differential is also caused by capital market imperfections, in which case it largely reflects pecuniary economies.
9. Empirical studies of entry barriers provide confirmation of all types, especially economies of scale, capital costs, and product differentiation. Advertising is associated with the last barrier, especially in consumer experience goods industries. Empirical evidence on economies of scale indicates their importance for some industries, but most seem more concentrated than necessary in this respect.

Behavioral and legal barriers have been saved for later treatment.

APPENDIX: CONTESTABLE MARKETS THEORY

Contestability theory was introduced in the early 1980s as an "uprising in the theory of industry," a "fundamental" contribution to industrial organization.[60] Moreover, its inventors claimed that this was not just a

---

[60] William J. Baumol, "Contestable Markets: An Uprising in the Theory of Industrial Structure," *American Economic Review* (March 1982), pp. 1–15; and W. J. Baumol, J. C. Panzar, and R. D. Willig, *Contestable Markets and the Theory of Industrial Structure* (San Diego, Calif.: Harcourt Brace Jovanovich, 1982).

theory. It was a theory that could "readily be applied" to governmental affairs, especially antitrust policy.[61] However, by the end of the 1980s it was clear that contestability theory was so far removed from reality that the influence it once enjoyed could not last.

A contestable market is one in which internal conditions, such as the number of incumbent firms or economies of scale, are utterly irrelevant to performance because three external conditions control all scenarios. First, *easy birth:* Entry is ultrafree. This freedom of entry derives from an assumption that all firms—actual and potential—have identical technologies, cost functions, production capacities, distribution opportunities, and product differentiation capabilities. Second, *easy life:* The entrant can fully establish itself before an existing firm can respond with price cuts. "If," as W. G. Shepherd explains, "the entrant obtains an advantage, even a tiny price difference, it will prevail absolutely and displace the existing firm, with no interaction or sequence of moves."[62] Third, *easy death*: Exit is absolutely costless. Sunk costs are assumed to be zero, which means that all costs incurred during entry can be fully recovered in the event of exit. All capital equipment, for instance, can be used elsewhere or readily sold without loss other than normal user cost and depreciation.

In brief, a contestable market is vulnerable to hit-and-run entry: "Even a very transient profit opportunity need not be neglected by a potential entrant, for he can go in, and, before prices change, collect his gains, and then depart without cost, should the climate grow hostile."[63] In a contestable market the force of potential competition alone is sufficient to produce the same performance as perfect competition.

- Excess profits attract hit-and-run entry so in equilibrium they never occur.

- Production inefficiencies would prompt hit-and-run entry, so they are eliminated in equilibrium.

However, contestability theory suffers three fatal debilities—internal inconsistencies, unbelievable assumptions, and complete collapse with even slight relaxation of its assumptions (nonrobustness).[64] One internal inconsistency stems from conflicting implications in the easy birth and

---

[61] Elizabeth E. Baily, "Contestability and the Design of Regulatory and Antitrust Policy," *American Economic Review* (May 1981), pp. 178–183.

[62] William G. Shepherd, "Contestability v. Competition," *American Economic Review* (September 1984), pp. 572–587.

[63] Baumol, "Contestable Markets" p. 4.

[64] Shepherd, "Contestability v. Competition;" A. Jacquemin, *The New Industrial Organization* (Oxford: Clarendon Press, 1987); J. Vickers, "Strategic Competition Among the Few," *Oxford Review of Economic Policy* (Autumn 1988), pp. 39–62; Marius Schwartz, "The Nature and Scope of Contestability Theory," in *Strategic Behavior and Industrial Competition*, edited by D. J. Morris et al. (Oxford: Clarendon Press, 1986), pp. 37–57; and J. E. Stiglitz, "Technological Change, Sunk Costs and Competition," *Brookings Papers on Economic Activity*, No. 3 (1987), pp. 883–937.

easy life assumptions. How can we have an immense hit-and-run potential entrant, one big enough to displace completely the incumbent monopolist, and at the same time have an incumbent unwilling or unable to respond expeditiously with price cuts in the event that such entry actually occurs? As for unbelievable assumptions, the assumption of zero sunk costs cannot stand against the fact that entry always entails sunk costs. And this observation brings us to nonrobustness. As sunk costs rise only slightly above zero, they obliterate the profitability of hit-and-run entry. Hence, only slight deviations from the theory's assumptions cause the theory to collapse.

These criticisms of contestability theory are, however, only theoretical themselves. The empirical evidence is equally important and, as it turns out, is equally unkind to contestability. If entry was ultrafree, the incidence of entry would not be responsive to the variables empirically tested in Table 9–3. Hence, the empiricism of Table 9–3 contradicts contestability. Moreover, contestability would prevent an association between high prices and profits on the one hand and high concentration and barriers to entry on the other. Yet such associations are found.[65] Of particular empirical interest is the airline industry because the originators of contestability theory claimed that the airline industry was an extremely close match for their theory. Contrary to the theory, however, studies have shown that market concentration ratios and numbers of airlines occupying markets make a significant difference in fares. T. G. Moore, for instance, found that markets with five or more air carriers had price levels 24–41% lower than more concentrated markets.[66]

An ideal empirical test of contestability's robustness would compare two segments of the same market, differing only slightly in sunk costs. If a small elevation in sunk costs in one segment produced markedly greater barriers in comparison to the other, then contestability's practical relevance would evaporate. The market for industrial gases, with separate bulk and small-lot segments having somewhat different barriers, illustrates the point.[67] The trucking industry provides further evidence. Barriers into the "truckload" segment are much lower than those into

[65] Richard J. Gilbert, "The Role of Potential Competition in Industrial Organization," *Journal of Economic Perspectives* (Summer 1989), pp. 107–127.

[66] Thomas Gale Moore, "U.S. Airline Deregulation," *Journal of Law and Economics* (April 1986), pp. 1–28. See also Samuel H. Baker and James B. Pratt, "Experience as a Barrier to Contestability in Airline Markets," *Review of Economics and Statistics* (May 1989), pp. 352–356; and G. D. Call and T. E. Keeler, "Airline Deregulation Fares and Market Behavior: Some Empirical Evidence," in *Analytical Studies in Transport Economics*, edited by A. Daughety (New York: Cambridge University Press, 1985).

[67] G. W. Brock, "Vertical Restraint in Industrial Gases," in *Impact Evaluations of Federal Trade Commission Vertical Restraint Cases*, edited by R. N. Lafferty (Washington, D.C.: FTC Bureau of Economics, 1984).

the "less-than-truckload" segment because the latter requires some minimal loading dock facilities and warehouse space for purposes of shipment aggregation and parcel routing.[68] In sum, one cannot say that contestability theory holds as a rough approximation. It simply does not hold.[69]

[68] Kenneth D. Boyer, "What Do We Understand About the Economics of Regulation," in *Mainstreams in Industrial Organization*, edited by H. W. de Jong and W. G. Shepherd (Dordrecht, The Netherlands: Martinus Nijhoff, 1986), pp. 317–346; and T. G. Moore, "Rail and Truck Reform," *Regulation* (November/December 1983), pp. 33–41.

[69] For still further evidence, see Timothy F. Bresnahan and Peter C. Reiss, "Do Entry Conditions Vary Across Markets?" *Brookings Papers on Economic Activity*, No. 3 (1987), pp. 833–869.

10

Barriers to Entry — Concentration and Monopoly: Practice and Policy

Everyday in our lives monopoly takes its toll.
— SENATOR ESTES KEFAUVER

Practically everything about monopolization is big. The companies are big. The cases are big. The stakes are big.

We begin by exploring the wording of the Sherman Act and its rule of reason interpretation. Next we trace the history of monopolization law through three eras — (1) 1890–1940, the era of dastardly deeds, (2) 1945–1970, the era of *Alcoa*, and (3) 1970–present, an era of refinement and retreat. The issue of entry enters repeatedly.

I. THE SHERMAN ACT: SECTION 2

The Sherman Act was passed in 1890 in response to public outcries that something ought to be done about the large "trusts" that were beginning to flourish at that time. The first big trust was Standard Oil, formed in 1882. It was followed quickly by the Whiskey Trust, the Sugar Trust, the Lead Trust, and the Cotton Oil Trust. Senator Sherman exclaimed that without federal action the country would soon have "a trust for every production and a master to fix the price for every necessity of life." Hence, his Sherman Act.

Broadly speaking, the act contains two main sections outlawing (1) collusive restraints of trade and (2) monopolization. The first refers to collective conduct such as price fixing and is governed by a "per se" rule. We postpone treatment of restraints of trade until Chapter 13.

A. The Rule of Reason

Section 2 of the Sherman Act declares that

> Every person who shall monopolize, or attempt to monopolize, or combine or conspire with any other person or persons, to monopolize any part of the trade or commerce among the several States, or with foreign nations, shall be deemed guilty of a felony. . . .

Although Section 2 covers those who "combine or conspire" to monopolize, it is primarily concerned with single-firm activities and structural conditions. Having said that, we must ask: Why the word "monopolize"? Why not "monopoly"? What is the test of monopolization? How large a market share is required? What is meant by a "part of the trade or commerce"?

Simple summary answers to these questions might seem feasible. The Sherman Act is, after all, 100 years old and several hundred cases have been brought by the Justice Department under Section 2. Most issues, it would seem, should be settled now. Unfortunately, they are not. Economic knowledge, political philosophies, and business practices change over time, much as fashion changes. Even more significant, the wording of the statute was left vague enough to invoke extensive judgment.

A Sherman Act Section 2 violation is not as clear cut as shoplifting or murder. Monopolizers cannot be caught in the act. They are never really caught at all. They are accused and judged by a "rule of reason." The result is drawn-out deliberations. Trials of five years are not unheard of.

Illegal monopolization is not established without proof of two factors: (1) substantial market power and (2) intent. As Justice William Douglas wrote in the *Grinnell* case, the offense of monopoly "has two elements: (1) the possession of monopoly power in the relevant market and (2) willful acquisition or maintenance of that power. . . . "[1] Reason is exercised to establish both elements. In appraising monopoly power, the courts have considered barriers to entry of various kinds—including patents, pecuniary and real economies of scale, product differentiation,

---

[1] *U.S. v. Grinnell Corporation,* 384 U.S. 563 (1966).

absolute capital costs, and several conduct-related barriers. Profits, too, have come under review. The one index of monopoly power consistently receiving greatest attention, however, is the market share of the accused. In this interpretation, reason must be called upon to answer two key questions: What is the relevant market? What market share is sufficient to establish unlawful power?

B. Market Definition: Power Question 1

Section 2 refers to "any part of the trade or commerce," a phrase now taken to mean "relevant market." As we now know, markets do not have bright-line boundaries as do nations or continents. Many factors, therefore, influence market determination:[2]

1. The physical characteristics of the products
2. The end uses of the products
3. The cross-elasticity of demand between products
4. The absolute level of various sellers' costs
5. The absolute level of product prices, apart from consideration of cross-elasticities
6. The geographic extent of the market

The diversity of judgments the relevant market has provoked may be illustrated by two contrasting cases.

In *Du Pont* (1956) a majority of the Supreme Court defined the market broadly to include *all* flexible packaging materials (cellophane, foil, pliofilm, polyethylene, and so on) instead of merely cellophane, which Du Pont dominated.[3] The decisive argument for the court's majority was cross-elasticity of demand, as may be seen from the opinion:

> If a slight decrease in the price of cellophane causes a considerable number of customers of other flexible wrappings to switch to cellophane, it would be an indication that a high cross-elasticity of demand exists between them; that the products compete in the same market. The court below held that the "great sensitivity of customers in the flexible packaging markets to price or quality changes" prevented Du Pont from possessing monopoly control over price. . . . We conclude that cellophane's interchangeability with other materials mentioned suffices to make it a part of this flexible packaging material market.

Although Du Pont produced 75% of all cellophane sold in the United States, this amounted to only 14% of all "flexible packaging." Hence the broad definition made a big difference, and Du Pont won acquittal.

Three dissenting justices had doubts. They felt that cellophane was

---

2 For an overview see Alvin M. Stein and Barry J. Brett, "Market Definition and Market Power in Antitrust Cases — An Empirical Primer on When, Why and How," *New York Law School Law Review*, Vol. 24 (1979), pp. 639–676.

3 *U.S. v. E.I. duPont de Nemours Company*, 351 U.S. 377 (1956).

virtually unique. Cellophane's price, in particular, had been two to seven times higher than that of many comparable materials between 1924 and 1950. Yet during this period "cellophane enjoyed phenomenal growth," *more* growth than could be expected "if close substitutes were available at from one seventh to one half cellophane's price." Further-more, they thought cross-elasticity was low, not high. The price of cel-lophane fell substantially while other prices remained unchanged. In-deed, "during the period 1933–1946 the prices for glassine and waxed paper actually increased in the face of a 21% decline in the price of cellophane." If substantial "shifts of business" due to "price sensitivity" had in fact occurred, producers of these rival materials would have had to follow cellophane's price down lest they lose sales.[4]

Ten years later, in the *Grinnell* case (1966) a majority of the Court spoke as the minority did in *Du Pont*. They defined the market narrowly to include only "accredited central station protective services" (whereby a client's property is wired for burglaries and fires, signals of which are then sent electronically to a continuously monitored central station accre-dited by insurance underwriters). Other means of property protection were excluded from the relevant market for various reasons:[5]

> Watchmen service is far more costly and less reliable. Systems that set off an audible alarm at the site of a fire or burglary are cheaper but often less reliable. They may be inoperable without anyone's knowing it. . . . Propri-etary systems that a customer purchases and operates are available, but they can be used only by a very large business or government. . . . And, as noted, insurance companies generally allow a greater reduction in pre-miums for accredited central station service than for other types of protection.

Because Grinnell had 87% of the market as defined, the Court could not let it off the hook like an undersized trout. Grinnell suffered some dismemberment.

C. Market Share: Power Question 2

The cases cited indicate that a market share of 14% does not amount to illegal monopoly but 87% does. What about the area in between? What market share makes an illegal "monopoly"? In two major cases the Su-preme Court ruled that 64% of the farm machinery industry and 50% of the steel industry did not amount to monopoly. An influential appeals court judge, Learned Hand, once expressed the opinion that, while any percentage over 90 "is enough to constitute a monopoly; it is doubtful whether sixty or sixty-four per cent would be enough; and certainly thirty-three per cent is not."[6] For these several reasons the consensus

---

[4] For an economic critique see, G. W. Stocking and W. F. Mueller, "The Cellophane Case and the New Competition," *American Economic Review* (March 1955), pp. 29–63. Note that when a monopolist raises price and thereby moves up its demand curve, elasticity will rise. Therefore high elasticity might signal the presence of monopoly instead of its absence.

[5] *U.S.* v. *Grinnell Corporation*, 384 U.S. 563 (1966).

[6] *U.S.* v. *Aluminum Company of America*, 148 F.2d 416 (1945), 424.

seems to hold that market shares below 60% lie snugly beneath the Court's reach. And even 70% or 75% may manage to escape its grasp.

Notice, this means that *relative* size, not absolute size, is the focus. Famous firms, huge in absolute size (like General Motors and Mobil Oil), may elude attack because their market shares are less than awesome, their markets being also huge. On the other hand, unknown firms, rather small in absolute size (like Griffith Amusement Company and Grinnell Corporation), may be challenged because they are giants relative to their markets.

D. Intent

Actually, there is even more uncertainty than the given figures suggest. The issue of intent is also important. Generally speaking, there is a trade-off between the market share and the degree of intent the prosecuting attorneys must prove to win a guilty verdict. A clear-cut case of 95% market share would now probably run afoul of the law with very little proof of intent. Conversely, intent would gain importance when a market share of less than 60% was involved.

Indeed, it will be recalled that Section 2 forbids mere *attempts* to monopolize as well as monopolization itself. Although the scope of this offense is much disputed and unclear, it seems safe to say that the requirements for proving a charge of "attempt" are now much more rigorous with respect to intent than they are in cases of pure monopolization. Traditionally, proof of an attempt to monopolize requires two elements: (1) a *specific intent* to monopolize and (2) a *dangerous probability of success*.[7] The requirement of specific intent—such as would be shown by clearly anticompetitive acts like blatant predatory pricing, coercive refusals to deal, sabotage, and gross misrepresentation—arises because in this context the monopolization is not actually achieved. Without indications of specific intent, a court could not be sure that monopolization was what the defendant had in mind. Moving beyond attempts to situations where monopoly has been achieved, only "general" intent need be proved because any specific intent is then largely manifest in the end result.[8]

Use of the word "monopolize" in the Sherman Act (rather than "monopoly") implies that simple possession of a large market share is not itself frowned upon, at least not enough to earn a conviction. An illegality requires more: some positive drive, some purposeful behavior, some "intent" to seize and exert power in the market. Only a moment's

[7] Lawrence Sullivan, *Handbook of the Law of Antitrust* (St. Paul, Minn.: West, 1977), pp. 134–140.

[8] The "dangerous probability" requirement has stirred controversy of late because some lower courts have recently held that near monopoly or a high probability of actual monopolization are necessary to a finding of dangerous probability. See especially *U.S. v. Empire Gas Co.* 537 F.2d 296 (8th Cir. 1976), *cert. denied*, 429 U.S. 1122 (1977).

reflection reveals the wisdom of this policy. What of the innovator whose creativity establishes a whole new industry, occupied at first by just his firm? What of the last surviving firm in a dying industry? What of the superefficient firm that underprices everyone else through genuine economies of scale or some natural advantages of location? To pounce on these monopolies would have to be regarded as cruel (since they are actually "innocent"), stupid (since it would be punishing good performance), and irrational (since no efficient structural remedy, such as dissolution, could ensue). Thus a finding of intent to monopolize is essential, even though it may not be easy.

In Section 2 cases a monopolist's intent is not determined by subjecting its executives to lie detector tests or psychoanalysis. Intent emerges from the firm's particular acts or its general course of action. With this statement we come to the point where, for pedagogical purposes, three more or less distinct eras of Section 2 interpretation may be distinguished depending on what the courts have required of plaintiffs to prove intent.

- *1890–1940:* In the early days, the Supreme Court usually held that an offensive degree of intent could be established only with evidence of abusive acts. This could be called the era of leniency because "well-behaved" monopolists with as much as 90% of the market were welcomed if not cherished.
- *1945–1970:* The *Alcoa* case of 1945 set a very stringent standard, excusing monopolists only when power was "thrust upon" them, as if by accident. Little was needed to show offensive intent because "no monopolist monopolizes unconscious of what he is doing."[9]
- *1970–Present:* Most recently the pendulum has swung back toward leniency. A string of lower court decisions gives monopolists spacious room for aggressive, if not abusive, conduct. Still, this era's record is mixed because the Supreme Court has not spoken clearly.

We shall take up each era successively.

II. THE EARLY DAYS: 1890–1940

A. An Overview

Before *Alcoa*, the Supreme Court usually held that an offensive degree of intent could be established only with evidence of abusive, predatory, or criminal acts. The types of conduct that qualified included the following: (1) predatory pricing, that is, cutting prices below costs on certain products or in certain regions and subsidizing the resulting losses with

---

[9] *U.S.* v. *Aluminum Company of America*, 148 F.2d 416 (1945).

profits made elsewhere; (2) predatory promotional spending or predatory pricing on "fighting brands" or "bogus independent" firms or upon new facilities or new products; (3) physical violence to competitors, their customers, or their products; (4) exaction of special advantages from suppliers, such as "railroad rebates"; (5) misuse of patents, copyrights, or trademarks; and (6) preclusion of competitive opportunities by refusals to sell, exclusive dealing arrangements, or anticompetitive tie-in sales.

For the most part, this list of "predatory tactics" is derived from the major early cases listed in Table 10–1. The first five cases mentioned there ended in convictions. The last five mentioned ended in acquittals. Notice from the center column that the market shares of the convicted monopolizers are not markedly greater than those of the acquitted firms, although in the latter group there are two with only 50% of industry sales. The big difference lies in the next column, where a "Yes" indicates that obviously predatory tactics were used by the defendant and a "No" indicates a fairly clean slate in this regard. With but one exception, those guilty of dirty tricks were also found guilty of monopolizing. Conversely, the "good" trusts managed to get off. The obvious implication must be qualified by the possibility that changes in court personnel could have made some difference, as suggested perhaps by the dates of the decisions in the last column. Another qualification that lessens the strength of the argument is the exclusion of several railroad cases from consideration. Between 1904 and 1922, the Supreme Court decided against three railroad combinations that did not employ predatory practices to gain substantial market shares.[10] Even so, we can buttress the message of Table 10–1 by consulting the Court's opinions.

B. Standard Oil of New Jersey (1911)

Standard Oil (now Exxon) was the most notorious monopoly of its time. First organized in Ohio in 1870, by 1872 it had acquired all but a few of the three dozen refineries in Cleveland. Additionally, it had garnered complete control of the pipelines running from oil fields to refineries in Cleveland, Pittsburgh, Philadelphia, New York, and New Jersey. Further transportation advantages were gained from the railroads through preferential rates and large rebates. From this strategic footing Standard Oil was able to force competitors to join the combination or be driven out of business. As a result, the combine grew to control 90% of the petroleum industry, a dominance that produced enormous profits. Under legal attack from authorities in Ohio, the company was reorganized in 1899 as Standard Oil of New Jersey, a holding company. The new combine continued to exact preferential treatment from railroads and to cut

10 Northern Securities Co. (1904), Union Pacific (1912), and Southern Pacific (1922).

TABLE 10–1.   Major Section 2 Cases, 1911 to 1927

Industry	Percentage of the Industry (%)	Predatory Tactics Present?	Date of Final Judgment
I. Unlawful monopolies			
Standard Oil of N.J.	Petroleum	85–90	Yes	1911
American Tobacco Co.	Tobacco products	76–97	Yes	1911
E. I. du Pont	Explosives	64–100	Yes	1911
Eastman Kodak Co.	Photo equipment	75–80	Yes	1915
Corn Products Refining Co.	Glucose	53	Yes	1916
II. Cases of acquittal			
United Shoe Machinery Co.	Shoe machinery	90	No	1917
American Can Co.	Packers' cans	50	Yes	1916
Quaker Oats Co.	Rolled oats cereal	75	No	1916
U.S. Steel Corp.	Steel	50	No	1920
International Harvester Co.	Harvesters	64	No	1927

Source: Milton Handler, *Trade Regulation*, 3rd ed. (New York: Foundation Press, 1960), pp. 378–379.

crude oil supplies to competing refiners. Business espionage, local price warfare, and the operation of bogus independents were also standard tactics. As the Supreme Court said, "The pathway of the combination . . . is strewn with the wrecks resulting from crushing out, without regard to law, the individual rights of others."[11]

In writing the Supreme Court's opinion, Chief Justice White emphasized intent, contrasting the tainted history of Standard Oil with what he called "normal methods of industrial development." Thus, by implication, the Court acknowledged that power alone was not enough, that monopoly in the concrete was condoned absent the willful drive. In applying this interpretation of Section 2 to the facts of *Standard Oil*, White said that the combine's merging and acquiring alone gave rise to a "prima facie presumption of intent." He went on, however, to state that this prima facie presumption was "made conclusive" by considering the rapacious conduct of the New Jersey corporation.

In sum, White gave birth to an infantile form of the rule of reason as we know it today. He found himself "irresistibly driven to the conclusion that the very genius for commercial development and organization which it would seem was manifested from the beginning soon begot an intent and purpose to exclude others . . . by acts and dealings wholly inconsistent with . . . normal methods." Given its context, White's "rule of reason" came to mean that a monopolist would not be forced to walk the plank unless he had *behaved unreasonably*.

Dissolution of the combine followed, yielding 34 separate companies. Historically, these offspring tended to be regionally and vertically specialized—for example, Standard Oil of California (now Chevron), Standard Oil of Ohio (Sohio), Standard Oil of New York (Mobil), Standard Oil of Indiana (American), and Standard Oil of New Jersey (Exxon).[12] With time, they spread into each other's territory to compete.

C. American Tobacco (1911)

The story in tobacco is similar to that in oil except that advertising and promotion were big weapons.[13] The story centers on James Duke, whose power play started in cigarettes, and then spread to other branches of the trade. By 1885 Duke had secured 11–18% of total cigarette sales for his company through an arduous promotional effort. He then escalated ad and promotional outlays to nearly 20% of sales, thereby forcing a

[11] *Standard Oil Company of New Jersey v. U.S.*, 221 U.S. 1 (1911). John McGee has argued that Standard's predatory pricing was less than alleged, even nonexistent, "Predatory Price Cutting: The Standard Oil (N.J.) Case," *Journal of Law & Economics* (October 1958), pp. 137–169. But his account has been questioned by F. M. Scherer, *Industrial Market Structure and Economic Performance* (Chicago: Rand McNally, 1970), pp. 274–276.

[12] Others included Atlantic Refining, Conoco, Marathon, Std. of Kentucky, Std. of Louisiana, and Std. of Nebraska.

[13] For a summary see D. F. Greer, "Some Case History Evidence on the Advertising-Concentration Relationship," *Antitrust Bulletin* (Summer 1975), pp. 311–315.

five-firm merger in 1889 and acquiring 80% control of all cigarette sales. His American Tobacco Company grew still further until he held 93% of the market in 1899. Coincident with this final gathering of power, cigarette ad expense as a percentage of sales fell to 11% in 1894, then to 0.5% in 1899. And cigarette profits swelled to 56% of sales in 1899.

With these stupendous profits Duke was able to launch massive predatory campaigns to capture other tobacco markets, which were at the time bigger than cigarettes. One measure of this effort is the American Tobacco Company's annual advertising and selling cost as a percentage of sales at crest levels in the target markets—28.9% for plug and twist, 24.4.% for smoking tobacco, 31.7% for fine-cut chewing, and 49.9% for cigars. Duke even went so far as to introduce deliberately unprofitable "fighting brands," one of which was appropriately called "Battle Ax." Losses ensued; mergers followed; and after the entire industry (except for cigars) was under American's thumb, advertising receded substantially to such relatively peaceful neighborhoods as 4% and 10% of sales.

Just before the Supreme Court's ruling against American in 1911 the combine controlled the following shares: smoking tobacco, 76.2%; chewing tobacco, 84.4%; cigarettes 86.1%; snuff, 96.5%; cigars 14.4%. Stressing the crude behavior of the combine, the Court found American's acts unreasonable. Dissolution ensued, creating oligopoly in place of monopoly.[14] Competition improved, but not markedly.

D. U.S. Steel (1920)

A chain of mergers occurred around the turn of the century, eliminating the independence of 170 steel companies and culminating in the formation of U.S. Steel Corporation in 1901. When formed, this behemoth accounted for 66% of all American steel production. Its market power is evident in the fact that U.S. Steel's capitalization was double the market value of the stock of its constituent companies. Still, the corporation's market share dwindled a bit by 1911, when, flush with success in *Standard Oil* and *American Tobacco*, the Justice Department filed suit. Its share fell further, and in 1920 U.S. Steel won acquittal.

In acquitting U.S. Steel the court held that the corporation's 50% market share (at the time of the case) did not amount to excessive power, and, even if it had amounted to excessive power, the corporation had not abused it: "It resorted to none of the brutalities or tyrannies that the cases illustrate of other combinations." The corporation "did not oppress or coerce its competitors . . . it did not undersell its competitors in some localities by reducing its prices there below those maintained elsewhere, or require its customers to enter into contracts limiting their purchases or restricting them in resale prices; it did not obtain customers by

[14] *U. S.* v. *American Tobacco Co.*, 221 U. S. 106 (1911).

secret rebates . . . there was no evidence that it attempted to crush its competitors or drive them out of the market. . . . " In short: "The corporation is undoubtedly of impressive size. . . . But the law does not make mere size an offense, or the existence of unexerted power an offense. It, we repeat, requires overt acts. . . . "[15] U.S. Steel was indeed a combination formed by *merger*. But merger was not then considered evidence of intent even though it is obviously an "overt act."

Allowing monopoly by merger was no mere oversight, for in a stinging dissent Justice Day reminds the majority that the Sherman Act expressly bans "combinations" and goes on to argue that the "contention must be rejected that the [U.S. Steel] combination was an inevitable evolution of industrial tendencies compelling union of endeavor." Nevertheless, the view that abusive "overt acts" were required to prove intent prevailed in this and other opinions of the day.

III. THE ALCOA ERA: 1945–1970

A. An Overview

Although the *U.S. Steel* interpretation may not have gutted Section 2, it certainly bloodied it a bit. Section 2 lay incapacitated until 1945, when the *Alcoa* decision brought recuperation.[16] In essence, *Alcoa* lengthened the list of intent indications beyond predatory and abusive tactics. According to *Alcoa*, unlawful intent can almost be assumed unless the defendant is a "passive beneficiary" of monopoly power or has had monopoly power "thrust upon" him. To *any* extent the monopolist reaches out to grasp or strives actively to hold his dominant position, he is denied the right to claim that he has no unlawful intent. This hard line is softened by other language in the opinion that exempts monopoly gained by "superior skill, foresight and industry." Subsequent cases changed the wording to permit monopoly grounded on "a superior product, business acumen or historic accident."[17] But the *Alcoa* interpretation remained fairly well intact for nearly three decades.

B. Alcoa (1945)[18]

The Aluminum Company of America provides many interesting economic lessons as well as legal lessons. For more than half a century it dominated all four stages of the U.S. aluminum industry: (1) bauxite ore

15 *U.S.* v. *U.S. Steel Corporation*, 251 U.S. 417 (1920).

16 *U.S.* v. *Aluminum Company of America*, 148 F.2d 416 (2d Cir. 1945).

17 *U.S.* v. *Grinnell Corporation*, 384 U.S. 563 (1966).

18 Primary sources for this section are L. W. Weiss, *Economics and American Industry* (New York: John Wiley, 1961), Chapter 5; Merton J. Peck, *Competition in the Aluminum Industry, 1945–1958* (Cambridge, Mass.: Harvard University Press, 1961).

mining; (2) conversion of bauxite into aluminum oxide or alumina; (3) electrolytic reduction of alumina into aluminum ingots; and (4) fabrication of aluminum products, such as cable, foil, pots and pans, sheets, and extrusions. Alcoa's dominance derived mainly from various barriers to entry:

1. Patents.   Until 1886, the processes for extracting pure aluminum were so difficult and costly that it was a precious metal like gold or platinum. In that year, just after graduating from Oberlin College, Charles Hall discovered electrolytic reduction of alumina into aluminum. His discovery was later duplicated by C. S. Bradley. Alcoa acquired the rights to both their patents, and thereby excluded potential entrants legally until 1909.

2. Resources Controlled.   Resource limitations also barred entry. Alcoa integrated backward into bauxite mining and electric power, the two key resources for producing aluminum. Although these resources were too plentiful to be fully preempted by a single firm, Alcoa vigorously acquired, developed, and built the lowest-cost sources of each.

3. Economies of Scale.   As if all that were not enough, economies of scale constituted an additional barrier. Of the several stages of the production process, the second stage—conversion of bauxite into alumina—yielded the greatest efficiencies from increased size. Until 1938 there was only *one* alumina plant in the entire United States. The unit costs of a 500,000-ton per year plant embodying 1940 technology were 10–20% below the unit costs of a 100,000-ton plant. And it was not until 1942 that U.S. consumption of alumina topped 500,000 tons. The dire implications for entry into alumina production during that era should be obvious. Economies were not nearly so pronounced for reduction and fabrication (there being four smelting plants in the United States during the 1930s and a goodly number of fabricators).

Nonetheless the barriers associated with alumina spilled over into these other stages because Alcoa was *vertically integrated*. However efficient a producer of ingot or fabricated products might be, he was ultimately dependent on Alcoa for his raw materials and simultaneously competing with Alcoa as a seller. This put independents in a precarious position. Alcoa could control the independents' costs *and* selling price. Were Alcoa unkind enough to raise its price of ingot and lower its price of foil, say, the foil fabricators would be in a bind. The "price squeeze" would pinch the margin between their costs and selling price. Just such a squeeze was alleged in 1926 and 1927, when Alcoa reduced the margin between ingot and certain types of aluminum sheet from 16 cents a pound to 7 cents a pound and then kept it there until 1932. Two independent rollers of sheet initiated an antitrust suit that was settled out of court.

4. The Antitrust Suit. The government lost its antitrust suit at the district court level in 1941. The district judge relied on the *U.S. Steel* case of 1920. He felt that mere size, unaccompanied by dastardly deeds, did not violate Section 2. The Supreme Court could not hear the Justice Department's appeal because four Court justices disqualified themselves on grounds of prior participation in the case, leaving less than a quorum. However, the New York Circuit Court of Appeals was designated court of last resort for the case. That three-judge panel, acting under the leadership of Judge Learned Hand, decided against Alcoa, thereby reversing the lower court and boldly overturning precedent.[19]

On the question of market power, the circuit court determined that Alcoa controlled over 90% of primary aluminum sales in the United States, the other 10% being accounted for by imports.[20] "That percentage," Hand said, "is enough to constitute a monopoly." On the issue of intent, the Court *rejected* the notion that evil acts must be in evidence. Lacking substantial judicial precedent for this position, the Court looked to congressional intent:

> [Congress] did not condone "good trusts" and condemn "bad" ones; it forbade all. Moreover, in so doing it was not necessarily actuated by economic motives alone. It is possible, because of its indirect social or moral effect, to prefer a system of small producers . . . to one in which the great mass of those engaged must accept the direction of a few.

By this interpretation a monopolist could escape only if its monopoly had been "thrust upon it," only if "superior skill, foresight and industry" were the basis for its success. Was this true of Alcoa? The Court thought not, emphasizing conditions of entry:

> It would completely misconstrue "Alcoa's" position in 1940 to hold that it was the passive beneficiary of a monopoly . . . There were at least one or two abortive attempts to enter the industry, but "Alcoa" effectively anticipated and forestalled all competition. . . . It was not inevitable that it should always anticipate increases in the demand for ingot and be prepared to supply them. Nothing compelled it to keep doubling and redoubling its capacity before others entered the field.

5. Assistance to Entrants. Today, partly as a result of this decision, Alcoa accounts for less than one-third of all U.S. aluminum ingot capacity. The government did not bring this about by breaking Alcoa into fragments. Instead, it encouraged new entry into the industry. Shortly after World War II, the government's war plants were sold at bargain-basement prices to Reynolds and Kaiser (two former fabricators). This move alone reduced Alcoa's market share to 50%. Later, during the Cold

---

[19] *U.S.* v. *Aluminum Company of America*, 148 F.2d 416 (1945).

[20] A debate over market definition centered on the question of whether scrap aluminum should be included in the market along with primary aluminum. Judge Hand's exclusion of scrap has been vindicated. See Robert E. Martin, "Monopoly Power and the Recycling of Raw Materials," *Journal of Industrial Economics* (June 1982), pp. 405–419.

and Korean wars of the 1950s, the government aided the entry of Anaconda, Harvey (now owned by Martin Marietta), and Ormet. These firms were the beneficiaries of rapid amortization certificates, government-guaranteed construction loans, long-term contracts to supply the government's stockpile of aluminum, and cut-rate government electricity. Changing economic conditions also helped. The demand for aluminum in the United States has increased 3000% since 1940 and 1000% since 1950. Simultaneously, costs as a function of plant size have not altered appreciably. As a consequence, economies of scale have shrunk to the point at which a minimum efficient-scale alumina plant would account for only about 8% of total U.S. capacity, and a minimum efficient-scale ingot plant would account for only about 3%. These developments enabled still further entry during the 1960s and 1970s.[21]

C. United Shoe Machinery (1953)

U.S. v. *United Shoe Machinery* was tried in 1953, was decided against United Shoe, and was affirmed per curiam by the Supreme Court in 1954.[22] United was found to supply somewhere between 75% and 85% of the machines used in boot and shoe manufacturing. Moreover, it was the only machinery producer offering a full line of equipment. United had many sources of market power, but the following are especially noteworthy:

1. Like Alcoa, United held patents covering the fundamentals of shoe machinery manufacture at the turn of the century. These basic patents were long expired by the 1950s, and with some effort competitors could "invent around" United's later patents. Still, at the time of the suit, United held 2675 patents, some of which it acquired and some of which impeded entry.

2. A logical strategy for a new entrant would have been to start with one or two machine types and then branch out into a more complete line. Indeed, this was the approach of United's major rival, Compo, which specialized in "cementing" machines. United's answer to the challenge, however, was a discriminatory price policy that fixed a lower rate of return where competition was of major significance and a higher rate of return where competition was weak or nonexistent.

---

[21] An interesting assessment of these events was given in 1984 by a prominent Alcoa executive involved in the case. When asked if the case was in the interest of society, he said, "Definitely. Definitely." He thought that "in the end," it was also in the interest of Alcoa because competition improved Alcoa's performance. George David Smith, *From Monopoly to Competition* (Cambridge: Cambridge University Press, 1988), p. 214.

[22] *U.S.* v. *United Shoe Machinery Corp.*, 110 F. Supp. 295 (D. Mass. 1953), aff'd per curiam, 347 U.S. 521 (1954). See also Carl Kaysen, *United States* v. *United Shoe Machinery Corporation* (Cambridge, Mass.: Harvard University Press, 1956).

3. Finally, United never sold its machines; it only leased them. This policy precluded competition from a secondhand market. Furthermore, the terms of the leases restricted entry into new machinery production. Ten years was the standard lease duration. If a lessee wished to return a machine before the end of his ten-year term, he paid a penalty that tapered down from a substantial amount in the early years to a small amount in the later years. If he was returning the machine for replacement, he paid a lower penalty if he took another United machine than if he switched to a rival manufacturer's machine. Moreover, service was tied in. No separate charges were made for repairs and maintenance, with the result that a newly entering firm had to build a service organization as well as manufacturing and marketing capabilities.

On the basis of these facts, the court ruled against United, saying that the "defendant has, and exercises, such overwhelming strength in the shoe machinery market that it controls that market." What is more, "this strength excludes some potential, and limits some actual, competition." Regarding intent, the court conceded that "United's power does not rest on predatory practices." However, United's lease-only system, its restrictive lease clauses, its price discrimination, and its acquisition of patents

> are not practices which can be properly described as the inevitable consequences of ability, natural forces, or law. They represent something more. . . . They are contracts, arrangements, and policies which, instead of encouraging competition based on pure merit, further the dominance of a particular firm. In this sense they are *unnatural* barriers . . . [italics added].

The court ordered United to sell as well as lease its machines, to modify the terms of its leases, and to divest itself of some assets.

Among other cases of the *Alcoa* era, *Grinnell* (1966) is notable for saying that monopolization based on "superior product, business acumen, or historic accident" would not be illegal. Grinnell Corp. did not pass the test.[23]

IV. 1970–PRESENT: REVISION AND RETREAT

The *Alcoa* era sputtered to an end during the 1970s and early 1980s. Cases against two giant firms that seemed vulnerable under *Alcoa* standards—IBM and Kodak—were won by the defendants. I say "sputtered to an end," however, for two reasons. First, the Supreme Court did not

---

[23] *U.S.* v. *Grinnell Corporation*, 384 U.S. 563 (1966). The case apparently stimulated competition substantially. See Don E. Waldman, *Antitrust Action and Market Structure* (Lexington, Mass.: Lexington Books, 1978), pp. 49–57.

explicitly decide to make the change, as the Court has not ruled on a major monopolization case for quite some time. Second, two giant firms, Xerox and AT&T, each had trouble with Section 2 of the Sherman Act, trouble serious enough to indicate that Section 2 remains alive. Still, these cases against Xerox and AT&T carry little meaning for legal trends on intent because both were settled by consent decrees and both involved market shares approaching 100%.

Let's begin discussion of this final era, then, with a glance at Xerox and AT&T. That is followed by details on Kodak and IBM.

A. Xerox and AT&T

In 1973 the FTC charged Xerox with monopolizing the copier industry, alleging that Xerox controlled 95% of the plain-paper copier business and 86% of the total office-copier market. The allegations of offensive conduct paralleled those of *United Shoe Machinery*. That is, Xerox's licensing, pricing, and patent policies were said to exclude competition artificially. Xerox responded by negotiating a settlement in 1975, one that provided for (1) licensing patents on reasonable royalties, (2) supplying "knowhow" to competitors, (3) modifying price policies, and (4) selling as well as leasing copy machines. The consent decree has been denounced for being ineffectual, but it may have helped the entry of Savin, IBM, and others—entries that jolted the industry with new competition.[24]

The American Telephone & Telegraph case was launched by the Justice Department in 1974. Admitting that AT&T's monopoly of most telephone service could be justified by "natural" economies of scale, the Justice Department claimed that AT&T should not be allowed to extend that monopoly power into contiguous fields where economies were significantly less consequential—equipment manufacturing in particular. Thus the government sought to split AT&T into portions representing regulated "natural" monopoly activities and *non*regulated, potentially competitive activities. Such a split would prevent AT&T from using its monopoly power in regulated markets to subsidize its operation in unregulated markets, hurting competition in the latter. The suit was settled in early 1982 by a consent decree that caused AT&T to shed its regulated regional phone service utility companies, leaving a unit comprised of AT&T Long Lines, Bell Laboratories, and Western Electric. This case is unique, however. It portends little for firms untouched by public utility regulation.[25]

---

24 Don E. Waldman, "Economic Benefits in the *IBM*, *AT&T*, and *Xerox* Cases: Government Antitrust in the 70's," *Antitrust Law and Economics Review*, No. 2 (1980), pp. 75–92.

25 *The Wall Street Journal*, January 11, 1982, pp. 1, 4; January 12, 1982, p. 3; January 21, 1982, pp. 1, 21.

B. Greater Leniency with Kodak and IBM

To set the scene for Kodak and IBM it may be noted that, despite *Alcoa*, *United Shoe*, and the other cases of the 1945–1970 era, some uncertainty remained about what kind of conduct would prove intent. The uncertainty stemmed from the difficulty of trying to curb monopoly without at the same time squashing business incentive. Indeed, the uncertainty could be seen in the *Alcoa* opinion itself. Tension separates two of Judge Hand's statements: (1) Congress "did not condone 'good trusts' and condemn 'bad' ones; it forbade all;" and yet (2) "The successful competitor, having been urged to compete, must not be turned upon when he wins." This tension, a circuit court recently complained, "makes the cryptic *Alcoa* opinion a litigant's wishing well, into which, it sometimes seems, one may peer and find nearly anything he wishes."[26]

In 1979 a blue-ribbon panel called the National Commission for the Review of Antitrust Laws and Procedures more than endorsed the first of these views. It urged congressional consideration of a "no fault" monopoly law. With such a law, government prosecutors would never need to prove intent, only "persistent monopoly power." The rationale? . . . "the Commission believes that persistent monopoly power, in all but the most exceptional instance, can only result from culpable conduct."[27]

At the same time, however, in 1979, the lower courts began issuing a series of opinions in the *Kodak* and *IBM* cases that moved in the opposite direction. These lower courts were busy exonerating Kodak and IBM of monopolization in major private suits. They found that many allegedly exclusionary practices merely reflected these firms' "superior product, business acumen," or "skill, foresight, and industry" — not the willful maintenance of monopoly power. As one commentator put it, these cases give a monopolist "greater freedom to fight off its competitors." And in so doing, "they invite comparison with the earliest Section 2 cases," which required "overt acts" for proof of intent.[28] Topping things off, a major U.S. government case against IBM was withdrawn in January 1982.

We first cover the private suits against Kodak and IBM, then the big *U.S.* v. *IBM* case.

1. Kodak (1979)[29] Kodak controls the photography industry, dominating the manufacture of still cameras, film, and paper used to

---

[26] *Berkey Photo* v. *Eastman Kodak Co.*, 603 F.2d 263 (2d Cir. 1979).

[27] National Commission for the Review of the Antitrust Laws and Procedures, *Report to the President and the Attorney General* (Washington, D.C., January 1979), p. 156.

[28] John A. Maher, "Draining the ALCOA 'Wishing Well,' the Section 2 Conduct Requirement After *Kodak* and *CalComp*," *Fordham Law Review* (December 1979), pp. 294–295.

[29] *Berkey Photo, Inc.* v. *Eastman Kodak Company* 603 F.2d 263 (2d Cir. 1979), cert. denied 444 U.S. 1093 (1980).

print color pictures. During the late 1960s and early 1970s its shares of these markets ranged from 64% to 94%. In photofinishing, however, it held about 10%.

Berkey is primarily a photofinisher, but between 1966 and 1978 it competed with Kodak in still cameras. Disappointed with its lack of success in still cameras, Berkey sued Kodak for monopolizing the camera and film markets. A jury favored Berkey, but the circuit court of appeals reversed, and the Supreme Court let the reversal stand.

Berkey's claims concerning Kodak's dominance were never questioned. As the court put it, "If a finding of monopoly power were all that were necessary to complete a violation of Section 2, our task in this case would be considerably lightened." Berkey's claims concerning intent were severely questioned, however. These claims centered on Kodak's introduction in 1972 of its 110 compact camera *system*. The word "system" needs stress because it was more than just a new camera, it included entirely new film (Kodacolor II), film format, and photofinishing. Kodak decided upon its package approach rather haltingly, in large part because of uncertainties as to the adequacy of its old film and the performance capabilities of its new film. Berkey challenged the introduction of the 110 system using essentially three arguments:

> *first*, that because Kodak set *de facto* standards for the photography industry, it had a special duty to refrain from surprise innovations and was required to make adequate predisclosure to enable rivals to stay competitive with it; *second*, that the introduction of Kodacolor II as part of the 110 system was not technically necessary for the new camera and was instead a use of Kodak's monopoly power in film to gain a competitive advantage in cameras; and *finally*, that limiting Kodacolor II to the 110 format unlawfully foreclosed competition by other manufacturers in existing formats.[30]

While rejecting Berkey's arguments the circuit court explicitly rejected *Alcoa's* "thrust upon" standard. Kodak, the Court said, may "compete aggressively," even to the point of using its *combined* film and camera capabilities to bolster its faltering camera sales. An integrated business does not "offend the Sherman Act whenever one of its departments benefits from association with a division possessing a monopoly in its own market."[31]

2. CalComp (1970)[32]   In 1969 and 1970 IBM began to suffer substantial competition from new "plug compatible" peripherals manufacturers,

---

30 Maher, "Draining the ALCOA 'Wishing Well,' " pp. 312–313 (emphasis added).

31 Many major innovations like miniature cameras and cartridge loading cannot be credited to Kodak. Indeed, diffusion of these innovations was delayed for decades because of Kodak's film monopoly. James W. Brock, "Structural Monopoly, Technical Performance, and Predatory Innovation," *American Business Law Journal* (Fall 1983), pp. 291–306.

32 *California Computer Products, Inc., et al.* v. *International Business Machines*, 613 F.2d 727 (9th Cir. 1979).

or PCMs. By May 1971 the PCMs had 14.5% of IBM's disk-drive market and 13.7% of its tape-drive market. Moreover, these shares would have been about 20% by 1976 had IBM not done something. But IBM did do something. On May 27, 1971, it introduced long-term leases coupled with price reductions of 20–35% on equipment vulnerable to such competition.

Within the year following, PCM equipment orders were off 44% from the previous year, despite deep defensive price cuts by the PCM companies. They lost money for the next two years. For its part, IBM made up its lost revenues by increasing prices in other product lines — central processing units, card equipment, and maintenance services — just two months after the May reductions. These increases varied from 4% to 8% on equipment, and some maintenance charges rose 25%.

This and related episodes sparked a rash of PCM suits charging IBM with monopolization of peripherals markets. CalComp's suit was typical, and all of CalComp's allegations of IBM wrongdoing were rejected by the circuit court. *First*, IBM's price cuts on peripherals were allegedly predatory. But this claim was rejected because CalComp failed to prove that IBM's prices were below cost. *Second*, CalComp argued that IBM's recoupment with price increases on other products was an unlawful use of IBM's power in the mainframe market. This claim also lost its wheels, however, because *complete* recoupment had not been shown and because rising costs may have justified those price increases (suspicious timing notwithstanding). In language reminiscent of *U.S. Steel*, the court concluded that IBM's conduct was not "*unreasonably* restrictive of competition."

C. Summary

Kodak and *CalComp* thus offer cover for a monopolist's "hard competition." *Berkey's* instructions seem especially solid. Monopolists may innovate significantly improved products without disclosure of trade secrets or provision of other aids to rivals. Monopolists need not restrain their research and development efforts. Furthermore, diversified monopolists may exploit benefits of association among their various divisions insofar as those benefits are based on "more efficient production, greater ability to develop complementary products, reduced transaction costs," and so forth (*not* including coercive acts like tying). The clear teaching from *CalComp* is that a monopolist may fend off rivals with price cuts as long as its prices remain profitable — that is, remain above average total cost.

Berkey and *CalComp* thus paved the way for Reagan's Assistant Attorney General William Baxter, who withdrew the government's big case against IBM even though it had been prosecuted for 13 years under four presidents previous to Reagan and was just months away from a district court opinion. This withdrawal was historic.

3. IBM (Dismissed 1982)[33]   As shown in Figure 10–1, a computer system has numerous components, much as a stereo system has. IBM, Unisys, and the other big companies are called systems suppliers, for they produce and market a full line of "hardware" equipment together with "software" programs and services to run their systems. A second sector is made up of **plug-compatible** or **peripherals** manufacturers. They produce printers, tape drives, disk drives, and other individual items of peripheral equipment that can be plugged into the central system. Third, there are a host of service bureaus, consulting groups, programmers, and leasing firms that deal primarily in services rather than manufacturing. They are often lumped together as software houses. Finally, the newest segment of the industry sells minicomputers. Responsibility for development of these devices rests not with the huge systems suppliers but with smaller firms like Data General, Hewlett-Packard, and Apple.

IBM's Market Share.[34]   Before Baxter, the Justice Department contended that the market should be defined narrowly to include "general purpose" computers and peripheral products compatible with IBM equipment—systems suppliers, essentially. Moreover, the department

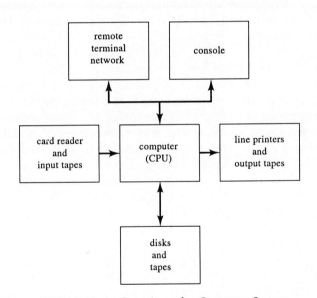

FIGURE 10–1. Overview of a Computer System.

---

[33] *U.S.* v. *International Business Machines Corp.,* 69 CIV 200, So. Dist. of N.Y.

[34] For brief discussion see Leonard W. Weiss, "The Structure-Conduct-Performance Paradigm and Antitrust," *Univ. of Pennsylvania Law Review* (April 1979), pp. 1124–1130.

measured market shares in terms of the lease value of computers *in-stalled*—that is, the rental value of all general-purpose systems in use whether leased or purchased. By this reckoning, IBM's annual market share ranged between 68% and 75% over the period 1964–1972.

In contrast, IBM argued the market should include practically every-thing having to do with computers. Inclusion of all electronic data pro-cessing businesses reduced IBM's market share to 33%. Moreover, this 33% figure threw together all annual revenues from sales and rentals. It was not based on installed equipment.

IBM's Intent.   IBM contended that, even if the 68–75% figures were accurate, its power derived from superior skill, foresight, and industry. But the historical record is far from clear on this point.

From 1924 IBM has supplied a broad line of business machines. Its early forte was punch card tabulating equipment. In 1935, IBM had under lease 85.7% of all tabulating machines, 86.1% of all sorting machines, and 82% of all punch card installations then used in the United States. IBM did not fully appreciate the computer's potential until 1951, when one of IBM's best customers, the U.S. Census Bureau, accepted delivery of the world's first commercial computer from Univac, a division of Remington Rand (now Unisys). At the time, IBM held 90% of the punch card tabulating machine market, and Remington Rand ac-counted for the remaining 10%. Hence, IBM rightly viewed Univac I as a threat to its existence.

Shortly after IBM entered the computer field (delivering its first machine in 1953), two other business machine manufacturers joined IBM and Sperry Rand—National Cash Register (NCR) and Burroughs. As it turned out, prior business-machine experience was a crucial determinant of success in computers. IBM's big advantage lay in its accumulation of tabulating machine customers who had vast amounts of data already coded on punch cards, plus a natural interest in any means of rapidly processing them. IBM catered to this group by designing its computers to read their cards. IBM had more than just good contacts, it had a good reputation; and during 1956, "IBM shipped 85.2% of the value of new systems, and Remington Rand only 9.7%—approximately the same rela-tive shares as then existing in the tabulating machine market.[35]

IBM's "lag-behind-then-recover-quickly" pattern of behavior became commonplace thereafter. Remington Rand and RCA were the first to introduce transistorized computers. Philco introduced the first large-scale solid-state system. Data General was the first with medium-scale integra-tion and complete semiconductor memories. Honeywell and Burroughs were the most innovative with operating systems and compilers. Gen-eral Electric developed time sharing. And so on. Attempted entry often

---

[35] Gerald Brock, *The U.S. Computer Industry: A Study of Market Power* (Cambridge, Mass.: Ballinger, 1975), p. 13.

motivated these efforts. What is more, these efforts nibbled away much of IBM's early market share, but IBM always managed a rebound by duplication. By contrast, many of these innovators are no longer producing computers.

Several barriers to entry into the general purpose field protected IBM from those innovative would-be competitors. In economies of scale, a 10% share of the market or thereabouts seems to have been necessary to achieve full production efficiency. In product differentiation, two interrelated factors fostered fairly intense brand loyalty when it came to complete systems—(1) buyer ignorance, and (2) a lack of standardization.[36] Finally, capital requirements for new entry amounted to about $1 billion, a princely sum.

Specific Charges.   On intent, the Justice Department levied a number of specific charges. It alleged that IBM tried to maintain control and to inhibit entry deliberately through a wide variety of questionable marketing, financial, and technical maneuvers. These included

> "Bundling," whereby IBM quoted a *single* price for hardware, software, and related support. (IBM unbundled in 1970).
> "Fighting machines," whereby IBM introduced selected computers with inordinately low prices in those sectors of the industry where its competitors appeared to be on the verge of success.
> "Paper machines," whereby IBM tried to dissuade computer users from acquiring or leasing Control Data's 6600 (an advanced, truly remarkable machine) by announcing that IBM would soon have a comparable and perhaps even superior product, when in fact IBM had no such thing.

After reviewing the evidence amassed against IBM, Assistant Attorney General Baxter was not convinced, so he withdrew the suit in January 1982. He said that several of the acts attributed to IBM "may have occurred." But he said the most persuasive instances took place outside the market covered by the lawsuit. He did not think IBM had committed any "serious business improprieties," so the case was "without merit."[37]

Several days later Judge Edelstein, who had presided over six years of trial only to be denied the chance to decide the case, was quoted as saying that Mr. Baxter suffered from "myopia and misunderstanding of the antitrust laws and this case specifically." "Even one with a prodigious intellect," Edelstein said, "couldn't be expected to come up with a reasoned evaluation" of the case in the four or five months Mr. Baxter spent studying it.[38]

36 *Ibid.*, p. 47, 51.
37 *The Wall Street Journal*, January 11, 1982, pp. 1, 6; January 26, 1982, p. 10.
38 *The Wall Street Journal*, January 26, 1982, p. 10. For the debate among economists see F. M. Fisher, et al., *Folded, Spindled, and Mutilated* (Cambridge, Mass.: MIT Press, 1983); Russell Pittman, "Predatory Investment: U.S. vs. IBM," *International Journal of Industrial Organization* (December 1984), pp. 341–365; Lee Preston, "Predatory Marketing," in

In short, the structural approach grounded on *Alcoa* and shaped into proposals for "no-fault" legislation thus seems forsaken. Illegal monopoly will apparently not be found without proof of *palpably anticompetitive conduct*, a conduct approach reminiscent of *U.S. Steel*. The structural approach could be faulted for possibly punishing some meritorious winners of the competitive battle, thereby casting a wet blanket on incentives.[39] On the other hand, the conduct approach of *Berkey*, *CalComp*, and Mr. Baxter might yield more artificial monopoly power than is desirable.

Table 10–2 sketches the resulting history. In the early days, dastardly deeds indicated intent. During the *Alcoa* era a large dominant firm could not do the same things as a smaller rival—for example, aggressively gain control of key inputs, accumulate acquired patents, restrictively license instead of sell goods, engage in tying, or vary price sharply depending on competitive conditions (even if pricing above cost). Though "normal" or "reasonable" for a small firm, such tactics could not be used by a dominant firm to maintain dominance—that is, drive smaller rivals from the field. Most recently, since 1970, several new tactics have been questioned but found permissible—for example, IBM's paper machines and preclusive product designs. Moreover, several things found unacceptable during the *Alcoa* era now seem to be excused as nothing more than "hard" competition. Just how far the law has retreated remains unclear. The Supreme Court has not clarified matters. Furthermore, it may be that the *IBM* and *Kodak* cases were to some degree special cases. Both involved industries with rather rapid technological change. And of the two, the case containing the most questionable conduct, *IBM*, was also the case posing the greatest difficulties for market definition. Still, there now appears to be greater freedom for a "monopoly" to defend its position.

SUMMARY

The Sherman Act outlaws monopolization. Establishing a violation requires proof of two elements: (1) substantial market power and (2) intent. Reason, estimation, and hunch make appraisal of these elements

---

Regulation of Marketing and the Public Interest, edited by F. E. Balderson et al. (New York: Pergamon, 1981), pp. 81–112; Alan McAdams, "The Computer Industry," in *The Structure of American Industry*, 6th ed., edited by Walter Adams (New York: Macmillan, 1982); and Richard T. DeLamarter, *Big Blue: IBM's Use and Abuse of Power* (New York: Dodd Mead, 1986). By the way, although IBM won a withdrawal, new entrants (like Tandem, Hitachi, and Amdahl) and new products (like laptops, workstations, and minis) have given IBM new competition. See *Business Week*, October 16, 1989, pp. 75–86.

[39] Defenders of the structural approach point out, however, that power meritoriously gained cannot justify an award of perpetual power. Patents, for instance, last only 17 years.

TABLE 10–2.   Summary of Conduct Indicating Intent to Monopolize (Illustrative Cases in Parentheses)

1890–1940 Early days	1. Predatory pricing and advertising (Standard Oil and American Tobacco)
	2. Bogus firms and fighting brands (Standard Oil and American Tobacco)
	3. Secret rebates from suppliers (Standard Oil)
1945–1970 Alcoa era	4. Mergers to achieve power (Grinnell)
	5. Preclusive acquisition of key inputs (Alcoa)
	6. Acquisition of patents (United Shoe)
	7. Restrictive licensing (United Shoe)
	8. Bundling or tying (United Shoe, IBM)
	9. Deep price cutting (Grinnell, United Shoe, IBM)
Refinement and retreat	10. Paper machines (IBM)
	11. Systems exploitation (Kodak, IBM)
	12. Preclusive product design (IBM, Kodak)

uncertain. Hence we find very big cases in this area. Just about everything is considered except the rainfall in Indianapolis.

When attempting to examine market power, the courts consider barriers to entry of various kinds and profits. The item receiving greatest attention, however, is market share. Broad definitions of the market tend to favor defendants; narrow definitions favor the prosecutors. Which way the court will turn in any particular case is often unpredictable. Once a market definition is established, percentage points become all important. The consensus is that a market share well below 60% lies beneath the reach of the law (unless abusive practices are present), whereas shares above 80% make Justice Department attorneys look good in court.

On the issue of intent, interpretations may be divided into three periods. (1) Before *Alcoa* in 1945, intent could be demonstrated only by evidence of predatory, exclusionary, or unfair acts. The rule of reason essentially meant condemnation of unreasonable behavior. (2) After *Alcoa* and until recently, intent could be demonstrated by evidence that a dominant firm's actions were not "honestly industrial," not "passive," not reflective of "superior skill," "superior product," "business acumen," or "historic accident." This reading of Section 2 left monopolists room to maneuver, but not much. (3) The period since about 1970 reveals conflicting strains and ambiguity. Contributing to the muddle is a basic tension in the law as inherited from *Alcoa*, a tension created by a willingness to condone monopoly (pure and simple) and a simultaneous desire to condemn monopolization (tainted and crude).

Thus the early portion of the current period witnessed efforts to confirm and even extend *Alcoa*. Big cases were brought against Xerox, AT&T, and IBM. In addition, "presumptive rules," or "no-fault" structural tests were proposed, whereby defendants would have to prove their innocence if they transgressed some previously specified criteria, such as having more than 60% of the market for three years running.

Most recently, however, these rumblings have been silenced. *Xerox* and *AT&T* were settled by stringent consent decrees. But the legislative proposals came to naught. More importantly, we have witnessed a substantial movement away from *Alcoa* toward *U.S. Steel. Kodak* and *Cal-Comp* led the way. Withdrawal of *IBM* capped the trend. Whether these developments take us too far in condoning monopolization is a much debated question.

Part III

CONDUCT

11

■ Introduction to Conduct

Ideally we should control a major portion of the [airline] traffic at each of the cities in the northeast. The beauty of the . . . strategy is not just the marketing identity and control that it gives us. In addition, it enables us to keep control of prices . . . thus insulating a significant portion of our traffic from the devastating effects of unbridled price competition.
—RANDALL MALIN, Executive Vice President
of USAir, 1985 (internal memo to the
president and CEO of USAir)

Conduct is behavior—what firms do with their prices, production levels, products, promotions, and other key operating variables. As suggested in the opening quote, market structure influences conduct. In particular, market power, or "control," allows some "control" over price. Now that we have studied structure, we are ready to tackle its implications for conduct.

When discussing structure we also noted a reverse flow of cause and effect in which conduct could influence structure. For example, established firms in highly concentrated markets might behave in ways that make new entry difficult, thereby causing the market to remain highly concentrated. As we shall see, airlines try to gain and maintain control of their markets by price discrimination, frequent flyer plans, and special ties to travel agents.

Thus our keen interest in market power and competition continues in the next eight chapters covering conduct. Recall the short definition of *market power*; it is *the ability to influence market price and/or subdue rivals.* The first part of this definition referring to influence over price reflects a causal flow from structure to conduct. (And we shall go beyond price to consider structure's impact on nonprice conduct as well.) Firms possessing market power may *exploit* that power by raising price above the competitive level to increase their profits. In contrast, the second part of this definition referring to weakened rivals reflects a reverse causal flow, one running from conduct to structure. (And here we include power over potential rivals who might enter the market as well as existing rivals already there.) Firms subdue rivals in order to augment or maintain their market power, as might be measured by increased market shares or heightened barriers to entry. This kind of conduct may be said to *extend* market power. In its most brutal forms, exclusionary tactics of various kinds are involved, tactics that powerful firms may use to eliminate, discipline, or injure their weaker rivals. Finally, our definition of market power has an "and/or" conjunction linking its reference to exploitation and extension. This indicates *three* possibilities for conduct rather than just two: (1) conduct that exploits market power, (2) conduct that extends power, and (3) *combination conduct* that may be *both exploitative and expansionary at the same time.*

These three categories of conduct serve as column headings in Table 11–1. While the column headings of Table 11–1 identify three broad classes of power-related conduct, the row headings identify three possible sources of market power—single-firm power, tacit collective power (based on tacit understanding), and explicit collective power (based on express collusion). Whereas the column headings broadly suggest *what* kinds of conduct will hold our attention, the row headings could be said to identify *who* is engaged in those behaviors. A single firm may be able to engage in exploitation or extension if it enjoys "dominance" (to be defined shortly). On the other hand, firms that individually lack dominance may collectively achieve dominance through tacit or express agreement. They collude instead of compete.

In fact, Table 11–1 summarizes this chapter. Section I below elaborates on *who* it is that engages in market conduct (the row headings) and *what* basic kinds of conduct are at issue (the column headings). Section II surveys some empirical evidence linking "who" and "what" in a simple but rather dramatic way, for it shows that, indeed, market power typically raises prices. Section III then discusses each cell of the matrix in Table 11–1 beginning with cell A and ending with cell I. Theories of what firms might do under these various conditions receive attention, but empirical examples will be emphasized. Section IV qualifies the analysis of section III and briefly introduces the remaining chapters on conduct. Finally, an appendix on the airline industry illustrates our findings.

TABLE 11–1.   Varying Sources of Power Cross Classified with the Exploitation and Extension of That Power

	Exploitation of Market Power (e.g., by raising price or following quiet life): Short-Run Profit, Long-Run Loss of Power	Extension of Market Power (either inhibiting or excluding rivals and potential rivals): Short-Run Profits Forgone, Long-Run Gains	Combination Conduct (which both exploits power and is exclusionary): Profitable in All Periods
Single-firm power	A. Monopoly or dominant firm raising price and restricting output (or otherwise exploiting power)	D. Single-firm exclusionary conduct (e.g., capacity preemption, limit pricing, predation)	G. Single-firm exclusive dealing, tying, price discrimination, and such
Tacit collective power	B. Tacit collusive restraint on supply in oligopoly, raising price	E. Tacit collective use of exclusionary devices (e.g., predation or product proliferation)	H. Uniform collective practice of these behaviors
Explicit collective power	C. Cartel activity to raise price or otherwise exploit power	F. Explicit collusion applied to exclude or check rivals	I. Aggregated rebate cartels, exclusive patent cross-licensing

I. INTRODUCTION: WHO AND WHAT?

A. Who Engages in the Conduct?

Research measuring market power with market shares divides into two basic approaches. The first approach tests for *collective* power as measured by, say, the four-firm concentration ratio or H index. The basic idea here is that the level of concentration will determine the degree of collusion in the market. In particular, higher concentration is expected to foster greater uniformity of behavior among firms in the market—a reluctance to compete vigorously for additional business once it is recognized that in the end, such competition hurts all sellers with low prices and profits.

The second approach focuses on the *individual firm* and commonly measures power by the individual firm's market share. As we have seen, firms differ in the products they sell, their organizational forms, the intensity of their advertising, and sometimes in the level of their prices, even when they are in the same market. This diversity often allows firms to achieve market power on their own, without relying on the collusive cooperation of others in the market. Pursuing efficiencies or innovations might yield this power, so dynamics often enter this single-firm approach.

Both approaches have generated substantial evidence of market power. For example, many researchers have found a positive association between marketwide concentration and profit levels, thereby lending support for the "collective" approach.[1] At the same time, however, profit levels have been found to be positively associated with individual firm market shares, which is consistent with the view that individual firms possess market power independent and apart from any collective effects.[2] When researchers pit the two possibilities against each other to test which approach is more representative of reality, the results are mixed. Some comparative studies favor the collective, marketwide approach.[3] Others find market power in individual firms rather than marketwide collectives.[4] Lodged between these one finds results supporting a compromise view, where market power seems to reside in some collective or strategic group of the very largest individual firms, such as those ranked first and second in the market or those among the largest accounting for 30% of total output.[5]

An *eclectic* approach would thus seem to be warranted. For some situations an individual firm analysis would be most accurate. For others, collective power among the leading firms—either tacitly or expressly established—will best explain conduct. Indeed, there are cases

[1] Leonard W. Weiss, "The Concentration-Profits Relationship and Antitrust," in *Industrial Concentration: The New Learning*, edited by Harvey J. Goldschmid et al. (Boston: Little, Brown 1974), pp. 201–220; and F. M. Scherer and David Ross, *Industrial Market Structure and Economic Performance*, 3rd ed. (Boston: Houghton Mifflin, 1990), pp. 411–430.

[2] See, for example, William G. Shepherd, "The Elements of Market Structure," *Review of Economics and Statistics* (February 1972), pp. 25–35; Steven Martin, *Market, Firm, and Economic Performance*, Monograph Series in Economics and Finance, New York University, 1983; and Steven A. Rhoades, "Market Share as a Source of Market Power: Implications and Some Evidence," *Journal of Economics and Business*, Vol. 37 (1985), pp. 343–363.

[3] Alice P. White, "Firm or Market Data: the Proper Test of the Structure-Performance Relationship," *Journal of Economics and Business*, Vol. 36 (1984), pp. 151–160; Richard Schmalensee, "Do Markets Differ Much?" *American Economic Review* (June 1985), pp. 341–351.

[4] David Ravenscraft, "Structure-Profit Relationships at the Line of Business and Industry Level," *Review of Economics and Statistics* (February 1983), pp. 22–31; Dennis C. Mueller, *Profits in the Long Run* (Cambridge: Cambridge University Press); and Frederick H. De B. Harris, "Market Structure and Price-Cost Performance under Endogenous Profit Risk," *Journal of Industrial Economics* (September 1986), pp. 35–55.

[5] John E. Kwoka, Jr., "The Effect of Market Share Distribution on Industry Performance," *Review of Economics and Statistics* (February 1979), pp. 101–109; and Michael E. Porter, "The Structure Within Industries and Companies' Performance," *Review of Economics and Statistics* (May 1979), pp. 214–227.

where firms behave collusively on some conduct variables but independently on others. In these cases the two approaches could both be applicable to a single industry. Following the order of the row headings in Table 11–1, we begin by discussing single-firm power and then consider tacit and explicit collective power.

1. Single-Firm Power. Significant single-firm power yields "dominance." A **dominant firm** *is one that is able to exercise, acquire, and maintain substantial market power unilaterally, without the need for group collusive agreements, either tacit or explicit.*[6] By this definition a dominant firm has certain advantages over those dominated, as a seller controlling 70% of supply will typically have advantages over buyers who are small and numerous, or as a low-cost established firm will have advantages over a high-cost potential entrant.[7] Quite often, market share is used by economists as a rough general measure of dominance, but the threshold share indicating dominance is not chiseled in granite. Oliver Williamson suggests that a market share over 60% typically establishes dominance.[8] Shepherd and Utton use a threshold of 50%.[9] Stigler, Scherer, Pascoe, Weiss, and Geroski all favor 40% (and Geroski judges this figure to be "the conventionally accepted cut-off point" for empirical work).[10] Still others opt for a 30% threshold to indicate dominance.[11]

Although specific numbers are needed for empirical work or factual examples, single-firm market power is a matter of degree rather than discrete jumps, so there is no solid basis in economics for a sharp dividing line between dominant firms and others. These numbers are therefore somewhat arbitrary. Still, they illustrate the fact that "dominance" occurs without a huge, bone-crushing market share in the 70–100% range. Single-firm dominance occurs "when there is a probability that

[6] Richard Schmalensee, "Standards for Dominant Firm Conduct," in *The Economics of Market Dominance*, edited by Donald Hay and John Vickers, (Oxford: Basil Blackwell, 1987), pp. 61–88.

[7] Advantages or "asymmetries" are stressed by P. A. Geroski and A. Jacquemin, "Dominant Firms and Their Alleged Decline," *International Journal of Industrial Organization* (March 1984), pp. 1–27.

[8] O. E. Williamson, "Dominant Firms and the Monopoly Problem," *Harvard Law Review* (June 1972), pp. 1512–1531.

[9] William G. Shepherd, "Causes of Increased Competition in the U.S. Economy, 1939–1980," *Review of Economics and Statistics* (November 1982), pp. 613–626; and M. A. Utton, *Profits and Stability of Monopoly* (Cambridge: Cambridge University Press, 1986).

[10] G. J. Stigler, "The Kinky Oligopoly Demand Curve and Rigid Prices," *Journal of Political Economy* (October 1947), pp. 432–449; F. M. Scherer, *Industrial Market Structure and Economic Performance*, 2nd ed. (Chicago: Rand McNally, 1980), p. 232; G. A. Pascoe, Jr., and L. W. Weiss, "The Extent and Performance of Market Dominance" (Washington, D.C.: FTC Bureau of Economics Working Paper, 1983); and P. A. Geroski, "Do Dominant Firms Decline?" in *The Economics of Market Dominance*, edited by D. Hay and J. Vickers (Oxford: Basil Blackwell, 1987), pp. 143–167.

[11] John Cubbin and Simon Domberger, "Advertising and Post-Entry Oligopoly Behavior," *Journal of Industrial Economics* (December 1988), pp. 123–140.

the other enterprises in the market will act in a way calculated not to affect adversely the dominant concern's short-term interests."[12] In other words, a dominant firm's rivals will behave more or less noncompetitively. Their motive for this need not be a trembling fear that they would otherwise be crushed (although that could be true of really strong dominance). Rather, the cooperation could be motivated by a recognition among the smaller rivals that following the dominant firm's leadership would best serve their own profit interests. In any case, examples of dominant firms (and their market shares) include Anheuser-Busch in beer (43% United States), Brush Wellman in beryllium-engineered products (65% worldwide), Eastman Kodak in consumer film (50% worldwide), and Loctite in anaerobic adhesives (80% worldwide).

2. Tacit Collective Power. Immediately adjacent to single-firm dominance on the continuum of market power depicted in Table 11–1 is collective power based on **tacit understanding**. Two, three, and even more firms, if dominant in their combined market shares, can frequently reach tacit understandings that curb competition between them. That is to say, *they restrain themselves without formal agreement, each firm choosing not to vie on price or some other variable that could otherwise be the focus of their rivalry.* They may also act uniformly for exclusionary purposes.

In many cases the resulting uniformity yields market conduct and performance approaching that of dominant-firm situations. For example, some concentration-profit studies contain evidence of a "critical" four-firm concentration ratio in the range of 40–60%, above which profits are significantly higher than otherwise, apparently because competition is significantly less when four-firm concentration enters that high range.[13] More qualitatively, Gribbon and Utton analyzed reports of the U.K. Monopolies Commission from 1960–1981 for evidence of "competitive" and "noncompetitive" pricing behavior.[14] They found that 16 of 20 "dominant-firm" industries priced noncompetitively and 18 of 21 "concentrated oligopoly" industries priced noncompetitively mainly by tacit collusion. The proportions of noncompetitive pricing are almost identical despite structural differences between the two classes.

---

12 G. DeQ. Walker, "Control or Dominate a Market: Developments in Australian Merger Law," *Antitrust Bulletin* (Summer 1979), pp. 371–393.

13 See, for example, S. A. Rhoades and Joe Cleaver, "The Nature of the Concentration-Price/Cost Margin Relationship for 352 Manufacturing Industries: 1967," *Southern Economic Journal*, Vol. 39 (1973), pp. 90–102; David Round, "Price-Cost Margins in Australian Manufacturing Industries, 1971–72," *Australian Journal of Management*, Vol. 1 (1976), pp. 85–93; and R. M. Bradburd and A. M. Over, "Organization Costs, Sticky Equilibria, and Critical Levels of Concentration," *Review of Economics and Statistics* (February 1982), pp. 50–58.

14 J. D. Gribbon and M. A. Utton, "The Treatment of Dominant Firms in the U.K. Competition Legislation," in *Mainstreams in Industrial Organization*, edited by H. W. de Jong and W. G. Shepherd (Dordrecht, The Netherlands: Martinus Nijhoff, 1986), pp. 243–272.

3. Explicit Collective Power. **Explicit collusion** *entails an express agreement not to compete in some way.* Although it may be a secret to outsiders, the agreement is reached after participating firms communicate with each other. "Cartel" is the word often used here, as in "OPEC cartel" (for the Organization of Petroleum Exporting Countries).

When market concentration and other structural conditions are such that tacit collusion is not feasible, but conditions are not so competitive that collusion is altogether impossible, tacit collusion may give way to high frequencies of express collusion or cartelization. For example, an analysis of 606 cases of illegal price fixing in the United States found that the highest frequencies of cartel activity occur in markets with approximately 4 to 10 firms. Below 4 firms, cartel activity is relatively rare because tacit collusion or single-firm dominance is controlling. At the other end of the continuum, in markets where firms number more than 10, and especially where they number more than 20, cartel activity is relatively rare because vigorous competition tends to prevail.[15]

B. What Conduct?

Conduct can be divided into price and nonprice categories, with subdivisions of the nonprice category for advertising, packaging, product quality, and so on. Conduct may also be divided into the column headings of Table 11–1. Those divisions emerge from the all-important matter of market power — its exploitation or extension, or both simultaneously. Review of these three cases reveals a different time pattern of profits for each case.

1. Exploitation of Market Power. In theory, the classic example of exploiting market power was examined earlier in Chapter 2 — that is, the pure monopolist raising price and restricting output in order to maximize profit (pages 35–37). Correspondingly, it is easy to imagine a cartel creating a monopoly situation by establishing a single sales agency, through which all firms in the market channel their sales and thereby allow buyers only one source of supply. Again theory would predict an elevated price and a restricted output.

There are several things to note about these situations. First, exploiting market power in this way offers the clearest case available of structure causing conduct. The monopoly structure is obviously what yields the monopolistic conduct. Second, exploitation can take nonprice forms insofar as they too may raise profits. Hence market power may be exploited by reducing product quality, or by curbing customer service, or by cutting back on investments in innovation — all of which may enhance profits by lowering costs while holding to some given price level.

---

[15] A. G. Fraas and D. F. Greer, "Market Structure and Price Collusion: An Empirical Analysis," *Journal of Industrial Economics* (September 1977), pp. 21–44.

Third, the exploitation of market power, with nothing more, may generate high excess profits in the short run, but those excess profits will often shrink in the long run. Why? In the long run new firms may enter the market seeking a piece of the high-profit action, or substitute products may be invented to attract buyers away from the pricey one, or some similar development may undermine the monopolistic power. Figure 11–1(a) illustrates this effect. Profits are high in the near term as exploitation occurs. But they fall and then level out in the long term as dynamic competition erodes the market power that enabled the exploitation in the first place.

2. Expansion of Market Power. Exploiting, which nothing more, may therefore invite the dynamic competition that weakens market power in the long run. On the other hand, those possessing market power can often take steps to extend or maintain their power in the long run. And the typical time pattern of profits associated with these tactics, as show in panel (b) of Figure 11–1, is exactly the opposite of that associated with exploitation shown in panel (a). Extensions of market power typically require some sacrifice of profits in the short run, perhaps even to the point of losses, because they commonly entail lower revenues or higher costs than otherwise in the short run. The payoff comes in the long run, though. Profits eventually rise as market power is extended because that greater power can eventually be exploited. The expectation here is that the rise in future profit will more than compensate for the short-run sacrifices (so the present value of the expected stream of profits will be attractive).

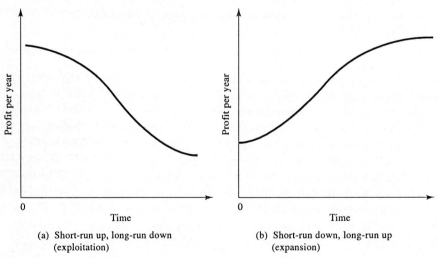

(a) Short-run up, long-run down
(exploitation)

(b) Short-run down, long-run up
(expansion)

FIGURE 11–1. Time pattern of profits corresponding to exploitative and expansionary conduct.

Conduct extending market power belongs to a larger class of conduct called strategic behavior. **Strategic behavior** is *positioning oneself physically or psychologically so as to discourage or thwart actions or reactions by rivals and potential rivals that would, if taken, impair one's own goal attainment.*[16] Product proliferation designed to block the expansion of rivals would be an example. Broadly speaking, strategic behavior entails long-run planning, it takes into account rivals' likely responses when evaluating alternative courses of action, and it uses tactics that depend on dynamic developments in the marketplace.[17] Through strategic behavior dominant firms (individually or collectively) can use their relatively large size, first mover positions, low-cost raw material supplies, or some other advantages to injure weaker existing rivals or discourage the entry of potential rivals.[18] As we shall see in detail later, strategic behaviors that entail some short-run sacrifice of profits include predatory pricing, entry limit pricing, and preemptive capacity expansion. And as may be seen now, these exclusionary tactics are examples of conduct influencing structure, a reversal of the classical causal flow from structure to conduct.

3. Combination Conduct (Exploitative and Expansionary). The two profit patterns of Figure 11–1 are rather extreme cases. Occasionally a dominant firm (or collective group) may employ strategic behaviors that are richly profitable in *both* the short run and the long run, conduct that is both exploitative and expansionary. as Steve Martin remarks,

> There are tactics a dominant firm can employ to influence fringe firms' costs and beliefs about the way the dominant firm will react to fringe behavior. In this way, a dominant firm can maintain market share *and* earn a high profit.[19]

Of the two methods Martin mentions—raising rivals' cost and altering their beliefs—the more readily understandable is the former. A dominant firm may raise its rivals' costs, for example, by imposing exclusive dealing contracts on its suppliers. This would prohibit its low-cost suppliers from selling their services or materials to the dominant firm's rivals, thereby forcing the excluded rivals to rely on higher-cost alterna-

[16] F. M. Scherer, "On the Current State of Knowledge in Industrial Organization," in *Mainstreams in Industrial Organization*, edited by H. W. de Jong and W. G. Shepherd (Dordrecht: Martinus Nijhoff, 1986), p. 13.

[17] Steven C. Salop, "Strategy, Predation, and Antitrust Analysis: An Introduction," in *Strategy, Predation, and Antitrust Analysis*, edited by Steven C. Salop (Washington, D.C.: Federal Trade Commission, 1981), p. 1.

[18] Indeed, by some definitions, the "dominance" we referred to earlier is grounded on just such advantages. Geroski and Jacquemin say that a dominant firm is one which has access to a "differential movement advantage" that "can be exploited by making some credible commitment which pre-empts rivals, and thus restricts the scope of their actions." See "Dominant Firms and Their Alleged Decline," p. 9. Alice P. White says a dominant firm "is able to control to a degree that competitive environment in which all other firms operate." See *The Dominant Firm* (Ann Arbor: University of Michigan Press, 1983), p. 3.

[19] Stephen Martin, *Industrial Economics* (New York: Macmillan, 1988), p. 79.

tive sources of supply. As Tom Krattenmaker and Steve Salop say, raising rivals' cost "need not entail sacrificing one's own profits in the short
run."[20] An example of this is U.S. Steel Corporation shortly after the
turn of the century. Through vertical acquisition of prime iron ore deposits beyond its own needs, U.S. Steel "managed *both* to protect its
market share *and* to earn handsome profits."[21]

This "combination" conduct shares some special similarities with
"expansionary" conduct. For one thing, both entail strategic behavior, as
defined earlier. Second, it is once again a case of conduct influencing
structure rather than the reverse because combination conduct has
exclusionary consequences for the number of rivals and the ease of their
entry. It should be noted, however, that in this present case the conduct
is exclusionary without significant sacrifice of profits because structural
conditions are very anticompetitive to begin with. Hence it is perhaps
best to say that in these instances, causal flow is not one way but is
simultaneously interacting, with anticompetitive structure and conduct
mutually maintaining each other.

A final similarity is related to the second. It is often difficult to tell
the difference between "expansionary" and "combination" conduct because behavior can sometimes be either one depending on the circumstances. In particular, there are practices that may have high costs
under most circumstances (and thereby lead to some sacrifices of profits
in the short run before long-run gains begin to mount), but may have
little or no cost in other circumstances (thereby qualifying for combination conduct). For example, a firm may exclude others by "patent
preemption." A patent is a legal monopoly over the use of a new idea,
so aggressively patenting the inventions that potential newcomers might
rely on as their means of entry can block their rivalry. Patent preemption normally incurs costs for the legal and scientific efforts involved,
but Gilbert and Newbery show theoretically that certain circumstances
reduce "the cost of preemption to nil" and make the preservation of
monopoly "costless and hence doubly attractive."[22] In general, firms and
strategic groups that are greatly dominant to begin with enjoy much
greater access to the costless practices of the combination category than
do nondominant firms and strategic groups.

Despite these close similarities between expansionary and combination conduct, it is useful to separate them in Table 11–1 and elsewhere.

---

20 T. G. Krattenmaker and S. C. Salop, "Anticompetitive Exclusion: Raising Rivals'
Cost to Achieve Power over Price," *Yale Law Journal* (December 1986), p. 224. On exclusive
dealing specifically, see W. S. Comanor and H. E. Frech III, "The Competitive Effects of
Vertical Agreements," *American Economic Review* (June 1985), pp. 539–546.

21 Naomi R. Lamoreaux, *The Great Merger Movement in American Business, 1895–1904*
(Cambridge: Cambridge University Press, 1985), p. 153 (emphasis added).

22 Richard J. Gilbert and David M. G. Newbery, "Preemptive Patenting and the Per-
sistance of Monopoly," *American Economic Review* (June 1982), p. 524.

Predatory pricing and entry-limit pricing typify expansionary conduct. However, we find that, in contrast, exclusive dealing, tying, loyalty rebates, and exclusive cross-licensing of patents typify combination conduct.

II. PRICE LEVEL AND MARKET POWER: AN ILLUSTRATED NOTE ON METHOD

Theories of business behavior abound. Their abundance is explained partly by the fact that *assumptions* are the seeds from which theories grow. Change a theory's underlying assumptions and (wham) you change the theory that sprouts. Because assumptions can be easily changed, theories of conduct mutate and multiply by the millions, or at least it seems so to someone who tries to stay abreast of new developments in industrial organization.

The abundance of conduct theories is also explained by the great *variety* of observable behaviors. There are, for instance, dozens of ways a firm may cut price if it want to—for example, grant a cash rebate after purchase, discount the posted price, add "free" goods into the bargain, and so on. Theories vary with the variety.

Unfortunately, theories prove nothing. By changing assumptions economists can reach conclusions with one theory that directly contradict those of another theory. For example, under one set of assumptions it may be argued that cartels are beneficial to society.[23] Under another set of assumptions theory supports the traditional conclusion that cartels are harmful.[24] Similarly, an abundant variety of theories may not be very helpful despite the fact that actual business behavior comes in abundant varieties. As F. M. Scherer has remarked, "A set of theories that can explain everything predicts nothing."[25] In sum, theories are helpful, but they suffer limitations. Economic knowledge ultimately rests on the empirical record.

An excellent way to illustrate this and at the same time further introduce conduct is to review briefly the evidence regarding market concentration and *price* level. As noted earlier, empirical studies commonly reveal a positive association between market concentration and *profit* levels. But theoretical interpretation of the positive concentration-profit relationship has been hotly disputed. Two interpretations are possible because profits depend on two variables—prices and costs. One interpretation, the market-power theory, is that profits rise with concen-

[23] Donald Dewey, "Information, Entry, and Welfare: The Case for Collusion," *American Economic Review* (September 1979), pp. 587–594.

[24] Don E. Waldman, "Welfare and Collusion: Comment," *American Economic Review* (March 1982), pp. 268–271.

[25] F. M. Scherer, "Reviewing the Economics of Market Dominance," *International Journal of Industrial Organization*, Vol. 6 (1988), p. 517.

tration because higher concentration yields greater market power, and the market power fosters *higher prices* and therefore the higher profits. The alternative interpretation, the efficient-market theory, holds that higher concentration reflects greater efficiency, not greater market power, and this greater efficiency *lowers costs*, thereby yielding the higher profits that are associated with higher concentration.[26] Under this latter theory prices might even be *lower* with higher concentration if these hypothesized lower costs are at least partially passed on to buyers in the form of lower prices.

Thus direct evidence on the relationship between concentration and price levels would settle this dispute over the positive concentration-profits relationship. The market-power theory would win support if concentration and prices were *positively* associated, whereas the efficient-market theory would be supported if concentration and prices were *inversely* related, with higher concentration being associated with lower prices (everything else being equal).

It turns out that the market-power theory deserves our greatest respect. *Price levels are positively associated with market concentration measured in a variety of ways* (e.g., four-firm concentration ratio or H index or a shrinking number of firms). Statistical tests of the price-concentration relationship are more difficult than are tests of the profit-concentration relationship because prices cannot be compared across markets as readily as profits. Still, price tests are possible, especially those that are *intra*industry, *inter*market, and cross-sectional. That is, they compare prices of a *given* product or service in diverse geographic markets at one point in time—the price of cement in Seattle, St. Louis, and Boston in March 1988, for instance. Upon occasion it is also possible to trace major price and concentration changes for a given product over time, such as the price of airline services in New England before and after a significant merger of two New England air carriers. Thus despite the difficulties, many dozens of empirical studies have been conducted, and all but a few of them show a positive relationship between concentration and price level. They therefore support the market-power hypothesis and refute the market-efficiency alternative.[27]

---

[26] Harold Demsetz, "Industry Structure, Market Rivalry, and Public Policy," *Journal of Law and Economics* (April 1973), pp. 1–9. Also see Samuel Peltzman, "The Gains and Losses from Industrial Concentration," *Journal of Law and Economics* (October 1977), pp. 229–263.

[27] Most of the studies that show contrary results can be faulted for not giving the hypothesis a fair test. One of the most serious problems is attenuated variance in the measure of concentration. Studies comparing one-firm markets with two-firm markets are unlikely to yield significant results because competition may be just as lacking in the latter as in the former. See, for example, Donald R. Fraser and Peter S. Rose, "Banking Structure and Performance in Isolated Markets," *Antitrust Bulletin* (Fall 1972), pp. 927–947; and Gary M. Fournier and Donald L. Martin, "Does Government-Restricted Entry Produce Market Power?" *Bell Journal of Economics* (Spring 1983), pp. 44–56.

Let's review the evidence in four steps: auction markets, geographic cross sections of markets, changes in concentration and prices over time, and miscellaneous cases.

A. Auction Markets

In auction markets, bidding determines who becomes the seller or the buyer. Those selling highway construction services, for instance, bid for highway building contracts as projects became available from government authorities. They submit asking prices. Conversely, those buying timber in the U.S. national forests bid for it by offering to pay prices that will win the business. As a consequence, auction markets tend to place sellers (or buyers) in competition with each other — price being determined by the lowest asking price among sellers (or the highest offering price among buyers, if they are the ones doing the bidding). There is a large body of theory that generally predicts higher selling prices as the number of bidding sellers falls (or lower buying prices as the number of bidding buyers falls).[28]

None of the 20,000 items you might buy in a supermarket is sold to you at auction. However, hundreds of goods and services are subject to bidding, and quite a few of them have yielded tests of whether the number of bidders affects price. Tax-exempt bond issues, offshore oil tracts, national forest timber, highway construction projects, defense weapon systems, and mass-transit construction projects — in all these cases the statistical results show that the number of bidders affects price in the direction that competition would suggest.[29] For example, a study of contracts for the construction of Bay Area Rapid Transit (BART) around San Francisco Bay found that, on average, each additional bidder added enough competition to lower price by 2%.[30]

Figure 11-2 presents a visual example. Each of the 44 dots represents a major drug purchase by the U.S. Military Medical Supply Agency (MMSA) during 1959 and early 1960. Two characteristics of each

---

[28] Lance Brannman, J. Douglass Klein, and Leonard W. Weiss, "The Price Effects of Increased Competition in Auction Markets," *Review of Economics and Statistics* (February 1987), pp. 24–32.

[29] Lance Brannman, J. Douglass Klein, and Leonard W. Weiss, "Concentration and Winning Bids in Auctions," *Antitrust Bulletin* (Spring 1984), pp. 27–31; Reuben Kessel, "A Study of the Effects of Competition in the Tax-Exempt Bond Market," *Journal of Political Economy* (July 1971), pp. 706–738; J. Douglass Klein and Lance E. Brannman, "The Effectiveness and Stability of Highway Bid-Rigging" (mimeo, 1987); John M. Kuhlman and Stanley R. Johnson, "The Number of Competitors and Bid Prices," *Southern Economic Journal* (July 1983), pp. 213–220; James L. Smith, "Risk Aversion and Bidding Behavior for Offshore Petroleum Leases," *Journal of Industrial Economics* (March 1982), pp. 251–269; and S. Sagawara, "Putting Adam Smith to Work in the Pentagon," *Washington Post,* National Weekly Edition, March 13–19, 1989, p. 31.

[30] Kenneth M. Gaver and Jerold L. Zimmerman, "An Analysis of Competitive Bidding on BART Contracts," *Journal of Business* (July 1977), pp. 279–295.

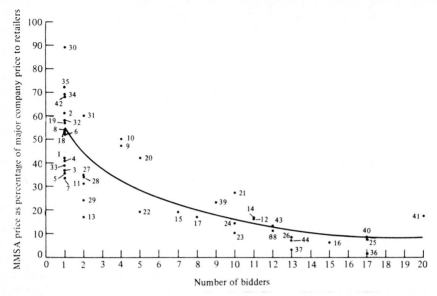

FIGURE 11–2. MMSA drug procurement: relationship of number of bidders to MMSA price expressed as percentage of commercial price, 1959 and early 1960. Source: U.S. Senate, Subcommittee on Antitrust and Monopoly of the Committee on the Judiciary, Administered Prices of Drugs: Report. 87th Cong., 1st Sess. (1961), p. 95.

sale are plotted there: (1) the number of firms bidding on the supply contract, as shown on the horizontal axis, and (2) the lowest price at which MMSA was able to buy the drug, which is expressed as percentage of the price charged to retail druggists for the same product sold under brand name. The diagram shows an inverse relationship between MMSA prices and the number of bidders.

B. Geographic Cross Sections

Concentration-price studies based on data from separate geographic markets have recently multiplied apace. Hence there is now a mountain of evidence indicating a positive concentration-price relationship concerning cement, gasoline retailing, life insurance, bank checking accounts, auto loans, business loans, personal loans, newspaper advertising space, legal services, beer, drug retailing, airlines, natural gas pipelines, hospital services, railroads, and grocery retailing.[31] For example:

- Results for commercial bank new auto loans may be seen by comparing the average interest rate on a standardized auto loan in the

[31] R. S. Thompson, "Structure and Conduct in Local Advertising Markets," *Journal of Industrial Economics* (December 1984), pp. 241–249; Roland H. Koller and L. W. Weiss, "Price Levels and Seller Concentration: The Case of Portland Cement," in *Concentration and*

Price, edited by L. W. Weiss (Cambridge, Mass.: MIT Press, 1989), pp. 17–40; James M. MacDonald, "Competition and Railroad Rates for the Shipment of Corn, Soybeans, and Wheat," *Rand Journal of Economics* (Spring 1987), pp. 151–163; John R. Schroeter, Scott L. Smith, and Steven L. Cox, "Advertising and Competition in Routine Legal Service Markets: An Empirical Investigation," *Journal of Industrial Economics* (September 1987), pp. 49–60; Daniel V. Gordon, "The Effect of Price Deregulation on the Competitive Behavior of Retail Drug Firms," *Applied Economics* (May 1988), pp. 641–652; Neela D. Manage, "Further Evidence on Estimating Regulated Personal Loan Market Relationships," *Quarterly Review of Economics and Business* (Winter 1983), pp. 63–80; Monica Noether, "Competition Among Hospitals," *Journal of Health Economics* (September 1988), pp. 259–284; Ronald W. Cotterill, "Market Power in the Retail Food Industry," *Review of Economics and Statistics* (August 1986), pp. 379–386; Allen N. Berger and Timothy H. Hannan, "The Price-Concentration Relationship in Banking," *Review of Economics and Statistics* (May 1989), pp. 291–299; Peter J. Meyer, "Concentration and Performance in Local Retail Markets," in *Industrial Organization, Antitrust, and Public Policy,* edited by John V. Craven (Boston: Kluwer, 1983), pp. 145–161; Stephen A. Rhoades, *Structure-Performance Studies in Banking: An Updated Summary and Evaluation,* Staff Study 119 (Washington, D.C.: Board of Governors of the Federal Reserve System, 1982); E. E. Baily, David R. Graham, and Daniel P. Kaplan, *Deregulating the Airlines* (Cambridge, Mass.: MIT Press 1985), pp. 155–165; G. D. Call and T. E. Keeler, "Airline Deregulation Fares and Market Behavior," in *Analytical Studies in Transport Economics,* edited by A. Daughety (New York: Cambridge University Press, 1985); J. D. Cummins, H. S. Denenberg, and W. C. Scheel, "Concentration in the U.S. Life Insurance Industry," *Journal of Risk and Insurance* (June 1972), pp. 177–199; John H. Landon, "The Relation of Market Concentration and Advertising Rates: The Newspaper Industry," *Antitrust Bulletin* (Spring 1971), pp. 53–100; B. M. Owen, "Newspaper and Television Station Joint Ownership," *Antitrust Bulletin* (Winter 1973), pp. 787–807; F. R. Edwards, "Concentration in Banking and Its Effect on Business Loan Rates," *Review of Economics and Statistics* (August 1964), pp. 294–300; P. A. Meyer, "Price Discrimination, Regional Loan Rates, and the Structure of the Banking Industry," *Journal of Finance* (March 1967), pp. 37–48; D. Jacobs, *Business Loan Costs and Bank Market Structure* (New York: Columbia University Press, 1971); F. W. Bell and N. B. Murphy, "Impact of Market Structure on the Price of a Commercial Bank Service," *Review of Economics and Statistics* (May 1969), pp. 210–213; George Kaufman, "Bank Structure and Performance: The Evidence from Iowa," *Southern Economic Journal* (April 1966), pp. 429–439; A. A. Heggestad and J. J. Mingo, "Prices, Nonprices, and Concentration in Commercial Banking," *Journal of Money, Credit and Banking* (February 1976), pp. 107–117; F. R. Edwards, "The Banking Competition Controversy," *National Banking Review* (September 1965), pp. 1–34; Douglas F. Greer and Robert P. Shay, *An Econometric Analysis of Consumer Credit Markets in the United States,* Technical Study Vol. IV, National Commission on Consumer Finance (Washington, D.C., 1973), Chapters 2 and 4; H. W. de Jong, "Industrial Structure and the Price Problem: Experience in the European Economic Community," in *The Roots of Inflation,* edited by G. C. Means et al. (New York: Burt Franklin, 1975), pp. 199–209; *Prescription Drug Price Disclosures,* Staff Report to the Federal Trade Commission (processed, 1975), part III; pp. 41–44; Almarin Phillips, "Evidence on Concentration in Banking Markets and Interest Rates," *Federal Reserve Bulletin* (June 1967) pp. 916–926; R. C. Aspinwall, "Market Structure and Commercial Bank Mortgage Interest Rates," *Southern Economic Journal* (April 1970) pp. 376–384; S. A. Rhoades, "Does the Market Matter in Banking?" Research Papers in Banking and Financial Economics (Washington, D.C.: Federal Reserve Board, 1977); H. P. Marvel, "Competition and Price Levels in the Retail Gasoline Market," *Review of Economics and Statistics* (May 1978), pp. 252–258; M. L. Marlow, "Bank Structure and Mortgage Rates," *Journal of Economics and Business,* No. 2 (1982), pp. 135–142; D. B. Graddy and R. Kyle III, "The Simultaneity of Bank Decision-making, Market Structure, and Bank Performance," *Journal of Finance* (March 1979), pp. 1–18; S. A. Rhoades and R. D. Rutz, "The Impact of Bank Holding Companies," *Journal of Economics and Business,* No. 4 (1982), pp. 355–365; and D. Hester, "Customer Relationships and Terms of Loans," *Journal of Money, Credit, and Banking* (August 1979), pp. 349–357.

ten states having the highest and the ten states having the lowest bank concentration as of 1971. The former was 10.7% interest, the latter 9.9%.[32]

- Regarding natural gas sales to industrial buyers it is estimated that, instead of monopoly, a second pipeline in a market lowers prices by $1.08 per thousand cubic feet (or about 27% on average), a third pipeline lowers prices by $0.36 per thousand cubic feet (or about 9%), and a fourth firm by $0.18 per thousand cubic feet (or about 4%).[33]

- Regarding railroad freight rates, it has been estimated that, on average, every 20% increase in concentration is associated with a 3% increase in price level.[34]

- An extensive study of grocery retailing in 1974 compared weighted average prices of a "grocery basket" comprised of 94 comparable products across 35 U.S. cities. The groceries were found to be 5.3% more expensive in cities with four-firm concentration ratios of 70 as opposed to 40. A retailer's large market share relative to others also had a positive impact on price. Translating the combined results for concentration and relative market share into "monopoly overchargers," the study's authors estimated $662 million in "excess prices" during 1974, with great variations across cities.[35]

C. Change in Concentration and Change in Price

Complementing these cross-section studies, before-and-after studies of *changes* in concentration and prices also find positive relationships. An example mentioned earlier in connection with mergers concerned Xidex Corporation. Xidex acquired two rivals in the microfilm market, raising its market share from 46% to 55% with the first acquisition and from 61% to 70% with the second. As a consequence Xidex's prices jumped first by 11% and then by an additional 23%.[36] Similarly, a study of the price impact of two airline mergers found that (1) the union of North-

[32] *Consumer Credit in the United States*, Report of the National Commission on Consumer Finance (December 1972), pp. 118–119.

[33] John Richard Morris, "The Relationship Between Industrial Sales Prices and Concentration of Natural Gas Pipelines," Working Paper 168 (Washington, D.C.: Federal Trade Commission Bureau of Economics, November 1988).

[34] Curtis M. Grimm, "Horizontal Competitive Effects in Railroad Mergers," in *Research in Transportation Economics*, Vol. 2, edited by T. E. Keeler (Greenwich, Conn.: JAI Press, 1985), pp. 27–53.

[35] B. W. Marion, W. F. Mueller, R. W. Cotterill, F. E. Geithman, and J. R. Schmelzer, *The Profit and Price Performance of Leading Food Chains 1970–74*, A Study for the Joint Economic Committee, U.S. Congress, 95th Cong., 1st Sess. (1977), p. 4. See also R. M. Lamm, "Prices and Concentration in the Food Retailing Industry," *Journal of Industrial Economics* (September 1981), pp. 67–78.

[36] David M. Barton and Roger Sherman, "The Price and Profit Effects of Horizontal Merger: A Case Study," *Journal of Industrial Economics* (December 1984), pp. 165–177.

west and Republic increased fares on flights out of Minneapolis–St. Paul by about 5.6% overall, and (2) the merger of TWA and Ozark increased the fares on flights out of St. Louis by about 1.5%.[37]

Dramatic changes of concentration in the opposite, downward direction are commonly followed by substantial price changes in the opposite, downward direction. New entry often triggers such events. By 1989, for example, MCI, Sprint, and other new entrants into the long-distance telephone market had reduced AT&T's former 100% market share to about 77%. Markedly lower prices on long-distance service resulted, prices usually led downward by MCI.

Table 11–2 gives another example of this. In 1972 Xerox had a monopoly on plain-paper copiers, a legacy from its creation of the market in 1959. Following the entry of IBM, Litton, and several others, Xerox's market share fell from 100% to 58.5%, then to 43.2%, and further. Prices fell in step, first by –6.9% in 1973 compared to 1972, then by –12.0% in 1974, and so on as indicated in Table 11–2.

Studies using Census data in an effort to estimate the influence of general changes in concentration, up or down, across numerous industries are hampered by several difficulties. For example, concentration typically does not change much from one Census to another. Still, despite these difficulties, a careful study using 1959–1977 Census data has produced results agreeing with those already reviewed. Kelton and Weiss found that a ten-percentage-point increase in concentration among consumer goods carried with it a 6% increase in price (on average). Their results for producer materials were also positive but weaker.[38]

D. Miscellaneous Evidence

Concentration's adverse consequences for prices sometimes appear indirectly from circumstantial evidence. For example, Nickell and Metcalf tested concentration's impact on price for a cross section of supermarket products. Because the price of cornflakes is not directly comparable to the price of coffee, they converted observed prices into comparable

[37] Gregory J. Werden, Andrew S. Jaskow, and Richard L. Johnson, "The Effects of Mergers on Economic Performance: Two Case Studies from the Airline Industry," U.S. Department of Justice, Antitrust Division Working Paper (October 2, 1989).

[38] Their results for producer capital goods were zero, apparently due to the heterogeneous nature of those goods. Christina Kelton and Leonard Weiss, "Change in Concentration, Change in Cost, Change in Demand, and Change in Price," in Weiss (ed.), *Concentration and Price*, pp. 41–66. For intensive studies of this type regarding single industries, with similar results, see Hideki Yamawaki, "Market Structure, Capacity Expansion, and Pricing," *International Journal of Industrial Organization* (March 1984), pp. 29–62; Marvin B. Lieberman, "The Learning Curve and Pricing in the Chemical Processing Industries," *Rand Journal of Economics* (Summer 1984), pp. 213–218; and Naomi R. Lamoreaux, *The Great Merger Movement in American Business, 1885–1904* (Cambridge: Cambridge University Press, 1985), pp. 126–138.

TABLE 11–2. Xerox Market Shares and Percentage Changes in
Rental Prices on Plain-Paper Copiers, 1972–1976

Year	Xerox's Market Share* (percent)	Xerox's Price Changes (percent)	All Firms' Price Changes, Annually (percent)
1972	100.0%	—	—
1973	58.5	−6.9%	−8.4%
1974	43.2	−12.0	−11.8
1975	14.1	−2.5	−5.9
1976	13.7	−8.2	−2.7

*Market share defined in terms of new new placements, that is, current sales plus new rentals minus returns of old rental machines.

Source: Timothy F. Bresnahan, "Post-Entry Competition in the Plain Paper Copier Market," *American Economic Review* (May 1985), pp. 15–19.

forms by using a price ratio for each product—namely, the price of the leading advertised brand (like Kellogg's cornflakes) relative to the price of the supermarket's private-label brand (like Safeway's cornflakes). They found that high concentration raises the price ratio substantially.[39]

That high concentration elevates price may also be inferred from findings that high price elasticities of demand are positively associated with high concentration. This is so because price elasticity of demand tends to rise as price level rises.[40] A similar inference might be drawn from studies showing that imports account for a higher share of the domestic market when concentration is relatively high (and other things are equal). Imports are relatively high in these industries presumably because the prices of domestic suppliers are elevated by the concentration.[41]

In some situations higher concentration leads to a deterioration in product quality or customer service while price level remains unaffected. In these instances the consequences for buyers are similar to those associated with price increases. Indeed, upon occasion, high concentration apparently causes quality or service to deteriorate even as price increases. In these cases high concentration is doubly troublesome.[42]

[39] Stephen Nickell and David Metcalf, "Monopolistic Industries and Monopoly Profits, or Are Kellogg's Cornflakes Overpriced?" *Economic Journal* (June 1978), pp. 254–268.
[40] Emilio Pagoulatos and Robert Sorensen, "What Determines the Elasticity of Industry Demand?" *International Journal of Industrial Organization* (September 1986), pp. 237–250.
[41] David I. Rosenbaum and Steven L. Reading, "Market Structure and Import Share: A Regional Market Analysis," *Southern Economic Journal* (January 1988), pp. 694–700; and E. Pagoulatos and R. Sorenson, "Domestic Market Structure and International Trade," *Quarterly Review of Economics and Business* (Spring 1976), pp. 45–59.
[42] Monica Noether, "Competition Among Hospitals," James C. Robinson, "Market

In sum, "Our evidence that concentration is correlated with price is overwhelming."[43] Moreover, we have substantial evidence that concentration is associated with curtailments in product quality and service, so that price effects are only part of the story. The evidence thus clearly sides with the market-power hypothesis rather than the efficient-market hypothesis.[44]

III. REVIEW OF THE SPECIFIC CASES IN TABLE 11-1

These empirical generalities are important. But many specifics also deserve attention. Is the impact of concentration the same if dominance is achieved by one firm or, in contrast, by a group of firms? How does a single-firm raise prices? How does a group achieve these results? Do high concentration and high prices last long? If so, why? Questions like these are the province of Table 11-1.

In this section we review each of the cells of Table 11-1, beginning with cell A, which covers the "exploitation" of power by dominant individual firms, and ending with cell I, which covers expressly collusive "combination" conduct.

A. Single-Firm Power Exploitation

The conventional theory of dominant, single-firm pricing is depicted in Figure 11-3. Line $D'D$ represents marketwide demand, while S is the supply curve of the competitive fringe of small firms, and MC is the dominant firm's marginal cost curve. Dominance is established because

---

Structure, Employment, and Skill Mix in the Hospital Industry," *Southern Economic Journal* (October 1988), pp. 315–325; Philip L. Hersch, "Competition and the Performance of Hospital Markets," *Review of Industrial Organization*, Vol. 1, no. 4 (1984), pp. 324–340; Michael Black and Douglas Greer, "Concentration and Non-price Competition in the Recording Industry," *Review of Industrial Organization*, Vol. 3, no. 2 (1987), pp. 13–37; Heggestad and Mingo, "Prices, Nonprices and Concentration in Commercial Banking," pp. 107–117; Gregory Werden, Andrew Joskow, and Richard Johnson, "The Effects of Mergers on Economic Performance: Two Case Studies from the Airline Industry," U.S. Department of Justice, Antitrust Division Working Paper (October 1989); and Jonathan Kwitny, "Wire Trouble," *The Wall Street Journal*, July 1, 1985, p. 1.

43 Weiss, *Concentration and Price*, p. 283.

44 Still further evidence concerns monopsony, that is, power among buyers. On January 4, 1990, for instance, *The Wall Street Journal* reported that large chicken processors like Tyson, Con Agra, and Perdue have monopsony power vis-à-vis chicken growers in many regions. The consequences? "In regions where competition [to buy] is intense, growers may gross 20% more than their counterparts in areas dominated by a single processor," says Paul Aho, a Cornell University economist," (p. A8). For more evidence see, for example, Gwen Quail, Bruce Marion, Frederick Geithman, and Jeffrey Marquardt, "The Impact of Packer Buyer Concentration on Live Cattle Prices," University of Wisconsin-Madison, NC-117 Working Paper No. 89 (May 1986); and W. J. Mead, *Competition and Oligopsony in the Douglas Fir Lumber Industry* (Berkeley: University of California Press, 1966), Chapters 11 and 12.

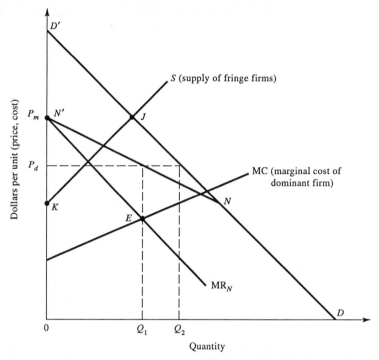

FIGURE 11–3. Dominant firm pricing model (exploitation).

MC lies below S. The dominant firm will set price to maximize its profit given the supply curve of the fringe firms. The dominant firm's demand curve will therefore be the marketwide demand curve *minus* the amounts supplied by the fringe firms at various possible prices. Curve $N'ND$ represents this *net* demand curve for the dominant firm. $N'ND$ is derived by horizontally subtracting S from $D'D$. Thus where S crosses $D'D$ the result is zero net demand at N'. And where S is zero at point K, the net demand will correspond to marketwide demand at point N on $D'D$. In order to maximize profits, the dominant firm sets the marginal revenue curve corresponding to this net demand, that is, MR_N, equal to its margin cost at point E. The result is an output for the dominant firm of $0Q_1$ with price $0P_d$. The fringe firms then supply an amount corresponding to the difference between Q_2 and Q_1, so total combined output is $0Q_2$, and the price of the fringe firms is also $0P_d$ as they follow the dominant firm.

Pure monopoly price would be higher than $0P_d$ at $0P_m$, and pure monopoly output would accordingly be lower than $0Q_2$. Hence, the competitive fringe of small firms leaves the dominant firm with less market power than a pure monopolist would have, but the dominant firm still has considerable power to exploit.

Empirical evidence on dominant firms does not support this theory in every particular, but much evidence is consistent with its general thrust. There is, for example, considerable evidence that a firm's market share and price level are positively correlated. Table 11–2 on Xerox is relevant in this respect. Moreover, a study of Maxwell House coffee, whose city-by-city market shares ranged from less than 30% to over 50%, revealed a significant positive correlation of .438 to .725 between the firm's market share and its price level during the 1970s.[45] Unlike the theory of Figure 11–3, however, Maxwell House's higher prices did not provide an "umbrella" for fringe firms to follow. Many in the coffee fringe had to price *below* Maxwell House in order to remain alive.

Similar share-price findings have been made for processed food products, light bulbs, pharmaceuticals, grocery retailing, and other goods and services.[46] Let's not linger, however. The last point to be made before departing independent exploitation by a dominant firm is this: such exploitation, *with nothing more*, commonly leads to the erosion of market power. The fringe expands as buyers eventually switch to lower-priced options and entry occurs. For example, after U.S. Steel Corporation was formed in 1901 by the merger of over 100 previously independent firms, the corporation raised prices substantially to exploit its new power. Thereafter it maintained relatively high prices, which slowly but eventually induced fringe firms to expand and newcomers to enter. Figure 11–4 reveals how U.S. Steel's market share fell as a consequence from over 65% in 1901 to less than 20% in 1983.[47] Federal Express, the king of overnight delivery services, also experienced a shrinking market share as fringe firms like UPS, Purolator, and Emery expanded under Federal's price umbrella. From a near 100% monopoly in the early 1980s, Federal's market share slipped to 52.8% by 1987 (and Federal's prices fell correspondingly, by 4% in 1985 and then by 7% in 1987).[48]

[45] John C. Hilke and Philip B. Nelson, "Strategic Behavior and Attempted Monopolization: The Coffee Case," in *The Antitrust Revolution*, edited by John E. Kwoka, Jr., and Lawrence J. White (Glenview, Ill.: Scott, Foresman, 1989), pp. 208–231.

[46] James J. McRae and Francis Tapon, "Some Empirical Evidence on Post-Patent Barriers to Entry in the Canadian Pharmaceutical Industry," *Journal of Health Economics* (March 1985), pp. 43–61; Robert L. Wills and Willard F. Mueller, "Brand Pricing and Advertising," *Southern Economic Journal* (October 1989), pp. 383–395; Ronald W. Cotterill, "Market Power in the Retail Food Industry: Evidence from Vermont," *Review of Economics and Statistics* (August 1986), pp. 379–386; Robert P. Rogers, *Development and Structure of the U.S. Electric Lamp Industry* (Washington, D.C.: FTC Bureau of Economics, 1980), pp. 90–92.

[47] Hideki Yamawaki, "Dominant Firm Pricing and Fringe Expansion: The Case of the U.S. Iron and Steel Industry, 1907–1930," *Review of Economics and Statistics* (August 1985), pp. 429–437.

[48] *Business Week*, March 30, 1987, p. 31. For further examples, see Robert Stobaugh, *Innovation and Competition: The Global Management of Petrochemical Products* (Boston: Harvard Business School Press, 1988), pp. 67–71; and R. E. Caves, M. Fortunato, and P. Ghemawat, "The Decline of Dominant Firms, 1905–1929," *Quarterly Journal of Economics* (August 1984), pp. 523–546.

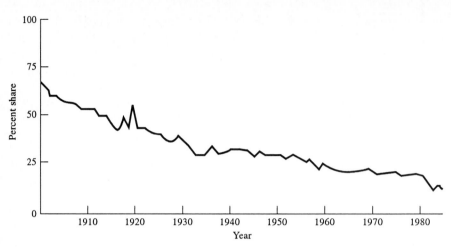

FIGURE 11–4. U.S. Steel's market share, 1901–1984. Source: Stephen Martin, *Industrial Economics* (New York: Macmillan, 1988), p. 74.

B. Tacit Collective Power Exploitation

Much theory of tacit collective behavior can be reduced to the following equation,

$$\frac{P - \text{MC}}{P} = \frac{H}{E}$$

where P is price level, MC is the industry-average marginal cost, H is the Herfindahl-Hirschman index of market concentration (with $H = 1.0$ being monopoly), and E is price elasticity of demand. This says that price will rise relative to cost as the H index rises or as price elasticity of demand falls. Firms in the market recognize their inter-dependence, so each restricts its own output without express agreement to do so. The more that sales are concentrated in the hands of a few large firms, the greater the curtailment of output and consequently the higher is price relative to marginal cost. Still, insofar as the H index falls below monopoly levels, there will be some independence, so the com-bined output of all the firms will exceed monopoly levels and price will therefore be below monopoly level.

The rewards of tacit collusion, on the one hand, and the competitive urges that may nevertheless persist, on the other hand, can both be seen in **game theory**. The basic idea in game theory you already know about. When playing a game you take account of what opponents are doing, and they take account of what you are doing. The game most illustrative of tacit collusion is the "Prisoners' Dilemma." Two firms are in this game, and they each may follow one of two strategies—"cooperation" or "defection," where cooperation is the same as holding price high in the market and limiting output while defection is aggressive price cutting. Cooperation by both firms yields tacit collusion. Defection by both creates all-out competition.

For example, imagine a market consisting of two firms, Ethyl and Du Pont. Each firm can select either a high price (P_H) or a low price (P_L), with consequences illustrated in Table 11–3.[49] The numbers in Table 11–3 represent the profit payoffs in a single period for the different possible pricing combinations in that period. The numbers entered first, in regular type, are for Ethyl, while those in italics are for Du Pont. Thus, when Ethyl's price is P_H and Du Pont's price is likewise P_H, Ethyl's profits are 100 and Du Pont's are *100*. With Ethyl cooperatively charging high price P_H and Du Pont defecting to low price P_L, Ethyl would lose business to Du Pont and thereby suffer a loss of −10 while Du Pont would gain profits of *140*.

If Ethyl and Du Pont were to confront each other *only once and operate independently*, there would be strong incentives for both to defect, resulting in a competitive payoff of only 70 for each firm. This is so even though mutual cooperation would clearly be more profitable for both, yielding 100 for each. The combined total from mutual cooperation, 200 (100 + *100*), is obviously better than the combined total under competitive defection, 140 (70 + *70*), and also better than the combined total of either of the two remaining options, 130 (140 − *10* or −10 + *140*), so the reasons behind the competitive defections are interesting.

Notice that each firm can assume that its rival will either cooperate or defect. If Ethyl assumes that Du Pont will cooperate by charging P_H,

TABLE 11–3. The Prisoners' Dilemma Payoff Matrix (Ethyl's payoffs in regular type: Du Pont's payoffs in italics)

		Du Pont's Price			
		P_H (cooperation)		P_L (defection)	
Ethyl's Price	P_H (cooperation)	100	*100*	−10	*140*
	P_L (defection)	140	*−10*	70	*70*

[49] This example comes from Steven C. Salop, "Practices that (Credibly) Facilitate Oligopoly Co-ordination," in *New Developments in the Analysis of Market Structure,* edited by J. E. Stiglitz and G. F. Mathewson (Cambridge, Mass.: MIT Press, 1986), pp. 265–290.

Ethyl's best strategy is to *defect* to P_L because its P_L payoff of 140 is greater than its P_H payoff of 100. If, on the other hand, Ethyl assumes that Du Pont will charge P_L Ethyl's best strategy is again to *defect* to P_L, because the payoff is then 70 instead of the -10 loss it would experience by charging P_H. Hence Ethyl will defect and charge P_L because that gives it the best result *regardless of the behavior it expects from Du Pont*. In turn, Du Pont would follow the same line of logic because it sees the same numbers as Ethyl, only from the other side. If Du Pont expects Ethyl to cooperate with a price of P_H, Du Pont favors P_L over P_H comparing *140* to *100*. If Du Pont assumes Ethyl will charge P_L, Du Pont again favors P_L over P_H comparing *70* to -10. Hence *both* firms defect despite the greater rewards for cooperation.

Note, however, the constraints we imposed on this situation at the outset — namely, *independent play only once*. Dropping the constraint of playing the game only once enhances the attraction of mutual cooperation. Why? With only one game, there are no future periods, so neither player would opt for a cooperative P_H hoping that *in future periods* such behavior would induce its rival into similarly cooperative behavior, with the resulting payoffs of 100 and *100*. However, with a repeated game extending over numerous periods cooperation between Ethyl and Du Pont will be in their *individual and their mutual interests* over the long run. This emerges from a strategy of "tit for tat," which is the best strategy to follow in repeated games of this sort.[50] In tit for tat you do to your opponent what he has just done to you. You cooperate a long as your opponent cooperates. If he betrays you and defects to P_L, then the next time you betray him to penalize him in retaliation. You charge P_L. If he responds to the penalty and cooperates, you reinforce that action. You cooperate again. And so on.

"Games" among rivals in a given market tend to be of this repeated variety because business continues from month to month and year to year. Hence tacitly collusive behavior is often logical for oligopolists even when the forces favoring competitive betrayal are strong. Tacit collusion is also attractive if the rewards for defection are small in comparison to those associated with cooperation. Table 11–4 illustrates this possibility. The payoffs for defection while the rival is cooperating have been reduced in Table 11–4 to 90 and *90* (down from 140 and *140* in Table 11–3). Once P_H is reached by both Ethyl and Du Pont, defection by either alone would reduce their payoff from 100 to 90, and defection by both would reduce their payoffs to 70. Hence P_H for each is a *stable equilibrium*. Once there, *neither player has an incentive to change strategy*,

[50] Robert Axelrod, *The Evolution of Cooperation* (New York: Basic Books, 1984). See also F. M. Scherer and David Ross, *Industrial Market Structure, and Economic Performance* 3rd ed. (Boston: Houghton Mifflin, 1990), pp. 216–219.

TABLE 11–4. Pure Tacit Coordination (Ethyl's payoffs in regular type: Du Pont's payoffs in italics)

		Du Pont's Price			
		P_H (cooperation)		P_L (defection)	
Ethyl's Price	P_H (cooperation)	100	*100*	−10	*90*
	P_L (defection)	90	*−10*	70	*70*

given the opponent's strategy. Such a stable solution is called a **Nash equilibrium**, after John Nash, who formalized the concept.[51]

Game theory thus illustrates the incentives for cooperation and competition. Beyond this, however, its contribution to industrial economics is limited. In particular it cannot predict real conduct accurately, partly because its predictions vary greatly with the assorted assumptions that can be fed into its many variations, and partly because of the fact that realistic assumptions tend to give a game many Nash equilibria rather than just one. With multiple equilibria, a game's predictive power is reduced considerably because it points in many directions instead of just one.[52] Direct empirical tests of the theory are mainly contrived experiments in hypothetical situations or computer simulations. These suggest that cooperative strategies often dominate competitive strategies, as likewise suggested by the positive associations between price and concentration reviewed earlier. But most of the real-world evidence concerning game theory is anecdotal rather than statistical.[53]

The exploitation of market power by tacit collusion may result in the eventual loss of market share for those involved (absent measures to extend their market power). The U.S. automobile industry during the 1970s offers an example. General Motors, Ford, and Chrysler, the "Big Three" of the domestic industry, were collectively dominant at the time.

[51] John F. Nash, Jr., "Noncooperative Games," *Annals of Mathematics* (September 1951), pp. 286–295.

[52] David M. Kreps and A. Michael Spence, "Modelling the Role of History in Industrial Organization," in G. R. Feinwel (ed.), *Issues in Contemporary Microeconomics and Welfare* (Albany: State University of New York Press, 1985), pp. 340–378.

[53] John McDonald, *The Game of Business* (Garden City, N.Y.: Doubleday, 1975); C. K. Harley, "Oligopoly Agreement and the Timing of American Railroad Construction," *Journal of Economic History* (December 1982), pp. 797–823. For an example of statistical confirmation of repeated game tacit collusion, see Margaret E. Slade, "Interfirm Rivalry in a Repeated Game," *Journal of Industrial Economics* (June 1987), pp. 499–516.

The Japanese producers constituted a competitive fringe. During the 1970s there were devaluations of the dollar relative to the yen which caused the prices of Japanese imported cars to rise. The "Big Three" could have held their prices constant and gained market share vis-à-vis the Japanese, or raised their prices for greater short-term profitability at the expense of their market share. They chose the latter course. For example, Toyota raised the U.S. price of its Corolla four times in the 1978 model year from $3048 to $3498, or about $400. GM and Ford followed each time for a cumulative jump of roughly $400 on their Chevette and Pinto, respectively. According to John Kwoka, "The domestic producers were taking every opportunity to raise prices, even though the clear effect would be to concede market share to the Japanese."[54] During the 1970s auto imports doubled their market share from 14% to 28%.

C. Explicit Collective Power Exploitation

When structural conditions are sufficiently competitive to prevent tacit collusion, but not sufficiently competitive to cause intense all out rivalry, cartels may emerge as a means to exploit market power. These explicit agreements take many forms. There are market allocation schemes, in which sellers are assigned to certain territories or certain buyers free from the rivalry of their co-conspirators. There are single sales agencies, through which colluders channel all their sales. There are also simple price-fixing agreements, by which each seller agrees to adhere to certain prices. In places and times where such conduct has been lawful, collusive agreements have flourished.[55] When clearly illegal, as in the United States since the last century, such conduct is discouraged but not absent because it can be quite profitable. Secrecy hides it.

The incentives for cartel members to defect are the same as those under tacit collusion. Indeed, the procompetitive forces are often stronger in cartel situations than those of tacit collusion. Nevertheless, the consequences for price are frequently similar. There are numerous instances of prices increasing from 30% to 60% under cartels, or of prices falling substantially with the breakup of cartels.[56] The most famous cartel of all time — the Organization of Petroleum Exporting Countries

[54] John E. Kwoka, Jr., "Market Power and Market Change in the U.S. Automobile Industry," *Journal of Industrial Economics* (June 1984), p. 514. This was repeated in the 1980s. See John Bussey, "Fateful Choice," *The Wall Street Journal*, April 13, 1988, pp. 1, 11.

[55] See, for example, Dennis Swann, et al., *Competition in British Industry* (London: Allen & Unwin, 1974), Chapter 1.

[56] Ibid., pp. 156–157; W. B. Erickson, "Price Fixing Conspiracies: Their Long-Term Impact," *Journal of Industrial Economics* (March 1976), pp. 189–202; W. F. Mueller, "Effects of Antitrust Enforcement in the Retail Food Industry," *Antitrust Law and Economics Review* (Winter 1968–69), pp. 86–87; and Robert M. Feinberg, "Strategic and Deterrent Pricing Responses to Antitrust Investigations," *International Journal of Industrial Organization* (March 1984), pp. 75–84.

(OPEC) — gained global notoriety by quadrupling the price of crude oil in 1973 and then tacking on further price increases at fairly regular intervals during the decade thereafter.

Once again, however, exploiting market power without also taking steps to extend or maintain that power may lead to its weakening. OPEC's price escalation was striking, and its subsequent loss of market power was equally striking. The cartel's share of world crude oil production fell from over 55% in 1973 to about 30% in 1985.[57]

D. Single-Firm Extension of Market Power

We have seen that exploitation of market power may invite its erosion, just as a boxer who comes out swinging hard in the early rounds may tire quickly. On the other hand, there is abundant evidence that market power, especially that possessed by dominant firms, usually lasts a very long time — decades, occasionally even centuries.[58] This durability implies that the second half of our definition of market power is as important as the first — the second half being the ability "to subdue competitors." As Alice P. White says, "The essence of market power is that it places several variables at the disposal of the firm for strategic competitive behavior rather than price alone."[59] More bluntly, *Fortune* explained G.E.'s constant striving to rank first or second in *every* market it serves (aircraft engines, broadcasting, lighting, electric motors, and so on) by saying that G.E. wants "to throw rocks down on its rivals from above."[60]

The contrast between simple exploitation of market power (in cases A, B, and C of Table 11–1) and strategic extensions of market power (in cases D, E, and F) may be illustrated in Figures 11–5 and 11–6.[61] Figure 11–5 represents a simple game in which, unlike before, *the order of the players' moves is specified*. The players are two firms — a dominant "incumbent" firm and a "potential entrant" contemplating entry into the market. The potential entrant can go IN the market or stay OUT. If the potential entrant remains OUT, the incumbent earns monopoly profits of 300. However, if entry occurs the incumbent can either FIGHT, which

---

[57] For other examples, see Don E. Waldman, "The Inefficiencies of 'Unsuccessful' Price Fixing Agreements," *Antitrust Bulletin* (Spring 1988), pp. 67–93.

[58] M. A. Utton, *Profits and Stability of Monopoly* (Cambridge: Cambridge University Press, 1986); Dennis C. Mueller, *Profits in the Long Run* (Cambridge: Cambridge University Press, 1986); and P. A. Geroski, "Do Dominant Firms Decline?" in *The Economics of Market Dominance*, edited by Donald Hay and John Vickers (Oxford: Basil Blackwell, 1987), pp. 143–167.

[59] Alice Patricia White, *The Dominant Firm: A Study of Market Power* (Ann Arbor: University of Michigan Research Press, 1983), p. 66.

[60] Stratford P. Sherman, "The Mind of Jack Welch," *Fortune*, March 27, 1989, p. 40.

[61] A. Dixit, "Recent Developments in Oligopoly Theory," *American Economic Review* (May 1982), pp. 12–17.

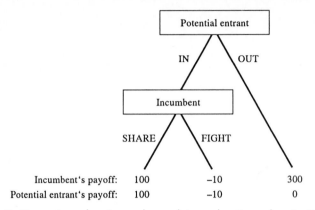

FIGURE 11–5. Game tree showing values of incumbent's and potential entrant's payoffs.

is costly to both firms (–10), or he can SHARE, acquiescing in the entry, which is more profitable for the incumbent than fighting (100), but not as profitable as monopoly. Clearly, the incumbent will hope that the potential entrant stays OUT. As the potential entrant sees it, staying OUT is better than a FIGHT (0 versus –10), but not as good as getting IN to gain a SHARE of the market (100 versus 0).

What will happen? This Figure 11–5 game has two possible Nash equilibria:

1. The incumbent threatens to FIGHT in the event of entry, so the potential entrant stays OUT.
2. The potential entrant goes IN, and the incumbent chooses to SHARE.

In each case, each firm will hold to its strategy given the strategy of the other. In (1) the incumbent will threaten to FIGHT as long as the potential entrant stay OUT (which it would do, given a FIGHT). If the potential entrant goes IN, however, as in (2), the incumbent will SHARE. Which Nash equilibrium will prevail?

Notice that the first, (1), is implausible. The incumbent's vow to FIGHT *lacks credibility* because it is in his interest to SHARE rather than FIGHT *if entry actually occurs*. The threat is an empty threat. Recognizing this, the potential entrant would choose to go IN. The second Nash equilibrium, (2), would thus prevail in Figure 11–5, and the monopolist's power would erode with the entry.

This result follows if, as implicitly assumed, the incumbent can do nothing to prevent entry. However, this assumption is too simplistic. As noted previously, incumbents can often act *strategically* to thwart entry and thereby *extend* their power. The game in Figure 11–6 allows such strategic behavior by adding an earlier stage of incumbent decision making than contained in Figure 11–5. If the incumbent is PASSIVE at that

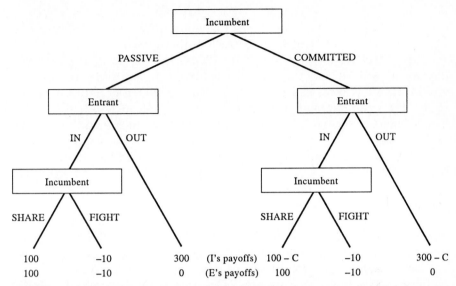

FIGURE 11–6. Game tree when incumbent can behave strategically precommitting resources to thwart entry.

earlier stage, Figure 11–6 shows the results to be the same as in Figure 11–5, and entry will occur. On the other hand the incumbent can take a COMMITTED stance. It can make a strategic move by investing early in resources that would only be useful in the event of a FIGHT after an attempted entry. Let's say this commitment costs "C." Thus if the incumbent commits C, its payoffs are reduced to 300 − C in the event of continued monopoly or to 100 − C in the event of SHARING, and its payoff remains at − 10 if there is a FIGHT. The strategic investment might be made to acquire excess production capacity that could be used to wage a price war against the entrant. Other possible commitments include especially heavy advertising or product proliferation. The main thing is that the incumbent's investment be an irreversible commitment that is visible to the potential entrant.

The new game thus has three stages. First, the incumbent decides whether or not to invest C. Second, the potential entrant decides whether or not to enter. Third, the incumbent decides whether to SHARE or FIGHT. What happens now that the incumbent can behave strategically?

The PASSIVE option not to invest gives the incumbent the same payoff as before in Figure 11–5—namely, 100 after entry occurs and SHARE is chosen. The COMMITTED option holds more promise. If C is spent and the potential entrant stays OUT, the incumbent gets 300 − C. On the other hand, if the entrant comes IN despite the commitment, the incumbent will choose to FIGHT as long as -10 is greater than $100 -$ C. For example, a C commitment of 130 would prompt the incumbent to FIGHT because the payoff to its SHARE option would then be -30 ($100 - 130$), which is much worse than FIGHT's -10. Realizing that the incumbent will FIGHT, the potential entrant will stay OUT and experience a payoff of 0 instead of -10. With the potential entrant OUT, the incumbent's commitment is rewarded with a payoff of 170, which is $300 - C$ in this case when $C = 130$. (And this 170 is much greater than the SHARE payoff $100 - C$, or -30.) Thus, as long as the incumbent can find some commitment C that is greater than 110 and less than 200 he will be able to keep the potential entrant OUT and yet gain a payoff that exceeds the PASSIVE option's payoff of 100 (which follows entry and SHARE). This entry deterring strategy is a Nash equilibrium.[62]

To what extent do dominant firms actually engage in strategic behavior to extend their monopoly power? According to the research of Robert Smiley, strategic entry deterrence is "surprisingly important." He conducted a questionnaire survey of executives in major American corporations, collecting 293 responses. The executives were asked to indicate the degree to which a particular entry deterring strategy was practiced on a five-point scale ranging from "frequently" to "never." Among the strategies inquired about were:

- *Product proliferation:* filling product niches so that new entrants would find no unmet demand
- *Intense advertising:* creating sufficient brand loyalty to discourage potential entrants
- *Patent preemption:* acquiring patents to block alternative innovations
- *Mean reputation:* giving the impression in the media and otherwise that the incumbent will compete especially rigorously against new rivals, lashing out against them
- *Limit pricing:* setting a lower price than would otherwise be most profitable in order to lead potential entrants to expect an especially low price after entry
- *Excess capacity:* building excess plant to meet all expected demand, thereby reducing the attractiveness of entry

Table 11–5 reveals that product proliferation and intensive advertising are the two most popular strategies. Over 50% of the respondents claim to use them more than occasionally. At the other extreme, limit pricing and excess capacity were said to be rarely or never used by well over

---

[62] In general, entry-deterring behavior is more likely to be profitable in comparison to passive, entry-permitting behavior when the payoff to monopoly is high relative to sharing and the cost of a fight is not so great as to heap doubt on the probability that the incumbent will actually fight. Here the monopoly payoff ($300-C$) is high relative to sharing (100), and the cost of fighting is modest (-10 instead of, say, -250).

TABLE 11–5. Frequency of Use of Entry Deterrence Strategies

Detterent Strategy	Prevalence				
	Frequently	Often	Occasionally	Rarely	Never
Product proliferation	26%	31%	22%	14%	6%
Intensive advertising	24	28	26	14	7
Patent preemption	11	20	16	31	23
Mean reputation	8	19	22	31	21
Limit pricing	7	15	21	32	25
Excess capacity	7	14	17	32	30

Notes: The labels for the categories "Often" and "Rarely" are different than those in Smiley's article. Also these are the results for existing products rather than new products. The results for new products show much higher frequencies on advertising and patent preemption.

Source: Robert Smiley, "Empirical Evidence on Strategic Entry Deterrence," *International Journal of Industrial Organization* (June 1988), pp. 167–180.

50% of respondents. Bracketed between these results are those for patent preemption and reputation building, which could be considered moderately popular entry-deterrent strategies. For an overall impression Smiley asked his respondents how they would rate entry considerations in importance compared to other strategic marketing and production decisions. "Surprisingly," he writes, "more than half of the respondents felt that entry considerations were at least as important as other strategic marketing and production decisions."[63]

Although Smiley kept his sources confidential, the business press and scholarly literature are replete with specific examples of dominant firm entry deterring efforts. They include Gillette in safety razors (product proliferation),[64] Du Pont in titanium oxide (excess capacity),[65] General Foods in coffee (intensive advertising and limit pricing),[66] United

[63] Robert Smiley, "Empirical Evidence on Strategic Entry Deterrence," *International Journal of Industrial Organization* (June 1988), pp. 167–180.
[64] White, *The Dominant Firm*, p. 71.
[65] Pankaj Ghemawat, "Capacity Expansion in the Titanium Industry," *Journal of Industrial Economics* (December 1984), pp. 145–163.
[66] John C. Hilke and Philip B. Nelson, "Strategic Behavior and Attempted Monopolization: The Coffee Case," in *The Antitrust Revolution*, edited by J. E. Kwoka, Jr. and L. J. White (Glenview, Ill.: Scott, Foresman, 1989), pp. 208–240.

Shoe Machinery Corporation in shoe machinery (patent preemption),[67] Alcoa in the aluminum industry (excess capacity),[68] Monsanto in chemical herbicides (limit pricing),[69] IBM in computers and computer peripheral equipment (limit pricing and perhaps reputation building),[70] Campbell's in condensed soups (product proliferation),[71] and Safeway in grocery retailing (geographic market preemption through excess store construction).[72] Little wonder, then, that evidence shows dominant firms typically remaining dominant for very long periods.

E. Tacit Collective Extension of Market Power

Next time you're in a supermarket, take a moment to study the shelves of ready-to-eat breakfast cereals. The immense variety of brands, shapes, and flavors is mind boggling. (In 1990 you could buy "Teenage Mutant Ninja Turtles Cereal" or "Breakfast with Barbie.") Yet the swarm of different cereals is the responsibility of just a few producers—Kellogg, General Foods (Post), General Mills, and Ralston. It could thus be said that the major cereal companies engage in product proliferation as an entry-deterring strategy. They do so collectively, in a tacit manner, as none of them except perhaps Kellogg individually qualifies as a dominant firm. Hence it provides a good example of tacit collective extensions of market power.[73]

Although it may seem that these oligopolists are simply competing against each other, with those countless product introductions yielding entry deterrence as a unintended by-product, such is probably not the case. Smiley's sample of corporate executives included many that were from tightly-knit oligopoly firms (like the cereal companies) rather than dominant firms.

Another example of these "category E" conditions concerns Coca-

---

[67] Carl Kaysen, *United States v. United Shoe Machinery Corporation* (Cambridge, Mass.: Harvard University Press, 1956).

[68] Leonard W. Weiss, *Economics and American Industry* (New York: John Wiley, 1961), Chapter 5.

[69] *The Wall Street Journal*, January 27, 1987, p. 10.

[70] Russell W. Pittman, "Predatory Investment, US vs IBM," *International Journal of Industrial Organization* (December 1984), pp. 341–365; Richard T. DeLamarter, *Big Blue: IBM's Use and Abuse of Power* (New York: Dodd, Mead, 1986).

[71] Bill Saporito, "The Fly in Campbell's Soup," *Fortune*, May 9, 1988, pp. 67–70; *Business Week*, January 26, 1987, pp. 64–69.

[72] Douglas S. West, "Testing for Market Preemption Using Sequential Location Data," *Bell Journal of Economics* (Spring 1981), pp. 129–143; and Paul K. Gorecki, *The Administration and Enforcement of Competition Policy in Canada, 1960 to 1975* (Ottawa: Consumer and Corporate Affairs, 1980), pp. 305–306, regarding *Regina v. Canada Safeway Ltd.* (1974) 1 W.W.R. 210, 12 C.P.R. (2d)3.

[73] F. M. Scherer, "The Welfare Economics of Product Variety," *Journal of Industrial Economics* (December 1979), pp. 113–134; Richard Schmalensee, "Entry Deterrence in the Ready-to-Eat Breakfast Cereal Industry," *Bell Journal of Economics* (Autumn 1978), pp. 305–327.

Cola and Pepsi Co. in the soft drink market. A *Wall Street Journal* article reveals that their preemptive efforts extend beyond product proliferation. Their activities

> are at odds with the public perception that Coke and Pepsi, which account for 70% of the $30 billion-a-year soft-drink market, are locked in a no-holds-barred struggle for American taste buds. David McFarland, a University of North Carolina professor who has studied soft-drink marketing, likens the competition to television wrestling. "They make a lot of sounds and groans and bounce on the mat, but they know who is going to win." Both Coke and Pepsi stand to benefit from this arrangement, he argues, but many smaller companies can't enter the ring to compete.
>
> In some markets, for instance, Atlanta-based Coca-Cola Co. and Pepsi Co., Inc., Purchase, N.Y., have each agreed with bottlers to make huge payments to grocery chains in return for crucial advertising and store displays. This practice tends to lock out rivals . . . from similar promotional advantages.[74]

Statistical evidence of entry-forestalling behavior in a large number of oligopolistic industries is available.[75] But case history evidence is more convincing. Two cases of tacit collusive exclusionary conduct that are especially interesting are those for cigarettes and motion pictures during the 1920s, 1930s, and 1940s.[76]

F. Explicit Collective Extension of Market Power

If dominant firms and tacitly collusive oligopolists engage in strategic behavior to extend their market power, it is easy to imagine cartels doing the same. Examples of such cartel behavior include watches, aluminum, quinine, red phosphorous, electrical equipment, and diamonds.[77] In some cases firms that are behaving tacitly to exploit their power (cell B in Table 11–1) may collude explicitly to extend that power. One strategy they may use is the "group boycott," in which case the colluding firms refuse to do business with others who do business with their rivals.[78]

[74] *The Wall Street Journal*, December 9, 1987, p. 6.

[75] A. Koutsoyiannis, "Goals of Oligopolistic Firms: An Empirical Test of Competing Hypothesis," *Southern Economic Journal* (October 1984), pp. 540–567.

[76] Simon N. Whitney *Antitrust Policies*, Vol. II (New York: Twentieth Century Fund, 1958), Chapters 11 and 15; and the papers by R. B. Tennant and W. F. Hellmuth in *The Structure of American Industry*, edited by Walter Adams 3rd ed. (New York: Macmillan, 1961), pp. 357–429.

[77] D. F. Greer, "United States of America," in *Restrictive Business Practices* (New York: United Nation Publication TD/B/390, 1973), pp. 39–84; Richard Newfarmer, *Transnational Conglomerates and the Economics of Dependent Development* (Greenwich, Conn.: JAI Press, 1980); and Edward J. Epstein, *The Rise and Fall of Diamonds* (New York: Simon & Schuster, 1982).

[78] Lawrence A. Sullivan, *Handbook of the Law of Antitrust* (St. Paul, Minn.: West, 1977), pp. 229–256.

A much more complicated tactic with the same effect has allegedly been practiced by Visa and MasterCard in order to exclude American Express, Discover, and other nonbank credit cards from the growing market in "debit cards" (which can take the place of cash by electronically transferring funds out a consumer's bank account at the time of purchase).[79]

G. Single-Firm "Combination Conduct"

Some strategies, *when practiced by dominant firms*, may both exploit and extend their dominance. Such "combination conduct" may enhance a dominant firm's profits in both the short and long run. Volume discount price discrimination, loyalty rebates, lease-only marketing, exclusive dealing, and tying are among these practices. Here we are confined to only a brief discussion with further details saved for later chapters.

1. Price Discrimination.   Rather than simply raise price *level*, as illustrated earlier in Figure 11–3, a dominant firm may occasionally be able to develop a price *structure* that generates excess profits while at the same time discouraging new entry. Figure 11–7 illustrates a volume discount structure having this effect.[80] Buyers purchasing 1 to 200 units per month pay $8 per unit. Buyers purchasing 201 to 400 units per month pay $7 per unit on *all* units (even units 1–200). Volumes in the 401–600 range yield per unit price of $6. And volumes in excess of 600 lower price to $5 per unit.

If this were the price structure of a dominant established seller, it could pose a barrier to entry to smaller but equally efficient potential sellers. Suppose, for example, that a small potential seller does not have the capacity to supply a big buyer with all his requirements of 500 units per month. Indeed, because of uncertainty, this big buyer may not want to buy all his 500 units per month from the newcomer even if the newcomer has the capacity. The buyer might prefer instead to purchase small trial quantities or to build ties with two suppliers, the old and the new. What price would the potential seller have to charge in order to get this big buyer to buy 200 units from him? Would it be the going price the buyer pays to the established supplier, namely, $6 per unit as shown in Figure 11–7? No. It would have to be a substantially lower price than $6. Why? Because the buyer's purchase of 200 units from the potential seller would drop the buyer's purchases from the established seller below 400 units to 300 (500 − 200 = 300), thereby causing the buyer to lose part of his discount from the established seller. Price on the 300 units from the established seller jumps from $6 to $7, costing the

---

[79] *The Wall Street Journal*, July 27, 1989, p. B3.

[80] Robert C. Brooks, Jr., "Volume Discounts as Barriers to Entry and Access," *Journal of Political Economy* (February 1961), pp. 63–69.

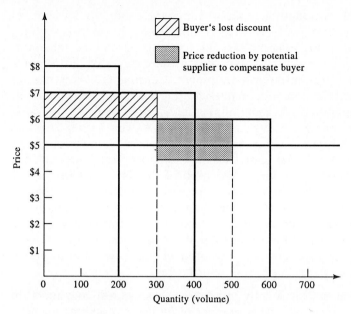

FIGURE 11–7. Volume discount structure.

buyer $300. Hence, the price the potential seller charges *must be low enough to compensate the buyer for this loss.* Otherwise he won't make the sale. The potential seller's price must be $4.50 per unit. This is derived by noting that, at a price of $6, the 200 units would cost the buyer $1,200. From this, the potential seller must subtract the $300 the buyer loses in dollar discounts, leaving the potential seller with $900 revenue on 200 units, which amounts to $4.50 per unit (900/200). The shaded areas in Figure 11–7 indicate the buyer's lost discount and the potential seller's price reduction below $6 per unit.

In sum, this price structure imposes **switching costs** on the buyers in the event they *switch* from the established, dominant firm to a small rival. Buyers are consequently discouraged from switching, just as you would be discouraged from switching to a new make of auto if you then had to pay much higher auto insurance or remodel your garage. Another price structure that can have a similar effect is the loyalty rebate, in which buyers are rewarded with a delayed rebate if they are loyal to a single seller.[81]

Perhaps the most commonplace examples of this are the "frequent flyer" programs major airlines use to build customer allegiance (see the appendix to this chapter).

[81] Paul Klemperer, "The Competitiveness of Markets with Switching Costs," *Rand Journal of Economics* (Spring 1987), pp. 138–150.

2. Lease-Only Marketing. Many dominant producers of durable machinery have refused to "sell" their equipment to "buyers," preferring instead to "lease" it to "lessees," usually for long durations—for example, five or ten years. Such has been true in the past of IBM in computers, AT&T in telecommunications equipment, Continental in can closing machinery, United Shoe in shoe manufacturing machinery, and Xerox in photocopying equipment. Leasing allows high prices while at the same time it may raise entry barriers in several ways.[82] The barrier effect of greatest present relevance is this: Leasing can attach buyers to an incumbent supplier for much the same reason that price discrimination can create switching costs. The longer the term of the lease and the higher the penalties imposed on the customer for early cancellation, the higher will be the customer's costs of switching from an established supplier to a new supplier. "First movers" may be especially adroit at using lease-only marketing to exploit and extend that market power because customers desiring the first mover's new product will have little incentive to refuse the lease given the lack of alternatives.

3. Tie-in Sales. Lease-only marketing also glues customers to suppliers when the leases "tie" a number of different machines together into a single "package" or "system," as when those renting from IBM before 1970 paid a single monthly fee for memory, CPU, disk drive, printers, and all the other parts of the computer system. Such tie-in selling extends beyond the durable capital equipment. Kodak formerly tied picture developing to the sale of its Kodak film (so shutterbugs then had to mail the exposed film to Kodak for processing). In this way Kodak controlled 90% of the film developing market as well as 90% of the market for film.[83] Thus tying—requiring the buyer of one article to also buy others from the seller—can sometimes be used by a dominant firm both to exploit and extend its market power.[84]

---

[82] P. Aghion and P. Bolton, "Contracts as Barriers to Entry," *American Economic Review* (June 1987), pp. 388–401; Jean Tirole, *The Theory of Industrial Organization* (Cambridge, Mass.: MIT Press, 1989), pp. 196–198; and White, *The Dominant Firm*, pp. 94–95.

[83] Don E. Waldman, *Antitrust Action and Market Structure* (Lexington, Mass.: Lexington Books, 1978), pp. 143–150.

[84] Jean Tirole, *The Theory of Industrial Organization*, pp. 333–336; J. Carbajo, D. de Meza, and D. J. Seidmann, "A Strategic Motivation for Commodity Bundling," *Journal of Industrial Economics* (March 1990), pp. 283–298. This includes "systems selling": Walter Adams and James W. Brock, "Integrated Monopoly and Market Power: Systems Selling, Compatibility Standards, and Market Control," *Quarterly Review of Economics and Business* (Winter 1982), pp. 29–42. Sometimes volume discounts across products can create ties. Regarding IBM in the mid-1980s,

> The most effective tactic [to subdue rivals] has been to offer volume discounts, which IBM has been extending to more and more items in its product line. If a customer will commit to buying, say, 20 IBM systems over 18 months, he may earn a published discount of 16%. On occasion, the company allows the buyer to reach the purchase target by picking among different items in the IBM catalogue; that helps lock out competitors who can offer deep discounts on just a few products. See Bro Uttal, "Is IBM Playing Too Tough?" *Fortune*, December 10, 1984, p. 37.

4. Evidence. Broadly based empirical evidence on these several practices has been compiled by J. D. Gribbon and M. A. Utton. They analyzed 50 detailed industry reports by Britain's Monopolies and Restrictive Practices Commission. In the process they identified 108 barriers to entry for the 50 industries. Of these barriers, two-thirds were behavioral, such as loyalty discounts in pricing, lease-only marketing policies, exclusive dealing, tying, and intensive advertising. Inclusion of intensive advertising means that Gribbon and Utton included cases of "extension" along with the "combination conduct" of current concern. Still, their results are instructive. They found that greater monopoly power was associated with a greater incidence of these behavioral barriers to entry. Dividing the 50 industries into three classes — "dominant firm," "concentrated oligopoly," and "loose oligopoly" — they calculated an average of 1.8 behavioral barriers per industry in the "dominant firm" group compared with 1.4 and 1.1 for the "concentrated" and "loose oligopoly" groups, respectively.[85] The positive association between behavioral barriers and single-firm dominance illustrates the importance of behavioral barriers to the exploitation/extension of monopoly power. It also underscores the fact that many of these behaviors are not seriously anticompetitive in the context of fluid competition. Tying or exclusive dealing by a pipsqueak firm is, for instance, no problem.

H. Tacit Collective "Combination Conduct"

During the mid-1980s newspapers around the United States had to battle to retain retailer display advertising, worth $15 billion annually. Retailers like K Mart and J. C. Penney were switching to direct mailers like Advo, which distributed printed advertising circulars to consumers through the postal service at less cost to the retailers and perhaps with greater promotional punch. In an effort to beat back these direct-mail upstarts the newspapers tried to raise their rivals' costs at little cost to themselves. They lobbied the Postal Rate Commission to increase third-class mail rates. They also allegedly "coerced" marketing research firms into charging Advo especially high rates for marketing research studies useful to Advo.[86]

Another example of this category of conduct is the cozy reciprocal buying under long-term contracts that goes on among chemical and petroleum companies. Assume, for example, that company A specializes in the production of X, company B specializes in Y, and company C specializes in Z. Then A will supply B and C with X, while those two companies reciprocate by supplying A with products Y and Z, and so

---

[85] J. D. Gribbon and M. A. Utton, "The Treatment of Dominant Firms in the UK Competition Legislation," in de Jong and Shepherd (eds.), *Mainstreams in Industrial Organization*, p. 243–272.

[86] *Business Week*, November 2, 1987, p. 122.

on. This enables each firm in the exchanges to carry a full line of products (or use them in their production process) while at the same time their specialization allows realization of economies of scale. In addition, this limits entry because it restricts a newcomer's sale and purchase opportunities—hence the "combination" effect.[87]

Finally, tacit collective use of certain pricing structures can have effects similar to those discussed previously in connection with Figure 11–7. The airlines, for instance, have "travel agent commission override programs" (or TACOs). An airline's TACO pays ever greater bonuses to any travel agent who generates ever greater specified volumes of revenues for the airline:

> Because the [bonuses] are increasing, the programs can effectively "attach" travel agents to certain airlines. . . . In a recent survey of travel agents, more than half reported that their choice of airline for a customer is "usually" (24%) or "sometimes" (27%) influenced by TACOs. . . . [An] airline offering the most opportunities for building up "points" (revenues in this case) and offering the most valued set of bonuses will be the most effective in industry loyalty, through a TACO program. These aids to inducing loyalty are likely to favor the airlines with more flights to and from a city.[88]

I. Explicit Collective "Combination Conduct"

An aggregated rebate cartel advances the basic idea of loyalty rebates and TACO bonuses one step farther. It is an agreement among a *group* of sellers to give their customers delayed rebates calculated in terms of the volume an individual customer purchases *from all members in the group* during a given period. The twist here is that the "loyalty" rebate is not based on loyalty to just one seller, but rather loyalty to a *group* of sellers during some time period. Although generally illegal in the United States, aggregated rebate cartels are common in countries with lenient antitrust policies and in international shipping.[89] Their intent is to exclude newcomers while also smothering competition among members of the group.

This dual purpose is especially evident in the case of "loyalty contracts" that are used by shipping "conferences" plying international waters:

[87] Alfred E. Kahn, "The Chemical Industry," in *The Structure of American Industry*, edited by Walter Adams, 3rd ed. (New York: Macmillan, 1961), pp. 250–251; and M. Fayad and H. Motamen, *Economics of the Petrochemical Industry* (New York: St. Martin's Press, 1986), pp. 66–67. For another example of reciprocal selling that had exclusionary effects while allowing the exploitation of market power, see William F. Hellmuth, Jr., "The Motion Picture Industry," in Adams (ed.), *The Structure of American Industry*, pp. 403–407.

[88] Severin Borenstein, "Hubs and High Fares: Dominance and Market Power in the U.S. Airline Industry," *Rand Journal of Economics* (Autumn 1989), p. 347.

[89] Committee of Experts on Restrictive Business Practices, *Aggregated Rebate Cartels* (Paris: Organization for Economic Cooperation and Development, 1972).

The common characteristic of loyalty contracts is that the conference [of steamship companies] offers a shipper a discount off the regular price if the shipper agrees to purchase exclusively from the conference. The point is to retain the loyalty of it customers by making it expensive to switch from conference vessels to nonconference vessels.

With a deferred rebate, if the shipper purchases exclusively from the conference in the first six months, he earns the discount, but does not actually receive it. The shipper receives the discount in the form of a rebate at the end of the second six months, but only if he continues to purchase exclusively from the conference during the second six months. If at any time the shipper purchases from another conference, he loses *both* the rebate he was building during that six months and the rebate from the previous six months.[90]

Loyalty rebates *induce* the loyalty of buyers toward sellers. Sometimes those in a buyer-seller relationship can *exchange commitments* of exclusivity to their *mutual* benefit. For example, the first cartel case ever prosecuted in the United States under Section 1 of the Sherman Act (1890) had such an arrangement. A cartel of mine operators supplying coal to Nashville agreed to sell only to a cartel of wholesale coal dealers in Nashville, while in return the colluding Nashville dealers agreed with the mine operators to buy their coal supplies only from those in the operators' cartel. The exclusionary effect of this *joint* exclusive dealing between the two cartels was critical to the rich profitability of their conspiracies:

> Although a cartel among wholesalers was attempted in 1887 and failed, and a cartel among mine operators alone was probably destined to a similar fate because of distrust and fierce competition among the mines, a combination of the principal mine operators with a cost advantage serving Nashville *and* established wholesalers could support supracompetitive prices for residential coal in Nashville.[91]

Combinations of exploitation and extension may also be achieved collectively by the collusive use of patents. Simple exploitation of a patent's monopoly power by an *individual* patentee would fall into category A of our Table 11–1 scheme, and so is legal. However, firms have been known to act collectively to exploit *and* enhance that power by means that are now largely illegal in the United States. Two or more firms holding patents on related technologies may "cross-license" each other exclusively so that between them they may use all the technologies involved while at the same time keeping these technologies out of the hands of would-be rivals. Alternatively, a group of firms may commit

[90] William Sjostrom, "Monopoly Exclusion of Lower Cost Entry: Loyalty Contracts in Ocean Shipping Conferences," *Journal of Transport Economics and Policy* (September 1988), p. 339 (emphasis added).

[91] John J. Siegfried and Michelle Mahony, "The First Sherman Act Case: Jellico Mountain Coal, 1891," *Antitrust Bulletin* (Winter 1990), pp. 801–832.

their patents to a "pool." The pool's managers would operate a cartel, assigning to each pool contributor licenses to produce certain products, directions to serve certain customers, instructions to change certain prices, and so on, all the while excluding potential competitors from access to the pooled technologies. One of the most notorious patent pools in American business history was Hartford-Empire, which effectively cartelized the glass container industry during the first half of this century until struck down by antitrust action in 1945.[92]

IV. QUALIFICATIONS

This cell-by-cell exploration of Table 11–1 might seem complicated, but it is a simplification of reality, in some ways an oversimplification. Hence a few brief caveats are needed.

First, specific instances of conduct are sometimes difficult to place in a single category. In 1989, for instance, *The Wall Street Journal* reported that coffin manufacturers refused to supply coffins to Hillmark Casket Gallery and other *discount* coffin retailers because funeral homes, the predominant sellers of coffins, threatened to boycott any coffin maker who supplied the discounters. As explained by Ronald Hast, a prominent funeral director and publisher of a trade magazine, "If a casket company is selling to a maverick, funeral directors won't buy from it."[93] This conduct seems like it would best fit in category F covering explicitly collusive exclusionary conduct. On the other hand, no great sacrifice of short-run profits is involved for either the funeral homes instigating the boycotts or the coffin makers, so it might be assigned to category I along with the Nashville coal cartel.

Second, a single industry can be operating in several different cells of Table 11–1 at the same time. Firms might be colluding on price (C) while simultaneously proliferating their products to exclude potential rivals (E). Another possibility is vigorous rivalry (off the chart) coupled with collusive endeavors of some sort (e.g., C or F). In 1988 Airbus Industrie and McDonnell Douglas were battling tooth and nail to sell jetliners to Delta Air Lines and British Airways while at the same time they were talking amiably of cooperating in a joint venture that would produce a new jumbo jet.[94]

---

[92] *Hartford-Empire Company v. United States*, 323 U.S. 386 (1945). See for a summary Don E. Waldman, *The Economics of Antitrust* (Boston: Little, Brown, 1986), pp. 217–225. For descriptions of international patent cartels, see Corwin D. Edwards, *Economic and Political Aspects of International Cartels*, U.S. Senate, Subcommittee on War Mobilization of the Committee on Military Affairs (1944), pp. 5–7; and H. Kronstein, *The Law of International Cartels* (Ithaca, N.Y.: Cornell University Press, 1973), pp. 276–303.

[93] *The Wall Street Journal*, July 5, 1989, p. B1.

[94] *The Wall Street Journal*, April 27, 1988, p. 20.

Third, the behavior of one industry in one category of conduct may facilitate the achievements of other industries in other categories. The Nashville coal cartels — combining mines and distributors (I) — were aided by the limit pricing of a railroad that dominated the local transportation market (D).

Fourth, conduct can change abruptly as circumstances change with time. During the 1920s the small cigarette companies selling at discount prices were tolerated by American, Reynolds, and Liggett & Meyers — the "Big Three" of the industry then, whose prices were at exceptionally profitable levels (cell B behavior). However, once the market share of the small companies reached 23% in the early 1930s, the "Big Three" cut price substantially to beat them back (E).

Finally, the chart of Table 11–1 ignores the vast realm of "procompetitive" conduct, such as the price discounting of the small cigarette companies during the 1920s and 1930s. Indeed, it is worth noting again that *much conduct is "anticompetitive" only when practiced by dominant firms or dominant collusive groups of firms.* Price discrimination may be procompetitive or anticompetitive, depending on the circumstances. The same could be said of exclusive dealing or tying. Hence a major task of the following chapters is to sort out the sheep from the wolves wearing sheepskins.

Although the ensuing conduct chapters are not organized precisely on the pattern of Table 11–1 (partly because of these several complications), they may be previewed with reference to those categories. Chapter 12 covers short-run pricing behavior that is nonstrategic (cells A, B, and C plus procompetitive pricing). Chapter 13 focuses on cartels in particular (cell C). Long-run or strategic pricing is the province of Chapter 14, including price discrimination (D, E, F, and G). U.S. policy governing price discrimination, as embodied in the Robinson-Patman Act, is tackled in Chapter 15. Conduct concerning product differentiation — advertising especially — comes next in Chapter 16 (many cells), followed by a discussion of misrepresentation policy in Chapter 17. Finally, Chapters 18 and 19 are devoted to various forms of multimarket conduct. Vertical integration and conglomeracy receive attention at that point, as well as exclusive dealing and tying, which may be the basis for "combination conduct" (cells, G, H, and I).

SUMMARY

Market power is the *ability* to influence price and/or subdue competition. Our previous discussion of structure focused on the trappings of *ability*; now we begin to focus on the *reality* as it is observed in actual conduct. In reality, the ability is often exercised. This is seen in (1) conduct that *exploits* market power, (2) conduct that *extends* market power, and (3) *combination conduct* that is both exploitative and expansionary. These constitute the three column headings of Table 11–1. Profit patterns over time typically vary across these categories — (1) exploitation yielding high short-term profits that then diminish, (2) extension producing low initial profits followed by riches, and (3) combination conduct reaping a good steady return from the start.

Market power of serious proportions stems from single-firm dominance, tacit collective action, or explicit collective action. These are the row divisions of Table 11–1. Competition prevails outside these conditions.

There is strong and abundant evidence that high prices are associated with high concentration. Studies of auction markets, geographic cross sections of markets, changes over time, and sundry miscellaneous cases stand behind this statement. These studies support market-power theories and refute efficient-market theories. They therefore also explain Table 11–1's emphasis on market power.

Exploring the cells of Table 11–1 reveals a wide variety of behaviors, including dominant firm price leadership, Prisoners' Dilemma game theory, cartel price fixing, strategic entry deterrence (e.g., product proliferation and patent preemption), group boycotts, volume discount price discrimination, loyalty rebates, tie-in sales, lease-only marketing, exclusive patent pooling, reciprocal collusive exclusive dealing, and aggregated rebates. Most of the items toward the end of this list are designed to "raise rivals' costs" or to create "customer switching costs." Perhaps the best summary of all these behaviors is found in the body of Table 11–1 itself.

Finally, a warning: Although Table 11–1 may seem complicated, it is a simplification. Future chapters will convince you that reality is considerably more complex.

APPENDIX: THE AIRLINE INDUSTRY

The airline industry of the 1980s exemplifies many of this chapter's main points. From 1938 to 1978, the airlines were regulated by the Civil Aeronautics Board, which severely restricted their conduct. However, during 1978–1984 the CAB's controls were relaxed, the CAB was disbanded, and competition burst upon the scene as two things happened: (1) United, American, Delta, Eastern, and the other established airlines expanded their operations beyond their formerly regulated territories, and (2) new carriers entered with cut-rate fares — People Express, Muse Airlines, and Presidential among them. The share of total domestic air traffic accounted for by the largest eight carriers fell from 80.4% in 1978 to 74.1% in 1983.[95] Prices fell sharply in most major city-pair markets.

[95] William G. Shepherd, "The Airline Industry," in *The Structure of American Industry*, edited by Walter Adams, 8th ed. (New York: Macmillan, 1990), p. 223.

Moreover, between 1978 and 1983 the operating profit margins of U.S. scheduled airlines plunged toward zero and actually became negative during 1980–1982.[96]

However, almost as quickly as competition blossomed, it withered after 1984. All but a few of the new entrants went bankrupt or were forced by troubled circumstances to sell out to established airlines. By 1989 American West and Midway were the only notable surviving newcomers, and they were not thriving. Meanwhile, a shopping spree of acquisitions and mergers consolidated the established carriers. These pairings included Delta and Western, American and Air Cal, Northwest and Republic, TWA and Ozark, plus a threesome—Texas Air acquiring Continental and Eastern. Nationwide eight-firm concentration rose from 74% in 1983 to more than 90% by the end of the decade. An airlines industry executive explained the merging and concentration succinctly: "Carriers are trying to achieve the market dominance that, among other things, will give them better control over their prices."[97]

Airline dominance is most clearly seen at the *local* and *regional* level. In particular, all the major airlines organized themselves into hub-and-spoke systems. As a consequence, air travel in and out of most hub cities became dominated by just one or two airlines. TWA accounted for 83% of all flights departing from St. Louis in 1985–1987. Similarly high shares went to USAir in Pittsburgh (83%), Northwest Airlines in Memphis (87%), and Continental in Houston (72%). United and Continental controlled Denver (87% together), while Eastern and Delta controlled Atlanta (88%).[98]

In turn, many city-pair markets, such as Detroit-Washington, D.C., and Pittsburgh-Philadelphia, have become dominated by just one or two carriers. Abundant evidence now indicates that structure in these markets greatly affects conduct. Conversely, individual and collective conduct by the dominant carriers has had a dramatic impact on the structure of these markets. Let's review the evidence under the three column headings of Table 11–1 (i.e., exploitation, extension, and combination conduct).

Exploitation of Power.   Prices are strongly associated with both single-firm dominance and, more generally, collective market concentration. Each association illustrates exploitation.

Table 11–6 reports 1987 data on airfares (cents per passenger per mile) for two situations of dominance—Northwest Airlines, which accounts for 77% of all passenger enplanements at Minneapolis–St. Paul airport, and Delta Airlines, which has a 55% market share in its "hub"

---

96 *The Economist*, September 9, 1989, p. 78.
97 *The Wall Street Journal*, September 17, 1986, p. 35.
98 Shepherd, "The Airline Industry," p. 222. See also, *The Wall Street Journal*, July 20, 1987, p. 1.

TABLE 11–6.   Comparisons of Average Airfares (Cents per Mile) for Flights to/from Dominated Airports, 1987

Nonstop Route Distance miles	Flights to/from Minneapolis/St. Paul		Flights to/from Atlanta	
	Northwest Airlines	Other Airlines	Delta Airlines	Other Airlines
Under 200	60.7¢	45.6¢	60.1¢	50.3¢
200–500	38.9	33.1	36.8	31.2
500–1000	22.1	18.7	21.9	19.2
1000–1500	13.9	11.1	13.9	12.9
1500–2000	10.8	8.4	10.5	9.0
Over 2000	8.9	7.9	8.2	8.4
All	17.6	14.9	19.8	17.4

Source: Severin Borenstein, "Hubs and High Fares: Dominance and Market Power in the U.S. Airline Industry," *Rand Journal of Economics* (Autumn 1989), p. 356.

city of Atlanta. Comparing the fares of these dominant airlines in these cities with those of other carriers in these cities shows markedly higher fares for Northwest and Delta. In general, including many other cases, Borenstein estimates that a carrier with 50% of an *airport's originations* will charge approximately 6% more than an airline with a small presence. Moreover, a carrier with a 70% share of traffic *on a given route* is able to charge 2% to 12% higher fares than its rivals on the same route having only 10% shares.[99]

The foregoing effects are separate from the adverse effects of high marketwide concentration, which have been found in numerous studies. For example, Thomas G. Moore compared two classes of city-pair markets — those served by one to four airlines and those served by five or more. He found that the unconcentrated markets, with five or more carriers, enjoyed price levels of 24–41% lower than the concentrated markets (other things being equal).[100] Similarly, Gloria J. Hurdle and her associates found much higher prices in markets of "high" as opposed to "low" concentration. Using a regression tree statistical technique on 1985 data from 867 city pairs, they found prices to be as much as 50% higher in highly concentrated markets.[101]

[99] Severin Borenstein, "Hubs and High Fares: Dominance and Market Power in the U.S. Airline Industry," *Rand Journal of Economics* (Autumn 1989), pp. 344–365. See also E. E. Bailey, D. R. Graham, and D. P. Kaplan, *Deregulating the Airlines* (Cambridge, Mass.: MIT Press, 1985), pp. 169–171.

[100] Thomas G. Moore, "U.S. Airline Deregulation," *Journal of Law and Economics* (April 1986), pp. 1–28.

[101] Gloria J. Hurdle, Richard L. Johnson, Andrew S. Jaskow, Gregory J. Werden, and

Although not as dramatic as these results, those of D. R. Graham, D. P. Kaplan, and D. S. Sibley are pictured in Figure 11–8. Airfares measured in cents per passenger per mile clearly rise with concentration measured by the Herfindahl–Hirschman index (especially up to an H index of 0.6).[102]

Extension of Power. Apart from their acquisitions of rivals, the leading airlines conducted themselves in other ways that extended (and maintained) their power. Alfred E. Kahn, a chief architect of deregulation while chairman of the CAB in the late 1970s, gives an example of predatory pricing:

> [In June, 1984] People Express announced a new air service between Minneapolis–St. Paul and Newark, New Jersey, at one way fares of $99 week days and $79 evenings and weekends. The lowest fare before that was $149, and it was available only with all sorts of restrictions; regular "economy" was $263. Immediately after, Northwest Airlines responded with full page ads, announcing unrestricted fares of $95 and $75, for

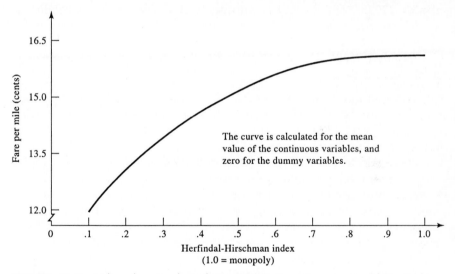

FIGURE 11–8. Airline fares and market concentration. Source: David R. Graham, Daniel P. Kaplan, and David S. Sibley, "Efficiency and Competition in the Airlines Industry," *Bell Journal of Economics* (Spring 1983), p. 135.

Michael A. Williams, "Concentration, Potential Entry, and Performance in the Airline Industry," *Journal of Industrial Economics* (December 1989), p. 135.

102 See also Bailey, Graham, and Kaplan, *Deregulating the Airlines*; S. A. Morrison and C. Winston, "Empirical Implications of the Contestability Hypothesis," *Journal of Law and Economics* Vol. 30 (1987), pp. 53–66; and G. D. Call and T. E. Keeler "Airline Deregulation, Fares and Market Behavior" in Daughety (ed.), *Analytical Studies in Airline Transportation*, pp. 65–83.

much better service — wider seating, free meals, free baggage handling and transfer — to all three New York airports. So Northwest not only cut its regular fares in this one market by two-thirds, it effectively undercut People's very substantially.

If predation means anything, it means deep, pinpointed, discriminatory price cuts by big companies aimed at driving price cutters out of the market, in order then to be able to raise prices back to their previous levels. I have little doubt that is what Northwest was and is trying to do.[103]

With time, price cutting by the majors became less obviously predatory. They would simply *match* the lower fares of the upstarts, not undercut them. The majors could then rely on their established reputation, more frequent flights, and service frills to run newcomers aground. Moreover, the majors developed tremendous sophistication at pinpointing where and under what restrictions airfares should be cut in order to subdue competitors at little sacrifice to themselves. Computers aided this "yield management" strategy. During *each day* of 1988 for instance, United Airlines filed about 30,000 fare changes, monitored advanced sales on 120,000 United flights, and made changes in seat availability at various discounts on about 15,000 of those flights.[104] Such "yield management" shot down the low-fare strategy of the entrants. Donald Burr, who founded People Express, says sadly, "I'm the world's leading example of a guy killed by the computer chip."[105]

Combination Conduct.   In addition, the large established airlines were able during the 1980s to extend and maintain their power with strategies of very little or no cost to themselves. These strategies therefore appear to have been almost immediately profitable even as they furthered collective and single-firm (city-pair) dominance.

Frequent flyer programs were one such strategy. Introduced in 1981 by American Airlines and since copied by the other majors, these programs give free travel to a customer after he or she has flown a certain number of miles on the airline. Customer allegiance is secured by a form of loyalty rebate. These programs put entrants and small airlines at a disadvantage because they create switching costs for frequent flyers who might otherwise switch to the upstarts. (And frequent flyers are mainly business travelers, the airlines' most lucrative class of customers.)[106]

A second strategy was to distort the computer reservation systems used by travel agents, the systems they rely on to obtain flight sched-

---

103 Alfred E. Kahn, "The Macroeconomic Consequences of Sensible Microeconomic Politics," address at AEA Meetings, December 1984, published by National Economic Research Associates, 1985.

104 *Washington Post*, National Weekly Edition, December 4, 1988, p. 21.

105 *The Wall Street Journal*, July 19, 1989, p. A8. See also *Business Week*, February 4, 1985, pp. 36–38, and *The Wall Street Journal*, November 26, 1985, p. 33.

106 For more discussion, see Borenstein, "Hubs and High Fares," pp. 345–346.

ules and price information. These computer reservation systems are "leased" by travel agents from the major airlines who own them—mainly American Airlines and United Airlines, whose Sabre and Apollo systems accounted for almost 80% of all the "lease" revenues paid in the mid-1980s.[107] During the 1980s the owner-airlines programmed these computer systems to display their own flight availabilities and airfares to travel agents, and therefore to customers, before displaying data on rivals. The resulting biases adversely affected the small airlines and discounting start-ups.[108]

Furthermore, as *The Wall Street Journal* explained in 1989, the large carriers gained control over the available airport gates, thereby raising their smaller rivals' costs:

> Today, a start-up can literally be blocked at the gate. The major carriers have locked up 20-year to 4-year leases on passenger loading gates at the big airports. New airlines wanting to sublease gates must haggle with the giants, the equivalent of a tiny new store trying to get floor space from Macy's. Not surprisingly, the big carriers drive hard bargains.
>
> In Detroit, Southwest Airlines pays giant Northwest Airlines $150 per flight to use two gates—about 19 times what Northwest pays the airport authority to lease the space . . . American West, as part of its lease agreement for one gate at New York's John F. Kennedy Airport, pays Trans World Airlines employees to service the planes, at rates twice what American West pays its own, nonunion ground-service workers.[109]

Finally, entry at four key airports (Chicago O'Hare, Washington-National, Kennedy, and LaGuardia) is discouraged by a severe scarcity of slots. These are the landing and takeoff rights corresponding to specific time periods. In 1969, when originally assigned by the Federal Aviation Administration (FAA), these slots were widely disbursed. But by 1989 that had changed, as explained by *The Wall Street Journal*:

> Thanks to mergers, the industry's eight remaining major airline companies now hold 95% of the slots. Some aren't being used, but FAA officials say carriers can easily manipulate their schedules to disguise unused slots. The result: Only 17 of 3,184 domestic slots have become available to small or new airlines in the past two years.[110]

A final note: Although these several strategies hamper small carriers and discourage the entry of new ones, they would be less harmful if the majors vigorously competed among themselves. Unfortunately, the evidence reviewed earlier on airline prices dampens our hopes in this re-

---

[107] Shepherd "The Airline Industry," p. 226; Margaret E. Guerin-Calvert, "Vertical Integration as a Threat to Competition: Airline Computer Reservation Systems," in Kwoka and White (eds.), *The Antitrust Revolution*, pp. 338–370.

[108] Ibid.

[109] *The Wall Street Journal*, July 19, 1989, p. A8.

[110] Ibid.

gard. Moreover, by 1989, some evidence of reciprocal forbearance was emerging. The majors were developing a respect for each other's hubs. "At times recently," stated *The Wall Street Journal* in 1989, "it's seemed as though the airlines have used the nation's air route system as a giant chess board in the sky, moving in and out of markets in an apparent attempt to avoid stiff competition."[111]

---

[111] *The Wall Street Journal*, March 10, 1989, p. A8.

12

Price and Production Behavior in the Short Run: Theory and Evidence

. . . true oligopoly is interdependence plus uncertainty.

—DONALD DEWEY

Of the several aspects of conduct mentioned previously, none have received greater attention than price and production policies. It is proper, then, that we take these up first. We begin with *short-run* price and production policies in this chapter and the next. *Long-run* aspects come later.

The principal short-run issues include price rivalry among "existing" sellers, price behavior during slumps in demand, supply control over the business cycle to stabilize price, and price fixing. Considering the long run, our scope will broaden to include not only existing competitors, but also potential and past competitors. That is, we shall consider how pricing influences the birth and death of firms.

Within the short-run context we have already presented simple theories of price determination under perfect competition and monopoly. The present chapter will focus on behavior associated with structural conditions that lie between those extremes — namely, oligopoly and monopolistic competition. The first section discusses interdependence, which is a prime determinant of how firms in these settings view their demand curves. The second section introduces complications and uncertainties, particularly those associated with cyclical swings of demand. Next we review several pricing mechanisms used to cope with these complications and uncertainties. The concluding section is devoted to cross-section empirical evidence of short-run price behavior.

I. INTERDEPENDENCE

A. The Cournot Model

Over a century ago, Augustin Cournot demonstrated the importance of interdependence in oligopoly with a clever theoretical model.[1] He assumed the following:

- There are two sellers (we call them **J** and **K**).
- The product is homogeneous, spring water to be exact.
- Each seller has zero marginal costs.
- Finally, and very importantly, he assumed that each seller in selecting his output level would believe that his rival's level of output would not change. This belief holds despite the fact that each rival's output does change as the theory unfolds. Hence sellers do not learn by experience and their actions center on quantity instead of price.

Cournot's model is illustrated in Figure 12–1, where $D'D$ indicates marketwide demand. We begin with firm **J**, who is the first to sell and who therefore assumes that **K**'s present output will remain at zero. **J** maximizes profit by producing 1000 units, which is determined by equating $D'D$'s marginal revenue R_o with marginal cost, which is zero. Firm **K** now starts selling. By assumption, **K** believes that **J** will continue to produce 1000 units. Hence **K** perceives its demand curve to be HD, which when shifted to the price axis becomes $E'E$. The marginal revenue curve associated with **K**'s demand $E'E$ is R_1, so firm **K** maximizes its profit by selling 500 units (where marginal revenue meets marginal cost).

With **K**'s output set at 500, **J**'s original output of 1000 is no longer best for **J**, however. So if **J** assumes that **K**'s output will remain at 500, it will now view its demand as $F'F$, which is demand when 500 units are

[1] A. Cournot, *Researches into the Mathematical Principles of the Theory of Wealth* (New York: Macmillan, 1897), first published in Paris in 1838.

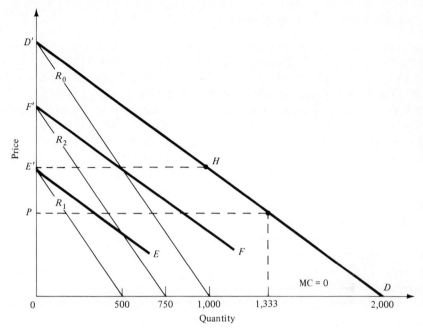

FIGURE 12–1. The Cournot model.

subtracted from $D'D$. Seeing $F'F$ as its demand, **J** then maximizes profit by equating marginal revenue R_2 with marginal cost at 750 units. Once **J** is set at 750, it is then **K**'s turn to react once more, triggering further rounds of action-reaction that are not shown in Figure 12–1.

Although these further rounds are not shown, it should be apparent from what has happened already that **J** and **K** are converging toward a common level of output. The first output pairs were 1000 **(J)** and 0 **(K)**, followed by 750 **(J)** and 500 **(K)**. In the end, they each wind up with outputs of 666⅔ units, which when combined yield 1333⅓ units total output and price P, as shown in Figure 12–1.

Under perfect competition, output would be higher at 2000 units and price would be lower at zero. Pure monopoly, on the other hand, would place output at 1000 and price at E'. Thus Cournot's model yields an equilibrium that is "in between" these structural extremes. Moreover, if we introduced additional firms into the model, moving from duopoly to triopoly to still more populous forms of oligopoly, market output and price would move in the direction of the perfect competition results.

The assumptions of Cournot's model are very unrealistic. Yet these implications of the model are not too misleading, in large part because they derive from seller interdependence. Turning to more modern theories we shall see that interdependence remains, but the focus is mainly on *price* behavior instead of quantity behavior.

B. Modern Theory: Two Demands

The interdependence of oligopolists and monopolistically competitive firms is reflected in the demand curves they confront. Whereas a pure monopolist sees the marketwide demand curve and the purely competitive firm sees a perfectly elastic demand curve, those in between may view *two* demand curves. Two curves are necessary to account for the possible reactions of rivals—followship or nonfollowship—given a change in the firm's price. The **followship** demand curve applies if a change in price is matched by rivals. A price reduction under followship conditions will gain added sales for the firm but not at the expense of rivals because they will have lowered prices too. The sales come from added *marketwide* sales, which, if distributed among all rivals according to their preexisting market shares, would leave each firm's market share unchanged. Conversely, a price increase curtails a firm's sales in proportion to the market's loss of sales, provided all firms act uniformly on the increase. The followship curve could therefore also be called a **constant market share** demand curve.

As indicated by the FD curves in Figure 12–2, followship demand varies depending on firm size. Each panel of Figure 12–2 assumes the *same* marketwide demand. But FD for the "Big" firm is drawn on the assumption of a 90% market share; that for "Middle" assumes a 50% market share; and "Little" assumes a 25% market share. The firms could not all be in the same market, but each FD is a reflection of the marketwide demand underlying the illustrations. This may be appreciated by noting that the elasticity of each FD curve at price P_0 is the same, and each such elasticity in turn matches marketwide elasticity. Price P_0 divides each FD curve into upper and lower portions. Elasticity is the same at P_0 because the length of the upper portion *relative* to the lower portion is the same in each case.

Although the followship curves are identical in elasticity, such is not true of the **nonfollowship** demand curves labeled NFD. They do vary in elasticity across firms within a given market because the assumption underlying their construction—that rivals do *not* match price changes—yields substantially different quantity results depending on firm size. Big firm's NFD will have an elasticity very similar to its FD though slightly higher. An unfollowed price cut below P_0 would cause customers to switch to Big. But the most Big could gain from competitors would be an additional 10 percentage points of market share, since at price P_0 Big already enjoys 90%. Comparing 10 to 90 implies a low elasticity for Big's NF curve. At the other extreme, an unfollowed price cut of similar magnitude on the part of Little could easily double Little's sales volume, implying that Little's nonfollowship demand curve at P_0 is highly elastic. Putting two and two together we may conclude that *the smaller the firm relative to its market, the greater the divergence between its followship and non-*

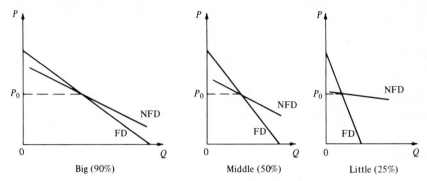

FIGURE 12–2. Followship (FD) and nonfollowship (NFD) demand curves for various sized firms.

followship demand curves and between their elasticities. Since product differentiation also influences demand, a related conclusion holds that the more differentiated the firm's product is, the less the divergence will be. Or the more standardized the product, the greater the divergence between FD and NFD and their elasticities.

A good example of the combined effects of market share and product differentiation comes from gasoline retailing in Vancouver, British Columbia. Margaret Slade found the nonfollowship elasticity of demand for small independent retailers, who do not rely on national advertising for "image" building, to be almost two times greater than the nonfollowship elasticity for large, "major" brand retailers like Shell, Texaco, and Chevron.[2]

As structure affects a firm's demand elasticities in this fashion, it will also affect the firm's opportunities for earning sales revenues and thereby its price behavior. The linkage between demand elasticity and total revenue is summarized in the two-part diagram of Figure 12–3. The horizontal axis of both parts is quantity. The vertical axis of the upper part is price; that of the lower part is total revenue. Because total revenue is price times quantity, the *area* under the demand curve at any point equals the vertical *distance* under the total revenue curve of the lower part. At point H, for example, total revenue is $OJHK$, and this corresponds to GF using the total dollars vertical scale of the total revenue diagram. It should be clear, then, that a price reduction will increase total revenue if demand is elastic, as it is in the AH range and below to $E = 1$. But a price reduction will decrease total revenue if demand is inelastic, as it is between $E = 1$ and B. Conversely, a price increase will boost the firm's

[2] Margaret E. Slade, "Conjectures, Firm Characteristics, and Market Structure," *International Journal of Industrial Organization* (December 1986), pp. 347–369.

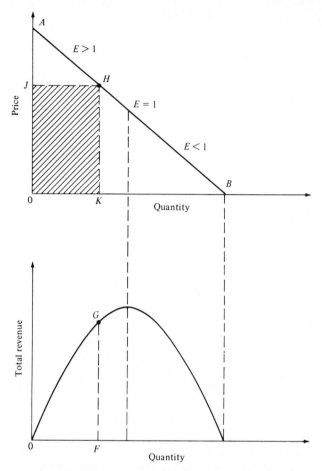

FIGURE 12–3. Relationship between demand elasticity and total revenue.

total revenue if demand is inelastic but trim total revenue if demand is elastic.[3]

These relationships tell us a great deal about which of the three firms of Figure 12–2 has the most to gain from a trip down its nonfollowship demand curve via price cuts below P_0. Little has the most elastic NFD; hence, it would gain the most, assuming that it could in fact move down its NFD. Conversely, Big has the least to gain from such behavior. We can therefore surmise that relatively small firms are more likely to cut prices and bestow bargains than are big firms. Turning the issue around, we may ask which firm is most likely to gain from a price *increase*. Big is

[3] In early 1980 IBM raised prices on its 4300 series equipment. *Business Week* reported that, as a result, IBM's revenue would increase by about $1 billion because, "No one expects the higher prices to reduce demand" (January 28, 1980, p. 84).

the most likely gainer in this case. We can expect, therefore, to find relatively large firms most frequently cast in the role of upside price leader.

These deductions are fair and proper, but they are nevertheless a bit premature. We have not considered two important factors that may affect their accuracy: (1) Costs are as important as revenues in determining behavior, for costs as well as revenues determine profits. (2) Just as we mortals cannot be in two places at one time, so too the firm cannot be on more than one demand curve at any one time (except where the curves intersect). A price cut will take it down either NFD or FD, not both. A price increase is an either/or journey in the opposite direction. Because the elasticities of NFD and FD differ, we must discover *which* curve the firm regards as its *actual* demand curve under various circumstances. The firm's view of its terrain determines what steps the firm takes, if it takes any at all. We shall demonstrate the significance of these additional considerations by exploring two classical models of firm conduct—"monopolistic competition" and the "kinky demand curve" of oligopoly.

C. Monopolistic Competition

Assume, as did the originator of this model, Edward Chamberlin,[4] that *all* firms in the market are small, smaller even than Little of Figure 12–2. Assume further that each firm has a negatively sloped, though highly elastic, nonfollowship demand curve because each has a differentiated product. These assumptions yield a model of shortsighted price cutting. In other words, the interdependence of the firms goes unrecognized in this case, with the result that price competition predominates.

Figure 12–4 depicts the situation as viewed by a typical small firm. We begin with all firms charging price P_1. The typical firm is earning excess total profits equal to the difference between P_1 and average total cost (ATC) directly below point A *times* the quantity produced (assuming that the average total cost curve includes a normal profit as a cost). Though adequate, the firm's profit could be increased if it cut price to P_2 without being followed by rivals. In that event, it would move down its nonfollowship demand curve NF_1 to a point such as *B*. Notice the very high elasticity of NF_1. Quantity nearly doubles. So this ploy yields a substantial increase in total revenue, while declining unit costs (ATC) keep total costs from rising by as much. However, the profit gains last only as long as rivals fail to follow, because these gains are procured at their expense. Their demand curves will have shifted to the left, leaving them with fewer customers, higher costs, and lower profits. To regain their former market shares, these rivals cut their prices to P_2 as well, an

4 Edward Chamberlin, *The Theory of Monopolistic Competition*, 8th ed. (Cambridge, Mass.: Harvard University Press, 1962).

action that shifts the firm of Figure 12–4 from point B to point C. After cut and countercut, the result is a movement down the followship demand curve from A to C and to a new nonfollowship curve NF_2. As the firm of Figure 12–4 is typical of all firms in the market, this descent carries all other firms with it. If our typical firm is shortsighted enough to try the same stunt again, the others will naturally follow and further downward shifts will ensue. Equilibrium is reached at point E, at which point any further price cutting takes the firm below average total cost. Here, theory posits a truce.

Of course the key to this scenario is the inability of the small firm to see beyond its first step down the nonfollowship curve. The firm does not consider the inelastic followship curve relevant. The temptations of NF's high elasticity are too great. The firm feels it is too small to have an impact on others in the market. The consequence is price competition. The pattern may be illustrated with an example taken from grocery retailing, which in the past in certain cities might qualify as monopolistically competitive. In 1975 and 1976 price wars broke out in several cities, despite the fact that industry executives unanimously decried them, saying that "price wars always hurt profits and rarely change market shares among the combatants — the supposed goal." Except for consumers, who obviously benefit, "everybody fights harder and everybody loses."[5] Here is the story of one of the bloodiest battles of this period:

> The Chicago price war, undoubtedly one of the longest and costliest in supermarket history, began abruptly. On a Saturday afternoon in April . . . the manager of Jewel Food Store heard from a visitor that a nearby Dominick's store was changing a lot of prices. Unusual for a Saturday, the manager thought. He sent an employee to check.

> The employee found Dominick's aisles swarming with stock boys repricing merchandise. *And all the prices were being reduced.* Within minutes, Jewel employees throughout the area were scouting Dominick's stores. Their reports were startling . . . . Dominick's was slashing prices as much as 15% on "hundreds and hundreds" of items.

> On Tuesday, Jewel's response was ready. Jewel was cutting prices on 3,327 items from 2% to 30%. On Friday, National Tea announced it was reducing prices . . . . Other competitors jumped in quickly.

> Mr. DiMatteo [the manager of Dominick's] says he thought he could batter the competition. So he ordered the price cuts . . . . However, "the competition jumped in a lot faster than I thought they would," he concedes, "I thought we'd be alone for a while."[6]

Although the followship demand curve was not wholly invisible to Mr. DiMatteo, it was certainly obscure and broken as depicted in Figure 12–4.

---

[5] "Supermarket Scrap," *The Wall Street Journal*, July 19, 1976.
[6] Ibid.

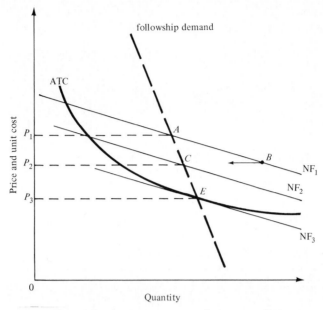

FIGURE 12–4. Shortsighted price cutting under monopolistic competition.

As for the ultimate effects on market share, "Progressive Grocer, a trade magazine, found that 95% of the Chicago shoppers it questioned at one point during the price war said they were going to the same store as they had before the battle broke out."

D. The Kinky Demand Curve of Oligopoly

Fewer firms in the market, with larger market shares, convert conditions to **oligopoly**, and the interdependence becomes *recognized*.[7] One way of demonstrating this conversion is the theory of "kinked demand." Let P_0 in Figure 12–5 represent the going market price. Q_0 is then the firm's output, and K indicates the firm's position on its demand curves. Given these conditions, what action is best for the firm? Is it likely to slash price, boost it, or leave it unchanged? If the firm thinks its prices below P_0 will be followed, then *below* point K the followship demand curve alone is relevant. The NF demand curve thus disappears below K. Conversely, if the firm is doubtful that its price increases will be followed, then above K only the NF demand curve is applicable, and the F curve does the vanishing act.

    [7] R. L. Hall and C. J. Hitch, "Price Theory and Business Behavior," *Oxford Economic Papers* (May 1939), pp. 12–45; and P. M. Sweezy, "Demand Under Conditions of Oligopoly," *Journal of Political Economy* (August 1939), pp. 568–573.

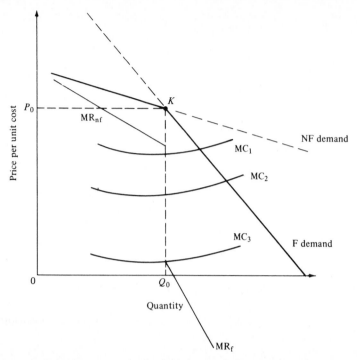

FIGURE 12–5. The kinked demand oligopoly model.

Now, a split personality may be fine for anyone with too many friends, but schizophrenic demand curves such as these put the firm in a straightjacket. Costs aside, it should be clear that a price cut below P_0 would substantially diminish total revenue because the F curve below K is inelastic. Moreover, things are just as bad the other way around. A price increase above P_0 would reduce total revenue substantially because NF above K is highly elastic. With total revenue falling from a step in either direction, the best strategy is to stand pat.

Furthermore, this rigidity of price may not be compromised by cost considerations. If the firm is operating under the MR = MC rule of profit maximization, marginal costs can vary over a spacious range without causing price to flutter from its P_0 perch because the marginal revenue curve is discontinuous. The discontinuity arises because the marginal revenue applicable to price increases is MR_{nf}, which is derived from the *nonfollowship* demand curve above K, whereas the marginal revenue applicable to price reductions is MR_f, which is derived from the *followship* demand curve below point K. Marginal cost is shown to vary from MC_1 to MC_3, but it always remains equal to marginal revenue.

A good example of kinked demand expectations was uncovered by Geir Gripsrud in the course of interviewing the managers of 129 independent grocery stores in Norway in the late 1970s. Oligopoly conditions for this sample are indicated by the fact that, on average, each manager perceived the presence of about three rival stores whose prices had to be taken into account. When asked whether or not their main competitor would follow a general price *reduction* of 3% if they (the respondent) cut prices, 61.0% of all respondents said "yes," they would expect to be followed down. On the other hand, when asked whether or not they expected their main competitor to follow if they initiated a general price *increase* of 3%, only 7.5% of all respondents said "yes," they expected to be followed up. Thus downside followship was commonly expected among these Norwegian grocers while, conversely, expectations of upside followship were rare, leading Gripsrud to conclude that "the kinked demand curve is prevalent" in the retail markets he sampled. (For later purposes it should be noted that each of the grocers expecting to be followed on the upside was quite large relative to its rivals, almost three times larger on average.)[8]

In sum, kinked demand theory yields two basic predictions: (1) Oligopolists will refrain from price cutting when their followship demand curves are inelastic; and (2), except in rapid inflation, oligopoly prices will tend to be rigid, despite moderate changes in costs. Although both predictions are consistent with the opinions of businessmen and much of their observed behavior, the model suffers several serious limitations.[9] In many respects it is a model of rigidity that, as presented above, is itself too rigid.

E. Criticisms and Modifications to the Kinky Model

Although kinked demand theory is inadequate in its simple form, it is useful when modified to account for real-world nuances. This section covers several criticisms and modifications that prove informative.

1. Firm Versus Marketwide Cost Changes: Consider, first, the matter of moderate increases in costs. The kinked demand theory is most applicable when the costs of an *individual* oligopolist rise but those of others in the market remain unchanged. A firm confronted with unique cost increments has no reason to expect that a price increase on its part will be followed by its less troubled rivals. But what about cost increases

[8] Geir Gripsrud, "Market Structure, Perceived Competition, and Expected Competitor Reactions in Retailing," *Research in Marketing*, edited by L. P. Bucklin and J. M. Carman, Vol. 8 (Greenwich, Conn.: JAI Press, 1986), pp. 251–271.

[9] For a critique, see G. J. Stigler, "The Kinky Oligopoly Demand Curve and Rigid Prices," *Journal of Political Economy* (October 1947), pp. 432–449. For critiques of Stigler, see C. W. Efroymson, "The Kinked Oligopoly Curve Reconsidered," *Quarterly Journal of Economics* (February 1955), pp. 119–136; R. B. Heflebower, "Full Costs, Cost Changes, and Prices," in *Business Concentration and Price Policy* (Princeton, N.J.: Princeton University Press, 1955), pp. 361–392; and J. M. Clark, *Competition as a Dynamic Process* (Washington, D.C.: Brookings Institution, 1961), pp. 287–289.

that confront *all* rivals simultaneously? A hike in the cost of steel to automakers, for example? Or a 15% rise in labor costs due to a newly signed collective bargaining contract? The oligopolist who attempts to initiate price increases to cover these costs is not really sticking his neck out very far. Followship is likely. Thus, the business press is riddled with news accounts of oligopolists raising prices after such across-the-board cost increases.

2. Price Level versus Price Changes: A second limitation is suggested by the first. Kinked demand theory may partly explain the rigidity of an *existing* price level, but it does not explain how prices reached that level in the first place. In other words, it is an instructive but *incomplete* theory of oligopolistic price behavior. Besides uniform cost increases, it ignores the possibility of price leadership and cartelization. It yields no solid predictions as to whether prices will be higher in concentrated markets as compared with unconcentrated ones. And it does not tell us whether profits will be greater where barriers to entry prevail.

3. Firm Size: These criticisms may be expanded into a third and somewhat different shortcoming of the theory. In its simple form, the theory imparts an impression of interfirm uniformity that is often unrealistic. A cursory reading of the theory conjures up notions of a market in which all firms are exactly the same size and weight (say, ten firms each with one-tenth of the market), all offer identical products, and all charge exactly the same price. Such an image must be rejected, however. Oligopolists usually differ in size, products, and prices—even within the same narrow market definition.

A very large and efficient firm may act as price leader, for instance. Because leadership implies followship, such a firm would usually see *only* the followship demand curve, upside and down. No kink would be visible, as the kink is created by a combination of nonfollowship and followship curves. Historically, General Motors has usually served as such a leader in the auto industry. The qualification "usually" is needed because GM's price increases have occasionally not been followed during severe slumps in demand, and Japanese producers have recently given GM some stiff competition. At the other size extreme, a very small firm, such as AMC in the auto industry, before its merger with Chrysler, would not see any kink if its price moves were never followed.

The most likely candidates for the kinky demand are therefore an industry's medium-sized firms, like Ford or Chrysler. They are big enough to usually be followed on the down side, too big to be ignored even by GM. Yet they are not qualified by size, efficiency, or historical reputation to be assured that their price increases will usually be honored by imitation.[10] In short, *the presence of a kinked demand curve for a firm is*

---

[10] L. J. White, *The Automobile Industry Since 1945* (Cambridge, Mass.: Harvard Univer-

TABLE 12–1.   Firm Price Changes by Alternative Methods (Explicit or Implicit) in the British Automobile Industry, 1956–1968

Method	Price Increases		Price Decreases	
	Number	Percent	Number	Percent
Explicit: Quality not changed	70	69.3%	8	17.4%
Implicit: Quality changed	31	30.7	38	82.6
Total	101	100.0%	46	100.0%

Source: John Cubbin, "Quality Change and Price Behavior in the United Kingdom Car Industry, 1956–1968," *Economica* (February 1975), pp. 43–58.

affected by its size relative to rivals, and especially large or small firms may see no kink even as their rivals perceive one.

4. Methods of Price Changes: Kinked demands may be present but obscured by different methods of changing prices as well as by a diversity of firm size. In particular, price increases might be achieved in ways that differ from price decreases. Why? In general, firms *will* want to be followed if they initiate price *increases*, but *will not* want to be followed if they initiate price *reductions*, for reasons just the opposite to those behind the kinked demand curve of Figure 12–5. Firms want price *in*elasticity on the upside in order to boost their total revenues. Conversely, firms want price elasticity on the downside in order to boost their total revenues.

In autos, for example, price can be changed *explicitly* by offering the same car at a higher or lower price than before. Price can also be changed *implicitly* by offering more quality (e.g., more "standard equipment") than before at the same price (in effect a price cut) or by offering less quality (e.g., less "standard equipment") than before at the same price (in effect a price hike). John Cubbin's study of the British auto industry during 1956–1968 came up with the data in Table 12–1. When raising price, the auto companies typically did so explicitly, without lowering quality. Roughly 70% of the 101 price increases observed were explicit price hikes. Quick followship was being encouraged. Price reductions, on the other hand, were almost always implemented implicitly through improvements in quality. Nearly 83% of all price cuts were done in this way, apparently

sity Press, 1971), pp. 111–135; and S. E. Boyle and T. F. Hogarty, "Pricing Behavior in the American Automobile Industry, 1957–71," *Journal of Industrial Economics* (December 1975), pp. 81–95.

[11] Richard E. Caves and Michael E. Porter, "From Entry Barriers to Mobility Barriers," *Quarterly Journal of Economics* (May 1977), pp. 241–261; and Michael E. Porter, *Competitive Strategy* (New York: The Free Press, 1980), pp. 126–155.

because this made followship more difficult or less likely. Hopes for a more elastic response from consumers, and correspondingly higher revenues, are therefore in evidence in this contrasting behavior.

5. Strategic Groups: A diversity of prices — with some firms charging more than others — may also obscure kinky demands among firms. Once the diversity is recognized, the kinks may appear in modified form. In particular, price diversity may be due to differences in firm size and product differentiation. The diversity will have a pattern to it if the industry's firms are clustered in strategic groups. A *strategic group*, it will be recalled, is a group of firms pursuing a similar strategy in terms of such things as advertising intensity, product quality, price policy, geographic scope, and breadth of product line.[11] In detergents, for example, Proctor & Gamble, Colgate, and Lever Brothers follow a high price, intensive advertising, consumer-oriented strategy. Less well-known firms sell under the private labels of retail chains and accordingly follow a low price, no advertising strategy. Still other firms specialize in bulk, industrial detergents.

The diversity of prices and strategic groups in many real-world markets is illustrated by Table 12–2, which presents data on retail gasoline prices in Washington, D.C., by brand, as of late 1969. The first column reports the number of stations selling each brand, except that independents are lumped in one category at the bottom. The second column converts these numbers of stations into estimates of market share. Thus, Exxon's 144 stations constitute 20.7% of all stations. In addition, the brands are arrayed from largest market share to smallest. Pricing is conveniently summarized by reporting the percentage of each brand's stations pricing above and below the reference price for regular gas in the market. For example, 53 Exxon stations, or 36.8% of Exxon's total, priced above reference. The "reference price" (which at that time was a mere 35.9 cents) is a kind of base or modal price that guides the actions of most gasoline retailers, especially the so-called "major brands." The majors are of course familiar to every driver and television viewer. They stress service, saturation of locations, credit cards, advertising, tires, batteries, accessories, clean restrooms, gasoline additives, and other nonprice forms of competition. As Table 12–2 suggests, they also have the lion's share of the business. They may be contrasted with the independents, which generally offer spartan accommodations, abbreviated service, very little advertising, and "competitive" prices. (Quite often they also carry quaint names like Hi-Rev, Rotten Robby's, and Stinker.)

Our earlier discussions of product differentiation led to expectations of the majors charging higher prices than the independents, and Table 12–2 bears out those expectations. The vast majority of major brand stations priced at or above reference. *All* independents priced below reference (by at least 4 cents a gallon or 11%). Moreover, theories concerning

TABLE 12–2. Price Levels of Gasoline Stations Located in Washington, D.C., Fall 1969

Brand	Number of Stations Surveyed	Total Stations (Market Share) (%)	Brand's Stations Pricing Above Reference (%)	Brand's Stations Pricing Below Reference (%)
Exxon	144	20.7%	36.8%	14.6%
American	90	12.9	20.0	15.6
Shell	73	10.5	15.1	13.7
Texaco	66	9.5	9.1	36.4
Sunoco	61	8.8	4.9	16.4
Gulf	59	8.5	10.2	23.4
Mobil	50	7.2	4.0	54.0
Sinclair	32	4.6	9.4	53.1
Citgo	28	4.0	7.1	42.9
Atlantic	26	3.7	0	84.6
Scott	15	2.2	0	100.0
Phillips	14	2.0	0	50.0
Hess	9	1.3	0	100.0
Independents	30	4.3	0	100.0
Total	697	100.0%		

Source: F. C. Allvine and J. M. Patterson, *Competition, Ltd.: The Marketing of Gasoline* (Bloomington: University of Indiana Press, 1972), p. 13.

nonfollowship elasticity and monopolistic competition suggest that firms with small market shares are more likely to charge lower prices than firms with large market shares. This, too, is borne out by these data. As one reads down Table 12–2, the percentage of stations pricing above reference dwindles as the percentage of stations pricing below reference grows. It should also be mentioned that this generalization holds not only for the majors within a *given* market, but also for a *given* major operating in *various* markets. Exxon, for instance, had the largest market share and highest prices in Washington, D.C. Yet at the same time in San Francisco, Exxon ranked ninth with only 3.8% of the market. There, 87.4% of its stations were pricing *below* reference. In other words, majors often behave like independents, at least with respect to price, when their market share is like that of independents.

As for kinks, they are somewhat ill defined and variable across firms and geographic markets, but they are not destroyed by price differentials. A price differential may not cause continual shifting of market share in favor of the low-priced brand because of product differentiation.

In the gasoline industry it is "customary" for independents to price a few cents below dominant majors. At that point the independents could very well see a kink. Cuts below the customary differential tend to be followed by the majors.

More generally, the pattern of small-share, low-price is common to many industries, in large part because of the elasticity differences outlined in Figure 12–2. During the 1970s and 1980s Kodak had 90% of the film market in the United States and set prices high, while Fuji, with only about 10%, priced 5–10% below Kodak. In Japan, it was the reverse. Kodak had a 12% share there and priced below Fuji, which then held 70% of the Japanese market.[12] Similarly, Campbell's dominates the canned soup market in the United States and refuses to supply retailers with "private-label" soups because that would constitute a price cut. Heinz, which is a pipsqueak in U.S. canned soups, is the one that supplies cut-rate private-label brands for Safeway and other giant retailers. In Britain it's the reverse. Heinz dominates canned soups in the United Kingdom and refuses to supply low-priced private-label soups. Campbell's is the small one there and competes with private-label brands.[13] Thus, in sum, kinked demands for different firms may not be all alike, as suggested in the simple theory of Figure 12–5. Rather they may appear as they do in Figure 12–6, varying from one firm to another with different "going" prices and elasticities while accompanied, perhaps, by

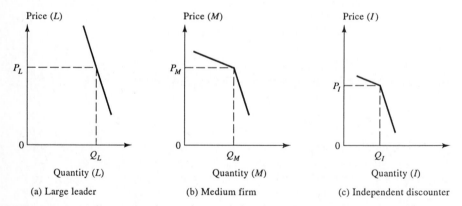

| (a) Large leader | (b) Medium firm | (c) Independent discounter |

FIGURE 12–6. Illustrative demand curves for three firms in the same market: A large price leader (L), a medium-sized firm (M), and an independent "off-brand" discounter (I).

[12] *Forbes*, November 22, 1982, pp. 55–56.
[13] *Business Week*, March 11, 1985, p. 49. For still further examples in grocery products, see *Fortune*, July 11, 1983, pp. 92–102. Note also that Gillette and Bic alternate roles in U.S. markets for disposable razors, pens, and lighters (*Fortune*, February 25, 1980, pp.

a dominant price leader in the same market that sees no kink because of upside followship.

6. Other Reasons for Price Rigidity: One final limitation of the simple kinked demand model is that prices may be rigid for reasons other than kinked demand.[14] Consider first the cost of changing prices. It may be high enough to inhibit frequent alterations, especially when price lists are voluminous and complex. What's more, buyers of certain products may prefer a stable price, even though it may on average be higher than a fluctuating price. A molder of plastic houseware products enunciated this point somewhat incoherently when he upbraided his suppliers at a trade convention:

> When you producers were selling polyethylene to us molders at the stable price of 41 cents a pound, my company made much more money than we do now, when price is much lower but bounces up and down with every deal. Why? Simply because I didn't have to spend all my time rushing around to see if I could make as good a deal as the next guy — and never be quite sure.[15]

Finally, the last factor worth mentioning helps to introduce our next section. Many changes of condition that would normally provoke price changes under pure competition do not do so under oligopoly because they are considered *temporary* changes, which, if responded to, might prove unsettling. Swings in the business cycle are the most important of these. Since frequent price revisions can shake up even the coziest nest of oligopolists and jostle them into occasional price wars, oligopolists tend to favor stable prices. As we shall see more clearly, recognized interdependence often leads to tacit collusion, cartelization, and other forms of pricing cooperation. But cooperation can be a delicate thing. And fluctuating prices may camouflage "chiseling" and provoke serious "misunderstandings" — two factors corrosive to cooperation.[16]

148–150). Weekly rental prices for autos in Orlando, Florida, followed market share very closely in the late 1980s: Hertz, $174; Avis, $159; Budget, $119; Dollar, $109; Alamo, $100; and Ugly Duckling, $69 (*Fortune*, August 31, 1987, p. 76). Small firms in the tractor industry have priced below the leading firms because of their perceived elasticity. See R. Kudrle, *Agricultural Tractors: A World Industry Study* (Cambridge, Mass.: Ballinger, 1975), pp. 86, 109.

[14] Stigler, "The Kinky Oligopoly Demand Curve"; and T. Scitovsky, *Welfare and Competition* (Chicago: Richard D. Irwin, 1951), Chapter XII.

[15] E. Marting, *Creative Pricing* (American Management Association, 1968), p. 37. For sellers' views see A. A. Fitzpatrick, *Pricing Methods of Industry* (Boulder, Colo.: Pruett Press, 1964), p. 67; and *The Wall Street Journal*, December 15, 1982, p. 1 (on auto sales).

[16] In light of the fact that the kinky demand curve has genuine but *limited* relevance, it is not surprising that sweeping tests of its existence *in general* come up empty handed. See Walter J. Primeaux, Jr., and Mickey C. Smith, "Pricing Patterns and the Kinky Demand Curve," *Journal of Law & Economics* (April 1976), pp. 189–199.

II. CYCLICAL COMPLICATIONS AND UNCERTAINTIES

On June 14, 1977, St. Joe Minerals Corporation announced a massive cutback in zinc refinery output from 95% to 65% capacity utilization. Why the cut? To keep prices from falling. As the company's spokesman put it, "We're hoping production restraint . . . will be sufficient to prevent further cuts and allow zinc price to move back toward a more healthy level."[17] On January 9, 1987, *The Wall Street Journal* reported that world oil prices had surged upward, "bolstered by a report that Saudi Arabia's daily crude output [had] plunged" from 5.1 million barrels a day to around 3.3 million barrels a day.[18]

These are two examples of a very important and fundamental rule of economics: *If prices are to be controlled in either the short or long run, one must control demand or supply, or both.* In the case of oligopolists coping with cyclical swings in demand, the only option usually open is supply control. Cyclical swings in demand are either inherent in the product[19] or a result of economywide difficulties. Both causes are beyond the control of individual firms.

A. A Bit of Theory

The principle is illustrated in Figure 12–7.[20] It depicts demand and unit costs for two firms. The underlying conditions are the same for each, except that 12–7 (a) assumes a kinked demand whereas 12–7 (b) assumes an elastic demand. The horizontal axis in each case is capacity use, which is simply an alternative way of expressing quantity. The vertical axis measures price and costs per unit of output. For simplicity, average variable costs (AVC) are assumed to be the same for each unit of output up to full capacity. (They are still "variable" in the sense that total dollar costs rise with added output.) When fixed costs per unit are added to AVC, the result is total unit costs, ATC (which in this case do not include a normal profit). Thus at price P_H the break-even point for each form is at point B, which corresponds to 40% capacity utilization.

---

17 *The Wall Street Journal*, June 15, 1977.

18 *The Wall Street Journal*, January 9, 1987, p. 26.

19 A curious example of this is textiles. For many decades this industry experienced a mysterious and never fully explained cycle of high demand in odd-numbered years and low demand in even-numbered years. J. W. Markham. *Competition in the Rayon Industry* (Cambridge, Mass.: Harvard University Press, 1952), pp. 112–115.

20 For a similar discussion, see R. Sherman, *The Economics of Industry* (Boston: Little, Brown, 1974), pp. 148–150; Markham, *Competition in the Rayon Industry;* and Robert E. Smith, "A Theory for the Administered Price Phenomenon," *Journal of Economic Issues* (June 1979), pp. 629–645. For still other theories see Howard N. Ross, "Oligopoly Theory and Price Rigidity," *The Antitrust Bulletin* (Summer 1987), pp. 451–469; and Joseph E. Stiglitz, "Price Rigidities and Market Structure," *American Economic Review* (May 1984), pp. 350–355.

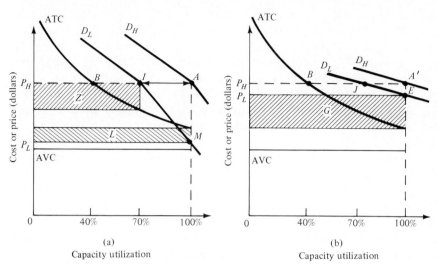

FIGURE 12–7. Price and quantity responses to fluctuations in demand.

Demand is shown to fluctuate cyclically between a high level, D_H, and a low level, D_L.

Looking first at Figure 12–7 (a), we can compare the implications of adjusting to slack demand by cutting price, as opposed to cutting quantity, when demand is price *in*elastic (which is typical below the kink in the short run). For demand D_H, the firm is at point A. Capacity utilization is 100%, and profit with price P_H is lucrative. As demand shifts back to D_L, full capacity can be maintained only by cutting price from P_H to P_L, moving the firm from A to M. However, unit costs exceed price at that point, yielding losses indicated by shaded area L. The firm would continue to produce in the short run, despite the loss, because it is covering its variable costs, AVC, and part of its fixed cost. In short, absorbing the slack by a move from A to M is distasteful to the firm (but not to its customers). Had the firm been able to maintain price at P_H by cutting back capacity use to 70%, it would be at point I. Even though this tactic boosts unit costs substantially, they are still less than P_H at I. Hence, total profits are indicated by shaded area Z. From the firm's viewpoint, the superiority of this A to I supply adjustment is quite plain. Profits are not only maintained over phases of the cycle, they are more stable over numerous cycles. Why, then, would any firm want to end up at M, as many often do? Although they do not want to, they may be *forced* to by price competition, which brings us to Figure 12–7(b).

Quantity curtailment plus price maintenance are the preferred combination only under the right circumstances—of which inelastic demand is the most important. If on the other hand short-run demand is very responsive to small price shadings, as is assumed in Figure 12–7(b), quantity maintenance, coupled with price cutting, would be the more profitable combination. In 12–7(b) demand shifts by the *same* magnitude as in 12–7(a). A constant price P_H begets 70% capacity use in both cases. Point J in 12–7(b) corresponds to point I in 12–7(a). Thus the profit consequences of maintaining price in 12–7(b) are the same — that is, total profit at J would equal are Z. Area Z may be compared to area G in 12–7(b) to see the greater rewards bestowed by cutting price to P_L and moving from J to E. Area G clearly exceeds area Z. Adjustment A' to E is superior to A' to J.

The only remaining question is *when* does each model apply? As already suggested, the inelasticity of Figure 12–7(a) seems typical of medium and large firms in most oligopolistic industries because their followship curves reflect marketwide demand, which itself is typically inelastic in the short run — especially in producer goods industries such as steel, zinc, aluminum, paper, and chemicals. These oligopolists will try to avoid price cuts in periods of declining demand, recognizing the likelihood of their detection and imitation by competitors, with a resulting loss of profits by all. Figure 12–7(b) on the other hand seems typical of (1) the small firms in these same oligopoly industries, (2) the small firms *wholly populating* monopolistically competitive markets, and (3) the few large oligopolists who just happen to be in markets with highly elastic short-run demands.

To small firms in monopolistically competitive industries, the high elasticity of Figure 12–7(b) is a tempting illusion of nonfollowship. The consequences of their price cutting copy those of Figure 12–4 seen earlier. Their price competition magnetically draws them down the followship curve to points like M in Figure 12–7(a). On the other hand, these elastic curves may *not* be illusory to the small firms that play in the yards of large oligopolists. If the large firms in an oligopolistic industry are intent on maintaining price for reasons defined in Figure 12–7(a), their smaller rivals may correctly see nonfollowship curves of the Figure 12–7(b) variety. At the very least, those who play at the knees of big oligopolists would be strongly tempted to test just how real their nonfollowship curves really were. Several predictions concerning the cyclical variability of prices and quantities naturally follow:

1. Within oligopolies, small "fringe" firms are more likely than large firms to be the sole price cutters or to lead the industry in a general round of price shading when demand flags.
2. Within oligopolies, the large firms are more likely than small firms to cut output in the face of slack demand.
3. Price stability and quantity variability should be associated with concentrated oligopolies — as opposed to unconcentrated oligopolies, monopolistic competition, or pure competition.

Although considerations of demand elasticity have led us to these hypotheses, cost considerations would bolster them, especially the first two. For various reasons the short-run cost curves of smaller firms are often higher and steeper in slope than the cost curves of large firms. The implications of this for price and output policy may be seen by mentally lifting the ATC curve of Figure 12–7(b) a little higher than it is, then giving it a slight clockwise twist. The break-even point shifts to the right. The firm then would want all the more to maintain full-capacity utilization.[21]

B. The Evidence

Evidence for the first two hypotheses comes mainly from *intra*industry experiences. The third hypothesis receives its greatest support from systematic *inter*industry statistical studies. Hence, we postpone our empirical exploration of the third hypothesis, and turn directly to the first two.

For small-firm price cutting during slumps we have space for only a few stories:

- During the 15 months prior to January 1975, the United States sank into a very severe recession; U.S. auto sales plunged 25% from mediocre 1973 levels; and the industry cut back capacity use close to 50%. Price reductions were resisted. Indeed GM led price increases averaging $1,000 per car. Then that January, Chrysler, the smallest of the big three, broke the ice by cutting price as much as $400 per car under its "Car Clearance Carnival" rebate program. For a while GM and Ford did not join the carnival: "It will be late in January before anybody really knows what's happening," said a Ford executive. Chrysler was sufficiently successful, however, that the Big Two and AMC soon followed.[22]

- The rebates lasted only six weeks. Thereafter, general recovery lifted *big* car sales substantially but *small* car sales only moderately. This created particular problems for "tiny" AMC. Hence, in November, 1976, AMC cut prices on Gremlins and Pacers by $253, or roughly 7%. AMC said it was hoping this would boost its sales 30%, which implies a high nonfollowship elasticity estimate of 4.3 (i.e., 30/7). Unfortunately for AMC, GM followed with a $200 rebate program for three of its small car models that were also in excess supply.[23]

- In 1980, after its market share had shrunk to about 2% in an industry of slipping sales, Liggett & Myers cut the price of its famous-name cigarette brands (L&M and Lark) by putting them in black-and-white packs, giving them each a generic name like "Flavor Lights," and selling them for 35% less. Its market share rose more than 100% in

[21] This point is stressed by Markham, *Competition in the Rayon Industry*, pp. 150–157.

[22] *Business Week* and *The Wall Street Journal*, various issues. Benefits to consumers were in the neighborhood of $100 million.

[23] *The Wall Street Journal*, November 5, 1976 and November 17, 1976.

three years, implying a high nonfollowship elasticity of almost 3. In 1984 Liggett was producing about 20 billion generic cigarettes a year, which was 65% of its total volume. By 1986 Philip Morris (Marlboro), R. J. Reynolds (Winston), and Brown & Williamson (Kool) had joined the discounting with their own generics.[24]

- In 1960–1961, capacity use in the steam turbine generator industry dropped to 60%. Allis-Chalmers, the industry's smallest producer, led a "dramatic plunge in price levels".[25]

- During the massive recession of 1981–1982, the airline industry fought intermittent price wars. One-way coach fares between New York and California, for example, plunged from $478 to $99. Relatively small carriers such as World Airways, Air Florida, Capitol International, and Continental Airlines triggered the discounting. The big guys had to follow, but they occasionally signaled for truce by attempting to lead fare increases. United Airlines said, "We didn't start it. We want to stop it."[26]

- During the recession of 1982, small-firm price cutting in the steel industry caused U.S. Steel Corporation's market share to drop from 21% to 16% in just a matter of months because U.S. Steel, the biggest seller, had been trying to hold prices up. The irony was that U.S. Steel's efforts were converting it to small-firm status. Hence the company began matching the discounts, explaining to *Business Week* that the effort to prop up prices during periods of weak demand "was destroying the company," although "thirty years ago [when the company was much bigger] we could do that".[27]

That should give you the idea.[28] Many similar illustrations of the second hypothesis are available,[29] but one clear case will suffice. Col-

---

[24] *Business Week*, April 14, 1986, p. 41; and *The Wall Street Journal*, March 5, 1990, pp. A1, A7.

[25] R. G. M. Sultan, *Pricing in the Electric Oligopoly, Vol. I* (Cambridge, Mass.: Harvard University Press, 1974), pp. 151, 211.

[26] *The Wall Street Journal*, October 19, 1981, p. 6; April 28, 1982, pp. 1, 24.

[27] *Business Week*, October 10, 1983, pp. 104–106.

[28] For more examples see Markham, *Competition in the Rayon Industry*, p. 75; W. T. Stanbury and G. B. Reschenthaler, "Oligopoly and Conscious Parallelism," *Osgoode Hall Law Journal*, Vol. 15, no. 3 (1977), pp. 681–682; Naomi Lamoreaux, *The Great Merger Movement in American Business, 1895–1904* (Cambridge: Cambridge University Press, 1985), pp. 126–138; and R. M. Grant, "Pricing Behavior in the UK Wholesale Market for Petrol 1970–1980," *Journal of Industrial Economics* (March 1982), pp. 271–292.

[29] For examples see Markham, *Competition in the Rayon Industry*, pp. 136–138; *Business Week*, October 28, 1972, pp. 39–40, and December 14, 1974, p. 27; D. O. Parsons and E. J. Ray, "The United States Steel Consolidation: The Creation of Market Control," *Journal of Law and Economics* (April 1975), pp. 214–215; and H. Yamawaki, "Market Structure, Capacity Expansion, and Pricing in Japanese Steel," *International Journal of Industrial Organization* (March 1984), pp. 26–60. On the other hand see David E. Mills and Laurence Schumann, "Industry Structure and Fluctuating Demand," *American Economic Review* (September 1985), pp. 758–767.

TABLE 12–3. Distribution of Aluminum Capacity and Capacity Utilization, 1975

Company	(1) Percent of U.S. Capacity (Dec. 1974)	(2) Percent Capacity Utilization Rate (May 1975)
Alcoa	32.0%	74%
Reynolds	19.8	67
Kaiser	14.7	73
Conalco	7.0	66
Anaconda	6.1	77
Howmet	4.4	85
Martin Marietta	4.2	80
Revere	4.0	62
National-South wire	3.7	100
Alumax	2.7	99
Noranda	1.4	100

Source: Council on Wage and Price Stability, Staff Report, *Aluminum Prices 1974–75* (Washington, D.C.: U.S. Government Printing Office, 1976), p. 122.

umn 1 of Table 12–3 presents the rated capacity of U.S. aluminum ingot producers in December 1974, expressed as a percentage of total industry capacity. These percentages would be market shares if all firms were producing at full capacity. The industry was not operating at full capacity during the first half of 1975, however, because of the severe recession. Thus, the second column of Table 12–3 reports each individual firm's percentage rate of capacity utilization in May 1975. It is not difficult to see that size and capacity utilization are *inversely* related. As the source of these data explains:

> The three smallest firms operated at full capacity for the year 1975. These are remarkably high levels . . . considering that the impact of the recession on the aluminum industry was the worst in magnitude since the Great Depression. The explanation for this disparity in capacity utilization across firms of different size appears to be that the smaller firms used small discounts from list price to operate at full capacity levels, while the majors were holding prices at list. The larger firms chose to hold price and cut back production. . . .[30]

[30] Council on Wage and Price Stability, Staff Report, *Aluminum Prices 1974–75* (Washington, D.C., U.S. Government Printing Office, 1976), p. 121. See also *Business Week*, November 17, 1975, pp. 151–153. In 1989 and 1990 Alcoa made news by refusing to cut price on aluminum can stock as sales slumped. *The Wall Street Journal*, April 9, 1990, pp. A1, A4.

Although these experiences indicate that concentration helps secure short-run supply control (and thereby price control), concentration is not a conclusive or even a necessary condition. **Linear cost curves**, such as those used in drawing Figure 12–7 are also helpful. If, for reasons of plant design or inherent technology, unit costs were to rise steeply on either side of 98% capacity utilization, the utilization rate would be much less flexible.[31]

Durability of product aids as well. Style change, organic decay, whatever shortens product life span: perishables tend to be marked down quickly if they are not moving briskly into the hands of consumers. Durability permits an alternating current of inventory accumulation and discharge that cushions the shock of abrupt swings in demand, thereby smoothing out the rough linkage between consumer's pantry and manufacturer's plant.[32] Indeed, the aluminum ingot industry usually relies more heavily on inventory variation than production variation because ingots are more than durable; they are cheaply storable. A measure of these ingot qualities is that the majors used to maintain 2 pounds of fabrication capacity for every 1 pound of ingot capacity.[33]

For related reasons, **vertical integration** also helps supply control, although in its case the linkage secured may run from the consumer all the way back to the mineral pit, as in petroleum and steel.[34] An example of a *lack* of vertical integration contributing to price combat arose in the paper linerboard industry. It started in January 1977, when a nonintegrated company, Great Northern Nekoosa, slashed prices from $215 a ton to $195 a ton:

> Most of the other major producers have integrated operations that produce both linerboard and the finished box. But Great Northern sells all its linerboard on the open market. Mr. Bellis said, "It is fine for the integrated producers to say don't cut price when half the time they're taking it out of one pocket and putting it into another." He added: "If we hadn't cut prices our customers would have deserted us."[35]

Finally, and perhaps most important, there are a variety of *pricing mechanisms* or *rules of thumb*, that, when either imposed or voluntarily

[31] G. Stigler, "Production and Distribution in the Short Run," *Journal of Political Economy* (June 1939), pp. 305–327. For examples of "go" or "no go" facilities, see J. M. Blair, *Economic Concentration* (New York: Harcourt Brace Jovanovich, 1972), p. 282; and Andrew Likierman, "Pricing Policy in the Texturising Industry, 1958–71," *Journal of Industrial Economics* (September 1981), pp. 25–38.

[32] F. M. Scherer, *Industrial Market Structure and Economic Performance* (Chicago: Rand McNally, 1970), pp. 149–156.

[33] M. J. Peck, *Competition in the Aluminum Industry, 1945–1958* (Cambridge, Mass.: Harvard University Press, 1961), Chapter 6.

[34] M. G. de Chazeau and A. E. Kahn, *Integration and Competition in the Petroleum Industry* (New Haven, Conn.: Yale University Press, 1959), Chapter 17; and W. Adams and J. B. Dirlam, "Steel Imports and Vertical Oligopoly Power," *American Economic Review* (September 1964), pp. 626–655.

[35] *The Wall Street Journal*, February 4, 1977.

adopted, contribute to price stability by providing guidance, uniformity, or centralization to what might otherwise tend to be a rather diffuse, chaotic, even competitive pricing process. These mechanisms or rules of thumb serve purposes other than cyclical price stabilization. Indeed, they are vital to daily decision making and they foster industry discipline in good times as well as bad. Therefore, they warrant special attention.

III. PRICING MECHANISMS AND RULES OF THUMB

One thing to remember while reviewing these pricing mechanisms and rules of thumb is that their incidence varies according to market structure. Their usage is not randomly distributed; their impact is not always trenchant. Incidentally, their names are not exactly catchy either; cost-plus pricing, target-profit pricing, price leadership, facilitating practices, cartelization, and government tampering.

A. Cost-Plus and Target-Profit Pricing[36]

Cost-plus or "full-cost" pricing usually involves estimating the average variable costs of producing and distributing the product, adding a charge for overhead, and then adding a percentage markup for profits. In retailing, adding a common percentage markup to the wholesale cost of goods sold is quite common. Target-profit pricing is a variant of cost-plus pricing with an important application in manufacturing. It was originally devised by GM executives to achieve a target rate of profit while maintaining price and flexing output. The technique is illustrated in Figure 12–8, which may be considered a total-dollars version of Figure 12–7(a).

Target profit is defined as a certain percentage of investment, not sales. Hence, the technique is not simply a matter of wedging a nice profit percentage into price. Multiplying the target of, say, 30% before taxes times total investment yields a "hoped-for" dollar target profit. When this target profit is added to total cost, the result is the top broken line of Figure 12–8. Notice that target profit does not vary with output, but total costs do. Since target-dollar profit does not vary with output, the apparent implication is that the firm will have to *raise* price in recessions and cut price in booms. But such actions would drive customers away just when they are most needed and attract them when already abundant. The trick is to set price in such a way that the firm earns its target *on average* over the cycle while holding price fairly constant.

The firm achieves this balance by calculating cost and profit per unit on the basis of **standard volume**, or average output, which in Figure

---

[36] For details, see Kent B. Monroe, *Pricing: Making Profitable Decisions* (New York: McGraw-Hill, 1979), pp. 51–102.

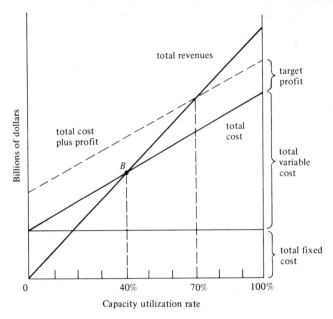

FIGURE 12–8. Target-profit pricing model.

12–8 is 70% of capacity. Thus, for example, if GM's standard volume is 5 million cars and its pretax target profit $5 billion, profit per standard volume car would be set at $1000 ($5 billion/5 million cars). If hypothetical overhead is $15 billion, fixed cost per standard volume car is then $3000 ($15 billion/5 million cars). With variable costs of $5000 per car, wholesale price comes to $9000 ($1000 + $3000 + $5000), and this price will determine the slope of the total revenue line in Figure 12–8. Of course, this example abstracts from the realities of many model lines, occasional rebate programs, and escalating costs of production over time.[37] But the idea is clear. In good years, with production above standard volume, realized profit will exceed target profit, as total revenues in Figure 12–8 exceed total cost-plus target profit. In slack years, the opposite holds. On average, the target will be grazed if not hit squarely.

Interview surveys, case studies, and econometric estimates reveal widespread use of these various techniques. R. L. Hall and C. J. Hitch canvassed 38 firms and determined that 30 of them followed some form of cost-plus or target pricing.[38] Fog's study of 138 Danish firms turned up evidence that the most usual method among them could be considered "flexible full-cost pricing."[39] A. Silberston concludes his review of British

37 *The Wall Street Journal*, October 23, 1981, pp. 1, 25.
38 Hall and Hitch, *Price Theory and Business Behavior*.
39 B. Fog, *Industrial Pricing Policies* (Amsterdam: North-Holland, 1960), p. 217. This

pricing studies by saying that "full cost can be given a mark of beta query plus".[40] A. D. H. Kaplan, J. B. Dirlam, and R. F. Lanzillotti interviewed officials in 20 large U.S. corporations, ten of which were apparently using target-profit techniques. Besides GM, the ten included such renowned companies as U.S. Steel, Du Pont, General Electric, Alcoa, and Union Carbide.[41] Finally, Robert C. Dolan concluded from his econometric analysis that 43 of the 50 industries he studied practiced full-cost or target-return pricing over 1959–1980.[42]

These studies touched off a heated debate over whether firms maximized profits. We shall not pursue this question here other than to note that target-profit and cost-plus pricing are not necessarily inconsistent with profit maximization, especially in the long run. As A. E. Kahn has observed, one should not confuse *procedures* with *goals*.[43] Some may use the target procedure to shoot for only 8%, but that may be the best they can do. One thing all successful target pricers share in common is a substantial ability to control supply in the short run.

B. Price Leadership

Many of the firms not classified as target or cost-plus pricers in the studies cited previously could be considered followers of larger "price leaders" who do employ such techniques. "The development of price leadership in large-scale industry," according to some experts, "has roots in the earlier experience of violent price fluctuation and cut-throat competition, which culminated in consolidation of competitors, as in steel, copper, oil production, tin cans, and farm equipment. Such experience has generated a distinct predisposition on the part of managements to avoid price changes except through periodic, well-considered, and well-publicized alterations in recognized *base* prices."[44] Under a diversity of

description also fits A. A. Fitzpatrick's finding for glass containers, paint, and furniture. *Pricing Methods of Industry* (Boulder, Colo.: Pruett Press, 1964).

[40] A. Silberston, "Price Behavior of Firms," *Economic Journal* (September 1970), p. 545.

[41] A. D. H. Kaplan, J. B. Dirlam, and R. F. Lanzillotti, *Pricing in Big Business* (Washington, D.C.: Brookings Institution, 1958); and R. F. Lanzillotti, "Pricing Objectives of Large Companies," *American Economic Review* (December 1958), pp. 921–940. An executive of U.S. Steel once explained that company's policy as follows: "If customers don't buy their steel [in a slump] there isn't too much you can do about it . . . I doubt that you would go out and buy two new cars instead of one if steel prices were cut . . . . Over the long pull, American steel mills have operated at about 75 percent average capacity. If you operate at 90 percent over a stretch, you've then got to figure on a stretch at 60 percent of capacity. Basically you must be able to make adequate profits at the average." See G. J. McManus, *The Inside Story of Steel Wages and Prices, 1959–1967* (Philadelphia: Chilton, 1967), p. 63.

[42] Robert C. Dolan "Price Behavior in Tight Oligopoly," *Review of Industrial Organization* (Fall 1984), pp. 160–188.

[43] A. E. Kahn, "Pricing Objectives of Large Companies: Comment," *American Economic Review* (September 1959), pp. 670–678. See also Kenneth G. Elzinga, "Pricing Achievements in Large Companies," in A. A. Heggestad, *Public Policy toward Corporations* (Gainesville: University of Florida Press, 1988), pp. 166–179.

[44] Kaplan, Dirlam, and Lanzillotti, *Pricing in Big Business*, p. 271.

structural conditions, price leadership takes many forms, but compressing them into three broad types will simplify the situation. These types are dominant-firm leadership, collusive leadership, and barometric leadership.[45] Table 12–4 summarizes the salient characteristics of each type.

1. Dominant-Firm Leadership. Dominant-firm price leadership is a giant/pygmy situation. One firm controls 50–95% of the market. Awed by its immense size and efficiency, the smaller firms willingly, if sheepishly, accept its leadership. Because unit costs of the fringe firms typically exceed those of the dominant firm materially, the small fry refrain from cutting prices below those set by the leader. Moreover, they virtually always follow the leader's upside price changes without hesitation. This means that the leader's disciplinary problems are few and far between. It also indicates that fringe firms probably prefer a higher level of price than the leader usually sets for the market. As with the other summary descriptions of Table 12–4, the illustration posits generalities that do not fit any particular industry perfectly, but there are several examples that fit the dominant-firm mold fairly well. Not surprisingly, many examples come from the annals of Section 2 Sherman Act prosecutions — United Shoe Machinery, IBM, and Alcoa.[46] In the case of Alcoa, we refer to the period of 1946–1965, during which time Alcoa did face some domestic competition but was still quite dominant. In those years Reynolds and Kaiser repeatedly expressed their preferences for prices higher than those Alcoa selected.[47] Of late, Alcoa's dominance has waned, as was implied by our earlier discussion of Table 12–3.

2. Collusive Price Leadership. This might better describe aluminum nowadays. Typifying this category are medium-to-high four-firm concentration ratios; a leader whose relatively large size (say, 20–40% of the market) and ancient lineage signify qualities befitting an industrial chieftain; a cost structure across firms that is uniform enough to generate fairly harmonious notions about what the industry's price level should be; widespread agreement among the oligopolists over long periods of time as to who their leader should be; few disciplinary problems with "chiselers"; and lags in followship short enough to save the leader from repeated embarrassment.

45 J. W. Markham, "The Nature and Significance of Price Leadership," *American Economic Review* (December 1951), pp. 891–905; Scherer, *Industrial Market Structure*, pp. 164–173.

46 For examples from U.K. antitrust actions, see J. D. Gribbin and M. A. Utton, "The Treatment of Dominant Firms in the U.K. Competition Legislation," in H. W. de Jong and W. G. Shepherd (eds.) *Mainstreams in Industrial Organization, Book II* (Dordrecht, The Netherlands: Kluwer, 1986), pp. 243–272. Of the 20 "dominant-firm" industries they studied (where the average market share of the top firm was 73%), 14 could be said to experience dominant-firm price leadership.

47 M. J. Peck, *Competition in the Aluminum Industry*, Chapter 4.

TABLE 12–4.   Outline of Three Broad Types of Price Leadership

Characteristic	Dominant Firm Leadership	Collusive Price Leadership	Barometric Price Leadership
Concentration ratio	Very high one-firm ratio	Medium to high four-firm ratio	Low four-firm ratio
Leader's qualification	Immense relative size and efficiency	Size, age, custom, efficiency	Forecasting ability, sensitivity
Cost across firms	Diverse	Roughly similar	Diverse
Changes in who leads?	Never	Occasionally	Often
Disciplinary problems	Never	Sometimes	Frequently
Followship lags	Never	Temporary	Leader "lags"
Examples	Aluminum (until recently), computers	Steel, cigarettes	Gasoline, turbines

The cigarette industry provides a classic example from the era when non-filtered regulars were all you could buy.[48] After the Sherman Act dissolution of American Tobacco in 1911, the industry came to be divided primarily between Reynolds, American, and Liggett & Myers. The popularity of Camels gave Reynolds a 40% share of the market by 1920, top spot, and rights to leadership. Between 1923 and 1941, American and Liggett & Myers stuck to Reynolds' prices like a Marlboro tattoo. There were eight list price changes during the period. Reynolds led six of them, five up and one down, with the others following usually not more than a day behind. The two Reynolds did *not* lead were price *cuts* initiated by American in 1933 that were necessitated by remarkable circumstances.

The circumstances were these: As the nation slid into the Great Depression and the prices of leaf tobacco and other cigarette materials were falling along with commodity prices in general, R. J. Reynolds led two bold increases in the wholesale price of cigarettes—7% in October 1929 and another 7% in June 1931. Consequently, retail prices of popular brands wound up at 15 cents. This gave the three companies profits that exceeded 30% of net sales less tax. At the time of the last of these 7% increases the so-called "10 cent" brands accounted for less than 1% of the total market. For obvious reasons, however, their sales thereafter skyrocketed to account for more than 20% of the market in the final two

---

[48] William Nicholls, *Price Policies in the Cigarette Industry* (Nashville, Tenn.: Vanderbilt University Press, 1951); and R. B. Tennant, *The American Cigarette Industry* (New Haven, Conn.: Yale University Press, 1950).

months of 1932. Upon feeling this slap, the three large companies retaliated. American led a 12% wholesale price cut on January 3, 1933, then initiated a second cut of 8% one month later, bringing the retail prices of the three companies down to 10 and 11 cents. This knocked the 10 cent brands' market share back to 7% almost immediately. After about a year the three large companies slowly began to raise their prices again. The renewed escalation enabled the 10 cent brands to regain a bit of their lost ground but never to recoup it completely.

More recent and more general data come from Great Britain because of that country's 1956 law against express collusion. Before 1956 over 2000 cartels operated in Britain. After 1956 most were abandoned. Ending the collusive agreements did not end the collusive behavior, however. A 1959 questionnaire survey of former cartel participants found that 41% of them continued to avoid price competition by relying on price leadership.[49] Given the circumstances, this would clearly be price leadership in lieu of collusion.

3. Barometric Price Leadership. Under barometric price leadership, conditions are substantially competitive. Use of the word "leadership" in this case may even by misleading. The leader is often no more than the first firm to announce formal revisions in *list* or *book* prices to reflect prevailing *realized* or *transactions* prices. In other words, the leader's main qualification in this case is his acute sensitivity to market pressures. The barometric leader "commands adherence of rivals to his price only because, and to the extent that, his price reflects market conditions with tolerable promptness."[50] If the firm actually does lead, it should be a good forecaster of the imminent trend, especially on the up side. International Paper Company illustrates the consequences of upside error. Its unsuccessful attempt to lead an increase in late 1976 cost it 100,000 tons of production, 1.4 percentage points off its 12.7% market share, and a bundle of profits.[51] Other indices that ironclad coordination is lacking under barometric leadership include a diversity of cost levels across firms, frequent changes in the identity of the leader, bigger disciplinary problems than are found under dominant firm and collusive leadership, and substantial lags in followship should the leader act more as a forecaster than as an announcer of prevailing reality.

Barometric leaders usually occupy unconcentrated industries as well, but not always. This last fact underscores the lack of precision in these three categories of leadership. For example, during the 1950s the steam turbine electric generator market was highly concentrated. General Electric (with a 60% share), Westinghouse (with 30%), and Allis-Chalmers

---

[49] J. B. Heath, "Restrictive Practices and After," *Manchester School of Economic and Social Studies* (May 1961), pp. 173–202.

[50] Stigler, *Production and Distribution in the Short Run*, pp. 445–446.

[51] *Business Week*, May 2, 1977, p. 54.

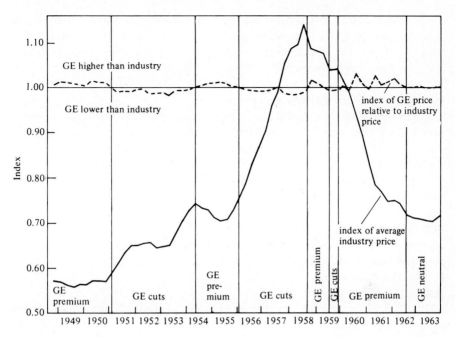

FIGURE 12–9. GE and industry prices of turbine electricity generators. Source: Ralph G. M. Sultan, *Pricing in the Electrical Oligopoly*, Vol. 1 (Boston: Division of Research, Graduate School of Business Administration, Harvard University, 1974), p. 282.

(with 10%) accounted for all U.S. production. Moreover, in book prices, GE was the undisputed leader. GE's price book was the Sears' catalog of the industry, and the others copied it to the letter.[52] Still, in *transactions* prices, GE appears to have been only a barometric leader. This is shown in Figure 12–9, which charts an index of the industry's transactions prices together with GE's transactions prices *relative* to those of its rivals. Notice that GE's transactions prices were slightly *below* its rivals' prices during periods of high demand and rising industry prices. Conversely, GE's transactions prices were slightly *above* its rivals' prices during periods of slack demand and falling industry prices. A partial explanation for this behavior was GE's desire to maintain a 60% market share while serving as leader. During slumps GE's share would diminish as rivals priced beneath it. During booms its share would be restored as rivals eagerly took advantage of the opportunity to advance their prices while GE acted in a more leisurely way.

C. Facilitating Practices

Sometimes firms facilitate their collusive behavior by adopting certain rules or customs concerning their pricing—often called "facilitating prac-

[52] Sultan, *Pricing in the Electric Oligopoly*, pp. 213–214.

tices." Information exchanges are a typical example. With these, firms regularly notify each other about price lists, discounts, future changes of prices, and so on. Information exchanges assist collusive understanding because they may discourage secret price cutting, which a firm may try in order to move down its elastic nonfollowship demand curve. Information exchanges eliminate secrecy.[53]

Another facilitating practice, under some circumstances, is advance notice to customers of price increases. This facilitated collusive price leadership among chemical companies producing lead-based antiknock gasoline additives during the 1960s and 1970s (a big market before the advent of lead-free gasoline).[54] Four-firm oligopoly prevailed. Market shares in 1977 were as follows: Du Pont 35.2%, Ethyl 34.6%, PPG 16.7%, and Nalco 13.4%. The role of price leader rotated between the market's two largest firms—Du Pont and Ethyl. Contracts required sellers to tell buyers *at least* 30 days in advance of changes in list prices, so Du Pont or Ethyl would typically lead the way by announcing price changes 35 to 39 days in advance. The extra days' notice gave rivals enough time to announce matching price changes, say, 31 days in advance, with the result that all four firms in the market could then charge identical list prices every day of the year, even on days when price changes became effective. There were 24 price increases from 1974 to 1979, and in 20 of these the antiknock oligopolists had identical list price changes effective on the same date. Figure 12–10 illustrates those increases occurring in 1976. The dates *above* the price line are the dates price changes went into effect, while those *below* it are the dates of announcement. For example, the increase from 60.5 to 62.3 cents a pound that became effective August 13, 1976, was first announced by Du Pont on July 9, then announced by Ethyl (July 13), PPG (July 13), and Nalco (July 14). Hence when August 13, the effective date, rolled around, all four sellers hiked their prices in unison. This method permitted more than uniformity. It permitted the leader, Du Pont or Ethyl, to know *in advance* whether everyone would be following. Adjustments could be made before commitments solidified. Rather than engage in price leadership, the firms could have jousted for additional market shares by price shading. But a Du Pont document explains why rivalry was resisted: "An alternative strategy would be [to] attempt to hold or increase market share by selective discounting to meet competitive situations. This has been rejected because the potential earnings gain from increased shares is small compared with the risk of earnings loss through a reduction in market price that would probably

---

[53] For evidence on the importance of information exchanges to tacit collusion, see Dennis Swann et al., *Competition in British Industry* (London: Allen & Unwin, 1974), pp. 74–75, 158–163.

[54] Federal Trade Commission, *In the Matter of Ethyl Corp. et al*, 101 F.T.C. 425 (1983).

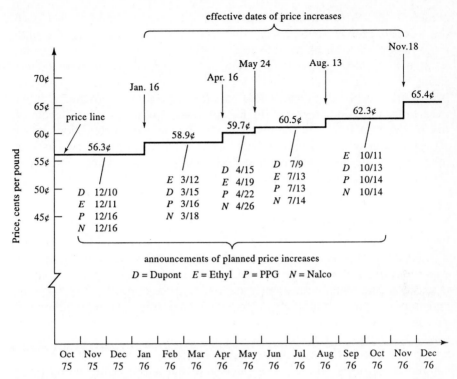

FIGURE 12–10. History of the price for tetraethyl lead antiknock gasoline additive, 1976. Source: *In the Matter of Ethyl Corp. et al,* 101 FTC 425 (1983), pp. 578–579.

result from competitive reaction."[55] In short, price leadership, aided by facilitating practices, was more profitable than price competition.[56]

D. Cartelization

Looking back at Figure 12–9 we can detect some evidence of cartelization, namely, the sharp rise in turbine generator prices after 1954, a rise that is followed by an equally sharp fall after 1959. During the years in between, GE, Westinghouse, and Allis-Chalmers conspired to fix prices—that is, they operated a loose-knit cartel. All in all, the price fixing extended to 19 other electrical equipment products, to 26 other firms, and in these broader respects, to many years before 1955. This is a fascinating bit of

---

[55] Ibid., p. 455.
[56] Profits for 1974–1977 were as follows: Ethyl, 40%; Du Pont, 26%; PPG, 20%; and Nalco, 20%. The all-manufacturing average at the time was, in contrast, less than 10%. Ibid., pp. 492, 586. For more on facilitating practices, see David M. Grether and Charles R. Plott, "The Effects of Market Practices in Oligopolistic Markets," *Economic Inquiry* (October 1984), pp. 479–507.

evidence drawn from a much larger topic than we can treat now. Hence the next chapter is devoted entirely to cartelization. Here we may note in passing that securing a uniformity of behavior among otherwise competitive firms is the essence of cartelization. Cooperation is refined, formalized, and often pursued with vigor. When cartelization is applied to pricing, the results can include less variation across firms, greater stability over time, and, as suggested in Figure 12–9, higher absolute levels of price. It will be shown in the next chapter that structural conditions affect the ease with which cartel agreements can be privately devised. As you might guess, fewness of firms and high market concentration are conducive to cartel conduct.

E. Government Intervention

With minor exceptions *private* cartelization is illegal in the United States. Cartelization nevertheless permeates many industries. Sanctioned and supervised by various governmental bodies, it has spread under the cover of more euphemistic names such as "parity price supports," "marketing agreements," "oil prorationing," "collective bargaining," and "regulation." The list could easily be expanded to include various forms of cartelization affecting U.S. foreign trade. In many instances, the government was pushed into these policies at the insistence of politically powerful commercial groups. These groups believed that supply control and price stability would be of dramatic benefit to them. They also perceived the possibility of gaining higher *absolute* prices, profits, and incomes as well, but they were not in a position to attain these several objectives without the government's help. Generally speaking, their industries and markets were *too* competitively structured to secure these ends by price leadership or similar informal cooperation (or even secret, illegal cartelization). Thus, stripped to its essentials, the government's agricultural price support program attempts to curtail production and keep "surplus" commodities off the market during periods of slack demand or inadvertently abundant production.

IV. CROSS-SECTION STATISTICAL EVIDENCE[57]

We are finally ready for the evidence concerning *inter*industry differences in cyclical price behavior. Figure 12–11 restates the main hypothesis. Its horizontal axis measures positive and negative percentage changes in

---

[57] Other surveys of the statistical evidence that have influenced this section are A. E. Kahn, "Market Power Inflation: A Conceptual Overview," in *The Roots of Inflation* (New York: Burt Franklin, 1975); and Dennis W. Carlton, "The Theory and the Facts of How Markets Clear," in *Handbook of Industrial Organization*, edited by R. Schmalensee and R. Willig, Vol. I (Amsterdam: North-Holland, 1989), pp. 909–946.

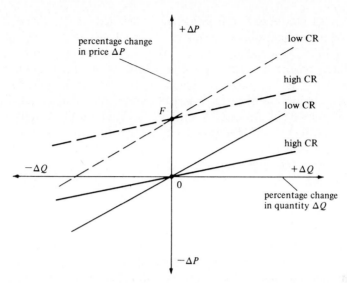

FIGURE 12–11. Price movements relative to quantity movements and concentration.

quantity, whereas its vertical axis indicates positive and negative percentage changes in price. Instances in which competitive industries have displayed almost perfect vertical movement along the vertical axis exist. In these cases quantity has remained fairly constant, while price has absorbed the cyclical swing. Conversely, there are also instances of highly concentrated industries moving horizontally along the $+\Delta Q - \Delta Q$ axis, displaying very little change in price for enormous variations in quantity.[58]

Although these are the extreme patterns our earlier theory may have suggested, the theory was deliberately oversimplified. A more realistic but still abstract view of the matter is depicted by the diagonal lines of Figure 12–11. The solid lines going through the origin show prices in unconcentrated industries (low CR) rising more during booms and falling more during slumps than prices in highly concentrated industries (high CR). So oligopolistic prices might not be absolutely "rigid"—merely "sticky," or, more precisely, "relatively sticky" as compared to competitive prices. The dashed lines of Figure 12–11 indicate that this hypothesis could still hold during broad-based secular inflation. In other words, both diagonals going through the origin have equal parts of plus and minus price change for an overall average of zero net change. We have of late experienced *general* inflation, with prices typically going up faster or slower but almost always going up. The dashed diagonals thus indicate the same degree of stickiness and variability amidst secular inflation as the solid diagonals do with no net inflation.

[58] F. C. Mills, *Price-Quantity Interactions in Business Cycles* (New York: National Bureau of Economic Research, 1946), pp. 29, 46–47.

The first evidence confirming the presence of relatively inflexible prices among oligopolistic industries was presented by Gardner C. Means in 1935.[59] He called them "administered prices." Since that time Means has presented further positive evidence for subsequent periods. Unfortunately, he has been overzealous in propounding his views and occasionally inconsistent in his interpretations. As a consequence, he has stirred up a string of formidable critics.[60] A blow-by-blow account of the debates is unnecessary. The lessons to be learned may be stated simply: (1) There are many factors, such as costs, that are more important than concentration in determining price changes, and (2) prices vary widely across industries for reasons too complex to pin down easily.

This is not to say, however, that concentration has no influence or that its influence is trivial. The weight of accumulated evidence now seems to rest on the side of Means. For example, David Qualls computed the year-to-year price change variance of 30 four-digit industries for which wholesale price data were available over the period 1957–1970. He then divided his sample into two groups, depending on whether the industry's four-firm concentration ratio was greater or less than 50%. Comparing the two groups, he found that average variance in the unconcentrated industries greatly exceeded average variance in the highly concentrated industries, 39.0% to 6.2%.[61]

Philip Cagan's comprehensive study of pricing during our post–World War II recessions also lends support to the pattern of Figure 12–11.[62] He used wholesale price indexes for over 1000 narrowly defined industries that he divided into three concentration categories—high, medium, and low. In all five recessions studied up through 1970, average prices in the high-concentration category decreased *less* than those in the low concentration category. Moreover, Cagan found a shift over time that would correspond to a shift of the solid diagonals of Figure 12–11 up toward the dashed diagonals. Thus, during the 1969–1970 recession, only the low-concentration category experienced any decline in average price levels. Prices in the medium and high groups actually increased.

More recently, Ralph Bradburd and Richard Caves explored cyclical variations in prices *and* quantities for 83 intermediate goods industries. Cleverly, they measured cyclical swings in demand by derivation—that is,

[59] *Industrial Prices and their Relative Inflexibility*, Senate Doc. 13, 74th Cong., 1st Sess., 1935.

[60] See, for example, G. J. Stigler, "Industrial Prices as Administered by Dr. Means," *American Economic Review* (September 1973), pp. 717–721; and J. F. Weston, S. Lustgarten, and N. Grottke, "The Administered-Price Thesis Denied: Note," *American Economic Review* (March 1974), pp. 232–234.

[61] P. D. Qualls, "Price Stability in Concentrated Industries," *Southern Economic Journal* (October 1975), pp. 294–298.

[62] P. Cagan, "Changes in the Recession Behavior of Wholesale Prices in the 1920's and Post–World War II," *Explorations in Economic Research NBER* (Winter 1975), pp. 54–104. See also Howard N. Ross, "Price and Margin Rigidity in Deflation: The Great Depression," *Review of Industrial Organization*, Vol. 3, no. 4 (1988), pp. 53–91.

from changes in the outputs of the customer industries these industries supplied (as the demand for steel, for instance, would be derived from the production of autos, appliances, and other final goods using steel). Among other things, Bradburd and Caves found that high concentration *reduced* the responsiveness of prices to changes in demand while at the same time high concentration *increased* the responsiveness of quantities — as pictured in Figure 12–11.[63] This finding on quantity is corroborated by studies showing a positive association between high concentration and high fluctuations in employment and inventories.[64]

These several multi-industry studies are supported by evidence that emerges from individual industries. It has been found, for example, that electricity prices are less flexible in local monopoly markets as compared to duopoly markets.[65] In aluminum, various fabricated products have historically fallen into three basic categories of price behavior: rigid, moderately flexible, and highly flexible. The first (covering, e.g., coil, foil stock, and sheet) has been the least competitive.[66] The nickel industry has changed from price stability to price variability as competition has increased in recent decades.[67] Further examples concern magazine advertising, pharmaceuticals, paper products, and tin plate.[68] (See also the appendix to this chapter.)

Instead of examining raw prices, some researchers have explored changes in prices *less* variable costs, otherwise known as **price-cost gross margins**. The foregoing findings with respect to price fluctuations do not rule out the possibility that gross margins might behave independently of market power. On the other hand, our theories concerning Figure 12–7 suggest that margins, like prices, should be more flexible in competitive industries than in oligopolies. That is, they should compress more during slumps and expand more during booms, everything else being equal. Evidence on this point goes as far back as the Great Depression, and much of it does seem to show an inverse relationship between con-

---

[63] Ralph M. Bradburd and Richard E. Caves, "Transaction-Cost Influences on the Adjustment of Industries' Prices and Outputs," *Review of Economics and Statistics* (November 1987), pp. 575–583.

[64] D. Stanton Smith, "Concentration and Employment Fluctuations," *Western Economic Journal* (September 1971), pp. 267–277; Robert M. Feinberg, "Market Structure and Employment Instability," *Review of Economics and Statistics* (November 1979), pp. 497–505; and Yakov Amihud and Haim Medelson, "Inventory Behavior and Market Power," *International Journal of Industrial Organization* (June 1989), pp. 269–280.

[65] Walter J. Primeaux and Mark R. Bomball, "A Reexamination of the Kinky Oligopoly Demand Curve," *Journal of Political Economy* (July/August 1974), pp. 851–862.

[66] George David Smith, *From Monopoly to Competition: The Transformation of Alcoa, 1888–1986* (Cambridge: Cambridge University Press, 1988), p. 283.

[67] Robert D. Cairns, "Changing Structure in the World Nickel Industry," *Antitrust Bulletin* (Fall 1984), pp. 561–575.

[68] Julio J. Rotemberg and Garth Saloner, "The Relative Rigidity of Monopoly Pricing," *American Economic Review* (December 1987), pp. 917–926; and Naomi R. Lamoreaux, *The Great Merger Movement in American Business, 1895–1904* (Cambridge: Cambridge University Press, 1985).

centration and margin flexibility. During cyclical *up*swings, margins tend to rise in competitive industries relative to those in oligopolistic industries; during *down*swings, the opposite occurs.[69]

Still, this finding is not rock solid. There are good theories and impressive evidence from recent data supporting the contrary view that price-cost margins in highly concentrated industries move procyclically relative to those in competitive industries. As indicated in Figure 12–12, which is based on evidence compiled by Domowitz, Hubbard, and Petersen, this would mean that margins in highly concentrated industries contract more sharply during recessions and expand more greatly during recoveries than do margins in relatively competitive industries. Several theories behind this possibility stem from something else that may be readily seen in Figure 12–12. The price-cost margins of highly concentrated industries (as reflected in the top line for industries with four-firm concentration ratios in the 80 to 100 range) are on average *higher* than the price-cost margins of unconcentrated industries (as represented by the bottom line of Figure 12–12 for industries with four-firm concentration ratios in the 0 to 20 range). The margin $(P-C)/C$ is about .32 for the former versus .23 for the latter, on average. David Qualls, for example, argues that strong market power allows these higher margins in highly concentrated industries and this power also allows "margins to be varied (in keeping with industrywide profit maximizing considerations) in the face of fluctuating demand."[70] In other words, profit maximizing would, in theory, require powerful oligopolists or monopolists to compress their margins when demand shifts left and expand them when demand shifts right. Profit-maximizing competitive firms, however, will not vary their margins cyclically because they are, by the force of competitive circumstances, *always low*. In other words, thin competitive price-cost margins are in effect *too thin* to fluctuate with booms and busts. Qualls found evidence like that of Domowitz, Glenn, and Petersen in Figure 12–12. Others supporting this view include Goldstein (with American data); Round (with Australian data); Neumann, Bobel, and Haid (with German data); and Bedrossian and Moschos (with Greek data).[71]

[69] A. C. Neal, *Industrial Concentration and Price Inflexibility* (Washington, D.C.: American Council on Public Affairs, 1942); L. W. Weiss, "Business Pricing Policies and Inflation Reconsidered," *Journal of Political Economy* (April 1966), pp. 177–187; P. Cagan, "Inflation and Market Structure," *Explorations in Economic Research* (Spring 1975), pp. 203–216; J. A. Dalton, "Administered Inflation and Business Pricing: Another Look," *Review of Economics and Statistics* (November 1973), pp. 516–519; and Howard N. Ross, "Price and Margin Rigidity in Deflation: The Great Depression," *Review of Industrial Organization*, Vol. 3, no. 4 (1988), pp. 53–91.

[70] P. David Qualls, "Market Structure and the Cyclical Flexibility of Price-Cost Margins," *Journal of Business* (April 1979), pp. 305–325.

[71] Jonathan Goldstein, "Markup Variability and Flexibility," *Journal of Business* (October 1986), pp. 599–621; David K. Round, "Intertemporal Profit Margin Variability and Market Structure in Australian Manufacturing," *International Journal of Industrial Organization* (June 1983), pp. 189–209; Manfred Neumann, Ingo Bobel, and Alfred Haid, "Business

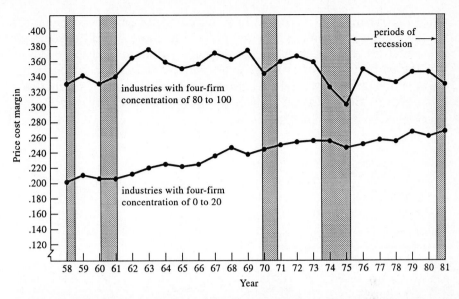

FIGURE 12–12. Price-cost margins over the business cycle by different degree of industrial concentration, 1958–1981. Source: Ian Domowitz, R. Glenn Hubbard, and Bruce C. Petersen, "The Intertemporal Stability of the Concentration-Margins Relationship," *Journal of Industrial Economics* (September 1986), p. 18.

These findings of price-cost behavior in the pattern of Figure 12–12 might seem to conflict with the substantial body of evidence indicating greater *price* rigidity in highly concentrated industries as depicted in Figure 12–11. But they may be consistent. Note first what was mentioned earlier. Much evidence on margins conflicts with the pattern of Figure 12–12, so the margin evidence of Figure 12–12 is less reliable than the price evidence supporting Figure 12–11. Second, and more important, consistency is easily possible even if the pattern of Figure 12–12 is accepted. This is because margins vary directly with *costs* as well as with prices, whereas prices move only with variations in prices. Figure 12–13 illustrates this point with simple sketches of prices and costs under conditions of low demand and high demand that would be compatible with both Figure 12–11 and Figure 12–12. In panel (a) of Figure 12–13, representing highly concentrated markets, the margin fluctuates procyclically. In panel (b) representing competitive markets, the margin remains constant over the cycle even though prices in panel (b) fluctuate more than they do in panel (a). The margin in panel (b) of Figure 12–12 remains constant because the costs of competitive firms are fluctuating as

Cycle and Industrial Market Power," *Journal of Industrial Economics* (December 1983), pp. 187–196; and A. Bedrossian and D. Moschos, "Industrial Structure, Concentration, and the Speed of Price Adjustment," *Journal of Industrial Economics* (June 1988), pp. 459–475.

much as prices. And it follows that the costs in competitive panel (b) are fluctuating much more over the cycle than the costs in noncompetitive panel (a). In fact, there is considerable evidence from post–World War II data that unit costs are relatively variable in low-concentration industries and relatively rigid in high-concentration industries, especially labor costs.[72] Hence Figure 12–13's reconciliation of Figures 12–11 and 12–12 may be on the mark.

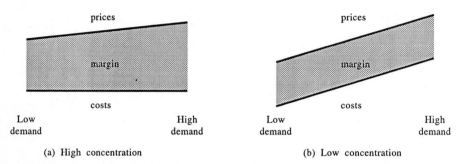

| (a) High concentration | (b) Low concentration |

FIGURE 12–13. Price, cost, and margin behavior over the business cycle (reconciling the evidence that supports Figures 12–11 and 12–12).

SUMMARY

Between August 1982 and February 1983 the wholesale price of gasoline fell about 16 cents a gallon. Reflecting their lower costs, gasoline retailers cut their price to motorists by about 14 cents a gallon. In contrast, the wholesale price of home heating oil fell about 15 cents a gallon during the same months, but the reduction was *not* passed on to consumers by heating oil retailers. Why the big difference? "One reason," according to *The Wall Street Journal*, "is that the gasoline business is more competitive than the heating oil business."[73]

Cournot would understand this contrast if he were still alive. Fortunately, his theory of interdependence is still alive to help us understand the contrast. His theory has been improved upon, however.

Analysis of short-run price and production policy under oligopoly and monopolistic competition now centers on the firm's twofold de-

---

[72] See, for example, Ian Domowitz, R. Glenn Hubbard, and Bruce C. Petersen, "Oligopoly Supergames: Some Empirical Evidence on Prices and Margins," *Journal of Industrial Economics* (June 1987), pp. 379–398; and D. F. Greer, "Market Power and Wage Inflation: A Further Analysis," *Southern Economic Journal* (January 1975), pp. 466–479.

[73] *The Wall Street Journal*, February 18, 1983, p. 19.

mand curves. These curves' price elasticities, shapes, visibilities, and shifts tell most of the story. The followship curve reflects marketwide demand and is typically rather inelastic. Conversely, the nonfollowship demand curve reflects switches of market share. The smaller the firm and the more standardized the product, therefore, the more price elastic the nonfollowship curve is. Under monopolistic competition all firms face highly elastic nonfollowship demand curves. The phoney promises these curves give price cutters of increased total revenue are too alluring to resist. Abundant small-firm populations also keep interdependence unrecognized and followship demand curves invisible. The result is price competition.

Under oligopoly, with its fewer and larger firms, interdependence is recognized. Kinked demand theory, though flawed, helps to explain why price cuts are resisted. To large firms the nonfollowship demand curve is less elastic and therefore less alluring than to small firms. Even more important, only the followship demand curve is visible to them on the downside. On the upside, only strong dominant price leaders see the followship demand curve. The theory's major implication is rigid prices, or, when amended by certain realities such as inflation, *relatively* rigid prices (especially on the down side).

This implication holds even in the face of fluctuating demand. Supply control facilitates the maintenance of prices and profits within a given cycle, plus greater stability across numerous cycles. Comparatively large firms (with relatively inelastic demand curves) appreciate this quality of supply control the most. The elastic nonfollowship demand curves of smaller firms often entice them into secret discounting or thinly veiled price cutting when demand is slack. Intraindustry experiences demonstrate the different views large and small firms have of the same market.

Short-run stability, guidance, coordination, and uniformity are furthered by various "mechanisms" or pricing procedures. The most important of these are cost-plus pricing, target-profit pricing, price leadership, facilitating practices, and cartelization. These techniques tend to be most highly refined, most consistently adhered to, and most commonly observed in markets displaying stronger as opposed to lesser market power. Those in markets of lesser market power must rely on government intervention, usually in some form of cartelization, to secure the discipline that cyclical supply control requires.

Finally, cross-section evidence is not altogether solid. Still, it seems to show relatively rigid prices in industries bearing ossified structures as compared to those displaying more competitive characteristics. Interindustry studies of output and employment corroborate this inference. The cyclical evidence on price-cost margins is less certain. Some of it is procyclical with concentration, as pictured in Figure 12–12. If so, it can be reconciled with the evidence on price rigidity by the fact that costs are relatively flexible under competition.

APPENDIX: TRANSACTION PRICES VERSUS LIST PRICES

The price data used by Gardner Means for his original study of price inflexibility, and also the data used by most other researchers in this area, derive from "list" prices rather than "transaction" prices. List prices are announced by sellers in notices or catalogs and reported to the Bureau of Labor Statistics for conversion into official price indexes. Transaction prices may differ from list prices because of secret discounts, special deals, or other modifications. Economists skeptical of the "administered price" hypothesis were for many years critical of the evidence supporting the hypothesis because it used list prices, the only ones generally available, instead of transaction prices. The critics argued that transaction prices would be the more flexible of the two. George Stigler and James Kindahl hoped to verify their skepticism by collecting transaction prices from buyers (not sellers) for 70 commodities over the period 1957–1966.[74] Although Stigler and Kindahl interpreted their data as showing an absence of "administered prices," careful subsequent studies of the same data now confirm the kind of behavior depicted in Figure 12–11. The work of Howard Ross and Joshua Krausz, for example, is summarized in Table 12–5. Stigler's and Kindahl's transaction-price data are labeled SK. The Bureau of Labor Statistics list price data go by BLS. Note that the results are quite similar for both sets of data. During recessions prices fall more in situations of low concentration than high concentration. Indeed, high-concentration prices rise in this sample instead of fall as they are "supposed" to when demand tumbles. Conversely, during recoveries, low-concentration prices rise, as expected, while high-concentration prices fall slightly. Overall, the competitive

TABLE 12–5. Average Price Changes, in Percent, as Reflected in SK and BLS Data, 1957–1966 (forty-eight commodities free of sharp trend)

Concentration	Recessions		Recoveries	
	SK (%)	BLS (%)	SK (%)	BLS (%)
Low	−4.44	−3.14	3.50	2.78
High	0.22	1.02	−0.38	−0.08

Source: Howard N. Ross and Joshua Krausz, "Buyers' and Sellers' Prices and Administered Behavior," *Review of Economics and Statistics* (August 1986), p. 377.

[74] George J. Stigler and James K. Kindahl, *The Behavior of Industrial Prices* (New York: National Bureau of Economic Research, 1970).

prices vary much more over the cycle, down and up, than do noncompetitive prices.[75]

Dennis Carlton measured transaction price rigidity by the number of months a given buyer pays a given seller the same price, on average. For example, if monthly prices paid were $5, $5, $5, $6, $6, $6, and $6, the average rigidity would be 3.5 months. By this approach, Carlton found a very strong positive correlation between concentration and price rigidity in the Stigler-Kindahl data. "The more highly concentrated an industry is, the greater is the likelihood that the industry has prices that remain unchanged for long periods of time."[76]

In short, the problem of transactions prices versus list prices was worth investigating. But the results appear to be quite similar in both.[77]

[75] For more extensive BLS data, see Howard N. Ross and Joshua Krausz, "Cyclical Price Behavior and Concentration: A Time Series Analysis," *Oxford Bulletin of Economics and Statistics* (August 1985), pp. 231–247.

[76] Dennis W. Carlton, "The Theory and the Facts of How Markets Clear," p. 922. See also "The Rigidity of Prices," *American Economic Review* (September 1986), pp. 637–658.

[77] See also Milton Moore, "Stigler on Inflexible Prices," *Canadian Journal of Economics* (November 1972), pp. 486–493; and Leonard W. Weiss, "Stigler, Kindahl, and Means on Administered Prices," *American Economic Review* (September 1977), pp. 610–619.

13

Price and Production Behavior: Cartel Practice and Policy

*Between 1969 and 1973 I saw the retail price of a
loaf of bread in Phoenix go from 35 cents to 69
cents. At least 15% of that increase could be traced
to our conspiracy. There's no question that price-
fixing is a cost factor for the consumer.*
— Confession of DONALD PHILLIPS, former vice
president of Baird's Bread Co.

In a word, the subject of this chapter is cartelization. Broadly defined, a
cartel *is an explicit arrangement among, or on behalf of, enterprises in the same
line of business that is designed to limit competition among them*[1]. The concept
includes price fixing, explicit collusion, and conspiracy. It might involve
no more than a sociable discussion of prices over cocktails, or it might
be so complex as to involve sales quotas, customer allocations, weekly

[1] G. W. Stocking and M. W. Watkins, *Cartels or Competition* (New York: Twentieth
Century Fund, 1948), p. 3.

388

meetings, enforcement committees, and penalty formulas. There are buyer cartels and seller cartels. They may be open or secret, governmental or private, legal or illegal, local or international.

Cartels fit within the short-run context of the preceding chapter for many reasons. When privately devised, they are often short-lived. Their purpose, moreover, is frequently price stabilization rather than flagrant price escalation. Then too, their popularity among businesspeople seems to vary inversely with the business cycle. But the fit is very imperfect. Cartels, it must be acknowledged, are not always "short-run" phenomena. As suggested by this chapter's opening quote, cartels may last for years. The British/Indian ocean liner shipping "conference" celebrated its centennial anniversary in 1975.

Cartels may also raise prices and profits sharply. Some recent evidence indicates that a sample of large U.S. firms involved in illegal price fixing had *lower* profits than other large firms, thus suggesting a short-run "preventive" purpose to their activity.[2] But there are also numerous instances of prices increasing from 20% to 60%, even hundreds of percents, under cartels.[3] The most famous cartel of all time — the Organization of Petroleum Exporting Countries, or OPEC — gained global notoriety by quadrupling the price of crude oil in 1973 and then tacking on price increases at fairly regular intervals during the decade thereafter.

In short, "the typical purpose and effect of cartelization is to set prices higher than would prevail under competition, to reduce them as seldom as possible, and to raise them further whenever the opportunity permits."[4] Attainment of these ends often requires restrictions extending beyond price and output. Advertising and product quality have felt the grasp of concerted business practices. Unavoidably, then, this chapter is more than just an elaboration of the preceding chapter's short-run pricing subjects. It introduces the long-run subjects of the next chapter and other aspects of conduct as well.

We begin by surveying U.S. government policy. A study of structural conditions favorable to cartelization follows. We then review the electrical equipment cases and conclude with an extended discussion of the crude petroleum industry and OPEC.

---

2 P. Asch and J. J. Seneca, "Is Collusion Profitable?" *Review of Economics and Statistics* (February 1976), pp. 1–12. But see on the other hand Robert M. Feinberg, "Antitrust Enforcement and Subsequent Price Behavior," *Review of Economics and Statistics* (November 1980), pp. 609–612.

3 See, for example, W. B. Erickson, "Price Fixing Conspiracies: Their Long-term Impact," *Journal of Industrial Economics* (March 1976), pp. 189–202; W. F. Mueller, "Effects of Antitrust Enforcement in the Retail Food Industry," *Antitrust Law & Economics Review* (Winter 1968–69), pp. 86–87; and J. J. Siegfried and M. Mahony, "The First Sherman Act Case: Jellico Mountain Coal," *Antitrust Bulletin* (Winter 1990), pp. 801–832.

4 Corwin D. Edwards, *Economic and Political Aspects of International Cartels* (Washington, D.C.: Subcommittee on War Mobilization of the Committee on Military Affairs, U.S. Senate, 1944), p. 13.

I. U.S. GOVERNMENT POLICY

A. Per Se Violation

"Every contract, combination . . . or conspiracy, in restraint of trade or commerce among the several States, or with foreign nations, is hereby declared to be illegal." So reads Section 1 of the Sherman Act of 1890. It is the backbone of U.S. antitrust policy. There are exemptions (regulated industries, export cartels, and milk among them), but this is the basic policy applying to most interstate commerce. As enforced, the law is rather empty of economic content, for violation is a *per se* offense. That is, explicit (albeit secret) collusion to fix prices, allocate territories, or otherwise rig the market is illegal *regardless* of the reasonableness or unreasonableness of the economic consequences. The only proof required is proof that conspiracy actually occurred. This dictum contrasts markedly with the "rule of reason" approach to monopolization cases.

Stringent interpretation of the law dates back to 1897, when the Supreme Court decided *U.S.* v. *Trans-Missouri Freight Association*. The Court's most explicit early expression of the per se doctrine is found in its 1927 opinion *U.S.* v. *Trenton Potteries*. Twenty-three corporations producing 82% of the vitreous pottery fixtures (bathroom bowls, tubs, and so on) in the United States were accused of conspiring to fix prices and limit production. The Court rejected their argument that the "reasonableness" of their prices should be considered, saying that

> The aim and result of every price-fixing agreement, if effective, is the elimination of one form of competition. The power to fix prices, whether reasonably exercised or not, involves power to control the market and to fix arbitrary and unreasonable prices. The reasonable price fixed today may through economic and business changes become the unreasonable price of tomorrow. Once established, it may be maintained unchanged because of the absence of competition secured by the agreement for a price reasonable when fixed. Agreements which create such potential power may well be held to be *in themselves* unreasonable or unlawful restraints. . . .[5]

This rigorous standard of illegality might lead you to think that businesspeople shun conspiracies for fear of being caught. Alas, life is not so simple. Well over a thousand civil and criminal prosecutions have been brought under Section 1 and many more will surely follow. Of late, the Justice Department has launched an average of 20 criminal cases a year. With bathroom bowls still fresh on our minds, we should mention that since *Trenton Potteries* in 1927, members of the vitreous plumbing

---

[5] *United States* v. *Trenton Potteries*, 273 U.S. 392 (1927), p. 397. (Emphasis added.) The wisdom of the per se rule is demonstrated by J. Douglass Klein, "Cooperation and the *Per Se* Debate: Evidence from the United Kingdom," mimeo, December, 1987.

fixture industry have twice been caught and found guilty of further price fixing (a most unsanitary record). The latest conspiracy, in the 1960s, came to light when Internal Revenue Service agents stumbled onto three tape recordings of price-fixing meetings stashed in the abandoned desk of a man they were investigating for income tax evasion. The 15 firms involved include American Standard, Borg-Warner, and Kohler Company. Estimates of impact indicate that prices were lifted roughly 7% on $1 billion worth of business. "Price fixing rather than competition has been a way of life in the industry," commented an industry official who testified as a key government witness.[6] Unfortunately, this example is not unique. Recidivism is quite common in antitrust.

B. Remedies

A major contributor to the problem of widespread and repeated offenses has been light penalties. Until very recently, criminal violations were merely misdemeanors; fines could be measured in peanuts ($50,000 at most); suspended sentences were fashionable; and jailings were rare and brief. In short, crime paid. Donald Phillips, the confessed price-fixer we quoted at the outset, put it this way: "When you're doing $30 million a year and stand to gain $3 million by fixing prices, a $30,000 fine doesn't mean much. Face it," he said, "most of us would be willing to spend 30 days in jail to make a few extra million dollars. Maybe if I were facing a year or more, I would think twice."[7]

A trend toward more deterrent penalties has developed. Of all the people who have gone to prison for price fixing between the passage of the Sherman Act in 1890 and the present, most of them served time after 1965. In addition, the act was amended in 1974 to make criminal violation a *felony*, punishable by as much as three years in prison, with fines as high as $100,000 for individuals and $1 million for corporations.

Violators not only face these criminal sanctions, they may be sued by their victimized buyers for *three times* the financial loss suffered from the conspiracy. In the plumbing fixture case, treble damages were reckoned at $210 million, but out-of-court settlements with the victimized plaintiffs brought actual payments down to $28 million. In broader terms, the popularity of treble damage suits has burgeoned since 1960.[8]

---

[6] See *The Washington Post*, June 6, 1971; and *Fortune*, December, 1969.

[7] *Business Week*, June 2, 1975, p. 48.

[8] For more on penalties see K. G. Elzinga and W. Breit, *The Antitrust Penalties: A Study in Law and Economics* (New Haven, Conn.: Yale University Press, 1976). On the economic consequences see Robert M. Feinberg, "The Timing of Antitrust Effects on Pricing," *Applied Economics* (June 1984), pp. 397–409; and M. K. Block and J. S. Feinstein, "The Spillover Effect of Antitrust Enforcement," *Review of Economics and Statistics* (February 1986), pp. 122–131.

C. "Reserved Cities," "Dancing Partners," and "Poker"

Given a punitive per se rule, the key remaining question is *what* constitutes "price fixing" or "collusive restraint." Businesspeople have demonstrated skill when it comes to colluding. Their artistry may be divided into two broad categories: (1) cases with clear evidence of anticompetitive collusion and (2) cases offering no more than circumstantial evidence. This section covers the first category. Subsequent sections handle the second.

For sheer simplicity of obvious evidence, no collusive technique tops the *single sales agency*, whereby producers refuse to sell directly to their customers and instead sell through a common central agency that sets price for all participants.[9] Equally obvious would be a short, written *contract* specifying minimum prices. Only a bit more complicated is the *market allocation* approach, whereby each cartel member is assigned exclusive access to certain geographic areas or customers.

The classic *Addyston Pipe & Steel* case of 1899 provides a good example of this last tactic. Six manufacturers of cast iron pipe, including Addyston, entered into an agreement that assigned certain southern and central U.S. cities to individual members of the cartel. These "reserved cities" were the exclusive province of the designated member. The price at which pipe was sold in each reserved city was determined jointly by the cartel, the member to whom the business was assigned paying a fixed bonus into the cartel's profit-sharing pool. In order to give appearances of continued competition other members submitted fictitious bids to customers in reserved cities, "fictitious" because these bids were always at prices higher than those charged by the designated member.[10]

Some forms of agreement involve no direct communications concerning price. Nevertheless, Justice Department lawyers have been able to ferret out many such offenses. One of their most celebrated victories was *U.S. v. Socony-Vacuum* (now called Mobil) in 1940. The defendants were major integrated oil companies accounting for 83% of all gasoline sales in the midwestern states. They instituted a "dancing partner" program in the Midwest, under which each major agreed to buy the "surplus" gasoline of some particular independent refinery. "Surplus" was gasoline that could not be disposed of except at "distressed" prices. The independents were small and lacked spacious storage facilities. They consequently sold their "surpluses" at whatever discounted price they could get.

The defendant majors were not accused of direct price fixing. In-

---

[9] To a large degree, this form governs the international diamond industry headed by De Beers. Even the USSR sells through De Beers. For fascinating accounts see Edward Jay Epstein, *The Rise and Fall of Diamonds* (New York: Simon & Schuster, 1982); *Fortune,* September 6, 1982, pp. 42–53; and *Business Week,* June 1, 1981, pp. 104–105.

[10] *Addyston Pipe and Steel Company* v. *U.S.,* 175 U.S. 211 (1899).

deed, their surplus purchases from "partners" were at prices determined by the force of competition in the other sales made by all refiners. The essence of the accusation was that removal of excess supply from the market *indirectly* propped up the price. To be sure, the defendants argued that their activities did not constitute price fixing. But the Court was not fooled:

> In this [oil] case, the result was to place a floor under the market—a floor which served the function of increasing the stability and firmness of market prices. . . . Under the Sherman Act a combination formed for the purpose and with the effect of raising, depressing, fixing, pegging, or stabilizing the price of a commodity in interstate or foreign commerce is illegal per se.[11]

A string of related cases from the late 1970s involved *bid rigging* among highway construction contractors in the South. In 1979, executives of five of Nashville's largest paving companies met at a hotel for what was supposed to be a poker game. In fact, the poker was just a cover. They met to rig the bids on three local highway projects. Nine months later one of the poker players pleaded guilty to price fixing, and, in exchange for a light sentence, divulged extensive information about the industry's bid rigging in general. The game then became dominoes, as the Justice Department's investigations soon led to indictments against 57 corporations and 80 of their officers in at least six southern states.[12]

D. Trade Associations

Notwithstanding the Court's strong per se stance, not all collective activity is forbidden. Competitors are still free to form, and to take active part in, trade associations. These associations raise problems, however. Because "education" is a prime purpose of trade associations, it is quite common for them to collect and disseminate information on a wide variety of subjects, prices included. Moreover, trade association meetings are conducive to talk of prices. As a former assistant manager for a textile firm said: "I don't know what people would do at a trade association meeting if not discuss prices. They aren't going to talk just about labor contracts and new technology."[13] Fortunately for the consumer, trade association cover cannot immunize outright conspiracies from prosecution. Approximately 30% of all cases brought by the government involve trade associations.

---

[11] *United States* v. *Socony-Vacuum Oil Co.*, 310 U.S. 150 (1940).

[12] "Highway Robbery?", *The Wall Street Journal*, May 29, 1981, pp. 1, 25.

[13] *Business Week*, June 2, 1975, p. 48. See also Jeffrey Sonnenfeld and Paul R. Lawrence, "Why Do Companies Succumb to Price Fixing?" *Harvard Business Review* (July–August 1978), pp. 145–157.

Still, the "information" activities of trade associations pose ticklish problems for drawing the legal line between what does and what does not constitute price fixing. On the one hand, it can be argued that enhanced knowledge on the part of industry members lessens market imperfections, thereby fostering more effective competition. On the other hand, too much knowledge may inhibit price competition. Recall from the previous chapter that price cutters often attempt to *conceal* their discounts in order to forestall followship. They know that their downside nonfollowship demand curves may disappear when exposed to the full light of day, leaving them only the inelastic, unattractive, and unprofitable followship demand curve to contend with.

Illegal information activities are illustrated by the *American Column and Lumber* case of 1921.[14] The hardwood flooring trade association involved required each of 365 participants to submit six reports to its secretary: (1) a daily report of all actual sales; (2) a daily shipping report, with exact copies of the invoices; (3) a monthly production report; (4) a monthly stock report; (5) current price lists; and (6) inspection reports. In turn, the trade association secretary supplied detailed reports to the firms from this information. The exchange was supplemented by monthly meetings where speakers urged cartel-like cooperation with exhortations such as, "If there is *no increase in production*, particularly in oak, there is going to be good business," and "*No man is safe in increasing production.*"

The Supreme Court decided this was "not the conduct of competitors." In subsequent cases the Court has frowned upon trade association programs involving elaborate standardization of the conditions surrounding sales, reports of future prices, and requirements that members must adhere to their reported prices. As regards *permissible* trade association activities, programs appear to be lawful "when they limit price reports to past transactions, preserve the anonymity of individual traders, make data available to buyers as well as sellers, and permit departure from the prices that are filed."[15]

E. Conscious Parallelism

We saw in the last chapter that cartelization was only one of a number of suppressors of price competition. Recognized interdependence produces cartels, but it also produces kinked demand curves, price leadership, and uniform cost-plus pricing, all of which — *despite the absence of any explicit agreement* — may yield behavior that closely resembles cartel behavior (namely, high and stable prices). Stated differently, "economic

---

[14] *American Column and Lumber Co. et al.* v. *United States*, 257 U.S. 377 (1921).

[15] C. Wilcox, *Public Policies Toward Business*, 3rd ed. (Homewood, Ill.: Richard D. Irwin, 1966), p. 129.

theory has suggested that this kind of noncompetitive behavior might well arise in an 'oligopoly' situation . . . without overt communication or agreement, but solely through a rational calculation by each seller of what the consequences of his price decision would be, taking into account the probable or virtually certain reactions of his competitors."[16] Such oligopolistic uniformity of behavior has been called **tacit collusion** or **conscious parallelism**.

How have the courts handled this problem? Does mere conscious parallelism fall within the meaning of "contract, combination, . . . , or conspiracy," which are specified by the Sherman Act? In short, is it illegal? The answer comes in two installments. First, *in and of itself*, conscious parallelism is *not* illegal. It does not provide conclusive circumstantial evidence of conspiracy. The Supreme Court's clearest statement to this effect is found in the *Theatre Enterprises* case of 1954:

> this Court has never held that proof of parallel business behavior conclusively establishes agreement or, phrased differently, that such behavior itself constitutes a Sherman Act offense . . ."conscious parallelism" has not yet read conspiracy out of the Sherman Act entirely.[17]

Second, and on the other hand, consciously parallel behavior may indicate an unlawful conspiracy or agreement *when viewed in conjunction with additional facts.* These additional facts may be subdivided into two categories

1. Additional independent evidence of a more formal agreement, as illustrated by the following:[18]
   a. Identical sealed bidding on nonstandard items (for example, large turbine generators)
   b. Basing-point pricing systems, whereby all sellers quote identical delivered prices to any given buyer despite substantial transportation costs and widely differing delivery distances
   c. Elaborate exchanges of information, such as those in trade association cases
   d. Unnatural product standardization or false denials of interfirm quality differences
   e. Simultaneous and substantial price increases (coupled with output reductions) unexplained by any increase in cost

---

[16] D. F. Turner, "The Definition of Agreement Under the Sherman Act: Conscious Parallelism and Refusals to Deal," *Harvard Law Review* (February 1962), p. 661. For elaboration see *The Journal of Reprints for Antitrust Law and Economics*, Vol. XIII, no. 2 (1982).

[17] *Theatre Enterprises, Inc.* v. *Paramount Film Distributing Corp.*, 346 U.S. 537 (1954). See also *United States* v. *National Malleable & Steel Castings Co.*, 1957 Trade Cases, para. 68,890 (N. D. Ohio, 1957), *affirmed per curiam*, 358 U.S. 38 (1959).

[18] Turner, "The Definition of Agreement Under the Sherman Act" and R. A. Posner, *Antitrust Law, An Economic Perspective* (Chicago: University of Chicago Press, 1976), pp. 62–70.

2. Additional independent evidence that the conduct is restrictive or *exclusionary*, such as
   a. Parallel buying up of scarce raw materials that are not, in fact, used
   b. Parallel and predatory price cutting
   c. Cross-licensing of patents

The *American Tobacco* case of 1946 discussed earlier on page 373 is illustrative.[19] Unlawful conspiracy was found in that case, even though there was no evidence of meetings in smoke-filled rooms or other rendezvous. Parallel pricing behavior was placed in the context of additional facts. In particular, (1) prices were raised despite cost reductions and a massive depression, (2) the three largest companies bought up cheap tobacco they did not use but the "ten cent" brands would have used, and (3) the three largest companies cut prices only after the "10 cent" brands won a healthy market share. The Court declared that "No formal agreement is necessary to constitute an unlawful conspiracy." In this case, conspiracy was proved "from the evidence of ɯe action taken in concert" and from "other circumstances."

F. Basing-Point Pricing

Of all the "plus" factors listed, perhaps the one in greatest need of further explanation is the item (b) in group 1 — basing-point pricing systems. A simple example of this is the old "Pittsburgh Plus" single basing-point system of the steel industry. Until 1924 all steel producers, regardless of their mill locations, quoted prices as if they were shipping from Pittsburgh. A steel company located in Gary, Indiana, when quoting a price to a buyer located in nearby Chicago, would add to the factory price the railroad freight cost from Pittsburgh to Chicago, rather than the slight freight cost from Gary to Chicago. The excess transportation charge pinned on the buyer was called "phantom freight."

Conversely, if the Gary plant was quoting a price to a buyer in New York, it would add to the factory price the freight cost from Pittsburgh to New York, rather than the larger and truer freight cost from Gary to New York. This undercharging of New York buyers meant that the seller had to "absorb freight." The mills located at the "base," in Pittsburgh, neither charged phantom freight nor absorbed freight on *any sale*. Their transport charges matched their transport costs. But sellers at all other locations dealt shamelessly in fictitious transport figures. When they were located closer to the buyer than the Pittsburgh mills, they

---

[19] *American Tobacco Co.* v. *United States*, 328 U.S. 781 (1946). For an interesting discussion of Australian cases, see Richard A. Miller and David K. Round, "Price-Fixing, Price Leadership, or Ordinary Associations," *Australian Business Law Review* (August 1982), pp. 251–269.

quoted phantom freight. When they were located farther from the buyer than the Pittsburgh mills, they absorbed freight.

The system is illustrated in Figure 13–1, where horizontal distance represents geographic distance (with Chicago, Pittsburgh, and New York located west to east) and vertical distance represents seller's cost—manufacturing cost first (which does not differ with location) and transportation cost second (which goes up with distance travelled). Thus the transportation cost of mill M_1 shipping to buyer B_1 is zero, but to buyer B_2 it is yx and to buyer B_3 it is vz. Under "Pittsburgh Plus," the double shafted line emanating from Pittsburgh would be the delivered price line for *all* sellers. Price x would be quoted to buyer B_2 by M_2 and M_3 as well as M_1, even though the transport costs of M_2 and M_3 would be quite different, as indicated by the single solid and broken lines, respectively. Delivered price to buyer B_1 would be u. To buyer B_3 it would be z. When M_2 charges buyer B_2 price x, it is charging phantom freight equal to xy. When M_2 charges buyer B_3 price z, it must absorb the wz portion of total freight cost wv.

The Pittsburgh Plus system achieved one particularly important result. As a given *buyer* saw it, *all sellers* were quoting exactly the same price to him. This did not mean that all buyers were quoted the same price, as buyers close to the base saw low identical quotes and buyers distant from the base saw high identical quotes. Yet each buyer saw but one price. The single-base system of Pittsburgh Plus was abandoned under pressure from the FTC in 1924. Yet this uniform result still held after the steel industry converted to a *multiple* basing-point system by introducing Gary and Birmingham as additional bases. The base closest to the buyer then provided the key to all quotes.

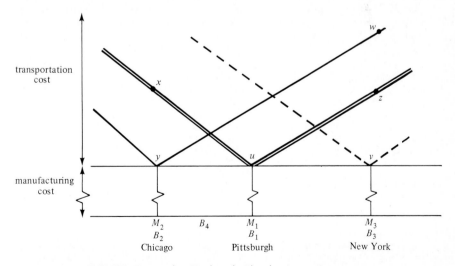

FIGURE 13–1. The Pittsburgh Plus basing-point system.

Why would the sellers want to quote identical prices to each buyer? To facilitate collusion and effective price leadership. These systems simplify the pricing of colluding firms. They nullify any interfirm cost advantages attributable to geographic location. They enable the leader to lead with ease from the base. They permit price discrimination as when in Figure 13–1 seller M_2 charges a high price x to low-cost buyer B_2 while charging a low price of u to high-cost buyer B_1. They have also been attacked on these grounds as indicative or supportive of restrictive agreements.[20]

Attacks against basing-point pricing in steel, cement, and corn oil were carried out in the late 1940s with the aid of evidence indicating artificially contrived support.[21] The circulation of uniform railroad rate books, the policing of shipments to prevent destination diversion or truck hauling, the creation of fictitious rail rates to places not served by railroads, the complete absence of f.o.b. pricing—all these and other facets of the systems revealed that they were not innocently natural competitive developments but rather conspiracies. Moreover, the products involved—steel, cement, and corn syrup—indicated that such systems are especially pertinent to homogeneous, bulky commodities with relatively high transportation costs. In steel, for instance, transportation averages 10% of buyers' total cost.

Official attention to basing-point pricing rekindled during the late 1970s when the plywood industry was caught in a scheme that was simultaneously simple and complex.[22] Prior to 1963 all construction plywood was produced from Douglas fir in the Pacific Northwest. The South had abundant yellow pine timber, but the peculiar resins and pitch of yellow pine prevented its bonding into a durable sandwich board. Development of a new glue solved this problem, giving birth to a southern pine plywood industry. This southern branch grew prodigiously from 1 producer in 1963 to 25 in 1973, nurtured in part by freight

[20] D. D. Haddock theorizes that basing-point pricing is the result of innocent competition, not collusion. ["Basing-Point Pricing: Competitive vs. Collusive Theories," *American Economic Review* (June 1982), pp. 289–306.] However, his theory is refuted by the historical record. The Pittsburgh Plus system was collusively established to curb price competition. See W. T. Hogan, *Economic History of the Iron and Steel Industry of the United States* (Lexington, Mass.: Lexington Books, 1971), pp. 1095–1101. Also, until the Supreme Court relaxed its standards of proof in *FTC* v. *Cement Institute* (1948), the FTC successfully challenged a number of basing-point systems by proving the presence of collusive agreements. See Alan M. Anderson, "Conscious Parallelism in the Use of Delivered Pricing Systems," *Cornell Law Review*, Vol. 66 (1981), p. 1202.

[21] *Corn Products Refining Company* v. *Federal Trade Commission*, 324 U.S. 726 (1945); *FTC* vs. *Cement Institute*, 333 U.S. 683 (1948); *Triangle Conduit and Cable Co.* v. *FTC*, 168 F. 2d 175 (7th Cir. 1948). In *Cement* price uniformity was strikingly illustrated when each of 11 companies, bidding for a 6000-barrel government order in 1936, submitted sealed bids of $3.286854 per barrel.

[22] For details see Samuel M. Loescher, "Economic Collusion, Civil Conspiracy, and Treble Damage Deterrents: The Sherman Act Breakthrough with Southern Plywood," *The Quarterly Review of Economics and Business* (Winter 1980), pp. 6–35.

cost advantages vis-à-vis the northwest industry. Southern plywood could be delivered in Chicago, for example, at half the transport cost of northwestern plywood, a potential saving of 10% to plywood purchasers off their total delivered price. Yet the full potential of this saving was not realized by buyers because the southern mills priced their plywood as if it had been shipped from a ficticious base mill in Portland, Oregon, discounting slightly so as to make southern pine plywood a bit more attractive pricewise. Georgia-Pacific initiated the system when it expanded beyond the northwest into the South but declined to offer f.o.b. mill prices at its southern mills for buyers desirous of providing their own transportation (although G-P did offer f.o.b. prices from its northwest mills). Subsequent southern producers, even those without northwest mills, followed Georgia-Pacific's lead, to the financial disappointment of southern and eastern plywood purchasers. The Federal Trade Commission concluded that the industry's pricing system illegally restrained price competition and maintained an undue amount of phantom freight for southern producers.[23]

G. Summary

To summarize the overall legal situation, we may call upon a panel of experts, the Supreme Court:

> [P]rice fixing is contrary to the policy of competition under the Sherman Act . . . its illegality does not depend on a showing of its unreasonableness, since it is conclusively presumed to be unreasonable. It makes no difference whether the motives of the participants are good or evil; whether the price fixing is accomplished by express contract or by some more subtle means; whether the participants possess market control; whether the amount of interstate commerce affected is large or small; or whether the effect of the agreement is to raise or decrease prices.[24]

II. DETERMINANTS OF CARTELS AND THEIR POTENCY

A pet theory of anti-antitrusters is that cartels cannot "really" get off the ground. Or if they do, their life is "short and turbulent."[25] In a related vein, a few economists believe that collusive behavior is unrelated to such important structural features as concentration and the number of firms in the market.

---

[23] *In the Matter of Boise Cascade Corp. et al.*, 91 FTC 1 (1978). The FTC ruling was later overturned on appeal, but a private case held up. *The Wall Street Journal*, September 9, 1981, p. 48.

[24] *United States* v. *McKesson & Robbins, Inc.*, 351 U.S. 305 (1956), pp. 309–310.

[25] For example, in *Newsweek*, February 17, 1975, p. 80, Milton Friedman predicted that the OPEC cartel would "begin to disintegrate" within a year. The cartel continued to earn approximately $80 billion a year throughout the 1970s, and despite problems during the 1980s, it still survives as this is written in early 1990.

The aim of the present section is to show that these views are wrong. They stem from preconceived notions and an empirical literature replete with instances of cartel collapse. This literature is useful, but it gets more respect that it deserves.[26] Many cartels endure, even as many fall apart. The feasibility, incidence, and endurance of collusion are all largely determined by structural and technological conditions.[27]

A. Feasibility and Necessity

Before considering specific conditions, we must make a few preliminary observations. Perhaps the most important thing to remember is that the purpose of all collusion is to maximize joint profits, for only if firms act together can they price and produce like a monopolist. Furthermore, common sense tells us that cartelization occurs only when it is both *feasible* and *necessary* to achieving the objective of joint-profit maximization. If cartelization were not feasible, it surely would not occur. If it were not necessary to achieving the objective, it would likewise not occur, especially if it is illegal and heavily penalized.

The trick, then, is to recognize that "feasibility" and "necessity" are determined by structure. In particular, they vary *inversely* with structure. This relationship is most readily seen through two extreme circumstances, both of which would preclude cartelization. First, where there are hundreds of small firms selling a standardized product (for example, wheat), cartelization is absolutely *necessary* to achieving joint maximization but it is *im*possible to bring off privately (without government approval and imposition). Recognized interdependence is too remote. The incentives for price cutting are too great. Private enforcement of an agreement is too costly. And, if collusion is illegal, detection by the antitrust authorities would be too easy. The result is *no* cartel (unless the government wants to use its police power to establish one). Second, moving to the opposite extreme, imagine a market occupied by just two sellers of a simple standardized product (for example, aluminum ingots). In this case, a private cartel is quite *feasible* but wholly *un*necessary to achieving the joint-profit maximization objective. Recognized interdependence is unavoidable. The incentives for price cutting are virtually nil. The opportunity for simple price leadership is clearly open. The chances that "conscious parallelism" will yield a monopoly outcome are very good. Again the result is *no* cartel. Tacit collusion prevails instead.

To repeat, only when cartelization is both *feasible* and *necessary* to achieving the profit objective are we likely to find it, given a hostile legal

---

26 G. J. Stigler, "A Theory of Oligopoly," *Journal of Political Economy* (February 1964), p. 46

27 Ibid; Posner, *Antitrust Law*, pp. 47–61; P. Asch, "Collusive Olipology," J. M. Kuhlman, "Nature and Significance of Price Fixing Rings," and W. B. Erickson, "Economics of Price Fixing," all in *Antitrust Law & Economic Review* (Spring 1969), pp. 53–122.

environment. When structural conditions are highly unfavorable, necessity and impossibility combine to produce competition. When structural conditions are highly favorable, possibility and a lack of necessity combine to produce *tacit* collusion. In between, necessity and feasibility blend, and cartelization is likely to occur.

B. Effect of Number of Firms

With respect to numbers of firms, these considerations of likelihood lead us to expect that cartel occurrence is least common in markets with either a very large or a very small number of firms. Some intermediate range of "fewness" seems most conducive, since it offers a combination of necessity and feasibility. The present author and Art Fraas tested this expectation by (1) compiling a usable sample of 606 illegal price-fixing conspiracies from the records of all Section 1 prosecutions dispatched between 1910 and 1973, (2) counting the number of firms involved in each of these cases, and (3) computing a frequency distribution for these cases based on the number of firms.[28]

The resulting frequency distribution is shown in Figure 13–2 by the solid line. The vertical axis there is percentage frequency of each number of firms, as given on the horizontal axis. (Note that no fewer than two firms can conspire.) For example, in roughly 10% of all the sampled cases of cartelization, four firms were party to the illegal conspiracy. If by contrast 50% of the sampled cases involved four firms and 50% involved five, the distribution would look like a limbless tree, 50 percentage points tall, rooted at 4 and 5 on the horizontal axis. But this is obviously an improbable vegetable. Rather, the distribution bears out expectation. It has an arched, positive-negative configuration. The positively sloped portion of the distribution (beginning with two firms and rising) seems to reflect a trade-off between tacit and express collusion, with the incidence of explicit collusion rising and the incidence of tacit collusion falling as the number of firms in the explicit conspiracies (and in the market)[29] rises. On the other hand, the negatively sloped portion of the price-fixing distribution (beginning at about six firms) reflects a region of trade-off between express collusion and competitive independence. As the number of firms rises over this range, express collusion becomes less and less feasible.

This plot may be compared to the dashed-line distribution of Figure 13–2. It represents all industries generally, not just instances of price

[28] Arthur G. Fraas and D. F. Greer, "Market Structure and Price Collusion: An Empirical Analysis," *Journal of Industrial Economics* (September 1977), pp. 21–44. See also G. A. Hay and D. Kelley, "An Empirical Survey of Price Fixing Conspiracies," *Journal of Law and Economics* (April 1974), pp. 13–38.

[29] Hay and Kelley, "An Empirical Survey of Price Fixing Strategies," report data on the number of firms in each of 34 conspiracies and the total number of firms in each of the 34 markets involved. The simple correlation between the two is .96.

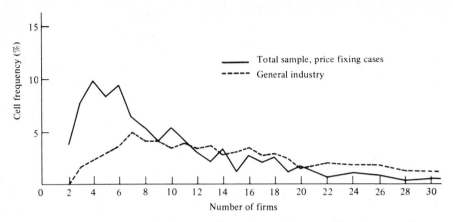

FIGURE 13–2. Frequency distribution of numbers of firms involved in price fixing.

fixing. Data for 1569 narrowly defined manufacturing markets of fairly uniform geographic scope underlie the distribution. A comparison of the two distributions indicates that a low number of firms is indeed conducive to collusion. The general industry distribution is spread out, whereas the price-fixing distribution is bunched toward the low numbers end.

We now have our first hint as to why many cartels are feeble and fragile while others are strong and durable. If the behavioral trade-off is between tacit collusion and cartelization — that is, if a cartel is set up because tacit collusion is not working well for profit achievement — then the cartel is probably built upon a fairly solid structural foundation. Its prospects appear promising. On the other hand, if the behavioral trade-off is between cartelization and competition — that is, if the cartel amounts to a last-gasp effort to pull the industry from the pit of vigorous competition — then the cartel's life expectancy and potential effectiveness naturally seem dim. One implication is that fewness of firms and *cartel effectiveness* go hand in hand. Although few data are available to test this notion systematically, the available evidence seems favorable to it.[30] One problem with any test of such a proposition is that many factors *other* than firm numbers have an influence. Even as few as two firms might compete wholeheartedly given the right surrounding circumstances.

[30] Fritz Voigt, "German Experience with Cartels and their Control during Pre-War and Post-War Periods," in *Competition, Cartels, and their Regulation*, edited by J. P. Miller (Amsterdam: North-Holland, 1962), p. 171; G. W. Stocking and M. W. Watkins, *Monopoly and Free Enterprise* (New York: Twentieth Century Fund, 1951), p. 112; Robert H. Porter, "On the Incidence and Duration of Price Wars," *Journal of Industrial Economics* (June 1985), pp. 415–426; and J. Douglass Klein and Lance E. Brannman, "The Effectiveness and Stability of Highway Bid-Rigging," mimeo, December 1987.

TABLE 13–1. Outline of Conditions Affecting the Incidence of Cartelization: Graded on the Basis of Feasibility and Necessity

Market Condition or Characteristic	(1) Feasibility: Excellent; Need: Unnecessary (Tacit Collusion)	(2) Feasibility: Good; Need: Helpful (Cartel)	(3) Feasibilty: Poor; Need: Essential (Competition)
Number of firms	Very few (2–5)	Several (5–25)	Many (30+)
Concentration ratio	Very high	High-medium	Low
Type of product	Standardized	Slightly different	Differentiated
Rate of techno- logical change	None	Slow-moderate	Rapid
Frequency (and size) of sales	Frequent (small)	Often (medium)	Lumpy (large)
Opportunity for secret deals	None	Some	Great
Rate of growth	Slow	Medium	Rapid
Elasticity of demand	Low (less 0.5)	Medium	High (2+)
Production costs across firms	Identical	Similar	Diverse

C. Other Structural Factors

The theoretical influence of other structural factors is outlined in Table 13–1. The format of the table is illustrated by inclusion of the number of firms in the market as the first condition listed. From left to right across the three columns, the number of firms mentioned rises from "very few" to "many." This pattern accords with the column headings that indicate a declining feasibility but a rising necessity of cartelization for joint-profit maximization as one reads from left to right.

Concentration. The second condition listed is concentration. The theory behind the table's specifications for this variable should be obvious because concentration is inversely correlated with the number of firms in markets and in conspiracies.[31] High to moderate four-firm concentration would seem to be most conducive to cartelization, as indicated in column (2). Extremely high concentration would of course foster tacit collusion, and vice versa for competition. Moreover, George Hay and Dan Kelley found that concentration and cartel stability are positively associated. For their sample of 65 cases "the preponderance of

---

[31] Using Hay and Kelley data again, ("An Empirical Survey of Price Fixing Strategies"), the correlation between concentration and the number of conspirators is −0.69.

conspiracies lasting ten or more years were in markets with high degrees of concentration."[32]

Firm numbers and concentration are listed first because they seem to be the most important variables mentioned. The other variables can be influential, however, as fewness of firms and high concentration are not sufficient in themselves to assure tacit collusion (although they appear to be essential to such a result). The other variables affect feasibility and necessity for the same basic reasons that numbers and concentration do. They affect the ease of reaching an agreement, the incentive to "cheat" or "double-cross" one's co-conspirators, and the ease of detecting double-crossers.

Type of Product and Technological Change.[33]   Type of product and rate of technological change are alike in their influences. Product differentiation or rapid change inject complexities that make it hard to reach an agreement in the first place. These complexities, moreover, make detection of double-crossers more difficult. Price cuts may be shrouded in the folds of product variations.[34] Double-crossing itself can take forms other than price cutting—namely, escalations in advertising or styling or research or some other nonprice variable. In light of these possibilities, it is not surprising that many cartels attempt to standardize their product, restrict advertising, and regulate technological change, for standardization and stagnation are most conducive to cooperation.[35]

Type of Sale and Opportunity for Secret Dealing.   If sales move in large lots over intermittent time intervals, then each sales transaction produces an important surge in the seller's revenue stream. The payoff to any given instance of price shading in this situation can be very lucrative. Temptations to cheat may therefore tug strongly here. This intermittent sales factor, plus healthy doses of rapid technological change and product differentiation, help to explain why the market for commerical airliners is intensely competitive despite its dominance by just three firms—Boeing, McDonnel-Douglas, and Airbus. Infrequent orders of multimillion-dollar denominations tend to knock airliner prices into tail

---

[32] Hay and Kelley, "An Empirical Survey of Price Fixing Conspiracies," p. 26.

[33] Sonnenfeld and Lawrence, "Why Do Companies Succumb to Price Fixing?," pp. 148–149; R. E. Caves and M. E. Porter, "Market Structure, Oligopoly, and Stability of Market Shares," *Journal of Industrial Economics* (June 1978), pp. 289–313.

[34] During the late 1970s, members of the European Economic Community's steel cartel cheated by adding "bonus" tonnage to deliveries and by deliberately "delivering late," which "tardiness" then permitted them to pay buyers a fine, that is, discount. Kent Jones, "Forgetfulness of Things Past: Europe and the Steel Cartel," *The World Economy* (May 1979), p. 150.

[35] In the first case prosecuted under the Sherman Act, members of a coal cartel adopted a classification scheme to account for differences in the quality of coal. This "simplified coal pricing and rid the market of the quality heterogeneity that existed between the coal of different mines." J. J. Siegfried and M. Mahony, "The First Sherman Act Case: Jellico Mountain Coal, 1891," *Antitrust Bulletin* (Winter 1990), pp. 801–832.

spins. As S. L. Carroll observed, "If any collusion, market sharing or market splitting has occurred among the airframe companies, it has been well hidden indeed. . . . The lumpy and discrete nature of orders makes competitive concessions quite tempting."[36] Conversely, an even flow of *frequent* and *small-sized* sales is most accommodating to colluders.

Much the same could be said of opportunities for secret dealing. Where these opportunities are slight, agreements are easy to police and the incentive to double-cross is considerably reduced. Conversely, a prevalence of secrecy enables price discounting under the table, which improves the downside viability of the seductively elastic nonfollowship demand curve.

Rate of Growth and Elasticity of Demand. A rapid rate of growth in industry demand can upset the best laid plans for several reasons. Perhaps the most important is that the gains to be had from collusion then appear less attractive to potential participants. This may explain why cartels are often called children of depressions. Rapid growth may also confound policing and enforcement efforts. With new customers flocking to the market and old ones expanding their buying, it is difficult to measure market shares and to detect diversions of business that may be caused by double-crossing. Conversely, shares can be pinpointed and diversions due to price shading can be more easily discovered under stable conditions.

Elasticity of demand enters the picture for related reasons. As Hay and Kelley put it, "The more inelastic is industry demand, the greater are the potential rewards to the price fixers. Concomitantly the smaller will be the sacrifice in terms of capacity utilization."[37]

Production Costs. Finally, it should be obvious why production costs might influence collusion. Widely divergent costs across firms would breed divergent opinions concerning what price should prevail, threatening the success of negotiations. When discussing costs and cartels F. M. Scherer has also stressed the unsettling impact of uneven cost *changes* across firms: "The more rapidly producers' cost functions are altered through technological innovation, and the more unevenly these pricing action is." He cites an example drawn from an industry previously mentioned: "In the sanitary pottery fixtures industry, conflicts attendant to the introduction of tunnel kilns (replacing more costly beehive oven processes) were in part responsible for the failure of pro-

---

[36] Sidney L. Carroll, "The Market for Commercial Airliners" in *Regulating the Product Quality and Variety*, edited by R. Caves and M. Roberts (Cambridge, Mass.: Ballinger, 1975), pp. 150, 163. See also John Newhouse, *The Sporty Game* (New York: Alfred A. Knopf, 1982); *Business Week*, May 8, 1989, pp. 34–35; and *Fortune*, July 17, 1989, pp. 40–45. For an interesting contrast of lumpy and nonlumpy sales of baby formula, see *Business Week*, January 25, 1988, p. 38.

[37] Hay and Kelley, "An Empirical Survey of Price Fixing Conspiracies," p. 15.

ducers to eliminate widespread price-cutting despite repeated attempts to reach collusive agreements."[38]

The Importance of Each Factor. The relative importance of these numerous conditions is difficult to test empirically. Aside from the obvious problems of measuring them and uncovering observations of them (cartelization is after all secretive), their effects in real life are not nearly so neat and straightforward as our simple outline in Table 13–1 implies. The conditions may interact on behavior. Various combinations may be potent or weak. In short, the factors do not willingly submit themselves to systematic analysis. For example, Table 13–1 says that rapid technological change nourishes spirited competition. But, if most other factors favor tacit collusion, rapid technological change may merely force cartelization upon the industry, something which can hardly be considered spirited competition. For another example, Table 13–1 suggests that ten firms are too plentiful to permit effective tacit collusion. But no one would strain oneself imagining a ten-firm industry in which nearly all the other conditions point in the direction of tacit collusion — with the result that tacit collusion consequently prevails.

Empirical work is also hampered by the fact the cartels differ in *design.* Two industries might have virtually identical structural conditions. Yet one industry might be successfully cartelized and the other not, despite very serious attempts in the latter case to smother competition. A researcher observing the two industries might well conclude erroneously that some obscure and irrelevant structural difference caused the disparity. However, the true explanation might rest instead on the particular design of the successful cartel.[39] Its penalty system, policing technique, and allocation mechanism might be works of art, with unique and seemingly unimportant details that make them masterpieces (if that is not too noble a word).

Notwithstanding the difficulties, there are many case studies that provide crude evidenciary support for the assertions of Table 13–1.[40] Further support may be found in a statistical analysis of the 606 cases of illegal price fixing mentioned earler.[41]

---

[38] F. M. Scherer, *Industrial Market Structure and Economic Preformance* (Chicago: Rand McNally, 1970), p. 192.

[39] Jones, "Forgetfulness of Things Past," gives a good example.

[40] F. Voight, "German Experience with Cartels," Stocking and Watkins, *Monopoly and Free Enterprise;* Siegfried and Mahony, "The First Sherman Act Case"; H. C. Passer, *The Electrical Manufacturers: 1875–1900* (Cambridge, Mass.: Harvard University Press, 1953); G. B. Richardson, "The Pricing of Heavy Electrical Equipment: Competition or Agreement?" *Bulletin of the Oxford University Institute of Economics and Statistics* (1966), pp. 73–92; S. M. Loescher, *Imperfect Collusion in the Cement Industry* (Cambridge, Mass.: Harvard University Press, 1959); Jones, "Forgetfulness of Things Past"; Sonnenfeld and Lawrence, "Why Do Companies Succumb to Price Fixing?"

[41] Fraas and Greer, "Market Structure and Price Collusion."

D. Summary

In short, evidence indicates that the structural conditions most favorable to tacit cooperation are a relatively small number of rival firms in a market setting relatively free of complications. Moreover, a variety of regimental or disciplinary devices facilitates tacit or explicit collusion under more adverse structural conditions. To state these results somewhat differently: Evidence suggests that, as the number of firms in the market or the complexity of structural conditions increases, conspirators must resort to arrangements of increasingly elaborate design or efficiency to achieve their joint profit-maximizing objectives. Indeed, this finding probably explains why many elaborately formal cartels are eventually undermined by double-crossing, bickering, and dissolution. Elaborate cartels probably arise most often where structural conditions are more favorable to *competition* than to collusion. However, to conclude from this that cartels are nearly always short-lived and feeble would be wrong. In the region of tradeoff between tacit and express collusion, at least, cartels probably yield stable and substantial gains for their organizers (as well as losses for their customers).

III. THE ELECTRICAL EQUIPMENT CASES[42]

The electric equipment cases are to American price fixing what Watergate is to American political corruption. The collusive activity began some time in the 1920s or 1930s (it was so long ago no one seems to know exactly when). At first it was a rather casual adjunct to the industry's trade association activities, involving just a few products. By the 1950s, however, conspiracy had spread to every corner of the trade. Table 13–2 gives some idea of the vast scope of the price fixing and of the structure of the markets involved. Roughly $7 billion of business was involved. The products ranged from $2 insulators to multimillion-dollar turbine generators. The average number of firms participating in each market was 6.6. Several of the larger participants—such as General Electric, Westinghouse, Allis Chalmers, McGraw-Edison, and I-T-E Circuit Breaker—operated and conspired in many of the markets. Smaller firms—like Moloney Electric and Wagner—were more specialized. In all, 29 firms and 44 individuals were indicted during 1960 for criminal conspiracies in 20 separate product lines.

Table 13–2 gives the impression that high concentration and a paucity of firms might have permitted tacit collusion in four or five of these

[42] This section draws from R. G. M. Sultan, *Pricing in the Electrical Oligopoly*, Vol. 1 (Cambridge, Mass.: Harvard University Press, 1974); C. C. Walton and F. W. Cleveland, Jr., *Corporations on Trial: The Electric Cases* (Belmont, Calif.: Wadsworth, 1964); and R. A. Smith, *Corporations in Crisis* (Garden City, N.Y.: Anchor Books, 1966), Chapters 5 and 6.

TABLE 13–2. Extent and Coverage of the Electrical Equipment Price Fixing Conspiracies

Product	Annual (1959) Dollar Sales ($ millions)	Number of Firms Indicted	Share of Market (%)
Turbine generators	$400*	3 (6)*	95 (100)
Industrial control equipment	262*	9*	75*
Power transformers	210	6	100
Power switchgear assemblies	125	5 (8)*	100
Circuit breakers	75	5	100
Power switching equipment	35*	8 (15)*	90–95*
Condensers	32	7	75–85
Distribution transformers	220	8	96
Low-voltage distribution equipment	200*	6 (10)*	95*
Meters	71	3	100
Insulators	28	8	100
Power capacitors	24	6	100
Instrumental transformers	16*	3 (4)*	95*
Network transformers	15	6	90
Low-voltage power circuit breakers	9	3 (5)*	100
Isolated phase bus	7.6	4	100
Navy and marine switchgear	7	3	80
Open-fuse cutouts	6	8	75
Bushings	6	4	100
Lightning arresters	16	7	100

* Includes companies named as co-conspirators but not indicted.

Source: Adapted from *Corporations on Trial: The Electric Cases*, by Clarence C. Walton and Frederick W. Cleveland, Jr., copyright 1964 by Wadsworth Company, Inc., Belmont, California 94002. Reprinted by permission of the publisher.

markets. But conditions not revealed in the table provided substantial competitive pull, thereby abetting explicit collusion. First, many of these products were not standardized but custom made and differentiable. Various collusive steps were taken to standardize product quality, especially in the early years. Second, many items of equipment were sold in big chunks, which amplified the incentive to cut prices to gain business. Even within given product lines, large orders received larger discounts off "book" price than small orders. A third factor was the volatility of the business cycle in the electrical apparatus field. These goods are durable capital equipment and experience fluctuations in demand far beyond those encountered by most other industries. Slack demand seems to have caused much price cutting, even when the conspiracies were in high gear. Finally, technological change was fairly brisk during the decades involved.

Collusive procedures and experiences varied from product to product, from sealed-bid sales to off-the-shelf transactions, and from higher to lower levels of management. One common thread, however, was the atmosphere of skullduggery surrounding all the conspiracies. Code names, pay-phone communications, clandestine meetings in out-of-the-way places, faked expense account records, and secret market allocations all entered the plot. Perhaps the most sensational technique devised was the "phase of the moon" system developed for sealed-bid switchgear sales:

> This system was intended to fix automatically the price each conspirator would quote, with a rotation of the low price among competitors to create the illusion of random competition. The contemplated range of bid prices was modest. According to the "moon sheet," which was in effect from December 5, 1958 through April 10, 1959, position would be rotated among the five major competitors every two weeks.[43]

Disclosure of the system inspired some jokester in General Electric to rewrite the words to the then popular song "Moonglow." Sung to the same tune, the first verse went like this: "It must have been Moonglow/ Way up in the blue/It must have been Moonglow/That brought that bid to you."[44]

Despite all the shenanigans, it is not clear that the conspirators were able to raise or stabilize prices appreciably in all product lines. Double-crossing was fairly commonplace. A "white sale" drove prices down to 60% of book in 1955. Many participants have made self-serving claims that their efforts failed, and it can be argued that supply and demand remained important determinants of price level.[45] On the other hand, a federal trial judge was persuaded by the evidence that prices of turbine generators would have been 21% lower were it not for the conspiracy. In addition, solid evidence indicates a substantial price impact in circuit breakers and insulators plus some indirect overall effect via stabilization of market shares.[46] In any event, economic consequences were relevant only to the treble damage suits, which yielded $400 million or thereabouts. The government's criminal suits were settled under the per se

---

[43] Sultan, *Pricing in the Electrical Oligopoly*, p. 39.
[44] J. G. Fuller, *The Gentlemen Conspirators* (New York: Grove Press, 1962), p. 66.
[45] Sultan is the industry's best defender, *Pricing in the Electrical Oligopoly*.
[46] Ibid., pp. 85, 210, 273: David F. Lean, Jonathan D. Ogur, and Robert P. Rogers, *Competition and Collusion in Electrical Equipment Markets: An Economic Assessment* (Federal Trade Commission Staff Report, July 1982); and Bruce T. Allen, "More on the Turbine Market," *Industrial Organization Review*, Vol. 7, (1979), pp. 61–72.

rule, with seven executives serving brief stints in the slammer and with fines totaling $1,954,000, the bulk of which was paid by the companies.[47]

IV. THE OIL INDUSTRY AND OPEC[48]

A. Introduction

Of the oil industry's several sectors, crude extraction (hereafter called "crude") is the most interesting to us here. Both in the United States and abroad that sector has spawned some rather remarkable cartels or "near" cartels. At the same time competition has not been altogether absent. For most of its history, the crude industry seems to have been caught in the region of trade-off between cartelization and competition. Calouste Gulbenkian, a pioneer of Iraqi oil development, may have said it best: "Oilmen are like cats; you can never tell from the sound of them whether they are fighting or making love."

This turbulent blend should lead anyone who has followed the discussion this far to anticipate at least two aspects of the oil story: (1) many oil cartels have been less than love-ins, and (2) the most enduring and significant cartels have been encouraged, supported, and run by government agencies (exempted thereby, or beyond the reach of the Sherman Act). The crude industry's habit of falling under collectivized or centralized control — either private or official — has led some observers to argue that "socially acceptable operation of the industry *necessarily requires* either government regulation of output or the domination of the industry by firms large enough to exercise control over total output and to keep competition, especially price competition, within very narrow limits."[49]

---

[47] An electrical equipment cartel currently operates outside the reach of U.S. law in international markets. For details see Barbara Epstein and Richard Newfarmer, *International Electrical Association: A Continuing Cartel*, Report, U.S. House of Representatives, Committee on Interstate and Foreign Commerce (June 1980).

[48] Main sources for this section are M. G. de Chazeau and A. E. Kahn, *Integration and Competition in the Petroleum Industry* (New Haven, Conn.: Yale University Press, 1959); M. A. Adelman, *The World Petroleum Market* (Baltimore: Johns Hopkins University Press, 1972); J. M. Blair, *The Control of Oil* (New York: Pantheon Books, 1976); N. H. Jacoby, *Multinational Oil* (New York: Macmillan, 1974); R. Engler, *The Brotherhood of Oil* (Chicago: University of Chicago Press, 1977); Anthony Sampson, *The Seven Sisters* (New York: Viking Press, 1975); U.S. Senate Subcommittee on Multinational Corporations of the Committee on Foreign Relations, *Report on Multinational Oil Corporations and U.S. Foreign Policy* (Washington, D.C.: U.S. Government Printing Office, 1975); U.S. Senate Subcommittee on Antitrust and Monopoly of the Committee on the Judiciary, *Hearings on Government Intervention in the Market Mechanism:* Petroleum, parts 1–5, 91st Cong., 1st and 2nd Sess. (1969, 1970); E. T. Penrose, *The Large International Firm in Developing Countries* (Cambridge, Mass.: The MIT Press, 1968); S. L. McDonald, *Petroleum Conservation in the United States* (Baltimore: Johns Hopkins University Press, 1971); James M. Griffin and D. J. Teece, *OPEC Behavior and World Oil Prices* (London: Allen & Unwin, 1982); and Dermot Gately, "OPEC and the World Oil Market," *Journal of Economic Literature* (September, 1984), pp. 1100–1114.

[49] Penrose, *The Large International Firm in Developing Countries*, p. 165.

Not all experts hold this view; many refute it. Although we cannot pursue the debate here, there seems to be enough truth to the instability argument to give industry leaders and governments an excuse to play the part of "eveners, adjusters, and organizers." (Of course governments have also been spurred to action by the strategic military and economic importance of oil.) Our discussion of these cartelization efforts is split between the domestic U.S. and foreign markets.

B. U. S. Domestic Crude Oil

Figure 13–3 reveals that prior to 1934 the price of domestic crude oil was highly unstable. The solid line shows peaks and valleys in price level of alpine proportions in those years. Moreover, the high frequency of change — as indicated by the dashed line — was equally unsettling. The data traced there actually understate the true volatility because they refer to a representative *posted* price, not to actual *transaction* prices, which fluctuated more wildly. For example, discovery of the immense East Texas Field in 1930 and the country's simultaneous slide into depression combined to press down the posted price shown in Figure 13–3 to 61 cents a barrel in 1933, but some transaction prices fell to the amazingly low figure of 10 cents a barrel. This instability may be attributed to a "law of capture" as well as to inelasticities and shifts of supply and demand. Under the "law of capture" crude oil belonged to whomever got it out first. Couple this law with (1) fragmented property ownership over a given oil reservoir, (2) the fluid nature of the stuff, plus (3) generous amounts of greed, and you have a mad rush to drain the reservoir. The goal of each owner was simply (and crudely): "get it out while the getting's good." The results were

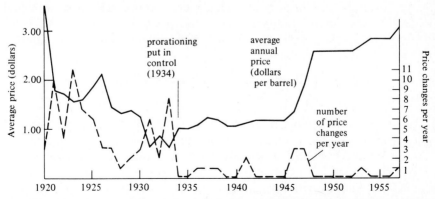

FIGURE 13–3. Price levels and changes for U.S. crude oil, Oklahoma 36° gravity. Source: M. G. de Chazeau and A. E. Kahn, *Integration and Competition in the Petroleum Industry* (New Haven, Conn.: Yale University Press, 1959), pp. 138, 148–149.

- Appalling *physical waste* because of reckless damage of the reservoir's natural drive pressures and loss of oil to evaporation in makeshift open-air storage vats.

- Enormous *"economic waste"* because of extraction and consumption of crude oil when its value was low and excessive investment in drilling.

- Added *instability* of prices and producer incomes.

Broad-based private cartelization was impossible, given the thousands of producers. Hence, during the depths of greatest difficulty in the early 1930s, remedial steps were taken by state and federal authorities that eventually led to a tablelike structure of price support resting on four legs: (1) demand prorationing, (2) the Connally "Hot" Oil Act, (3) the Interstate Oil Compact, and (4) import quotas.

State Controls. **Demand prorationing** was a system of flexible production control first instituted by state authorities in Oklahoma and Texas, later emulated in Louisiana, Kansas, and New Mexico (thus including the states most bountifully blessed with oil). Its effects on prices may be seen in Figure 13–3, where after 1934 prices are much less volatile than before. Moreover, those changes that do occur thereafter are almost always increases.

Operation of the system is illustrated in Figure 13–4. In essence, supply was restricted or expanded to whatever level was necessary for price to be at or above the "administered price" level. The supply curve looked like an L lying down. This configuration means that supply was perfectly price elastic up to full capacity use (at the corner of the L). Thereafter, the supply curve that prevailed in the absence of prorationing took over. Not all wells were subject to regulation, the main exemptions being "discovery" wells and inefficient "strippers," the latter being wells physically incapable of producing more than a few barrels a day. Moreover, state authorities had no control over imports into the United States. Hence, exempt and import supplies were subtracted from projected demand before determining the output allowed from the regulated wells. In short, the fraction of allowed capacity utilization was reckoned monthly by the following formula:

$$\frac{\text{fraction of capacity utilization for regulated wells}}{} = \frac{\text{demand} - (\text{exempts} + \text{imports})}{\text{total capacity of regulated wells}}$$

Allowable utilization therefore decreased with decreased demand or increased imports, exempt capacity, and total regulated capacity. In Figure 13–4 the fraction for "low demand" is about 0.7, whereas that for "high demand" is 1.0. Competitive drilling was limited indirectly through regulations defining what constituted "total capacity" for each producer. These definitions embodied well spacing formulas, which for many years were faulty in not eliminating law-of-capture competitive drilling completely.

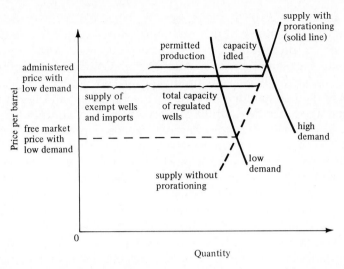

FIGURE 13–4. Restriction of supply under demand prorating, lifting prices to "administered level" above free-market level.

Federal Controls. As for the three other legs of price support, all were federal measures. The Connally "Hot" Oil Act of 1935 prohibited the interstate shipment of crude oil (or products refined from crude oil) produced in excess of the state allowables. Without this law, state officials doing the prorationing were handicapped. Cheating was easy. The year 1935 also saw passage of the Interstate Oil Compact Commission Act, providing a forum for the prorationing agencies of producing states. There they could collude and coordinate their efforts lest they compete with each other at the state level for ever larger shares of national output. Finally, mandatory import quotas came much later, beginning in 1959.

During the early years of prorationing, restrictions on imports were not needed. The United States dominated world oil in those days, being the richest in then known reserves, the most productive, and the largest exporter. As late as 1949 the United States accounted for 36% of the world's reserves and 55% of its production. Until World War II, moreover, all international shipments of crude were priced according to a "Houston-plus" single basing-point system. Thereafter, U.S. fortunes began three decades of decline. Development of superabundant and cheap mideastern supplies threatened the U.S. industry. A new basing point was established in the Persian Gulf, and U.S. prices rose relative to those of the new base. As this price differential widened, U.S. imports multiplied several times over, gushing in at a rate of 18.3% of total U.S. crude consumption by 1958, the year before mandatory quotas.

The consequences for U.S. production were enormous. In that year capacity utilization of Texas's regulated wells was only 33%, down from

100% utilization in 1948. Imports were not the sole cause of this, however. Ample exemptions from prorationing in states with prorationing, an absence of prorationing in less nicely endowed and more costly crude-producing states (such as Mississippi, Colorado, Wyoming, and Montana, which in 1958 were producing at 86% to 100% of capacity), some unchecked competitive drilling in several states, and tax incentives that encouraged needless drilling everywhere also contributed to the problem. These several factors raised U.S. costs, precluding a painless price cut to meet the foreign competition.

Bloated by high costs (which pinched consumers $2.15 billion a year) but flush with political clout (owing to campaign contributions and bribes as well as popular votes), the industry escaped threat when the federal government set quotas to limit imports (quotas of sufficient magnitude that they cost consumers an additional $7–$8 billion a year). "National defense" was proclaimed the reason. The regrettable influence of factors other than imports may be seen by the fact that later, in 1964, after the quota program was in full swing, regulated wells in Texas were held to only 28% of their full capacity. Those in Louisiana and Oklahoma were also working only 32% and 28% of the time.

Prorationing allowables are now pegged at 100%, and they have been since 1972. Import quotas have been discontinued since 1973. The Connally "Hot" Oil Act and Interstate Compact Commission Act are still on the books but superfluous. The first sign of change occurred without popular notice in 1969; ominously, U.S. productive capacity began to decline. At current rates of consumption the United States will probably run very short of crude petroleum within 20 years.

C. The International Crude Oil Market

Prior to about 1950 the foreign sector was rife with the cartel handiwork of the major companies, the eldest of the Seven Sisters in particular. Between 1950 and 1970 the power of the Seven Sisters diminished. And finally, since 1970, OPEC, a cartel comprised of the *governments* of 13 of the world's leading crude exporting countries, has taken command.

Before 1950. The **Seven Sisters** were Exxon, BP (British Petroleum), Shell, Gulf, Texaco, Socal (Standard of California), and Mobil. They came by their collective name because, like mortal sisters, they fought and competed with each other while preserving a family affinity.[50]

The Seven Sisters stood virtually (but not virtuously) alone in foreign trade prior to 1950. They controlled crude prices and output in the producing countries through cartel arrangements among themselves and by concession agreements with foreign producing country governments. Under "concessions" these governments ceded to the oil companies

---

[50] Sampson, *The Seven Sisters*, p. 59.

authority to engage in the exploration and exploitation of certain territories, which in the early days amounted to entire countries. In exchange, the companies paid royalties and taxes on oil extracted.

We shall skip over the "Red Line" and "As Is" agreements, two cartels of the pre-World War II era. Instead, we shall focus on the post-war origins of Aramco, which brought Socal, Texaco, Exxon, and Mobil together in what eventually proved to be the richest concession of all—Saudi Arabia. Strictly speaking Aramco was a joint venture, not a cartel, but it neatly illustrates the competitive-cooperative behavior of the Sisters.

Here is the story.[51] As of 1947 the Saudi Arabian concession was entirely in the hands of Socal and Texaco, two newcomers to the international scene of the times, who had developed it from scratch beginning in 1936. They operated Aramco through a joint venture called "Caltex." More important, their exclusive ownership of those enormous oil reserves made the industry more competitive by threatening the market power of the then more well-established international majors—Exxon, Mobil, and BP:

> By 1947, Caltex had tripled its market share both East and West of Suez. With 33 cents a barrel production costs, Caltex could market Arabian crude for as little as 90 cents a barrel while the older international majors were selling for $1.30 and up. . . . Exxon and Mobil rightly concluded that their longterm market prospects in Europe were unfavorable if they failed to get a share of the vast low-cost reserves of [Aramco].

Exxon and Mobil launched a two-part plan: (1) buy into Caltex's Aramco, and (2) once in, secure a 50% price increase for Aramco's crude. Part one went through first, Exxon buying 30% and Mobil buying 10% leaving Caltex 60%. When drawing up the papers, Exxon and Mobil were able to insert technical language, which went unnoticed by Caltex, to facilitate the price increase part of their plan. Hence, "No sooner had the Aramco merger contracts been signed than a major fight erupted between Caltex and Exxon/Mobil over the price of Arabian Oil". The fight was bitter. Caltex felt cheated. But Exxon and Mobil pressed hard. A Mobil representative even turned sarcastic. "I hope and trust," he said, "our Texas friends will . . . turn to Webster's and look up the definition of 'partnership.' I am quite sure it does not define it as 'a combination of people welshing on their original agreement because it temporarily does not suit their own self-interest." In the end Exxon and Mobil won. Aramco's price jumped 40% to $1.43.

From 1950 to 1973. Table 13–3 outlines the shifting balance of power from 1950 to 1973, a period of "recognized interdependence" rather than cartelization. As of 1950, OPEC had not yet been formed. The Seven Sisters dominated with 88% of all foreign production and a seamless web

---

[51] Distilled from *Report on Multinational Oil Corporations*, Chapters II and IV.

TABLE 13-3.   Outline of the Shift of Power from the Seven Sisters to OPEC, 1950-1973

Index of Power	Year			
	1950	1960	1970	1972/3
A. Power of the Seven Sisters				
1. Market share abroad (%)	88	72	71	71
2. Strength of collusive agreements	Joint ventures	Independents arrive	Independents a problem	Disarray
3. U.S. production as percent of world (%)	54	36	23	21
4. Spare capacity (U.S. imports percent of consumption) (%)	9	13	23	36
B. Power of OPEC				
1. "Free" world production (%)	(No OPEC)	45	61	65
2. Knowledge	—	Poor	Good	Very good
3. Unity of interest	—	Weak	Moderate	Strong

of joint ventures (such as Aramco) binding them together. However, as the first two lines of Table 13-3 indicate, their power thereafter declined. Among the many "independent" companies entering the foreign market during the 1950s and 1960s were ARCO, Citgo, Occidental, Phillips, Marathon, and Sun.

The entry of the independents plus several other developments combined to lower transactions prices first, then posted prices. By 1959, some discounts off the posted price of $2.08 ran as high as 40 cents. To the oil companies the "posted" price was essentially fictional. However, the posted price was not fictional to oil-producing country governments, for their revenues were keyed to that price. Hence, when the majors unilaterally reduced posted prices in 1959 and 1960 to better reflect transactions prices, Saudi Arabia, Iran, Iraq, Kuwait, and Venezuela threw tantrums. More important, they formed OPEC to make their views felt and protect their interests.

Turning to the bottom half of Table 13-3, we see that at first, in 1960, OPEC was not much to look at. Accounting for less than half of "free" world production, OPEC lacked full knowledge of the trade, solidarity, and boldness. However, with time, and with the addition of Indonesia, Nigeria, Libya, Algeria, Qatar, United Arab Emirates, Gabon, and Ecuador to its membership, OPEC grew powerful in measurable and unmeasurable ways. Its shares of world production and exports burgeoned, while the world's dependency on oil reached addictive dimensions.

In such intangibles as knowledge and solidarity, changes occurred that can only be touched upon here. For example, one of OPEC's first acts was to commission an independent research study of the profits the Sisters were earning on their investments in the Middle East and Venezuela. They found that "between 1956 and 1960, the rate of return on net assets was 71 percent in Iran, 62 percent in Iraq, 14 percent in Qatar, 61 percent in Saudi Arabia, and 20 percent in Venezuela."[52] (These amazing profits are partly explained by the fact that unit costs amounted to no more than about 25 cents a barrel in the Middle East.)

The eagerness of newly entering independents to bid high for concessions taught other lessons. For example, oil reserves were more rapidly developed by granting a number of concessions instead of just one and by encouraging independent entry. Still other lessons were learned when reports of the Sister's pre-1950 cartel activities were made public. As one Kuwaiti said: "OPEC couldn't have happened without the oil cartel. We just took a leaf from the oil campanies' book. The victim had learned the lesson."[53] Capping these lessons, OPEC members expanded their experience by gaining increased control of their concessions.

Things came to a head in October 1973. U.S. demand had far outstripped its domestic supplies, forcing abandonment of import quotas and 100% capacity use in prorationing states. Moreover, European consumption reached an all-time high. In fact, for the first time in more than 14 years the transactions price of oil rose *above* the posted price, which was $3.01 a barrel. In sum, events could not have put OPEC in a more powerful position. Then war broke out between Israel and the Arabs. A partial oil embargo followed, lifting the auction prices of crude oil as high as $17 a barrel, way above the $3 posted price. With a hop and a skip, OPEC lifted the posted price. Hopping first to $5.11, then skipping to $11.65 within a few months time, OPEC shocked the United States and the world. (See Figure 13–5.)

OPEC Since 1973. For the rest of the 1970s OPEC managed things in an orderly fashion. As shown in Figure 13–5, the cartel's price continued to rise by small steps—5% here, 10% there. Output varied to support price. And just as Texas carried the main burden of supply control in the United States, Saudi Arabia served as the main "evener and adjuster" in OPEC. Its role was based on its vast oil reserves. Its philosophy was explained by its oil minister, Sheik Zaki Yamani: "Usually any cartel will break up, because the stronger members will not hold up the market to protect the weaker members. But with OPEC, the strong members do not have an interest to lower the price and sell more."[54] The cartel's success during this period yielded hundreds of billions of dollars in profits, some

---

[52] Mana Saeed Al-Otaiba, *OPEC and the Petroleum Industry* (New York: John Wiley, 1975), p. 109.
[53] Sampson, *The Seven Sisters*, p. 162.
[54] Ibid., p. 295. For further details on OPEC at this time, see *OPEC: Twenty Years and*

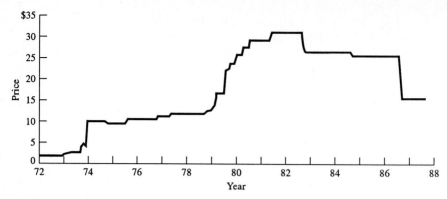

FIGURE 13–5. Official (posted) price of Saudi Arabian light (34°) crude oil, 1972–1988. Source: *Basic Petroleum Data Book*, Vol. VIII, no. 1 (January 1988), Section VI, Table 11; *Petroleum Economist*, various issues.

of which was spent by OPEC countries to nationalize the oil assets they contained, thereby ending the concessions of the oil companies.

Thereafter, however, the cartel fell into disarray, partly because of revolution in Iran and war between Iraq and Iran. Prices doubled during 1979, but not uniformly, with the result that for a while member prices ranged from over $35 per barrel to under $30. Order was restored temporarily with posted prices eventually clustering around $34 a barrel in 1981. The order was only temporary, however, because 1979's price escalations aggravated two forces that had been building for some time:

- First, the output of *non*-OPEC oil burgeoned as the high prices fostered discovery and development. The new oil came from Mexico, the North Sea, Egypt, and elsewhere.

- Second, the world's demand for oil plummeted as conservation efforts took hold and the world fell into a deep recession. Oil consumption of western countries dropped 10% between 1980 and 1985.

With worldwide demand contracting and non-OPEC supply expanding, there was only one way that OPEC could continue to hold price above $30 a barrel. OPEC cut output drastically, from 31.0 million barrels a day in 1979 to 16.6 million barrels a day in 1985. All OPEC members contributed cutbacks, but Saudi Arabia's contribution was especially noteworthy — an enormous drop in production of 65% between 1980 and 1985. Hence, Figure 13–6 shows OPEC's share of world oil output falling from about 50% in 1979 to little more than 30% in 1985, with non-OPEC producers outside the United States and communist countries being the biggest beneficiaries.

Beyond, edited by Ragaei El Mallakh (Boulder, Colo.: Westview Press, 1982); and Ian Seymour, *OPEC Instrument of Change* (New York: St. Martins, 1981).

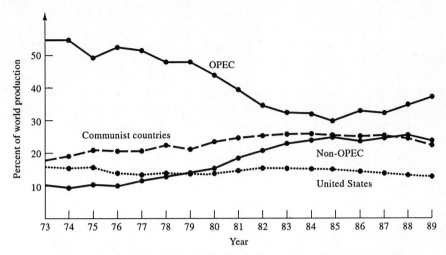

FIGURE 13–6. Shares of total world oil output by groups, 1973–1989.

These events imitated oil prorationing in the United States during 1930–1970. Figure 13–4 illustrates OPEC's attempt to hold price up if non-OPEC supply is represented by the "supply of exempt wells and imports" and OPEC's potential supply is represented by the "total capacity of regulated wells." The enormous drop in OPEC output was "capacity idled," as demand fell to "low" levels with recession plus elevated prices and as non-OPEC supplies expanded. Figure 13–4 indicates that the "free-market price" would have been greatly below the "administered price" at OPEC. Moreover, the distribution of output between low-cost and high-cost producers was like that under U.S. prorationing. Recall that low-cost, prorationed Texas wells were operating at only 30% of their capacity in the late 1950s and early 1960s while high-cost wells in non-prorationing states like Wyoming and Montana were at 100% of capacity. By the mid-1980s Saudi Arabia, whose production costs were far below $1 a barrel at the time, was operating at one-third its capacity while high-cost non-OPEC producers, like Norway, Britain, and the United States were producing every barrel they could at 100% capacity.

By 1985 OPEC lost patience with non-OPEC suppliers because they did not respond to OPEC's pleas for production restraint. Among OPEC members Saudi Arabia became especially irate, as its yearly oil revenues plummeted from $113 billion in 1981 to $34 billion in 1985.[55] Saudi Arabia was disappointed in the cheating of some OPEC members as well as the aggressiveness of non-OPEC producers. No longer was Saudi Arabia saying that the "strong would support the weak." They began shouting,

[55] *The Wall Street Journal*, April 8, 1986, p. 34.

"We intend to preserve our share in the market and protect it."[56] Hence, Saudi Arabia led OPEC in a massive expansion of output. Between August 1985 and August 1986 Saudi Arabian output more than doubled and other OPEC output rose 20%. By early 1986 transaction prices on oil collapsed to as low as $7 a barrel! *In short, prices collapsed for two simple reasons. First at $35 a barrel worldwide capacity to produce oil exceeded worldwide demand by at least 25%. Second, one group of producers (the OPEC countries) was no longer willing to give its share of a shrinking market to another group (the non-OPEC countries).*[57]

The price war ended almost as quickly as it began. In August 1986, OPEC members hammered together a new set of production quotas that, if honored, would reduce OPEC output over 20% below pre-war output levels.[58] Moreover, shortly thereafter the Soviet Union, Mexico, Norway, Brunei, Malaysia, and other non-OPEC producers announced that they would either cut their oil exports or make some other show of support.[59] Figures 13–5 and 13–6 indicate what happened next. First, transactions prices tended to level out at posted levels of about $18 a barrel. Second, OPEC's world market share recovered somewhat while that of non-OPEC producers stopped climbing at about 25%. The curtailment of non-OPEC supplies was not achieved because non-OPEC producers turned especially cooperative, although in 1989 they were holding meetings and pledging restraint.[60] Rather, their output has been discouraged by the lower $18 price compared to the earlier $34 price. At $18 a barrel many of the world's most costly wells were closed. Indeed, when adjusted for inflation, the $18 price in real terms was only slightly greater than prices in 1972 before OPEC's first big jolts.

As this is written (in late 1990) turmoil prevails because of the war with Iraq. Oil prices have gyrated up and down. Their future is uncertain. Still, we may conclude that those who have argued that OPEC has been irrelevant or ineffectual have been proven wrong. Two key indicators of the cartel's impact have been the industry's chronic excess capacity and a marginal cost of OPEC production that lies far below price.[61]

---

[56] *The Wall Street Journal*, December 9, 1985, p. 3.

[57] Daniel Yergin, "A Good Sweating," *The New Republic*, February 17, 1986, pp. 8–10; and Dermot Gately, "Lessons from the 1986 Oil Price Collapse," *Brookings Papers on Economic Activity*, No. 2 (1986), pp. 237–268.

[58] *The Wall Street Journal*, August 6, 1986, p. 1.

[59] *The Wall Street Journal*, September 2, 1986, p. 2

[60] *The Wall Street Journal*, February 22, 1989, p. A3.

[61] For evidence of cartel impact, see James M. Griffin, "OPEC Behavior: A Test of Alternative Hypotheses," *American Economic Review* (December 1985), pp. 954–963; and M. A. Adelman, "Scarcity and World Oil Prices," *Review of Economics and Statistics* (August 1986), pp. 387–397. Assertions by MacAvoy and a few others that the market is competitive are thus wrong. Paul W. MacAvoy, *Crude Oil Prices: As Determined by OPEC and Market Fundamentals* (Cambridge, Mass.: Ballinger, 1982).

SUMMARY

When successful, cartels stifle competition. They restrict and regulate output, thereby raising and stabilizing price. U. S. antitrust law generally forbids such "restraints of trade" on a per se basis. Violators face civil or criminal prosecution (or both), regardless of the reasonableness of their intentions or the success of their efforts. Given a per se rule, the key question then becomes: What constitutes a "contract, combination . . . or conspiracy, in restraint of trade," as specified by Section 1 of the Sherman Act? Certain fairly obvious activities clearly come within reach of these words, activities such as market allocations, explicit price fixing, and single sales agencies. In addition, prosecutors have tracked down, and courts have found guilty, some more devious undertakings, including concerted purchases of "distressed" surpluses and certain trade association information schemes. Plain and simple "conscious parallelism" lies beyond the clutches of the law. But "conscious parallelism" has been found in violation when coupled with either (1) additional circumstantial evidence of conspiracy (for example, basing-point pricing) or (2) concerted activities of an exclusionary or predatory nature.

Public records of prosecuted conspiracies and other evidence enable study of the incidence and endurance of private cartels. Conceptually, the ground most fertile for cartelization lies between the spacious acreage where competition thrives and the narrow plots where tacit collusion grows. Thus private cartelization requires that the number of firms in the market be few, but not "too" few. Likewise, concentration must be high but not "too" high. And so on. Other conditions favorable to private collusion, either tacit or explicit, comprise a standardized product, slow growth, slow technological change, smoothly flowing sales, little opportunity for secret deals, low elasticity of demand, and uniform production costs among competitors. Of course cartels can be established by the government even in market environments harsh on private cartelization.

Our case studies of electrical equipment and crude oil illustrate these points. Scarcity of firms and high concentration in some sectors of the former industry might have permitted tacit collusion were it not for large and "lumpy" sales, some product differentiation, and fairly rapid technological change. Confronted with these impediments to tacit collusion, formal cartelization seemed the only means of securing stability and better profits. In the case of crude oil, the domestic and foreign industries present somewhat different pictures. Stateside, a diffuse market structure and an unsteady record of price and output led to a form of government cartelization that was particularly important from 1933 to 1973. Dwindling domestic supplies and unquenchable demand have since set the control machinery on "idle." Abroad, the Seven Sisters alternated between cartelization and competition, the former predominating prior to 1950, the latter breaking through more and more regularly with the entry of vigorous independents between 1950 and 1973. Since 1973, the Organization of Petroleum Exporting Countries, or OPEC, has established itself as the greatest and wealthiest cartel of all time. Ever-present undercurrents of competition may eventually sink OPEC, but for now it is only floundering.

14

Price and Production Strategy in the Long Run: Theory and Evidence

It was always our idea to carry on the business in such a manner that the inducement (to outsiders) to go into the aluminum business would not be inordinately great.
—A. V. DAVIS, CEO of Alcoa when it was a monopoly

Like the anatomy of an insect, our prior discussion of short-run price and output behavior can be reduced to three segments:

1. *Objectives* (stability and avoidance of falling profits)
2. *Conditions* affecting achievement of these objectives (number of firms, concentration, lumpiness of sales, and so on)
3. *Mechanisms* used (cartelization, price leadership, and so on)

The issues in this chapter's long-run analysis may be similarly seg-mented. Regarding firm *objectives,* long-run profit maximization heads the list. Other objectives — such as long-run supply control or market share maintenance — can be considered translations of this main objec-tive. *Conditions* affecting the achievement of long-run profits include many factors from our short-run analysis, namely, the number of firms, concentration, product differentiation, and technological change. But two additional conditions distinguish long-run analysis — the condition of entry and long-run price elasticity of demand. Finally, we may list *mechanisms* in order of their treatment hereafter:

1. Entry limit pricing
2. Dynamic pricing
3. Price discrimination
4. Predatory pricing

These items deserve special notice not only because they have long-run use in exploiting a given degree of market power but because they may affect market power itself. That is, they may influence the life and death of rivals as well as observed prices, outputs, and profits. We therefore acknowledge that structure-to-conduct is not the only possible direction of causal flow. Conduct may determine structure as well, providing a feedback effect. Still another way of contrasting the present long-run and the more limited short-run contexts involves the scope of recognized interdependence. In the short run, recognized interdependence extends only to *existing* rivals. In the long run, recognized interdependence ex-tends also to *potentials* — the potential entry of a new rival or the poten-tial demise of an old rival. To a large degree, short-run pricing is *in-clusionary* (as in a cartel) while long-run pricing is *exclusionary* (in an attempt to deter entry, for instance). This being the case, strategic be-havior is an important part of our discussion.

I. ENTRY LIMIT PRICING

A. The Theory of Entry Limit Pricing

Barriers to entry are crucial to any discussion of long-run price strategy, for without them excessive prices and profits could not endure. The theory of "limit pricing" reflects this nicely: sellers in concentrated mar-kets will set prices high enough to make excess profits but not so high as to attract new entry. Three assumptions underlie the theory:[1]

[1] D. K. Osborne, "On the Rationality of Limit Pricing," *Journal of Industrial Economics* (September 1973), pp. 71–80; J. S. Bain, *Barriers to New Competition* (Cambridge, Mass.: Harvard University Press, 1956); P. Sylos-Labini, *Oligopoly and Technical Progress* (Cam-

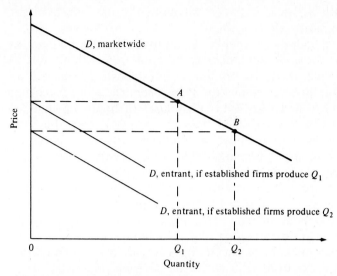

FIGURE 14–1. Derivation of postentry demand facing a potential entrant.

1. Established sellers and potential entrants seek maximum profits over the long run.
2. Established sellers think potential entrants will expect them to maintain their outputs in the event of new entry, letting price fall with the entrant's added output.
3. Established sellers have no difficulty colluding to determine and set the entry-limiting price.

The first postulate explicitly recognizes that anticipated profitability guides both classes of decision makers — entrants and established firms. Potential entrants calculate prospective profits from expected postentry demand and cost conditions. In turn, the entrant's postentry demand and cost conditions depend on the postentry behavior of established sellers. The dependency is most readily seen with respect to postentry demand. In essence, the more the established firms produce after the new firm's entry, the lower the entrant's demand will be at any given price. Figure 14–1 depicts this with a set of three demand curves. The long, uppermost curve is marketwide demand. The two shorter and lower curves represent the *entrant's* postentry demand given two specific levels of postentry output by *established* firms — Q_1 and Q_2. Given postentry output Q_1, the entrant's demand curve is that segment of the market's demand curve extending southeast of point A. Given Q_2, the entrant's demand curve is that segment of the market's demand curve

bridge, Mass.: Harvard University Press, 1962); and F. Modigliani, "New Developments on the Oligopoly Front," *Journal of Political Economy* (June 1958), pp. 215–232.

to the right of point B. These segments are shifted to the vertical axis to accord with the entrant's view of them.

These entrant demands are merely illustrative. Others are obviously possible. And the theory would now come to a halt without further specification as to what the postentry output of established firms will be. This is where assumption 2 comes in. It is essential to much existing theory and is often called the "Sylos postulate" in honor of an entry theorist, P. Sylos-Labini, who relied heavily upon it. Given the Sylos postulate, the potential entrant must contend with a demand curve derived from that segment of the marketwide demand curve extending to the right of the *preentry* quantity produced by existing firms. In other words, established firm output is assumed to be fixed in the event of entry. We shall explore the reality of this assumption shortly. Present acceptance of it permits immediate consideration of the cost side of the potential entrant's profit calculations. For given the Sylos postulate demand curve, the potential entrant need only compare his cost conditions to this demand in order to reach a yes or no decision on entry.

Most entry barriers may be categorized as either (1) absolute cost differences between established firms and potential entrants or (2) economies of scale. Figure 14–2 illustrates the first of these possibilities. It is like Figure 14–1, except that average total costs (ATC) have been added in simplified form for both the entrant and established firms. As depicted, the potential entrant, compared to established firms, suffers an absolute cost disadvantage at every level of output. Distance xz indicates the extent of disadvantage per unit of output.

Now, if established firms set price at P_{max} in hopes of maximizing their short-run profits, they would be inviting entry. Given the Sylos postulate, the entrant's postentry demand curve would then be D_1, which exceeds the entrant's unit cost (ATC, entrant) over a substantial range. Entry would be profitable for the newcomer. Entry would also cut the price and profit of established firms, however, so they may attempt to prevent the entry. The key question is what preentry combination of price and quantity will block the newcomer? According to assumption 3, the established firms know the answer and act together to implement the impediment. Price P_{ed} corresponds to output Q_{ed}, and, given the Sylos postulate, the combination will deter the entry. With Q_{ed}, the entrant's postentry demand curve lies below D_1. More important, it lies below the entrant's unit costs at every level of output, preventing the entrant from earning any postentry profit. In other words, P_{ed} is the highest price the established firms can charge without attracting entry. If the extent to which industry price can exceed average cost of the established firms is used to measure the height of entry barriers, then distance xz is the barrier premium in this case.

Barriers attributable to economies of scale add complexities to the theory because the barrier premium will then be a function of (1) the

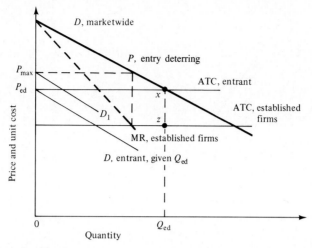

FIGURE 14–2. Entry limit pricing with absolute cost differences.

size of the market, (2) the elasticity of marketwide demand at any given price, (3) the scale at which economies of scale are exhausted, and (4) the rate of decline in the unit cost curve when moving from zero output to minimum efficient output. At least two diagrams are called for in this case — Figures 14–3 (a) and 14–3(b). Their solid-line average total cost curves (ATC) display identical economies up to a minimum efficient scale (MES). Furthermore, it is now assumed that existing firms and potential entrants confront the *same* ATC curves. Thus, everyone is equally efficient or inefficient at a given level of output.

Figure 14–3(a), then, illustrates the effect of differing elasticities of demand. When the solid-line marketwide demand applies, P_{ed} and Q_{ed} are the entry-deterring price and output. The resulting entrant's demand of D_{ent} is insufficient to cover cost at any output. And vw is the barrier premium associated with this particular solution. Note, however, that demand is inelastic at point v. In contrast, the dashed demand curve of lesser slope is elastic. Were it applicable, P_{ed} and Q_{ed} would no longer deter entry because the entrant's dashed demand curve would then exceed entrant's cost. Given the Sylos postulate, established firms must cut price to G and expand output beyond Q_{ed} to deter entry in this instance. As a result, their barrier premium would shrink to less than one-half the value of vw. Conversely, if we imagined a *lower* elasticity than that displayed by the solid line demand at v, entry deterring price would be higher than P_{ed} and the premium would be greater than vw.

Turning to Figure 14–3(b), we see that for a given level of minimum efficient scale, MES, the barrier premium will be greater the more rapidly unit cost rises at less than MES scale. Entry-deterring price as-

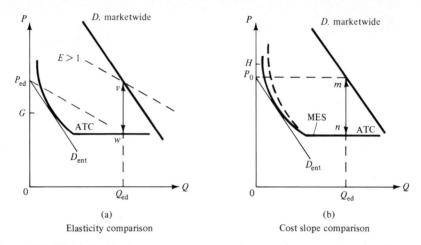

FIGURE 14–3. Maximum price-cost premiums with economies of scale.

sociated with the solid unit cost curve is P_0, and the resulting barrier premium is mn. A more rapid ascent of unit costs, as indicated by the dashed curve, would permit an even higher preentry price at point H plus a correspondingly larger barrier premium. Conversely, a flatter, less sharply rising unit cost curve would force the entry-deterring price and barrier premium below P_0 and mn.

The reader should be able to see the similar effects ensuing from a shift right or a shift left of the MES, holding everything else about the cost curve constant (that is, its height and shape). The reader should also be able to work out the effects of market size, which may be accounted for by shifts of the marketwide demand curve. Lest your efforts go sour, however, we shall include the implications of such moves in the following summary of limit pricing theory: Entry-deterring price and barrier premium will be higher (1) the greater the absolute cost disadvantage of potential entrants, (2) the lower the marketwide elasticity of demand at any price, (3) the sharper the increase in entrant's unit costs below minimum efficient scale output, (4) the larger the level of output at minimum efficient scale, and (5) the smaller the absolute size of the market.

B. Critique of the Theory

However tidy these conclusions may seem, they can be misleading. The theory underlying them is too tightly bound by assumptions to give us any more than a vague prediction of actual behavior. Our brief critique following will center on the Sylos postulate of identical pre- and postentry established-firm output.

Can the preentry conduct of established firms be predicted? . . . No.   The thinking of potential *entrants* is fairly straightforward. Their behavior depends on their expectations of postentry established-firm reaction. But the theory is not based on entrant behavior. It is primarily grounded upon a very delicate balance of established-firm mental reasoning that may or may not be true. Established firms are presumed to *think* that potential entrants *think* not in terms of postentry reactions but rather in terms of *preentry* policy. To be sure, preentry policy may signal something about postentry reaction, but the meaning of such signals is not chiseled in granite on Wall Street. Moreover, the gap between signal senders and receivers is large, and the number of parties involved great enough to foul up communications. Indeed, the signal that the theory postulates seems unrealistic. Established firms set price at the blocking point *and keep it there indefinitely.* A more realistic theory might have established firms reducing price when entry is imminent and raising it when the threat has subsided. Take, for example, Shop-Rite's attempted entry into the Washington, D.C., grocery retailing market in 1967:

> This chain came into the Washington market by opening three stores. It has since closed two of them. *Just prior* to this chain's entry into the Washington market, the stores of two leading Washington area chains [Safeway and Giant] located near the stores of the new entrant cut their prices substantially below those charged in the rest of the metropolitan area.[2]

Thus, contrary to the theory, established firms are often capable of identifying specific entry threats as they arise, especially where substantial plant and equipment purchases must precede entry. Moreover, established firms might deliberately maintain excess capacity, which capacity could be used to increase output and depress price at the appearance of an entrant on the horizon. This approach is not always optimal, but when it is profitable, it invalidates the Sylos postulate.[3]

Can the postentry conduct of established firms be predicted? . . . No. Theorists who rely on the Sylos postulate like to argue that a constant output policy is plausible because it is most unfavorable to entrants. As we have just seen, however, this conclusion is unwarranted. Postentry reactions of established firms can be much more nasty than this. On the other hand, they can also be rather accommodating. Established firms often cut back output to make room for entrants. Established firms are not necessarily moved to this action by benevolence; it may be better for their profits to see that price is maintained. Several examples are provided by the large electrical equipment manufacturers, who, during the

---

2 Federal Trade Commission, *Economic Report on Food Chain Selling Practices in the District of Columbia and San Francisco* (Washington, D.C.: FTC, 1969), pp.4, 23. For a related example see J. B. Dirlam and A. E. Kahn, *Fair Competition* (Ithaca, N.Y.: Cornell University Press, 1954), pp. 213–214.

3 J. T. Wenders, "Excess Capacity as a Barrier to Entry," *Journal of Industrial Economics* (November 1971), pp. 14–19. See also A. M. Spence, "Entry, Capacity, Investment, and Oligopolistic Pricing," *Bell Journal of Economics* (Autumn 1977), pp. 534–544.

great price-fixing conspiracies, allocated market shares of certain product lines to smaller rivals who had not produced in those submarkets before. To accommodate the entrants, General Electric and Westinghouse gave up some of their market shares.[4] In short, the postentry behavior of established firms is largely unpredictable.

Can potential entrant conduct be predicted? . . . No. Entry will not necessarily occur even if price is maintained well above the so-called "entry-deterring" level. Potential entrants know that it is postentry price that counts, and nightmares of bloody postentry price wars may keep them out. Conversely, entry may very well occur despite the diligent efforts of established firms to keep preentry price below the probable unit costs of potential entrants. Inexperienced entrants may be overly optimistic about their cost prospects or about the mood of existing sellers.

An interesting possibility in this regard is this: an entrant might try the "gnat strategy" to heighten its prospects of success. That is, the entrant limits its capacity and signals its intention of remaining small, hopeful of convincing incumbent firms to accommodate the entry rather than fight it. For example, in 1984, when Braniff reentered midwestern airline markets after a bout with bankruptcy, Braniff's prices were below those of American Airlines, Delta, and other established "big boys," but it followed a strategy of offering no more than just *two* flights a day on any route. Braniff felt that any more flights would provoke a nasty reaction: "A gnat is too small to be hit with a sledge hammer—and the big boys carry sledgehammers."[5] In sum, limit price theory provides predictions about the behavior of potential entrants that often seem no more solid than those concerning established firms.

Does limit pricing theory explain maximum long-run price level? . . . No. Despite appearances, it can be argued that the theory does not really explain maximum long-run price level.[6] The theory predicts a price level low enough to ward off entry, and presents this prediction as the more plausible of two possible options: (1) an especially high price, such as P_M in Figure 14–4, that invites entry, and (2) a lower entry-deterring price, such as P_E in Figure 14–4. Because theory chooses the lower of these two options, P_E, it appears that this conduct establishes the *utmost* long-run price. But there really is no such price option in the *long run*. Under either option, price will end up at the *same* level. If price is initially set high enough to attract entry, then a multiplication of com-

---

[4] C. C. Walton and F. W. Cleveland, Jr., *Corporations on Trial: The Electric Cases* (Belmont, Calif.: Wadsworth, 1964), p. 52.

[5] Ruth Simon, "The Eagles and the Gnat," *Forbes*, November 4, 1985, pp. 104–107. Another name for this is "judo economics." See Judith R. Gelman and Steven C. Salop, "Judo Economics: Capacity Limitation and Coupon Competition," *Bell Journal of Economics* (Autumn 1983), pp. 315–324.

[6] D. K. Osborne, "The Role of Entry in Oligopoly Theory," *Journal of Political Economy* August 1964, pp. 396–402.

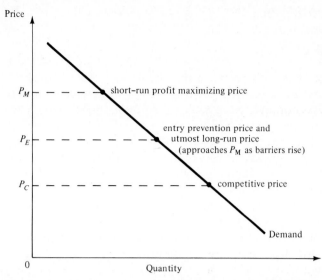

FIGURE 14–4. Alternative price levels and the theory of limit pricing.

petitors will drive price down until it equals the entry-deterring price P_E (at which point entry stops). If price is initially set at entry-deterring level, P_E, it obviously ends at the entry-deterring level. The only long-run difference in these two options is the number of firms eventually in the market and the likely level of concentration, with the first distinction obviously yielding the more competitive structure of the two. Since the high initial price option yields a more competitive structure, a further unwinding of the theory might produce predictions concerning different long-run price levels, but only indirectly. That is, the more competitive of the two structures might foster a relatively lower price level in the long run, a level *below* entry-deterring price and near P_C in Figure 14–4. Aside from this possibility, however, the theory of limit pricing conduct is more important from the standpoint of *concentration* than of price.

Notice we are *not* saying that barriers to entry themselves are unimportant to price level. We are saying that, in theory, barriers to entry *alone* explain *utmost possible* long-run price (and the higher the barriers, the higher this maximum long-run price P_E will be relative to the purely competitive price P_C). Simple price setting does not determine that maximum. We are also saying that pricing conduct can, and does, affect *actual* long-run price level, but only through two channels: (1) As already suggested, conduct together with concentration will determine *where* observed price actually lies between utmost long-run (entry-deterring) price P_E and purely competitive price P_C. (2) Conduct other than simple price setting may affect the height of barriers to entry, thereby *indirectly* affecting utmost long-run price.

II. DYNAMIC PRICING

A. Theory

Disenchantment with limit pricing theory has led many theorists to devise models of "dynamic pricing." Early theories of dynamic pricing stressed the notion that established firms might actually earn higher profits by pricing high and inducing entry than by holding prices down. By dynamic pricing, established firms deliberately give up part of the market to newcomers; however, they earn hefty profits in the short run before entries divide demand. Of course established firm profits will fall as entry proceeds; their market share will shrink and market price will fall. This profit trend is shown by the declining curve in Figure 14–5. Lucrative early profits turn into skimpy profits with time. By contrast, the profit stream associated with a limit pricing strategy is fairly steady over time and may actually rise slightly if the market is growing. This too is shown in Figure 14–5.

Although the limit pricing profit stream is below the dynamic pricing profit stream at the start, it eventually supersedes the latter. This raises a pertinent question: Is dynamic pricing therefore a model of *short-run* profit maximizing and limit pricing a model of *long-run* profit maximizing? Despite your eyeball's affirmative answer, your mind should be telling you "No, both models are similar in that both assume *long-run* profit maximization as the goal of established firms." Both models can

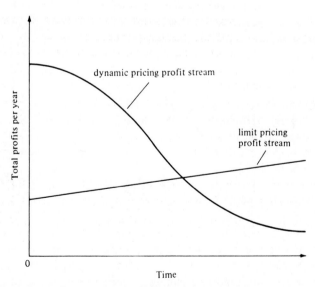

FIGURE 14–5. Profit streams of established firms under two price strategies.

be put on the same footing for long-run comparison by (1) properly *discounting* each profit stream to reduce the value of distant and therefore less useful dollar revenues, (2) adding up the discounted values in each resulting series, and (3) thereby converting the profit stream to *present values*. Given a common objective of long-run profit maximization, the strategy yielding the highest present discounted value will be chosen.

Advocates of the dynamic pricing model argue that "the present value of a series of declining profits . . . may exceed the present value of a perpetual profit rate . . . "[7] Not surprisingly, advocates of the limit price model think the opposite. Actually, recent dynamic theorists have refined and elaborated this basic issue until it is now inaccurate to regard it as a stark either-or matter. Their models do not speak in terms of a flood of immediate entry versus a drought induced by limit pricing. Theorists no longer think of entry as an all or nothing affair. By assumption, incumbent firms control the entry spigot. A high price attracts "more" entry, a low price "less" entry. Hence incumbents try to control entry, permitting an intermediate and varying rate of entry that maximizes the present value of incumbent firm profits.[8]

B. Empirical Evidence on "Dynamic" and "Limit" Pricing[9]

Empirical tests of these theories are extremely difficult. For one thing, their empirical implications are similar. Under both limit pricing and dynamic pricing firms earn supranormal profits. Under both theories potential competition moderates those profits, but not completely. For another thing incumbent firms may *attempt* one strategy while actual *events* give appearances that another strategy is being practiced. Hence, an established firm may attempt limit pricing with the intent of preventing any entry and earning persistently high profits. Yet, as we have already noted, entry may nevertheless occur, reducing incumbent profits over time and giving misleading appearances that dynamic pricing, not limit pricing, is the strategy being followed. Limit pricing is not, in other words, a perfect tool for blocking new entrants or preserving excess profits.

Hence, the evidence is mixed. Interindustry evidence shows entry generally occurring and excess profits eroding in the long run, observations consistent with dynamic pricing. Yet this entry is also commonly

[7] G. J. Stigler, *The Theory of Price* (New York: Macmillan, 1952), p. 234.

[8] D. W. Gaskins, "Dynamic Limit Pricing: Optimal Pricing Under Threat of Entry," *Journal of Economic Theory* (September 1971), pp. 306–322; D. P. Baron, "Limit Pricing, Potential Entry, and Barriers to Entry," *American Economic Review* (September 1973), pp. 666–674, and M. Kamien and N. Schwartz, "Limit Pricing and Uncertain Entry," *Econometrica* (May 1971), pp. 441–454.

[9] For a review, see Richard J. Gilbert, "The Role of Potential Competition in Industrial Organization," *Journal of Economic Perspectives* (Summer 1989), pp. 107–127.

meager or ineffectual, and excess profits decline only at a *very slow* pace, so this evidence does not rule out limit pricing.[10] Richard Gilbert concludes that these interindustry studies "need not contradict either the classical limit pricing model or the model of dynamic limit pricing."[11]

Other evidence, especially case study evidence, is available. This is clearer for individual cases. But limit pricing and dynamic pricing both make appearances, so the evidence remains mixed, and sweeping generalizations cannot stand.

Prominent examples that appear to fit the dynamic pricing mold include the steel, chemical, and copper markets. U.S. Steel's early high-price policy and continued loss of market share received earlier mention. In a study of 39 chemical product markets, Lieberman found that entry into markets of high concentration was typically followed by an expansion of capacity by the established firms. This suggests dynamic pricing because the incumbents are not behaving in a manner that prevents entry, but they are investing to retard the expansion of new entrants once they enter.[12] Caves, Fortunato, and Ghemawat analyze the experiences of several dozen dominant firms formed in the merger movement around 1900 and conclude that most of them adopted dynamic pricing during the period 1905–1929.[13]

On the other hand, one does not have to look far for equally valid examples of what appear to be limit pricing. During the first half of this century Alcoa reported no more than moderate profits despite its considerable power. Similarly, General Foods Corporation is said to price its specialty products at low to moderate levels in "full realization that a high price will restrict the volume and . . . speed up the process of developing competition."[14] Another example from the food industry is Campbell Soup, which "has steadfastly refused to raise prices far enough above costs to reap a short-term deluge of profits, thereby discouraging any real competition."[15]

Some firms have switched from limit pricing to dynamic pricing as circumstances changed. For example, Du Pont, United Shoe Machinery, and Kodak apparently employed limit pricing during the first half of this century to help maintain monopoly power in cellophane, shoe machin-

[10] W. G. Shepherd, *The Treatment of Market Power* (New York: Columbia University Press, 1975), pp. 113–129; Dennis C. Mueller, *Profits in the Long Run* (Cambridge: Cambridge University Press, 1986); and P. A. Geroski, "Do Dominant Firms Decline?" in *The Economics of Market Dominance*, edited by D. Hay and J. Vickers (Oxford: Basil Blackwell, 1987), pp. 143–167.

[11] Gilbert, "The Role of Potential Competition in Industrial Organization," p. 117.

[12] M. Lieberman, "Post-Entry Investment and Market Structure in the Chemical Processing Industries," *Rand Journal of Economics* (Autumn 1987), pp. 533–549.

[13] Richard E. Caves, Michael Fortunato, and Punkaj Ghemawat, "The Decline of Dominant Firms, 1905–1929," *Quarterly Journal of Economics* (August 1984), pp. 523–545.

[14] A. D. H. Kaplan, J. B. Dirlam, and R. F. Lanzilotti, *Pricing in Big Business* (Washington, D. C.: Brookings Institution, 1958) p. 216.

[15] T. Horst, *At Home Abroad* (Cambridge, Mass.: Ballinger Co., 1974) p. 16.

ery and film processing. But they switched to dynamic pricing after anti-trust actions induced them to encourage entry.[16]

Finally, there are examples of single firms demonstrating *both* theories at the *same time* in different markets. One is Xerox. It appears to have engaged in limit pricing for its very-high-volume market (serving customers making more than 100,000 copies per machine per month); simultaneously it vigorously encouraged entry using dynamic pricing in the low-volume market (below 5000 copies per machine per month). In the middle-volume range, Xerox followed an "in between" policy. Who threatened entry? Patents prevented any "dry process" entry in the early years of Xerox's success. But electrofax technology was developed at about the same time and was liberally licensed to all comers by RCA. Thus the impact of Xerox's pricing policies may be gauged in terms of electrofax firm entry into these submarkets up through 1967. Limit pricing held entry down to just 3 firms. Open dynamic pricing brought in 25. In between, 10 newcomers entered the middle volume segment of the copy machine market.[17]

Of all the empirical studies, one by Masson and Shaanan is the most interesting. They get mixed results, too. Yet their mixed results seem to reveal an interesting pattern. First, in terms of Figure 14–4, relatively few firms raise price to the very high short-run profit maximizing level of P_M, and these few are typically protected by very high barriers to entry, so that entry-deterring price P_E is pretty close to P_M in these cases. Stated differently, extreme instances of "dynamic" pricing seem rare. Second, extreme instances of "limit" pricing seem equally rare. In terms of Figure 14–4, most firms with discretionary pricing power choose to price somewhat above P_E rather than below, thereby inducing *some* entry but preventing floods of newcomers. Thus, actual price typically lies somewhere between P_M and P_E, falling further below P_M as P_E falls further below P_M toward P_C when entry is easy.[18]

In sum, theories of an intermediate sort — those hypothesizing that firms price to maximize the present value of their profit stream by allowing an *intermediate and varying rate* of entry — have received support. Still, there are exceptions where entry is barred for many decades or gushes in rather rapidly or expansively.

The foregoing evidence relates primarily to the behavior of *incumbent* firms. That is, do incumbents actually try to exclude entry or regulate entry by using relatively low preentry prices? Equally interesting is the

---

[16] Don E. Waldman, *Antitrust Action and Market Structure* (Lexington, Mass.: Lexington Books, 1978), pp. 41–49, 146–149; Waldman, "The du Pont Cellophane Case Revisited," *Antitrust Bulletin* (Winter 1980), pp. 805–830.

[17] E. A. Blackstone, "Limit Pricing and Entry in the Copying Machine Industry," *Quarterly Review of Economics & Business* (Winter 1972) pp. 57–65.

[18] Robert T. Masson and Joseph Shaanan, "Stochastic-Dynamic Limiting Pricing: An Empirical Test," *Review of Economics and Statistics* (August 1982), pp. 413–422.

observed behavior of *potential entrants*. Are they, in fact, discouraged by relatively low preentry prices? Apparently they are. Very little direct evidence on this question is available, but it indicates that potential entrants usually respond to preentry prices as theories of limit pricing and dynamic pricing predict.[19]

C. Nonprice Behavioral Barriers

The evidence for staunch "limit pricing" is thus certainly detectable, but on the whole it is rather weak. The main reason for the weakness seems to be a simple one—namely, there are better alternative strategies. In pricing, "dynamic pricing" is apparently a better strategy in many instances. Entry is curbed by dynamic pricing but not blocked. Still other pricing options include loyalty discounts, which allow incumbent firms to charge fairly high prices while at the same time discouraging entry by imposing "switching costs" on buyers who switch from incumbents to newcomers (see pages 330–335 of Chapter 11 and Section IV of this chapter). Nonprice alternatives are of even greater importance.

Glance back to Table 11–5 on page 327. Robert Smiley's poll of business executives discloses that only 22% of his respondents relied on limit pricing to deter entry "frequently" or "often." In contrast, alternative strategies—product proliferation, intense advertising, and patent preemption especially—are much more popular among Smiley's respondents.

Alice Patricia White's detailed study of nine dominant firms (including Kodak, IBM, Coca-Cola, and Procter & Gamble) reaches a similar conclusion. Her case histories revealed some evidence of strategic pricing to maintain market power, dynamic pricing especially. But she found nonprice strategies to be of immensely greater importance as devices to manage market structure. Product proliferation, research and development, vertical integration, and exclusionary marketing tactics such as tying were especially evident.[20]

Still other references to empirical work along these lines are possible.[21] But we need not belabor the point. We *should not expect* to find a mountain of empirical evidence of strategic pricing to control entry— especially not "limit" pricing. The rich availability of possibly more profitable substitute strategies limits the chances here. Indeed, it is interesting to find the evidence as supportive as it is.

[19] Timothy H. Hannan, "Prices, Capacity, and the Entry Decision: A Conditional Logit Analysis," *Southern Economic Journal* (October 1983), pp. 539–550.

[20] Alice Patricia White, *The Dominant Firm: A Study of Market Power* (Ann Arbor, Mich.: UNI Research Press, 1983).

[21] J. D. Gribbon and M. A. Utton, "The Treatment of Dominant Firms in the UK Competition Legislation," in *Mainstreams and Industrial Organization*, edited by H. W. de Jong and W. G. Shepherd, (Dordrecht, The Netherlands: Martinus Nijhoff, 1986), pp. 243–271; and Robert Stobaugh, *Innovation and Competition* (Boston: Harvard Business School Press, 1988), pp. 17–19.

III. PRICE DISCRIMINATION

Like a pesky housefly, price discrimination unavoidably invaded the foregoing discussion. Safeway and Giant Foods, for example, used it to repulse Shop-Rite's entry into Washington, D.C. Indeed, most every enterprise and market provides examples. For *price discrimination occurs whenever a seller sells the same commodity or service at more than one price.* Moreover, even if the sale items are not exactly the same, but only related, price discrimination is said to occur if the seller sells very similar products at different price-cost ratios.[22] IBM, for instance, used to rent two disk drive systems that differed only slightly in cost and model number (the 2314 and 2319) but immensely in price ($1455 a month versus $1000). The broad definition includes cases in which costs differ and identical prices are charged.

A. Essential Conditions

Three conditions are essential for price discrimination: (1) The seller must have some *market power*. A purely competitive firm does not have sufficient control over price to engage in discrimination. (2) The seller must confront buyers who have *differing price elasticities of demand*. These elasticity differences among classes of buyers may be due to differences in income level, differences in "needs," differences in the availability of substitutes, differences in use of the product, and so on. Without different elasticities, buyers would not willingly pay different prices. To practice price discrimination, of course, the seller must be able to identify these different demands. (3) These various buyer elements must be kept *separate*. Without separation, low-price customers could resell their purchases to the high-price customers, subverting the seller's ability to identify and segregate the different demands. A grisly example of the importance of market separation was furnished during the early 1940s by Röhm & Haas in connection with its sale of methyl methacrylate plastic. General industrial users were charged 85 cents a pound, whereas dental laboratories and dentists who used the plastic for making dentures were charged 45 *dollars* a pound. After many dental buyers discovered the difference, "bootlegging" or, more technically, arbitrage, became a problem. To stifle bootlegging the company considered poisoning the industrial plastic. The Food and Drug Administration would have then unwittingly enforced separation of the markets for Röhm & Haas. To quote from company correspondence,

---

[22] Stated differently, price discrimination occurs when "*varieties* of a commodity are sold to different buyers at different *net* prices." Louis Phlips, "Price Discrimination: A Survey of the Theory," *Journal of Economic Surveys*, Vol. 2, no. 2 (1988), pp. 135–167. (Emphasis original.)

> A millionth of one percent of arsenic or lead might cause them [the FDA] to confiscate every bootleg unit in the country. There ought to be a trace of something that would make them rear up.[23]

Röhm & Haas eventually rejected the idea, but it started rumors that the industrial material had been adulterated.[24]

B. Analysis of Price Discrimination

Theoretically, price discrimination is usually analyzed in three categories: first degree, second degree, and third degree.

First-Degree Discrimination. This is perfect discrimination. Each and every unit sold goes for the very highest price above cost it can fetch. Each and every buyer pays as much as he or she is willing to pay for the quantity he or she wants. Figure 14–6 compares first degree price discrimination with single, uniform pricing. With a single price of $0B$, $0Q$ units would be purchased, yielding total revenues equal to $0BCQ$, which is price times quantity. Given constant total unit costs of $0B$, including a normal profit, the seller earns no more than a normal profit. Buyers willingly pay $0BCQ$. Indeed, by definition of the demand curve, they would actually be willing to pay $0BCQ$ *plus* the shaded area ABC, or $0ACQ$. The difference between what they actually pay and what they are willing to pay is called "consumers' surplus," which in this case is $0ACQ - 0BCQ$ or ABC. Under first degree price discrimination, the seller varies prices over the AC range to capture this consumers' surplus as well as the $0BCQ$ revenue obtained from the single price. Seller's total revenue then equals the entire area under the demand curve between A and C, and profits bulge.

For obvious reasons, such perfect discrimination is extremely difficult in the real world and is never achieved in practice. However, Xerox may have come pretty close to perfection, at least during the 1960s.[25] The company did not at first sell its 914 copy machines. It *leased* them and *metered* the intensity of their use, charged $25 per month plus 3.5 cents per copy. Low-intensity users paid little; high-intensity users paid

[23] Corwin D. Edwards, *Economic and Political Aspects of International Cartels*, U.S. Senate, Subcommittee on War Mobilization of the Committee on Military Affairs, 78th Cong., 2nd Sess. (1944), p. 19.

[24] During 1988 sales of coffee beans to countries that did not belong to the International Coffee Agreement were about 11 million bags, while *actual consumption* in those countries was only about 6 million bags. (A bag weighs 132 pounds.) What was going on? Prices to nonmember countries, like Japan, were so low compared to the prices charged to member countries, like the United States, that buyers in nonmember countries could sell to "unscrupulous" coffee roasters in member countries at prices $50 a bag less than the price levels the roasters would normally pay. The bootlegging, worth hundreds of millions of dollars, threatened the life of the international agreement. *The Wall Street Journal*, May 1, 1989, p. C12.

[25] E. A. Blackstone, "The Copying-Machine Industry: Innovations, Patents and Pricing," *Antitrust Law and Economics Review* (Fall 1972), pp. 105–122.

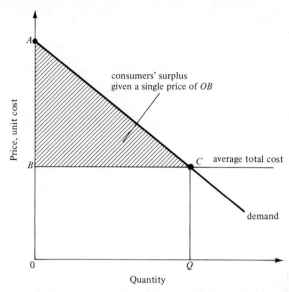

FIGURE 14–6. First-degree price discrimination.

a lot. In this way price was tailored to each individual customer's will-ingness to pay and elasticity of demand. Was this profitable? Absolutely!

> The estimated cost of producing the original 914 copier was approximately $2500. Some users, because of the large number of copies they make on their leased Xerox machines, have paid Xerox an *annual rental* of more than $20,000 per machine or—assuming at least a five-year machine life—a total "purchase price" of more than $100,000 for each such machine.[26]

The key to the system was the meter. Most sellers cannot practice first-degree discrimination because they cannot measure the depth of each buyer's desire and ability to pay. In addition, leasing kept buyers sepa-rate from each other. Had Xerox *sold* its machines at widely differing prices, bootleggers could have undermined its discrimination.

   Second-Degree Discrimination. Second-degree price discrimination is illustrated in Figure 14–7. Demand is partitioned into three blocks. Quantity $0Q_1$, is sold at price $0G$. Quantity $Q_2 - Q_1$ is sold at price $0K$. And, finally, quantity $Q_3 - Q_2$ is sold at price $0J$. Total revenues obtained are $0JHQ_3$ plus the shaded area. In other words, this system is like first-degree discrimination only less refined. Much less consumers' surplus is captured by the seller from the buyers. Standard examples include "quantity discounts" and "block rate" pricing of electricity and gas. Xerox used such a scheme during the late 1960s for its copier-duplicators

[26] Ibid., p. 112.

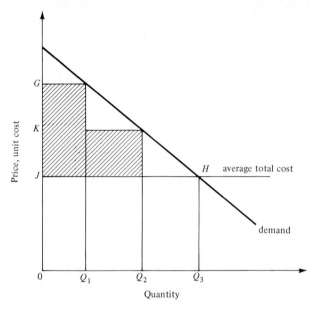

FIGURE 14–7. Second-degree price discrimination.

(not its 914s). Its charges were 4 cents each for the first three copies from the same original, 2 cents each for the fourth through the tenth copies, and 1 cent each for every copy above 10. (This too was profitable. Overall, Xerox earned 21–30% after-tax return on net worth during the period 1962–1970.)

Third-Degree Discrimination. This is depicted in Figure 14–8. The negatively sloped demand curves indicate monopoly power. Differences in their angles of descent and intercepts indicate differing elasticities of demand at each possible price, with the result that buyers in market X have the relatively more elastic demand. Total unit cost (ATC) is the same in both markets because the product is basically the same. Moreover, ATC is again assumed to be constant. This means that ATC and marginal cost (MC) are identical. Following the conventional profit maximizing formula of MR = MC, we find that P_x and Q_x are the optimal combination in market X, whereas P_y and Q_y are the optimal combination in market Y. Shading again indicates excess profits. Notice that price in the relatively elastic market, P_x, is substantially below price in the relatively inelastic market, P_y. Indeed, nothing would be sold in market X at price P_y. Notice also that if these markets could not be kept separate, their demands, their elasticities, and of course their buyers, too, would blend, leaving only one market for the seller instead of two.

Third-degree discrimination is considerably more widespread than second degree and much more so than first degree. Examples abound. The auto industry alone provides many interesting illustrations:

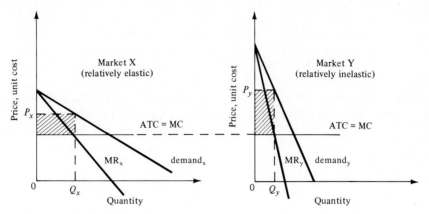

FIGURE 14–8. Third-degree price discrimination.

1. Fleet buyers have frequently been able to buy new cars at unit prices considerably below those paid by individual consumers.
2. Manufacturers' markups vary across model lines. In the past, big luxury cars carried the greatest spread between wholesale price and direct manufacturing cost. Ford, for example, charged the following markups as a percentage of manufacturer's price in 1966: Ford "Custom" two-door sedan, 6.7%; "Galaxie 500" sedan, 13.4%; and "LTD" two-door hardtop, 21.1%.[27] More recently, relative elasticities of demand seem to have shifted with the skyrocketing popularity of small cars as compared to big cars, and the auto manufacturers have modified the size of these profit margins accordingly. GM took the lead in 1980 by *lowering* the price of its luxury cars 2.4% while *raising* the price of its subcompacts 10.1%.[28]
3. Manufacturers gain much larger markups on cars loaded with optional equipment in comparison to stripped-down cars. For example, in 1987–1988 GM and Ford were charging $120 extra for tinted windshields that cost only $18 more than normal, and $78 for digital clocks costing $4.[29]
4. Manufacturers charge a much higher profit markup on repair parts than on parts in the form of fully assembled new vehicles. Two key factors help to explain the difference: (a) parts generally have a very low price elasticity of demand, and (b) assemblers may try to use parts sales to "meter" each consumer's intensity of auto use.[30]

[27] U.S. Senate, Select Committee on Small Business, *Hearings on Planning, Regulation, and Competition: Automobile Industry—1968*, 90th Cong., 2nd Sess. (1968), pp. 273–321.

[28] *Business Week*, September 22, 1980, pp. 78–88.

[29] *The Wall Street Journal*, October 1, 1987, p. 33.

[30] R. W. Crandall, "Vertical Integration and the Market for Repair Parts in the U.S. Auto Industry," *Journal of Industrial Economics* (June 1968), pp. 212–234.

5. When selling repair parts, the Big Three vehicle manufacturers have apparently discriminated against their own dealers. Rough estimates from the late 1960s indicate that independent warehouse distributors paid about 30% less for assembler brand parts than what franchised dealers paid.[31] Independent wholesalers enjoyed bargain prices because, to some degree, they could turn to alternative parts suppliers. In fact, only about 40% of all parts moving through independent channels at that time came from vehicle producers; the other 60% came from independent parts manufacturers. By contrast, franchised dealers were "persuaded" to buy at least 75% of their parts from the vehicle manufacturers. Instruments for producer persuasion included threat of franchise cancellation, delayed shipment of new vehicles at the beginning of the new model year, and so on. The dealers' burden is lightened somewhat by the manufacturers' efforts to "persuade" consumers through advertising and warrantee stipulations that "factory authorized service" is the only kind of service they should get. GM's massive "Mr. Goodwrench" campaign is a good example of this.

6. Finally, discrimination occurs in dealers' showrooms, as cars are one of the few (legal) commodities still available to consumers at negotiated and therefore variable prices. No more than about 40% of all buyers pay full "sticker" price. Those not paying sticker, dicker. And some dicker better than others.

Other common examples of third-degree price discrimination relate to firms selling in several product lines, with differing degrees of market power across those product lines.

C. Social Effects

Actually, the catch-as-catch-can price discrimination of auto showrooms fits none of the theoretical models just outlined. Other real-life forms also fail to fit, such as discrimination associated with basing-point pricing, or with secret "off-list" discounting during recessions, or with predatory pricing. Even so, the social desirability of all forms of price discrimination may be judged by three criteria—income distribution effects, efficiency effects, and competitive effects. In each case blanket labels of "good" or "bad" are inappropriate.

With respect to income distribution, for instance, price discrimination quite clearly adds to profits at the expense of consumers. Since this may contribute added inequality to society's unequal distribution of income, many would say that is bad. On the other hand, profit-enhancing price discrimination may occasionally make the difference between profit

---

[31] R. W. Crandall, "The Decline of the Franchised Dealer in the Automobile Repair Market," *Journal of Business* (January 1970), pp. 22–23.

and loss, in which case the very existence of the enterprise in question depends on its ability to discriminate. Suppose, for example, that some small town could not attract the services of a physician unless it allowed her to charge the rich higher prices than the poor, there not being much income from that particular practice under a flat fee system. The profit-enhancing properties of discrimination in this instance would be good.

The picture is also mixed for efficiency effects. In some cases price discrimination may foster allocation efficiency. For instance, the first-degree price discrimination of Figure 14–6 would be more efficient than a monopolist's single price well above unit costs (represented by distance $0B$). With first-degree discrimination the price on marginal sales at point C would match marginal benefit, and this in turn would match marginal cost. On the other hand, price discrimination may not foster efficiency, depending on such things as the shapes of the cost and demand curves.[32]

With respect to competition, elaboration is necessary.

IV. PRICE DISCRIMINATION AND COMPETITION

The competitive implications of price discrimination need elaboration because they illustrate two key points made earlier—(1) that market power affects price level and (2) that entry can be discouraged by pricing techniques other than "limit" or "dynamic" pricing—techniques yielding hefty profits in the short run (as with dynamic pricing) *while at the same time* securing profits in the long run (as with limit pricing). We shall discuss price discrimination and competition under two categories that correspond to these points, namely, "exploitation" of market power and "extension/exploitation." (See Table 11–1, pp. 299.)

It should first be acknowledged, however, that price discrimination can be procompetitive. A small firm, for example, may charge different buyers different prices unsystematically in its attempts to "make a sale." Auto dealer dickering illustrates this, and we shall discuss this further in the next chapter.

A. Exploitation of Market Power

Earlier, in Chapter 11 (pp. 316–317), we saw that price levels and market shares are commonly correlated. Previously, however, we were looking mainly at *different firms* with different prices and different shares. Here we are interested in how the *same firm* prices in different markets.

Abundant evidence of this relates to a single firm charging different prices for the same product in different geographic markets according to

---

[32] Louis Phlips, *The Economics of Price Discrimination* (Cambridge: Cambridge University Press, 1983).

differing degrees of market power. In Europe, in the 1970s, for instance, United Brands Company was charging its banana customers in Belgium 80% more than its customers in Ireland. And price differentials between Germany, Belgium, and The Netherlands ranged from 18% to 54%, all apparently due to diversity in United's power across these markets.[33]

In the United States, General Foods has priced its Maxwell House coffee differently in different cities according to its market share. During the 1970s the brand's city-by-city market share in the East and Midwest ranged from less than 30% to over 50%. The correlation between this variance and the brand's price level ranged from .438 to .725 over different years of the 1970s.[34]

Finally, Figure 14–9 shows a scatter diagram for data on a large grocery store chain during the late 1950s—National Tea Company. Each dot represents a share/net profit pairing for a city served by the chain. It is easy to see that market share and net profit (net price) are positivity related. In Indianapolis, for instance, both variables are relatively high, while in Memphis they are both relatively low.[35]

B. Extension/Exploitation of Market Power

Price discrimination may be used strategically to extend market power— that is, to discourage new entry or expand market share. Discrimination to effectuate limit pricing is an obvious possibility here. And such is illustrated by the Electric Reduction Company (ERCO). During the 1950s and 1960s, ERCO enjoyed a monopoly on industrial phosphates in Canada. On the buyers' side of the market were three large soap makers who together purchased 80% of ERCO's output. Nearly two dozen smaller firms purchased the remaining 20% of the output. ERCO's price to the "big three" was much lower than its price to the small companies. The lower price was, in effect, a limit price. It kept the big three from entering the phosphate business themselves, or from acting in concert to guarantee 80% of the market to any new entrant who would offer prices lower than ERCO's.[36]

Equally interesting is the case of Rentokil, a pest control firm that has dominated the United Kingdom with branches everywhere and a

[33] *United Brands Company* v. *The Commission of European Communities* (1978) 1 Common Market Law Reports, pp. 429–508. These are "weekly" price differences. Annual average differences were less pronounced. Note: To prevent bootlegging, United prohibited ripeners (who buy bananas green) from reselling.

[34] John C. Hilke and Philip B. Nelson, "Strategic Behavior and Attempted Monopolization: The Coffee Case," in *The Antitrust Revolution*, edited by J. Kwoka and L. White, (Glenview, Ill: Scott, Foresman, 1989), p. 220.

[35] For more elaborate evidence of this sort concerning Grand Union in New England, see Ronald W. Cotterill, "Market Power in the Retail Food Industry: Evidence from Vermont," *Review of Economics and Statistics* (August 1986), pp. 379–386.

[36] D. G. McFetridge, "The Emergence of a Canadian Merger Policy: The ERCO Case," *Antitrust Bulletin* (Spring 1974), pp. 1–11.

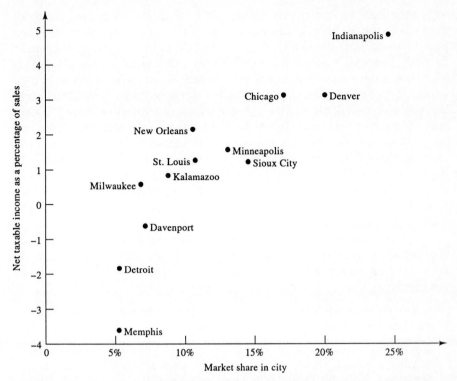

FIGURE 14–9. Relationship between market share and net profit (net price) for grocery retailing, National Tea Company, 1957–1959. Source: *Economic Report on the Structure and Competitive Behavior of Food Retailing* (Washington, D.C.: Federal Trade Commission, 1960), p. 94.

national market share exceeding 60% during the 1980s. Two facts would normally imply that Rentokil's huge market share would not last long—its colossal profits (92% return on capital invested) and the absence of *technical* barriers to entry or expansion in the industry (e.g., high minimum efficient sale). Indeed, there were over 200 *other* firms in the industry during the 1980s, but none of them had more than a 3% market share and none of them operated nationally throughout the United Kingdom. Most of these small firms specialized in "job work" (such as disposing of a wasp's nest in Mrs. Smith's backyard). They did not compete effectively against Rentokil for "contract work," under which long-term pest control services were provided to large commercial clients (such as infested bakeries or canneries), and by which Rentokil earned 79% of its total sales revenues in 1985.[37] Rentokil used three strategies

37 United Kingdom Monopolies and Mergers Commission, *Pest Control Services* (London: Her Majesty's Stationery Office, 1988), pp. 3–8.

to exterminate or control its competitors when they pestered Rentokil too much (when, that is, they grew bigger than gnats). First, Rentokil bought them out. Between 1970 and 1985 Rentokil acquired 18 rivals.[38] Second, Rentokil refused to supply other U.K. pest control companies with the rodentcide "bromadiolone," which it imported from a foreign chemical producer under an exclusive arrangement. Substitute compounds were available to rivals, but only more expensive ones.[39] Third, and of greatest relevance here, Rentokil engaged in selective price cutting. When rivals were on the verge of winning a big contract away from Rentokil, the company would cut price, sometimes "drastically," in order to obtain or keep the business.[40] This was price discrimination of the sort that Safeway used against Shop-Rite in Washington D.C., rather than the steady, systematic, limit–price sort of discrimination ERCO used in Canada.

Volume discounts and loyalty rebates are still further forms of price discrimination that could under certain conditions extend market power (even as that power may also be exploited). In general, these strategies are similar:

Volume discounts are reduced prices for ever larger volumes purchased during some given time period such as a year.[41]

Loyalty rebates give delayed rewards to buyers purchasing more than specified amounts, which amounts might be large absolutely or large as a percentage of the buyer's total purchase requirements.

Volume discounts were illustrated earlier in Figure 11–7 on page 330. Loyalty rebates were illustrated earlier in connection with ocean shipping conferences on page 335 and airline frequent flyer programs on page 342.

Each technique entails price discrimination for the same reason. Certain buyers pay relatively high prices while others pay low prices (albeit the low prices may be delayed). The buyers most favored by the seller are precisely the ones behaving most favorably toward the seller. It follows that the anticompetitive feature of each of these techniques is also the same—namely, a "switching cost" imposed on buyers who shift

---

[38] Company documents, for instance, reveal Rentokil's motive for acquiring Pestoxin in 1982:

They are at present our only competitor capable of offering service nationally. They hold pest control contracts with several of our multiple customers and have affected our price negotiations by our customers being able to threaten to give them the contract if we increased our price and in some instances, if we did not in fact reduce our price. (Ibid., p. 26)

[39] Ibid., p. 45.

[40] Ibid.

[41] Note: These are not quantity discounts, which reduce price as large quantities are purchased at one time. If you buy two pairs of shoes and get the second one at half price that is a quantity discount. Competitive problems primarily concern volume discounts.

their business to small rivals or new entrants. This switching cost obviously discourages switching, and thereby deters entry and small-firm expansion. Finally, these two techniques are not always anticompetitive, but the circumstances under which they are anticompetitive happen to be the same. When used by relatively large firms or by a cartel they tend to be anticompetitive.[42]

Before being attacked by antitrust authorities in 1979, Hoffmann-LaRoche & Company used loyalty rebates to maintain its dominance in vitamins in the European Economic Community.[43] Commonly called Roche (not roach), this company enjoyed the following EEC market shares during the 1970s:

Vitamin A	47%
Vitamin B_2	86%
Vitamin B_3	64%
Vitamin B_6	95%
Vitamin C	68%
Vitamin E	70%
Vitamin H (biotin)	95%

(Roche offered a full line. It did not manufacture vitamins B_{12}, D, K, and M, but acquired them for resale from other manufacturers in "swap" arrangements.) Roche offered two purchasers two different prices for an identical quantity of the same product depending on whether those two buyers would agree or not agree to buy most or all of their vitamin requirements from Roche. For example, Roche's contract with Beecham, a large bulk buyer, gave Beecham a loyalty rebate of 1% if Beecham bought 60% of its requirements from Roche, a 1.5% rebate if 70%, a 2% rebate if 80%, and so on. Most loyalty rebates ranged from 1% to 5%, but they went as high as 20%. Moreover, the rebates applied to each customer's total purchases from Roche *regardless of the type of vitamins involved.* Hence a customer who felt compelled to buy Roche's B_2, B_6, and H (because alternative sellers were lacking) would also be pressured to buy Roche's other vitamins, where Roche's market shares were not in the 86% to 95% range. Given Roche's dominance, the European Court of Justice found that loyalty rebates "deny other producers access to the market."[44]

---

[42] For formal theory, see Paul Klemperer, "The Competitiveness of Markets with Switching Costs," *Rand Journal of Economics* (Spring 1987), pp. 138–150. Theories softening the anticompetitive consequences of switching costs are possible. See J. Farrell and Carl Shapiro, "Dynamic Competition with Switching Costs," *Rand Journal of Economics* (Spring 1988), pp. 123–137. It is worth noting that Farrell and Shapiro's procompetitive conclusion depends heavily on the existence of "unattached" customers—who do not incur any switching costs and who therefore might counteract the anticompetitive effects of switching costs. This to some degree assumes away the problem.

[43] *Hoffmann-LaRoche & Co.* v. *Commission of the European Communities*, 3 C.M.L.R. 211 (1979).

[44] Ibid., p. 290. Prior to a 1975 consent decree with the FTC, Xerox had a pricing

In sum, price discrimination can be used to extend market power. Simple examples include the limit prices of ERCO and the selective price cuts of Rentokil. More elaborate schemes, such as volume discounts and loyalty rebates, may allow a dominant firm or cartel to exploit power while simultaneously extending it. These price structures (i.e., their terms and conditions) may allow a high average level of price while at the same time curbing market share erosion to fresh newcomers or small fringe firms.

V. PREDATORY PRICING[45]

A. Definition

There are two elements common to all phenomena called "predatory pricing." First, predatory pricing involves temporary price cuts, not for purposes of enlarging demand but rather for purposes of eventually restricting supply. Once the predator is in a position to restrict supply (either by himself or with the cooperation of others), price is then increased. Since "predation" usually requires price to be cut at least below total unit cost, and since the eventual increase carries price well above total unit cost, the stream of profits generated by this ploy is the opposite of that generated by dynamic pricing, as depicted in Figure 14–5. That is, losses lead profits. Predatory pricing would make no sense if the losses incurred during the predatory campaign were not rewarded by profits after the campaign was over.

The second element of predatory pricing is the predator's "staying power," or "deep pocket," which must be greater or deeper than that of the rivals who are to be preyed upon. As with Nature's great predator *Felis leo*, large absolute size is an advantage. "If such a concern finds

---

schedule that gave discounts to customers who leased several Xerox machines. According to Kodak's Mike Murray, the FTC's ban "did make it easier for us to get our one machine in at a time." Gary Jacobson and John Hillkirk, *Xerox: American Samurai* (New York: Macmillan, 1986), p. 72. For other examples, see Karin Wagner, "Competition and Productivity: A Study of the Metal Can Industry in Britain, Germany, and the U.S.," *Journal of Industrial Economics* (September 1980), p. 32; and M. Fayad and H. Motamen, *The Economics of the Petrochemical Industry* (New York: St. Martins, 1986), p. 67. For examples of loyalty rebates by Sears, Proctor & Gamble, and others dealing with consumers see *The Wall Street Journal*, June 21, 1989, p. B1. The report says that firms use them in hopes of "locking out all competitors."

[45] For surveys, see Paul Milgrom and John Roberts, "New Theories of Predatory Pricing", in *Industrial Structure and The New Industrial Economics*, edited by G. Bonanno and D. Brandolini, (Oxford: Clarendon Press, 1990), pp. 112–137; Janusz A. Ordover and Garth Saloner, "Predation, Monopolization, and Antitrust," in *Handbook of Industrial Organization*, edited by R. Schmalensee and R. Willig, Vol. 1, (Amsterdam: North-Holland, 1989), pp. 537–596; and Joseph F. Brodley and George Hay, "Predatory Pricing: Competing Economic Theories and the Evolution of Legal Standards," *Cornell Law Review*, Vol. 66 (1981), pp. 738–803.

itself matching expenditures or losses, dollar for dollar, with a substantially smaller firm, the length of its purse assures it of victory".[46]

In short, **predatory pricing** is charging particularly low prices temporarily in order to increase long-run profitability by (1) driving competitors from the field, (2) disciplining uncooperative competitors or (3) hindering entry.

B. Driving Competitors Out

Use of predatory pricing to drive competitors out is obviously what gives the practice its name:

> The most extreme form of predatory pricing takes place when a seller holds price below the level of its rivals' costs (and perhaps also its own) for protracted periods, until the rivals either close down operations altogether or sell out on favorable terms. The predator's motivation is to secure a monopoly position once rivals have been driven from the arena, enjoying long-run profits higher than they would be if the rivals were permitted to survive.[47]

Of the two forms of victim liquidation, *bankruptcy* and *merger*, the one more favorable to the profit positions of both predator and prey is merger. Unless the victimized rival is very weak to begin with, or unless the predator applies nonprice harassments such as sabotage or patent infringement suits, a price war to the finish can be very expensive for both combatants. As Lester Telser puts it, "Since both firms can benefit by agreeing on a merger price, and both stand to lose by sales below cost, one would think that rational men would prefer merger."[48]

Indeed, the attractions of merger may be great enough to make price cutting of any kind seem superfluous. But merger is often illegal, and selective and controlled price cutting can serve several purposes even when merger is legal and the ultimate goal. The price the predator must pay to acquire rivals will be lower according to the vigor of the warfare or the *threat* of warfare. If mere threat can cause victims to sell out cheaply, so much the better. But a threat is hollow unless occasionally carried out. Malcolm Burns found that the old American Tobacco Company systematically used predatory pricing to reduce the cost of acquiring its competitors just before and after 1900: "Other things being equal, the estimated direct savings range up to 60 percent of what some targeted rivals would have cost if they had not been preyed on, and

---

[46] Corwin D. Edwards, "Conglomerate Bigness as a Source of Power," in *Business Concentration and Price Policy* (Princeton, N. J.: Princeton University Press, 1955), p. 334.

[47] F. M. Scherer, *Industrial Market Structure and Economic Performance* (Chicago: Rand McNally, 1970), p. 273.

[48] L. G. Telser, "Cutthroat Competition and the Long Purse," *Journal of Law & Economics* (October 1966), pp. 259–277.

[American's] reputation produced an additional discount averaging 25 percent [merely by threatening predation]."[49]

Another purpose served by combining predatory pricing and merger, as opposed to simply buying up rivals, is that it discourages entry. A predation-free policy of merger at attractive prices to those selling out would stimulate the entry of new firms, thereby foiling plans for eventual monopolization.

The best examples of fatal predation by large firms occurred around the turn of the century when antitrust policy was not clear. Tobacco, sugar, oil, and business machines are among the industries with skeletons in their closets.[50] More recent examples (from the United States, Canada, and the United Kingdom) involve matches, industrial gases, bread, oil, and newspapers.[51]

A common strategy in all cases is the "fighting brand" or "bogus independent." These are artificial creations of the predator, whose funding and control are often kept secret in order to protect the reputation of the predator and the quality image of his "regular" brands, creations that are *expected* to lose money. Once the victim is gone, the losses end by withdrawal of the fighting brand or closure of the bogus independent. Here, for instance, is part of a letter dated July 30, 1903 from the manager of a bogus independent tobacco company to his boss in the old American Tobacco Company:

> I do not believe for the present that we should attempt to make any money out of this business. . . . [If] we hold our prices down to where there is little or no profit, it will make some of our friends [rivals] very sick. They are not in business for the fun or it. . . .[52]

C. Disciplining Uncooperative Competitors

A leading firm may slash prices temporarily in order to punish mavericks whose price discounting is eroding the market share of the

---

[49] Malcolm R. Burns, "Predatory Pricing and the Acquisition Cost of Competitors," *Journal of Polical Economy* (April 1986), pp. 266–296.

[50] Besides the preceding references, see U. S. Bureau of Corporations, *Report of the Commissioner of Corporations on the Tobacco Industry* (Washington, D. C., 1909, 1915) Parts I, II, and III; A. S. Eichner, *The Emergence of Oligopoly* (Baltimore: Johns Hopkins University Press, 1969); and William Rodgers, *Think: A Biography of the Watsons and IBM* (New York: Stein and Day, 1969), Chapters 2, 3, 4.

[51] M. A. Utton, *Diversification and Competition* (Cambridge: Cambridge University Press, 1979), pp. 61—65; *Continental Baking Company* v. *Old Homestead Bread Co.*, 476 F. 2d 97 (10th Cir.) *cert. denied*, 414 U. S. 975 (1973); Robert J. Bertrand, *The State of Competition in the Canada Petroleum Industry*, Vol. 1; *Findings Issues and Remedies* (Ottawa: Minister of Supply and Services Canada, 1981), pp. 52–55; and *The Wall Street Journal*, January 4, 1988, p. 6.

[52] Malcolm R. Burns, "New Evidence on Predatory Price Cutting," *Managerial and Decision Economics* (December 1989), pp. 327–330. There are many other "smoking gun" quotes in this article.

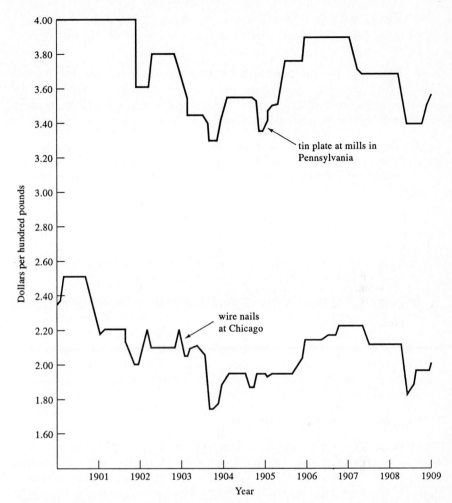

FIGURE 14–10. Prices of tin plate and wire nails, by months, 1901–1908. Source: Noami R. Lamoreaux, *The Great Merger Movement in American Business, 1895–1904* (Cambridge: Cambridge University Press, 1985), p. 137.

would-be price leader. If the discipline works, the price leadership (or cartel cooperation) is solidified.

For example, after its formation in 1901, U.S. Steel tried to lead the steel industry toward a producers' paradise of high and stable prices. Small independents were slow to follow, however, taking advantage of U.S. Steel's price umbrella to discount and maintain full capacity. U.S. Steel's resulting discipline is illustrated at the top of Figure 14–10 for tin plate. Nearly

all the independent firms had been running full in October 1902, whereas [U.S. Steel's tin plate] subsidiary was turning out less than half its potential product. After [U.S. Steel] slashed its prices, the situation was completely reversed. By January, 1903, most of the independents' mills were idle.[53]

Once chastised, the independents became cooperative. U.S. Steel could then raise its prices anew. Figure 14–10 shows similiar disciplinary cuts for wire nails around 1901–1902. The figure also shows that some maverick behavior persisted but was eventually subdued:

> Over the next few years this pattern was repeated. The Steel Corporation maintained prices until its officers felt that competitors were obtaining too large a share of the business. Then (typically during downturns) U.S. Steel suddenly reduced its [price] quotations. As Figure [14–10] shows, over time, the periods of price maintenance grew longer and bouts of price cutting less frequent. In part, this was a result of U.S. Steel's success in forestalling further entry, but it was also a result of the increase in discipline that U.S. Steel's periodic price cuts had fostered among the manufacturers. By mid-decade, the independent firms had, for all practical purposes, joined U.S. Steel in a cartel to restrain production and support prices.[54]

In sum, this is an example of predatory pricing for disciplinary purposes. It has both the main elements of predation — deep, temporary price cuts plus an imbalance of power. But the objective is not one of driving rivals from the market. Other examples could be drawn from gasoline retailing, grocery retailing, cement, building materials, and sugar.[55]

D. Predatory Pricing to Deter Entry

The price of 1000 5-mg Valium tablets to Canadian hospitals in 1969 was $42.70. Shortly thereafter, it fell to *zero* as Hoffman-LaRoche Limited (Roche), who held a monopoly on diazepam (Valium's generic name), tried to fend off the entry of Vivol, Horner Company's brand of diazepam.[56] Roche thought its monopoly was worth preserving because Valium, a tranquilizer, had become very profitably the most heavily prescribed drug in Canada after oral contraceptives. Horner's attempted entry followed on the heels of a change in Canadian patent law, which

---

[53] Naomi R. Lamoreaux, *The Great Merger Movement in American Business, 1895–1904* (Cambridge: Cambridge University Press, 1985), p. 135.

[54] Ibid., p. 136.

[55] Federal Trade Commission, *Economic Report on the Structure and Competitive Behavior of Food Retailing* (January 1966), pp. 121–142, *Federal Trade Commission* v. *Cement Institute, et al.*, 333 U. S. 683 (1948); C. D. Edwards, *Maintaining Competition* (New York: McGraw-Hill, 1964), pp. 169–170; A. S. Eichner, *The Emergence of Oligopoly*, pp. 243–246; and F. C. Allvine and J. M. Patterson, *Competition, Ltd.: The Marketing of Gasoline* (Bloomington: Indiana University Press, 1972), Chapters 5–7.

[56] What follows comes from "Reason for Judgment in *Her Majesty the Queen* v. *Hoffmann-LaRoche Limited*," released on February 5, 1980, mimeo, Supreme Court of Ontario.

brought the compulsory licensing of drug patents. The battle centered on the hospital market rather than the retail market because the hospital market was the easiest door by which to enter. Once a product gained a foothold there, hospital doctors and interns would prescribe it in their private practice.

Knowing of Horner's plans to launch Vivol in early 1970, Roche officials decided in late 1969 that an extended giveaway of Valium would be wise:

> It is our feeling that this tactic will not only abort Horner's efforts but serve as a warning to [other drug manufacturers] who seem to be showing an interest in this product.

In May 1970, after Horner's first shipments to hospitals, Roche personnel agreed that "the pipeline would be kept filled" by giving away Valium. So in June, Roche began giving Valium away free to hospitals, a program that lasted one year and dispensed a total of 82 million pills, the market price of which would have been about $2,600,000.

Horner, as you might well guess, did not make much headway in the hospital market during Roche's giveaway. Indeed, it may be that some of Horner's personnel began taking their Vivol tranquilizers to stay calm. Still, Roche's strategy was not completely successful because Horner enjoyed surprising success in the nonhospital market, selling over $12,000,000 worth of Vivol between 1970 and 1974.

Predatory pricing may thus affect entry as much as limit pricing. Further instances of predatory pricing to deter entry concern grocery retailing, computers, gypsum products, trash collection services, concrete, roasted coffee, roofing tiles, and organic peroxides.[57]

E. Skeptics, Asymmetries, and Raising Rival's Cost

John McGee is predatory pricing's most noted skeptic. His influential articles in 1958 and 1980 argued that predatory pricing is irrational and

---

[57] Russell W. Pittman, "Predatory Investment U.S. vs. IBM," *International Journal of Industrial Organization* (December 1984), pp. 341–365; G. W. Brock, *The U.S. Computer Industry* (Cambridge, Mass.: Ballinger, 1975), pp. 109–134; Richard T. DeLamarter, *Big Blue: IBM's Use and Abuse of Power* (New York: Dodd, Mead, 1986); Lee E. Preston, "Predatory Marketing," in *Regulation of Marketing and the Public Interest*, edited by F. E. Balderston et al. (New York: Pergamon Press, 1981), pp. 81–112; *Recent Efforts to Amend or Repeal the Robinson–Patman Act*, Hearings before the Ad Hoc Subcommittee on Antitrust . . . and Related Matters of the Committee on Small Business, U.S. Congress, House, 94th Cong., 2nd Sess. (1975–1976), Part 1, pp. 514–520; Part 2, pp. 36–57; *Business Week*, March 27, 1989, p. 54; *D & S Redi-Mix vs. Sierra Redi-Mix and Contracting*, (1983) Daily Journal D.A.R. 60; John C. Hilke and Philip B. Nelson, "Strategic Behavior and Attempted Monopolization: The Coffee Case," in Kwoka and White (eds.) *The Antitrust Revolution*, pp. 208–240; and Robert Merkin, "Predatory Pricing or Competitive Pricing," *Oxford Journal of Legal Studies* (Summer 1987), pp. 182–214. For examples in grocery retailing besides Shop-Rite, see Willard F. Mueller, "Alleged Predatory Conduct in Food Retailing," N.C. Project 117, Working Paper No. 78 (1984).

therefore extremely rare, so rare that we should have no policy to discourage it.[58] His arguments may be summarized as follows:[59]

1. Merger is a less costly means of doing away with rivals.
2. Predatory pricing should not force exits once the intended victims recognize that the price cutting is temporary. The prospects of higher profits later should entice them to stay in and also entice investors and leaders to finance their persistence.
3. He argued that even if victims do leave the market, they can easily reenter after the predator raises prices.

We have discussed the first argument previously. Merger is not a good substitute for predatory pricing because it is illegal to lessen competition substantially by merger, and even if it were legal, predatory pricing can be a useful means of lowering the aquisition price paid by the predator.

McGee's *second argument* is grounded on an implicit assumption that the predator and prey stand on an equal footing. There is, in a word, "symmetry" between them in their knowledge, financial strengths, and motives. McGee assumes that predators cannot "bluff" their way to victory and their prey can easily defend themselves.

The problem with this assumption is its lack of reality. Male lions do not prey solely on other male lions, and the same could be said of commercial carnivores. Apart from asymmetries of size and strength, there may be information asymmetries. The best metaphor in this respect is poker.[60]

In poker, information symmetry (as implicitly assumed by McGee) would require that each poker player be dealt five cards face up for all to see followed by betting, with the best hand winning. In contrast, information asymmetry would occur if each player were dealt three cards face up and two cards face down in the hole (known only to each player), followed by betting and disclosure of the hidden cards to determine the winning hand among all those remaining in play by betting support. Only in the latter game could "bluffing" occur. A player with two kings face up, for instance, might bluff (with heavy betting) that a third is in the hole, thereby defeating a superior hand having three fives.

In the real world of business, asymmetries abound. Hence theories based on symmetries seem irrelevant. Among the asymmetries we have

[58] J. S. McGee, "Predatory Price Cutting: The Standard Oil (N. J.) Case," *Journal of Law & Economics* (October 1958), pp. 137–169; and J. S. McGee, "Predatory Pricing Revisited," *Journal of Law & Economics* (October 1980), pp. 289–330.

[59] Paul Milgrom and John Roberts, "New Theories of Predatory Pricing," in *Industrial Structure in the New Industrial Economics* edited by G. Bonanno and D. Brandolini (Oxford: Clarendon Press, 1990), pp. 112–137.

[60] Paul Milgrom and John Roberts, "Informational Asymmetries, Strategic Behavior, and Industrial Organization," *American Economic Review* (May 1987), pp. 184–193.

encountered so far in this book, there are market share mismatches, first mover advantages, absolute product cost differences, and varying strengths of brand image under product differentiation.[61]

The third argument — that victims of predation may easily reenter the market once the predation is over — can also be questioned. Apart from the fact that technical entry barriers like economies of scale may deter reentry, there is the matter of expectations. A firm's decision about entering or reentering will be based on its expectations of profit or loss. And a predator may be able to influence those expectations. In particular, predatory behavior may give the predator a reputation for aggressiveness that, in turn, generates expectations of prospective losses among victims if they contemplate reentry (and among those considering first-time entry).[62]

Very impressive evidence of reputation's impact has been found in grocery retailing in Edmonton, Canada.[63] Safeway's vigorous attacks on new entrants during the 1950s and 1960s intimidated potential rivals to such a degree that they would not enter "Safeway's territory" even during a period when Safeway itself could not build added capacity because of a temporary court order. Hence the benefits of a mean reputation extend beyond the ability to charge especially profitable prices over the long run. Its nasty reputation allowed Safeway to build new stores in new areas at a (leisurely) pace that was most profitable. Safeway did not have to build far ahead of demand in a costly effort to preempt the market. Indeed, this evidence on reputation is so robust as to suggest that

> there are conditions under which predation will dominate pre-emption as an entry-deterring strategy. It might even pay an incumbent firm to allow new entry to take place in its expanding market so that an ensuing predatory attack will be correctly interpreted as an aggressive response to incursion into its market. Entry deterred in this manner may entail lower cost than the persistent opening of new stores before it pays new firms to enter.[64]

In other words, a predator needs some prey in order to terrify potential entrants. It may therefore pay the predator to allow some en-

[61] See, for example, G. S. Carpenter and K. Nakamoto, "Consumer Preference Formation and Pioneering Advantage," *Journal of Marketing Research* (August 1989), pp. 285–298; S. J. Hoch and J. Deighton, "Managing What Consumers Learn From Experience," *Journal of Marketing* (April 1989), p. 1–20; and T. F. Bresnahan and P. C. Reiss, "Do Entry Conditions Vary Across Markets?" *Brookings Papers on Economic Activity* (No. 3, 1987), pp. 833–871.

[62] Paul Milgrom and John Roberts, "Predation, Reputation and Entry Deterrence," *Journal of Economic Theory*, Vol. 27 (1982), pp. 280–312; and D. M. Kreps and R. Wilson, "Reputation and Imperfect Information," *Journal of Economic Theory*, Vol. 27 (1982), pp. 253–279.

[63] Balder Von Hohenbalken and Douglas S. West, "Empirical Tests for Predatory Reputation," *Canadian Journal of Economics* (February 1986), pp. 160–178.

[64] Ibid., pp. 176–177.

trants who will, once squashed, serve as object lessons. This contrasts sharply with McGee's argument that potential predators are paralyzed by a fear of potential entrants.

Thus, in the end, McGee's several arguments seem unpersuasive. Predatory pricing sometimes pays. It therefore sometimes occurs. Still, it is important to recognize, in the spirit of McGee's arguments, that price predation has its risks, often to the point of being irrational. It burdens the predator in the short run. And its prospects of securing long-run power may be slim. Hence dominant firms often resort to nonprice methods of injuring rivals.[65] Dominance may be achieved or extended by raising rivals' costs rather than lowering rivals' revenues.[66] Indeed, victims may sometimes be "squeezed" by a simultaneous reduction of revenue and increase in cost. We shall pursue these possibilities later. They deserve mention new merely because dominant firms may find them to be good substitutes for predatory pricing, just as they are often good substitutes for entry-limit pricing.

SUMMARY

The principal objective assumed for this chapter's analysis is long-run profit maximization. Under very favorable structural conditions, this may be achieved simply by *exploiting* market power. On the other hand, the *extension* of market power may be profitable, and a combination of exploitation and extension would perhaps be still more profitable. This chapter looks at long-run price strategies of exploitation and extension, mainly the latter.

An entry limit price is high enough to reap excess profits while being low enough to warn potential entrants away. Short-run profits may be sacrificed, but preservation of established market shares boosts long-run profit. Entrants may not heed the warning, and incumbents may use alternative signals, so for these and other reasons, the theory is not completely convincing. Theories of dynamic pricing postulate higher near-term prices and profits inviting more entry than limit pricing theory. The empirical evidence on these strategies is mixed, as both make their appearance. And extreme instances of either one alone seem unusual.

65 J. A. Ordover and R. D. Willig, "An Economic Definition of Predation: Pricing and Product Innovation," *Yale Law Journal* (November 1981), pp. 8–53.

66 T. Krattenmaker and S. Salop, "Anticompetitive Exclusions: Raising Rivals' Costs to Achieve Power Over Price," *Yale Law Journal* (November 1986), pp. 209–295; S. C. Salop and D. T. Scheffman, "Cost-Raising Strategies," *Journal of Industrial Economics* (September 1987), pp. 19–34.

Price discrimination occurs when different varieties of a commodity (or service) are sold to different buyers at different prices, net of costs. It requires some market power, differing price elasticities of demand, and market separation. Under first-degree price discrimination, price varies to the point of capturing all the consumers' surplus. Second-degree price discrimination treats different buyers differently depending on their purchase quantities, with price falling in a "block" structure. Third-degree discriminaiton is most common, with low prices in elastic markets and high prices in inelastic markets.
with monopoly power. Selective discounting, as illustrated by Rentokil, can extend market power. Volume discounts and loyalty rebates are yet more subtle means to the same end.

Predatory pricing, a sister of price discrimination, is charging particularly low prices temporarily in order to increase long-run profitability by (1) driving competitors from the market, (2) disciplining uncooperative competitors, or (3) hindering entry. Theories grounded on restrictive assumptions pooh-pooh predatory pricing. Theories acknowledging asymmetries, reputation effects, and other features of reality comport better with the empirical evidence, which shows price predation occurring occasionally. Legal constraints (covered in the next chapter) and the attractiveness of nonprice predation help to explain why the incidence is no more than occasional.

15

■ Price and Production Strategy in the Long Run: Public Policy

That the Robinson–Patman Act . . . is the most controversial of our antitrust laws may be the understatement of the century.

—FREDERICK ROWE

There are many things in life that can be either good or bad depending on the circumstances—wealth and wine, for instance. The same applies to price discrimination. Under some circumstances, it increases competition. At times it lessens competition. This good/bad dichotomy makes public policy a delicate exercise. Indeed, public policy itself can be pro-competitive or anticompetitive. Public policy governing predatory pricing likewise has problems.

The purpose of this chapter is to review and assess public policy governing price discrimination and predatory pricing. Apart from the Sherman Act of 1890, statute law in these areas began in 1914 with Section 2 of the Clayton Act concerning price discrimination. This was

458

greatly altered by the Robinson–Patman Amendment of 1936. Now, more than a thousand enforcement actions later, we confront a large body of case law that requires summary consideration. Controversy sparked by predatory pricing policy also receives attention.

I. PRICE DISCRIMINATION

The Clayton Act's original Section 2 outlawed only flagrantly predatory price discrimination. Its limited scope yielded few prosecutions. While this law lay idle, chain stores revolutionized grocery, drug, and department store merchandising. Small, single-shop, "mom-and-pop" stores suffered and, during the Great Depression, began dropping like blighted apples. The outcries of their owners caused the Federal Trade Commission (FTC) to study and report. Although the FTC's report found much virtue in chain stores, it also found that "a most substantial part of the chains' ability to undersell independents" could be attributed to the chains' ability to buy goods from manufacturers more cheaply than independents could. The chains' **oligopsony** buying power "forced" manufacturers to discriminate in favor of chains. Moreover, their large size enabled chains to buy directly from manufacturers, thereby sidestepping independent brokers, wholesalers, jobbers, and other middlemen as well as underselling independent retailers. So Congress went to bat for small business. In the words of Congressman Patman in 1935:

> The day of the independent merchant is gone unless something is done and done quickly. He cannot possibly survive under that system. So we have reached the cross road; we must either turn the food . . . business of this country . . . over to a few corporate chains, or we have got to pass laws that will give the people, who built this country in time of peace and who saved it in time of war, an opportunity to exist . . .[1]

In short, the purpose of the Robinson–Patman Act of 1936 went well beyond the traditional antitrust purpose of maintaining competition. It injected two new objectives: *protection* of small business and maintenance of "*fair*" or "equitable" price relationships between buyers who compete with each other as sellers.

A. Subsection 2(a) of Robinson–Patman

The aims of protection and equity lurk beneath the tortured language of all six main subsections in the act, especially 2(a). Subsection 2(a) prohibits a seller from charging different prices to different purchasers of

---

[1] Hearings Before the House Committee on the Judiciary on *Bills to Amend the Clayton Act*, 74th Cong. 1st Sess. (1935), pp. 5–6.

"goods of like grade and quality" where the effect "may be substantially"

1. "to lessen competition or tend to create a monopoly in any line of commerce," or
2. "to injure, destroy, or prevent competition with any person" (or company)
   a. "who either grants or"
   b. "knowingly receives" the benefit of the discrimination, or
   c. "with customers of either of them."

Thus, there are two definitions of **illegal competitive effect:** (1) a *broad* definition that refers to substantial lessening of competition in the *market as a whole* and (2) *a narrow* definition that refers to injury to *particular competitors.* The broad definition reflects the traditional antitrust aim of maintaining competition, and its language matches that applying to mergers. In contrast, it is the narrow definition that reflects the aims of protection, equity, and fairness.

Either of these two forms of competitive damage may occur in

a. the seller's market, which is called **primary level injury**
b. the buyers' market, which is called **secondary level injury**
c. the market containing customers of the buyers, which is called **tertiary level injury**.

If, for example, a manufacturer cuts price to one wholesaler but not to others, it might damage competition among manufacturers (primary level), or among wholesalers (secondary level), or among retailers who buy from the wholesalers (tertiary level). If it were a matter of direct sales to retailers, then retailers would be the buyers of the discriminating seller, and they would then be considered "secondary" level. If this sounds confusing to you, you are not alone, as indicated by itemization of the first common criticism of the act.

Common Criticism 1: The act is "a roughly hewn, unfinished block of legislative phraseology," a "masterpiece of obscurity," a source of "crystal clear confusion."[2]

Compounding the confusion, several types of price discrimination have been found injurious to competition. They are (1) volume or quantity discounts, (2) territorial price discrimination, and (3) functional discounts. These are outlined in Table 15–1, together with indications of the level at which they are said to damage competition and the specified breadths of injury typically used in the past by the FTC and appellate courts when enforcing the statute. The dashes in the table identify combinations of level and type that are rarely if ever attacked under the law.

---

[2] "Eine Kleine Juristische Schlummergeschichte," *Harvard Law Review* (March 1966), p. 922.

TABLE 15-1. Summary Outline of Injury Definition Applied, Given the Basic Types of Discrimination Found to be Illegal and Market Level of Reference

	Type of Price Discrimination		
Level of Injury	Volume or Quantity Discounts	Territorial Price Discrimination	Functional Discounts
Primary level	Broad or narrow	Broad or narrow	—
Secondary level	Narrow	Narrow	Narrow
Tertiary level	—	—	Narrow
Main Line of possible defense	Cost	Good faith	Cost or good faith

These blank combinations are eligible for illegality, but the authorities tend to ignore them. The bottom row of Table 15-1 shows the defenses discriminators of each type occasionally use to fend off FTC attorneys. These defenses—"cost" and "good faith"—are explicitly recognized by the Robinson–Patman Act:

- *Cost defense:* "nothing herein . . . shall prevent differentials which make only due allowance for differences in the cost of manufacture, sale, or delivery resulting from [differing methods of sale or delivery]."

- *Good faith defense*, Subsection 2(b): "nothing herein . . . shall prevent a seller rebutting the prima-facie case . . . by showing that his lower price . . . was made in good faith to meet an equally low price of a competitor."

Often, these defenses do not offer much protection in practice. The cost defense has fallen into disuse because the FTC and appellate courts have been stingy in allowing its application. They require elaborate proofs and reject justifications based on reallocations of overhead costs. The meeting competition in good faith defense is much more useful. It allows a low price to match competition. This defense has recently been expanded to allow low prices that obtain new customers as well as retain old ones and low prices that unwittingly or unknowingly beat a rival's prices.[3] Still, critics of the Robinson–Patman Act favor further liberalization of the good faith defense as well as the cost defense.

Common Criticism 2: By amendment or reinterpretation, the defenses open to discriminators ought to be liberalized.

[3] Richard A. Whiting, "R–P: May It Rest in Peace," *Antitrust Bulletin* (Fall 1986), pp. 709–732.

Before delving into the case law concerning the act, we may note in its language two major anomalies. First, despite its origins, the statute's fire is focused not on the power or conduct of oligopsonistic *buyers* but rather on the conduct of *sellers*. As Corwin Edwards observes,

> The avowed purpose of the Congress was to use the law of price discrimination to curb the buying power of chain stores and other large buyers. However, the means to be employed consisted primarily in forbidding sellers, the presumed victims of that buying power, from granting the concessions that were exacted from them. . . . If the statute was an effort to protect competition from the pressure of powerful buyers on weak sellers, it was anomalous to provide that protection primarily by action against weak sellers who succumbed to the pressure. Such a process bears some resemblance to an effort to stamp out mugging by making it an offense to permit oneself to be mugged.[4]

Our roster of antitrust defendants has so far been dominated by giants like IBM and Alcoa. The roster of Robinson–Patman defendants, however, introduces a population largely composed of midgets such as Samuel H. Moss, Inc., and Fruitvale Canning Company. The possibility that this oblique approach on sellers might backfire is illustrated by the *Jens Risom* case of 1967, in the office furniture field. Furniture manufacturers such as Risom sold to retailers at a discount off list price amounting to as much as 50%, whereas their sales to interior decorators, who competed with the retailers, were at no more than 40% discount. As a result of the FTC's order ending the discrimination, Risom and some other manufacturers eliminated interior decorators as direct buying customers. These decorators thereafter had to buy furniture for their clients through retailers. Thus, although the intent of the FTC's order was to place decorators on an equal competitive footing with retailers, decorators ended up at the mercy of the retailers with whom they competed. Subsequent to the order, several decorators reported that their clients' costs had increased — one giving estimates of increases ranging from 10% to 20%, depending on which retailer supplied the decorator's clients with furniture.[5]

A second notable quirk concerns the statute's definition of price discrimination. Price differences unjustified by cost differences are "discriminatory," but cost differences unaccompanied by price differences are not. In other words, the economic definition of discrimination — differing price-cost ratios, even if prices are identical — is rejected by the statute in favor of a definition that hinges almost entirely on price differences

---

[4] Corwin D. Edwards, *The Price Discrimination Law* (Washington, D.C.: Brookings Institution, 1959), p. 63.

[5] *Recent Efforts to Amend or Repeal the Robinson–Patman Act*, Part 1, Hearing before the Ad Hoc Subcommitttee on Antitrust . . . and Related Matters of the Committee on Small Business, U.S. Congress, House, 94th Cong., 1st Sess. (1975), pp. 282–312.

alone. The consequences of this approach are illustrated by the *Binney & Smith* case. Binney & Smith, Co., was found by the FTC to have sold school supplies at a uniform price to both jobbers, who are middlemen, and large retail chains. This price uniformity, though obviously injurious to jobbers, was not questioned by the FTC.[6]

> Common Criticism 3: Even accepting the act's purposes as proper, the statute is ill-conceived. Indeed, many proponents of protection and fairness are disappointed with it.

Before discussing the types of discrimination listed in Table 15–1, we should first specify the kinds of evidence that indicate "broad" or "narrow" injury, the two designations constituting the body of Table 15–1. **Broad** (or **marketwide**) **injury** to competition is indicated by substantial reductions in the number of competitors in the market, elevated barriers to entry, a lack of competitive behavior in pricing, or foreclosure of substantial parts of the market to existing competitors. **Narrow** (or **competitor**) **injury** is indicated by simple price differences among customers, or a price difference coupled with diversion of business from the disadvantaged buyer toward the favored buyer, or diversions away from a nondiscriminating seller toward a discriminating seller. Injuries embraced by this narrow definition are clearly more personal than those embraced by the broad definition. That is, the discrimination appears to cripple a *single* firm or particular *class* of firms. Obviously, the broad definition coincides more nearly with a purely economic definition of competion, while the narrow definition coincides with some notions of fairness.

A quick glance at Table 15–1 also reveals that narrow evidence of injury is more commonly used by the FTC, especially when judging injury at secondary and tertiary levels. At primary level, broad injury has been found only in cases concerning volume or quantity discounts and territorial price discrimination.[7]

Volume and Quantity Discounts.   These are first cousins to second-degree price discrimination. Quantity discounts are based on the amount purchased in a *single* transaction, with large quantities lowering price. Volume discounts are based on *cumulative* purchases, involving numerous transactions, during some stated period of time, such as one year. Of the two, volume discounts are least likely to be cost justifiable and more anticompetitive in the broad sense. For these reasons the FTC has attacked volume discounts much more vigorously than it has quantity dis-

---

6 Edwards, *The Price Discrimination Law*, p. 311.

7 See also R. C. Brooks, Jr., Testimony, *Small Business and the Robinson–Patman Act*, Hearings before the Special Subcommittee on Small Business and the Robinson–Patman Act of the Select Committee on Small Business, U.S. Congress, House, 91st Cong. 2nd Sess. (1970), Vol. 2, p. 657.

counts. At primary level, volume discounts can heighten barriers to entry or foreclose small sellers from substantial segments of the market.[8]

Although such discounts may have genuine anticompetitive effects at primary (seller's) level, very few cases have actually been argued on these grounds. The rarity may be due to a dearth of situations causing broad injury at primary level. Then again, it may also be a consequence of the fact that, under the act, volume and quantity discounts are more easily prosecuted on grounds of narrow injury at the secondary or buyer level. Recall that a major purpose of the act was to make such prosecutions as these easier.

The classic case here is *Morton Salt*, decided by the Supreme Court in 1948. Morton sold its table salt at $1.60 a case in less-than-carload lots, at $1.50 a case for carload lots, and at still lower prices of $1.40 and $1.35 for annual volumes exceeding 5,000 and 50,000 cases, respectively. In defense of these prices, Morton claimed that they were equally available to all, that salt was just one tiny item in grocers' inventories, and that therefore competitive injury could not arise. Rejecting these arguments the court concluded as follows:

> The legislative history of the Robinson–Patman Act makes it abundantly clear that Congress considered it to be an evil that a large buyer could secure a competitive advantage over a small buyer solely because of the large buyer's quantity purchasing ability. . . . Here the Commission found what would appear to be obvious, that the competitive opportunities of certain merchants were injured when they had to pay [Morton] substantially more for their goods than their competitors had to pay. . . . That [Morton's] quantity discounts did result in price differentials between competing purchasers sufficient to influence their resale price of salt is shown by the evidence. . . . Congress intended to protect a merchant from competitive injury attributable to discriminatory prices on any or all goods sold in interstate commerce, whether the particular goods constituted a major or minor portion of his stock. . . . [In] enacting the Robinson–Patman Act Congress was especially concerned with protecting small business. . . . [9]

This narrow, numerical interpretation of injury was later carried to extremes during the 1950s. Since then, this hard line has softened, but a fairly stringent interpretation of secondary line injury still prevails.

Critics of this policy argue that although individual *competitors* may suffer, *competition* may not. Such discrimination in favor of large buyers is said to "introduce flexibilty into the distributive system, helping to compress traditional markups, and prevent or disrupt a rigid stratification of functions." Moreover, a large buyer "which does indeed make possible cost savings on the part of its suppliers may yet, in facing impure markets, have to coerce suppliers into giving it the concessions

---

[8] R. C. Brooks, Jr., "Volume Discounts as Barriers to Entry and Access," *Journal of Political Economy* (February 1961), p. 65.

[9] *Federal Trade Commission* v. *Morton Salt Co.*, 334 U.S. 37 (1948).

which its greater efficiency justifies."[10] In short, price discrimination may increase price flexibility and rivalry at primary and secondary levels; it may also contribute to efficiency. Even so, enhanced competition is not automatic. Price concessions are not always passed on to consumers or spread throughout the market. Moreover, loss of even a few competitors diminishes competition where there are only a few to begin with. The ultimate effect depends heavily on the circumstances. Hence controversy will continue.[11]

Territorial Price Discrimination. This type of discrimination takes two forms: (1) selective geographic price cutting and (2) fictional freight charges imposed under basing-point pricing systems. Both received earlier mention. The former has produced many illegal primary line injuries, whereas the latter has been charged with injuring competition at secondary level. As indicated in Table 15–1, neither can be defended by cost justifications. Because geographic price cutting includes "predatory pricing," several primary line cases of this sort cast a good light on the Robinson–Patman Act. In fact, they give the FTC its finest hours of enforcement.[12] These cases contain poignant examples of genuine broad injury to competition; they also contain striking evidence of predatory intent. Some excerpts from business correspondence follow:

> So by continuing our efforts and putting a crimp into him wherever possible, we may ultimately curb this competition if we should not succeed in eliminating it entirely.

> Don't try to follow me. If you do, we will put you out of business.

The latter message was no idle threat; ensuing below-cost prices ultimately throttled the smaller competitor.[13]

Still, geographic price discrimination may also be procompetitive. It may be used for promotional purposes; for entering new geographic markets; or for further penetrating established markets to spread overhead costs. When used for these laudable purposes, it is usually less systematic than the "sharpshooting" associated with predation. Nevertheless, procompetitive territorial pricing has occasionally been attacked by the FTC. In the *Page Dairy* case, for instance, the FTC myopically went after a firm whose unsystematic price discrimination was actually undermining its competitors' efforts at cartelization:

---

[10] J. B. Dirlam and A. E. Kahn, *Fair Competition* (Ithaca, N.Y.: Cornell University Press, 1954), pp. 204–205.

[11] For a good discussion of the circumstances, see ibid, Chapters 7 and 8. See also L. S. Keyes, "Price Discrimination in Law and Economics," *Southern Economic Journal* (April 1961), pp. 320–328.

[12] E. B. Muller & Co. v. FTC, 142 F. 2d 511 (6th Cir. 1944); Maryland Baking Co. v. FTC, 243 F. 2d 716 (4th Cir. 1957); Forster Manufacturing Co. v. FTC, 335 F. 2d 47 (1st Cir. 1964). Among private cases see Volasco Prods. Co. v. Lloyd A. Fry Roofing Co., 346 F. 2d 661 (6th Cir. 1965); Moore v. Mead's Fine Bread Co., 348 U.S. 115 (1954); and Continental Baking Co. v. Old Homestead Bread Co., 476 F. 2d 97 (10th Cir. 1973).

[13] *Forster Manufacturing Co.*

From the trial record it appears that before the complaint against Page Dairy, other dairies had made an unsuccessful effort to draw it into agreement to fix prices. . . . It is a reasonable inference that the competitors of the company brought its prices to the Commission's attention, not because the local discrimination was unusual, but because Page Dairy was a price-cutter and would not co-operate with other dairies.

The Commission's order in 1953 required Page Dairy to cease selling to any buyer at a lower price than to any other buyer where it was in competition with any other seller. The immediate effect of the order was a price increase by Page Dairy, as a result of which various dairies that had been troubled by price competition of the company felt that their problems had been met.[14]

The line between geographic price cutting that is predatory or destructive of competition and that which promotes or expands competition is obviously difficult to draw. "But," according to the critics, "one thing is certain: it cannot be drawn merely at the point where a price reduction diverts trade from a competitor."[15]

Common Criticism 4: As interpreted, the law stifles genuine price competition, thereby raising and stiffening price levels.

Returning to the bright side of the coin, the FTC put the Robinson–Patman Act to good use in attacking collusive basing-point price systems in the *Corn Products Refining* case of 1945 and others.[16] As we have seen, basing-point systems are price-fixing mechanisms, but the FTC's initial assault was based on narrow secondary line injury under Subsection 2(a). (Later, in *Cement Institute*,[17] a restraint of trade approach was applied.) The defendant in *Corn Products* produced glucose in Chicago and Kansas City plants, but maintained Chicago as a single basing point. Thus, both plants sold only at delivered prices computed as if all shipments originated in Chicago. Kansas City candy manufacturers who bought glucose from the Kansas City plant were charged phantom freight, as if the sweetening had come all the way from Chicago. After hearing the case on appeal, the Supreme Court accepted the FTC's finding that the candy manufacturers located in Kansas City competed with those in Chicago. The Court also agreed that, though small, the price differentials on glucose would affect the candy makers' costs and final prices. The cost differences were said to be "enough to divert business

---

14 Edwards, *The Price Discrimination Law*, pp. 443–444. For a related example see William K. Jones, Testimony, *Small Business and the Robinson-Patman Act*, Hearings before Special Subcommittee on Small Business of the Select Committee on Small Business, House, 91st Cong., 1st Sess. (1969), Vol. I, p. 109.

15 Philip Elman, "The Robinson-Patman Act and Antitrust Policy: A Time for Reappraisal," *Washington Law Review*, Vol. 42 (1966), p. 13.

16 *Corn Products Refining Company* v. *FTC*, 324 U.S. 726 (1945).

17 *FTC* v. *Cement Institute*, 333 U.S. 683 (1948).

from one manufacturer to another." Consequently, narrow competitive injury was adjudged at the secondary or buyer level (between candy manufacturers), and the price system was banned.

Functional Discounts.   As indicated by Table 15–1, primary level injury is not usually associated with functional discounts, but findings of narrow injury at secondary and tertiary levels have been frequent. By definition, functional discounts are determined not by amounts purchased or buyer location but rather by the functional characteristics of buyers. Functions in the "traditional" distribution network are well known: Producers sell to wholesalers, who sell at a higher price to jobbers, who in turn sell at a higher price to retailers, who finally sell at a still higher price to consumers. Other functional differences may be based on other buyer classifications, such as government versus private.

The problem of illegal price discrimination arises when people of different functions compete. Most commonly, "traditional" channels get jumbled, as when resale competition crops up between resellers in different classifications, or when a producer sells at various levels in the distribution network to someone's disadvantage. In other words, discrimination between buyers who are *not* in competition with each other is *not* a violation. The FTC has never ruled against a functional discount per se; somebody down the line must be disadvantaged relative to his competitors.

For example, if a producer charges a lower price to its direct-buying retailers than to its independent wholesalers, competition may be injured at the *retail* level between its direct buyers and the *customers* of the independent wholesalers. In *Tri-Valley Packing Association* v. *FTC*, a processor of canned fruits and vegetables sold its canned goods at lower prices to certain retail chains with buying agencies in San Francisco than it charged retailers and wholesalers who did not have buying agencies in San Francisco. The FTC and appellate court found violation of Subsection 2(a) because the direct buying retailers had an advantage over their competitors who had to buy from the higher-paying wholesalers.[18]

A different problem arises when a buyer performs a dual role, say, wholesaling *and* retailing, in which case he may get a large wholesaler's discount that gives him a competitive advantage when reselling as a retailer but not when reselling as a wholesaler.[19] Critics point out that compliance with the Robinson–Patman Act in these instances often raises a serious inconsistency. Compliance implies that the producer must control the prices at which his independent middlemen resell. But such control involves the producer in "resale price maintenance," or ver-

---

[18] *Tri-Valley Packing Ass'n* v. *FTC*, 329 F. 2d 694 (9th Cir. 1964).

[19] *FTC* v. *Standard Oil Co.*, 355 U.S. 396 (1958) and 340 U.S. 231 (1951); *Mueller Company* v. *FTC*, 323 F. 2d 44 (7th Cir., 1963).

tical price fixing, which is generally illegal under Section 1 of the Sherman Act.[20]

Common Criticism 5: Compliance with the price discrimination law in this and other respects is inconsistent with other antitrust policies.

An Overview.   Critical analyses of the Robinson–Patman Act suggest that procompetitive discriminations may be distinguished from anticompetitive discriminations by whether they are perpetrated by firms with small or large market shares. *Systematic, large-firm discriminations tend to be anticompetitive, whereas unsystematic, small-firm discriminations tend to be competitive.* But there are exceptions.

The criticism may give the added impression that enforcement zealous enough to crush many small-firm discriminations must have also stamped out large-firm discriminations altogether. But this inference would be fallacious. Discrimination can take many forms not reached by the law. A powerful seller may favor particular buyers by making uniform price reductions upon that part of his product line most important to those particular buyers. Moreover, a powerful seller can sometimes refuse to sell to those he disfavors. Similarly, a powerful buyer, deprived of discriminatory price concessions, can nevertheless obtain substantial advantages in acquiring goods:

> It can (a) take a seller's entire output at a low price; (b) obtain low prices from sellers who are meeting some other seller's lawful competition; (c) buy goods cheaply abroad; (d) obtain low prices upon goods so differentiated from what bears higher prices that the prohibition of the law is inapplicable; (e) obtain goods of premium quality without paying a premium price; (f) buy large amounts under long-term contract when prices are unusually low; or (g) produce goods for itself.[21]

For these many reasons, chain stores have thrived despite the law.[22] The shrewd reader may think up other avenues of evasion. Brokerage payments and preferential promotional services or allowances cannot be among them, however. Discrimination via these routes is foreclosed by Subsections 2(c), (d), and (e) of the Robinson–Patman Act, each of which warrants a few words.

B. Subsections 2(c), (d), and (e)

As may be seen from Table 15–2, these portions of the Robinson–Patman Act are *not* simple extensions of Subsection 2(a) governing seller's price differences. Whereas some kind of probable competitive injury must be

[20] Edwards, *The Price Discrimination Law*, p. 312.

[21] Corwin D. Edwards, "Control of the Single Firm: Its Place in Antitrust Policy," *Law & Contemporary Problems* (Summer 1965), p. 477.

[22] Stanley C. Hollander and Mary Jane Sheffet, "The Robinson-Patman Act: Boon or Bane for Retailers," *Antitrust Bulletin* (Fall 1986) pp. 759–795.

TABLE 15-2. Comparative Outline of Subsections 2(a), (c), (d), (e), and (f), of the Robinson–Patman Act

Subsection	(1) Competitive Injury Required?	(2) Cost Defense Available?	(3) Good Faith Defense Available?	(4) Violator Is Buyer or Seller?
2(a) General	1. Yes	2. Yes	3. Yes	4. Seller
2(c) Brokerage	1. No	2. No	3. No	4. Both
2(d) Promotional pay	1. No	2. No	3. Yes	4. Seller
2(e) Services	1. No	2. No	3. Yes	4. Seller
2(f) Buyer inducement	Buyer liability for knowingly inducing violation of one of the above.			

shown under 2(a), such is not the case for (c), (d), and (e). Furthermore, whereas 2(a) discriminators may defend themselves by cost justifications or demonstrations of meeting competition in good faith, those running afoul of Subsections 2(c), (d), and (e) may not, except for (d) and (e) with respect to good faith. In other words, these additional provisions of the act specify what could be considered per se violations.

Subsection 2(c), the **brokerage provision**, outlaws payment or receipt of brokerage fees that cross the sales transaction from seller to buyer. It also prohibits any compensation *in lieu* of brokerage. Brokers (whose job it is to match up buyers and sellers without ever taking title to the goods) are quite active in the grocery game plus a few other distributive trades. Subsection 2(c) was aimed primarily at a practice in the food industry by which chain stores large enough to buy direct, without benefit of brokers, got price reductions equivalent to the brokerage fees that sellers would have otherwise paid. In practice, however, this provision outlawed *all* brokerage commissions, large or small, except those paid to a truly independent broker. At times, 2(c)'s rigorous application has harpooned marketing arrangements that helped small concerns. In the *Biddle* case, for instance, Biddle sold market information services to 2400 grocery buyers — placing their orders with sellers, collecting brokerage from sellers, and then passing some brokerage on to the buyers in the form of reduced information fees.[23] This practice was declared illegal, however, as were others equally beneficial to small independents.[24] The courts held that "The seller may not pay the buyer brokerage on the

---

[23] *Biddle Purchasing Co., v. FTC*, 96 F.2d 687 (1938).

[24] See for example, *Quality Bakers* v. *FTC*, 114 F.2d 393 (1940); and *Southgate Brokerage Co.* v. *FTC* 150 F.2d 607 (1945).

latter's purchases for his own account" (period). The Supreme Court's *Broch* opinion of 1960[25] has since introduced a modicum of flexibility into brokerage cases, but a modicum is not a magnum.

Subsection 2(d) makes it unlawful for a seller to make any **payment to a buyer** in consideration of the buyer's promotion of the seller's goods, unless similar payments are made available on "proportionately equal terms" to *all* competing buyers. Subsection 2(e) makes it unlawful for the seller himself to **provide promotional services** to or through a buyer unless he provides opportunity for such services on "proportionally equal terms" to *all* other competing buyers.

For example, if Revlon were to provide Macy's, Bullock's, and Sears with in-store demonstrators of Revlon cosmetics, or if they *paid* these large retailers to conduct these demonstrations, then Revlon would have to make equal-proportionate opportunities of some kind open to all retailers who compete with Macy's, Bullock's, and Sears in cosmetics. You may ask proportionate to what? And in what way? Does that mean that Revlon must circulate a midget giving one-shot, 15-minute demonstrations among independent corner drug stores for every fully developed model it sets up in Macy's for a weekend visit?

The FTC and the courts have chopped through a thick jungle of questions such as these during the past 50 years. And, in order to guide the ordinary, time-pressed businessperson through the treacherous path so cleared, the FTC has kindly drawn up a long "Guide for Advertising Allowances and Other Merchandising Payments and Services" that attempts to clarify the case law for laymen. Among other things, it states that a seller's burden under the law is heavier than mere selection of the appropriate allowances or services. He must (1) know which customers compete with each other, (2) notify each competing buyer that these aids are available, and (3) police the destination of any payments to make sure they are properly spent.[26] Although the general economic effect of these regulations is unclear, a multitude of small merchants seems to support them on grounds of fairness and equity. Interviews with apparel merchants, after intensive FTC activity concerning 2(d), turned up the following typical response: "It cleaned up the problem of individually negotiated advertising allowances which was inherently unfair to the small guy."[27] Although most economists do not ridicule such sentiments, they tend to be skeptical.

Common Criticism 6: Subsections 2(c), (d) and (e) should not pose per se violations. Discriminations of any kind should be subjected to tests of competitive injury and be allowed liberal cost and good faith defenses.

---

[25] *FTC v. Henry Broch & Co.*, 363 U.S. 166 (1960).
[26] P. Areeda, *Antitrust Analysis* (Boston: Little, Brown, 1974), p. 951–960.
[27] *Recent Efforts*, p. 346.

C. Subsection 2(f), Buyer Inducement

Subsection 2(f) makes it unlawful for any buyer "knowingly to induce or receive a discrimination in price which is prohibited by this Section." Here Congress finally addressed the problem it was really most worked up about—the big buyer who pressures his suppliers for discriminatory concessions. However, this subsection has been used more sparingly than a spare tire because the Supreme Court has made it difficult for the FTC to apply. The FTC's attorneys have the burden of proving (1) that an illegally injurious discrimination occurred, (2) that it was not cost justified, and (3) that the buyer *knew* it was not cost justified.

D. Declining Robinson–Patman Enforcement

On the one side we have seen corrective action appropriate to antitrust policy. On the other side we have seen official applications of dubious merit—attacks on harmless trade practices, protective interventions where injury was slight, and even anticompetitive proceedings. The controversy between those seeing Dr. Jekyll and those seeing Mr. Hyde reached a particularly high pitch during the late 1960s and early 1970s. Two task forces on antitrust policy appointed by two successive presidents (Johnson and Nixon), plus a blue-ribbon committee appointed by the American Bar Association, severely criticized the act and the FTC's enforcement of it. Later, President Ford's people in the Justice Department proposed radical modifications in the statute. Central to this and similar proposals is abolition of the narrow-injury test, but some critics have urged *complete abolition* of the Robinson–Patman Act. In response to these developments, Congress held three sets of hearings,[28] but no new legislation came of them, primarily because small-business trade associations mobilized to thwart reform. Small-business merchants seem to revere the current law with religious fervor, despite the fact that it has often been used to their disadvantage. "Please don't let the Robinson–Patman Act die," they plead. "All small businesses need it to survive."[29] Admittedly, the act's principal achievements lie in the realms of protection and fairness (though not necessarily fairness to consumers).

For its part, the FTC seems to have responded to the criticism by drastically altering its enforcement policies. In 1961 the FTC issued 105 complaints and 90 orders under the act; in 1971 it issued just 12 complaints and 15 orders; and between 1976 and 1982 the FTC averaged only 1 complaint and 1 order per year. During the mid-1980s the FTC

---

[28] *Recent Efforts to Amend or Repeal*, Parts 1, 2, and 3; *Small Business and the Robinson-Patman Act*, 3 vol.; *Price Discrimination Legislation*—1969, Hearings before the Subcommittee on Antitrust and Monopoly of the Committee on the Judiciary, U.S. Senate, 91st Cong. 1st Sess. (1969).

[29] *Recent Efforts to Amend or Repeal*, Part 3, p. 207.

issued no complaints.[30] Of late, the FTC's most notable action was taken in late 1988 against six of the nation's largest book publishers (including Macmillan). They allegedly violated the law by selling books at lower prices to major bookstore chains, like Waldenbooks, and at higher prices to independent stores.[31] Given the sharp decline in official Robinson–Patman activity, a former FTC commission said that "Robinson–Patman is being slowly anesthetized."[32]

Aside from official enforcement, however, private suits are also possible and quite common. In truth, a private treble damage suit, *Utah Pie Co.* v. *Continental Baking Co.*,[33] was the fuse that ignited much of the recent debate. The Utah Pie Company, a small Salt Lake City purveyor of frozen pies, sued three formidable pie opponents—Continental, Carnation, and Pet—for injuriously cutting prices below cost in Salt Lake City while maintaining prices elsewhere. In 1967, the Supreme Court held that the three national firms had violated Subsection 2(a) despite the fact that Utah Pie had enjoyed the largest share of the local market and had maintained profits throughout the price war. According to one critic, the Supreme Court used subsection 2(a) "to strike directly at price competition itself."[34]

Although private suits continue, they too are apparently declining. The main reason for this is a shift against potential plaintiffs. The Supreme Court gave price discriminators greater freedom in cases decided during the 1980s. The good faith defense was expanded, for instance. And the *Morton Salt* test was relaxed. According to one observer of the Court, "The decisions show a definite trend toward avoiding pricing rigidity and promoting pricing flexibility."[35]

Hence, the critics may now be less critical, even though the Robinson–Patman Act remains on the books.

II. PREDATORY PRICING

As the debate concerning Robinson–Patman cooled down, a debate about predatory pricing policy heated up. Two Harvard law professors, Phillip Areeda and Donald Turner, triggered the debate when they proposed what may be called the "AVC rule" in a 1975 article.[36] AVC refers

[30] Whiting, "R–P: May It Rest in Peace," p. 711.
[31] *The Wall Street Journal*, December 23, 1988, p. B6.
[32] "Robinson-Patman Is not Dead—Merely Dormant," address by Paul Rand Dixon, May 21, 1975 (mimeo).
[33] *Utah Pie Co.* v. *Continental Baking Co.*, 386 U.S. 685 (1967).
[34] W. S. Bowman, "Restraint of Trade by the Supreme Court: The Utah Pie Case," *Yale Law Journal* (November 1967), p. 70.
[35] Harry L. Shniderman, "The Robinson-Patman Act and the Supreme Court, 1978–85," *Antitrust Bulletin* (Fall 1986), p. 708.
[36] Phillip Areeda and Donald F. Turner, "Predatory Pricing and Related Practices Under Section 2 of the Sherman Act," *88 Harvard Law Review* (1975), pp. 697–733.

to average variable cost. Succinctly stated, the AVC rule would permit monopolists to cut price down to average variable costs but no further. As shown in Figure 15–1, which shows two cost configurations depending on technology, the AVC curves mark the threshold. Price-quantity combinations below the AVC lines (below the gray areas) would be illegal; price-quantity combinations anywhere above the AVC lines would be legal. The main justification for such a standard is short-run allocative efficiency. That is, AVC approximates marginal cost (MC) and static welfare economics theorizes that prices equal to marginal cost are allocatively efficient. Proponents of the AVC rule also claim it is simple and practical to employ. (Indeed, the original formulation of Areeda and Turner referred to marginal cost, not average variable cost, but they shifted to AVC because of the extreme difficulty of estimating MC.)

Criticisms of the AVC rule have been diverse and numerous.[37] Its service to allocative efficiency and its alleged ease of application have both been questioned. Morever, the use of short-run data to detect long-run strategic behavior has been challenged as illogical. Of greatest interst to us here, however, is a criticism that is easily appreciated, namely, the AVC rule produces a defendant's paradise, a monopolist's heaven. Notice from Figure 15–1 that *any* price below average *total* cost (ATC) is one that generates losses. If price falls below ATC *and* AVC, then the

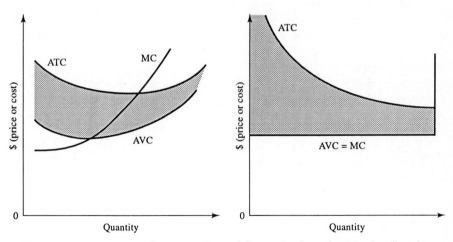

FIGURE 15–1. Cost curves for comparison of the AVC rule and ATC rule of predatory pricing.

[37] F. M. Scherer, "Predatory Pricing and the Sherman Act: A Comment," *89 Harvard Law Review*, 869 (1976); Oliver Williamson, "Predatory Pricing: A Strategic and Welfare Analysis," *87 Yale Law Journal*, 284 (1977); Paul L. Joskow and Alvin K. Klevorick, "A Framework for Analyzing Predatory Pricing Policy," *89 Yale Law Journal*, 213 (1979); and Roland H. Koller II, "When Is Pricing Predatory?" *Antitrust Bulletin* (Summer 1979), pp. 283–306.

losses are so great that in the short run the firm would normally shut down to minimize its losses.[38] If price falls below ATC but is above AVC so as to be in the gray area, the firm will not shut down immediately, but eventually it will. Thus a monopolist with abundant financial reserves could, under the AVC rule, drive less financially secure but equally efficient rivals from the market without fear of prosecution merely by pricing *below ATC* and *above AVC*. The requirement of a "deep financial pocket" does not detract from the point. Monopolists are often if not usually well heeled. The point is that the AVC rule is inaccurate. Under it, wolves are mistaken for sheep. Given this bias, the AVC rule fails to maintain competition (whatever its merits in short-run allocative efficiency).

What is a better rule? Together with numerous others, the present author advocates a two-part standard keyed to average *total* cost, or ATC rule.[39] That is, offensive monopolistic conduct would be shown by (1) pricing below average total cost, plus (2) substantial evidence of predatory intent. The call for explicit evidence of intent is necessary because prices fall below ATC all the time for wholly innocent reasons (i.e., drastically flagging sales, short-term promotions, spoiling perishables, and so forth). Pricing below AVC as well as ATC would be one possible indicator of intent because such very deep pricing cannot be loss minimizing. Other indicators include (1) documents revealing long-term business plans of injurious price cutting activity, (2) bribing distributors to refuse service to victims, (3) building immense new capacity in a market which is clearly not large enough to utilize fully that capacity at a profitable price, and (4) extremely sharp escalation of advertising outlays for a prolonged period of time.

In terms of Figure 15–1, pricing in the gray area may or may not be predatory, so indicators of intent are needed to sort out the wolves from the sheep, the anticompetitive from the procompetitive. Really deep price cutting, below AVC, is itself indicative of intent.

There is currently no consensus regarding a possible legal rule on predatory pricing. The AVC rule received early support in a number of court decisions.[40] More recently, however, the AVC has been abandoned by a number of courts in favor of some form of ATC rule. In 1988 for instance, the 11th Circuit Court of Appeals rejected the AVC rule saying

---

[38] The most a firm should ever lose (if it is loss minimizing) is its total fixed cost. Prices not covering average variable cost by, say, one dollar per unit lead to loss equal to all fixed cost *plus* $1 for every unit produced and sold.

[39] D. F. Greer "A Critique of Areeda and Turner's Standard for Predatory Practices," *Antitrust Bulletin* (Summer 1979), pp. 233–261; and Richard A. Posner, *Antitrust Law: An Economic Perspective* (Chicago: University of Chicago Press, 1976), pp. 184–195.

[40] See, e.g., *Janich Bros. Inc.* v. *American Distilling Co.*, 570 F.2d 848 (9th Cir. 1977); and *International Air Industries* v. *American Excelsior Co.*, 517 F.2d 714 (5th Cir. 1975).

it was "like the Venus de Milo: much admired and often discussed, but rarely embraced."[41]

Apart from these cost tests there is a growing consensus that significant monopoly power is a prerequisite to successful predation so it should be proven in a successful plaintiff's case. Large market shares and barriers to entry are thus relevant here.[42]

SUMMARY

The Robinson–Patman Act has been called the "Magna Carta" of small business. Others have named it "Typhoid Mary." Ever since it amended Section 2 of the Clayton Act in 1936, it has stirred controversy. Perhaps *any* law governing price discrimination would be controversial. Price discrimination always entails a high price somewhere and a low price somewhere else. Those who see evil in price discrimination tend to see the high price more readily than the low price. Those who see goodness in price discrimination seem to have reverse viewing capabilities. In addition to viewer attitudes, circumstances make a difference.

In any event, the Robinson–Patman Act outlaws price differences where the effect may be broad or narrow competitive injury at any one of three levels — primary, secondary, or tertiary — unless the difference can be defended on grounds of "cost justification" or "good faith" price mimicry. Three major classes of price discrimination have been found to violate these standards at least occasionally: (1) volume or quantity discounts, (2) territorial discrimination, and (3) functional discounts. The first two are particularly prone to true anticompetitive effects, and a number of these cases cast the FTC in good light. On the other hand, attacks against all three have produced instances of ill-advised enforcement.

Subsections 2(c), (d), and (e) prohibit any discrimination that takes the form of brokerage payments, discounts in lieu of brokerage, payments for promotion or other services, and direct provision of promotion or other service. These are generally per se prohibitions because potential competitive injury need not be shown and, for the most part, these practices cannot be defended on grounds of cost or good faith. Finally, Subsection 2(f) addresses the problem that Congress was most concerned about, for it bans knowing inducement or receipt of an unlawfully discriminatory price. Despite the efforts of Congress and the FTC, the act has apparently not stemmed the advance of chain stores. Chains

---

[41] *McGahee v. Northern Propane Gas Co.*, 858 F.2d 1487 (11th Cir. 1988), at p. 1495. See also *William Inglis & Sons Baking Co. v. ITT Continental*, 668 F.2d 1014 (9th Cir. 1981); James D. Hurwitz and William E. Kovacic, "Judicial Analysis of Predation: The Emerging Trends," *Vanderbilt Law Review* Vol. 35 (1982), pp. 63–157; and Chris S. Courtroulis, "Developments in Robinson-Patman Land," *Antitrust Law Journal*, Vol. 58, Issue 2 (1989), pp. 443–456.

[42] Daniel M. Wall "Antitrust Developments," *Antitrust* (Fall/Winter 1989), pp. 40–43.

have found ways around the law. In addition, the FTC has recently eased up on the act's enforcement, and court interpretations have grown more accepting of price variations.

Finally, the law governing predatory pricing has bounced around a bit lately. Areeda and Turner's AVC rule won temporary acceptance in the late 1970s and early 1980s. Now a number of courts have accepted some form of ATC rule, which considers evidence of intent as well as price-cost relationships.

APPENDIX TO CHAPTER 15: SMOKING GUNS IN CIGARETTES

Its sales slipping and its market share languishing at little more than 2%, Liggett Group, Inc., broke sharply with cigarette industry tradition in 1980. It cut price by 35%. It did so by placing its L&M and Lark cigarettes in simple black-and-white packs carrying generic names, like "Flavor Lights," and discounting heavily. In an industry noted for its potent brand images, huge profit margins, and ever-rising prices, this was a radical move, but a good one for Liggett. Rebound followed. Liggett shelved its plans to shut down after its market share more than doubled in three years. By early 1984, Liggett was selling 20 billion generic cigarettes annually, about 65% of its total volume.

The rival hardest hit by this was Brown & Williamson (B&W), whose Barclay, Kool, Belair, and other brands gave the company third place in the industry. B&W responded with Project G. (as in generic). It lashed out at Liggett with such force that Liggett eventually defended itself by suing B&W under the Robinson–Patman Act. The resulting trial was the most intriguing one in recent years.

Under Project G. B&W brought out its own generic cigarettes in packs designed to look almost exactly like Liggett's. Since cigarette wholesalers tended to carry only one generic brand, B&W's plan was to have its generic replace Liggett's in the inventories of wholesale distributors. As regards pricing:

> The problem was how to knock out Liggett without setting off a price war that would stimulate demand for bargain smokes—and jeopardize the monopoly-level profits flowing from name brands because of copycat pricing. The B&W task force hit on its ingenious—and according to the jury, illegal—solution: It would create a rebate system to induce cigarette wholesalers to stock its new black-and-whites instead of Liggett's, with the biggest bonuses going to the biggest-volume wholesalers. The retail price of B&W black-and-whites would be the same as Liggett's, but wholesalers would earn more by stocking B&W's. "Our goal is to capture existing demand, not create new consumer demand," the B&W plans emphasized.[43]

[43] Stephen J. Adler and Alix M. Freeman, "Smoked Out," *The Wall Street Journal*, March 5, 1990, pp. A1-A7.

For example, a broker that accounted for 40% of Liggett's generic volume switched to B&W for rebates of $20 million. B&W's intent, as revealed in company documents, was to force Liggett from the field or at least cause it to abandon its generics. Its intent was so clearly revealed that the judge in the case later called the documents "smoking guns."[44]

Liggett's share of the budget segment fell from 88.9% in 1983 to 14.4% in 1989. It lost share to RJR and Philip Morris as well as B&W because they entered the fray with their own budget brands (Doral, Cambridge, and Alpine). Liggett's situation was helped by the budget segment's rapid growth, up to 15% of all cigarette sales in 1989. Still, Liggett apparently suffered injury. It was able to persuade the trial jury to award it damages of $49.6 million, which under the antitrust laws were automatically trebled to $148.8 million, the largest damage award ever made under the Robinson–Patman Act. As this is written, the case is on appeal to higher court. In addition, the loyalty of those who puff on Marlboros, Camels, and the other "image" brands is being tested as the budget segment continues to grow. According to one distributor

> The industry is deathly afraid . . . that as these low prices proliferate, "people will figure out that cheap cigarettes are exactly the same" as famous brands.[45]

---

[44] Ibid., p. A1.

[45] Ibid., p. A7. Although Liggett readily admits that its generics are the same, the other companies deny that their generics are the same as their branded cigarettes.

16

Product Differentiation Conduct: Theory and Evidence

[We] try to keep a very high share of "voice" in the marketplace to maintain the ability to charge a price that is higher than competition because most of our products sell at a higher price than competition.
— AUGUST A. BUSCH III, Chief Executive,
Anheuser-Busch, Inc. (1989)

What is the relationship between concentration and advertising? To what extent does product differentiation contribute to market power? How do business rivals wield advertising as a weapon of competition? These are some of the grand mysteries of industrial organization economics, and recent research has yielded solutions. The job of this chapter is to sift through these solutions and reach some tentative conclusions.

The scene is set by Figure 16–1. The double-shafted arrows indicate causal connections we have already explored. Of those connections, the most important for our present purposes is that between product differ-

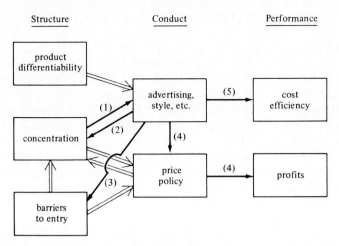

FIGURE 16–1. Product differentiation issues in the context of structure, conduct, and performance.

entiability and advertising, style, and other forms of product differentiation. Chapter 5 disclosed that advertising intensity corresponds positively to product differentiability. In particular, advertising as a percentage of sales tends to be higher for consumer goods as compared with producer goods, for "experience" goods as opposed to "search" goods, for nondurable "convenience" goods as compared with durable "shopping" goods, for goods susceptible to promotion by strong emotional appeal, and so forth. Much the same was said of other forms of product differentiation, though less rigidly.

Those conclusions provide a base upon which we now build. We shall take differentiability as "given" when postulating various swellings and contractions of differentiation effort.

The numbered, single-shafted arrows of Figure 16–1 indicate causal connections discussed in this chapter. Their numbers specify sequence of treatment. After a few preliminary remarks about profit-maximizing theory, we consider

1. Concentration as a cause of advertising intensity
2. Advertising as a cause of concentration
3. Advertising as a barrier to entry
4. Advertising's influence on prices and profits
5. The cost efficiency implications of advertising activity

Advertising is emphasized throughout because data for other forms of differentiation effort are scarce. Still, these other forms will not be ignored. The sketchy evidence concerning them is intriguing.

I. PROFIT MAXIMIZATION AND OVERVIEW

A. Simple Theory

Advertising can be profitable because it can enlarge sales volume or permit price increases. But advertising costs money, and its potency as a generator of revenues during a single year is limited. Hence, each firm confronts the question of how much should be spent on advertising to maximize profits. A simplified theoretical answer assumes (1) a short-run time horizon with no lagged effects to advertising, (2) constant advertising outlays on the part of all rival firms, (3) constant product quality, and (4) full knowledge of certain elasticities. Under these conditions the firm's profit-maximizing advertising-to-sales ratio would be[1]

$$\frac{A}{S} = \frac{\dfrac{(\%\Delta \text{ in } Q)}{(\%\Delta \text{ in } A)}}{\dfrac{(\%\Delta \text{ in } Q)}{(\%\Delta \text{ in } P)}}$$

where A/S is advertising outlay relative to sales revenue, Q is quantity of product sold, P is price, Δ is change, $(\%\ \Delta \text{ in } Q)/(\%\ \Delta \text{ in } A)$ is advertising elasticity of demand, and $(\%\ \Delta \text{ in } Q)/(\%\ \Delta \text{ in } P)$ is price elasticity of demand. Lurking beneath this maximization equation is the familiar rule of MR = MC. And this equation gives a simplified view of the impact of market structure on advertising intensity.

Consider first the upper term on the right-hand side, namely, advertising elasticity of demand, $(\%\ \Delta \text{ in } Q)/(\%\ \Delta \text{ in } A)$. This is a measure of sales response to advertising, and it is largely determined by product differentiability. The greater the advertising elasticity, the greater the sales responsiveness. Hence the greater the advertising elasticity, the greater the firm's A/S, everything else being equal.

So much, of course, is not really new. What is new concerns the lower term on the right-hand side. That is *price* elasticity of demand $(\%\ \Delta \text{ in } Q)/(\%\ \Delta \text{ in } P)$. This term's placement indicates an inverse relationship between the firm's advertising intensity, A/S, and the firm's price elasticity of demand (holding advertising elasticity constant). The greater the price elasticity, the lower the firm's ad outlay relative to sales. Conversely, the lower the price elasticity, the greater the ad effort. Because a firm's price elasticity of demand is a function of its market share, this discovery leads to a simple theory connecting concentration to ad intensity at marketwide levels. As a firm's market share rises, its demand curve becomes more and more like marketwide demand and

---

[1] Robert Dorfman and Peter Steiner, "Optimal Advertising and Optimal Quality," *American Economic Review* (December 1954), pp. 826–836.

thereby becomes less and less elastic. Hence, rising market share might be associated with rising *A/S* for the market as a whole. And rising market concentration might likewise be associated with rising *A/S*.

This theory is most clearly seen in the extreme case of purely competitive firms selling a perfectly standardized product in a market of very low concentration. With $(\%\Delta$ in $Q)/(\%\ \Delta$ in $P)$ being infinitely high for each firm, *A/S* will be zero. Or, in terms of real-world inquiry: Do wheat farmers advertise? (Do hermits fraternize?).

This reasoning, unqualified, yields a "linear hypothesis," with advertising intensity and market concentration positively related throughout their range, as depicted in Figure 16–2. A few economists believe this to be the true relationship between advertising and concentration.[2] We do not pursue their position now, however, because the linear hypothesis is plagued by various problems. Although there is some evidence supporting the positive linear hypothesis,[3] there is also much evidence to the contrary.[4] Differing samples and differing perspectives have produced these differing results, thereby igniting controversy. All in all, this author is convinced that the linear hypothesis sits on thin ice.

B. Problems and Complexities[5]

The main problem with the linear hypothesis as presented is that its underlying assumptions are unrealistic. For one thing, advertising *has* lagged effects, so the assumption of a short-term time horizon is myopic. For another, the theory assumes that business executives have good estimates of the effect of advertising and price variation on sales volume. To credit most executives with such insight would be fanciful. Estimates are clouded by a vast array of other variables affecting sales volume, such as general economic trends, tastes, and competitive activity.

---

[2] For example, H. M. Mann, J. A. Henning, and J. W. Meehan, Jr., "Advertising and Concentration: An Empirical Investigation," *Journal of Industrial Economics* (November 1967), pp. 34–45.

[3] Ibid.; S. I. Ornstein, J. F. Weston, M. D. Intriligator, and R. E. Shrieves, "Determinants of Market Structure," *Southern Economic Journal* (April 1973), pp. 612–625; R. M. Bradburd, "Advertising and Market Concentration: A Re-examination," *Southern Economic Journal* (October 1980), pp. 531–539; and R. W. Ward and R. M. Behr, "Revisiting the Advertising-Concentration Issue," *American Journal of Agricultural Economics* (February 1980), pp. 113–117.

[4] Leading papers are L. G. Telser, "Advertising and Competition," *Journal of Political Economy* (December 1964), pp. 537–562; and R. B. Ekelund, Jr., and W. P. Gramm, "Advertising and Concentration: Some New Evidence," *Antitrust Bulletin* (Summer 1970), pp. 243–249. For reviews of these and other papers see James M. Ferguson, *Advertising and Competition: Theory, Measurement, Fact* (Cambridge, Mass.: Ballinger, 1974), Chapter 5; and Richard A. Miller, "Advertising and Competition: Some Neglected Aspects," *Antitrust Bulletin* (Summer 1972), pp. 467–478.

[5] For details see K. Cowling, J. Cable, M. Kelly, and Tony McGuinness, *Advertising and Economic Behavior* (London: Macmillan, 1975).

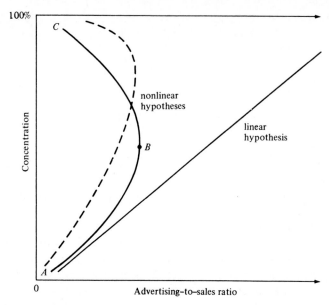

FIGURE 16–2. Hypothetical relations between advertising intensity and concentration.

Mention of competitive activity raises a third and more significant shortcoming in the simple theory, namely, the theory's unrealistic assumption of constant rival firm advertising. What one firm does will often affect the behavior of others, in advertising as well as price strategy. This interaction is illustrated by the estimate that, on average, a 1% increase in advertising by one cigarette company provokes a 1.12% increase in the advertising of its competitors.[6] Similarly, a statistical study of 60 firms showed that the most important determinant of each firm's advertising outlay was the A/S ratio of the industry it occupied.[7]

There are other problems as well, and, on the whole, a "nonlinear" hypothesis seems more tenable. Two versions of the nonlinear hypothesis are depicted in Figure 16–2—the line labeled ABC and the dashed line. In contrast to the linear hypothesis, it is assumed that concentration and advertising intensity are positively related only up to a point, after which point, in the region of high concentration, the relationship becomes negative. The implication is that advertising as a percentage of sales will *not* be highest where concentration is highest but rather where concentration is moderately high, such as at point B. Cross-section statistical tests of the nonlinear hypothesis using four-digit industries suggest that A/S reaches a maximum where four-firm con-

---

[6] H. G. Grabowski and D. C. Mueller, "Imitative Advertising in the Cigarette Industry," *Antitrust Bulletin* (Summer 1971), pp. 257–292.

[7] D. C. Mueller, "The Firm's Decision Process: As Econometric Investigation," *Quarterly Journal of Economics* (February 1967), pp. 58–87.

TABLE 16-1. Estimated Advertising-to-Sales Ratios (in Percent) for Industries Differing by Concentration and Share of Sales Going to Consumer

Share of Sales to Consumers (%)	Four-Firm Concentration Ratio (%)				
	15	30	43	64	85
0 (producer good)	0.36	0.36	0.36	0.36	0.36
50 (mixed good)	1.55	2.43	2.93	3.24	2.93
100 (consumer good)	2.74	4.49	5.50	6.11	5.50

Source: A. J. Buxton, S. W. Davies and B. R. Lyons, "Concentration and Advertising in Consumer and Producer Markets," *Journal of Industrial Economics* (June 1984), p. 460.

centration is from 36% to 72%.[8] Other estimates peg the maximum at still higher levels of concentration—dashed line in Figure 16-2.[9]

The nonlinear relation has been found only for consumer goods, not producer goods. This makes sense. Buxton, Davies, and Lyons discovered this with a clever statistical approach that recognized some goods are *both* producer goods and consumer goods. Sugar, for example, is sold to bakeries and candy makers as well as to consumers directly. Table 16-1 shows their results for 51 U.K. industries. As indicated by the row headings on the left, the type of good is identified by the share of sales going to consumers, with zero such sales in the case of a pure producer good. Reading the estimated *A/S* ratios of the table horizontally from left to right, we see that concentration has no impact on advertising intensity for pure producer goods. It is 0.36% of sales over the entire range of concentration. At the other extreme, when 100% of the sales are going to consumers, the nonlinear relationship stands out. Advertising as a percentage of sales at first rises with concentration, then peaks at 6.11% when four-firm concentration is 64%, and finally falls as concentration continues to rise. In between, for "mixed" goods, the nonlinear relationship appears, but it is much less pronounced compared to the pure consumer good. (Esposito, Esposito, and Hogan corroborate these results using American data for 129 industries. Moreover, they show that the nonlinear relationship is stable over time from 1963 to 1977.)[10]

[8] Allyn D. Strickland and Leonard W. Weiss, "Advertising, Concentration and Price-Cost Margins," *Journal of Political Economy* (October 1976), pp. 1109–1121; Stephen Martin, "Entry Barriers, Concentration, and Profits," *Southern Economic Journal* (October 1979), pp. 471–488; L. W. Weiss, George Pascoe, and Stephen Martin, "The Size of Selling Costs," *Review of Economics and Statistics* (November 1983), pp. 668–672; Noel D. Uri, "A Re-examination of the Advertising and Industrial Concentration Relationship," *Applied Economics* (April 1987), pp. 427–435; and John T. Scott, "Nonprice Competition in Banking Markets," *Southern Economic Journal* (January 1978), pp. 594–605.

[9] Cowling, Cable, Kelly, McGuinness, *Advertising and Economic Behavior*; and Stephen Martin, "Advertising, Concentration, and Profitability," *Bell Journal of Economics* (Autumn 1979), pp. 639–647.

[10] Frances F. Esposito, Louis Esposito, and William V. Hogan, "Interindustry Differ-

The next several sections elaborate on this nonlinear relationship. Of particular interest is the possibility that, given nonlinearity, *two* directions of causality prevail, not one. Causation may flow from advertising to concentration as well as from concentration to advertising. As suggested by the following outline, this will be taken into account as we further discuss the theories and evidence surrounding the nonlinear hypothesis:[11]

1. Concentration as a cause of advertising
   a. Positive range
   b. Negative range
2. Advertising as a cause of concentration
   a. Positive range
   b. Negative range

II. CONCENTRATION AS A CAUSE OF ADVERTISING

A. Positive Range (Concentration as a Cause)

What was said previously about elasticities and advertising could be reapplied here as one explanation for a positive relation between concentration and advertising where concentration is low to moderate. That is, rising concentration reduces individual firm price elasticity of demand, thereby boosting A/S at firm and industry levels.

In addition, there may be a trade-off between price and nonprice competition as concentration rises. At low levels of concentration, price competition seems preeminent. Firm survival and expansion depend mainly upon efficiency and price shading. However, at moderate levels of concentration, firms begin to appreciate the financial dangers and futility of price rivalry. In this range of concentration firms may therefore shift their emphasis from price to *non*price competition. Indeed, if tacit or explicit collusion in price is easier to achieve than collusion in non-

---

ences in Advertising in U.S. Manufacturing: 1963–1977, *"Review of Industrial Organization*
(Spring 1990).

[11] Principal sources are ibid; Strickland and Weiss, "Advertising Concentration and
Price-Cost Margins"; D. F. Greer, "Advertising and Market Concentration," *Southern Economic Journal* (July 1971), pp. 19–32; D. F. Greer, "Some Case History Evidence on the
Advertising-Concentration Relationship," *Antitrust Bulletin* (Summer 1973), pp. 307–332;
John Cable, "Market Structure, Advertising Policy and Intermarket Differences in Advertising Intensity," in *Market Structure and Corporate Behavior*, edited by K. Cowling (London:
Gray-Mills, 1972), pp. 105–124; C. J. Sutton, "Advertising, Concentration, and Competition," *Economic Journal* (March 1974), pp. 56–69; N. Kaldor and R. Silverman, *A Statistical
Analysis of Advertising Expenditure and of the Revenue of the Press* (Cambridge: Cambridge
University Press, 1948), pp. 34–35; and R. E. Caves, M. E. Porter, A. M. Spence, and J.
T. Scott, *Competition in the Open Economy* (Cambridge, Mass.: Harvard University Press,
1980).

TABLE 16–2.   Payoff Matrix Depending on Advertising Intensities

		Pepsi	
		Low Advertising	High Advertising
Coke	Low Advertising	A 30 30 P 40 40	A 30 50 P 0 70
	High Advertising	A 50 30 P 70 0	A 50 50 P 20 20

A = Advertising expenditure in, say, millions of dollars.
P = Profits in, say, millions of dollars.

price factors, price combat may well lapse while advertising warfare rages. Collusion over price policy is likely to be easier than collusion over nonprice policy because price "double-crossing" is often more readily detectable and more quickly countered than *non*price "double-crossing." Whereas price policy is often clearly definable and highly visible, nonprice policy usually entails myriad subtle dimensions, lags and complexities. Thus, even though equal advertising outlays might be mutually agreed upon, media mix, message content, timing, and other important factors remain potentially corrosive to collusion.

Unrestrained nonprice rivalry may be more clearly seen in a simple *game theory* example of the Prisoner's Dilemma type. Table 16–2 presents hypothetical data for two rivals called "Coke" and "Pepsi." Assume that only two strategies are open to each—a *low* (restrained) strategy, "in which case the firm spends $30 million on advertising, and a *high* (intense) strategy, in which case the firm spends $50 million on advertising. These outlays are labeled "A" on the top line of each of the four cells in the matrix (with Pepsi's figures always shown in italics on the right.) The profit payoffs associated with these advertising outlays are labeled "P." Note that each firm earns profits of $40 million when they both advertise at $30 million (in the "low-low" upper left-hand corner). But each firm earns profits of only $20 million when they both advertise at $50 million (in the "high-high" cell). This implicitly suggests that the added expenditures of the high-high case ($50 million versus $30 million) come out of profits ($40 million minus the $20 million in extra advertising leaves only $20 million in profit). In other words, it is assumed that advertising intensity will not affect the overall, marketwide sales of the two firms taken together. However, *disparities* in the advertising outlays of Coke and Pepsi will dramatically affect the *distribution* of sales (and profits) between them.

What will be the outcome of these circumstances? Assuming a one-time game, unrestrained "high-high" advertising will occur (50, *50*) with profits suffering as a consequence (20, *20*). To see this, let's first consider Coke's reasoning. If Coke thinks Pepsi will adopt a "low" effort, then the profits Coke compares are 40, if it follows a "low" strategy, and 70, if it follows a "high" strategy. "High" would thus be the choice. A "high" outlay for Coke is especially profitable when Pepsi's outlays are "low" because Coke will then be taking market share away from Pepsi. If, on the other hand, Coke assumes that Pepsi will follow a "high" advertising strategy for the period, Coke will be comparing profits of 0 and 20 (0 for a "low" Coke outlay and 20 for a "high" Coke outlay). The very low 0 profits would occur because Coke would be losing sales to Pepsi in the case of a "high" for Pepsi and a "low" for Coke. With Coke's "high" strategy paying off more than its "low" strategy (20 versus 0), Coke will obviously choose the "high" option. Hence, Coke will choose the "high" option *regardless of the strategy it anticipates from Pepsi*.

What about Pepsi? What strategy will it pick? Given the payoff matrix of Table 16–2, which is symmetrical in its payoffs to the two firms, Pepsi will also choose "high" and spend heavily on advertising. Its numbers are in italics. If Pepsi assumes a "low" for Coke, it will expect profits of *40* and *70* for its own "low" and "high" strategies, respectively. If, however, Pepsi assumes a "high" for Coke, it compares profits of *0* and *20* for its "low" and "high" strategies, respectively. Regardless of what Pepsi anticipates from Coke, Pepsi will find the "high" option to be the most attractive (just as Coke did).

With both Coke and Pepsi opting for "high" advertising expenditures, the prisoner's dilemma problem emerges clearly. Spending 50 and *50*, their profits of 20 and *20* are relatively low compared to what they would be if they constrained themselves to "low" advertising outlays. With low outlays of 30 and *30*, they would realize profits twice as high at 40 and *40*. What takes the fizz out of their profits is fairly evident, however. It would be dangerous for one rival to initiate a de-escalation in outlays as long as it was vulnerable to losing business and a profits to its rival.

As noted earlier in Chapter 11, Prisoner's Dilemma games may also occur in pricing. But most real-world applications seem to relate to non-price competition.[12] A nice example of excessive advertising in oligopoly concerns cigarettes. It is estimated that a $2.2 million reduction in cigarette advertising in 1961 would have led to only a $1.25 million decline in total sales revenue.[13]

---

[12] John McDonald, *The Game of Business* (Garden City, N.Y.: Doubleday, 1975); and Willard G. Manning and Bruce M. Owen, "Television Rivalry and Network Power," *Public Policy* (Winter 1976), pp. 33–57.

[13] Julian Simon, "The Effect of the Competitive Structure Upon Expenditures for Advertising," *Quarterly Journal of Economics* (November 1967), p. 621.

B. Negative Range (Concentration as a Cause)

When concentration reaches really lofty heights, a negative relation (such as in the *BC* range of Figure 16–2) may be expected for at least two reasons. The higher industry price levels implied by ever-higher concentration raise the industry's price elasticity of demand. And, according to the profit-maximizing formula outlined earlier, rising price elasticity should shrink the industry's advertising-to-sales ratio. More obviously, ever-higher concentration makes tacit or explicit collusion in nonprice activities more and more feasible.

An especially interesting example of the collusive aspect of concentration concerns advertising in the British soap industry.[14] At the turn of the century a loose oligopoly prevailed with the largest firm, Lever Brothers, holding a 20% market share. Advertising competition throbbed painfully. So in 1906 William Lever openly tried to organize a cartel, arguing that some "measures must be adopted by the leading soap-makers in conference to allay the fierce competition which has arisen amongst them, to terminate the frenzied competitive advertising which was daily becoming more intolerable. . . . " But the newspapers would have none of this. After receiving their first advertising contract cancelations, they editorially attacked the "Soap Trust" with such fervor that it soon had to be disbanded. Lever slowly alleviated his frustration, however, by acquiring one competitor after another until in 1920 he could claim control of 71% of the industry. Advertising appropriations declined concurrently. Other examples of express collusion cover a wide variety of products and a diversity of nonprice activities, including trading stamps, coupon offers, and product quality as well as advertising.[15]

Just as rising concentration should eventually reduce nonprice competition, so, too, falling concentration in this region should increase it. Falling concentration reduces the ability of oligopolists to hold differentiation outlays down to joint profit-maximizing levels. Deteriorating collusion is important in this respect, but there are other factors as well. Examples of such inverse relations abound in both time-series and cross-section forms:

---

[14] See Greer, "Some Case History Evidence . . . " (1973), pp. 318–319.

[15] *Government Intervention in the Market Mechanism, The Petroleum Industry, Part 1,* Hearings before the Subcommittee on Antitrust and Monopoly, U.S. Senate, 91st Cong., 1st Sess. (1969), pp. 569–570; L. P. Bucklin, *Competition and Evolution in the Distributive Trades* (Englewood Cliffs, N.J.: Prentice-Hall, 1972), p. 131; T. A. Murphy and Y. K. Ng, "Oligopolistic Interdependence and the Revenue Maximization Hypothesis," *Journal of Industrial Economics* (March 1974), pp. 229–230; Corwin D. Edwards, *Cartelization in Western Europe* (Washington, D.C.: Bureau of Intelligence and Research, U.S. Department of State, 1964), pp. 10, 14; and C. L. Pass,"Coupon Trading—An Aspect of Non-price Competition in the U. K. Cigarette Industry," *Yorkshire Bulletin of Economic and Social Research* (November 1967), pp. 124–136.

- In 1911, when tobacco was chewed as often as smoked, an antitrust decree fractured the monopolistic American Tobacco Company into several successor companies. Comparing *A/S* during the two years preceding the decree with *A/S* during the two years following, we find that *A/S rose* 32% for navy plug tobacco, 15% for flat plug, 148% for plug-cut smoking, 41% for long-cut smoking, 81% for granulated smoking, and 93% for domestic blend cigarettes.[16]

- Cross-section evidence on advertising in the drug industry is shown in Figure 16–3. The observations are supplied by John Vernon, who found an inverse relationship between concentration and advertising intensity. The beginnings of a nonlinear form are evident as well.[17]

- Two cross-section studies of the electric utility industry show that pure monopoly has lower advertising outlays than duopoly — where the duopoly occurs because of a second supplier of electricity[18] or because of an independent supplier of natural gas.[19]

To summarize, concentration of intermediate orders seems most conducive to vigorous nonprice competition. Concentration of either high or low extremities seems least conducive.

III. ADVERTISING AS A CAUSE OF CONCENTRATION

A. Positive Range (Advertising as a Cause)

There are three ways in which advertising may foster high degrees of concentration. First is the existence of economies of scale to advertising. As stated earlier in Chapter 9 the incidence of such economies varies across industries. Where such economies do prevail, they contribute to concentration, but only up to the point of their exhaustion.

Second, and aside from scale effects, one or several of the largest firms in an industry might consistently maintain greater advertising outlays relative to sales than smaller firms maintain. The big spenders could possess larger financial resources, greater foresight, or predatory designs. A striking instance of predatory advertising occurred in the tobacco industry around the turn of the century, before the antitrust action of 1911.[20] The story centers on James Duke, whose power play started in

---

[16] Greer, "Some Case History Evidence . . . " (1973), p. 327.

[17] John M. Vernon, "Concentration, Promotion, and Market Share Stability in the Pharmaceutical Industry," *Journal of Industrial Economics* (July 1971), pp. 246–266. See also J. J. Lambin, *Advertising, Competition and Market Conduct in Oligopoly over Time* (Amsterdam: North Holland, 1976), p. 135, Table 6.23, lines 4 and 6.

[18] W. J. Primeaux, Jr., "An Assessment of the Effect of Competition on Advertising Intensity," *Economic Inquiry* (October 1981), pp. 613–625.

[19] William H. Collins and Carol B. Collins, "Advertising and Monopoly Power: The Case of the Electric Utility Industry," *Atlantic Economic Journal* (September 1984), pp. 45–53.

[20] Greer, "Some Case History Evidence . . . ", pp. 311–315

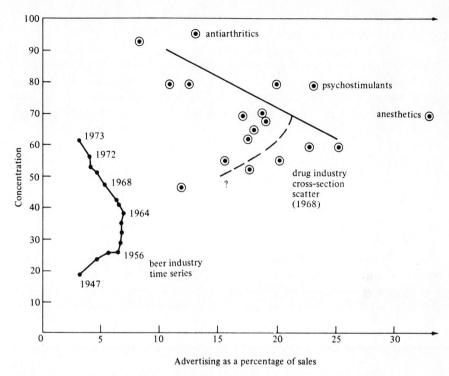

FIGURE 16–3. Concentration and advertising intensity. Source: D. F. Greer and J. M. Vernon in *Journal of Industrial Economics*, July 1971, updated.

cigarettes, then spread to other branches of the trade. By 1885 Duke had secured 11–18% of total cigarette sales for his company through an arduous promotional effort. He then escalated ad outlays to nearly 20% of sales, thereby forcing a five-firm merger in 1889 and acquiring 80% control of all cigarette sales. His American Tobacco Company grew still further until he held 93% of the market in 1899. Coincident with this final gathering of power, cigarette ad expense as percentage of sales fell to 11% in 1894, then to 0.5% in 1899. And cigarette profits swelled to 56% of sales in 1899.

With these stupendous profits Duke was able to launch massive predatory campaigns to capture other tobacco markets. One measure of this effort is the American Tobacco Company's annual advertising and selling cost as a percentage of sales at crest levels in the target markets— 28.9% for plug and twist, 24.4% for smoking tobacco, 31.7% for fine-cut chewing, and 49.9% for cigars. Duke even went so far as to introduce deliberately unprofitable "fighting brands," one of which was appropriately called "Battle Ax." Losses ensued; mergers followed; and after the entire industry (except for cigars) was under American's thumb, advertising receded substantially to such relatively peaceful neighborhoods as

4% and 10% of sales. Thus the episode traces a full nonlinear course (*ABC* in Figure 16—2), illustrating more than mere predation.

A third positive force of advertising on concentration is similar to predation in that it produces an escalation of outlays; it is different in that no single firm plays the role of "heavy." How might innocent escalation come about? There are any number of possibilities. Some firms, large or small, might have outstanding success in their advertising campaigns or might establish initially favorable *A/S* ratios, thereby inadvertently or advertently enjoying unusually rapid growth at the expense of rivals. But, after suffering losses in market share, most of the rivals attempt to emulate these successful companies through increased advertising outlays. Then everyone is off to the races. Competitive rounds of escalation could continue, resulting in cost-price squeezes, losses, bankruptcies, mergers, and ever-higher concentration. Prisoners' Dilemma game theory is obviously applicable here.

Fantastic as this scenario may seem, the beer industry played it just recently.[21] The traces are sketched in Figure 16–3 in terms of five-firm concentration ratio and advertising as a percentage of sales. (The concentration ratio is based on national sales, thereby understating the "true" level of concentration, which would be based on regional, not national, markets. You may compensate, however, by mentally shifting the Figure 16–3 curve up a bit.) Beginning in 1947, concentration was low to moderate, and advertising was just slightly above 3% of sales revenue. Promotion expense rose rapidly thereafter, as one firm after another leapfrogged ad outlays relative to sales. The process was apparently aggravated by the advent of TV advertising, a decline in tavern sales, the rise of package sales, the geographic expansion of many brewers, and a massive labor strike that closed down Schlitz, Pabst, and Miller for over two months in 1953. By the early 1960s, advertising relative to sales was hovering near the 7% level. As a result, profits wilted. Profits after taxes as a percentage of equity fell from 19% in 1947 to 6% in 1960 and 1961. *All firms*, big and small alike, were pulled down financially, as if by quicksand. Most of those eventually engulfed were small, however, suggesting that economies of scale may have been at work as well. In 1947 there were 404 brewing companies, in 1974 only 58. Many disappeared by merger (distress sales). Other simply folded. As concentration continued to climb, advertising activity eventually subsided and profits recovered.

The sources underlying Figure 16–3 show this subsidence of advertising during the early 1970s. But they are not current enough to show the advertising scuffle touched off by Miller in the late 1970s. Miller has had remarkable success in gaining market share by spending on advertising three times as much per barrel as the other brewers (its parent

---

21 D. F. Greer, "Product Differentiation and Concentration in the Brewing Industry," *Journal of Industrial Economics* (July 1971), pp. 201–219.

company, Philip Morris, subsidized the early losses of this strategy), and by "segmenting" the market with different buyer images for each of its labels — "Miller High Life," "Lite," and "Löwenbräu." Between 1972 and 1982, Miller quintupled its market share from 4% to 23% and punched its way into second place behind Anheuser-Busch. Miller's rivals retaliated vigorously, or, as William Coors put it, the industry went "berserk with advertising expenditures." Ad outlays as a percentage of sales in 1981 approached the peak level of 1964, so the outburst alters the neat nonlinear pattern of Figure 16–3, but probably only temporarily (as the concentration trend continues).[22] Advertising wars are like price wars: They can erupt and subside almost any time.

B. Negative Range (Advertising as Cause)

In the range of inverse relationship, advertising may push up concentration as long as advertising outlays exceed the industry (or monopoly) optimum level. The heavy cost burden, particularly in the region of most intensive nonprice competition, may provoke mergers and failures, as just illustrated in the case of beer.

A still more interesting possibility entails rising advertising as a cause of *decreasing* concentration, where concentration is initially very high. Most obviously, advertising may assist new entry. In fact, entry can sometimes be accomplished through little or nothing more than an ingenious or lavishly financed advertising campaign. It can also be achieved through product differentiation generally, in which advertising plays only a part. Even if technological innovation rather than advertising is the means of a newcomer's entry into a highly concentrated market, his or her eventual success could be endangered if he or she did not vigorously promote his or her sales. In any event, it is not likely that entry will dent concentration appreciably unless the entrant spends considerably more on advertising relative to sales than established firms spend. This expenditure in turn hoists the marketwide A/S ratio. Thus, in a study of 34 new brands of grocery and drug products that were successful enough to gain 2–39% market shares within two years after introduction, the entrants had advertised much more intensively than established firms. On average, the entrants' share of total industry advertising exceeded their share of total sales by 70%.[23] And these were not just "me too" products.

[22] D. Greer, "The Causes of Concentration in the U.S. Brewing Industry," *Quarterly Review of Economics and Business* (Winter 1981), pp. 87–106; *Advertising Age*, August 2, 1982, p. 41; *Beverage Industry*, September 24, 1982; and C. M. L. Kelton and W. D. Kelton, "Advertising and Intraindustry Brand Shift in the U.S. Brewing Industry," *Journal of Industrial Economics* (March 1982), pp. 293–303.

[23] James O. Peckham, "Can We Relate Advertising Dollars to Market Share Objectives?" in *How Much to Spend for Advertising?* edited by M. A. McNiven (National Association of Advertisers, 1969), pp. 23–30.

Pepsi-Cola provides a good example. During the 1930s Coca-Cola enjoyed 60% of all soft drink sales and Pepsi-Cola was languishing in receivership. Pepsi was successfully revived after some modification of its flavor and an exuberant ad campaign financed at a cost per case nearly three times greater than Coke's cost per case. By 1940 Pepsi had 10% of the market to Coke's 53%. Pepsi's market share continued to grow and Coke's continued to wither as long as Pepsi held a substantial edge in ad cost per case. By the early 1960s, Pepsi held about 20% to Coke's 38%. At that point Coke's share began to stabilize. Coke had by then escalated its ad outlays per case to match those of Pepsi more closely, and it has since yielded no further ground. (In 1987 Coke's share was 40% compared to Pepsi's 31%, so Pepsi has continued to grow, but at the expense of smaller firms like 7-Up and RC, not at the expense of Coke.[24]) The result now is less power for Coke and the Pepsi generation of a threefold increase in industry ad cost per case. Notice that this example illustrates more than the entrant's contribution to a rising industry *A/S* ratio. Coke's reaction to Pepsi's entry illustrates a *second* source of rising *A/S*. Established firms are not likely to stand idly by and watch their market shares evaporate. They retaliate, counterpunch, throw "empties," whatever. This observation brings us once again to entry barriers.

To recap briefly before continuing, an escalation in advertising may cause concentration to rise or fall. Which alternative results usually depends on the initial level of concentration.

IV. ADVERTISING AS ENTRY BARRIER

Earlier, in Chapter 9, we considered the possibility that product differentiation could pose a barrier to entry. That discussion, however, was mainly confined to *static* barriers, such as the barrier implied by large economies of scale. Here we acknowledge a *dynamic* advertising barrier. When Coke suffered insults at the hands of Pepsi, its response was slow and moderate. But such is not always the case. Established firms may lash out at newcomers, uncoiling massive barrages of advertising, promotion, and other nonprice artillery. Here are a few examples:

- Between 1900 and 1902 a tremendous jump in the popularity of Turkish tobacco cigarettes trimmed 16 percentage points off the American Tobacco Company's 93% market share. The company rushed its own Turkish brands to market and raised its cigarette ad outlay from 0.5% to 20.3% of sales.[25]

---

[24] *Beverage Industry* (March 1988), pp. 39–40.
[25] Greer, "Some Case History Evidence . . . ," p. 326.

- In 1961 a new firm entered the Australian soap market, which was then essentially split between two dominant firms. The two old-timers inflated their ad outlays 45% to 100% within a year.[26]

- In 1980 Procter & Gamble launched "High Point" instant decaffeinated coffee, challenging General Foods' "Sanka," the age-old leading brand. In response, promotional spending on "Sanka" soared seven-fold to an annual rate of $90 million.[27]

- In 1983 Procter & Gamble introduced Citrus Hill ready-made orange juice, pouring an estimated $100 million into advertising. Minute Maid and Tropicana, the two dominant brands, responded with dramatic increases in their own advertising outlays. Their retaliatory escalations preserved their market shares, but squeezed their profits severely. (Citrus Hill gained at the expense of smaller firms.)[28]

A study of the new entry reactions of 42 companies in 18 U.K. consumer goods markets proved intriguing.[29] Significant advertising escalations in response to the new entries were found for 16 incumbents in 11 of the markets. As proportions, then, significant retaliations occurred in 61% of the markets and involved 38% of all the incumbents sampled. Moreover, strategic behavior could be observed. Sharp advertising responses occurred more frequently in *static markets* than rapidly growing ones. And *dominant firms* (those with market shares over 30%) were much more likely to react aggressively than others. (This helps to explain why high concentration is associated with relatively *low* frequencies of successful entry. See Table 9–3 on page 249.)[30]

In short, product differentiation may pose a barrier to entry for reasons other than those mentioned in Chapter 9—lagged carryover, economies of scale, and static capital costs. Moreover, these examples help to explain the emphasis businesspeople give to product differentiation when voicing their opinions on barriers.

V. DIFFERENTIATION OTHER THAN ADVERTISING

Variations of differentiation effort *other* than advertising often follow nonlinear patterns like advertising. Data on other aspects of product dif-

---

[26] M. A. Alemson and H. T. Burley, "Demand and Entry into an Oligopoly Market: A Case Study," *Journal of Industrial Economics* (December 1974), pp. 109–124.

[27] *Business Week*, January 26, 1981, p.65.

[28] *Business Week*, October 31, 1983, p.50; January 23, 1989, p. 38; *The Wall Street Journal*, August 17, 1984, p. 14.

[29] John Cubbin and Simon Domberger, "Advertising and Post-Entry Oligopoly Behavior," *Journal of Industrial Economics* (December 1988), pp. 123–140.

[30] For a different twist in the entry response, see Charles F. Mason, "Predation by Noisy Advertising," *Review of Industrial Organization*, Vol. 3, no. 1 (1986), pp. 78–93; and John C. Hilke and Philip B. Nelson, "Noisy Advertising and the Predation Rule in Antitrust Analysis," *American Economic Review* (May 1984), pp. 367–371.

ferentiation are more difficult to obtain than advertising data, so the empirical record in this regard is sketchy. Still, it is illuminating. Complete nonlinear patterns like those in Figure 16–2 have been found in cross-section studies of hospital services (e.g., the number of nurses per patient's bed),[31] industrial excess capacity (which could be a proxy for speed of service, but which may also reflect entry deterring efforts),[32] and product proliferation.[33]

The last of these studies—on product proliferation—is the most relevant. In it, John Connor developed data for 419 new food products introduced into each of 102 product markets during 1977–1978. New flavors (e.g., honeynut cornflakes), new formulas (e.g., diet Coke), and new brands (like Citrus Hill orange juice) were among the fresh offerings tallied for purposes of the study. Connor found that the rate of new product introductions varied with four-firm concentration in the nonlinear pattern of Figure 16–2. According to his estimates, product proliferation reached a peak between concentration levels of 60% and 70%, when roughly 12 new food brands per year (per product type) were introduced. Firms in soft drinks, alcoholic beverages, and pet foods were among the top product launchers.

More common are studies that, because of data limitations and historical circumstances, cover only the positive or negative range of the relationship (the *AB* or *BC* range of Figure 16–2). Here are some examples:

- For a sample of 40 highly concentrated city banking markets, Lawrence White found a very robust inverse relationship between commercial bank concentration and the intensity of *branching activity*. He estimated there were 47.5% more banking offices in the least, as compared with the most, concentrated market in his sample (everything else being equal).[34]

- In another cross-section study of local banking markets, which are generally highly concentrated, Arnold Heggestad and John Mingo found inverse relationships for a wide assortment of nonprice variables, including extraordinary banking hours and the availability of trust services and overdraft privileges.[35]

[31] James C. Robinson, "Market Structure Employment and Skill Mix in the Hospital Industry," *Southern Economic Journal* (October 1988), pp. 315–325.

[32] Frances F. Esposito and Louis Esposito, "Excess Capacity and Market Structure in U.S. Manufacturing: New Evidence," *Quarterly Journal of Business Economics* (1986), pp. 3–14.

[33] John M. Connor, "Food Product Proliferation: A Market Structure Analysis," *American Journal of Agricultural Economics* (November 1981), pp. 607–617.

[34] Lawrence J. White, "Price Regulation and Quality Rivalry in a Profit-Maximizing Model," *Journal of Money, Credit and Banking* (February 1976), pp. 97–106. The most and least concentrated markets in his sample had Herfindahl indexes of .48 and .15, respectively. In terms of number-equivalence this is two and seven firms.

[35] A. A. Heggestad and J. J. Mingo, "Prices, Nonprices, and Concentration in Selected Banking Markets," *Bank Structure and Competition* (Chicago: Federal Reserve Bank of Chicago, 1974), pp. 69–95.

- Several cross-section studies show hospital bed supplies and special services to be much higher in oligopoly markets as compared to monopoly or duopoly markets.[36]
- In 1987 the *Times* newspaper of St. Petersburg, Florida, invaded the turf of the Tampa *Tribune*. The *Tribune*, in turn, invaded the turf of the *Times*. The resulting nonprice competition from these entries was quite costly "requiring extra editions, bigger staffs, new marketing campaigns, and increasingly high-tech color printing presses (for full-color graphics and photos)."[37]

The rock and roll revolution of the 1950s and 1960s yields the most rousing example of this.[38] Newly issued records of the dominant companies like CBS and RCA were sedate and serious in the late 1940s and early 1950s. So the rise of rock and roll music was left to small independents like Sun Records and Atlantic, which introduced most of the legendary rock artists, including Jerry Lee Lewis, Elvis Presley, and Ray Charles. As indicated in Figure 16–4, the independents were sufficiently successful that by the early 1960s concentration in the industry had fallen markedly (measured by the share of *Billboard* charted hits accounted for by the four leading firms). The major companies reacted by recruiting rock stars away from the independent companies, by acquiring the independent companies, by "covering" successful independent records with their own versions, and by eventually innovating on their own. Thus the lower concentrations and increased competition resulted in vastly greater product diversity. Figure 16–4 shows this in the much greater number of records reaching the weekly top ten of *Billboard* during 1962, 1963, and the other years of lowest concentration. Once the majors beat out the independents and recovered their dominance during the 1970s, this diversity diminished. (And during the late 1970s and early 1980s, when concentration continued to climb, new record releases by the industry fell substantially, down 45% for LPs and 18% for cassettes.)[39]

In short, the behavior of nonprice variables other than advertising often imitates the behavior of advertising.

---

[36] Paul L. Joskow, "The Effects of Competition and Regulation on Hospital Bed Supply and the Reservation Quality of the Hospital," *Bell Journal of Economics* (Autumn 1980), pp. 421–447; and George W. Wilson and Joseph M. Jadlow, "Competition, Profit Incentives, and Technical Efficiency in the Provision of Nuclear Medicine Services," *Bell Journal of Economics* (Autumn 1982), pp. 472–482.

[37] *The Wall Street Journal*, April 26, 1988, p. 20.

[38] Michael Black and Douglas Greer, "Concentration and Non-price Competition in the Recording Industry," *Review of Industrial Organization*, Vol. 3, no. 2 (1987). pp. 13–37.

[39] Ibid., p. 30. For related evidence on concentration and diversity in motion pictures, see Barry R. Litman, "The Motion Picture Industry," in *The Structure of American Industry*, edited by Walter Adams, 8th ed. (New York: Macmillan, 1990), p. 212.

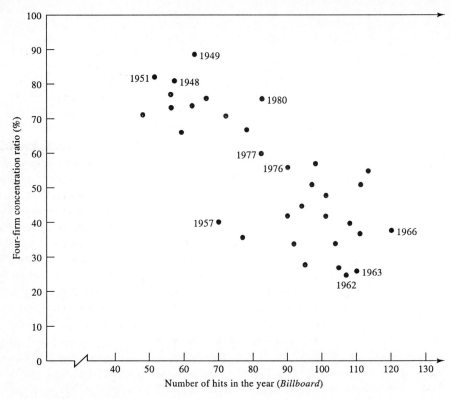

FIGURE 16–4. Relationship between concentration and product diversity in the record industry. *Sources:* R. A. Peterson and D. G. Berger, "Cycles in Symbol Production: The Case of Popular Music," *American Sociological Review* (April 1975), pp. 160–161; E. W. Rothenbuhler and J. W. Dimmick, "Popular Music Concentration and Diversity in the Industry, 1974–1980," *Journal of Communication* (Winter 1982), p. 145. The original data came from *Billboard* various issues.

VI. ADVERTISING, PRICES, AND PROFITS

Given the flip-flop nature of our preceding remarks, you might suspect that advertising (and perhaps other nonprice actions) can either increase or decrease prices and profits. You would be right. One of the main factors determining whether it is an increase or a decrease is the *source level* in the stream of production and distribution. *Manufacturers'* advertising frequently *raises* prices and profits for manufacturers as it builds brand loyalties and market power. Conversely, *retailer's* advertising frequently *lowers* prices and profits among retailers because at that level advertising tends to be informative, procompetitive, and effective at creating efficiencies.

A. Manufacturers' Advertising, Prices, and Profits

Although manufacturers' advertising frequently raises prices and profits, such is not always the case. Table 16–3 attempts an oversimplified summary by distinguishing two realms: one in which advertising displays anticompetitive traits and one in which it acts neutrally or perhaps even procompetitively. On the anticompetitive side, where intensive advertising tends to raise prices, profits, and entry barriers, we find experience goods whose qualities cannot be assessed before purchase, especially nondurable "convenience" goods of this type, such as soap, aspirin, soft drinks, breakfast cereals, and many other low-priced grocery and drug items. (Beer fits this category, too, so the rising ad costs and falling profits in that industry during the 1950s may be considered a transitory, disequilibrium development.) Exhortative TV advertising typifies their promotion, building relatively strong (and mindless) brand allegiances among consumers. On the neutral or procompetitive side, where advertising intensity is less closely associated with price and profit levels, we find search goods whose qualities can readily be assessed before purchase, and what may be called "big-ticket," durable shopping goods, like furniture and appliances. Compared to the anticompetitive realm, advertising for these goods tends to be more informative and more reliant on print media—newspapers and magazines in particular. Also, the retailers of these goods play a key part with demonstrations, credit, repair services, and the like. The economic consequences are in the end more favorable for consumers.

This is an oversimplified summary because most products carry some characteristics from both realms, as a continuum, not a gap, bridges the two sides. Moreover, there are some obvious exceptions, such as cigarettes and liquor, which belong in the anticompetitive first realm but which by law cannot be advertised on television. Still, the broad classification helps to reveal the basic pattern that emerges from a wide range of evidence.

Formal statistical analyses have confirmed the message of Table 16–3 in several ways:

- A study of advertising-profit correlations found (1) a significant *positive* correlation of .78 for *nondurable experience* goods, (2) a significant *negative* correlation of − .65 for *durable experience* goods, and (3) a nonsignificant *negative* correlation of − .02 for *search* goods such as clothing, hats, and furniture.[40]

- More sophisticated statistical studies have discovered: (1) A strong *positive* association between advertising intensity and profits for nondurable *"convenience"* goods. The explanation is that these goods are

[40] Philip Nelson, "The Economic Consequences of Advertising," *Journal of Business* (April 1975), p. 237.

TABLE 16–3.   Summary of the Effects of Advertising on Prices, Profits, and Barriers to Entry in Manufacturing: Two Broad Classes of Goods

Nature of Division	Anticompetitive Realm, Advertising **Raises** Prices, Profits, and Barriers	Neutral or Procompetitive Realm, Advertising Has **No** **Effect** on or **Lowers** Prices, Profits, and Barriers
Type of *product*	Experience goods, nondurable convenience goods (e.g., soap, beer, soda)	Search goods, durable shopping goods* (e.g. furniture, appliances, autos)
Type of *advertising* (chief message and media)	Exhortative, broadcasting media (TV especially)	Informative, print media exhortation
Type of *consumer* effect	Brand loyalty, reduced price elasticity of demand	Mixed effects, but brand switching and increased price elasticity

*Note: Nonprice activities other than advertising (for example, styling) may have anticompetitive effects for these products.

"presold" and inexpensive, so manufacturers have tremendous influence over brand choice and persuasive advertising is especially effective. (2) *No* association between advertising intensity and profits for durable *"shopping"* goods. The explanation: Manufacturers' exhortative advertising is of little influence here because of hefty product prices, heavy retailer influence, and an emphasis on other forms of differentiation.[41]

• When advertising expenditures on television, magazines, and local newspapers are analyzed separately, it appears the *television* advertising has the most potent *positive* impact on profits, especially for convenience goods. Local newspaper advertising is at the opposite pole, with a mild inverse (procompetitive) association.[42]

• The frequency with which advertisers disclose prices in their ads probably measures two things: the intensity of price competition and the level of information content in their advertising. A very interesting study of magazine advertising found that (1) in *convenience* goods industries, high overall ad outlays are associated with a *lack* of price competition and information content, while (2) in *shopping*

[41] Michael E. Porter, "Consumer Behavior, Retailer Power, and Market Performance in Consumer Goods Industries," *Review of Economics and Statistics* (November 1974), pp. 419–436; and David K. Round, "Advertising and Profitability in Australian Manufacturing," *Australian Economic Papers* (December 1983), pp. 345–355.
[42] Michael E. Porter, "Interbrand Choice, Media Mix and Market Performance," *American Economic Review* (May 1976), pp. 398–406.

TABLE 16–4.   Relative Prices and Sales of Distributors' and
Manufacturers' Brands, 1966

Product	Average Retail Price per Case		Percentage of Sales Accounted for by	
	Distributors' Brands ($)	Advertised Brands ($)	Distributors' Brands (%)	Advertised Brands (%)
Frozen orange juice	8.74	11.57	79	20
Frozen green beans	4.94	6.42	77	21
Canned green peas	4.76	5.54	29	60
Canned peaches	6.24	6.54	47	53
Catsup	4.46	5.51	28	70
Tuna fish	12.72	15.46	31	63
Evaporated milk	6.52	7.49	45	54

*These data are for a typical advertised brand. All others are averages.
Source: National Commission on Food Marketing, *Special Studies in Food Marketing*, Technical Study 10 (Washington, D.C.: The Commission, 1966), pp. 66, 70–71.

goods industries, high overall ad outlays seem to *stimulate* price competition and information disclosure.[43]

More concretely, the positive relationship between advertising and price for many products is shown in price differences between "distributor" (or private-label) brands and "advertised manufacturer" brands. Table 16–4 shows the retail prices and market shares of these two types of brands for seven food products, as estimated by the National Commission on Food Marketing. In every instance, price of the advertised brand exceeds average price of the distributors' brands, by a low of 5% for canned peaches to a high of 32% for frozen orange juice. On average, these advertised brands are 21% more costly to consumers than the distributors' brands. A similar study of British markets found price differences of 18%, 16%, and 29% for instant coffee, margarine, and tooth-

[43] Alfred Arterburn and John Woodbury, "Advertising, Price Competition, and Market Structure," *Southern Economic Journal* (January 1981), pp. 763–775. Further pertinent findings are in P. W. Farris and D. J. Reibstein, "How Prices, Ad Expenditures, and Profits Are Linked," *Harvard Business Review* (November 1979), pp. 173–184, Exhibit IV; E. Pagoulatos and R. Sorensen, "A Simultaneous Equation Analysis of Advertising, Concentration and Profitability," *Southern Economic Journal* (January 1981), pp. 728–741; Blake Imel, Michael R. Behr, and Peter G. Helmberger, *Market Structure and Performance* (Lexington, Mass.: Lexington Books, 1972); J. J. Lambin, *Advertising, Competition, and Market Conduct in Oligopoly over Time* (Amsterdam: North-Holland, 1976); and James A. Zellner, "A Simultaneous Analysis of Food Industry Conduct," *American Journal of Agricultural Economics* (February 1989), pp. 105–115.

paste.[44] To conduct your own research, make a quick visit to the nearest Safeway, A&P, or other large chain. (For really whopping price differences, check out the drug and detergent shelves.)

At this point the defenders of advertising cry "Foul! These are unfair comparisons! As any fool can see, heavily advertised, higher-priced brands are of higher quality than those cheap brands." Indeed, some defenders claim that people get *more* for their money by buying advertised brands, inflated prices notwithstanding.

Well, what about this quality claim? As you might guess, rigorous research into this question is very difficult to conduct. Nevertheless, a few bits of reliable evidence are available, and they yield a tentative, three-part answer: (1) On the whole, advertising intensity is apparently *not* positively associated with product quality. But (2) there is sufficient variance across products to include many instances where a correspondence between advertising intensity and quality is indeed the case. (3) When quality and advertising are positively correlated, it appears that the price premium associated with advertising exceeds that which might be justified by quality. *In brief, quality variations do not explain the positive price-advertising correlations.*

Consider the following:

1. One of the most notorious instances of price difference concerns prescription drugs, where unadvertised "generic" products are dirt cheap compared to advertised brand names — for example, for reserpine $1.10 versus $39.50, for meprobamate $4.90 versus $68.21, tetracycline $8.75 versus $52.02, and penicillin G $1.75 versus $10.04 (in 1972). Yet drug quality is very closely regulated by the U.S. Food and Drug Administration, and no notable quality differences between "generic" and "brand" name drugs has been found despite extensive testing.[45]

2. Regarding distributor versus highly advertised manufacturer brands, many come off the *same* assembly line to the *same* technical specifications. They differ only in label and perhaps "trim." Thus, more than half of all tires sold in the United States under distributor labels are produced by Goodyear, Firestone, Goodrich, Uniroyal, and General. And according to the editor of *Modern Tire Dealer Magazine*, "there is no noticeable quality difference among nationally advertised tires, the associate brands made by the smaller companies, and private-label brands made by both."[46]

[44] David Morris, "Some Aspects of Large-Scale Advertising," *Journal of Industrial Economics* (December 1975), pp. 119–130. See also Stephen Nickell and David Metcalf, "Monopolistic Industries and Monopoly Profits," *Economic Journal* (June 1978), pp. 254–268.

[45] Milton Silverman and Philip R. Lee, *Pills, Profits and Politics* (Berkeley: University of California Press, 1974), pp. 138–189, 334; and *Drug Product Selection*, Staff Report to the Federal Trade Commission (January 1979), pp. 51–53, 236–256.

[46] *Washington Post*, April 20, 1975, pp. M1, M3. On TV sets, see *Washington Post*, June

3. Holding product quality constant by sampling 133 processed food products with competing brands of similar quality (e.g., canned peas and dried rice), R. L. Wills and W. F. Mueller found a strong positive correlation between a brand's price and its advertising outlays. At maximum impact, "advertising resulted in prices that were elevated about 13 percent at wholesale and 10 percent at retail above the price of an unadvertised manufacturer's brand."[47]

4. Estimating the extent to which interbrand variations in prices could be explained by advertising and quality for a sample of heterogeneous food products rated by *Consumer Reports*, Robert Wills found a positive association between price and advertising after accounting for quality. Advertising had a positive effect on price that was four times greater than the effect of quality. (And this was due chiefly to electronic media.)[48]

5. H. J. Rotfeld and K. B. Rotzoll studied 12 product classes, including drain cleaner, laundry detergent, cooking oil, and toothpaste.[49] They correlated quality rank (as determined by *Consumer Reports* and *Consumers Bulletin*) with brand advertising intensity (as measured by absolute dollars spent on national media) for each product. They concluded that quality and advertising intensity were not positively related when comparing advertised brands.

It appears, then, that the quality argument has many weak spots.[50] However, defenders of advertising have a further argument debunking the notion that advertising inordinately raises prices and profits. This is the "subjectivist" argument. This holds that advertising adds a "value" not in the product, for which the consumer may rightfully wish to pay extra. The housewife pays more for the highly advertised brand, thinking that she thereby gets more for her money. Since she *thinks* she is getting more, she *must* be getting more, or so it is argued. Perhaps the

---

8, 1975, pp. F1, F8. Principal TV suppliers for Sears, Wards, and J.C. Penney have been General Electric, Sanyo, Panasonic, RCA, and Admiral. For both tires and TVs, private-label prices apparently average 8–10% less than manufacturer label prices. On the quality of private-label canning in Table 16–4, see National Commission on Food Marketing, *Fruit and Vegetable Industry*, Study No. 4 (June 1966), p.191.

[47] Robert L. Wills and Willard F. Mueller, "Brand Pricing and Advertising," *Southern Economic Journal* (October 1989), pp. 383–395.

[48] Robert L. Wills, "Advertising and Quality as Sources of Price Heterogeneity Among Brands of Food Products," Working Paper No. 77, NC 117 Project, University of Wisconsin (1984).

[49] H. J. Rotfeld and K. B. Rotzoll, "Advertising and Product Quality: Are Heavily Advertised Products Better?" *Journal of Consumer Affairs* (Summer 1976), pp. 33–47.

[50] For still further evidence, see Y. Kotowitz and F. Mathewson, "Advertising and Consumer Learning," in *Empirical Approaches to Consumer Protection Economics*, edited by P. M. Ippolito and D. T. Scheffman, (Washington, D.C.: Federal Trade Commission, 1986), pp. 109–134; and K. B. Monroe and R. Krishnan, "The Effect of Price on Subjective Product Evaluations," in *Perceived Quality*, edited by J. Jacoby and J. Olson (Lexington, Mass.: Lexington Books, 1985), pp. 209–232.

"security" of the advertised brand warms her heart. Perhaps she feels that her family will love her more for using a familiar brand. In other words, advertising sells hope, confidence, elation, and faith with each unit of canned milk, detergent, soda, aspirin, and drain cleaner. The problem with this argument is that it is tautological.[51] By *definition*, the consumer is *always* right and rational, even if he or she continues to pay extra after being informed that to do so is foolish. *By definition*, higher prices are *always* justified by higher "quality." But arguments by definition are dead-end streets.

In sum, advertising by manufacturers lifts prices, profits, and barriers to entry over a wide range of consumer products—in particular, nondurable experience goods or "convenience" goods. Though such adverse effects are sometimes observed for other products, the record is mixed, occasionally being favorable.

B. Retailers' Advertising, Prices, and Profits

The impact of retailer advertising is quite different from manufacturer advertising. At retail level it generally seems to foster *lower* prices and *lower* profit margins (and perhaps *easier* entry too).

Lee Benham, for instance, examined retail prices of eyeglasses in states that legally restricted merchant advertising and retail prices in states that had few or no restrictions on advertising. Comparing the most and least restrictive states, he discovered a $20 difference in average prices in 1963. Where advertising was prohibited, the price of eyeglasses averaged $37.48. Conversely, where advertising was wholly unrestricted, prices averaged $17.98.[52] Moreover, Benham surveyed several large "commercial" retailers, such as Sears, asking which states they felt were the most and least difficult to enter with respect to eyeglass merchandising. According to Benham, "The states ranked as most difficult were classified as 'restrictive,' those ranked least difficult were classified as 'nonrestrictive,' and the remaining states were classified as 'other.'"[53]

Similarly, prescription drug retail prices have been analyzed for the effects of state restrictions on retail drug *price* advertising. The retail prices of ten representative prescription drugs vary across states such that restrictions on price advertising *raised* prices an average of 4.3%, with the highest differential being 9.1% for one sampled product.[54]

---

[51] William Breit and K. G. Elzinga, "Product Differentiation and Institutionalism: New Shadows on an Old Terrain," *Journal of Economic Issues* (December 1974), pp. 813–826; and Paul W. Farris and Mark S. Albion, "Reply," *Journal of Marketing* (Winter 1982), pp. 106–107 (indeed, for an interesting comparison between reality and theory read pages 94–105 in the same journal).

[52] Lee Benham, "The Effect of Advertising on the Price of Eyeglasses," *Journal of Law & Economics* (October 1972), pp. 337–352.

[53] L. Benham and A. Benham, "Regulating Through the Professions: A Perspective on Information Control," *Journal of Law & Economics* (October 1975), pp. 426–427.

[54] John F. Cady, "An Estimate of the Price Effects of Restrictions on Drug Price

Broad statistical studies corroborate these. Kenneth Boyer, for instance, analyzed two separate subsamples, one of which was retail and service enterprises (such as grocers, drugstores, auto dealers, laundries, and hotels). He compared their behavior with that of consumer goods manufacturers generally. He discovered

1. A strong *positive* correlation between advertising intensity and profits for *manufacturers* (as usual, when all consumer goods are included).
2. A weak *negative* correlation between advertising intensity and profits in *retail and service trades*.[55]

Why these favorable results for retail advertising? There seem to be several related reasons. First, retailing tends to be a "search" service— that is, consumers have powers of prepurchase assessment, and price receives great emphasis. This is particularly true of drug and eyeglass retailing, where the beneficial effects of advertising are most thoroughly documented. Once a doctor prescribes the drugs or glasses needed, the question of where to buy them can be answered by fairly simple search, a search focusing mainly on price. Availabilities and convenient location also carry weight; hence, they too receive attention in retailer advertising.

Second, as suggested by the first point, retailer advertising tends to be informative, just like "search good" advertising. Information on price heightens price competition, which in turn encourages retailer efficiency:

> In general, large-volume low-price sellers are dependent upon drawing consumers from a wide area and consequently need to inform their potential customers of the advantages of coming to them. If advertising is prohibited, they may not be able to generate the necessary sales to maintain the low price.[56]

C. Manufacturers and Retailers Together

A simplified summary of our findings for manufacturers and retailers taken together is shown in Figure 16–5, where RP is the retailer's price to consumers, MP is the manufacturer's price to retailers, and the

---

Advertising," *Economic Inquiry* (December 1976), pp. 493–510. See also W. Luksetich and H. Lofgreen, "Price Advertising and Liquor Prices," *Industrial Organization Review*, Vol. 4, no. 1 (1976), pp. 13–25. See also Alex Maurizi and Thom Kelly, *Prices and Consumer Information* (Washington, D.C.: American Enterprise Institute, 1978), p. 40; Amihai Glazer, "Advertising, Information, and Prices—A Case Study," *Economic Inquiry* (October 1981), pp. 661–617; John E. Kwoka, Jr., "Advertising and the Price and Quality of Optometric Services," *American Economic Review* (March 1984), pp. 211–216; and John Schroeter, Scott Smith, and Steven Cox, "Advertising and Competition in Routine Legal Service Markets," *Journal of Industrial Economics* (September 1987), pp. 49–60.

[55] Kenneth D. Boyer, "Information and Goodwill Advertising," *Review of Economics and Statistics* (November 1974), pp. 541–548.

[56] Benham, "The Effect of Advertising on the Price of Eyeglasses," p. 339.

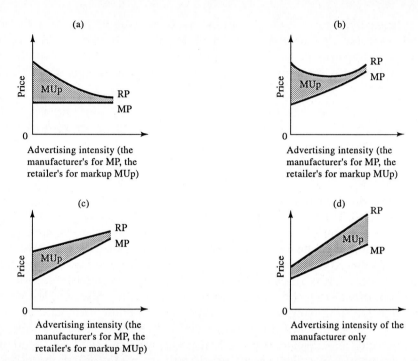

FIGURE 16–5. Advertising and price level. RP = retailer's price to consumer; MP = manufacturer's price to retailer; shaded area denotes retailer's markup margin MUp.

shaded area, MUp, indicates the retailer's markup over cost of goods sold. Thus, vertically, each diagram in Figure 16–5 represents some component of consumer price. Horizontally, panels (a), (b), and (c) register advertising intensity *either* by the manufacturer (for MP) *or* by the retailer (for MUp). Hence, panels (a), (b), and (c) summarize the possibilities that derive directly from our preceding discussion. If it is assumed that greater advertising intensity at *retail level* usually reduces retailers' markups, then the vertical distance between MP and RP will shrink as indicated by all three shaded areas in panels (a), (b), and (c). What happens to price to consumers then depends largely on what happens to price at manufacturer's level in response to *manufacturer's advertising*: (1) Consumer's price falls with greater advertising intensity in panel (a) where manufacturer's advertising is neutral, as appears to be the case for search goods and shopping goods. (2) Consumer's price falls and then rises if, as in panel (b), retailer's markup at first falls *more* rapidly and then falls *less* rapidly in comparison to the rising manufacturer's price MP. This ambiguous collection of possible consumer prices might hold for many consumer convenience goods. (3) Finally, other consumer convenience goods seem to fit the pattern of panel (c), with consumers' price rising steadily.

Panel (d) recognizes a complication, however. Whereas panels (a), (b), and (c) assume that the retailer's markup is *independent* of the *manufacturer's* advertising, being determined only by retailer advertising, panel (d) allows for interdependence. In particular, its horizontal axis measures only manufacturer's advertising. Thus, in accord with several recent studies of grocery retailer markups, panel (d) shows a positive impact for manufacturer's advertising on both manufacturer's price, MP, and retailer's markup, MUp.[57] It has sometimes been argued that heavy promotion by the manufacturer leads to strong consumer loyalties to particular brands (e.g., Tide detergent) but weak loyalties to particular retailers as retailers vie with each other to sell the brand. If this were true, retail margins might be *lower* where manufacturer's advertising was greater.[58] But the weight of evidence regarding groceries shows the opposite, as indicated in Figure 16–5 (d). Grocery retailers apparently place higher margins on heavily advertised branded products, not lower margins, thereby compounding the price effects of much manufacturer advertising.

A mixed picture thus emerges. It's this author's guess, for example, that video games and refrigerators fit (a) of Figure 16–5. Some prepared foods and candies probably illustrate (b), with different products occupying different positions on the horizontal axis. Finally, soft drinks, breakfast cereals, aspirin, detergents, beer, cigarettes, and liquor appear to be among the products in (c) and (d) of Figure 16–5. Relationships between advertising and profits may follow analogous patterns to these for price.

VII. IS ADVERTISING EXCESSIVE?

The last item on our agenda alludes to the possibility that advertising may be burning up more scarce productive resources than is socially optimal. Early debate of this issue tended to lump all advertising together and assume an "either-or" answer—either it was excessive or it was not. More recently the debate has entered a new and more refined phase, pushed by the discoveries outlined in the preceding discussion and by the work of William Comanor and Thomas Wilson, whose theories cast fresh light in this old corner.[59]

---

[57] John M. Connor and Scott Weimer, "The Intensity of Advertising and Other Selling Expenses in Food and Tobacco Manufacturing," *Agribusiness*, Vol. 2, no. 3 (1986), pp. 293–319; and L. W. Weiss, G. Pascoe, and S. Martin, "The Size of Selling Costs," *Review of Economics and Statistics* (November 1983), pp. 668–672. For limited contrary evidence, see M. S. Albion, *Advertising's Hidden Effects* (Boston: Auburn House, 1983).

[58] L. W. Weiss, *Case Studies in American Industry* (New York: John Wiley, 1980), pp. 257–258; and Robert L. Steiner, "Marketing Productivity in Consumer Goods Industries—A Vertical Perspective," *Journal of Marketing* (January 1978), pp. 60–70.

[59] W. S. Comanor and T. A. Wilson, *Advertising and Market Power* (Cambridge, Mass.: Harvard University Press, 1974), pp. 16–21.

To appreciate the current view, we must recognize that there are *two* demand curves for advertising messages — one generated by advertisers who seek to make sales and one representing the desires of consumers seeking information. Of course, these demands may vary from one market to another, and the type of messages demanded by the sellers may be quite different from the type of messages demanded by consumers. If we grant that social welfare is measured by the extent to which consumers' demands are met, "excessive" advertising may be measured by the extent to which the sellers' demand for messages in any given market exceeds the consumers' demand for messages in the market.

Although real-world measurement of this potential divergence is impossible, a few educated guesses are feasible. First, as we have seen, interbrand rivalries may rocket advertising intensity to stratospheric levels, especially in the middle range of market concentration. It seems safe to say that such cross-canceling "competitive" advertising is excessive from the social point of view. Indeed, it is excessive from the sellers' point of view as well as the consumers' because the sellers' hyperactive demand for messages stems from a "Prisoners' Dilemma," and escape via collusion would presumably curtail this demand.[60]

A second broad class of excesses probably occurs where intensive advertising permits firms to raise prices, reap supernormal profits, and bar entry. Under such conditions (outlined in Figure 16–5), sellers' demand for messages is likely to far outdistance that of consumers. "It is in such markets," Comanor and Wilson explain, "that one can infer that advertising is clearly excessive from a social standpoint, since those benefits to the firm that are not benefits to consumers accrue precisely because of the anticompetitive effects of the advertising."[61]

Finally, it is not preposterous to suppose that markets thick with exhortative advertising also inflict excesses detrimental to the social interest. Such markets are substantially the same as those just mentioned, but they deserve this slightly different acknowledgment because the message demands of sellers and consumers may differ in *quality* as well as *quantity*. Consumers would probably prefer a maximum of information and a minimum of exhortation in the messages they demand of the media. (Consumers' demand, if known, would indicate their willingness to pay money for the ads.) Conversely, sellers often find it profitable to maximize exhortation and minimize information, even to the

---

[60] For specific evidence of excess advertising see Lambin, *Advertising, Competition, and Market Conduct in Oligopoly over Time*; Henry G, Grabowski, "The Effects of Advertising on Intraindustry Shifts in Demand," *NBER Explorations in Economic Research* (Winter–Spring 1977–1978), pp. 375–401; and Jeffry M. Netter, "Excessive Advertising: An Empirical Analysis," *Journal of Industrial Economics* (June 1982), pp. 361–373.

[61] Much the same might be said of product proliferation in some industries. See F. M. Scherer, "The Welfare Economics of Product Variety: An Application to the Ready-to-Eat Cereals Industry," *Journal of Industrial Economics* (December 1979), pp. 113–134.

point of lying. Thus, wherever persuasion predominates there is again a big gap between the two demands and an indication that society's scarce resources are being squandered.

In markets *other* than those identified, advertising quantity and quality should be more nearly optimal. Although this is not a happy ending, it is at least a mitigating circumstance.

SUMMARY

The foregoing discussion went well beyond what is usually considered "conduct." Profits and cost efficiencies are not yet fully fair game, since they are more comprehensively treated later under "performance." Still, limited consideration of them is appropriate here, and it certainly cannot be claimed that we have ignored conduct.

Having discussed the close connection between product differentiability and nonprice activities earlier, we focus in this chapter on the relationship between concentration and advertising. The causal flow between these latter variables is two way; just about everyone agrees on that. There is less agreement concerning the nature and form of the relationship. Of the several competing theories, the "nonlinear" hypothesis is preferred here. It holds that peak nonprice activity occurs where concentration is neither extremely high nor especially low but rather somewhere in the middle or upper-middle region. As for causality, the nutshell view of the present author is this:

Concentration as a cause: (1) Firm-level price elasticities fall with rising concentration, thereby initially boosting industry A/S. However, as concentration reaches very high levels, price level is likely to rise, which, in turn, increases price elasticity and lowers A/S. (2) At moderate concentration, price competition wanes while nonprice competition rages. With greater market power, however, collusive understandings may hold even nonprice competition in check.

Advertising as a cause: Economies of scale to advertising, predation, and inadvertent ad warfare are three ways by which this causal flow may operate in low to moderate ranges of concentration. Indeed, whenever nonprice costs are significantly excessive from the industrywide standpoint, there is pressure for coalescence. In the range of negative relationship, advertising may assist entry, and this added A/S may reduce concentration. Of course the prospect of retaliation always poses a barrier to entry, too. So advertising is not unambiguously pro-entry.

This last observation is reflected in the discussion of prices and profits. Persistent advertising of promiscuous intensity is positively associated with prices and profits, but only under certain circumstances. These are outlined in Table 16–3 and Figure 16–5.

Finally, there seems to be a number of markets where advertising is unsatisfactory on a scale of social optimality (or cost efficiency). These markets may be grouped in three not necessarily exclusive classes: (1) those in the throes of white-hot nonprice rivalry of the Prisoner's Dilemma type, (2) those in which advertising makes a major contribution to market power, and (3) those saturated with persuasive, exhortative advertising.

We know much less about nonprice variables other than advertising. But limited data reveal close correspondences, especially on the relationship between concentration and product offerings (e.g., product proliferation and new record releases).

17

Deceptive and Unfair Practices: Policy

It is a basic tenet of our economic system that information in the hands of consumers facilitates rational purchase decisions.

—FEDERAL TRADE COMMISSION

A TV ad says that you can buy a Midas muffler for $18.95. But once you have it installed, you're charged $6.00 extra for clamps and hangers. Midas shops in California charged at least $24.95 on every $18.95 muffler sold in the mid-1980s, prompting state charges of deceptive advertising and $500,000 in fines.[1]

For seven years during the 1980s, Hertz Rental Car charged customers and insurance companies higher prices for repairs to rental cars damaged by customers than it actually paid to have the repairs made, collecting more than $13 million in the process. Would you say this was unfair or deceptive?[2]

This chapter reviews state and federal policies governing deceptive and unfair practices. Federal policy centers on Section 5 of the Federal Trade Commission Act (as amended by the Wheeler–Lea Act of 1938), which states that "Unfair methods of competition in commerce, and un-

---

[1] *San Jose Mercury News*, July 1, 1989, p. 1B
[2] *San Jose Mercury News*, January 26, 1988, p.2A.

fair or deceptive acts or practices in commerce, are declared unlawful." Since passage of the FTC Act in 1914, more than 3300 cases of deception have been prosecuted by the FTC.

Our survey of what is illegal comes in five parts and focuses primarily on advertising: (1) the criteria applied to determine deception, (2) specific examples of advertising that have collided with the criteria, (3) FTC procedures, (4) remedies applied to cleanup, and (5) miscellaneous unfair practices.

1. WHAT IS DECEPTION?

A. A Bit of History

Prior to the FTC Act, common law governed misrepresentation and deception. Successful prosecution was very difficult. The common law was rigged in favor of the con artist because conviction required a showing of *actual* deception in the mind of an *injured* buyer and *deliberate* intent in the mind of the seller. Common law cases were consequently very rare. Perhaps the only justification for this approach was the fact that sellers could suffer harsh penalties if convicted.

The FTC Act, as amended by the Wheeler–Lea Act of 1938, changed all this. Thereafter none of these elements—actual deception, buyer injury, and deliberate intent—had to be proven for the FTC to reach a guilty verdict. Until recently the Commission's decision hinged solely on whether or not a sales claim

1. possessed the *capacity or tendency* to deceive
2. a *substantial number* of buyers
3. in some *material respect* regarding the purchase decision

These three criteria for a violation were repeatedly endorsed by the courts for over 45 years. Moreover, they also became the main standard for regulating deception at the state level, partly because many states enacted statutes almost identical to the Federal Trade Commission Act (often called "Little FTC Acts").

In 1983, however, there was a change, a retreat toward the old common law. President Reagan's conservative appointees to the FTC adopted a new and less stringent enforcement strategy. By it, Reagan's FTC considered a sales claim unlawful if the claim

1. was *likely* to deceive
2. consumers *acting reasonably* in the circumstances
3. the result was *detrimental or injurious* to consumers[3]

---

[3] FTC enforcement policy letter October 14, 1983, reprinted in *Deception: FTC Oversight*, Hearings, U.S. Congress, House Subcommittee on Oversight and Investigations of the Committee on Energy and Commerce (March 26, 1984), pp. 184–185.

Our review of policy will take up the "old" FTC standard in some detail before turning to the "new" standard. Several advantages attend this approach. First, at the federal level, neither statutory language nor court interpretation have been altered substantially to adopt the "new" standard. The "old" standard persists. So far only the FTC's enforcement practices have changed (e.g., case selection), and the Commission might revert to its "old" ways under the Bush administration. Second, at the state level, state attorneys general and state courts presently continue to apply the "old" standard. Indeed, state attorneys general have overwhelmingly rejected the "new" approach, so the "old" approach is being enforced, often with national consequences. Finally, there is the simple matter of learning. A full understanding of the "new" approach requires some background knowledge of the "old" approach.

In short, we begin with the "old" standard of (1) a *capacity or tendency* to deceive (2) a *substantial number* of consumers (3) in a *material* way. We next take up the "new" standard requiring (1) a *likely* deception of (2) consumers acting *reasonably* (3) with *detrimental* results.

B. The "Old" Standard[4]

1. Capacity or Tendency to Deceive. The "old" standard attacks acts or practices having a *capacity or tendency* to deceive. Those acts or practices may be express or implied, oral or written, representations. They may omit pertinent facts. They may be in advertisements or personal sales pitches.

Let's elaborate for advertising. Under this standard the law attacks the ad, not the advertiser. Proof of intent is not required. Likewise, proof of actual deception is not required. The Commission or the court may examine an advertisement and determine on the basis of its own expertise whether there is a potential for deception. The Commission need not poll consumers, or hear from complaining witnesses.[5] Even if suspected deceivers defend themselves by providing a parade of witnesses who say they have not been misled, the FTC can still find a violation.[6] (Despite the power of the FTC to rely upon its own expertise under this "old" standard, it nevertheless supplemented its intuitive judgment with consumers' testimony, public opinion polls, and outside experts.[7])

Notice, too, the heavy emphasis on the word "deception" rather than something else, like "falsehood" (an emphasis that is in the "new" standard as well). Innocent souls tend to think in simple terms: truth

---

4 For an excellent brief explanation, see Patricia P. Bailey and Michael Perschuk, "Analysis of the Law of Deception," reprinted in *Deception: FTC Oversight*, pp. 1040–1166.

5 *Montgomery Ward* v. *FTC*, 379 F.2d 666 (7th Cir. 1967).

6 *Double Eagle Lubricants Inc.* v. *FTC*, 360 F.2d 268 (10th Cir. 1965).

7 M. T. Brandt and I. L. Preston, "The Federal Trade Commission's Use of Evidence to Determine Deception," *Journal of Marketing* (January 1977), pp. 54–62.

should be legal, falsity illegal. But this rule would be impractical, the controversies over truth being what they are. A better rule, the one actually applied by law, centers on the *deception* of potential buyers: "that which is not deceptive is legal, and that which is deceptive is illegal." This rule is different because falsity and deception are *not* necessarily the same. Although most false claims are deceptive, a claim may be false but not deceptive. Conversely, although most true claims are not deceptive, some true claims may be deceptive. These divergences arise because of the gap between any message's sender and receiver. Whereas truth and falsity hinge upon the literal content of the message sent, deception depends upon what goes on in the minds of folks receiving the message — that is, the potential buyers.

Take, for example, the remarkable claim of potency made by "Newman's Own Virgin Lemonade" in 1989 — that it restores virginity. (In a testimonial Whoopi Goldberg said, "Just seeing it being poured makes me feel virginal.") The claim was patently false. Yet no one was deceived. So the FTC did not flinch.

Examples of literal truth that actually deceive are equally easy to come by. In 1971 the FTC found deception in nonfalse television ads showing Hot Wheels and Johnny Lightning toy racers speeding over their tracks. To the TV viewer, the racers seemed to move like bullets. But this was merely a "special effect," which was achieved by filming the racers at close range from clever angles. The representation was technically accurate but nevertheless misleading.[8]

Many further examples relate to "half-true" advertisements that, although literally true, leave an overall impression that is quite incorrect. Profile Bread previously advertised that Profile was good for dieters because it had fewer calories per slice than other breads. This was true, but only half-true. The ads gave the impression that Profile was a low-calorie bread, with fewer calories per loaf. And this was not true. Profile had fewer calories per slice only because it was *sliced thinner* than regular bread. Hence the FTC and circuit court found deception.[9] (Profile was so bold as to claim that eating two slices before every meal would help weight loss.)

2. A Substantial Number of Deceived People. Given that deception lies in the mind of the observer rather than in the body of the advertisement, the next question is who among observers is to be protected? If one gullible person is misled, does that constitute illegal deception? What about 3%, or 15%, of the population? When reviewing a case in 1927 the Supreme Court held that Section 5 was "made to protect the trusting as well as the suspicious." Accordingly, the FTC and the appellate courts adopted a fairly stringent rule under the "old" standard, one

[8] Mattel, 79 FTC 667 (1971); Topper 79 FTC 681 (1971).
[9] *National Bakers Services Inc.* v. *FTC*, 329 F.2d 365 (7th Cir. 1964).

that protected the ignorant, the unthinking, and the trusting as well as the suspicious and hard headed.[10] The authorities decided, for example that a hair coloring could not claim that it colored hair "permanently."

Still, the authorities did not go so far as to protect the "foolish or feeble minded." They permitted obvious spoofs, such as a rampaging bull that is released merely by uncorking a malt liquor (Schlitz). Moreover, the authorities permitted generous amounts of "puffery."

Thus it could be said that the "old" standard asked only whether a *substantial number* of consumers had been misled. As two former FTC commissioners put it,

> The appropriate test has been variously stated as whether a "substantial segment," a "substantial percentage," "substantial numbers," or "some reasonably significant number" of consumers have been or could be misled.[11]

3. Materiality. Not long ago, former football star Joe Namath was often seen on TV hawking Hamilton Beach popcorn poppers. In the midst of his sales pitch he would leeringly tell us that his favorite off-the-field pleasure was making popcorn. Now we all know that Joe was fibbing. But this misrepresentation was "immaterial." It could not really influence the consumer's decision whether to buy the product. According to the "old" standard, deceptions had to be *material*. That is, they would have to refer to price, performance, durability, or the like, and thereby potentially affect the average purchase decision.

Here's a more recent example drawn from *Newsweek*:

> Who *are* Frank Bartles and Ed Jaymes? To many consumers they are a folksy pair of aging entrepreneurs hawking their new Bartles & Jaymes wine cooler in humorous TV ads. Watching the bucolic duo as they sit on their sagging front porch and spin their tale . . . it's easy to get caught up in their quest for fame and fortune. . . .
>
> Frank and Ed tell the public why they got into the cooler business (Ed owns an orchard, Frank a vineyard), where they got the snazzy label (Ed ordered it by mail from France) or how they get their cooler to stores in major markets (in an old pickup truck). . . . In every ad, Frank pokes fun at big business, marketing, or advertising.[12]

The ads have been so convincing that "dozens of people wrote in offering financial help after watching an ad in which Frank urged viewers to buy more Bartles & Jaymes because Ed had to make a big balloon payment on the second mortgage he took out to start the company." Yet, Bartles and Jaymes are fictitious characters. Their stories are tall tales. And their company is a "dummy" corporation actually owned and

---

10 *Charles of the Ritz Dist. Corp.* v. *FTC*, 143 F.2d 676 (2d Cir. 1944). See also Ira M. Millstein, "The Federal Trade Commission and False Advertising," *Columbia Law Review* (March 1964), pp. 457–465.

11 Bailey and Perschuk, "Analysis of the Law of Deception," pp. 140–141.

12 *Newsweek*, August 5, 1985, p. 44.

operated by the largest wine producers in the country—Ernest and Julio Gallo, Inc. Why aren't these blatant misrepresentations challenged? To be sure, they *are* deceptive. But the deceptions are considered "immaterial" by enforcement authorities even though they are obviously "material" to Gallo's marketing efforts.

To summarize the "old" standard, *an act or practice is deceptive if it has the capacity or tendency to mislead a substantial number of customers in a material way.*

C. The "New" Standard

When testifying before a congressional committee in 1984, James C. Miller III, the main proponent of the "new" standard and chairman of the FTC at the time, said emphatically that "the Commission's [new] policy statement does not represent a departure, radical or otherwise, from precedent."[13] This is partly true because there appears to be considerable overlap between the "old" standard and the "new".

On the other hand, this defense of the FTC's new enforcement policy is a bit deceptive for several reasons. *First,* in 1982, a year before the FTC's action, Chairman Miller called upon Congress to amend the FTC Act by rewriting it with the same language that appears in the "new" standards. Congress rejected the proposed amendment. But the mere fact that Miller sought a statutory change suggests that this "new" standard is really something new. And in defending his proposed amendment before Congress Mr. Miller identified numerous instances of deception under the "old" standard that would be allowed under the "new."

Second, most commentators on the "new" standards argue that they represent a substantial move toward greater leniency, a shift toward the common law standards that preceded the FTC Act.[14]

Finally and most important, after the FTC adopted the "new" standard in late 1983 the Commission's enforcement efforts altered noticeably. For example the FTC failed to act in the following instances:

- When the remarkable new sugar substitute NutraSweet became available, Coca-Cola advertised that Diet Coke was flavored "Now with NutraSweet," failing to mention that it also contained saccharin.
- The National Coffee Association promoted its caffeine-filled beverage with the message, "lets you calm yourself down."[15]

---

[13] *Deception: FTC oversight*, p.174.

[14] See, e.g., *Deception: FTC Oversight;* and L.D. Dahringer and D.R. Johnson, "The Federal Trade Commission Redefinition of Deception and Public Policy Implications: Let the Buyer Beware," *Journal of Consumer Affairs* (Winter 1984), pp. 326–342. Indeed, while defending his proposed amendment Miller himself said, "It tracks common law."

[15] *Business Week*, December 2, 1985, pp. 136–140; *Washington Post*, National Weekly Edition, July 1, 1985, p.22.

These claims have now been yanked from circulation under pressure from those still operating under the "old" standard—namely, state enforcement agencies and some private review organizations. But the FTC remains the main source of national enforcement, so its "new" policy deserves brief review.

1. Likelihood of Deception. Under the "new" standard, *"likely to mislead"* language replaces the "capacity or tendency" concept. The full implications of this substitution are not yet clear. However, it poses a more difficult burden of proof on plaintiffs and therefore a more lenient rule for advertisers. Proof that a claim is more likely to deceive than not would seem to require some showing of *actual deception*. And that is definitely not required by the "capacity or tendency" concept.

2. The Reasonable Consumer. Rather than protect a "substantial number" of consumers, the new policy protects those *"acting reasonably in the circumstances."* The rationale for this change is that, acting under the "old" standard, previous commissions squandered the taxpayers' money by prosecuting cases in which only a "few" consumers were likely to be misled. For example, the claim that a dye colored hair "permanently" should not have been attacked.

Critics of the new "reasonable" consumer criteria worry about trusting and unthinking souls. They also wonder about what could and could not be considered "reasonable" in today's age of exploding technology. Are people acting "reasonably" when they plunk down their money for the following?

- An electrical device emitting an ultrasonic sound (unhearable by humans) that allegedly irritates mice, fleas, roaches, and other pests, thereby driving them away.
- A pair of mail-order field binoculars said to have a 50-mile range ("actually tell time on a clock a full mile away!") and priced at only $9.
- A set of tires that purportedly stop 25% quicker.
- Packets of common herbs such as cayenne pepper, which are claimed to cure a wide variety of diseases, including cancer.
- A mouth wash that claims to prevent common colds or lessen their severity.

These examples come from actual cases of deception. And critics are concerned that advertisers may be able to evade the "new" standard simply by making their claims sufficiently preposterous that prosecutors would then not be able to prove that consumers were acting "reasonably" when they fell for the swindle.

3. Detrimental Results. In place of the materiality requirement of the "old" standard, the "new" standard substitutes the requirement that consumers suffer some *"detriment."* In the words of former FTC Chairman Miller, "this means that consumers are likely to suffer injury," monetary or otherwise.

An example covered by the "old" standard but exempt from the "new" illustrates this change. Suppose that a retailer of stereo equipment advertises a "going-out-of-business liquidation sale," offering name brand receivers, speakers, and other audio equipment at alleged savings of 60% off "regular" prices. Suppose further that the so-called "regular" prices are fictitiously inflated so that the "discount" prices are actually the same or even higher than the regular prices charged by more honest retailers. Still, folks flock to buy. The "new" standard ignores such scams, the reason being that consumers are not actually "injured." If a consumer willingly pays the offered price to buy the product, he or she cannot rightfully complain. The fact that the difference between the "sale" price and the "regular" price is misrepresented is irrelevant. Willing payment by the consumer absolves the seller of wrongdoing, or so it is argued.

Critics of the injury test contend that honesty in the marketplace is desirable for its own sake. Moreover, they argue that exemptions such as this have adverse economic side effects because they force consumers to intensify their vigilance, to spend more time price shopping or product testing, and to develop greater doubts about the reliability of advertising generally.

In sum, the FTC's "new" standard of enforcement covers claims (1) *likely* to mislead (2) *reasonable* consumers (3) with *detrimental results*. This represents a retreat from the "old" standard that attacks claims having (1) the *capacity or tendency* to deceive (2) *substantial numbers* of consumers (3) in a *material way*. Still, there is a large overlap between the two standards.[16]

The annual number of FTC cases dropped dramatically under the new standard. However, the FTC's resources also dropped dramatically at the same time, so assessing the impact of the new standard is difficult. Work years budgeted by Reagan's FTC for consumer protection fell about 40% "on the sometimes questionable premise that the marketplace ultimately will penalize purveyors of false and misleading claims."[17] Thus the decline in enforcement might be attributed to financial changes as well as policy changes.

The significance of the new standard can be questioned for other reasons also. First, state attorneys general filled the vacuum left by the

---

[16] For an argument of very little change, see Gary T. Ford and John E. Calfee, "Recent Developments in FTC Policy on Deception," *Journal of Marketing* (July 1986), pp. 82–103.

[17] William J. Baer, "At the Turning Point: The Commission in 1978," *Journal of Public Policy & Marketing*, Vol. 7 (1988), p.19. On resources, see the article by Andrew J. Strenio, Jr., in the same journal.

FTC. Texas challenged Kraft for calling Cheez-Whiz "real cheese." New York took action against Del Monte for claiming its canned vegetables were "as nutritious as the vegetables you buy fresh and cook at home." And so on. One attorney general explained the flurry of state enforcement by saying that the FTC had become a "toothless watchdog asleep at the switch."[18] Second, early indications (in 1989 and 1990) suggest a possible return to the old standard and stepped-up enforcement by the FTC under President Bush. Big new cases have been filed. And the advertising industry itself is pressuring the FTC to restore vigorous enforcement out of fear that diverse state-by-state regulations would become chaotic. Says Daniel Jaffe, spokesman for the Association of National Advertisers,

> We think it's totally counterproductive for the attorneys general to push the FTC aside in regulation. It's inevitable that they'll have inconsistent decisions.[19]

The main point here is this: The cases discussed next fit the "old" standard. Whether they would also meet the "new" standard is uncertain. But given the importance of the "old" standard to state enforcement activities, and given the hints of rejuvenation at the FTC, we can deepen our understanding of deception with the following review of examples without misleading anyone in the process.

II. EXAMPLES OF DECEPTION

There is a rich variety of illegal deceptions. Unfortunately, we have space for only a few broad classes:[20] (1) claims of composition, (2) claims of function or efficacy, (3) endorsements, and (4) mock-ups.

A. Claims of Composition

The Fair Packaging and Labeling Act, and similar acts governing textiles, furs, and woolens, now regulate ingredient claims for many products. Those claims not so covered are subject to a host of FTC precedents under Section 5. Naked lies, such as calling pinewood "walnut," are out. Many more slippery representations are now explicitly defined by the FTC. Here is a sampling:

> "Down" indicates feathers of any aquatic bird and therefore excludes chicken feathers.

---

18 *The Wall Street Journal,* April 17, 1989, p. B6.

19 Ibid.

20 For more complete surveys, see E. W. Kintner, *A Primer on the Law of Deceptive Practices* (New York: Macmillan, 1971); and G. J. Alexander, *Honesty and Competition* (Syracuse, N.Y.: Syracuse University Press, 1967).

"Linoleum" designates a product composed of oxidized oil and gums mixed "intimately" with ground cork or wood flour.

"Vanilla" unqualified describes only that which is obtained from the vanilla bean.

In 1983 the FTC decided against a leading advertising agency for its misleading promotion of a rubbing ointment used against arthritis pain. The product was called "Aspercreme." TV commercials said, "Now, with amazing Aspercreme, you can get the strong relief of aspirin directly at the point of minor arthritis pain." Magazine ads said it "concentrates all the strong relief of aspirin directly at the point of pain." You would think that aspirin was the active ingredient in this product, wouldn't you? Well, it wasn't. It contained no aspirin whatever, so the name and the advertising were found to be illegal.[21] (The present author's favorite example of a crooked name is that attached to Taiwan's best-selling cigarette — Long Life — which has 50% more tar than Marlboro.[22])

B. Claims of Function or Efficacy

During the late 1960s, Firestone advertised that its "Super Sports Wide Oval" tires were

> built lower, wider. Nearly two inches wider than regular tires. To corner better, run cooler, stop 25% quicker.

When sued by the FTC, Firestone presented evidence that cars with these tires traveling 15 miles per hour *did* stop 25% quicker than those with ordinary width tires. However, the tests were done on very low-friction surfaces, equivalent in slickness to glare ice or waxed linoleum. Thus "Wide Ovals" might enable some poor soul who crashes through the end of his garage to stop short of the kitchen refrigerator. But slippery surfaces and slow speeds are obviously not typical of U.S. highway conditions. Hence the FTC decided that Firestone's ads were deceptive.[23]

Deceptive claims of efficacy or function may even run afoul of the law when they are less explicit, when, that is, they enter the realm of innuendo and suggestion. A good example concerns "Vivarin," a simple but costly tablet containing caffeine and sugar in amounts roughly equivalent to those in a half-cup of sweetened coffee. The offending ad, which ran in 1971, had a middle-aged woman speaking as if she had discovered a surefire aphrodisiac:

---

[21] *In the Matter of Ogilvy & Mather International, Inc.* 101 F.T.C. 1 (1983). The ads also claimed Aspercreme was a "remarkable breakthrough," but its active ingredient had been in existence for nearly 30 years previous to the ad campaign.

[22] *Forbes*, December 11, 1989, p. 92.

[23] *Firestone Tire and Rubber Co.*, 81 FTC 398 (1972).

One day it dawned on me that I was boring my husband to death. It wasn't that I didn't love Jim, but often by the time he came home at night I was feeling dull, tired and drowsy. [Then I began taking Vivarin.] All of a sudden Jim was coming home to a more exciting woman, me. We talked to each other a lot more. . . . And after dinner I was wide-awake enough to do a little more than just look at television. And the other day — it wasn't even my birthday — Jim sent me flowers with a note. The note began: "To my new wife. . . ."[24]

More mundane but equally misleading in the judgment of the FTC was a "Wonder Bread" campaign of the 1960s, which included compelling TV commercials showing bread-eating children growing from infancy to adolescence before the viewer's very eyes while a narrator intoned that since Wonder Bread was "enriched," it "Helps build strong bodies 12 ways." The FTC charged that the ads deceptively represented Wonder Bread as an "extraordinary food for producing dramatic growth in children."[25] (Though no different from and no cheaper than other common breads, Wonder built a strong market share in this way, ranking number one nationally and accounting for as much as 30–40% of bread sales in some states.)

Health claims have become a special problem in recent years, as new and often incomplete research on nutrition gives selling points to food processors. As *Business Week* puts it, you could swear you're in a drugstore when strolling through a supermarket:

Cereal boxes proclaim that a bowl a day will help ward off cancer and heart disease. Vegetable oils vow to keep your arteries free of unhealthy deposits. Orange juice with added calcium aims to prevent brittle bones.[26]

Among other actions, legal challenges have been launched against Campbell's Soup Company (for low-cholesterol, healthy-heart claims on soups that were high in sodium, which contributes to high blood pressure, a leading cause of heart failure) and against Sara Lee Corporation (for its "Light" line of desserts, which at 200 calories per serving were no less fattening than regular desserts).

C. Endorsements

Mention of endorsements brings to mind athletes like Joe Montana, Chris Evert, Jack Nicklaus, and Bo Jackson. These are certainly very important people in advertising, and the FTC has several rules of thumb governing star testimonials. Thus, for example, an endorser must be a

---

[24] *Advertising of Proprietary Medicines, Hearings,* U.S. Senate, Subcommittee on Monopoly of the Select Committee on Small Business, 92nd Cong., 1st Sess. (1971), Part I, pp. 24, 229.

[25] *ITT Continental Baking Co.,* 83 FTC 865 (1973).

[26] *Business Week,* September 25, 1989, p. 42.

"bona fide" user of the product unless such would be clearly inappropriate (as was true of Joe Namath's peddling pantyhose). Moreover, the Commission urges that *ex*-users not be represented as current users, although this is obviously difficult to enforce.

But celebrity endorsements are not the only kind, or even the most important kind. There are "lay" endorsements, "expert" endorsements, "institutional" endorsements, "cartoon character" endorsements, and more, all of which have at one time or another reached the FTC's attention. The flavor of the Commission's thinking in these and related matters may be tasted by quoting Section 255.3, Example 5, from the FTC's "Guides Concerning Use of Endorsements and Testimonals in Advertising":

> An association of professional athletes states in an advertisement that it has "selected" a particular brand of beverage as its "official breakfast drink." [The] association would be regarded as expert in the field of nutrition for purposes of this section, because consumers would expect it to rely upon the selection of nutritious foods as part of its business needs. Consequently, the association's endorsement must be based upon an expert evaluation of the nutritional value of the endorsed beverage [rather than upon the endorsement fee]. Furthermore, . . . use of the words "selected" and "official" in this endorsement imply that it was given only after direct comparisons had been performed among competing brands. Hence, the advertisement would be deceptive unless the association has in fact performed such comparisons . . . and the results . . . conform to the net impression created by the advertisement.[27]

D. Mock-ups

When filming TV commercials, technicians often substitute whipped potatoes for ice cream and wine for coffee. The "real thing" melts under the hot lights, or fades, or looks murky on TV screens. Such artificial alterations and substitutions for purposes of picture enhancement are called **mock-ups**. Although these mock-ups are obviously innocuous (indeed, they may often reduce deception rather than produce it), advertisers have not confined their "doctoring" to innocent, nondeceptive, and prudent dimensions.[28]

- When Libby-Owens-Ford Glass Company wanted to demonstrate the superiority of its automobile safety glass, it smeared a competing brand with streaks of vaseline to create distortion, then photographed it at oblique camera angles to enhance the effect. The distortionless marvels of the company's own glass were "shown" by taking photographs with the windows rolled down.

[27] *Code of Federai Regulations*, Vol. 16, "Commercial Practices," p. 347.
[28] Quoting from I. L. Preston, *The Great American Blow-up* (Madison.: University of Wisconsin Press, 1975), pp. 235, 243. The cases referred to are *Libby-Owens-Ford* v. *FTC*, 352 F.2d 415 (6th Cir. 1965), and *Carter Products* v. *FTC*, 323 F.2d 523 (5th Cir. 1963).

- Carter Products promoted its Rise shaving cream with a mock-up that was equally fair to poor old brand X. A man was shown shaving with an "ordinary" lather, which dried out quickly after application. He then switched to Rise and demonstrated how it fulfilled its slogan. "Stays Moist and Creamy." Unbeknownst to the TV audience, the substance he used on the first try was not a competing brand nor a shaving cream at all. It was a preparation specially designed to come out of the aerosal can in a big attractive fluff and then disappear almost immediately.

In 1965, the Supreme Court voiced its opinion of such behavior in *Colgate-Palmolive Co.* v. *FTC.*[29] The TV commercial in question purported to show that Colgate's Rapid Shave shaving cream was potent enough to allow one to shave sandpaper with an ordinary blade razor. The ad's action and words went together: "apply . . . soak . . . and off in a stroke." But it was a hoax. What appeared to be sandpaper was actually loose grains of sand sprinkled on plexiglas. And the soak was a 2-second pause. Curious consumers who tried real sandpaper informed the FTC that it couldn't be done. So the Commission asked Colgate to come clean. It its defense, Colgate claimed that you *could* shave sandpaper with very small grains of sand, soaked for over an hour. It said the mock-up was necessary because such fine-grain sandpaper looked like plain paper on TV, and the true soak could not be captured in a few seconds. Indeed, Colgate felt so adamant about defending its ad that it fought the FTC all the way to the Supreme Court. The key questions addressed by the Court were as follows:[30]

1. Were undisclosed mock-ups of *mere appearance* acceptable? That is, could whipped potatoes stand in for ice cream? The Court said yes.
2. Were undisclosed mock-ups demonstrating *un*true performance acceptable? That is, could Rapid Shave be "shown" shaving the ribs off a washboard? The Court said no, clearly not.
3. Were undisclosed mock-ups demonstrating *true* performance acceptable? That is, assuming Rapid Shave *could* easily shave any sandpaper, was an undisclosed mock-up of this acceptable? The Court again said no. When the appearance is *central* to the commercial, and the clear implication is that we are seeing something real when, in fact, we are not, then the mock-up is illegal unless disclosed by saying "simulated" or something similar. Of course, if the real performance is possible and a real performance is shown, there is no problem.

[29] *Colgate-Palmolive Co.* v. *FTC*, 380 U.S. 374 (1965).
[30] Preston, *The Great American Blow-up*, p.238.

Absolute truth is thus not required. Inconsequential mock-ups for appearance's sake are permitted without an admission of fakery to the audience. Simulations are also allowed with disclosure. But mock-ups that materially deceive cannot be defended. Now, given your newly acquired knowledge of the law, let's test it. How would you react if you were an FTC commissioner and you caught Campbell's Soup Company putting marbles in the bottom of its televised bowls of soup, thereby making the vegetables and other solid parts of the soup appear attractively and abundantly above the surface? Is this mere appearance? Or is it a material deception? (Your test is not a mock-up test. The case actually came up in 1970. For the FTC's answer, see footnote 31.)

III. FEDERAL TRADE COMMISSION PROCEDURES[32]

When attacking problems of deception (or other problems within its jurisdiction), the FTC may proceed in one of three ways: (1) complaint plus prosecution, (2) guides, or (3) trade regulation rules.

A. Complaint Plus Prosecution

This is a case-by-case approach in the sense that a particular ad or ad campaign is assailed. The complete chain of formal process is as follows: The advertiser is issued a "complaint"; his case is tried before an "administrative law judge"; the judge renders an "initial decision"; the initial decision is reviewed by the full FTC; the Commission's decision may then be appealed by the "respondent" to federal courts of appeal on questions of law, perhaps even ending up like the *Colgate-Palmolive* case in the lap of the Supreme Court. This procedure may be cut short at the outset by consent settlement, in which instance a remedy is

---

[31] Consent settlement, *Campbell's Soup*, 77 FTC 664 (1970). The FTC thought this was deceptive. The July 11, 1985 issue of *The Wall Street Journal* gives us this update on food (p. 29):

> While fewer ads are downright misleading these days, companies still fudge a lot. For example, maraschino-cherry syrup is painted on ham for appetite appeal. Some products are sprayed with glycerin to make them glisten. Cigarette smoke and humidifiers are used to simulate steam for baked goods. And plastic sometimes substitutes for ice. Director Lee Howard even vacuums individual corn flakes and applies a chemical fixative so that when they are poured from a box and collide in midair, little pieces don't break off.

[32] Much of this and the next section is based upon M.J. Trebilcock, A. Duggan, L. Robinson, H. Wilton-Siegel, and C. Massee, *A Study on Consumer Misleading and Unfair Trade Practices*, Vol. 1 (Ottawa: Information Canada, 1976), Chapter III; U. S. Congress, House, *Oversight Hearings into the Federal Trade Commission — Bureau of Consumer Protection, Hearings*. Committee on Government Operations, 94th Cong., 2nd Sess. (1976); and G. G. Udell and P. J. Fischer, "The FTC Improvement Act," *Journal of Marketing* (April 1977), pp. 81–85.

reached without formal trial. The consent decree binds the advertiser to its provisions.

B. Guides

Whereas such case-by-case proceedings are ad hoc, piecemeal, and particular, industry guides and trade regulation rules are broader, more general, and less judical. Their more sweeping scope often improves the efficiency and efficacy of enforcement. Industry guides are distillations of case law, usually promulgated without formal hearings. They are issued to summarize and clarify case law for the benefit of the individuals regulated. These guides are nonbinding; they do not directly affect case-by-case procedure.

In short, industry guides are merely an expression of the FTC's view as to what is and what is not legal. There are guides for advertising fallout shelters, advertising shell homes, advertising fuel economy for new autos, advertising guarantees, and many others. In all, there were approximately 100 guides as of 1980. One — *Guides Concerning Use of Endorsements and Testimonials in Advertising* — we quoted earlier.

Since the Reagan administration's deregulation, the most noteworthy guides have been developed by the National Association of Attorneys General for state-level enforcement. Under their airline guidelines, for instance, airlines are supposed to point out when an advertised low fare applies only to one airport in a city. Moreover, any surcharges must be included in advertised prices, and restrictions on flight times and the like have to be prominently disclosed.[33]

C. Trade Regulation Rules

These are, in contrast to guides, much more serious. Like legislation, they embody the full force of law. Respondents may be prosecuted for violating the rule itself, rather than for violating the vague prohibitions of Section 5. Rules ease the burden of proof borne by the FTC's prosecuting attorneys because, once a transgression is detected, the respondent's only defense is to prove that the rule does not apply to his case. Since trade regulation rules carry so much force, the Commission formulates them by following an elaborate set of procedures:

> Rule-making proceedings consist of two parts — a preliminary private study conducted by the Commission and the final formulation of the rule with public participation. At the first stage, the Commission gathers through investigation, studies, and discussion information sufficient to support the rule, and then formulates a tentative version of the rule. Upon completion of these preliminary steps, a hearing is initiated: the procedures provide

[33] *The Wall Street Journal*, December 14, 1987, p.25.

for notice of the proposed rule-making to be published in the Federal Register and for opportunity to be given to interested parties to participate in the hearing through submission of written data or views or oral argument. After due consideration has been given to all relevant matters of fact, law, policy and discretion . . . a rule or order is adopted by the Commission and published in the Federal Register.[34]

Since these rule-making procedures were first established in 1962, more than 20 rules have been enacted. Rules now govern door-to-door sales, grocery store stocking of sale merchandise, gasoline octane disclosure, mail-order merchandise, and warranty disclosure.[35]

The Magnuson–Moss Federal Trade Commission Improvement Act of 1975 greatly strengthened the FTC's authority to issue trade regulation rules. The FTC's efforts prior to 1975 were challenged by litigation, but Section 202 of the Act of 1975 gave the FTC express authority to devise rules defining specific acts or practices as unfair or deceptive. The first rule issued under the act was the "Eyeglass Rule," of 1978, which among other things prohibits restraints on the advertising of optometrists. Such restraints (many imposed by state regulation) were found to *increase* the price of eyeglasses to consumers.[36]

On the other hand, the Federal Trade Commission Improvements Act of 1980 weakened FTC authority. And President Reagan's FTC, preferring a case-by-case approach, was very reluctant to use its rule-making authority and was eager to rescind some old trade regulation rules.

IV. REMEDIES

The product of these and other procedures is a variety of remedies designed to quash current violations, discourage future violations, and, in rare instances, erase the ill effects of past violations. The remedies include cease and desist orders, affirmative disclosure, corrective advertising, advertising substantiation, and restitution.

A. Cease and Desist Orders

The traditional and in most instances the *only* remedy applied is an order to cease and desist. This simply prohibits the offender from engaging further in practices that have been found unlawful or in closely similar practices. Thus Firestone was ordered to stop advertising that its tires could stop 25% quicker, and Colgate was ordered to cease "shaving"

[34] Trebilcock et al., *A Study on Consumer Misleading and Unfair Trade Practices*, pp. 153–154.

[35] Leaf through *Code of Federal Regulations*, Title 16.

[36] In re FTC Trade Regulation Rule, Advertising of Ophthalmic Goods and Services, *Trade Regulation Rep.* No. 335 (June 1978). For background, see Lee Benham, "The Effect of Advertising on the Price of Eyeglasses," *Journal of Law & Economics* (October 1972), pp. 337–352.

sand off plexiglas amid ballyhoo about sandpaper. By themselves, such orders are of course little more than slaps on the wrist. No penalties are levied. Penalties may be imposed only if the errant behavior persists *after* the order is issued. (Under the FTC Improvement Act of 1975, the Commission may ask a federal court to impose civil penalties of up to $10,000 per day of violation against those who breach its cease and desist orders.) But since penalties do not apply to original violations, it is often argued that advertisers are not significantly deterred from dealing in deception.

In support of the argument, it has been estimated that *one-third* of the members of the Pharmaceutical Manufacturers Association have at one time or another engaged in illegally deceptive advertising.[37] Moreover, recidivism is common. Once one deceptive campaign is stopped, another with different deceptions may be launched. Firestone's 25% quicker claim, for instance, was Firestone's third violation in 15 years. These considerations illuminate a major advantage of relying more on the other remedies mentioned, as they are harsher.

B. Affirmative Disclosure

This remedy is especially appropriate for two particular types of deception — misrepresentation by silence and exaggerated claims of brand uniqueness. To check the problem of deceptive silence, an affirmative disclosure order prohibits the advertiser from making certain claims unless it discloses at the same time facts that are considered necessary to negate any deceptive inferences otherwise induced by silence. Perhaps the most familiar example of affirmative disclosure is the FTC's requirement that cigarette advertisers disclose the dangers inherent to smoking: "Warning: The Surgeon General Has Determined That Cigarette Smoking Is Dangerous to Your Health."

C. Corrective Advertising[38]

Whereas cease and desist orders may prevent the *continuance* of misleading claims into the future, the purpose of corrective advertising is to wipe out any *lingering ill effects* of deception. What do we mean by lingering ill effects? There are several possibilities. From a purely economic point of view, deceptive advertising continues to generate sales even after it has stopped because of the "lagged effect" of advertising. As long as the ill-gotten gains in sales continue, the deception will return a

---

[37] R. Burack, "Introduction to the Handbook of Prescription Drugs," in *Consumerism*, edited by Aaker and Day (New York: The Free Press, 1974), p. 257. The regulations referred to here are actually those of the FDA, not the FTC, but they are similar.

[38] W. L. Wilkie, D. L. McNeill, and M. B. Mazis, "Marketing's 'Scarlet Letter:' The Theory and Practice of Corrective Advertising," *Journal of Marketing* (Spring 1984), pp. 11–31.

profit and the deceiver's more truthful competitors will suffer a disadvantage. Moreover, deceptive claims may be dangerous to consumer welfare where issues of health and safety are involved. If some folks continue to believe their tires stop 25% quicker, even after this claim is taken out of circulation, there is a problem of lingering ill effect. Accordingly, the typical corrective advertising order has had two parts:

1. Cease and desist making the deceptive claim.
2. Cease and desist *all* advertising of the product in question unless a specified portion of that advertising contains, for a specified time period, a statement of the fact that prior claims were deceptive.

Until 1977, the legal status of corrective advertising was shaky. Appellate courts did not pass on its legality until the *Listerine* ligitation. Listerine, which has been the nation's largest selling mouthwash (with about 40% of the market), was for decades promoted as a cold preventative as well. From 1938 to late 1972 Listerine labels declared that the stuff "KILLS GERMS BY MILLIONS ON CONTACT . . . For General Oral Hygiene, Bad Breath, Colds and Resultant Sore Throats." Moreover, countless TV commercials showed mothers extolling the medicinal virtues of gargling with Listerine twice a day. "I think," they would crow, "we've cut down on colds, and those we do catch don't seem to last as long."

Although the makers of Listerine denied that their ads ever suggested that Listerine would prevent colds, millions of folks got that message. The company's own polls showed that nearly two out of every three shoppers thought Listerine was a help for colds. Medical experts testifying at the FTC trial thought otherwise. Except for some temporary relief from sore throat irritation more easily achieved by gargling with warm salt water, Listerine was, in the experts' eyes, worthless. Believing the experts and taking into account the prevalence of this particular deception, a unanimous Commission ordered the company to include the following statement in a portion of its future ads: "Contrary to prior advertising, Listerine will not help prevent colds or sore throats or lessen their severity."

The *Listerine* case remains the high water mark for this remedy. To this writer's knowledge President Reagan's appointees to the FTC never imposed corrective advertising on any violator.

D. Advertising Substantiation[39]

In 1971 the FTC announced that from time to time it would thereafter drop a net into selected industries in hopes of fishing out schools of

---

[39] This section draws upon *Advertising 1972*, U.S. Senate, Committee on Commerce, 92nd Cong., 2nd Sess. (1972), pp. 336–483; and Dorothy Cohen, "The FTC's Advertising Substantiation Program," *Journal of Marketing* (Winter 1980), pp. 26–35.

deceptions. The net? . . . a requirement that advertisers in the target industries *substantiate* their current claims by submitting to the FTC, on demand, such tests, studies or other data concerning their advertising promises as they had in their possession *before* their claims were made.

The first substantiation orders were lowered on manufacturers of automobiles, air conditioners, electric shavers, and television sets. The resulting wave of submissions covered 282 claims made by 32 different firms. FTC analysis of these 282 revealed some good news and some bad news. First, the good news: A majority of the claims were adequately substantiated. Next the bad news: "Serious questions" arose with respect to substantiation "in about 30% of the responses." To quote some examples from the FTC Staff Report,[40]

> *Automobiles:* General Motors' advertising announced "101 advantages" designed to keep Chevrolet Chevelle from "becoming old before its time." As documentation for the claim General Motors listed such advantages as "full line of models," "Body by Fisher," and such safety items, already required by law, as "two front head restraints" and "back up light." . . .
>
> *Air Conditioners:* Fedders, ordered to document its claims that its model ACL20E3DA alone had "extra cooling power," admitted that the claim was incorrect and stated that the claim would not be made in future advertising.

Abetted by such discoveries as these, the program led to numerous formal complaints of violation. And in this light ad substantiation might not, strictly speaking, be considered a "remedy" at all, for these formal proceedings resulted in the same kinds of remedies as already mentioned — that is, cease and desist orders, corrective ads, and disclosures. Moreover, in 1984, Reagan's FTC relaxed the ad substantiation program considerably. Industrywide "rounds" of requests have been abandoned. Selection of any claims to be challenged is now based on the routine monitoring generally used for deception. Moreover, less demanding evidence now seems to suffice for substantiation.

Even so, the Commission clings to the principle that advertisers are expected to have a "reasonable basis" for their claims *before* placing them in the media. Substantiation thus lives on in a limited way.

E. Restitution

The FTC Improvement Act of 1975 empowered the FTC to seek equitable relief for consumers through (1) recision or reformulation of contracts, (2) refund of money, or (3) payment of compensatory damages. If effectively used, such measures of restitution can reduce the economic incentive for behaving badly because they can extract the ill-gotten gains from offenders. They obviously can also help to make victims whole. Thus, for example, some of the FTC's largest awards of restitution to date have

---

[40] Reprinted in *Advertising 1972*, pp. 412–442.

involved misrepresentation and fraud in land sales, one case yielding $8 million in refunds to more than 7600 people who bought lots in Colorado.

Several limitations apply to restitution. For one, there is a three-year statute of limitations. For another, punitive damages are not allowed. Beyond these statutory limitations, there are some practical constraints that make this remedy most applicable to especially fraudulent and corrupt business practices.

Having reviewed remedies, you can now see that, with rare exceptions, such as those for corrective advertising and restitution, these remedies are innocuous. Those dealing in deception suffer no penalties. Typically they are simply told to "cease and desist." Furthermore, by the time the FTC gets after them, they frequently want to change their ad campaigns anyway. This may sound too lenient, but it should be kept in mind that, at least in the past, proof of violation was fairly easy. "Capacity or tendency" plus "substantial number" and "materiality" could be considered pieces of cake for most prosecuting attorneys. Hence, although even the harshest of these remedies may seem light, it can be argued that none should be heavier if the burden of proof of misdeeds is also light. What is interesting is that President Reagan's FTC adopted a heavier burden of proof ("likelihood," etc.) while simultaneously lightening up on the remedies.

V. MISCELLANEOUS UNFAIR PRACTICES

A. Consumer Protection

The FTC's enforcement of Section 5 extends considerably beyond "advertising" and "deception." Misleading claims may be dispersed toe to toe, just as easily as over the airwaves or on the printed page. Furthermore, our emphasis on deception should not obscure the fact that many practices are banned for being "unfair," even if not deceptive. In the abstract, the FTC has said that "unfair" cannot be narrowly defined, that a number of factors would influence its judgment — such as, whether the questioned act or practice is immoral, unethical, oppressive, unscrupulous, or financially injurious to buyers. In the concrete, the FTC frowns upon:

1. *Bait and switch*, in which the seller lures the buyer into the store with some kind of "bait," like a sale price for a cheap model, then "switches" the buyer to something else.
2. *Merchandise substitution*, like the sale of 1980 model trucks as 1981 model trucks.
3. *High pressure*, door-to-door sales without a three-day "cooling off" period for buyer cancellation.

4. *Silent warranties*, where a manufacturer follows a secret policy of extending warranties to some but not all customers.

The last of these arose when in the late 1970s the FTC accused automakers of waging so called "secret warranty" campaigns as a means of paying for repairs to troublesome cars on an individual basis (for individuals who were troublesome in their complaints), without formally notifying the general public. Ford's alleged campaign was especially massive, involving more than 6 million Ford cars and trucks produced between 1974 and 1978 that were susceptible to premature engine wear and cracked blocks. Under a consent order in 1980, Ford agreed to (1) notify affected car owners by mail whenever it offers extended warranty coverage, (2) offer customers "technical service bulletins" describing in plain English the existence of any engine or transmission problems that could cost over $125 to repair, and (3) set up a toll-free 800 telephone number for owners to use in requesting service bulletins. FTC action to end Ford's secrecy prior to this order reportedly saved consumers more than $30 million in repairs.[41]

Other FTC efforts to eradicate unfairnesses sparked stormy protests from the affected industries during the late 1970s. A proposed trade regulation rule to restrict advertising aimed at young children, particularly TV advertising of sugared cereals and candy, provoked shrill opposition from cereal and candy manufacturers, TV networks, grocers, and others in the business community. They derided the FTC for brazenly becoming a "National Nanny." They maintained that, as easy as it might be to sell candy to a baby (or, more accurately, to the baby's parents through the baby's prompted appeals), it was not "unfair."

Equally controversial was a proposed rule regulating funeral parlors. After lengthy and costly study, the FTC's staff accumulated substantial evidence indicating that funeral homes frequently if not regularly took financial advantage of bereaved survivors. They apparently did this by (1) refusing to provide adequate price information, (2) embalming without permission, (3) needlessly requiring a casket for cremation, (4) harassing "discount" funeral homes, (5) misrepresenting local health requirements, (6) refusing to display inexpensive caskets, (7) disparaging customers who showed a concern for funeral costs (which now average over $2,000), and by other means.[42]

Waging an intense lobbying campaign against the FTC, the Commission's business foes succeeded in securing congressional passage of the Federal Trade Commission Improvements Act of 1980. The Senate

41 *The Wall Street Journal*, February 22, 1980, p. 12.
42 *Funeral Industry Practices*, Final Staff Report to the Federal Trade Commission, June 1978. For lively accounts of the politics on these issues see Michael Pertschuk, *Revolt Against Regulation* (Berkeley: University of California Press, 1982); and Susan Tolchin and Martin Tolchin, *Dismantling America: The Rush to Deregulate* (New York: Oxford University Press, 1983).

version of this bill would have terminated the FTC's investigation of children's advertising while the House bill would have killed the funeral proceedings. The final version did not go this far, but some shackles were imposed.

For example, the final bill trimmed the scope of any FTC rule regulating funeral home practices. The FTC's revised funeral industry rule merely

- Requires the availability of price lists, including price quotations over the telephone.
- Prohibits funeral directors from saying that a deceased person must be embalmed (unless local law requires embalming).
- Prohibits claims that a casket is required for cremation.

This legislation of 1980 and the Commission's new conservative complexion have resulted in retrenchment. The irony of this turn of events is that, just a few years before the FTC Improvements Act of 1980, the FTC was being lambasted with criticism that it was *not* doing enough for consumer protection. Indeed, it was this criticism that eventually resulted in the proconsumerist FTC Improvements Act of 1975.

B. Businessperson Protection

While hostility was curbing FTC trade regulation rules protecting *consumers*, an important new rule protecting *businesspeople* had clear sailing. This was the rule on "Disclosure Requirements and Prohibitions Concerning Franchising," which became effective in late 1979. The feverish growth of franchising during the 1960s and 1970s, especially in such fields as fast food, real estate, motels, hotels, hair salons, and rental services, resulted in total franchise sales of about $338 billion in 1980 from approximately 488,000 franchise establishments.[43] It also resulted in much fraud and misrepresentation by businesspeople against other businesspeople as many franchisors bilked franchisees.

Under the franchise system, one party (the franchisor) grants another party (the franchisee) the right to distribute or sell certain branded goods or services. In turn, the franchisee pays the franchisor for this privilege and agrees to operate his business according to the marketing plan of the franchisor. Duping prospective franchisees became commonplace during the 1960s and 1970s, prompting the attorney general of New York to complain that "franchising literally abounds with deceptive selling practices." These practices include franchisors

(1) misleading prospective franchisees about the potential profitability of their franchises, (2) refusing to show actual profit and loss statements to

[43] U.S. Department of Commerce, *Franchising in the Economy 1978–1980* (Washington, D.C.: U.S. Government Printing Office, 1980), p. 1.

potential franchisees, (3) having "hidden charges" in the prices franchisees are charged for services and supplies, (4) using a celebrity's name to deceptively promote the franchise, (5) overpromising on their aids to franchisees, and (6) using high pressure tactics in closing the sale of a franchise.[44]

The FTC's trade regulation rule was patterned after 16 state laws in existence at the time. It calls for the *disclosure* of such information as the business experience of the franchisor; the financial health of the franchisor; the total funds which must be paid to the franchisor; the recurring obligations of the franchisee; the rights of franchisees in contract terminations, cancellations, and renewals; and the restrictions franchisees face in purchasing supplies, selecting locations, and selling their goods and services. In addition, the rule *prohibits* the franchisor from making claims of potential earnings such as "make $50,000 profit" or "earn $70,000 per year" *unless* those claims are backed up by material facts sufficient to substantiate their accuracy, facts that are relevant to the prospective franchisee's business. Such supporting material must be disclosed to prospective franchisees before they commit themselves.[45]

Although the FTC's rule is perhaps too new to assess, study of the antecedent state laws suggests substantial improvement. Noting that Wisconsin's law reduced the apparent incidence of exaggerated prospective earnings from 37% to 15%, and noting other examples of heightened honesty in Wisconsin, S.D. Hunt and J.R. Nevin concluded, "The overall benefits of the full disclosure laws seem to outweigh their costs."[46] On the other hand, a 1985 estimate by *Investor Alert* indicated that tens of thousands of individuals were bilked out of about $500 million annually in franchise and business opportunity frauds. Thus the FTC can do only so much. According to a recent FTC survey of franchisees, 95% of them remembered getting the disclosure documents required by the trade regulation rule, but only 69% could remember taking the time to study them.[47] (Sometimes, doing one's homework pays.)

SUMMARY

In April 1972, the American Association of Advertising Agencies released the results of a poll of some 9000 students from 177 universities and colleges. The students took a dim view of advertising. Fifty-three percent told the AAAA that they considered advertising believable only "some of the time."[48] Was their skepticism unfounded?

[44] Shelby D. Hunt and John R. Nevin, "Full Disclosure Laws in Franchising: An Empirical Investigation," *Journal of Marketing* (April 1976), p. 54.
[45] *Code of Federal Regulation*, Title 16, FTC, Part 436.
[46] Hunt and Nevin, "Full Disclosure Laws in Franchising," p. 62.
[47] *San Jose Mercury News*, January 19, 1986, p. 1F (New York Times Wire Service).
[48] *Business Week*, June 10, 1972, p. 48.

Section 5 of the Federal Trade Commission Act (as amended by the Wheeler–Lea Act of 1938) bans "Unfair methods of competition in commerce, and unfair or deceptive acts or practices in commerce. . . . " The word "deceptive" is tricky. Truth and falsity are relevant but not conclusive, for true claims may deceive and false claims may not. Overall impressions in the buyer's mind count more than the literal meaning of claims.

Beyond this common thread, two standards of deception now prevail — an "old" standard used by the FTC, the courts, and state authorities for over 45 years, and a "new" standard used in FTC enforcement since 1983. Under the "old" standard, practices are illegal if they (1) have the *capacity* or *tendency* to deceive (2) *a substantial number* of consumers (3) in a *material* way. The FTC's "new" standard bans practices that are (1) *likely* to mislead (2) consumers *acting reasonably* (3) to their *detriment or injury*. The "old" standard is more stringent because it protects the ignorant, the hasty, and the trusting as well as those acting reasonably.

Of the many specific types of deception that have collided with the "old" standard and might run afoul of the "new," four were presented — those concerning (1) claims of composition, (2) claims of function or efficacy, (3) endorsements, and (4) mock-ups. A never-ending chain of cases under Section 5 has, over the years, outlined certain standards or rules in each of these areas. With respect to mock-ups, for instance, the Colgate Rapid Shave case is a particularly important link in the law. The Supreme Court reaffirmed what advertisers already believed — that undisclosed mock-ups of mere appearance were acceptable, and that undisclosed mock-ups demonstrating *un*true performance were unacceptable. The Court broke new ground by also ruling that undisclosed mock-ups demonstrating *true* performance were unacceptable insofar as the demonstration was central to the commercial. Ever since, the word "simulated" has appeared frequently on TV.

The FTC relies on three main procedures and four principal remedies to enforce the Act. The procedures are (1) complaint plus prosecution or consent decree, (2) advisory guides, and (3) compulsory trade regulation rules. The first is a case-by-case approach. The last two are broader in scope, reaching entire industries or complete categories of deceptive acts.

The principal remedies are (1) cease and desist orders, (2) affirmative disclosure, (3) corrective advertising, (4) advertising substantiation, and (5) restitution. The first is the traditional mainstay. The other four are recent innovations that may be considered a little more stringent.

Finally, the FTC's zealous efforts to curb "unfairness" during the late 1970s sparked angry charges from industry that it was being overbearingly unfair to business. The agency's staff was developing some of the most far-reaching proposals on record just at the time deregulation generally was coming into vogue. The result was the FTC Improvements Act of 1980 and, with the election of President Reagan, a decidedly more conservative group of commissioners. In addition to adopting a "new" standard of deception, this FTC has (1) forsaken trade regulation rules in favor of a case-by-case procedural approach, (2) dropped the corrective advertising remedy, and (3) weakened the ad substantiation program while still holding to the view that advertisers must have a "reasonable basis" for their claims prior to using them.

At this writing (early 1990) it is uncertain how far President Bush's appointees to the FTC will go to restore the Commission's old vigor and philosophy. Events hint of some restoration. In any case, state attorneys general, acting almost unanimously, have stepped in to fill the gap left by Reagan's reluctant FTC. They have launched many challenges to deception under their "Little FTC Acts," and they have formulated guides of proper conduct to coordinate their enforcement activities nationwide in industries with special problems, like the airline industry.

18

■ Multimarket Strategies

*In the past we have been characterized as a company
that was not absolutely committed to any activity.*
—CARL N. GRAF,
President,
W. R. Grace & Co.

What do Ball Park hot dogs, Hanes underwear, Isotoner gloves, and
Kiwi shoe polish have in common? They are all products of Sara Lee
Corporation, which also produces a leading European coffee, the top-
rated insecticide in Spain and France, and the best-selling mayonnaise in
the Benelux countries (among many other things and places). What do
Farmers Insurance, Firestone Tires, Pillsbury Foods, and CBS Records all
have in common? Each is owned by a foreign multinational corporation.

To this point our analysis of conduct has focused on single markets
or industries. However, the typical large corporation is not so confined.
Its operations span many markets, extending to everything under the
sun. Multimarket spread includes **vertical integration** (i.e., operation at
several stages of the production process), **conglomeracy** (i.e., diversity
of all kinds), and **multinationalism** (i.e., foreign as well as domestic
operation).

This chapter surveys these three multimarket forms—the reasons
for each and the conduct associated with each. We may introduce them
by noting that multimarket forms typically result from a firm's long-run
strategic planning. As P. F. Drucker has remarked, strategic planning

534

relates to "size and complexity, diversity and diversification, growth, change and innovation."[1]

I. VERTICAL INTEGRATION

A. Introduction and Definition

Exxon explores for crude oil, extracts it, transports it to refineries, refines it into gasoline and other products, and then finally ships and sells these products to ultimate consumers like you. Exxon is thus vertically integrated because it combines under single ownership several stages of the production-distribution process.

The opposite of vertical integration is the open market, where buyers and sellers act independently. For example, unlike Exxon, many independent oil refiners buy crude oil on the open market rather than supply it themselves internally.

Between these extremes are various intermediate cases where buyers and sellers in the chain of production and distribution are linked by specialized contracts to achieve various forms of "quasi-integration." Examples include long-term supply contracts, franchise agreements, and reciprocal sales arrangements. These bind a buyer and a seller together less rigidly than common ownership, but they bind more closely than open-market exchange.

The fact that many enterprises are not vertically integrated, or only quasi-integrated, tells us that vertical integration has certain disadvantages. Indeed contractual quasi-integration supposedly reduces the disadvantages while retaining the advantages. These disadvantages vary from one industry to another, but a few generalities come readily to mind.[2]

First, when a firm integrates either backward or forward, its added ownership stakes require added financial capital, which may be costly. Borrowed capital carries interest costs. Internally generated capital has opportunity costs. Either way the added capital can be an added burden.

A second disadvantage to vertical integration is reduced flexibility. Ownership of an in-house supplier or customer implies a concrete commitment to that particular supplier or customer. Changes in technology might sharply reduce the costs of open market alternatives, thereby making the in-house source a costly mistake. Changes in consumer fads, mineral deposits, labor contracts, and other potentially momentous factors can likewise create situations in which "the in-house supplier is providing a high-cost, inferior, or inappropriate product or service or the

---

[1] P. F. Drucker, *Management: Tasks, Responsibilities, Practices* (London: Heinemann, 1974), p. 603.
[2] Michael E. Porter, *Competitive Strategy* (New York: The Free Press, 1980), pp. 309–314.

in-house customer or distribution channel is losing position in its market and thus its suitability as a customer."[3]

Still, on the other hand, vertical integration abounds, so its advantages are considerable. Indeed, they are noteworthy enough to discuss in detail. Hence separate sections cover each of the following explanations for vertical integration: (1) technical-cost savings, (2) transaction–cost savings, (3) exploitation of market power, and (4) extension of market power (or a combination of extension and exploitation, as indicated in Table 11–1 on page 299).

B. Technical-cost Savings

Vertical integration may cut production costs for technical reasons. Integrated production of steel, for instance, enables the metal to remain hot from blast furnace to carbon burnoff to rolling and drawing. Costly reheating at each stage is eliminated.

Technical-cost savings usually warrant integration within one plant, or integration of adjacent plants at the same location. Hence these cost savings are usually not achieved by vertical integration that is attained by merger or acquisition.

Moreover, these cost savings tend to be of little interest to economists because they are typically grounded on engineering considerations more than economic ones. Let's therefore move on.

C. Transaction-cost Savings

Briefly, transaction costs are the costs of doing business in the open market. We encountered these earlier when discussing theories of the firm (pages 62–64). The most obvious of these costs that can be reduced by vertical integration are those associated with the mechanics of buying and selling—that is, marketing costs. Thus a "merchant" manufacturer of integrated circuits like AMD or National Semiconductor will incur costs for advertising, sales promotion, sales force, and market research. But a company like IBM, which produces integrated circuits solely for its own use to manufacture finished products, runs its integrated circuit operation without these marketing costs.

Oliver Williamson stresses the possibility that vertical integration can save transactions costs associated with asset *specificity*. This means that an asset is specifically committed to a buyer by its location or physical makeup or some other characteristic. This specificity makes the seller vulnerable to transaction costs unless continuity is established by integration (or quasi-integration) of some sort.[4] Imagine, for example, that

---

3 Ibid., p. 310.
4 Oliver E. Williamson, *The Economic Institutions of Capitalism* (New York: The Free Press, 1985), pp. 85–96.

Coors convinced a can manufacturer to build a large can manufacturing plant next to its huge Coors brewery in Golden, Colorado. This can plant would then be "site specific," as it would be located a long way from any alternative can buyers, such as other brewers or soft drink producers. Once the can plant is built, Coors might try to drop the original agreement and renegotiate terms in its favor because it would then have the can manufacturer "over a barrel" (beer barrel, of course). This recontracting would obviously raise the transactions costs associated with the independent supply of cans to the brewery, costs that would be eliminated by vertical integration, with Coors owning the plant. Note that the attraction of vertical integration here does not hinge on the actual occurrence of this recontracting for the specific assets. The *possibility* of it happening is often enough. (And Coors does supply its own cans.)

Given our broad definition of transactions costs, still further savings of this sort are possible from vertical integration. In particular, *uncertainty* can be costly, and vertical integration may cut the costs of dealing with uncertainty. Quality, for instance, is often of great importance. Assuring the quality of inputs coming from independent suppliers might require that the buyer as well as the seller engage in extensive sample testing, supplier factory inspections, and other actions in order to reduce uncertainty regarding input quality. These duplications of effort toward quality assurance could be considered transactions costs that might be reduced through vertical integration.

Coordination activities raise further possibilities. Dealing at arm's length with independent downstream distributors may be costly if highly coordinated national marketing efforts are regularly attempted. For example, the major record companies—for example, Warner Communications, CBS, and RCA—are vertically integrated into wholesale distribution in order to roll out new record releases in harmony with major concert tours, motion picture premiers, radio promotions, and other entertainment events that complement the marketing of records. Likewise, in the mid-1980s Coke and Pepsi bought out a number of their affiliated (but formerly independent) bottlers to amass 35% control of their bottling networks. *The Wall Street Journal's* explanation makes Coke and Pepsi look like record companies:

> Coca-Cola and Pepsi, trying to increase the shares of the market by filling every conceivable niche, have introduced new products at a bewildering pace—and some bottlers can't handle it. By increasing control at their bottling networks, Coca-Cola and Pepsi improve their ability to get new products onto store shelves quickly.[5]

Hence, vertical integration can sometimes reduce the transaction costs

[5] *The Wall Street Journal*, July 3, 1986, p. 6.

that would otherwise arise when coordinating marketing activities, especially those associated with product introductions.

Finally, transaction costs may also be particularly high when a buyer or seller is dealing with just a few independent counterparts on the other side of their market (a few sellers for the buyer or a few buyers for the seller). Fewness implies market power. And that power may create transactions costs to the extent it makes negotiations more difficult. For example, your transaction costs of buying a new car in a big city with many auto dealers clustered together are likely to be lower in this respect than if you have to negotiate with only one or two auto dealers in a small town. With many alternatives your bargaining position is good. But to improve your bargaining position vis-à-vis the two small-town dealers, you might have to resort to such relatively costly tactics as delay (until the end of the model year perhaps) or driving some distance to the next town in hopes of finding better prices. In short, and in business, vertical integration may reduce transactions costs by solving *small numbers bargaining problems*.

Empirical support for these theories of transaction-cost savings is impressive but limited. Several case studies of vertical integration indicate that it frequently occurs when opportunities for these cost savings loom large. For example, an interesting comparative study of the aluminum and tin industries reveals sharply contrasting degrees of upstream vertical integration associated with sharply contrasting conditions. In aluminum, vertical integration prevails, directly linking bauxite mining and aluminum oxide production. Here, high capital costs and economies of scale reduce the number of potential players to create small numbers bargaining problems, while at the same time high transportation costs and other factors create substantial asset specificity. Hence the extensive vertical integration in aluminum accords with big opportunities for transaction-cost savings. In contrast, there is very little vertical integration between tin mining and smelting. And the conditions in these several respects are just the opposite of those for aluminum.[6]

Several recent cross-section statistical studies further buttress theories of transaction-cost savings.[7] They show that interindustry variations in vertical integration are associated with interindustry variations in conditions that may reflect transactions costs. Of these conditions, the one

[5] *The Wall Street Journal*, July 3, 1986, p. 6.

[6] Jean-Francois Hennart, "Upstream Vertical Integration in the Aluminum and Tin Industries," *Journal of Economic Behavior and Organization*, Vol. 9 (1988), pp. 281–299.

[7] James M. MacDonald, "Market Exchange or Vertical Integration: An Empirical Analysis," *Review of Economics and Statistics* (May 1985), pp. 327–331; David T. Levy, "The Transactions Cost Approach to Vertical Integration: An Empirical Examination," *Review of Economics and Statistics* (August 1985), pp. 438–445; Stephen Martin, "Causes and Effects of Vertical Integration," *Applied Economics* (July 1986), pp. 737–755; and Richard E. Caves and Ralph M. Bradburd, "The Empirical Determinants of Vertical Integration," *Journal of Economic Behavior and Organization*, Vol. 9 (1988), pp. 265–279.

displaying greatest statistical significance is fewness of firms, as measured by concentration ratios among buyers or sellers or both. The transaction-cost interpretation of this finding is that fewness implies small numbers bargaining problems, which are reduced by vertical integration.

This interpretation may be largely true. However, concentration ratios *also* measure market power, and it may be that vertical integration is positively associated with concentration because it is a means of *exploiting* or *extending* market power, or some combination of the two. (See Table 11–1, page 299.) This does not mean that concentration's positive effect has no relationship whatever with transaction cost. It simply means that interpretation of this finding is somewhat muddled because vertical integration may be associated with concentration (and other measures of market power) for reasons that have nothing to do with transaction costs.

Our next two sections cover these reasons. The way in which vertical integration may be used to exploit market power are taken up first, followed by consideration of ways in which it may be a means for extending market power.

D. Exploitation of Market Power

The question of whether vertical integration could be used to exploit or extend market power is a much debated one. At first glance, it might seem that *vertical* integration could not add anything to market power derived from *horizontal* conditions, such as a single market's concentration level or barriers to entry. The horizontal conditions are what seem to matter. Therefore any vertical ties might seem irrelevant. And indeed, the dominant theories of the 1940s and 1950s held that vertical integration added nothing to market power.

In fact, it was believed that, if anything, a pure monopolist's acquisition of monopolistic downstream buyers would improve matters rather than make them worse. The basic idea was simple: Independence for successive monopolists would create a problem of "double marginalization," whereas their integration, with its resulting "single marginalization," would eliminate the problem. For example, given independence between a manufacturer and a distributor, the distributor's monopoly profit margin would be placed on top of its costs of goods sold, and those costs would *already include* the manufacturer's monopolistic profit margin. With these margins compounded, consumers' price level would be much higher than otherwise and output much lower. Vertical integration, with both the manufacturer and distributor under the same ownership, would eliminate the double markups for monopoly, and consumer's price level would then be lower with vertical integration and output higher. In other words, consumers have only so much consumers' surplus for a given product. And if two successive monopolists grab for that surplus, the consequences for consumers can be worse than if there was only one (vertically integrated) monopolist taking the surplus.[8]

Now, after much further theorizing and a considerable accumulation of empirical evidence, it is generally recognized that vertical integration is *not* necessarily neutral or beneficial. It can be used to exploit market power more thoroughly than otherwise. That is, it can be the means by which those with some market power can extract *more* consumers' surplus than otherwise possible. Two key assumptions propelled the old theories to their benign view of vertical integration, neither one of which corresponds closely with reality: (1) the manufacturer upstream is a *pure monopolist*, and (2) its product is being combined with other inputs by downstream buyers in fixed proportions. Once these assumptions are abandoned, vertical integration looks much less delightful from the consumers' perspective.[9] In particular, vertical integration may assist the exploitation of market power by (1) *curbing downstream input substitution*, (2) *enabling price discrimination*, and (3) *facilitating collusion*.

1. Curbing Downstream Input Substitution.   The theory of double marginalization, as just described, assumes that downstream buyers of the monopolist's product use that product in fixed proportions with other inputs. For example, tires are used in *fixed* proportions with a car's chassis in auto assembly because every car must have a chassis and four tires plus a spare. In contrast, steel is an input that comprises a variable fraction of an auto's makeup, as aluminum, plastics, and other materials may substitute for steel if the price of steel rises relative to the price of these other inputs.

A monopolist of a fixed proportion input (like tires) may exploit its market power by raising its price without worry that its higher price will cause downstream buyers to substitute other cheaper inputs for the monopolist's input. On the other hand, a monopolist of a variable-proportion input (like steel in autos) could not raise its price heedless of the prospect that its higher price would cause downstream buyers to switch to relatively cheaper substitute inputs. Given substitutes, the monopolist would be constrained. It could not extract the full monopoly profit that would be possible in the event the input were used in fixed proportions.

[8] Joseph T. Spengler, "Vertical Integration and Antitrust Policy," *Journal of Political Economy* (August 1950), pp. 347–352; and Roger D. Blair and David L. Kaserman, *Law and Economics of Vertical Integration* (New York: Academic Press, 1983), pp. 31–36.

[9] See, for example, James L. Hamilton and Soo Bock Lee, "The Paradox of Vertical Integration," *Southern Economic Journal* (July 1986), pp. 110–126; Willard F. Mueller, "Public Policy Toward Vertical Mergers," in *Public Policy Toward Mergers*, edited by J. F. Weston and S. Peltzman (Pacific Palisades, Calif.: Goodyear, 1969); George Hay, "An Economic Analysis of Vertical Integration," *Industrial Organization Review*, Vol. 1 (1973), pp. 188–198; and Oliver Hart and Jean Tirole, "Vertical Integration and Market Foreclosure," *Brookings Papers on Economic Activity: Microeconomics*, (1990), pp. 205–276.

However, if the upstream monopolist gained control of its downstream buyers, its problem of downstream input substitution would be solved. It could then, in effect, raise the price of its monopolized input without inducing profit-robbing downstream substitution away from its product because it would control downstream operations. Hence we have there a market power motive for vertical integration. If used to curb downstream input substitution, vertical integration assists the exploitation of market power.[10]

2. Enabling Price Discrimination. In 1985, physicians who were referring their patients to radiologist William Birnbaum for X rays and other tests began asking him for a share of his profits. They said they would stop referring patients to him if he refused to pay. Dr. Birnbaum refused, and in 1988 they carried out their threat by vertically integrating:

> In a building next door, they created a separate radiology practice in which they each owned investment shares. As owners of the new Irvine Imaging Center, they will divvy up the income from tests on their patients for such ills as broken bones, tumors, heart problems, back-aches, migraines and chest pains. The more tests, the more revenue, and the higher the dividends to physicians.[11]

Physician ownership of laboratories, X-ray centers, and other medical facilities has grown immensely in recent years, with results illustrated in Table 18–1. According to a Blue Cross–Blue Shield survey of Michigan, diagnostic laboratories owned by referring physicians charged almost double the fees of independent labs and did nearly twice as many tests on the average patient. Similarly, a 1989 study of this behavior from the physician's side rather than the lab's side found that, in Maryland, "physicians with an ownership interest in laboratories prescribe .53 services per visit to their office at a cost of $9.93 per lab service [while physicians] without an ownership interest ordered .27 lab services per visit at a cost of $8.68 per service."[12]

It should come as no surprise to learn then, that physicians apparently earn annual profits of 25%-100% on their investments in referral facilities. Moreover, such ownerships are spreading. Critics of the practice say the exorbitant profits amount to "kickbacks" arising from a conflict of interest. We merely note here that they arise from price discrimination made possible by vertical integration. Physicians are extracting more consumers' surplus from some patients than others by virtue of their ownership ties.

10 John M. Vernon and D. A. Graham, "Profitability of Monopolization by Vertical Integration," *Journal of Political Economy*, Vol. 79 (1971), pp. 924–925; and F. R. Warren-Boulton, "Vertical Control with Variable Proportions," *Journal of Political Economy*, Vol. 82, (1974), pp. 783–802.
11 *The Wall Street Journal*, March 1, 1989, p. A1.
12 *The Wall Street Journal*, June 2, 1989, p. B4.

TABLE 18–1.   Prices and Quantities of Medical Laboratory Services Depending on Lab Ownership, 1983, Michigan

Measures of Comparison	Physician-Owned Labs	Independent Labs
Average payment	$44.82	$25.48
Range of payments	$21.33–$123.18	$7.15–$30.33
Average number of tests per patient	6.23	3.76
Range of tests per patient	3.42–20.72	1.67–4.68

Source: *The Wall Street Journal*, March 1, 1989, p. A6.

Less interesting but more traditional forms of price discrimination also emerge from vertical integration. For example, Alcoa, which had a monopoly on aluminum production in the United States from 1888 to 1930, integrated downstream into fabricated products like foil wrap in order to price discriminate. Different potential end uses of aluminum had different price elasticities of demand depending on the availability of substitutes like steel or copper, and also depending on the technical attributes of aluminum versus the substitutes. To exploit these intermarket variations with price variations, Alcoa integrated downstream. This allowed Alcoa to separate its various markets, something necessary to prevent buyer arbitrage (i.e., bootlegging).[13]

3. Facilitating Collusion. Figure 18–1 illustrates four integrated and four independent firms operating three stages of a production process — crude materials, C, manufacturing, M, and retailing, R. The first two stages are linked by vertical integration, whereas manufacturing and retailing are free of ownership connections. Quite clearly, the singular ties of vertical integration suggest order, whereas the many trade ties of independence look like the work of a mad spider.

The implications for competitive conduct should be obvious. The independence of retailers tends to undermine any collusion among the manufacturers because (1) the retailers may compete among themselves, eroding prices at retail level and drawing manufacturers into price rivalry, and (2) retailers may maintain final prices, but manufacturers might still have an incentive to offer the retailers secret price concessions

[13] Martin K. Perry, "Forward Integration by Alcoa: 1888–1930," *Journal of Industrial Economics*, (September 1980), pp. 35–53. For another example of integration and price discrimination, see Robert W. Crandall, "Vertical Integration and the Market for Repair Parts in the U.S. Auto Industry," *Journal of Industrial Economics* (June 1968), pp. 212–234.

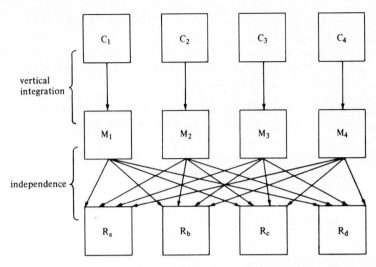

FIGURE 18–1. Vertical integration versus vertical independence.

to induce them to shift their buying patterns. An absence of vertical integration, moreover, tends to undermine collusion among the retailers themselves, because cartel-like agreements at the retail level are then complicated by the need to cover buying as well as selling practices. In short, thoroughgoing, effective cartelization of the industry as drawn in Figure 18–1 would require agreement among eight firms (1, 2, 3, 4, a, b, c, d). Complete vertical integration throughout would cut the number of agreeing parties to four. (For the acme of chaos, complete independence everywhere would raise the number of firms to 12.) Since fewness of firms simplifies collusive agreement, vertical integration may do likewise.

Once agreement is reached, vertical integration also eases the problem of enforcement. This is explained by William Adams:

> One reason for increased adherence to the collusive scheme is the heightened probability that cheating in any one market is more likely to be detected when all participating firms interact in the same economically related markets. As a result, if those colluding in one market find that a colleague has enhanced his market position in other economically related markets they share, they are less likely than otherwise to ascribe the result to chance, and will retaliate accordingly.[14]

---

[14] William J. Adams, "Market Structure and Corporate Power: The Horizontal Dominance Hypothesis Reconsidered," *Columbia Law Review* (November 1974), p. 1284.

Examples of vertical integration's contribution to tacit or explicit collusion include light bulbs,[15] petroleum,[16] steel,[17] textiles,[18] and drugs.[19] Moreover, statistical analysis shows that vertical integration seems to foster market share stability within an industry, something which also suggests a contribution to collusion.[20]

4. Summary. In each of the foregoing instances, vertical integration is being used simply to exploit some preexisting market power. Vertical integration is a machine for harvesting the fruits of power, not a machine for planting or cultivating that power in the first place. Some forms of quasi-integration—like resale price maintenance and tying—may under certain circumstances yield similar results. These are discussed in Chapter 19. Our next task is to explore vertical integration's use in planting and cultivating market power.

E. Extending Market Power

A key trait to any behavior that extends a firm's market power is that it maintain or expand that firm's market share at the expense of rivals, or it pushes rivals from the market altogether, or it deters newcomers from entering the market. There are three basic ways in which vertical integration might have these consequences. It can (1) *reduce rivals' revenues,* (2) *raise rivals' costs,* or (3) *simultaneously reduce rivals' revenues and raise their costs.* As we discuss each of these in turn, it will become apparent that reducing rivals' revenues and raising their costs are often related, and in some instances they are two sides of the same coin. Still, for our purposes, it is best if we take these in three separate steps.

1. Reducing Rivals' Revenues. Each year now auto manufacturers sell about 1 million cars to rental car companies. Consequently, their interest in the rental car business has gone from "0 to 60" very quickly. In 1987 GM helped to finance an employee buyout of Avis. Later, GM bought a 25% stake in the company. These moves toward integration

---

[15] Lester G. Telser, "Why Should Manufacturers Want Fair Trade," *Journal of Law & Economics* (October 1960), pp. 96–104.

[16] M. A. Adelman, "World Oil and the Theory of Industrial Organization," *Industrial Organization and Economic Development*, edited by J. W. Markham and G. F. Papanek (New York: Houghton Mifflin, 1970), p. 145. See also M. G. de Chazeau and A. E. Kahn, *Integration and Competition in the Petroleum Industry* (New Haven, Conn.: Yale University Press, 1959), pp. 428–449.

[17] W. Adams and J. B. Dirlam, "Steel Imports and Vertical Oligopoly Power," *American Economic Review* (September 1964), pp. 626–655.

[18] Irwin M. Stelzer, "The Cotton Textile Industry," in *The Structure of American Industry*, 3rd ed., edited by W. Adams (New York: Macmillan, 1961), pp. 42–73.

[19] Peter M. Costello, "The Tetracycline Conspiracy," *Antitrust Law & Economics Review* (Summer 1968), pp. 13–44.

[20] R. E. Caves and M. E. Porter, "Market Structure, Oligopoly, and Stability of Market Shares," *Journal of Industrial Economics* (June 1978), pp. 289–313.

with Avis gave GM assured annual sales of 60% of the rental company's fleet. Within days of GM's Avis deal, Ford acquired 80% of Hertz, its largest customer. This gave Ford "rights" to supply 70% of Hertz's fleet. In 1988 GM struck again, acquiring a 49% ownership interest in National Auto Rental. That gave GM 75% of National's fleet purchases. Ford then added to its vertical ties in 1988 by locking up 65% of Budget's car purchases (acting as a source of financing for a leveraged buyout of Budget). At this point Chrysler's revenues from this huge segment of the auto market were threatened. According to *The Wall Street Journal*

> All this left Chrysler feeling somewhat naked . . . So, in May [1989], the auto maker turned a quick double play. It agreed to buy Thrifty, cementing its 75% of Thrifty's 33,000-car corporate fleet. Four days later, Thrifty agreed to buy Snappy, which specializes in renting to people whose cars are damaged, stolen or under repair. "It's purely defensive," says Bennett E. Bidwell, Chrysler Motors unit's chairman. "We can't allow ourselves to be squeezed out."[21]

Complex theories of reducing rivals' revenues are available,[22] but the principle is easily seen in Figure 18–2 as a matter of downstream *foreclosure. Without* vertical integration, all sellers — A, B, and C — have open access to the buyer, "Outlet." *With* vertical integration between A and the "Outlet," rivals B and C find their revenues threatened by downstream foreclosure, as their sales to the "outlet" drop, being supplanted by A.

Anticompetitive foreclosure of this sort need not occur, and it has its skeptics. For example, look back at Figure 18–1. If manufacturer M_1 were to acquire retailer R_a and then turn M_2, M_3, and M_4 away from R_a, the consequences would be minimal if at the same time M_1 stopped selling to R_b, R_c, and R_d to concentrate its sales through outlet R_a. As M_1 "foreclosed" subsidiary R_a and shifted its supplies away from the remaining retailers, M_1's rivals would not lose revenues to M_1 because they would expand their sales to the remaining independent retailers R_b, R_c, and R_d as M_1 shifted.[23]

What is the difference between Figure 18–2 (where anticompetative foreclosure can be observed) and Figure 18–1 (where there is no threat to the revenues of M_1's rivals after M_1's downstream vertical integration)? One obvious difference is the degree of market power involved. In Figure 18–2 there is only one outlet. In Figure 18–1 there are four retailers of equal size, so M_1's vertical move closed 25% of the retail

---

21 *The Wall Street Journal*, June 29, 1989, p. A4.

22 David T. Levy and David Reiffen, "Vertical Integration as Strategic Behavior in a Special Setting: Reducing Rivals' Revenues," Working Paper #165, Federal Trade Commission Bureau of Economics, 1988.

23 This kind of argument is used by Bork and others to pooh-pooh the idea that vertical integration could ever cause anticompetitive foreclosure. *The Antitrust Paradox* (New York: Basic Books, 1978) pp. 304–309.

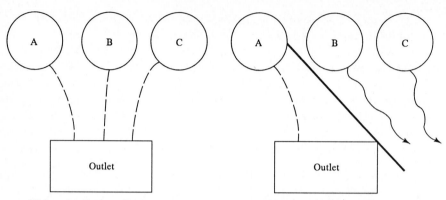

Without foreclosure, all sellers
A, B, and C have equal access to buyer.

With foreclosure, seller A captures the
buyer, forcing sellers B and C to look
elsewhere.

FIGURE 18–2. Downstream foreclosure from vertical integration by A that threatens the revenues of rivals B and C. Source: Adapted from Eugene M. Singer, *Antitrust Economics and Legal Analysis* (Columbus, Ohio: Grid, 1981), p. 94.

opportunities to the other manufacturers, not 100%. Another difference is an implicit assumption regarding supplier capacity — A's capacity in Figure 18–2 and M_1's in Figure 18–1. In Figure 18–2 it is implicitly assumed that A can easily expand capacity to fill all of outlet's requirements. On the other hand, it is assumed for Figure 18–1 that M_1's capacity is limited, so as it closes R_a to its rivals it fills R_a's shelves by shifting its sales away from R_b, R_c, and R_d (instead of expanding its sales to R_a while maintaining its sales to the others).

In short, reducing rivals' revenues by downstream foreclosure typically requires that the instigators of the foreclosure have substantial market power and sufficient capacity to supplant rivals' sales with their own rather than simply realign sales. These conditions apparently applied in the rental car market, as both GM and Ford together accounted for the lion's share of total supply there, and they also had the capacity to completely supplant Chrysler.[24] In criticism of the rental car example skeptics might argue that Chrysler's revenues would *not* be threatened even if GM and Ford had bought up all the leading car rental companies — Thrifty and Alamo as well as Hertz, Avis, Budget, and National. Skeptics might contend that Chrysler could *start its own* car rental company if it wished, thereby recapturing its lost revenues in that segment.

[24] These conditions also held when United Airlines and American Airlines used their vertical ties to computer reservation systems to reduce the revenues of rivals. See, for example, Margaret E. Guerin-Calvert, "Vertical Integration as a Threat to Competition: Airline Computer Reservation Systems," in *The Anti-Trust Revolution*, edited by J. E. Kwoka, Jr., and L. J. White (Glenview, Ill: Scott, Foresman, 1989), pp. 338–370. For related evidence of "channeling" in hospital supply, steel, and other markets, see Peter Petre, "How to Keep Customers Happy Captives," *Fortune*, September 2, 1985, pp. 42–46.

Well, what about this entry alternative? Admittedly, Chrysler *could* enter the car rental business. But it should be clear that it could do so only at extremely high cost in comparison to the established leading companies like Hertz. Given severe limits on airport parking acreage, on counter space, and on other such car rental inputs, and given also the huge investment that would be necessary for advertising and other reputation-building efforts, it seems that Chrysler's costs for such a venture would be prohibitively high. If so, GM's and Ford's efforts at *reducing* Chrysler's *revenues* by buying up all the major car rental companies would also have the effect, by this alternative interpretation, of *raising* Chrysler's *costs*. But there are more direct means of raising rivals' costs than this, so let's skip over this roundabout interpretation and consider raising rivals' costs expressly.

2. Raising Rivals' Costs.   Houston's refuse dump has two entrances:

> Through one gate, the big blue garbage trucks of Browning-Ferris Industries, Inc., breeze in and out, often without a wait. But at the other entrance, trucks from every other disposal company in town have to line up, sometimes waiting hours to get through the gates to dump their loads.

> The Browning-Ferris trucks have their own entrance because Browning-Ferris owns and operates the dump. The other garbage collectors say they can't compete, not only because of long waits but, they say, because Browning-Ferris increases the outsiders' dumping charges every six months or so.[25]

This is an example of raising rivals' costs, a strategy for extending market power that can be especially effective. Steven Salop and David Scheffman have shown that strategies designed to raise rivals' costs have significant advantages over predatory pricing. In particular, cost-raising strategies do not have an inherent problem of credibility. Such strategies may be profitable whether or not the rivals exit, since higher-cost rivals have an incentive to cut back output and raise prices immediately, which may make it possible for the predator to reap gains even in the short run.[26]

How could vertical integration raise rivals' costs? It can foster various forms of upstream foreclosure, in which case prime inputs are controlled by dominant firms, so their rivals consequently incur relatively higher costs or go without. (First mover control with economies of scale has this effect, for instance.) Besides the Browning-Ferris example, we earlier encountered U.S. Steel's extensive overbuying of iron ore and Alcoa's acquisition of the best hydroelectric sites for its production of aluminum. Similarly, backward vertical integration was undertaken by a

25 *The Wall Street Journal*, February 15, 1985, p. 33.
26 Steven C. Salop and David T. Scheffman, "Cost-Raising Strategies," *Journal of Industrial Economics* (September 1987), pp. 19–34.

number of the giant combines formed during the merger movement of 1895–1904 in attempts "to limit competitors' access to raw materials."[27]

Figures 18–3 and 18–4 illustrate this when potential entrants are the rivals whose costs are being raised. The market of a key input is pictured (not the output). Hence new rivals of the dominant incumbent firm would have to compete with the incumbent over this input. Figure 18–3 shows conditions before and after entry when there is *no* vertical integration and therefore *no* disproportionate raising of rivals' costs. Before entry, in 18–3(a), the demand and supply for the input are what they would be when seen by the incumbent firm alone. Setting aside the effects of monopsony, the firm's costs per unit would then be C_I. After entry, in panel (b) of 18–3, the entrants' demand for the input is added to the incumbent's demand, shifting the demand curve rightward. Without vertical integration by the incumbent firm, the costs of *both* the incumbent and the entrants end up being the same at $C_{I=E}$, as all firms compete equally for inputs. Here the incumbent cannot raise the entrants' cost relative to its own. Indeed, the competition for inputs and the upward sloping supply curve result in the incumbent paying higher costs than before entry.

In contrast, Figure 18–4 depicts the same situation except that, before entry, the incumbent locks up Q_0 of the input for its exclusive use

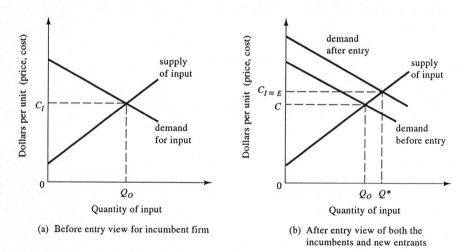

(a) Before entry view for incumbent firm

(b) After entry view of both the incumbents and new entrants

FIGURE 18–3. Input market before and after entry *without* vertical integration and *without* raising rivals' costs relative to incumbent.

[27] Naomi R. Lamoreaux, *The Great Merger Movement in American Business, 1895–1904* (Cambridge: Cambridge University Press, 1985), p. 155. For further examples, see Thomas G. Krattenmaker and Steven C. Salop, "Anticompetitive Exclusion: Raising Rivals' Costs to Achieve Power over Price," *Yale Law Journal* (December 1986), pp. 209–293.

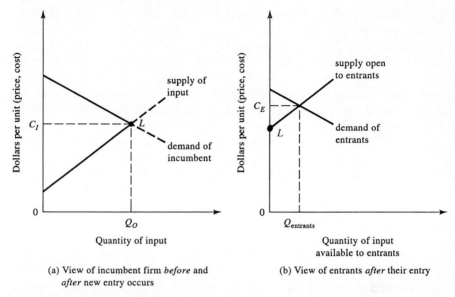

(a) View of incumbent firm *before* and *after* new entry occurs

(b) View of entrants *after* their entry

FIGURE 18–4. Input market before and after entry *with* vertical integration that raises rivals' costs relative to incumbent.

by upstream vertical integration. Panel (a) now depicts the incumbent's view both before *and* after entry, because vertical integration by the incumbent precludes postentry competition over the input, at least not over the quantity Q_0. Panel (b) now shows the extrants' view. Note that the horizontal axis of panel (a) represents *only* that quality of input that is available to the extrants after accounting for the fact that the incumbent has captured Q_0 of the input. Hence the input supply curve available to the entrants is limited to that portion which extends above point L and to the right of Q_0 in panel (a)—i.e., the input supply not already committed to the incumbent. In other words, only high-cost input supplies are available to potential entrants. If they actually enter, they will have an input cost per unit of C_E, which is substantially higher than the incumbent's cost, C_I, both before and after entry. Hence in this case vertical integration with backward foreclosure have been used by the incumbent to raise its (potential) rivals' costs, thereby keeping them at bay.

A form of quasi-integration called exclusive dealing can yield these results by contract instead of by ownership.[28] For example, during the 1970s and 1980s Anheuser-Busch and Miller Brewing Company obtained sponsorships to most live, network sports events, like Monday Night

[28] William S. Comanor and H. E. Frech III, "The Competitive Effects of Vertical Agreements," *American Economic Review* (June 1985), pp. 539–546; and John T. Hoven, "Exclusive Dealing Can Sustain a Monopoly," U.S. Dept. of Justice, Economic Analysis Group Discussion Paper 87–13 (1987).

Football, that were exclusive as regards beer. In the case of Anheuser-Busch, for instance, cars, computers, and other products could be advertised along with Bud or Michelob during a football or basketball game, but other brewer's brands of beer could not be advertised during the game. These live, network sports "exclusivities" were obtained by contracts, not vertical integration. But because they covered nearly all such programming, brewers other than Anheuser-Busch and Miller suffered. The others could advertise their brands on newscasts, soap operas, and still other TV programs, if they wished, but the costs of reaching the people who are the most gluttonous beer guzzlers in America—21- to 40-year-old males—by these alternatives were much greater than the costs associated with live, network sports events. This helps explain the rapid growth of Anheuser-Busch and Miller during the 1970s and 1980s relative to other brewers.[29]

Note that this instance of "raising rivals' costs" could also have a "reducing rivals' revenues" interpretation. To the extent that brewers like Stroh and Pabst could not reach beer buyers at a reasonable cost, their revenues were reduced. Note also that the anticompetitive consequences in this case of beer arose because of a "bottleneck" effect. An essential (or at least very important) ingredient to the beer business (live network TV sports sponsorships) was snared by Anheuser-Busch and Miller to the exclusion of others. Similar consequences may occur if there are economies of scale in the production of the input. Then dominant firm vertical control of the large-scale production facilities for the input forces smaller rivals' to contend with more costly small-scale input sources.

Some of the best evidence that vertical integration may raise rivals' cost comes from cases of exclusive dealing and related contractual ties. This is U.K. evidence. Shaw and Simpson studied dominant firms in 28 highly concentrated U.K. markets. Dominant firms that were forced by antitrust action to drop their vertical ties experienced a much greater loss of market share than otherwise—an average loss of -12.4% versus changes of -3.8% and +2.0% for two control groups.[30] Note once again that anticompetitive effects occur only if there is some dominance by those instigating the upstream foreclosures. (For more on exclusive dealing, see the appendix to this chapter.)

---

[29] *The Wall Street Journal*, May 22, 1985, p. 25; and *Advertising Age*, August 5, 1985, p. 1. Even though Anheuser-Busch and Miller paid premiums to the networks for these exclusivities, the audience demographs of live, network sports broadcasts were such as to seriously disadvantage the other brewers in terms of cost per thousand male viewers aged 21 to 40. The vast majority of all beer is consumed by these people, and much of it while they watch live sports events on T.V.

[30] R. W. Shaw and P. Simpson, "The Persistence of Monopoly: An Investigation of the Effectiveness of the U.K. Monopolies Commission," *Journal of Industrial Economics* (June 1986), pp. 355–372.

3. Reducing Rivals' Revenues and Raising Rivals' Costs Simultaneously. This simultaneous pinch is most clearly seen in the so-called *"price squeeze."* The classic example occurred in aluminum when Alcoa had a monopoly on ingots prior to 1940. Alcoa did two things with its ingots. Some it rolled and fabricated internally; others it sold to independent rollers and fabricators, such as Reynolds, who at the time had no ingot capacity. Survival of these independents obviously depended on prices at two levels: (1) the price they paid for ingots and (2) the price at which they sold their sheets and fabrications.

Alcoa clearly controlled the price of ingots. Alcoa was also big enough in downstream markets to influence the price of sheets and fabrications. Hence, Alcoa could, and allegedly did, raise the price of ingots and use the proceeds to lower its prices for sheets and fabrications. This pinched the independents, who had to cut their prices to retain customers. With their ingot costs rising and their final fabrication prices falling, their profits were disappearing. Alcoa, for its part, presumably suffered losses at fabrication stage, but these could be covered by its ingot profits.[31]

4. Summary. Now we know how vertical integration or quasi-integration may help to extend market power (or extend it while also exploiting it). Used by dominant firms, vertical integration may injure rivals, not because the dominant firms are more efficient but because of their strategic positions and behaviors. By contracting for exclusive rights to prime market outlets, by overbuying scarce ore deposits, and by achieving various other forms of downstream and upstream foreclosure, dominant firms may reduce rivals' revenues, raise rivals' costs, or do both at the same time, adversely affecting rivals' profits and viability. Combining these findings with our earlier ones on technical-cost savings and transaction-cost savings, it may be concluded that vertical integration can be either a boon or a bane depending on the circumstances.

II. CONGLOMERATES

A. The Benefits Of Conglomeration

The benefits claimed for conglomerate diversification are much less substantial than those that can be attributed to vertical integration. They include:[32]

---

[31] *U.S.* v. *Aluminum Company of America*, 148 F.2d 416 (2nd Cir., 1945) and 91 F. Supp. 333 (S.D.N.Y., 1950). More recently see *Greyhound Computer* v. *International Business Machines*, 559 F.2d 488 (1977), pp. 498–505. For an interesting case in Europe, see Roberto Zaratta, "The Paper Industry in the EEC," in *The Structure of European Industry*, edited by H. W. de Jong (Dordrecht, The Netherlands: Kluwer, 1988), p. 115.

[32] C. J. Sutton, *Economics and Corporate Strategy* (Cambridge: Cambridge University Press, 1980), pp. 51–76.

1. *Reduced instability and uncertainty:* If a firm draws its profits from a number of products experiencing different cyclical peaks and valleys, it can smooth its profit flows. Moreover, a firm's stability might be improved if it deals in products that vary by stage of product life cycle. Products in "decline" can be counterbalanced by those experiencing rapid "growth."
2. *Efficiency:* According to some commentators, conglomeracy enables the exploitation of "synergy" or managerial economies. A beer company may thus branch out into snack foods, as Anheuser-Busch has done, because these products may be distributed and perhaps marketed together
3. *New entry:* Conglomerate expansion is a source of new entry, provided it is achieved by internal expansion or "toehold" acquisition. For example, Sears and AT&T have recently entered the credit card business, giving stiff new competition to Visa and MasterCard.

Realization of these several benefits depends partly on the size and diversity that a firm has already achieved. That is to say, the magnitude and chaotic diversity of the country's 20 leading conglomerates seem to be way beyond the levels of size and diversity that could reasonably be justified by these several rationales. Indeed, many huge conglomerates seem to be admitting this when they engage in extensive self-dismemberment. Recent divestiture programs exceeding $1 billion in sales or assets have been adopted by ITT, W. R. Grace, Beatrice Foods, and Gulf & Western. (Moreover, heavy costs may be incurred instead of benefits. Shortly after American Can bought Sam Goody, Inc., a record store chain, Goody and its officers were indicted for racketeering, interstate shipment of stolen property, and dealing in counterfeit recordings. The record business thus gave American Can a record headache.[33])

As for the anticompetitive possibilities of immense conglomeracy, they include mutual forbearance, reciprocity, and cross-subsidization.

B. Conglomerates And Forbearance

Mutual forbearance among conglomerates is similar to tacit collusion among firms in the same market. Rather than compete vigorously by invading each other's bailiwicks, conglomerates may follow a strategy of "live and let live." As the size and diversification of conglomerates expand, they meet each other in more and more markets, they become more fully aware of each other's special concerns, and they grow to appreciate their mutual interests.

What motivates this? Conglomeracy raises the possibility of massive

---

[33] *Business Week*, March 24, 1980, pp. 130–132.

retaliatory attack in one market as punishment for competitive transgressions in another market. Corwin Edwards outlines the implications:

> A large concern usually must show a regard for the strength of other large concerns by circumspection in its dealings with them, whereas such caution is usually unnecessary in dealing with small enterprises. The interests of great enterprises are likely to touch at many points, and it would be possible for each to mobilize at any one of these points a considerable aggregate of resources. The anticipated gain to such a concern from unmitigated competitive attack upon another large enterprise at one point of contact is likely to be slight as compared with the possible loss from retaliatory action by that enterprise at many other points of contact.[34]

Circumspection finds expression in much business lore. ITT has in the past been so diligent about avoiding the wrath of IBM that a highly paid man was hired by ITT to do nothing more than stop ITT's companies from moving into computers.[35] Less dramatic but no less revealing is the case of National Bank of Commerce of Seattle, which turned down large prospective customers in western Washington on grounds that "our bank did not wish to fish in the Old National's fishing hole. . . ."[36]

Failure to forbear may have consequences illustrated by Clorox and Procter & Gamble (P&G) during the late 1980s. For decades Clorox held over 50% of the bleach business and P&G controlled over 50% of the detergent trade (Tide, Cheer, etc.). Each was also diversified — Clorox into bottled water, charcoal briquets, etcetera, and P&G into paper products, cake mixes, toothpaste, and many other grocery items. Yet their paths never crossed contentiously until Clorox ceased its circumspection vis-à-vis P&G and entered the detergent market in a big way in 1988. Its "Clorox Super Detergent" was not on grocers' shelves more than a few months, however, before P&G retaliated by escalating its detergent promotions and by entering the bleach market. Not only did P&G strike back with its own bleach, it launched an especially intense campaign against Clorox in the same western states where Clorox was first trying to establish itself in detergents. Thus P&G did much more than raise its detergent defenses, it aggressively blasted Clorox by counterattacking on the bleach front.[37]

[34] Corwin D. Edwards, "Conglomerate Bigness as a Source of Power," in *Business Concentration and Price Policy* (Princeton, N.J.: Princeton University Press, 1955), p. 335.

[35] Anthony Sampson, *The Sovereign State of ITT* (Greenwich, Conn.: Fawcett, 1974), p. 103.

[36] From company correspondence, government's exhibit, *U.S.* v. *Marine Bancorporation, Inc.*, 94 S. Ct. 2856 (1974). For very interesting recent examples in airlines see *The Wall Street Journal*, July 11, 1989, p. B1.

[37] *Forbes*, November 28, 1988, p. 138; and *Business Week*, May 2, 1988, p. 36. For related examples see Federal Trade Commission, *Economic Report on the Structure and Competitive Behavior of Food Retailing* (1966) pp. 145–146; Federal Trade Commission, *Economic Report on Corporate Mergers* (1966), pp. 458–471; and F. M. Scherer, A. Beckenstein, E. Kaufer, and R. D. Murphy, *The Economics of Multi-Plant Operation* (Cambridge, Mass.: Harvard University Press, 1975), pp. 137, 165, 314.

Rigorous statistical studies of the importance of mutual forbearance are nearly impossible because the necessary data rarely exist. Nevertheless, several studies have demonstrated the significance of such behavior in banking and manufacturing. A study of banking, by Arnold Heggestad and Steve Rhoades, is easiest to describe because the conglomeracy in that case was based on geographic spread. Because commercial banking is primarily a local market activity, and because many banks operate in more than one local market, the following inquiry was pursued: Is competitive intensity within a given local market determined solely by the *internal* structural conditions in that market, such as concentration and barriers to entry, or is it also determined by the frequency with which the firms in that market confront each other on the *outside*, in other local markets? Using a variety of measures for "competitive intensity" — including market share turbulence, price levels, and profit rates — Heggestad and Rhoades found that frequent outside contact *does* make a significant difference in the direction of mutual forbearance. In particular, if the firms in a local market have *no* competitive encounters in other markets, that local market tends to be vigorously competitive (other things equal). Conversely, if the firms in a local market encounter each other extensively and frequently elsewhere, then competition in that local market tends to be muted, puny, and lethargic. Hence, Heggestad and Rhoades conclude that "multimarket meetings do adversely affect the degree of competition within markets."[38]

C. Reciprocity In Conglomerates

Simply stated, **reciprocal buying** is "the use by a firm of its buying power to promote its sales."[39] "I'll buy from you if you'll buy from me," expresses the philosophy. As old as barter and often as trifling, reciprocity may nevertheless have anticompetitive consequences when used by giant firms.

Conglomeracy is an important factor because diversification is often associated with reciprocity. In Figure 18–5, for instance, conglomerate C owns subsidiary U. Firm S is a supplier to C and also a potential buyer of U's product. Thus C can coax S into buying from its subsidiary U by

[38] Arnold A. Heggestad and Stephen A. Rhoades, "Multi-Market Interdependence and Local Market Competition," *Review of Economics and Statistics* (November 1978), pp. 523–532; and "Multi-Market Interdependence in Banking: a Further Analysis," mimeo (1978). See also, John T. Scott, "Multimarket Contact and Economic Performance," *Review of Economics and Statistics* (August 1982), pp. 368–375; Robert M. Feinberg, "Sales-at-Risk: A Test of the Mutual Forbearance Theory of Conglomerate Behavior," *Journal of Business* (April 1985), pp. 225–241; and Donald L. Alexander, "An Empirical Test of the Mutual Forbearance Hypothesis: The Case of Bank Holding Companies," *Southern Economic Journal* (July 1985), pp. 122–140.

[39] G. W. Stocking and W. F. Mueller, "Business Reciprocity and the Size of Firms," *Journal of Business* (April 1957), p. 75.

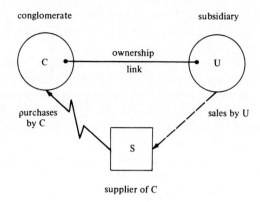

FIGURE 18–5. Reciprocity.

pointing out to S the fact that C and U are essentially the same company and that C is a big buyer of S's goods. Conglomeracy plays its part because C and U would not be linked without it.

To what extent is reciprocity actually practiced? Survey evidence from the early 1960s indicates that, at least in the past, the practice was quite popular. When asked, "Is reciprocity a factor in buyer-seller relations in your company?" 100% of all sampled purchasing agents in chemicals, petroleum, and iron and steel answered "yes." Purchasing agents from services and consumer goods industries reported significantly less reliance on reciprocity, but over one-third of them admitted that it was "a factor" in their trade relations.

Reciprocity has now declined. Questionnaire surveys from the 1970s reveal substantially lower reported rates of practice. For example, fewer than 20% of the large firms responding to a Harvard University survey gave any indication of reciprocal dealings.[40] Between 1963 and 1971 the antitrust authorities criticized reciprocity as being anticompetitive and cracked down with a string of hostile suits that were supported in federal courts by trial or consent settlement. Although reciprocity is not now per se illegal, these major events may have produced a genuine reduction in its usage.[41]

Because reciprocity can be quite innocuous, the picture of its competitive effects is cloudy. Even so, the antitrust authorities' past hostility toward the practice was not altogether unwarranted. Any attempt here to sort out the circumstances of harmless and harmful reciprocity would involve tortuous reasoning.[42] We shall therefore simply stress its offensive potentials.

[40] J. W. Markham, *Conglomerate Enterprise and Public Policy* (Cambridge, Mass.: Harvard University Press, 1973), pp. 77–82.

[41] But see F. R. Finney, "Reciprocity: Gone But Not Forgotten," *Journal of Marketing* (January 1978), pp. 54–59.

[42] Peter O. Steiner, *Mergers: Motives, Effects, Policies* (Ann Arbor: University of Michigan Press, 1975), pp. 218–254.

Once again the key to understanding anticompetitive effects is a recognition that competition in one market may not depend solely on conditions inside that market. Conditions outside, in other markets, may have decisive impact. In the case of reciprocity, competition among sellers and potential sellers in one market (that in which U sells in Figure 18–5) is affected by the monopsony buying power of a firm in another market (that in which C buys in Figure 18–5). Note that the monopsony buying power *might* be exploited entirely within the confines of the market where it lodges. The firm with buying power, C, might negotiate preferential price discounts from its supplier S, or might insist that supplier S throw some extra goods into the bargain. If the monopsony power were so confined, there would then be no adverse competitive consequences in any other market. However, there are some good reasons why the monopsonist might prefer to exploit its monopsony power via reciprocity, thereby entangling other markets where (in the form of U) it acts as a *seller* instead of a buyer:

1. Supplier S may not be able or willing to offer special price discounts to the big buyer because to do so might put pressure on the supplier to reduce prices to *all* buyers.
2. Conglomerate buyer C may not have true monopsony power in the sense of not buying a preponderant portion of all the product sold by supplier S and S's rivals. Rather, the conglomerate may merely be buying a large *dollar volume* of the product, a form of buying power that might be exploited most effectively through reciprocity.
3. Supplier S might *itself* have monopsony power in the market where the conglomerate's subsidiary U operates as seller. In this case reciprocity might not represent the exploitation of S by C. Instead, reciprocity might be *mutually* advantageous to both conglomerate C and supplier S. Whereas single market monopsony might lead to seller's price concessions, linked monopsony might find expression in reciprocity.

Whatever the reason for shifting buying power across markets into selling power (from the left-hand side to the right-hand side of Figure 18–5), the market of final resting place may suffer competitively. What are these potentially adverse competitive effects? Basically, there are three possibilities: (1) greater concentration, (2) augmented barriers to entry, and (3) greater price rigidity or higher prices. We have enough space to illustrate the last of these.

Price Effects. General Dynamics is an enormous company best known for its manufacture of major weapon systems. It is also a large and diversified purchaser. In 1957, when it took control of Liquid Carbonic Company (LC), General Dynamics had roughly 80,000 industrial suppliers from whom it purchased about $500 million annually. LC was a manufacturer of carbon dioxide and other industrial gases, with a market share equal to about 35% in 1957. Shortly after LC was taken into General Dynamics' corporate family, a "trade relations" program was instituted in hopes of selling LC gases to General Dynamics' many suppliers. As one LC official put it, "Let's not kid ourselves, the ultimate reason for establishing a trade relations department is to increase sales through the proper application of your purchasing power."[43]

The program proved successful by almost any measure. Over the period 1960–1962, "there was a 33 per cent increase in reciprocity sales, whereas general sales of LC increased only 7 per cent. In addition, prior to merger, LC's market share had declined by about 2.7 per cent. After merger and the reciprocity program, LC's market share regained its earlier position."[44] What is more, these gains were made without price reductions. Quite the contrary. In at least three instances LC gained reciprocity customers at prices *higher* than those charged by its rival gas suppliers.

Simply stated, prices are affected in the conglomerate's target market because *nonprice* considerations, emanating from other markets, lessen the potency of price as a competitive weapon. For the conglomerate seller pursuing reciprocity, buying power elsewhere is the key weapon.

D. Conglomerate Cross-subsidization

Cross-subsidization includes certain forms of price discrimination and predation (recall IBM versus the plug-compatible producers). It also includes a good deal more. Generally speaking, cross-subsidization is best thought of as a *dynamic* strategy — unlike forbearance and reciprocity, which are rather more static. Short-run losses, covered by short-term intrafirm transfers, may yield *future* power and *future* profits.

Conglomerates may cross-subsidize in a variety of ways for a variety of reasons. Long ago, American Tobacco cross-subsidized advertising for predatory purposes. More recently, Philip Morris Corporation has subsidized a massive advertising campaign for its Miller Brewing Company.[45] Yet Miller apparently wanted only a larger market share, not a full-fledged monopoly. Indeed, most modern cross-subsidization might best be thought of as a "power investment" rather than a predatory strategy. Short-run losses may be ultimately profitable because, as William Adams argues, "The power presently enjoyed by a firm depends heavily on the firm's conduct in the past. The greater was yesterday's advertising, the greater is today's product differentiation. The greater was yesterday's

[43] Erwin A. Blackstone, "Monopsony Power, Reciprocal Buying, and Government Contracts: The General Dynamics Case," *Antitrust Bulletin* (Summer 1972), p. 460.

[44] Ibid., p. 461.

[45] *Business Week*, November 8, 1976, pp. 58–67.

research and development activity, the greater is today's patent control. And so on."[46]

Adams goes on to point out that large diversified firms have a significant advantage over small specialized firms because internal funds are the prime source of capital for "power investments," and giants possess the deepest pools of internal funds. Outside capital from banks and other lenders is relatively scarce for these purposes because power investments are especially high in lender's risk. "Since such investments involve little physical asset creation, there may be nothing for the creditors to appropriate if a power bid fails. The prospect of an Edsel trademark as sole surviving asset from a power bid will not attract lending institutions."[47]

Obviously, the main headwaters of internal pools of funds are likely to be those markets where the conglomerate's monopolistic power is well established. You will not be startled to learn that as of the late 1980s, blades and razors accounted for only 32% of Gillette's total *sales* revenue, but blades and razors earned 61% of Gillette's overall *profit*[48].

Such cross-market disparities do not always indicate power grabs. Indeed, they occasionally reflect an effort at new entry. Gillette used its blade and razor profits to finance ill-fated entries into pocket calculators and digital watches. Still, this seems to be only occasionally true.

III. MULTINATIONAL CORPORATIONS

Multinational corporations distinguish themselves with wholly owned foreign subsidiaries, partially owned foreign joint ventures, or patent and trademark licensing agreements abroad. Coca-Cola, IBM, GM, Exxon, and Mobil are prominent examples among those calling the United States "home." Foreign multinationals include Michelin, Volkswagenwerk, Royal-Dutch Shell, and Unilever. From the perspective of these foreign firms, the United States is a "host" country. In aggregate terms, roughly 400 multinational enterprises produce perhaps as much as one-third of the free world's industrial output. They are, in short, vastly powerful. Table 18–2 lists some of those with especially high percentages of their sales and assets outside their home country.

A. Why Do Firms Become Multinationals?

Multinational enterprises exist for many reasons. Some, like Rio Tinto Zinc, go abroad to secure raw material supplies. Others, like National

---

46 Adams, "Market Structure and Corporate Power," p. 1287.
47 Ibid., p. 1289.
48 *Business Week*, February 29, 1988, p. 36.

TABLE 18–2. Selected Multinational Corporations with High Portions of Total Sales and Assets Outside Their Home Country

Company	Home Country	1989 Total Sales ($ billions)	Sales Outside Home Country (%)	Assets Outside Home Country (%)
Nestlé	Switzerland	$32.9	98%	95%
Hoffman-LaRoche	Switzerland	6.7	96	60
Philips	Netherlands	30.0	94	85
Electrolux	Sweden	13.8	83	80
ICI	Britain	22.1	78	50
Unilever	Britain/Netherlands	35.3	75	70
Colgate	United States	5.0	64	47
Honda	Japan	26.4	63	36
IBM	United States	62.7	59	NA
Coca-Cola	United States	9.0	54	45
Siemens	Germany	36.0	51	NA

NA = Not available.
Source: *Business Week*, May 14, 1990, p. 103.

Semiconductor, locate assembly plants abroad in order to lower their labor costs. The principal reason of interest to us here, however, is *monopolistic advantages.*[49] In particular, direct foreign investment frequently occurs in industries where monopolistic advantages prevail both at home and abroad. These advantages may be grounded in advanced technology (chemicals and computers, for example), potent product differentiation (as in the case of soft drinks and drugs), and economies of scale (as in autos). Note that many of these advantages are protected by "industrial property" rights at home and abroad—that is, patents, proprietary know-how, and trademarks. The basic idea is that these monopolistic advantages give the multinational enterprise an advantage over host country rivals, or at least give the multinational's foreign subsidiaries an equal chance in host country markets. Without such special advantages the foreigner would be at a *dis*advantage because local firms would naturally tend to be more familiar with local market conditions, local laws, local customs, and other local mysteries important to business success. A nice illustration of this is provided by Tandy Corporation, whose Radio Shack store in Holland geared its first Christmas promotion to December 25, unaware that the Dutch customarily ex-

[49] Richard E. Caves, *Multinational Enterprise and Economic Analysis* (Cambridge: Cambridge University Press, 1982), pp. 94–97.

change holiday gifts on December 6, St. Nicholas Day. They badly missed the market.[50]

Numerous statistical studies support this theory of direct foreign investment by finding high correlations between direct foreign investment on the one hand and four-firm concentration or advertising intensity or R&D expenditure on the other. In Mexico, for instance, foreign firms accounted for 100% of 1970 industry sales in transportation equipment, rubber, electrical equipment, and office equipment—all of which evince special advantages for member firms. In contrast, 1970 sales of foreign firms accounted for very small percentages in leather, textiles, and apparel—4.6%, 7.1%, and 4.0% respectively.[51]

From the home country's perspective, multinationals likewise come from oligopolistic industries. Indeed, it has been found that industrial concentration influences U.S. firm foreign investment in a way similar to that shown earlier for advertising in Figure 16–2 (line ABC on page 482). The *timing* of foreign investment and the *intensity* of foreign investment both seem to be keyed to "loose-knit" oligopoly.[52]

B. Adverse Multimarket Conduct

The economic consequences of multinationalism may be viewed from home and host country perspectives. From both perspectives, the consequences are mixed—some good and some bad. We cannot review the entire scene, so we shall limit the discussion to conduct especially pertinent to multimarket spread. In the main, this boils down to several host country adversities.

1. Mutual Forbearance.   If firms of potential international scope declined to compete against each other completely, there would be no multinationals, or they would be severely stunted. Becoming a multinational implies thrusts into territories of foreign rivals. So multinationalism is certainly not synonymous with forbearance.

Still, instances of explicit and tacit collusion abound. Formal or informal allocations of territories and price fixing may be the result. The recently documented activities of the International Electrical Association, an international cartel in heavy electrical equipment, illustrates the formal possibilities:

---

50 "Radio Shack's Rough Trip," *Business Week*, May 30, 1977, p. 55.

51 John M. Connor and Willard F. Mueller, "Manufacturing, Denationalization, and Market Structure: Brazil, Mexico, and the United States" *Industrial Organization Review*, No. 2 (1978), pp. 86–105.

52 F. T. Knickerbocker, *Oligopolistic Reaction and Multinational Enterprise* (Boston: Division of Research, Graduate School of Business Administration, Harvard University, 1973); and R. E. Caves, M. E. Porter, A. M. Spence, and J. T. Scott, *Competition in the Open Economy* (Cambridge, Mass.: Harvard University Press, 1980), pp. 86–87.

The cartel comprises over 50 European and Japanese producers and covers sales in most of the markets of the non-Communist world outside the United States, Western Europe, and Japan (amounting to almost $2 billion annually). . . . These cartel arrangements directly harm importing countries because of the onerous markup on cartelized sales as well as common policies among members restricting technology transfers to nonproducing countries. On the basis of data from one product section, it is estimated that successful collusive agreements may raise prices 15 to 25 percent above the competitive rate.[53]

Other examples, both formal and informal, concern tobacco, metal containers, and automobiles.[54]

2. Transfer Pricing.   Transfer pricing is like cross-subsidization in that it permits a multinational to vary its earnings across different divisions. The variations are achieved differently here, however, as they arise from transactions among the multinational's various geographic members. In particular, when a subsidiary abroad buys raw materials, technology, or services from its parent multinational company, it is charged an arbitrary intracompany price that might well be exorbitant. For example, the multinational oil companies apparently overcharged their Canadian subsidiaries $3.2 billion on crude oil imported into Canada over the years 1958–1970.[55] Investigations in Colombia for the late 1960s disclosed that drug giant Hoffman-LaRoche was overcharging its subsidiary (as a percentage of world market prices) by 94% for Atelor, by 96% for Trimatoprium, by over 5000% for Chlordiazepoxide, and by over 6000% for Diazepam.[56] A major motive for this kind of behavior is taxes. By manipulating intracompany prices, multinationals can cause profits to show up in nations whose tax bite is least burdensome. Moreover, they can take profits out of a host country in a way that evades regulation.

3. "Vertical" Restraints of Trade.   "Vertical" restrictions arise in the distribution or licensing process. These include exclusive dealing, tying, and territorial allocations among foreign distributors. Evidence concerning restraints such as these comes from studies of contracts transferring technology from multinational corporations to producers in less developed countries. Table 18–3 summarizes the results of several such studies by the United Nations Conference on Trade and Develop-

---

[53] Barbara Epstein and Richard S. Newfarmer, *International Electrical Association: A Continuing Cartel*, Report for the Committee on Interstate and Foreign Commerce, U.S. House of Representatives (June 1980), p. 12.

[54] See the citations in Caves, *Multinational Enterprise and Economic Analysis*, pp. 104–108.

[55] Director of Investigation and Research, Combines Investigation Act, *The State of Competition in the Canadian Petroleum Industry*, Vol. I (Ottawa, 1981), pp. 18–19, 61–70.

[56] S. Lall, "The International Pharmaceutical Industry and Less-Developed Countries," *Oxford Bulletin of Economics and Statistics* (August 1974), p. 161.

TABLE 18–3.   Percentage of Contracts Studied Imposing
Restrictions on Licensees, India, Philippines, and Spain

Type of Restriction	India (pre-1964)	India (1964–1969)	Philippines (1970)	Spain (1950–1973)
Global ban on exports	3.4%	0.9%	19.3%	44.4%
Partial ban on exports	40.0	46.2	13.0	25.9
Tied purchases	14.6	4.7	26.4	30.6
Minimum royalty restriction	5.2	1.2	5.1	NA

NA = Not available.
   Source: United Nations, Conference on Trade and Development, *Restrictive Business Practices* U.N. doc. TD/B/C.2/104/Rev. 1 (1971); *Major Issues Arising from the Transfer of Technology: A Case Study of Spain,* U.N. doc. TD/B/AC.11/17 (1974).

ment covering license agreements in India, the Philippines, and Spain. It may be seen that restrictions limiting the exports of licensees have been quite common. Tying provisions requiring licensees to purchase specified materials from the licensor or from other designated suppliers have been less frequent but common nevertheless. Still other restraints, such as minimum royalty payments, post-termination limitations, and restrictions on production methods appear very infrequently, but in certain individual instances they can be important.

SUMMARY

Today's typical large corporation is not limited to a single product and geographic market. It is more like an octopus, with tentacles probing vertical, conglomerate, and multinational crevices. The motives guiding these various forms of expanse may be harmless, and the results may be equally harmless. They may even be beneficial. Still, there are occasional problems.

   Vertical integration can be beneficial when it promotes technical efficiency or transaction-cost savings. On the other hand, vertical integration, when coupled with high concentration, can produce adverse economic consequences. It may greatly assist the exploitation of market power by (1) curbing downstream input substitution, (2) enabling price discrimination that would otherwise be impossible, and (3) facilitating collusion. Under certain circumstances vertical integration can also be used to extend market power by (1) reducing rivals' revenues (mainly through downstream foreclosure), (2) raising rivals' costs (mainly through upstream foreclosure), and (3) simultaneously reducing rivals' revenues and raising rivals' costs (with, e.g., the price squeeze).

Conglomerate spread across various product and geographic markets may reduce firm risk, gain efficiencies, and serve as a means of new entry. However, at especially large sizes, these benefits tend to fade and the possibilities of several adverse effects grow. Conglomerates, threatened by multimarket retaliations, may compete in certain markets less vigorously than nonconglomerates, a phenomenon called mutual forbearance. Reciprocal sales, or simple "reciprocity," is another possibility, one that may lessen price competition as nonprice factors become controlling. Finally, cross-subsidization may disadvantage rivals.

Multinational enterprises gain their multimarket stance through international operations. These firms typically come from highly concentrated industries, such as computers and autos, because their multinationalism often stems from certain monopolistic advantages—for example, technical prowess, brand image, and economies of scale. Some forms of multinational conduct bear close similarity to forms associated with vertical and conglomerate firm structures, namely, mutual forbearance and cross-subsidy. In addition, multinationals have been found to engage in "vertical" restraints of trade. These include export restrictions and tying provisions imposed on foreign licensees.

APPENDIX:
VERTICAL EXCLUSIVE DEALING IN NEW ZEALAND

For nearly four decades before 1990 the firm of Fisher & Paykel (F&P) dominated New Zealand's appliance industry. Until the 1980s F&P was snuggly protected by import tariffs and quotas. These locked the door to the New Zealand market. Nearby Australian companies—as represented by two appliance manufacturers in particular, Email and Hoover—could not get in to any significant degree. Beginning in 1984, however, those import barriers were reduced, unlocking the door to Email and Hoover. Their products were of good quality and their prices competitive. Even so, as late as 1988 F&P still dominated New Zealand's market with 90% of all refrigerator sales, 95% of freezer revenues, 80% in washing machines, 85% of the clothes dryer business, and 80% in dishwashers. Overall, its weighted average market share was 85% in 1988.

How did F&P hang on to its power once the door to imports was unlocked? F&P kept it shut by vigorously enforcing exclusive dealing contracts with its retailers. Any retailer wishing to carry the F&P line of appliances had to agree not to carry any competing appliances. All the major appliance dealers in New Zealand were bound by these contracts except for a few who tested F&P's sincerity and vigilance by marketing some rival appliances, and they were thereafter cut off by F&P. Given

F&P's vertical control of New Zealand's prime retailers, entry and expansion were made difficult for Email and Hoover and others also. Corner grocery stores and door-to-door sales were open to entrants, but effective appliance retailing obviously requires suitable display space, good locations, alluring store layouts, knowledgeable salespeople, and a favorable public reputation, so these alternatives were unattractive, and the alternative of establishing a new network of effective retailers from scratch was extremely costly. From the viewpoint of the established retailers who might switch to the imports, they were understandably reluctant to give up a well-known long-established line of appliances representing 85% of the market to risk everything with newcomers unproven in New Zealand.

When challenged by New Zealand's antitrust authorities in 1988, F&P defended itself by claiming its exclusive dealing was not anticompetitive and was wonderfully efficient (saying, for instance, that it was needed for effective communications between itself and its retailers). However, there were several signs that F&P was using its exclusive dealing for purposes of foreclosure:

- F&P did not impose exclusive dealing in New Zealand when its market share was low (i.e., stoves, microwaves, VCRs, and televisions).

- F&P did not impose exclusive dealing on its Australian retailers. Its market share on major appliances there was about 5%

- Some evidence showed New Zealand's whiteware appliance prices to have been much higher than Australia's, which didn't have exclusive dealing. This evidence was disputed by F&P, but F&P claimed that its hefty profits in New Zealand hinged on its exclusive dealing, so the price evidence could not have been too far wrong.

Hence, we have here an example of anticompetitive multimarket control (F&P's exclusive dealing) hampering the procompetitive multimarket spread of rivals (Email and Hoover branching into New Zealand from Australia).[57]

---

[57] This appendix is based on material submitted to New Zealand's Commerce Commission in connection with its case—"In the matter of Fisher & Paykel Limited," Decision No. 225, April 4, 1989. Interestingly, the main economic experts testifying in the case were imported—Benjamin Klein of UCLA for F&P and David Round of Australia for the opposition.

19

Vertical Market
Restrictions:
Practice and
Policy

*The sensitive focal points of the competitive general
market system are, as the name implies, in marketing
by individual enterprises and in the buying choices of
their customers.*

— E. T. GRETHER

Antitrust policy does not curb vertical integration achieved by internal
expansion. However, several important rules govern quasi-integration
achieved by anticompetitive vertical restraints. The practices at issue include tying, exclusive dealing, territorial restrictions, and resale price
maintenance.

1. *Tying* occurs when the seller allows the buyer to buy one line of
   the seller's goods *only* if the buyer also buys other goods too, as
   would be true if Xerox "tied" paper to its copiers.
2. *Exclusive dealing* binds a buyer (usually a retailer) to make *all* its

purchases of a given line of goods from a particular seller (usually a manufacturer). This differs from tying in that it may cover a considerable range of goods and it limits buyers to a single source of supply. This would be true for instance if an appliance store agreed with General Electric to carry only GE appliances.

3. *Territorial restrictions* give distributors exclusive territories or assigned locations. Thus Coca-Cola might assign Boston to one bottler, Providence to another bottler, and still other areas to other bottlers, prohibiting each bottler from raiding the territories of others.

4. *Resale price maintenance* occurs when manufacturers or other suppliers set the prices that their distributors may charge. Were Pontiac to insist that its auto dealers stick to the suggested retail prices given on window stickers, it would be practicing resale price maintenance.

Businesspeople offer various justifications for these practices, and some justifications are good enough that public interests are served as well as private business interests. Such goodness depends on the structural circumstances, however. When *small firms* in highly *competitive markets* engage in these practices, the results may tilt toward *goodness*. On the other hand, when used by *large dominant firms* in *oligopolistic settings* these vertical restraints tend to be *anticompetitive*.

Table 19–1 summarizes these potential competitive problems with simple labels. Tying and exclusive dealing tend to be *exclusionary* because they discourage new entry or handicap small rivals. Territorial restraints and resale price maintenance are said to be *collusive* because they may have cartel-like consequences. They may promote oligopolistic interdependence, thereby aiding tacit or explicit price collusion. Table 19–1 also indicates the main statutory laws and judicial rules governing these practices. Thus Table 19–1 outlines this chapter.

I. TYING

A. Business Justifications For Tying

The sale of one item is often tied to the sale of another with innocuous purpose and effect—multigame season tickets for instance. An understanding of policy is therefore best grounded on an understanding of some of the main purposes served by tying.

1. Economies and Conveniences. Shirts sold with buttons, autos with tires, and pencils with erasers illustrate combinations more efficiently manufactured and distributed together than apart. These ties are so close that we think of each as being one product, the parts of which

TABLE 19–1.　Outline of Vertical Restraints

Restrictive Practice	Potential Anticompetitive Effect	Main Statute Law	Judicial Rule Applied
1. Tying	Exclusionary	Clayton, Sec. 3 and Sherman, Sec. 1	Mixed: per se, rule of reason
2. Exclusive dealing	Exclusionary	Clayton, Sec.3	Rule of reason
3. Territorial restrictions	Collusive	Sherman, Sec. 1	Rule of reason
4. Resale price maintenance	Collusive	Sherman, Sec. 1	Per se rule

come in fixed proportions, such as nine buttons to a shirt. Since consumers would probably have to pay more for the privilege of buying separate parts, these ties are economically "natural."

2. Goodwill.　A franchisor of fast food might require that its franchisees purchase their chickens, cooking equipment, and packaging materials from the franchisor, thereby tying these materials to use of a trade name. In this way the franchisor could assure standardization of quality (not necessarily high quality) among his many franchisees. Without such assurance, one fast-food outlet might exploit the general reputation of the trade name by offering poor quality while charging rich prices.

3. Price Discrimination.[1]　A machine's consumption of materials, such as paper, ink, staples, or film, may, like a meter, measure intensity of use. Thus, when meters are impractical, easily tampered with, or prohibitively expensive, manufacturers of machines may try to sell or lease their machines at a low rate and tie in the sale of materials priced well above cost. In this way, customers with intense demands would pay more than marginal users. More over, profits would be greater than those obtained without such price discrimination, especially if the producer has monopoly power in the machine's market. Notice that this tie-in may merely *exploit* more fully some already existing monopoly power. It does not necessarily entail and *extension* of market power into the tied good's market. For example, even in the absence of antitrust policy, Xerox could not monopolize the paper industry if it tied copy paper to its machines because very little paper is used for that specific purpose.

However laudable these several justifications may be, they do not

---

[1] M. L. Burstein, "A Theory of Full-Line Forcing," *Northwestern University Law Review* (March–April 1960), pp. 62–95; and Arthur Lewbel, "Bundling of Substitutes or Complements," *International Journal of Industrial Organization* (March 1985), pp. 101–107.

necessarily justify a lenient policy on tying. Where economies are present, the lower costs could be reflected in a lower price for the combination product as compared to the constituent parts. Where goodwill is an issue, quality specifications and surveillance may substitute for forced ties. And where price discrimination is at stake, untying would reduce monopoly profits, but buyers would not feel hurt by this.[2]

B. Adverse Competitive Effects

To some, a major problem with tying is that it can be anticompetitive. It can raise barriers to entry in the market of the tied good or seriously disadvantage smaller tied-good competitors. Both effects are exclusionary, but neither effect necessarily occurs. It depends on the circumstances. If a firm has a monopoly in the tying good, and the tying and tied goods are complements used in varying proportions, such as bread and butter, the problem is particularly pernicious. William Baldwin and David McFarland explain:

> Assume that a seller with a complete monopoly on bread ties sales of his brand of butter to the bread, where butter was formerly sold in a perfectly competitive market. If there is no use for butter except to spread on bread, the tie-in will lead to a complete monopoly in the butter market. In any event, the bread monopolist will achieve some degree of monopoly power in the butter market.[3]

A different but more concrete example is offered by Kodak, which a while back tied film processing (developing) to its sale of film. When tied, Kodak enjoyed a 90% share of the amateur film and film processing industry. As a result of a 1954 antitrust consent decree, however, Kodak severed the tie, licensed its processing technology to new entrants, and agreed to substantial divestiture of its processing facilities. A flood of new entry followed, which combined with the divestiture to cause Kodak's processing market share to tumble 55 percentage points in just five years. With entry, prices of film processing fell substantially. Although Kodak retained its near monopoly on film, and even raised prices on film, it appears that the newfound competition in processing benefited shutterbugs.[4]

---

[2] James M. Ferguson, "Tying Arrangements and Reciprocity: An Economic Analysis," *Law and Contemporary Problems* (Summer 1965), pp. 553–565.

[3] W. L. Baldwin and David McFarland, "Tying Arrangements in Law and Economics," *Antitrust Bulletin* (Sepetmber–October 1963), p. 769. See also Jean Tirole, *The Theory of Industrial Organization* (Cambridge, Mass.: MIT Press, 1988), pp. 333–336; Timothy J. Brennan and Sheldon Kimmel, "Joint Production and Monopoly Extension Through Tying," *Southern Economic Journal* (October 1986), pp. 490–501; and Michael D. Whinston, "Tying, Foreclosure, and Exclusion," *American Economic Review* (September 1990), pp. 837–859.

[4] Don E. Waldman, *Antitrust Action and Market Structure* (Lexington, Mass.: Lexington Books, 1978), pp. 143–150. It should be noted that tying's anticompetitive effect need not be limited to exclusion. It may, for instance aid cartel discipline. See F. J. Cummins and

C. The Law on Tying

Section 1 of the Sherman Act covers tying, but the most explicit prohibition is found in Section 3 of the Clayton Act, which bans tie-in sales "where the effect . . . may be to substantially lessen competition or tend to create a monopoly." Judicial interpretation of these Acts approaches a per se rule. Ties are, in the Supreme Court's opinion, "*unreasonable in and of themselves* whenever a party has sufficient economic power with respect to the tying product to appreciably restrain free competition in the market for the tied product and a 'not insubstantial' amount of interstate commerce is affected."[5] This statement discloses, however, certain *rule-of-reason* elements, particularly for judgments about "sufficient economic power." Thus it is best to summarize by saying that violations will be found when the answers to all the following questions are "yes":

1. Are two products (or services) involved?
2. Does the seller possess sufficient economic power in the market of the tying product?
3. Is there substantial commerce in the tied goods?
4. Are defenses of "reasonableness" absent?

Of these questions, the first and third rarely raise thorny problems. The first is needed merely to prevent single products, like shirts with buttons, from being considered two products. The third is easily answered because "substantial commerce" seems to mean to the Court anything over a million dollars worth of business.

As regards "sufficient economic power" in the tying good, question 2, the Supreme Court has found a variety of conditions providing yes answers: (a) a large market share or "market dominance" in the tying good; (b) patents, copyrights, or trademarks for the tying good; (c) high barriers to entry in the tying-good market; and (d) uniqueness or "special desirability" of the tying good.

For example, a landmark case in patents is *International Salt* of 1947.[6] International had a "limited" patent monopoly over salt dispensing machines used in food processing. Users of the machines had to buy their salt from International or find other machines. International argued that preservation of goodwill required the tie-in, that only its own salt was of sufficient purity to provide top-quality dispensing. The Supreme Court rejected this assertion, observing that no evidence had been presented to show "that the machine is allergic to salt of equal quality pro-

---

W. E. Ruhter, "The *Northern Pacific* Case," *Journal of Law and Economics* (October 1979), pp. 329–350. Cases like these undermine the position of Bork and others who argue that tying is never anticompetitive. See Louis Kaplow "Extension of Monopoly Power Through Leverage" *Columbia Law Review*, Vol. 85 (1985) pp. 515–556.

[5] *Northern Pacific Railroad Co.* v. *United States*, 356 U.S. 1 (1958). Emphasis added.

[6] *International Salt Co.* v. *U.S.*, 332 U.S. 392 (1947).

duced by anyone except International." Moreover, the presence of the patents caused the Court to dispense some salty per se references, such as, "it is unreasonable, per se, to foreclose competitors from any substantial market."

Requisite power based on copyrights and uniqueness is illustrated by *U.S.* v. *Loew's, Inc.* (1962), which involved "block booking." When selling motion pictures to television stations, Loew's had "conditioned the license or sale of one or more feature films upon the acceptance by the station of a package or block containing one or more unwanted or inferior films." Put bluntly, the practice could tie *Gone With the Wind* and *Getting Gertie's Garter*. On the question of economic power, the Supreme Court decided that each film "was in itself a unique product"; that feature films "were not fungible"; and that "since each defendant by reason of its copyright had a 'monopolistic' position as to each tying product, 'sufficient economic power' to impose an appreciable restraint on free competition in the tied product was present."[7] On this precedent the distributors of *Star Wars* had to back down when caught tying a mediocre film to that biggest money-maker of all time.

When potent patents, copyrights, or trademarks do not conveniently show tying-good power, the courts can get bogged down in matters that plague monopolization cases. What is the relevant market? What market share constitutes market power? In *Times-Picayune* the Court defined the relevant tying-good market as all newspaper advertising in New Orleans, a definition that let the defendant off the hook.[8] In the Supreme Court's most recent case on tying, *Jefferson Parish Hospital District* v. *Hyde*, it was found that a 30% share of the tying-good market was not enough to establish tying-good power.[9]

Finally, the fourth question concerning reasonable defenses has on rare occasions been answered in favor of defendants. The defendant in *U.S.* v. *Jerrold Electronics*, for instance, was an early 1950s pioneer in the development of community television antenna systems. Rather than sell separately its bits and pieces of equipment and technical services, Jerrold sold only on a full systems basis, including services for layout, installation, and maintenance as well as equipment. There was no question that Jerrold had hefty market power in the tying good — equipment — given its 75% market share. Nor was there any question of substantial business in the tied services. Nevertheless, Jerrold successfully defended its tying with proof that the industry was at the time very young, that these antenna systems were extremely delicate, and that full control through tying was required in order to build customer confidence in the industry

    [7] *U.S.* v. *Loew's Inc.*, 371 U.S. 38 (1962).
    [8] *Times-Picayune Publishing Co.* v. *U.S.*, 354 U.S. 594 (1953). This definition was erroneous, however. See J. Dirlam and A. E. Kahn, *Fair Competition: The Law and Economics of Antitrust Policy* (Ithaca, N.Y.: Cornell University Press, 1954), pp. 106–108.
    [9] *Jefferson Parish Hospital District No. 2* v. *Hyde*, 104 S. Ct. 1551 (1984).

and preserve Jerrold's reputation. In short, this was a goodwill defense in an infant-industry context. The court agreed, but granted only a *temporary* waiver, as these special conditions would evaporate with the passage of time — the industry maturing and the equipment toughening.[10]

In sum, tying is virtually a per se violation when there is power in the tying good. Still, in the absence of patents or such, rule-of-reason judgment enters the determination of power. Indeed, the Department of Justice issued "Vertical Restraints Guidelines" in January 1985 which say that "tying will *not* be challenged if the party imposing the tie has a market share of *thirty percent or less* in the market for the tying product," unless it can be positively proven that the tying "unreasonably restrains competition" in the tied-good market.[11]

Certain rule-of-reason defenses grant further freedom even though they are rarely acceptable. Hence, the law here is a mixture of per se and rule-of-reason elements, with the rule-of-reason elements gaining ever greater ground over time.

II. EXCLUSIVE DEALING

Under an exclusive dealing agreement, the buyer obtains the seller's product on condition that he will not deal in the products of the seller's rivals. The buyer, say, a sugar wholesaler, agrees to secure its total requirements of sugar from one supplier, say, Amstar.

A. Business Justifications for Exclusive Dealing

From the supplier's point of view, exclusive dealing assures that distributors will devote their undivided energy to the supplier's products, something particularly important where personal sales, repair service, and promotion are required. Moreover, exclusive dealers often represent the manufacturer's interests more religiously. In 1974, for instance, Amstar stopped selling its sugar through general sugar brokers who served as agents for more than one sugar refiner. The stated reason for this action was that these general brokers acted with such "customer orientation" toward *their* buyers that "they at times acted more nearly as purchasing agents" for their buyers than sales agents for Amstar, causing Amstar lost profits. Thereafter Amstar sold only through exclusive dealing "direct brokers," who carried only Amstar sugar, and through its own sales force.[12]

---

10 *U.S.* v. *Jerrold Electronics*, 187 F. Sp. 545 (E.D. Pa. 1960), affirmed per curiam 365 U.S. 567 (1961). For another successful use of the goodwill defense, see *Dehydrating Process Co.* v. *A. O. Smith Corp.*, 292 F.2d 653 (1st Cir. 1961).

11 U.S. Department of Justice, Antitrust Division, "Vertical Restraints Guidelines" (January 23, 1985), p. 41 (emphasis added).

12 *Fuchs Sugar and Syrups, Inc., et al.* v. *Amstar Corp.*, CCH para 62,700 (CA-2, June

From the buyer's or distributor's point of view, there are a number of reasons for accepting exclusive dealing:

- Supplies may be more certain and steady, especially in times of shortage.
- Specialization entails lower inventories than would be required with several brands of the same product.
- If exclusive dealing is rejected, the buyer may no longer be a buyer (that is, the seller forces acceptance).
- Acceptance may be conceded in exchange for a commitment from the seller that protects the buyer-dealer from the competition of other buyer-dealers handling the same brand (for example, territorial assignments or limits on the number of dealerships in an area).

Recognizing that exclusive dealing offers advantages for buyers as well as sellers the Supreme Court has been a bit more lenient toward exclusive dealing as compared to tying, which the Court views as being a boon only to sellers.

B. Adverse Competitive Effects

Exclusive dealing may foreclose new entrants or small suppliers from main distribution channels, especially when used singly or collectively by dominant manufacturers or franchisors. Anticompetitive effects may ensue:

> Once a large or dominant supplier in a market obtains for his exclusive use a correspondingly large share of available outlets on a lower level of distribution, he has probably imposed prohibitive cost disadvantages on existing or potential rivals, since they are likely to have to create new outlets in order to participate in the market. The same is true where a group of suppliers collectively (if not collusively) obtain exclusive obligations from dealers — and thus produce an aggregate foreclosure.[13]

A recent example comes from the market for industrial gases (e.g., oxygen, nitrogen, and acetylene). That market has two segments — (1) a *bulk* segment, where producers of industrial gas sell directly to large customers like U.S. Steel, and (2) a *small-lot* segment, where producers sell to independent distributors who in turn sell to welding supply stores serv-

1979). For yet another explanation applicable to some cases see Howard P. Marvel, "Exclusive Dealing," *Journal of Law and Economics* (April 1982), pp. 1–25.

13 Donald N. Thompson, *Franchise Operations and Antitrust* (Lexington, Mass.: Heath/Lexington Books, 1971), p. 59. See also Oliver Williamson, "Assessing Vertical Market Restrictions" *University of Pennsylvania Law Review* (April 1979), pp. 960–966; and William S. Comanor and H. E. French III, "The Competitive Effects of Vertical Agreements?" *American Economic Review* (June 1988), pp. 539–546.

ing small customers like construction companies. During the 1960s the dominant established producers like Union Carbide and Airco encountered growing competition at the gas manufacturing level because of changing technology and fresh entrants. This new competition spread rapidly in the bulk segment of the industry. Union Carbide and Airco consequently experienced fizzling sales and profit margins in their dealings with direct buyers. However, the new competition did not reach small-lot sales because Union Carbide and Airco were able to foreclose that segment of the market. A combination of exclusive dealing and tying kept the new rivals away from small-lot distributors:

> Union Carbide and Airco both responded to the changed market conditions by strengthening and formalizing the ties between manufacturer and distributor. Both companies imposed formal contractual requirements that all gases used by a distributor must be purchased from the franchising manufacturers. In addition, informal but implicit ties between the sale of gases and the sale of welding equipment were imposed [because of the strong market power these firms enjoyed in welding equipment].[14]

FTC action finally ended these practices in 1979.

Quite often, the power behind the anticompetitive use of exclusive dealing is a popular brand name. During the 1980s, Pillsbury Company tried to maintain market share for its Häagen Dazs ice cream by imposing exclusive dealing on its distributors. This hurt the sales of Ben & Jerry's ice cream, so Ben & Jerry sued Häagen Dazs and launched a public relations campaign that produced some clever bumper-sticker slogans—"What's the Doughboy afraid of?" and "Häagen, your Dazs are numbered."[15] In the beer industry Anheuser-Busch discourages its wholesale distributors from carrying rivals' brands, especially in major metropolitan areas where Anheuser-Busch has huge market shares and its distributors can boast of immense marketing clout. Dennis Long, former president of Anheuser-Busch, said the company's intent in this strategy was to deprive rivals: "We discourage them from carrying other brands. We want to keep the advantage of size in-house."[16]

C. The Law on Exclusive Dealing

Section 3 of the Clayton Act covers exclusive dealing as well as tying, for it bans sales or leases conditioned on an "agreement or understanding that the lessee or purchaser . . . shall not use or deal in the [goods or wares] of a competitor" of the seller or lessor, where the effect "may

---

14 Gerald Brock, "Vertical Restraints in Industrial Gases," in *Impact Evaluations of Federal Trade Commission Vertical Restraints Cases*, edited by R. N. Lafferty, R. H. Lande, and J. B. Kirkwood (Washington, D.C.: Bureau of Economics, Federal Trade Commission, 1984), pp. 400–401.

15 *Business Week*, December 7, 1987, p. 65.

16 *The Los Angeles Times*, December 15, 1985, Part IV, p. 9.

Step 1: Safe Harbor   Step 2: Easy Entry?   Step 3: Further Study

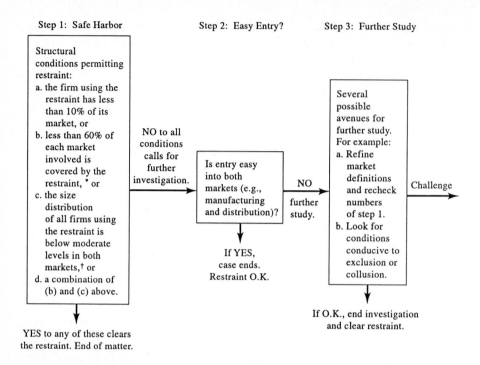

[*] This is measured by a "coverage ratio."
[†] This is measured by a "vertical restraint index" patterned after the H-index used in merger analysis.

FIGURE 19–1. Diagram of vertical restraint guidelines for exclusive dealing and territorial restraints. Source: U.S. Department of Justice, "Vertical Restraints Guidelines," January 23, 1985.

be to substantially lessen competition." According to the Supreme Court's interpretation of Section 3, exclusive dealing is not per se illegal. Hence the Court has considered economic conditions and purposes when determining illegalities. Two main factors are the seller's market share and the prevalence of the practice among all sellers.[17]

Most recently, in 1985, the Antitrust Division of the Justice Department stated its position in its "Vertical Restraints Guidelines." According to those guidelines, "Uses of vertical restraints by firms with small market shares, those restraints operating in unconcentrated markets, and those that do not cover a substantial percentage of the sales or capacity in the secondary (foreclosed) market, are unlikely to effectively facilitate collusion or to foreclose competitors from the market."

How small a market share? How unconcentrated? How extensive the coverage? The answers are spelled out in a multistep process of review, as shown in Figure 19–1. Under step 1, structural conditions are

---

[17] *Standard Oil of California and Standard Stations, Inc.* v. *U.S.*, 337 U.S. 293 (1949).

reviewed. If the firm imposing the restraint has less than 10% of its market, *or* if any of three other structural thresholds are favorably met, then the restraint will be permitted. If on the other hand *all* structural thresholds are violated, step 2 commences. This second step considers the condition of entry in the affected markets. If entry is thought to be easy, then again the restraint is permitted. Finally, if the structural tests of step 1 and the entry tests of step 2 make the restraint look bad, it may still escape challenge if further study can find some way to excuse it.

On the whole, these guidelines seem quite lenient. For example, if three manufacturers with 19% market shares and five dealers with 15% market shares were engaged in vertical restraints, they would be safe from challenge according to the "safe harbor" structural standards of step 1. As regards easy entry—step 2—it appears that the exclusive dealing arrangements in industrial gases would have been allowed by the guidelines' standard even though substantial economic evidence indicates that those restraints were anticompetitive. Indeed, the leniency of the guidelines is suggested by the fact that all 50 state attorneys general have banded together to issue conflicting, more stringent guidelines of their own.

Thus exclusive dealing is governed by a rule of reason which in some versions could be considered rather lenient. Moreover, difficulties of detection can occasionally offer further freedom for the practice. It need not be written into contracts. Manufacturers can reach *tacit* understandings with their distributors, understandings enforced by the manufacturers' refusals to deal. Although *collective* refusals to deal (boycotts) are essentially per se illegal, the courts have a long-standing tradition of recognizing the right of a manufacturer or other supplier to choose his distributors. Thus dominant firms have been able to impose exclusive dealing by using refusal to sell as their cat's paw.[18]

III. TERRITORIAL RESTRICTIONS

The Justice Department's "guidelines" on exclusive dealing also apply to vertical territorial restrictions. These come in many forms—exclusive territories, areas of "prime responsibility," exclusive franchising, and limited outlet franchising among them. The basic result of all such restraints is the same, however—more or less restrictive allocations of territories to the distributors or franchisees of a given brand, limiting intrabrand

---

[18] *Fuchs Sugar*; Thompson, *Franchise Operations and Antitrust*, Chapter 4; and A. R. Oxenfelt, *Marketing Practices in the TV Set Industry* (New York: Columbia University Press, 1964), p. 123. This is perhaps especially true under the "Guidelines" given their leniency. For a critical review of the guidelines, see Alan A. Fisher, Frederick I. Johnson, and Robert H. Lande, "Do the DOJ Vertical Restraints Guidelines Provide Guidance?" *Antitrust Bulletin* (Fall 1987), pp. 609–642.

competition. If such restrictions were devised *horizontally* among distributors and franchisees, they would obviously be per se violations of Sherman Section 1. If *vertically* imposed by manufacturers and franchisors,
Sherman Section 1 is still the only applicable statute, but these restraints
are not so obviously dangerous as to warrant per se treatment.

A. Business Justifications for Territorial Restrictions

Broadly stated, the main business justification for territorial restrictions
is that they promote *inter*brand competition even though they may stifle
*intra*brand competition. If, for example, the maker of Sylvania TV sets
allocated territories among its distributors, these distributors could not
compete against each other but they could channel their competitive efforts toward outselling RCA, Zenith, and Sony. There are a number of
reasons why this might be so:

1. Distributors or franchisees may have to make considerable invest-
    ments in their enterprise for facilities, advertising, inventory, and
    so on. If the brand promoted is weak, the high risks facing distrib-
    utors can be lessened by territorial protection. This would then aid
    in attracting new outlets.
2. For products needing full-service retailing, such as demonstration,
    service, and credit, territorial isolation protects distributors who
    provide these costly services from the raids of price discounters
    who do not provide such services.
3. Territorial isolation may aid quality maintenance if it facilitates the
    tracing and recall of faulty products and removes incentives one
    outlet may have for exploiting through adulteration the good
    reputation built up by other outlets of the same brand.

It should be noted that these justifications are most valid in instances where the manufacturer or franchisor is in a weak position vis-à-
vis its rival manufacturers or franchisors. Moreover, these justifications
are weakened by the fact that in many instances less restrictive means
of attaining the same ends are available.[19] Still, these rationales cannot
be dismissed lightly.

B. Adverse Competitive Effects

The potentially adverse competitive consequences of territorial restrictions are fairly obvious—cartel-like restraint, especially at distributor
level where intrabrand competition is shackled. The greater the concentration at manufacturer or franchisor level, the more serious the problem. If for instance Chevorlet happened to capture 90% of all U.S. auto

---

[19] Thompson, *Franchise Operations and Antitrust*, Chapter 7.

sales, intrabrand competition among Chevy dealers would be the main form of competition remaining in the industry. And restraints on this competition could prove costly to consumers.

Even where concentration is relatively low, interbrand competition might be muted by strong product differentiation. Consumers loyally attached to their preferred brand would then probably benefit substantially by vigorous intrabrand competition. Intrabrand competition in soft drinks has been curbed as Coke, Pepsi, and the other major syrup manufacturers have allocated exclusive territories among their bottlers. And in 1973 FTC economists estimated that removal of these territorial restrictions would save soda pop drinkers approximately $250 million a year.[20] (Congress prevented removal, however, when it later passed legislation specifically exempting the soda pop industry. Intense industry lobbying paid off.)

The problem for wise policy in this area now becomes clear. Territorial restrictions blunt *intrabrand* competition, but they may foster *interbrand* competition.

C. The Law on Territorial Restrictions

Given the ambiguous character of this practice it is not surprising that a rule of reason now applies in assessing its legality. What is a bit surprising is that such a rule emerged under Section 1 of the Sherman Act, a section notorious for its per se interpretations.

The Supreme Court first fully confronted vertical territorial restraints in *United States* v. *White Motors* (1963).[21] White was a relatively small manufacturer of trucks that had assigned territories to its distributors and dealers. Recognizing that White might thereby be better able to compete with such giants of the industry as GMC and International Harvester, the Supreme Court held that a rule of reason should apply and remanded the case for lower-court trial. Four years later in *Schwinn* the Supreme Court waffled a bit by judging a portion of Schwinn's plan under a per se rule and the rest under a rule of reason.[22] The ensuing confusion was cleared up in 1977 with *Continental TV* v. *GTE Sylvania*, which confirmed the rule of reason approach.[23]

The facts of *Sylvania* were simple: Suffering from lagging TV set sales, Sylvania shifted its marketing strategy in the early 1960s to a program that included greater selectivity in choosing retailers. These franchised retailers were bound by contract not to sell except from locations approved by Sylvania. The strategy encouraged retailers to prompte Syl-

---

20 Cited by Barbara Katz, "Competition in the Soft Drink Industry," *Antitrust Bulletin* (Summer 1979), p. 280.

21 *U.S.* v. *White Motor Co.*, 372 U.S. 253 (1963).

22 *U.S.* v. *Arnold Schwinn & Co.*, 388 U.S. 365 (1967).

23 *Continental TV, Inc., et al.* v. *GTE Sylvania, Inc.*, 433 U.S. 36 (1977).

vania sets more aggressively than before, thereby boosting Sylvania's market share from about 2% in 1962 to 5% in 1965. A fracas erupted, however, between Sylvania and one of its main San Francisco retailers, Continental TV, who fought Sylvania with a treble damage suit claiming the restrictions on dealer locations were illegal under the *Schwinn* decision.

Upon hearing the case the Supreme Court abandoned the per se portion of *Schwinn*, sided with Sylvania, and came out foursquare for a rule of reason. Such was necessary, the Court held, to balance the harm of lessened intrabrand competition with the benefits of heightened interbrand competition:

> Vertical restrictions reduce intrabrand competition by limiting the number of sellers of a particular product competing for the business of a given group of buyers . . . [But] . . .
>   Vertical restrictions promote interbrand competition by allowing the manufacturer to achieve certain efficiencies in the distribution of his products. These "redeeming virtues" are implicit in every decision sustaining vertical restrictions under the rule of reason.

Although the Court felt the facts favored Sylvania, the Court offered little guidance on how the rule of reason should be applied in subsequent cases. Nevertheless, in light of what was said previously, we can conclude that the harm of lessened intrabrand competition is more likely to outweigh the benefit of heightened interbrand competition (1) the greater the market power of the manufacturer, (2) the greater the overall market concentration, (3) the stronger the tethers of product differentiation, (4) the older and richer the manufacturer in question, and (5) the more tightly drawn the constraint. As already suggested, several of these factors are found in the 1985 Justice department guidelines summarized in Figure 19–1.

IV. RESALE PRICE MAINTENANCE

Resale price maintenance, in pure form, is *vertical* price fixing. A manufacturer specifies to its downstream wholesalers or retailers the minimum prices they may charge when reselling to their customers. A toaster manufacturer, for instance, might require its retailers to price its toasters at $35 or more. To assure adherence to such resale prices, manufacturers typically must discipline mavericks by cutting off their supplies, delaying their shipments, or threatening some similar penalty.

What makes resale price maintenance especially interesting is the heated controversy that has surrounded it for decades. This is reflected in its roller-coaster legal history—being illegal in the United States from 1911 to the 1930s, legal from the 1930s to roughly 1975, and then illegal again since 1975. Controversy is also reflected in sharply divided opinions. During the Reagan administration, those who were supposed to prosecute offenders (the Department of Justice and the FTC) wanted to legalize resale price maintenance at least partially and they refused to file cases. Conversely, Congress and the courts persisted in their opposition, thankful that private antitrust suits could make up for the lack of official enforcement. The acute controversy might seem overly dramatic to sideline spectators like yourself. After all, when resale price maintenance was legal it never covered more than about 4–10% of all retail sales in the United States. Still, the potential is immense. It covered 30–40% of all retail sales in Britain when previously legal there. Its use has also been heavily concentrated on relatively few products for which it can be immensely important — drugs and medicines, cosmetics and perfumes, small electrical appliances, and alcoholic beverages.[24]

A. Business Rationale for Resale Price Maintenance and Anticompetitive Effects

Although many manufacturers apparently like to engage in resale price maintenance, even though now largely illegal, it is not altogether clear why they like it. Casual reasoning would lead us to expect that once a manufacturer has set its own price, its interests would best be served by having the lowest price possible charged to final consumers, as that would maximize sales given the manufacturer's price. An efficient, competitive distribution system, earning the minimum distribution markup possible, would then seem most desirable. And resale price maintenance would not encourage distributor competition, efficiency, or markup minimization. Still, there are a few explanations deserving mention, because they help us assess whether a per se rule is justifiable.

First, it may be that the manufacturer is responding to the blandishments of his retailers, who use the manufacturer's resale price maintenance as a means of maintaining a retailer cartel. Here the manufacturer is not initiating the program, and the program is actually *horizontal* price fixing at retail level enforced by the manufacturer, not vertical price fixing. A rule preventing this seems quite acceptable. While passing this judgment, we should acknowledge that retailers need not engage in full-fledged cartelization to find comfort in resale price maintenance. In particular, it tends to shield small retailers from the price competition of larger, more efficient merchants. Numerous empirical studies have shown that prices of many commodities tend to be higher with resale price maintenance than without; that these elevated prices preserve *inef-*

---

[24] Thomas R. Overstreet, Jr. *Resale Price Maintenance: Economic Theories and Empirical Evidence* (Washington, D.C.: Bureau of Economics, Federal Trade Commission, 1983), especially pp. 6–7, 114–115, 151–155.

ficiency; and that discount retailing is hampered.[25] Thus if society wished to nurture small businesses for the sake of furthering some populist value judgments, resale price maintenance might win acceptance. But such value judgments seem to be losing favor of late.

Second, resale price maintenance may be used to facilitate a cartel at manufacturers' level. The practice cements vertical relationships and aids cartel discipline by readily disclosing "cheaters" and "double-crossers." This too would actually be horizontal price fixing, unworthy of saving by legalizing resale price maintenance.

Third, it is often argued that some manufacturers want the retail price of their wares to be kept high because consumers equate a high price with high quality. In the absence of the support resale price maintenance offers, prices would fall, pulling down with them the brand's quality image. This justification is weak, however, because there is another way the same result could be attained. If a manufacturer wants a high retail price for his product he can simply jack up his own price. When downstream distributors pay the manufacturer more, they will in turn charge more. Still, if manufacturers cannot control retail prices the retailers can cut their prices *below cost*. They might engage in "loss-leader" selling, discounting a few familiar brands drastically in order to attract customers whose purchases of other goods might more than compensate for the loss. Thus some manufacturers claim that resale price maintenance protects their products from loss-leader degradation.[26]

Fourth, resale price maintenance may serve the interests of both manufacturers and resellers simultaneously if *both* have some monopoly power. The reasoning is complex, and it entails some of the "quality" elements of the foregoing, but it makes sense of numerous cases that would otherwise be inexplicable. Resale price maintenance is said to grow out of "mutual dependence between two insecure partial monopolists" at different levels — production and distribution — where "the existence of the monopoly power of each depends in some significant degree upon the monopoly power of the other."[27] When producers of

---

[25] See S. C. Hollander's summary in B. S. Yamey (ed.), *Resale Price Maintenance* (Chicago: Aldine, 1966), pp. 67–100; Leonard Weiss, *Case Studies in American Industry*, 3rd Ed. (New York: John Wiley, 1980), pp. 282–288; and J. F. Pickering, "The Abolition of Resale Price Maintenance in Great Britain," *Oxford Economic Papers* (March 1975), pp. 120–146.

[26] Take General Motors, for example. High-volume "megadealers" have sometimes priced Cadillacs so low as to cause GM to worry about the car's luxury cachet. In 1985 magadealer Victor Potamkin took out full-page newspaper ads in New York City announcing "no-profit sales" of some Cadillacs at $200 under invoice. Complaining that Mr. Potamkin's cut-rate come-ons were "bad for Cadillac's image," the head of GM's Cadillac division flew to New York "to urge Mr. Potamkin to stop the ads but failed to get any assurances." *The Wall Street Journal* explained why Mr. Potamkin wanted to continue his discounting: "Selling some models below cost is a marketing tactic dealers often use to increase their sales and to attract new customers" (July 1, 1985, p. 6).

[27] Ward Bowman, "Resale Price Maintenance — A Monopoly Problem," *Journal of Business* (July 1952), pp. 141–155.

prominent brands engage in resale price maintenance and are selective in their choice of distributors, the power of selected distributors is enhanced by the reduced intrabrand competition, by the limited retail availability of the product, and by the "quality" image that may result. Conversely, retailers reward the price maintaining producers by stocking their brands in preference to others, by steering consumers toward their brands, and by boosting the producer's "quality" image. Levi's jeans, Florsheim shoes, and Russell Stover candies seem to provide examples.[28]

Finally, some products, like appliances, may be most effectively promoted through the provision of retailer services—such as demonstrations, fittings, bridal registers for wedding gifts, and repairs. Resale price maintenance may thus operate to protect retailers who offer these services from the poaching of discounters who do not offer these services. Full-Service-Sam would not last long if the customers he convinces to buy go down the street to consummate their purchases with Cut-Rate-Carl. So, the argument goes, Sam must be protected.[29]

B. The Law on Resale Price Maintenance

Under Section 1 of the Sherman Act, resale price maintenance is now regarded illegal per se. In light of the full-service dealer rationale just noted, however, a per se rule may seem too crude and too destructive of a laudable business practice (as compared with a rule of reason). Still, it can be argued in defense of the per se rule that these laudable ends can be reached by other, less restrictive means. A manufacturer, for instance, can require its retailers to provide certain services as a condition for continuing as its retailers. Even where such alternatives are limited, the present per se rule offers manufacturers much room to maneuver, enough room to achieve some degree of resale price maintenance. In other words, there is a rather large loophole in the law, a hole punched by what may be called legal rights of unilateral refusal to sell.

To the extent resale price maintenance is *totally and completely a unilateral* undertaking on the part of an *individual manufacturer*, it is *not* considered a restraint of trade. Such legality is clearest in two situations: *First*, if the wholesalers and retailers down the line are wholly owned and operated by the manufacturer, as are some tire retailers, then resale price maintenance is internal to the firm and therefore perfectly permissible. Indeed, *r*esale, as such, doesn't even occur. This exemption can be broadened a bit into a gray area, where distributors are not owned by

---

28 In general, see Robert L. Steiner, "The Nature of Vertical Restraints," *Antitrust Bulletin* (Spring 1985), pp. 143–197. In particular, see the articles by Sharon Oster and Timothy Greening in *Impact Evaluations of Federal Trade Commission Vertical Restraint Cases* (FTC 1984), pp. 48–180.

29 Roger D. Blair and David L. Kaserman, *Antitrust Economics* (Homewood, Ill.: Richard D. Irwin, 1985), pp. 349–353.

the manufacturer, through the legal device of consignment sales. Here the manufacturer *retains title* to the goods and thereby bears certain risks. Resale is again avoided, the only sale being the final sale to consumers.

Second, resale price maintenance meets the legally unilateral standard if the manufacturer does *nothing more* than announce its desire that resale prices be maintained at or above some specified level and then refuses to sell to those who defy that desire. Anything beyond this unilateral program invites prosecution. Anything that smacks of multilateral agreement stands exposed. Retailers cannot agree to adhere to the suggested prices. Rebellious retailers cut off from supplies cannot be reinstated through an understanding with the manufacturer that they will not shade price again. Still, the manufacturer can engage in resale price maintenance through unilateral refusal to deal.

Each of these two avenues to unilateral legality has its own justification. The first is a technicality—that is, resale price maintenance cannot occur if there is no resale. The second stems from a tradition of business practice—that is, enterprises have a wide-ranging right to choose those with whom they will do business, including the right of refusal to sell (even if they are choosy in the process).

Beyond these limits of unilateralism, however, resale price maintenance is per se illegal. Civil suits have confronted such firms as Pendleton Woolen Mills, Lenox Company (producers of fine china), and Levi Strauss. And although the Reagan administration did not prosecute in this area, some state attorneys general were active. In 1989 New York State settled a suit against Panasonic after the company agreed to pay consumers $16 million in damages. VCRs, camcorders, and cordless telephones were among the products involved.[30]

The saga of per se illegality begins with *Dr. Miles Medical Co.* v. *John D. Park and Sons Co.* in 1911.[31] The Dr. Miles company manufactured proprietary medicines and sought to prescribe the resale prices of both its wholesalers and retailers. Wholesaler Park and Sons refused to enter a resale contract with Dr. Miles and undermined the program by cutting prices on Dr. Miles drugs it obtained from other wholesalers. Dr. Miles sued, but without success, because the Supreme Court decided that a manufacturer parts with control once he parts with the goods. "Where commodities have passed into the channels of trade and have been sold by complainant to dealers at prices satisfactory to complainant, the public is entitled to whatever advantage may be derived from competition in the subsequent traffic."

A lengthy interlude of legality occurred when, during the Great Depression, many states responded to the urgings of retailers by enacting so-called "fair trade laws," which made resale price maintenance permis-

---

[30] *The Wall Street Journal*, January 19, 1989, p. B1.
[31] *Dr. Miles Medical Co.* v. *John D. Park and Sons Co.*, 220 U.S. 373 (1911).

sible. Notice it was *retailers*, not manufacturers, who lobbied most vehemently here, suggesting that retailers are shielded from competition when resale price maintenance is effective. Federal enabling legislation was needed to iron out the conflict between these fair trade laws and the Sherman Act, so Congress complied with the Miller–Tydings Act of 1937. This act missed a stitch by failing to grant specific clearance to "nonsigner clauses," without which resale price maintenance was ineffectual. Nonsigner clauses bound *all* retailers in a state to maintain prices, those who signed contracts with manufacturers *and* those who did not sign (hence "nonsigners"). Miller–Tydings was therefore patched up with the McGuire Act of 1952, which approved nonsigner clauses. This interlude ended, however, in 1975 with passage of the Consumer Goods Pricing Act of 1975. This act removed these enabling exemptions, thereby locking legal fair trade pricing into the small cage of unilateral action already outlined.

As regards the first unilateral boundary—vertical ownership of the goods—the main early precedent is the *General Electric* case of 1926.[32] GE escaped the *Dr. Miles* rule by retaining title to its light bulbs, selling on consignment to independent dealers who agreed to resell at GE's specified prices. Later, this consignment escape hatch was partially closed by the Court in *Simpson* v. *Union Oil Co.* (1964). Union Oil tried to maintain resale prices by selling on consignment to dealers like Simpson. But the Court found the consignment program to be a sham. "The risk of loss," it said, is on the dealers. "Their return is affected by the rise and fall in the market price." Hence the Court ruled that a "clever manipulation of words" could not camouflage a per se violation. A "consignment device" used to cover a vast "distribution system, fixing prices through many retail outlets" is illegal.[33] A gap thus opened between the "yes" of *GE* and the "no" of *Simpson*. We have neither the space nor patience to explore this gap here, but readers interested in contorted legal topography may look up *Alfred H. Hardwick* v. *Nu-Way Oil Co.* (1979).[34]

As regards the second boundary of unilateralism—simple announcement plus cutoffs—the leading precedent is *U.S.* v. *Colgate*,[35] decided only eight years after *Dr. Miles*. Colgate practiced resale price maintenance, disciplining maverick dealers with refusals to sell. But the Court was favorably impressed by Colgate's circumspection: "In the absence of any purpose to create or maintain a monopoly" a firm is free "to exercise his own independent discretion as to parties with whom he will deal;

---

[32] *United States* v. *General Electric Co.*, 272 U.S. 476 (1926).

[33] *Simpson* v. *Union Oil Co.*, 377 U.S. 13 (1964).

[34] *Alfred H. Hardwick* v. *Nu-Way Oil Company*, 589 F.2d 806 (1979), *cert. denied* 444 U.S. 836 (1979).

[35] *United States* v. *Colgate & Co.*, 250 U.S. 300 (1919).

and of course, he may announce in advance the circumstances under which he will refuse to sell."

More recently, in *Russell Stover Candies* (1983), it was found that dealer acquiescence in a manufacturer's suggested resale price policy was well within the protection of *Colgate*.[36] As one commentator put it,

> *Russell Stover* shows that a manufacturer may suggest resale prices, pre-ticket his goods, terminate price-cutters, effectively prevent dealers who wish to cut price from doing so out of fear of termination, and succeed in having 97.4% of his products retailed at or above their designated resale price — all while remaining within the safe harbor of *Colgate*.[37]

In the currently controlling case, *Monsanto Co.* v. *Spray-Rite* (1984), the Supreme Court reaffirmed the *Colgate* doctrine, saying that a man-ufacturer would be permitted to terminate price cutters even if "that termination came about 'in response to' complaints" from distributors hurt by the maverick. Such complaints "arise in the normal course of business and do not indicate illegal concerted action." Unfortunately for Monsanto, the Court went on to say that if such complaints are accom-panied by some "plus factors," then one can conclude that a manufac-turer is conspiring with its dealers to fix resale prices. Those "plus fac-tors" were found in *Monsanto*, so Spray-Rite, Monsanto's recalcitrant dealer, won its suit. Hence a manufacturer may announce a policy of resale price maintenance and enforce it.[38] Still, the manufacturer should *act unilaterally*, (1) not requiring the express agreement of its distributors and (2) not referring to distributor complaints even if acting in response to those complaints. Further, the manufacturer should *avoid coercion*: (1) not harassing distributors into compliance and (2) not terminating mavericks only to reinstate them once they agree to adhere to suggested resale prices.[39]

To conclude, the *Colgate* loophole takes the teeth out of the per se rule against resale price maintenance. "Only the stupidest manufacturer will get caught with specific agreements on prices," says Diane Wood, University of Chicago law professor.[40]

Still, there might be a good argument for some minor relaxation of the law. There may be manufacturers who cannot take advantage of the loophole and that would use resale price maintenance for efficient, pro-competitive reasons. A new entrant selling a product that could use

---

[36] *Russell Stover Candies, Inc.* v. *FTC*, 718 F.2d 256 (1983).

[37] Robert L. Steiner, "The Nature of Vertical Restraints." p. 193. See also Victor Goldberg, "Enforcing Resale Price Maintenance: The FTC Investigation of Lenox," *American Business Law Journal* (Summer 1980), pp. 225–256.

[38] *Monsanto Co.* v. *Spray-Rite Service Co.*, 104 S. Ct. 1464 (1984).

[39] For detailed instructions to manufacturers see Mary J. Sheffet and Debra L. Scam-mon, "Resale Price Maintenance: Is It Safe to Suggest Retail Prices?" *Journal of Marketing* (Fall 1985), pp. 82–96.

[40] *The Wall Street Journal*, May 3, 1988.

retailer services, for instance, might use resale price maintenance as an aid to establishing itself in the market. Personal computer companies like Hewlett-Packard and Eagle come to mind. Thus a few factual defenses could be grafted onto the per se rule without much loss and perhaps substantial gain. This would move the law in the direction of the rule of reason applying to territorial restraints.[41]

SUMMARY

Tying, exclusive dealing, territorial restrictions, and resale price maintenance constitute vertical restrictions. Tying is the sale of two or more products contractually bound. Exclusive dealing prevents a buyer-distributor from dealing in more than one brand of a given line of wares. Territorial restrictions insulate distributors from intrabrand competition, and resale price maintenance is vertical price fixing.

Tying may gain efficiencies, preserve business goodwill through the preservation of quality, or aid price discrimination. Tying may also be used to leverage monopoly power from the tying-good's market into the tied-good's market, and therein lies the rub. It can be exclusionary. Under Section 1 of the Sherman Act and Section 3 of the Clayton Act, tying is judged illegal if (1) there really are two products involved, (2) the seller possesses sufficient economic power in the tying good, (3) there is substantial commerce in the tied good, and (4) no defenses of reasonableness afford themselves. Though laced with rule of reason potential, these criteria boil down to a per se rule in some instances, such as tie-ins to patented products.

Exclusive dealing is also potentially exclusionary and also covered by Clayton Section 3. Nevertheless, given the possible benefits of this practice for distributors and ultimate consumers as well as instigating manufacturers, it is appropriate that a rule of reason prevail. The two main factors determining its legality are the seller's market share and the prevalence of the practice. If either or both are quite large, the exclusionary effect will be magnified and, with it, the likelihood of illegality.

Territorial restraints and resale price maintenance curb intrabrand competition among distributors, thereby inviting scrutiny under Section 1 of the Sherman Act. A main business justification for both is that they nourish incentives for vigorous "full-service" retailing and wholesaling.

---

[41] Robert Pitofsky, "Why *Dr. Miles* Was Right," *Regulation* (January/February 1984), pp. 27–30; and Terry Calvani and Andrew Berg, "Resale Price Maintenance After *Monsanto*," *Duke Law Journal*, Vol. (1984), pp. 1163–1204. Despite this suggestion, the rule of reason treatment of territorial restraints is not necessarily wise for resale price maintenance also. Resale price maintenance differs from territorial restraint in significant ways. See Michael Waterson, "On Vertical Restraints and the Law," *Rand Journal of Economics* (Summer 1988), pp. 293–297.

Such incentives may foster interbrand competition if used by the weak against the strong. On the other hand, both practices have anticompetitive potentials. Territorial restraints are therefore susceptible to challenge if used by a dominant firm or if used by most firms in a tightly-knit oligopoly with high concentration. Resale price maintenance is at present per se illegal. But it has been legal in the past and there are pressures to make it legal again, or at least rule-of-reason illegal.

Regardless of law, many vertical restraints escape through the use of tacit arrangements that are cemented by an ample freedom of choice in the selection of distributors and franchisees. This "out" is especially noteworthy for resale price maintenance, where the *Colgate* doctrine has held sway since 1919.

Part IV

PERFORMANCE

20

Introduction to Performance

Winning isn't everything. It's the only thing.
                                    —VINCE LOMBARDI

Just as the last lap of a long race tests the runner's early strategy, so a study of market performance will prove our survey of industrial organization. To be sure, structure and conduct are momentous and memorable in their own right. They are the economic equivalent of anatomy and action. As stated at the outset in Chapter 1, structure and conduct reflect the setting and process by which we obtain answers to the fundamental economic questions of what, how, who, and what's new. And, as we have seen, structure and conduct are sufficiently important to be the focus of many policies—policies whose main objectives are competitive, decentralized structure and fair, unrestrictive conduct.

Given that structure and conduct reflect *how* the game is played, performance reflects *how well* it is played. Performance consists of the achievements, outcomes, and answers provided by the market.

A few economists look upon performance as Vince Lombardi looked upon winning. They see it as the *only* source of thrill.[1] Most industrial organization economists, the present author included, do not share this view.[2] Nevertheless, performance is important, so the remaining four chapters give performance its due. The main topics covered are, in order of their appearance:

[1] John S. McGee, *In Defense of Industrial Concentration* (New York: Praeger, 1971).
[2] For elaboration, see H. H. Liebhafsky, *American Government and Business* (New York:

1. Allocation efficiency
2. Income distribution
3. Technical efficiency
4. Technological progress

The first two items are often measured in profit performance, excessively high profits indicating poor allocation and distorted income distribution. The remaining concepts are largely self-explanatory.

The odd-numbered chapters that follow — Chapters 21 and 23 — treat these topics theoretically and empirically. Their collective message is simple: *structure and conduct vitally influence performance.* What is more, there is for the most part substantial correlation between good structure, good conduct, and good performance, where "good" means conformity with the value judgments specified in Chapter 1. This is an important message. It means that structures displaying low concentration, easy entry, and well-informed buyers are desirable not only because they in and of themselves further such goals as freedom, decentralized decision making, and equal bargaining power, but because such structures also foster fair and vigorous competitive conduct. In addition, these structures and modes of conduct usually foster appropriate allocation of resources, low-cost methods of production, brisk technological advancement, and fairly equitable distributions of income.

Were these blanket statements *always* true, everything would be coming up roses, and the odd-numbered chapters would be all that were needed. However, these statements are qualified with words like "usually" and "for the most part," words that warn of exceptions. Unfortunately, for some industries, workably competitive structures do *not* always provide good performance. A classic exception is the so-called "natural monopoly," where economies of scale are so significant that a healthy number of competing rivals could exist only with horrendous inefficiencies. Low-cost performance in such cases requires monopoly structure. Other structural quirks, such as centralized interconnection (for example, telephone service), enormously high capital costs relative to total production costs (for example, sewage disposal), and physical singularities (for example, seaports), also nourish "natural monopolies." Zealous pursuit of competitive structures in these cases would be futile (because their attainment is impossible) or stupid (because, if attained, they yield poor performance). Hence, government typically approaches these unruly beasts by condoning and to some extent even encouraging monopolistic structures. In the hopes of serving the public interest, gov-

John Wiley, 1971), Chapter 13; Charles E. Lindblom, *Politics and Markets* (New York: Basic Books, 1977), especially Chapter 19; Corwin Edwards, *Maintaining Competition* (New York: McGraw-Hill, 1949); and F. M. Scherer, "The Posnerian Harvest: Separating Wheat from Chaff," *Yale Law Journal* (April 1977), pp. 974–1002.

ernment either (1) *takes over* ownership and operation or (2) *regulates* performance directly if private ownership is permitted. In short, if monopoly is inevitable, it is preferable that such monopoly be publicly owned or publicly supervised. The latter option, which is the subject of Chapter 22, is called "public utility" regulation.

Regrettably, the exceptions are not limited to a few specific industries whose "good" performance requires "bad" structures. Disharmonies between structure and performance arise under other conditions as well. Hence exceptions concerning specific aspects of performance warrant discussion.

In particular, governmental awards of *temporary, unregulated monopoly* may be deemed the best way of rewarding and encouraging good performance. Patents provide the main example of this. A patent gives its owner 17 years of monopoly control over an invention. Because unregulated monopoly often yields handsome profits, patents in theory reward deserving inventors, thereby spurring technological progress that would not otherwise occur. This policy is explored in Chapter 24.

Thus our passage into performance analysis does not put policy behind us. For a variety of reasons, government does not rest content with whatever desirable aspects of performance may be derived indirectly from its extensive (though often less than diligent) attention to structure and conduct. Government often dabbles and deals in performance directly. Whereas most policies governing structure and conduct may be called "antitrust" or "affirmative disclosure" policies, most of those governing performance typically entail "regulation" or "subsidization." Labels aside, you will find one even-numbered chapter on performance policy for each odd-numbered chapter on performance economics.

21

■ Profits, Wages, and Technical Efficiency: Theory and Cross-section Evidence

The creation of a monopoly involves a principle which can be generally applied . . . when in need of money.
— ARISTOTLE

Observations on the ill effects of market power date back to Aristotle. He tells of a Sicilian who monopolized the iron trade, thereby profiting 100%.[1] More recently, over the past 30 years, there have been more than a hundred empirical studies of the profitability of market power. These studies are more sophisticated, more scientific, and more thorough than Aristotle's. But most of them reach the same conclusion—market power

[1] Ernest Barker (ed.), *The Politics of Aristotle* (New York: Oxford University Press, 1962), p. 31.

boosts profits. The first purpose of this chapter is to review this mountain of empiricism and explain its implications for two measures of economic performance, namely allocation efficiency and wealth distribution.

The second purpose of this chapter is to show that market power can affect worker wage rates as well as profits. For this purpose we shall explore power in labor markets (as measured by unionization) as well as power in product markets.

As a third consideration, a growing body of empirical literature indicates that market power spawns technical inefficiency or X-inefficiency. X-inefficiency may economically be more costly to society than either excess profits or exorbitant wages.

I. PROFITS AND MARKET POWER

A. Theory

Figure 21–1 depicts the simple theory of excess profits and resource misallocation under monopoly. With pure competition, industry price would be $0P_c$, which equals marginal cost. Marginal cost includes a normal profit, one just big enough that investors are content to leave their capital committed to this industry. Competitive quantity Q_c will then be supplied in the long run. Moreover, with price equal to marginal cost, resources are optimally allocated to the production of this commodity.

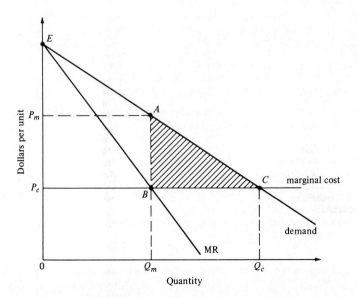

FIGURE 21–1. Social welfare loss due to monopoly.

Price indicates resource value "here," whereas marginal cost indicates resource value "elsewhere." Since value here just equals value elsewhere at the margin, any shift of resources will reduce consumer welfare. Consumers' welfare is measured by consumers' surplus, which is the greatest sum consumers are willing to pay for consuming quantity $0Q_c$ less the amount they actually pay. In Figure 21–1, assuming pure competition, $0ECQ_c$ is the sum they are willing to pay, whereas $0P_cCQ_c$ is the sum they actually pay. Hence triangle ECP_c is the consumers' surplus associated with pure competition.

Monopolization of the industry has at least two effects. First, **distribution inequity**. The monopolist maximizes profit by producing Q_m, where marginal revenue (MR) matches marginal cost. Price jumps to P_m and the monopolist takes part of what would be consumers' surplus under pure competition. This area, rectangle P_cP_mAB, is the monopolist's excess profit. How markedly the excess profit contributes to an unequal distribution of income and wealth depends on the relative financial condition of (1) those who pay the higher price and thereby lose the surplus and (2) those who earn the excess profit and thereby gain the surplus. If those who pay are generally poorer than those who receive (in the United States only about 2% of all households control over 50% of all business ownership claims), then income distribution is made more unequal than otherwise (Robin Hood in reverse, that is). Regardless of the distribution effect, area P_cP_mAB *should be considered a transfer* from one group to another. It is not a direct measure of allocation inefficiency.

The second effect of monopoly seen here is welfare loss caused by **misallocation of resources**. When price rises above the marginal cost to P_m, a portion of what used to be consumers' surplus disappears completely. This is triangular area ABC, which is neither retained by consumers nor transferred to the owners. In simple terms, misallocation occurs because monopolization underallocates resources to here, as production is cut back; production cutbacks also force overallocations elsewhere. The fact that price P_m exceeds marginal cost indicates that value here exceeds value elsewhere. And society would therefore be better off if resources were moved from elsewhere into here. But monopolization, with entry barred, prevents the necessary reshuffling. Welfare is lost just as welfare would be lost if seismic violence suddenly obliterated our coal resources. From Figure 21–1 it may be seen that welfare loss will be a positive function of profit as a percentage of sales and price elasticity of demand.

In short, if market power generates excess profit, two adverse economic effects could arise — allocation inefficiency and maldistribution of wealth or income. To understand these effects by analogy, imagine a playground bully grabbing a two-scoop ice cream cone from a little girl who has already eaten half of the top scoop. The other half of the top scoop falls to the dusty ground during the tussle, so the bully ends up with just the bottom scoop and the cone. In terms of Figure 21–1, the deadweight loss of area ABC would be symbolized by the grimy remains of the top scoop melting in the dirt. The transfer of P_mABP_c would be represented by the bully's gain. And the unmolested consumers' surplus, area EAP_m, would be expressed by the half-scoop the little girl ate before the assault.

Still, this is theory. Nothing is certain about these theoretical effects or the extent of actual harm. Research has tried to dispel some of the uncertainty by focusing on three questions raised by Figure 21–1:

1. Is there a positive association between market power and profitability?
2. Given a yes answer to question 1, what is the total welfare loss due to monopolistic misallocation?
3. Given a yes answer to question 1, what is market power's contribution to the above average wealth of the wealthy?

We shall take up each question in turn. It should be kept in mind throughout that pure monopoly and pure competition are extreme cases. Research actually centers on varying degrees of market power that lie between these extremes.

B. Does Market Power Increase Profit?

The relationship between market power and profit performance is the most thoroughly studied of all structure-performance relationships. New evidence appears almost monthly. One reason for the intense attention paid to this issue is the immense policy influence it carries. Another is the wide diversity of possible research approaches. "Profit," for example, can be measured in a number of ways, each of which has a variety of data sources.[2]

An ideal measure of "profit" would be comparable across industries and free from biases that varied with market power. For purposes of comparability, all measures are actually **profit rates**, computed by dividing dollar profit (either pretax or posttax) by some base figure. There are two broad classes of bases commonly used: (1) balance sheet data and (2) sales revenues. Accordingly, all measures can be divided into two groups.

The first group uses **stockholders' equity** or **assets** as the base. Indeed, the most widely used measure of profit is **rate of return on stockholders' equity after tax**. Symbolically, this is $(P - T)/E$, where P is total

---

[2] For reviews, see Leonard W. Weiss, "The Concentration-Profits Relationship," in *Industrial Concentration: The New Learning*, edited by H. Goldschmid, M. Mann, and F. Weston (Boston: Little, Brown, 1974), pp. 196–201; and Richard Schmalensee, "Inter-Industry Studies of Structure and Performance," in *Handbook of Industrial Organization*, Vol. II, edited by R. Schmalensee and R. Willig (Amsterdam: North-Holland, 1989), pp. 960–965.

dollar profit, T is tax on profit, and E is stockholders' equity. This measure has the desirable property of corresponding closely with the profit that stockholders seek to maximize. Moreover, this measure would be the same in the long run for all industries if pure competition prevailed throughout the economy. When assets instead of equity are used as the base, an adjustment must be made because debt capital as well as equity capital stands behind total assets, and debt capital is paid interest rather than profit, which is paid to equity capital owners. Accordingly, the formula for the **rate of return on assets after tax** is $(P - T + I)/A$, where P is dollar profit, T is tax, I is total dollar interest paid, and A is asset value. As compared with return on equity, this measure is probably less affected by irrelevant variances in debt/equity ratios, but most experts nevertheless consider it to be inferior to $(P - T)/E$.

A major problem with this class of measures is that they may bias all firms toward equal profit rates because the numerator and denominator tend to move together directly rather than independently. That is,

> assets are apt to be written up or down according to their profitability. For instance, plant and equipment that have changed hands since they were installed are apt to be valued at their purchase prices rather than at their original costs, and those purchase prices will reflect their income earning prospects. Even when assets do not change hands, investments that turn out badly are sometimes written down to reflect their income potential more realistically. The result of such revaluations is [also] to increase the equity of highly profitable firms and reduce it in unprofitable firms, thus biasing all firms toward equal profit rates.[3]

Another shortcoming of these measures is that available data for them are *firm* specific, not *market* specific. Because many firms are highly diversified, their reported profits are a mix of profits from a number of markets. By contrast, most measures of market power are market specific. The disparity often prevents a precise matchup of observations on market structure and observations on profit.

The most obvious of the second group of measures, which use sales, is **profit after tax relative to sales**, or $(P - T)/S$, where S is total sales revenue. This is not the form of profit that stockholders seek to maximize, but it has the advantage of measuring allocation inefficiency more directly than does profit relative to equity or assets. Moreover, it is not biased by asset revaluations. $(P - T)/S$ is not trouble free, however. It varies across industries for reasons wholly unrelated to market power. In particular, $(P - T)/S$ is largely determined by the capital intensity of the production process. Greater capital intensity implies a greater capital investment per unit of sales, and this in turn requires a greater profit per dollar of sales in order to reward investors with a

---

[3] Weiss, "The Concentration-Profits Relationship," p. 196.

given level of return on their investments. Letting E/S indicate investment per unit of sales, this may be seen in the following identity:

$$\frac{P - T}{S} = \frac{E}{S} \times \frac{P - T}{E}$$

For a given level of $(P - T)/E$, say, 9%, $(P - T)/S$ will be a direct function of E/S. Thus when using $(P - T)/S$, researchers must allow for capital intensity.

To summarize, there is a variety of profit measures and a variety of data sources, but imperfections affect each of them. If these imperfections spuriously generated positive associations between market power and profit, they would seriously reduce the validity of the measurements. Doubt would be cast on the meaning of such positive findings. However, most known errors work in the opposite direction. They either lessen the strength of any positive correlation between profits and power or bias it toward zero. Given this direction of error, "we can be pretty sure that if any positive relation does appear there is something there and it is understated. On the other hand, if no relationship is detected, one may still exist."[4]

Concentration and Profits.   Earlier chapters theorized that concentration fostered market power. They also reviewed evidence of a positive association between concentration and price level. It will not come as a jolt, then, to learn that most of the many statistical studies correlating profit and concentration find a *similar positive and significant relationship.* Figures 21–2(a) and 21–2(b) depict examples of these results. Such positive effects have been found for all measures of profit, for many different measures of concentration (four-firm and eight-firm ratios plus the Herfindahl–Hirschman index), and for vastly different time periods (from 1936 to the present). Moreover, the positive relationship holds for broad interindustry samples (including all manufacturing industries), narrow interindustry samples (limited to producer goods or food prod-

---

[4] Weiss, "The Concentration-Profits Relationship," p. 201. For a statistical demonstration of this conclusion, see J. A. Dalton and D. W. Penn, *The Quality of Data As a Factor in Analyses of Structure-Performance Relationships* (Federal Trade Commission Economic Report, 1971). A few economists go so far as to say that accounting rates of return are worthless and therefore any "examination of absolute or relative accounting rates of return to draw conclusions about monopoly profits is a totally misleading enterprise." See F. M. Fisher and J. J. McGowan, "On the Misuse of Accounting Rates of Return to Infer Monopoly Profits," *American Economic Review* (March 1983), pp. 82–97. This, however, is now a discredited view. Indeed, if it were true, businesspeople would be utterly lost. See the debate that followed in the *American Economic Review* (June 1984) and also J. A. Kay and C. P. Mayer, "On the Application of Accounting Rates of Return," *Economic Journal* (March 1986), pp. 197–207; Henry McFarland, "Evaluating q as an Alternative to the Rate of Return in Measuring Profitability," *Review of Economics and Statistics* (November 1988), pp. 614–622; and Stephen Martin, "The Measurement of Profitability and the Diagnosis of Market Power," *International Journal of Industrial Organization* (September 1988), pp. 301–321.

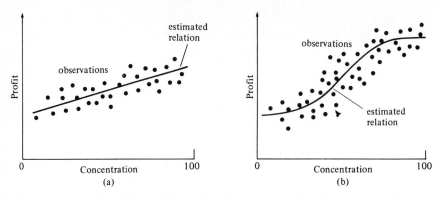

FIGURE 21–2. Positive relationships between profit and concentration.

ucts, for instance), and *intra*industry samples across diverse geographic markets (such as those in banking, grocery retailing, and bread).[5] As if this were not enough, the positive relationship emerges from data gathered from every corner of the world—England, West Germany, Canada, Japan, Pakistan, India, Mexico, Brazil, Australia, Taiwan, Kenya, Belgium, and France, as well as from the United States.[6] Given this wide variety of tests, the general consistency of a positive concentration-profit relationship is impressive.

Two brief numerical examples based on U.S. data convey the message. Robert Kilpatrick computed the correlation between concentration and three different measures of pretax profit for 91 industries using 1963 Internal Revenue Service data. The correlation coefficients are .388, .442, and .506 for profits as a percentage of equity, assets, and sales, respec-

[5] For surveys see Weiss, "The Concentration-Profits Relationship," and Stephen A. Rhoades, "Structure-Performance Studies in Banking: A Summary and Evaluation," Staff Economic Studies, No. 92 (Board of Governors of the Federal Reserve System, 1977); Rhoades, "Updated," Staff Economic Studies, No. 119 (Board of Governors of the Federal Reserve System, 1982). Among the many studies not mentioned in these surveys are David Qualls, "Concentration, Barriers to Entry, and Long Run Economic Profit Margins," *Journal of Industrial Economics* (April 1972), pp. 146–158; S. A. Rhoades and Joe M. Cleaver, "The Nature of the Concentration–Price/Cost Margin Relationship for 352 Manufacturing Industries: 1967," *Southern Economic Journal* (July 1973), pp. 90–102; James A. Verbrugge and R. A. Shick, "Market Structure and Savings and Loan Profitability," *Quarterly Review of Economics and Business* (Summer 1976), pp. 79–90; A. D. Strickland and L. W. Weiss, "Advertising, Concentration, and Price-Cost Margins," *Journal of Political Economy* (October 1976), pp. 1109–1123; Lana Hall, Andrew Schmitz, and James Cothern, "Beef Wholesale-Retail Marketing Margins, and Concentration," *Economica* (August 1979), pp. 295–300; and Michael Salinger, "The Concentration Margins Relationship Reconsidered," *Brookings Papers: Microeconomics*, 1990, pp. 287–321.

[6] J. Khalilzadeh-Shiraz, "Market Structure and Price-Cost Margins: A Comparative Analysis of U.K. and U.S. Manufacturing Industries," *Economic Inquiry* (March 1976), pp. 116–128; J. C. H. Jones, L. Laudadio, and M. Percy, "Profitability and Market Structure: A Cross-section Comparison of Canadian and American Manufacturing Industry," *Journal of Industrial Economics* (March 1977), pp. 195–211; Richard E. Caves and Masu Uekusa, *Industrial Organization in Japan* (Washington, D.C.: Brookings Institution, 1976), pp. 92–96; Law-

tively.[7] All are statistically significant at the 95% level or better. All indicate a relationship like Figure 21–2(a).

In another study, one limited to 97 firms producing food products, William Kelly used regression analysis to explain interfirm variance in profit rates as a percentage of stockholders' equity. A summary of his results is presented in Table 21–1. Reading the table horizontally discloses the estimated impact of advertising on profit. As advertising intensity increases, profit likewise increases, a result explained earlier in Chapter 16. The estimated impact of concentration is seen by scanning down the columns. For example, when advertising is held constant at 1% of sales, a profit rate of 6.3% is associated with concentration of 40, and a profit rate of 11.5% is associated with concentration of 70. Notice that most of the increase in profit occurs in the range of concentration between 40 and 60. Added concentration above 60 adds very little to profit (regardless of advertising intensity). The table does not present results for concentration ratios less than 40 because the sample did not include observations for low levels of concentration. Still, on the basis of other evidence, it can be assumed that profit would not vary greatly over the low range of concentration, in which case these results would trace the pattern depicted in Figure 21–2(b).

The exact *form* of the concentration-profits relationship is a much debated issue. Some evidence reveals a linear relation like Figure 21–2(a). Other evidence indicates a nonlinear or discontinuous form, one example of which is Figure 21–2(b). The present author is open minded on the subject of form, but he suspects that a nonlinear form *does* hold under some circumstances, and theory and evidence suggest a form like Figure 21–2(b). That is, it is in the *middle* range of concentration that the

---

rence J. White, *Industrial Concentration and Economic Power in Pakistan* ((Princeton, N.J.: Princeton University Press, 1974); P. K. Sawhney and B. L. Sawhney, "Capacity-Utilization, Concentration, and Price-Cost Margins: Results on Indian Industries," *Journal of Industrial Economics* (April 1973), pp. 145–153; John M. Connor and Willard F. Mueller, *Market Power and Profitability of Multinational Corporations in Brazil and Mexico*, Report to the Subcommittee on Foreign Economic Policy of the Committee on Foreign Relations, U.S. Senate (1977); William J. House, "Market Structure and Industry Performance: The Case of Kenya," *Oxford Economic Papers* (November 1973), pp. 405–419; F. Jenny and A. P. Weber, "Profit Rates and Structural Variables in the French Manufacturing Sector," *European Economic Review* (January 1976); Stephen Nickell and David Metcalf, "Monopolistic Industries and Monopoly Profits or, Are Kellogg's Cornflakes Overpriced?" *Economic Journal* (June 1978), pp. 254–268; David K. Round, "Price-Cost Margins, Industry Structure, and Foreign Competition in Australian Manufacturing," *Industrial Organization Review* (No. 3, 1978), pp. 151–168; M. Neuman, I. Bobel, and A. Haid, "Domestic Concentration, Foreign Trade, and Economic Performance," *International Journal of Industrial Organization* (March 1985), pp. 1–19; Tein-Chen Chou, "Concentration and Profitability in a Dichotomous Economy: The Case of Taiwan," *International Journal of Industrial Organization* (December 1988), pp. 409–428; and E. de Ghellinck, Paul Geroski, and Alexis Jacquemin, "Inter-Industry Variations in the Effect of Trade on Industry Performance," *Journal of Industrial Economics* (September 1988), pp. 1–17.
[7] Robert W. Kilpatrick, "The Validity of the Average Concentration Ratio as a Measure of Industrial Structure," *Southern Economic Journal* (April 1976), pp. 711–715.

TABLE 21–1.   Profit Rates of Food Manufacturing Firms
Associated with Levels of Industry Concentration and
Advertising to Sales Ratios

Four-Firm	Advertising to Sales Ratio (%)				
Concentration	1.0	2.0	3.0	4.0	5.0
40	6.2	7.4	8.5	9.6	10.7
45	8.0	9.1	10.2	11.3	12.4
50	9.3	10.4	11.5	12.6	13.7
55	10.3	11.4	12.5	13.6	14.7
60	11.0	12.1	13.2	14.3	15.4
65	11.4	12.5	13.6	14.7	15.8
70	11.5	12.6	13.7	14.8	15.9

Source: William H. Kelly, *On the Influence of Market Structure on the Profit Performance of Food Manufacturing Companies* (Washington, D.C.: Federal Trade Commission, 1969). p. 7

greatest transformation from competitive to collusive conduct is likely to occur. Therefore it is in the middle range that concentration and profit are most likely to move positively and significantly together, as shown in Figure 21–2(b).[8]

To summarize, it appears that, in general, there is a positive association between profitability and market concentration over a wide variety of measures and circumstances. Nevertheless, there are two sets of problems with this massive body of research. In turn, these raise two important qualifications to this conclusion. The first set of problems has to do with the *significance and magnitude* of the relationship, while the second set concerns *interpretation.*

Significance and Magnitude.   Regarding *significance and magnitude* a noteworthy minority of studies finds *no* positive association between concentration and profits, or only a weak one in the sense that profits do not rise much with increases in concentration. Three observations should be made here.

First, *reasonable explanations are available for many of these aberrant studies*, explanations which cast doubt on their validity or generality. It has been found, for example, that the relationship is weak or nonexis-

[8] See Norman R. Collins and Lee E. Preston, *Concentration and Price-Cost Margins in Manufacturing Industries* (Berkeley: University of California Press, 1968); A. A. Heggestad and J. J. Mingo, "The Competitive Condition of U.S. Banking Markets and the Impact of Structural Reform," *Journal of Finance* (June 1977), pp. 649–661; Ralph M. Bradburd and A. Mead Over, Jr., "Organizational Costs, 'Sticky Equilibria,' and Critical Levels of Concentration," *Review of Economics and Statistics* (February 1982), pp. 50–58; and Stephen A. Rhoades, "Does Market Structure Matter in Commercial Banking?" *Antitrust Bulletin* (Spring 1981), pp. 155–181.

tent during rapid spurts of economic expansion or price inflation.[9] Studies drawing data from such periods are likely, therefore, to produce contrary results. Another problem is multicollinearity. This means that computerized statistical procedures cannot sort out the independent contributions that the correlated variables make to profit.[10] Still another group of explicable contrary results arises from the use of limited samples of industries or markets, samples so limited that they do not include observations over a wide range of concentration. As we have just seen, if observations are limited to either high or low values, positive significant associations are less likely to be detected.[11] The contrary results of studies such as these need not be given great weight.

Our second point regarding these odd results is this: A number of them are genuine. *The statistical relationship between concentration and profits is indeed occasionally nonexistent or feeble.* This does not mean, however, that high concentration is a harmless phenomenon. Recall that a positive association between concentration and *price* level is quite firmly established in the empirical literature (see pages 307–314). We also know that fewness of firms fosters *collusion* (pp. 400–407). It thus appears that concentration's impact on price or collusive conduct is not always reflected in profits. A key factor that may cause a divergence between the results for profits and prices is illustrated in Figure 21–3. Expecting a positive concentration-profit relationship implicitly assumes that *costs do not rise* with concentration. This is pictured in panel (a) of Figure 21–3. With costs held constant, the higher price implied by the higher concentration (on the horizontal axis) will be translated into higher profit margins. However, the assumption of constant costs could be wrong. If costs rise with concentration as indicated in panel (b) of Figure 21–3, then concentration can lift prices without at the same time raising profits (or by raising profits only weakly depending on the degree to which costs rise with concentration). As will be shown a few pages later, costs *do indeed* rise with concentration because of rent seeking, X-inefficiencies, and labor wage variations, so the occasional finding of a nonexistent or weak association between concentration and profits is in this light to be expected.

Finally several of the best studies finding no relationship between concentration and profits do so only when a measure for *individual firm*

---

[9] G. Gambeles, "Structural Determinants of Profit Performance in the United States Manufacturing Industries, 1947–1967," Ph.D. dissertation, University of Maryland, 1969.

[10] The added variable most commonly at fault is economies of scale computed from data entering the concentration ratio. When an independent measure of scalar economics is used, the problem disappears and concentration attains significance. See R. E. Caves, J. Khalilzadeh-Shirazi, and M. E. Porter, "Scale Economies in Statistical Analyses of Market Power," *Review of Economics and Statistics* (May 1975), pp. 133–140.

[11] In the highs, see D. R. Fraser and P. S. Rose, "Banking Structure and Performance in Isolated Markets: The Implications for Public Policy," *Antitrust Bulletin* (Fall 1972), pp. 927–947. For examples of lows, see Collins and Preston's results for textiles and apparel, (*Concentration of Price-Cost Margins in Manufacturing Industries*, pp. 94–97).

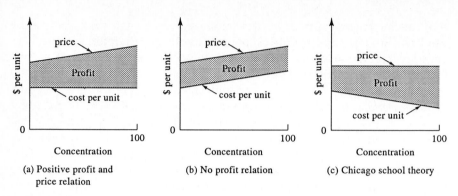

FIGURE 21–3. Price, cost, and profit margin relationships to concentration.

market share is included in the analysis.[12] This raises a problem of measurement. Concentration may not be as good a measure of market power as individual firm market shares, although concentration is, of course, related to market shares by definition. Recall from Table 11–1 in Chapter 11 (page 299) that there are two forms of market-power—*single-firm power*, which can be measured by individual firm market share, and *collective/collusive power*, which can be measured by concentration ratios (or the H index). To the extent that single-firm market power is the *only* type of power that counts, concentration ratios will be positively associated with profits *only* because the concentration ratio is positively associated with high market shares. And once individual firm market shares are expressly included in the statistical analysis, they will supplant the concentration ratio, reducing it to insignificance or weakness. It is now well established that single-firm market power *is* extremely important, independent of collusive behavior, and this is especially true of the top one or two firms in a market.[13] So it is not surprising that concentration, which best measures collusion, frequently loses significance once individual market shares are accounted for, because those individual shares best measure single-firm market power. Still, collusive behavior cannot be ruled out. There are a number of excellent studies that reveal positive significance for concentration once market share is taken into account.[14] Hence concentration is not harmless. It frequently contributes to collusive power quite apart from (noncollusive)

---

[12] David J. Ravenscraft, "Structure-Profit Relationships at the Line of Business and Industry Level," *Review of Economics and Statistics* (February 1983), pp. 22–31.

[13] William G. Shepherd, "The Elements of Market Structure," *Review of Economics and Statistics* (February 1922), pp. 25–37; John E. Kwoka, Jr., "The Effects of Market Share Distribution on Industry Performance," *Review of Economics and Statistics* (February 1979), pp. 101–109; Stephen A. Rhoades, "Market Share as a Source of Market Power," *Journal of Economics and Business*, Vol. 37 (1985), pp. 343–363; and Frederick H. de B. Harris, "Market Structure and Price-Cost Performance," *Journal of Industrial Economics* (September 1986), pp. 35–55.

[14] See, for example, Weiss, "The Concentration-Profits Relationship," pp. 225–230;

single-firm power. Moreover, concentration ratios rise with increases in the top firms' market shares, so concentration likewise measures single-firm market power at the marketwide level, albeit imperfectly.[15] Between single firms and marketwide collusion there is also the intermediate element of strategic groups. Accounting for strategic groups improves the statistical performance of concentration while qualifying that of market share.[16]

Interpretation Problems. Assuming there *is* a relationship between concentration and profits (as qualified by the foregoing considerations), its meaning has been disputed. Skeptics of the market power hypothesis, especially those associated with the "Chicago School," interpret this finding in ways that rule out any contributions from market power. They claim the positive correlation between concentration and profit is entirely spurious, that it is due to some fundamental flaw in the data or to factors unrelated to market power that just happen to be positively correlated with both concentration and profit.[17] This is not the proper place to review the entire debate. Still, we should mention some points made by the skeptics and indicate how each has thus far been answered:

1. Skeptics argue that accounting procedures may differ across firms, making the positive association meaningless. It has been shown,

Blake Imel, Michael R. Behr, and Peter G. Helmberger, *Market Structure and Performance* (Lexington, Mass.: Lexington Books, 1972); J. A. Dalton and Stanford L. Levin, "Market Power: Concentration and Market Share," *Industrial Organization Review*, No. 1 (1977), pp. 27–35; and D. F. Lean, J. D. Ogur, and R. P. Rogers, *Competition and Collusion in Electrical Equipment Markets: An Economic Assessment* (Washington, D.C.: Federal Trade Commission Staff Report, 1982).

15 Simulations on hypothetical data that artificially incorporate collusion reveal that concentration imperfectly measures collusion as well. Gregory J. Werden and Michael A. Williams, "Can the Concentration-Collusion Hypothesis Be Refuted Empirically," Department of Justice, Antitrust Division, EPO Discussion Paper 84–11 (1984). This underscores the point made earlier that biases against finding positive, significant results are such that failed tests do not really refute the market power hypothesis. For qualifiers on the share studies, see W. F. Mueller and D. F. Greer, "The Effect of Market Share Distribution on Industry Performance-Reexamined," *Review of Economics and Statistics* (May 1984), pp. 353–358.

16 Michael E. Porter, "The Structure Within Industries and Companies' Performance," *Review of Economics and Statistics* (May 1979), pp. 214–227; and Ralph M. Bradburd and David R. Ross, "Can Small Firms Find and Defend Strategic Niches?" *Review of Economics and Statistics* (May 1989), pp. 258–262.

17 John McGee, *In Defense of Industrial Concentration* (New York: Praeger, 1971), pp. 93–95; Yale Brozen, "The Antitrust Task Force Deconcentration Recommendation," *Journal of Law and Economics* (October 1970), pp. 279–292; Richard B. Mancke, "Causes of Interfirm Profitability Differences: A New Interpretation of the Evidence," *Quarterly Journal of Economics* (May 1974), pp. 181–193; Harold Demsetz, "Two Systems of Belief About Monopoly," in *Industrial Concentration: The New Learning*, edited by H. Goldschmid, M. Mann, and F. Weston (Boston: Little, Brown, 1974), pp. 164–184; Almarin Phillips, "A Critique of Empirical Studies of Relations Between Market Structure and Profitability," *Journal of Industrial Economics* (June 1976), pp. 241–249; and George J. Stigler, *Capital and Rates of Return in Manufacturing Industries* (Princeton, N.J.: Princeton University Press, 1963).

however, that accounting practices do not differ systematically between firms in concentrated and unconcentrated industries.[18]

2. Skeptics argue that the positive association is due merely to short-run disequilibrium conditions, that over the long run it disappears under the pressure of dynamic competition brought by new entry, product innovation, and the like. On the other hand, it has been demonstrated repeatedly that the relationship holds across decades of time, not merely months or years.[19] Moreover, study of the market value of firms indicates that investors behave as if firms with market power will keep that power into the distant future. "No indication has appeared that anticipations of entry will erode future excess profits."[20]

3. Skeptics claim that once risk is accounted for, the positive relationship will disappear, partly because risk is a major (and positive) determinant of both profit and concentration. Yet a number of studies have shown that even after profits are adjusted for risk-reward, the positive relationship remains.[21] Indeed, concentration and risk are *inversely*, not directly related, so the weakness of the concentration-profit relationship discussed earlier seems to be due partly to the fact that firms located in highly concentrated markets give up some of their monopoly profits in exchange for reductions in risk.[22]

4. Skeptics claim that small firms' profits are understated because their owner-officers take profit in the form of salaries. In turn, this allegedly understates the profits of unconcentrated industries. However, proper adjustment for this effect leaves the positive relation unscathed.[23]

[18] Robert L. Hagerman and Lemma W. Senbet, "A Test of Accounting Bias and Market Structure," *Journal of Business* (October 1976), pp. 509–514.

[19] David Qualls, "Stability and Persistence of Economic Profit Margins in Highly Concentrated Industries," *Southern Economic Journal* (April 1974), pp. 604–612; R. H. Litzenberger and O. M. Joy, "Inter-Industry Profitability Under Uncertainty," *Western Economic Journal* (September 1973), pp. 338–349; Dennis Mueller, "The Persistence of Profits Above the Norm," *Economica* (November 1977), pp. 369–380; and S. J. Liebowitz, "Measuring Industrial Disequilibria," *Southern Economic Journal* (July 1982), pp. 119–136.

[20] Stavros B. Thomadakis, "A Value-Based Test of Profitability and Market Structure," *Review of Economics and Statistics* (May 1977), pp. 179–185.

[21] William G. Shepherd, *The Treatment of Market Power* (New York: Columbia University Press, 1974), pp. 109–110; James L. Bothwell and Theodore E. Keeler, "Profits, Market Structure and Portfolio Risk," in *Essays on Industrial Organization*, edited by R. T. Masson and P. D. Qualls (Cambridge, Mass.: Ballinger, 1976), pp. 71–88; and S. A. Rhoades and R. D. Rutz, "Market Power and Firm Risk," *Journal of Monetary Economics* (1982), pp. 73–85.

[22] Jeffery A. Clark, "Market Structure, Risk, and Profitability," *Quarterly Review of Economics and Business* (Spring 1986), pp. 45–56; J. C. H. Jones and L. Laudadio, "Risk, Profitability, and Market Structure: Some Canadian Evidence," *Antitrust Bulletin* (Summer 1983), pp. 349–377; R. Charles Moyer and Robert Chatfield, "Market Power and Systematic Risk," *Journal of Economics and Business*, Vol. 35 (1983), pp. 123–130; and Frank J. Fabozzi et al, "Market Power as a Determinant of Systematic Risk," *Review of Business and Economic Research* (Spring 1986), pp. 61–70.

[23] Robert W. Kilpatrick, "Stigler on the Relationship Between Industrial Profit Rates

5. Skeptics argue that the relationship can be explained by nothing more than luck, luck being the source of both high concentration and high profit. Yet this, too, has been answered by both counterargument and evidence.[24]

6. Skeptics claim that interindustry or intermarket comparisons of profits are irrelevant because they indicate nothing about what would happen to profits if concentration *within* an industry or market *changed*. Policy, they say, brings changes, not comparisons. In reply, it appears that cross-section results are not deceiving. Direct estimates of the effects of change support the positive relationship.[25]

7. Finally, and most important, skeptics claim that the positive relationship arises *not* because concentration *raises prices* relative to costs, but rather because concentration is fostered by *efficiencies* which *reduce costs* relative to prices. This "efficiency hypothesis" is depicted in panel (c) of Figure 21–3, where profit margins rise with greater concentration because cost per unit falls. This hypothesis is sharply refuted by the abundant evidence of *positive* associations between concentration and *price* level reviewed earlier (pages 307–314). That evidence supports relations of the (a) or (b) variety in Figure 21–3, not (c). Still, this hypothesis has received such great attention that two specifics regarding it deserve elaboration.

   a. *First*, there is some evidence that the positive association between profits and concentration holds for large firms but not small firms. If one *assumes* that *all* firms within a given concentrated industry would benefit proportionately from any price collusion, then it can be argued that *all* firms — big and small — should experience a positive association between concentration and profits. The evidence of different profit experiences by size of firm thus allegedly supports the efficiency hypothesis. There are several problems with this line of argument, however: (i) Even if we accept the evidence of differences by size as valid, the assumption of equal proportionate benefit from collusion can be stoutly challenged. Price collusion may retard the exit of inefficient small firms or attract their entry, yielding size differences in observed profit rates without supporting the efficiency hypothesis.[26] (ii) The profit differences favoring large size may be ques-

and Market Concentration," *Journal of Political Economy* (May/June 1968), pp. 479–488.

[24] R. E. Caves, B. T. Gale, and M. E. Porter, "Interfirm Profitability Differences: Comment," *Quarterly Journal of Economics* (November 1977), pp. 667–675; and P. S. Albin and R. E. Alcaly, "Stochastic Determinants of Interfirm Profitability Differences," *Review of Economics and Statistics* (November 1979), pp. 615–618.

[25] Keith Cowling and Michael Waterson, "Price-Cost Margins and Market Structure," *Economica* (August 1976), pp. 267–274; and Maury N. Harris, "Entry and Long-Term Trends in Industry Performance," *Antitrust Bulletin* (Summer 1976), pp. 295–314.

[26] L. Hannah and J. A. Kay, *Concentration in Modern Industry* (London: Macmillan, 1977), p. 21; Robert J. Stonebraker, "Corporate Profits and the Risk of Entry," *Review of Economics and Statistics* (February 1976), pp. 33–39; M. E. Porter, "The Structure Within

tioned directly. Much evidence indicates *no* systematic differences by size for most industries. And where the differences do favor the largest firms, concentration does not commonly follow.[27]

b. A *second* brand of evidence said to support the efficiency hypothesis is the finding, noted earlier, that concentration's impact on profits often fades when data for individual firms are used and when *market shares* of the firms are included in the analysis. High market share generates high profits, draining concentration of significance. This might suggest that high profits are not due to high concentration but rather to high market shares based on economies of scale, superior products, and good management—for example, efficiency. However, problems plague this evidence, too. In particular, to the extent market share is positively associated with profitability, *market power* is usually the explanation for that positive effect, not efficiency. Earlier we reviewed evidence confirming a positive association between *price* and market share (pages 443–445), something inconsistent with the efficiency hypothesis.[28] Statistical analyses of what determines market shares find little association between cost efficiency and market share.[29] On the contrary, market share appears to be more heavily determined by factors indicative of market power—for example, advertising intensity, product proliferation, image, and innovation. Hence the positive correlation between market share and profit, to the extent there is one, appears to be due to market power reflected in market share

---

Industries and Companies' Performance," *Review of Economics and Statistics* (May 1979), pp. 214–227; and R. T. Masson and J. Shaanan, "Stochastic-Dynamic Limit Pricing: An Empirical Test," *Review of Economics and Statistics* (August 1982), pp. 413–422.

[27] M. Marcus, "Profitability and Size of Firm," *Review of Economics and Statistics* (February 1969), pp. 104–107; Ronald S. Bond and Warren Greenberg, "Industry Structure, Market Rivalry, and Public Policy: A Comment," *Journal of Law & Economics* (April 1976), pp. 201–204; F. M. Scherer, "The Causes and Consequences of Rising Industrial Concentration: A Comment," *Journal of Law & Economics* (April 1979), pp. 191–208; and Richard E. Caves and Thomas A. Pugel, *Intraindustry Differences in Conduct and Performance*, Monograph 1980-2, Series in Finance and Economics (New York: New York University, Graduate School of Business Administration, 1980); Louis Amato and Ronald P. Wilder, "The Effects of Firm Size on Profit Rates in U.S. Manufacturing, *Southern Economic Journal* (July 1985), pp. 181–190; and Louis Amato and Ronald P. Wilder, "Market Concentration, Efficiency, and Antitrust Policy: Demsetz Revisited," *Quarterly Journal of Business and Economics*, Vol. 27 (1988), pp. 3–19.

[28] See especially, John C. Hilke and Philip B. Nelson, "Strategic Behavior and Attempted Monopolization: The Coffee Case," in *The Antitrust Revolution*, edited by John E. Kwoka, Jr., and Lawrence J. White, (Glenview, Ill.: Scott, Foresman, 1989), pp. 208–231; Ronald W. Cotterill, "Market Power in the Retail Food Industry: Evidence from Vermont," *Review of Economics and Statistics* (August 1986), pp. 379–386.

[29] Robert Jacobson and David A. Aaker, "Is Market Share All That It's Cracked Up to Be?" *Journal of Marketing* (Fall 1985), pp. 11–22; and Robert F. Allen and Allan Scott Hagin, "Scale Related Efficiencies as a (Minor) Source of Profit-Market Share Relationship," *Review of Economics and Statistics* (August 1989), pp. 523–526.

rather than efficiencies underlying market share[30] For example, Gillette's sparkling image and 65% share of the shaving market give it profit margins of 32% on Atra and Trac II razors. But Gillette's deodorants have only 16% of their market plus fierce competition from Mennen, Procter & Gamble, and others, so there its profits margins stink.[31] To be sure, efficiency may be part of the cause, and in some cases the main cause, but, as a general proposition, the efficiency hypothesis cannot overthrow the market power hypothesis on the basis of available evidence.[32] In short, the positive concentration-profit relationship stands up under scrutiny (so Aristotle can rest in peace). Still, two qualifications attend it. *First, high concentration does not always produce high profits, largely because market power finds expression in higher costs and lower risk as well as higher prices, and these shrink monopoly profits. Second, to the extent single firm market power is at work instead of collective/collusive power, firm market share is a better measure for the profit relationship than concentration. Market share apparently embodies power in product differentiation, first mover position, and the like, although efficiencies contribute sometimes.*

The Effect of Other Elements of Market Power on Profit. It has already been shown that, besides concentration, advertising intensity is often positively associated with profits. What about other elements of market power? They too have been tested. They too make big contributions.

Barriers to Entry. If entry were free and easy, excess profits would evaporate regardless of concentration level. Thus, in theory, high barriers should boost profits (everything else being equal).

This expectation has been borne out by the data. One early study, for instance, found that among 21 highly concentrated industries those with "very high barriers" averaged 16.4% profit on equity, whereas those with "moderate-to-low" barriers averaged only 11.9% profit on equity.[33]

30 Ibid., Dennis C. Mueller, *Profits in the Long Run* (Cambridge: Cambridge University Press), pp. 50–84; Ariel Pakes, "Mueller's Profits in the Long Run," *Rand Journal of Economics* (Summer 1987), pp. 319–332; Margaret E. Slade, "Conjectures, Firm Characteristics, and Market Structure: An Empirical Assessment," *International Journal of Industrial Organization* (December 1986), pp. 347–370; Paul K. Gorecki, "The Importance of Being First," *International Journal of Industrial Organization* (December 1986), pp. 371–395; and Stephen A. Rhoades, "Market Share as a Source of Market Power: Implications and Some Evidence," *Journal of Economics and Business*, Vol. 37 (1985), pp. 343–363.

31 *Business Week*, April 25, 1988, p. 85.

32 For evidence of mixed effects, see Roger Clarke, Stephen Davies, and Michael Waterson, "The Profitability-Concentration Relation: Market Power or Efficiency?" *Journal of Industrial Economics* (June 1984), pp. 435–450; and Stephen Martin, "Market Power and/or Efficiency?" *Review of Economics and Statistics* (May 1988), pp. 331–335. See also Louis Amato and Ronald Wilder, "Firm and Industry Effects in Industrial Economics," *Southern Economic Journal* (July 1990), pp. 93–105.

33 H. Michael Mann, "Seller Concentration, Barriers to Entry, and Rates of Return in Thirty Industries, 1950–1960," *Review of Economics and Statistics* (August 1966), pp. 296–307.

More recent studies have used more refined measures of entry barriers. All in all, they also indicate that high barriers hoist profitability.[34]

One of the most fascinating recent studies is by Robert Stonebraker.[35] He hypothesizes that the risk faced by the small firms occupying market fringes "can be thought of as the vehicle through which entry barriers work." He reasons that "Most entry occurs on a small scale and entrepreneurs are likely to estimate the risk of entering an industry on the basis of the performance of existing small firms." To test this hypothesis Stonebraker devised two measures of risk for the small firms in each of 33 industries: (1) the *percentage* of observed small-firm profit rates falling below normal competitive profit, multiplied by the average *distance* these returns fall below the competitive profit rate and (2) an index of failure frequency. As it turns out, these measures of small-firm risk plus industry growth "explain" more than 60% of the interindustry differences in large, established-firm profits. Simply stated, the *worse* the profit experience of small firms, the *better* the profit experience of their rival large firms. In other words, small-firm risk apparently protects large-firm profit from entry erosion by serving as a warning beacon to would-be entrants. (Stonebraker also probed the causes of small-firm risk. Interestingly, advertising intensity was the single most important factor — higher advertising causing greater risk.)

Imports. As anyone who has "priced" Japanese television sets or purchased a foreign car knows, imports provide competition for domestic producers. Indeed, they are a form of entry. To see whether such competition affects profit performance, researchers have included import volume in statistical analyses of profits. The results? In general, heavy inbound ocean traffic does seem to mean greater competition because domestic industry profits are inversely related to import volume.[36] (The converse is also true; exports are often positively associated with profit performance.)

Summary. It appears that the answer to our first question is "yes."

See also Joe Bain, who pioneered this kind of research, *Barriers to New Competition* (Cambridge, Mass.: Harvard University Press, 1956).

[34] Harris, "Entry and Long-Term Trends in Industry Performance"; Caves, Khalilzadeh-Shirazi, and Porter, "Scale Economies in Statistical Analyses of Market Power"; Masson and Shaanan "Stochastic-Dynamic Limit Pricing"; William S. Comanor and Thomas A. Wilson, "Advertising, Market Structure, and Performance," *Review of Economics and Statistics* (November 1967), pp. 423–440; and Dale Orr, "An Index of Entry Barriers and its Application to the Structure Performance Relationship," *Journal of Industrial Economics* (September 1974), p. 39–49.

[35] Stonebraker, "Corporate Profits and the Risk of Entry," pp. 33–39.

[36] L. Esposito and F. F. Esposito, "Foreign Competition and Domestic Industry Profitability," *Review of Economics and Statistics* (November 1971), pp. 343–353; Gambeles, "Structural Determinants of Private Performance"; E. Pagoulatos and R. Sorensen, "International Trade, International Investment and Industrial Profitability," *Southern Economic Journal* (January 1976), pp. 425–434; and H. P. Marvel, "Foreign Trade and Domestic Competition," *Economic Inquiry* (January 1980), pp. 103–122.

There is a positive association between market power (variously measured) and profitability. This does *not* mean you should rush to telephone your stockbroker. Your purchase of ownership shares in GM, IBM, or some other behemoth will not guarantee you fantastic returns. More than likely your rate of return will be no more than normal because the prices of powerful firms' stocks are inflated. Expected excess profits are quickly *capitalized* into higher market prices for equity shares.[37] Riches arise mainly in the *process* of this capitalization. Hence, only early-bird owners (and their heirs) catch the worms of wealth. However, this *does* mean that the questions still pending concerning allocation efficiency and wealth distribution deserve careful attention.

C. What Is the Welfare Loss Due to Monopolistic Misallocation?

When the shaded triangle in Figure 21-1 is calculated for individual industries then tallied across the economy, what is the result? Arnold Harberger, over 30 years ago, was the first to attempt an estimate. Using 1920s data for the manufacturing industries and a series of bold assumptions, he concluded that welfare loss amounted to a piddling 0.06% of that portion of gross national product coming from manufacturing. For the economy as a whole, his estimate was a mere 0.1% of GNP.[38] These calculations led many to dismiss the monopoly problem as trifling. As one commentator quipped, this welfare loss would only be "enough to treat every family in the land to a steak dinner at a good (monopolistically competitive) restaurant."[39].

Subsequent researchers have criticized Harberger's procedures and assumptions as being biased downward. Among other things, it has been argued that Harberger's assumed price elasticities of demand were too low, that his assumed normal profit rate of return was too high, and that his study was limited to partial equilibrium conditions. Subsequent researchers have attempted to correct these shortcomings in various ways, and virtually all subsequent estimates of welfare loss are substantially greater than Harberger's. Most are 10 to 20 times greater. Yet, Harberger's estimates were so tiny that these multiples likewise yield relatively low numbers. Check the following estimates expressed as a percentage of GNP — Scherer's, 0.5–2%; Shepherd's, 2–3%; Worcester's, 0.4–0.7%; Carson's, 3.2%, at most; and Bergson's 2–4% (as interpreted by Worcester).[40]

---

[37] Timothy G. Sullivan, "A Note on Market Power and Returns to Stockholders," *Review of Economics and Statistics* (February 1977), pp. 108–113.

[38] Arnold C. Harberger, "Monopoly and Resource Allocation," *American Economic Review* (May 1954), pp. 77–87.

[39] F. M. Scherer, *Industrial Market Structure and Economic Performance* (Chicago: Rand McNally, 1970), p. 402.

[40] Ibid., p. 404; William G. Shepherd, *Market Power and Economic Welfare* (New York: Random House, 1970), p. 198; Dean A. Worcester, Jr., "New Estimates of the Welfare Loss

These more recent estimates are still small, but they should be qualified by three observations. First, *by its very nature* the percentage computation yields small estimates. Only a *portion* of industry suffers any loss at all. Furthermore, within the noncompetitive portion, the percentage loss is computed by comparing a fairly small triangle to a typically large total revenue. Table 21–2 presents a numerical example assuming unit elasticity, a price increase of 25% due to oligopoly, and constant costs equal to the purely competitive price of $1.00. Under oligopoly, price is $1.25; quantity is 800,000 units; total industry revenue is $1,000,000; and excess profit is the price differential, $0.25 times 800,000. The welfare loss triangle is one-half of the price differential (½ × 0.25) times the quantity differential (1,000,000–800,000 = 200,000), or $25,000. Dividing this by the oligopoly's total revenue of $1,000,000 to reckon loss in percentage terms yields 2.5%. If this hypothetical oligopoly amounted to as much as half of the total economy, then loss as a percentage of GNP would be only half of that, or 1.25%. Thus the percentage loss is *inherently* small. But our second observation is that a small percentage loss can be quite large when translated into absolute dollars; 1% of a $4 trillion GNP would be $40 billion per year (enough to keep college students, or even their colleges, out of rags). Finally, these are merely *static* losses. The *dynamic* losses due to monopoly power — losses like reduced invention, innovation, and economic growth — could well be much greater.[41] (See Chapter 23.)

D. What Is Market Power's Contribution to the Above-Average Wealth of the Wealthy?

William Comanor and Robert Smiley have done more than anyone "to estimate the impact of the past and current enterprise monopoly profits on the distribution of household wealth in the United States."[42] The task is not an easy one. The distributive consequences of excess profit depend on a number of complex factors — on, among other things, (1) how

---

to Monopoly, United States: 1956–1969," *Southern Economic Journal* (October 1973), pp. 234–245; and R. Carson, D. A. Worcester, Jr., and Abram Bergson, "On Monopoly Welfare Losses: Comments and Reply," *American Economic Review* (December 1975), pp. 1008–1031. The highest estimates, 4–13% of gross corporate product, are by Keith Cowling and Dennis Mueller, "The Social Costs of Monopoly Power," *Economic Journal* (December 1978), pp. 727–748; see also *Economic Journal* (September 1981), pp. 721–725. Interestingly, Masson and Shaanan find *actual* losses for their sample of industries to be 2.9%, and they estimate losses of 11.6% *if pure monopoly* prevailed. Hence, the beneficial effect of competition in these industries, to the extent it's present, is a welfare savings of 8.7%. See Robert T. Masson and Joseph Shaanan, "Social Costs of Oligopoly and the Value of Competition," *Economic Journal* (September 1984), pp. 520–535.

[41] For a good book on this point, see Mancur Olson, *The Rise and Decline of Nations* (New Haven, Conn.: Yale University Press, 1982); See also F. M. Scherer, "Antitrust, Efficiency, and Progress," *New York University Law Review* (November 1987), pp. 995–1019.

[42] William S. Comanor and Robert H. Smiley, "Monopoly and the Distribution of Wealth," *Quarterly Journal of Economics* (May 1975), pp. 174–194. See also Smiley's "Survey"

TABLE 21–2.　Computation of Welfare Loss in a
Hypothetical Industry

	Pure Competition	Oligopoly
Price	$P_c = \$1.00$	$P_m = \$1.25$
Quantity	$Q_c = \$1,000,000$	$Q_m = 800,000$
Total revenue	$P_c \times Q_c = \$1,000,000$	$P_m \times Q_m = \$1,000,000$
Excess profit	zero	$\$0.25 \times Q_m = \$200,000$
Dollar welfare loss	zero	$\frac{1}{2} \times 0.25 \, (Q_c - Q_m) = \$25,000$
Loss as percentage of revenue	zero	2.5%

much profit is excessive, (2) who pays the excess profit, (3) who receives
the excess profit, and (4) duration of monopoly. Accordingly, Comanor
and Smiley draw heavily upon certain estimates of others and several
simplifying assumptions. Examples follow:

1. They estimate that excess profit (not welfare loss) amounts to 3%
   of GNP and assume this to have held since 1890, the first year of
   their cumulative computation. As an alternative they also use 2%.
2. They make two alternative assumptions concerning who pays: (a)
   payments are proportional to the distribution of consumption expenditure, or (b) the rich spend relatively *more* of their budget on
   monopolistic goods.
3. As regards who receives, they assume that monopoly gains are
   distributed in proportion to the distribution of business ownership claims. This means that wealthy owners are no more or less
   likely to be monopoly owners than poor owners, a conservative
   assumption.
4. They assume that the gains are quickly capitalized and perpetu-
   ated to some degree by inheritance.

The results are striking. The wealthiest 2.4% of all households *actually* accounts for slightly more that 40% of total wealth. Under the 3%
excess profit assumption, an *absence* of monopoly power would reduce
this share to "somewhere between 16.6% and 27.5%, which would represent *a decline of nearly 50%* in their share of total household wealth."[43]
In addition, an absence of monopoly would elevate the wealth of the
poorest families by significant multiples. Comanor and Smiley conclude

---

in J. J. Siegfried (ed.), *The Economics of Firm Size, Market Structure, and Social Performance*
(Washington, D.C.: Federal Trade Commission, July 1980), pp. 90–103; and S. A. Rhoades,
"Welfare Loss, Redistribution Effect, and Restriction of Output due to Monopoly in Bank-
ing," *Journal of Monetary Economics* (1982), pp. 375–387.

[43] Comanor and Smiley, "Monopoly and the Distribution of Wealth," p. 191, emphasis added.

therefore that "past and current monopoly has had a major impact on the current degree of inequality in this distribution [of wealth]."

Converting these numbers into something concrete, we may note that the monopoly power of the old Standard Oil Company of New Jersey (broken up in 1911) generated a fortune for John D. Rockefeller that in today's dollars would be more than *$9 billion*.[44]

II. MARKET POWER AND LABOR EARNINGS

A. General Introduction

Excess profits are not the only source of higher prices and lost consumers' surplus. Other price-increasing excesses are associated with market power. Table 21–3 illustrates the point with data from grocery retailing. Column (1) is four-firm concentration in local markets. Columns (2) and (3) give a price index and profit as a percentage of sales. The last two columns are not perfectly comparable because the data underlying them differ. Nevertheless, to the extent these columns are comparable, they are instructive. Prices clearly rise with concentration. But they rise *much more* than profit. If the price increase of 5.3% associated with an increase in concentration from 40 to 70 were due entirely to profit, then profit would have gone from 0.37 to 5.4% of sales. But this is *not* the case. The observed jump in profit is from 0.37 to 1.28% of sales. Quite clearly, *costs* are rising with concentration as well as *profit*.

The separate cost and profit effects may be illustrated theoretically in Figure 21–4. Let $0P_m$ and $0C_m$ be a monopolist's price and cost per unit, respectively. Then profit per unit is the difference between P_m and C_m. With monopoly output equal $0Q_m$, total excess profit is area P_mABC_m. The deadweight welfare loss associated with this excess profit is shaded triangle ABH. Thus, in terms of lost consumers' surplus, the combined **profit effect** is represented by trapezoid P_mAHC_m, part of which is transfer and part of which disappears. The preceding sections discussed these profit effects. Were there nothing more in monopoly power, the establishment of competition would merely reduce price to C_m and expand output to Q_n, adding P_mAHC_m to consumers' surplus.

The **cost effect** is seen by first drawing a distinction between monopoly cost C_m and competitive cost C_c. If monopoly power raises costs as well as profits, then establishment of competition will reduce price from P_m to C_c, since competitive price will match competitive cost C_c. This is obviously a much greater price reduction than from P_m to C_m. The social gains from competition are correspondingly greater. Elimination of the

---

[44] *The Wall Street Journal*, February 11, 1983, p. 38.

TABLE 21–3. Estimated Index of Grocery Prices and Pretax Profit to Sales Ratios Associated with Various Levels of Concentration*

(1) Four-Firm Concentration Ratio	(2) Index of Grocery Prices	(3) Profits as Per Cent of Sales
40	100.0	0.37
50	101.0	0.99
60	103.0	1.22
70	105.3	1.28

* This assumes "relative firm market share" of 10.

Source: B. W. Marion, W. F. Mueller, R. W. Cotterill, F. E. Geithman, and J. R. Schmelzer, *The Profit and Price Performance of Leading Food Chains, 1970–74*, A Study for the Joint Economic Committee, U.S. Congress, 95th Cong., 1st Sess. (1977), p. 77.

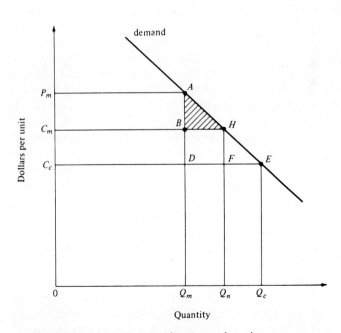

FIGURE 21–4. Cost implications of market power.

excess cost adds to consumers' surplus an area represented by trapezoid C_mHEC_c in Figure 21–4.

In sum, introduction of competition adds P_mAHC_m from the profit effect *plus* C_mHEC_c from the cost effect. Together these represent a total gain in consumers' surplus amounting to area P_mAEC_c. Stated in terms of loss rather than gain, this area represents the total loss in consumers' surplus due to monopoly, when both cost and profit effects are present. As before, this total welfare loss can be divided into different kinds of losses depending on the *destination* of the loss. Generally speaking, there are four possibilities, two of which should by now be familiar:

1. *Deadweight loss:* First and most obvious is a deadweight loss represented by triangle ADE in Figure 21–4. This is much greater than the deadweight loss associated with excess profit alone (which is ABH), because there is an additional deadweight loss due to higher cost (represented by trapezoid $BHED$). Estimates of this loss are therefore *under*estimates if based on profit alone. As explained earlier, this deadweight loss arises from *allocation inefficiency*. Quantity Q_m is less than the optimal quantity Q_c.

2. *Profit transfer:* A portion of the lost consumers' surplus again goes to excess profit. This is represented by P_mABC_m. Our earlier discussion and estimates of this effect could be reapplied here. Though a loss to consumers, this represents a gain to owners with *distributive consequences*.

3. *Cost that is transfer:* The added total cost of producing $0Q_m$, represented by C_mBDC_c, can take two possible forms. One is excess factor remuneration. Management or labor (or some other factor) may be overpaid at the expense of owners or consumers or both. The overpayments, or "rents," are analogous to excess profit. They are higher than what is necessary to keep the favored factor committed to the industry. Thus, managers may take advantage of the imperfect control stockholders have over the typical large firm to raise managerial salaries or pad expense accounts. On labor's side, it has been argued that unionized workers extract higher pay from concentrated than from unconcentrated industries. As in the case of excess profit, these several excesses may have significant *distributive consequences* depending on the financial strengths of the beneficiaries and the financial weaknesses of the owners or consumers who ultimately pay the higher costs.

4. *Cost that is waste:* A second cost element and the final destination of lost consumers' surplus is *technical inefficiency* or *X-inefficiency*— that is, the use of more labor, more materials, and more resources than are necessary to produce a given output. This X-inefficiency also shows up in space C_mBDC_c. Monopoly could easily give rise to such waste because, in a word, market power permits "slack."

Moreover, it has been argued that monopoly power fosters waste because those who seek such power must expend resources to get it and keep it. Thus resources are burned up when established oligopolists escalate their advertising outlays to fight off new entrants. And labor time spent running cartels is a real cost. (These are often called "rent-seeking" expenses.)[45]

Of these four destinations of lost consumers' surplus, the first two have already been traced. The remainder of this chapter is about the last two, which share area C_mBDC_c in Figure 21–4. Excess wages are taken up first, then X-inefficiency. We shall not explore managerial salaries further, so we should at least mention here that high concentration and high barriers to entry apparently do boost top executives' compensation.[46]

B. Unions, Concentration, and Wages

To some degree labor markets are much like product markets. They have demands and supplies; they have power problems, and so on. What, then, causes the wage rate of a steelworker to exceed the combined hourly earnings of a Greek philosopher and a McDonald's counter attendant? Researchers have uncovered a vast array of variables affecting relative wage earnings. These include skill level, productivity, geographic location, plant size, value of product produced, education, scholastic achievement, work conditions, race, sex, risk to life and limb, and legal regulations. To determine the influence of unionism on the labor supply side or concentration on the labor demand side, these and other factors must first be accounted for. As with price and profit research, there are many ways to skin this cat. Most of them are variants of multiple regression analysis, which allows researchers to control for "other" factors.

The market power hypotheses that have been so tested may be divided into three classes: (1) the wage impact of unionism; (2) the wage impact of product market concentration; and (3) the *interactive* effect of unions *and* product market concentration.

1. Impact of Unions on Wages. The hypotheses concerning unionism alone are most obvious. Workers unionize, that is, join together, to speak with one voice, threaten to walk out as one group, and restrict labor supply to one source so that they can demand and obtain higher wages than would otherwise be paid. To the extent unions succeed in raising members' wages they may be simultaneously *reducing* nonunion wages. The usual measure of union impact is therefore *relative* wage, the

45. R. A. Posner, "The Social Costs of Monopoly and Regulation," *Journal of Political Economy* (August 1975), pp. 807–827.

46 Oliver E. Williamson, *The Economics of Discretionary Behavior: Managerial Objectives in A Theory of the Firm* (Chicago: Markham, 1967), pp. 129–134.

union wage compared to nonunion wage (everything else held constant).

The most widely cited estimate of union impact is that of H. G. Lewis, who reckoned that for the period 1957–1958 unions enjoyed a relative wage advantage somewhere in the neighborhood of 10–15%.[47] Subsequent studies using better data have estimated still larger union-nonunion wage differentials.[48] One, for example, estimated average differentials for "craftsmen" and "operatives" of about 30%.[49] Another estimated union-nonunion wage differentials ranging between 16% and 25%.[50] Of course not all unions are equally powerful, and these estimates must be qualified by the observation that weak unions, such as the United Farm Workers, tend to gain very little, whereas particularly strong unions, such as the United Steelworkers, may achieve relative wages even above the 25–30% range.[51]

2. The Wage Impact of Product Market Concentration.   The impact of concentration is more complicated. Theories concerning the impact of product market concentration yield ambiguous indications. On the one hand, high concentration might foster high wages for reasons of "ability to pay." These reasons are (1) the ability of concentrated industries to pass excess wage costs on to customers and (2) the ability to pay excess wages out of excess profits. On the other hand, ability to pay does not necessarily dictate actuality. Many oligopolists may be able but *un*willing to pay extra. In particular, concentration in the product market often means there is concentration on the employer's side of the labor market as well—that is, there are few purchasers of that type of labor. And conventional theory predicts that monopsony (or oligopsony) power will depress wage rates rather than lift them. Thus with conflicting theories, it boils down to an empirical question.

Empirically, a few studies show no association between concentration and wage rates. A few show a positive association only at certain

[47] H. G. Lewis, *Unionism and Relative Wages in the United States* (Chicago: University of Chicago Press, 1963).

[48] Frank Stafford, "Concentration and Labor Earnings: Comment," *American Economic Review* (March 1968), pp. 174–180; Victor Fuchs, *The Service Economy* (New York: National Bureau of Economic Research, 1968), Chapter 6; and Adrian Throop, "The Union-Nonunion Wage Differential and Cost Push Inflation." *American Economic Review* (March 1968), pp. 79–99.

[49] Leonard W. Weiss, "Concentration and Labor Earnings," *American Economic Review* (March 1966), pp. 96–117.

[50] Sherwin Rosen, "On the Interindustry Wage and Hours Structure," *Journal of Political Economy* (March 1969), pp. 249–273; "Trade Union Power, Threat Effects and the Extent of Organization," *Review of Economic Studies* (April 1969), pp. 185–196. See also Lawrence M. Kahn, "Unionism and Relative Wages: Direct and Indirect Effects," *Industrial and Labor Relations Review* (July 1979), pp. 520–532.

[51] For surveys, see Belton M. Fleisher and T. J. Kniesner, *Labor Economics*, 3rd ed. (Englewood Cliffs, N. J.: Prentice-Hall, 1984), Chapter 7; and H. G. Lewis, *Union Relative Wage Effects: A Survey* (Chicago: University of Chicago Press, 1986).

times or under certain conditions.[52] Most studies of this sort, however, show wages rising significantly with concentration after accounting for all other factors influencing wages, including personal characteristics of the workers like age and education level.[53] Perhaps the most interesting of these studies is by Dale Belman and Leonard Weiss. They find a direct and indirect effect on wages from concentration. The direct effect is the effect of concentration alone. The indirect effect arises because high concentration fosters a higher incidence of unionism than otherwise, and as we have just seen unionism raises wages. Belman and Weiss estimate that, directly, a 10% increase in concentration raises wages between 1% and 2%. The added, indirect effect of concentration nearly matches these numbers. So the combined total effect of a 10% increase in concentration could be an increase in wages of almost 4%.[54]

What about the few studies showing no effect on concentration on wages? These may be muddled by monopsony effects, where the concentration ratio is not only reflecting product market power but also some monopsony power in the labor market. Careful studies of monopsony show that it can have a negative wage impact in some instances.[55]

3. Interactive Impact. A moment's reflection reveals why the preceding discussion of unionism and product market concentration is incomplete. It treats unionism and concentration independently. In fact, they are not independent. They are interactive. The influence of one often depends on the strength of the other. Consider unionization first. *The positive wage impact of unions is likely to be meager where concentration is low but great where concentration is high.* The main reason for this is that competitive firms tend to lack both the ability and the inclination to pay

[52] L. W. Weiss, "Concentration and Labor Earnings," *American Economic Review* (March 1966), pp. 96–117; Charles T. Haworth and Carol Reuther, "Industry Concentration and Interindustry Wage Determination," *Review of Economics and Statistics* (February 1978), pp. 85–95; and Thomas A. Pugel, "Profitability, Concentration, and Interindustry Variation in Wages," *Review of Economics and Statistics* (May 1980), pp. 248–253.

[53] Ira Horowitz, "An International Comparison of the Effects of Concentration on Industry Wages, Investment, and Sales," *Journal of Industrial Economics* (April 1971), pp. 166–178; J. A. Dalton and E. J. Ford, Jr., "Concentration and Labor Earnings in Manufacturing and Utilities," *Industrial and Labor Relations Review* (October 1977), pp. 45–60; John Kwoka, Jr., "Monopoly, Plant, and Union Effects on Worker Wages," *Industrial and Labor Relations Review*, Vol. 36 (1983), pp. 251–257; C. Lawrence and R. Lawrence, "Relative Wages in U.S. Manufacturing: An Endgame Interpretation," *Brookings Papers on Economic Activity* (1985), pp. 47–106; and William T. Dickens and Lawrence F. Katz, "Inter-Industry Wage Differences and Industry Characteristics," in *Unemployment and the Structure of Labor Markets*, edited by Kevin Lang and Jonathan S. Leonard (New York: Basil Blackwell, 1987), pp. 48–89.

[54] Dale Belman and Leonard W. Weiss, "Concentration and Wages: Direct and Indirect Effects," *Review of Economics and Statistics* (August 1988), pp. 391–397.

[55] John H. Landon, "The Effect of Product-Market Concentration on Wage Levels: An Intraindustry Approach," *Industrial and Labor Relations Review* (January 1970), pp. 237–247; and J. H. Landon and R. N. Baird, "Monopsony in the Market for Public School Teachers," *American Economic Review* (December 1971), pp. 966–971.

excess wage rates. Even if all existing firms in a competitive industry are unionized, the threat of fairly easy nonunion entry may check the union's power. Hence, unions are likely to have greater positive wage impact in oligopoly industries, where employers act more nearly in unison, have the financial means to meet union demands, and enjoy substantial protection from interlopers.

Turning things around, the impact of product market concentration probably depends on the presence or absence of a strong union on the labor side. Assuming the incidence of monopsony power is positively associated with product market concentration, high concentration is more likely to depress wages in the absence of a union than in the presence of a union. Substantial buyer power, when unchecked by countervailing seller power, could have this effect. Introduction of a union, however, places power on *both* sides of the labor market. In the extreme, this creates "bilateral monopoly." And, in theory, the resulting wage is logically indeterminant. The union wants a high wage. The monopsonistic employers want a low wage. The resulting wage could be anywhere in between, depending on relative bargaining power. This suggests that the impact of concentration may be largely indeterminant, given union presence. On the other hand, it could be argued that wages will be positively associated with concentration under unionism. For reasons given earlier, such as "ability to pay," high concentration plus unionism is more likely to yield higher wages than is low concentration plus unionism.

Empirical exploration of these complex interactive effects is very difficult. One of the best studies to date is that of Wallace Hendricks.[56] He used disaggregated plant-level data on wage rates paid by 450 manufacturing firms in 47 different industries during 1970–1971. The wage rates used were wages per hour for specific occupations (for example, electrician, machinist, and painter). The results were broadly similar for all nine occupations studied, but Hendricks gives janitors special attention because the impact of market power was better isolated for them than for any other group. These results are summarized in Table 21–4. Concentration and unionism are each divided into three groups—low, moderate, and high. The numbers in the body of the table are *percentage* comparisons, where the low concentration and low unionism category is used as the basis for comparison. Thus, where unionism and concentration are both high, wages are 19.5% higher, on average, than those under low-low conditions. The interactive effects may be seen by comparing the effects of unionism under alternative concentration conditions, then comparing concentration effects under alternative unioniza-

[56] Wallace Hendricks, "Labor Market Structure and Union Wage Levels," *Economic Inquiry* (September 1975), pp. 401–416. For European corroboration, see A. P. Jacquemin and H. W. de Jong, *European Industrial Organization* (New York: John Wiley, 1977), p. 145. For a Canadian study see Wayne Simpson "Unions, Industrial Concentration and Wages: A Re-examination," *Applied Economics* (March 1986), pp. 305–317.

TABLE 21–4.   Impact of Product Market Concentration
and Unionism on Hourly Wage Rates: Percent Comparisons

| Concentration | Unionism | | |
	Low	Moderate	High
Low	0% (base)	0.9%	9.3%
Moderate	7.0	14.1	13.6
High	−8.0	10.6	19.5

Source: Calculated from Wallace Hendricks, "Labor Market Structure and Union Wage Levels," *Economic Inquiry* (September 1975), pp. 401–416.

tion conditions. Thus, unionism generally has a *positive* impact, but the *magnitude* of impact is much smaller where concentration is low than where it is high. High unionism raises wages 9.3 percentage points where concentration is low. But where concentration is high, the difference between high and low unionism is 27.5 percentage points (moving from −8.0 to +19.5).

As for concentration, it carries a positive then ultimately *negative* impact on wages where unionism is low, suggesting that monopsony power dominates where concentration is really high and unionism is low. On the other hand, concentration has an unambiguously *positive influence* on wages where unionism is high. In this latter case, wages are about 10 percentage points greater for high over low concentration (19.5 versus 9.3).

It appears from these data, then, that interactive effects do prevail. Although this makes generalizations hazardous, it can be concluded that *union power usually raises wages.* As regards concentration, it can go either way. But because concentration seems to foster unionism (the positive correlation in manufacturing runs in the 0.4–0.7 range), and because more often than not concentration's direct impact is positive, it may be concluded that, on balance, *high concentration produces relatively high wages.*

With high wages being associated with high concentration and unionism in this manner, it appears that *unionized labor could be capturing some of the excess profits that would otherwise be going entirely to owners in highly concentrated industries.* This was suggested earlier in our comparison panels (a) and (b) in Figure 21–3 and in our discussion of Figure 21–4. Now the data of Table 21–5, which summarizes several recent studies of this issue, confirm this possibility.[57] These results reveal that

[57] For another study corroborating these results, but not comparable, see Michael A. Salinger, "Tobin's q, Unionization, and the Concentration-Profits Relationship," *Rand Journal of Economics* (Summer 1984), pp. 159–170.

TABLE 21–5.   The Effects of Unionism on Profitability (Price-Cost Margin) Depending on Concentration Level

| | Approximate Percentage Reduction in Profitability Due to Unionization (Versus No Union) | |
Study and Sample	Low Concentration	High Concentration*
All industries (Freeman & Medoff)	−7%	−21%
Manufacturing (Freeman & Medoff)	−1	−17
Manufacturing (Karier)†	−0	−34
Grocery retailing (Voos & Mishel)	−13	−66

*Definition of high concentration varies.

†To make Karier's estimate comparable to the others, it is assumed that, with high concentration, monopoly profits are one-half of total profits, measured in price-cost margins.

Sources: Richard B. Freeman and James L. Medoff, *What Do Unions Do?* (New York: Basic Books, 1984), p. 186; Thomas Karier, "Unions and Monopoly Profits," *Review of Economics and Statistics* (February 1985), pp. 34–42; and Paula B. Voos and Lawrence R. Mishel, "The Union Impact on Profits in the Supermarket Industry," *Review of Economics and Statistics* (August 1986), pp. 513–516.

when concentration is low, unionization of workers typically has very little negative impact on firm profits. However, when concentration is high, unionization has a substantial negative impact. *Price-cost margins in highly concentrated industries are 17–66% lower in the presence of labor unions than they would otherwise be.*

This is important. This means that *big chunks of the excess profits generated by product market monopoly power are going to workers in higher wages rather than to firms in excess profits (unionized workers in particular).* This is what Tables 21–4 and 21–5 say in English. Moreover, given the positive association between unionism and concentration, *studies of profits that do not take unions into account seriously underestimate the impact of monopoly on resource misallocation and resource transfers.* According to one estimate, "profit equations which omit the union variable are likely to underestimate the effect of concentration on profits by as much as 65%."[58] Little wonder, then, that many of the studies of concentration and profits referred to earlier found little or no positive association between concentration and profit despite the positive concentration-*price* relationship. The higher prices of market power go into higher costs for wages as well as higher profit. It appears that concentration's X-inefficiency causes higher costs too.

[58] Thomas Karier, "Unions and Monopoly Profits," *Review of Economics and Statistics* (February 1985), pp. 34–42.

III. X-INEFFICIENCY LOSSES DUE TO MARKET POWER

A. Introduction and Theory

X-inefficiency is a form of deadweight loss. Value is not merely transferred from one party to another; it is lost to all. This deadweight loss is, in a word, *waste*. According to Harvey Leibenstein, who coined the term, **X-inefficiency** means "the extent to which a given set of inputs do not get to be combined in such a way as to lead to maximum output."[59] When inputs are not producing the maximum output possible, there is error, inertia, spoilage, slovenliness, disorder, delay, ineptitude, or something similar. As a result, costs are higher than otherwise.

It should be stressed that the X-inefficiency concept is not necessarily, or even usually, applied to cost problems that could be cured by massive alterations of plant scale, by adoption of new technology, or by invention of new technology. Think of it rather as a problem of weak motivation and resource misallocation *internal* to the firm. Leibenstein points to the vast efficiency gains that plants and firms have achieved by "simple reorganizations of the production process such as plant-layout reorganization, materials handling, waste controls, work methods, and payments by results."[60] Viewed more broadly, X-inefficiency could reasonably include all forms of pure resource waste: excessive advertising, superfluous packaging, redundant plant capacity, and so on.

How does this dimension of performance relate to competition? We have already answered the question as it pertains to advertising and nonprice competition generally. As regards other forms of waste, theory postulates on at least two grounds that costs are *lower* whenever firms face intense competition:

> In the first place, the process of competition tends to eliminate high-cost producers, while the existence of substantial market power often allows such firms to remain in business. . . . Second, the process of competition, by mounting pressures on firm profits, tends to discipline managements *and employees* to utilize their inputs, and put forth more energetically and more effectively than is the case where this pressure is absent.[61]

In other words, the "carrot" of greater profits may dangle before all firms seeking to minimize cost, but only the "stick" swung by competition *forces* firms to pursue that objective.

---

[59] Harvey Leibenstein, "Competition and X-Efficiency," *Journal of Political Economy* (May 1973), p. 766.

[60] Harvey Leibenstein, *Beyond Economic Man* (Cambridge, Mass.: Harvard University Press, 1976), p. 37.

[61] W. S. Comanor and H. Leibenstein, "Allocative Efficiency, X-Efficiency and the Measurement of Welfare Losses," *Economica* (August 1969), p. 304.

B. Evidence

Tales of business woe constitute some of the most engrossing evidence to this effect. Large, powerful firms often coast merrily along until new entry, flagging demand, or some similar contingency leads to the discovery that costs can be cut drastically without cutting output by so much as one unit. You could build a bulky file of such evidence merely by reading *Business Week* and *Fortune*, from which the following examples are taken:

- Suffering from the slap of new entry and slipping profits, Xerox launched a cost-cutting drive for the *first time* in its history in 1975. Its chairman admitted that Xerox was suffering from "sloppy" internal practices and corporate "fat" that had developed during the easy days. Among other things the company fired 8000 employees, deferred construction of a lush new headquarters, sharpened its inventory control, and scrapped plans for a new plant, all while sales grew.[62]

- When Don Burnham took over as chief executive officer of Westinghouse in 1963, "the company was languishing on a five-year plateau of $2 billion in sales and earning only 5% on equity. By breaking organizational bottlenecks at the top, introducing more productive manufacturing processes, and slashing overhead, including more than 3000 people, Burnham doubled Westinghouse's return on equity within two years to 10%."[63]

- Shell Oil Company sustained some profit setbacks on worldwide operations during the 1960s, whereupon it discovered it could eliminate job duplication by consolidating its British and Dutch head offices and reduce its work force from 214,000 to 170,000 while increasing output. The result: labor cost savings of 32% per barrel.[64]

- For decades before the 1980s, Caterpillar dominated the heavy equipment industry: "Cat could push, crush, or roll over just about anything that got in its way. Competitors were too weak to be taken seriously. Customers were willing to pay fat premiums." Then in 1982 a slump in sales and a jump in Japanese competition shook the company. Cat closed factories, pruned payrolls, eliminated levels of

---

[62] *Business Week*, April 5, 1976, pp. 60–66. In 1980 Japanese competition forced Xerox into *another* cost-cutting campaign. By 1983 it had squeezed $176 million out of excess inventory, reduced overhead spending by $200 million annually, and trimmed its work force to 12,000, down from 18,000 in 1980, all while output remained unchanged. See Gary Jacobson and John Hillkirk, *Xerox: American Samurai* (New York: Macmillan, 1986), pp. 233–235.

[63] *Business Week*, July 20, 1974, p. 56.

[64] *Business Week*, March 8, 1969, pp. 56–57.

hierarchy in its management, and otherwise revamped. By 1988 it was earning record-breaking profits on higher sales.[65]

Further examples of competitive impact come from cartel case studies. A study of price fixing in the gymnasium seating, rock salt, and structural steel industries found cost increases of 10–23% due to competition's strangulation.[66] A massive study of cartel records concluded that available evidence "indicates that the characteristic purposes of cartels point away from efficiency and that their activities tend to diminish efficiency."[67] A research team headed by F M. Scherer recently uncovered numerous examples of excessive costs due to cartelization in Europe. Citing cases from cigarettes, steel, paint, glass bottles, and cement, Scherer's group concluded, "Our interviews provided *considerable* qualitative evidence that pure X-inefficiency was a *significant* cause of productivity differentials."[68]

Intermarket statistical assessments of X-inefficiency are difficult to devise. Although data on market structure are commonplace, data isolating efficiency are not. Data on costs offer a substitute for data on efficiency, but only a very imperfect substitute because costs are influenced by factors other than efficiency—factors such as wage rates, materials prices, and plant location. Nevertheless, statistical studies have conquered these problems. So far they all indicate that *X-inefficiency is positively associated with market power*. The data shown earlier in Table 21–3 provide one example. Costs of grocery retailing rise with local market concentration, as indicated by the discrepancy between price and profit behavior. And the authors of the study from which those data were taken could find no explanation other than X-inefficiency for the rise in costs.[69] Further examples follow:

[65] *Fortune*, December 19, 1988, pp. 69–76. During the mid-1980s Ford, Kodak, Du Pont, AT&T, Union Carbide, and many other big, top-heavy companies shed excess management personnel. Quinn Mills, a Harvard Business School professor and consultant to industry attributed this to "competition both domestically and internationally." *The Washington Post*, National Weekly Edition, September 16, 1985, p. 20. See also *Fortune*, October 28, 1985, pp. 46–49. For further examples involving big companies, see *Fortune*, March 4, 1985, pp. 70–78; *Forbes*, September 19, 1988, pp. 41–52; *The Wall Street Journal*, August 25, 1989, p. A4; *Fortune*, February 29, 1988, pp. 34–42; *Business Week*, July 10, 1989, pp. 50–55; and *Forbes*, April 8, 1985, pp. 94–95.

[66] W. Bruce Erickson, "Price Fixing Conspiracies: Their Long-Term Impact," *Journal of Industrial Economics* (March 1976), pp. 189–202.

[67] Corwin D. Edwards, *Economic and Political Aspects of International Cartels*, U.S. Senate, Subcommittee on War Mobilization of the Committee on Military Affairs, 78th Cong., 2nd Sess. (1944), p. 40.

[68] F. M. Scherer, A. Beckenstein, E. Kaufer, R. D. Murphy, *The Economics of Multi-Plant Operation* (Cambridge, Mass.: Harvard University Press, 1975), pp. 74–75, 168–169, 314–315 (emphasis added). For further evidence concerning European cartels see D. Swann, D. P. O'Brien, W. P. J. Maunder, and W. S. Howe, *Competition in British Industry* (London: Allen & Unwin, 1974).

[69] Besides the source of Table 21–3, see *Prices and Profits of Leading Retail Food Chains, 1970–74*, Hearings, Joint Economic Committee, 95th Cong., 1st Sess. (1977), especially pp. 88–89. Excess wages were a part of this too. Also see Voos and Mishel in Table 21–5.

- Several studies of the commercial banking and savings and loan industries disclose that high concentration raises expenses for excess staff, furniture, equipment, and facilities.[70]

- Measuring X-inefficiency as the extent to which firms make more than justifiable use of capital-intensive means of production, and drawing upon data for Pakistani industries, Lawrence White found that "firms with market power do seem to be 'indulging' in more capital-intensive methods than are firms facing more competition."[71]

- Walter Primeaux carefully compared costs of electricity production in two separate sets of cities — those with electric utility *monopolies* and those with direct competition between *two firms* (of which there were 49 cities). He found "that average cost is reduced, at the mean, by 10.75 percent because of competition. This reflects a quantitative value of the presence of X-efficiency gained through competition."[72] Related estimates of Rodney Stevenson show cost differences of 6% to 8%.[73]

- Weapon systems bought by the Department of Defense from two sources ("dual sourcing") are much less costly than those bought from one source ("single sourcing").[74]

- Several studies of costs in health care services find large cost savings associated with competition.[75]

---

[70] Jerry L. Stevens, "Bank Market Concentration and Costs: Is There X-Inefficiency in Banking?" *Business Economics* (May 1983), pp. 36–44; Franklin R. Edwards, "Managerial Objectives in Regulated Industries: Expense-Preference Behavior in Banking," *Journal of Political Economy* (February 1977), pp. 147–162; C. A. Glassman and S. A. Rhoades, "Owner vs. Manager Control Effects on Bank Performance," *Review of Economics and Statistics* (May 1980), pp. 263–270; T. H. Hannan and F. Mavinga, "Expense Preference and Managerial Control," *Bell Journal of Economics* (Autumn 1980), pp. 671–682; and J. A. Verbrugge and J. S. Jahera, Jr., "Expense-Preference Behavior in the Savings and Loan Industry," *Journal of Money, Credit, and Banking* (November 1981), pp. 465–476.

[71] Lawrence J. White, "Appropriate Technology, X-Inefficiency, and A Competitive Environment: Some Evidence from Pakistan," *Quarterly Journal of Economics* (November 1976), pp. 575–589.

[72] Walter J. Primeaux, "An Assessment of X-Efficiency Gained Through Competition," *Review of Economics and Statistics* (February 1977), pp. 105–108.

[73] Rodney Stevenson, "X-Inefficiency and Interfirm Rivalry: Evidence from the Electric Utility Industry," *Land Economics* (February 1982), pp. 52–65.

[74] Everett Pyatt, "Procurement Competition at Work: The Navy's Experience," *Yale Journal on Regulation* (Summer 1989), pp. 319–331.

[75] Howard P. Tuckman and Cyril F. Chang, "Cost Convergence Between For-Profit and Not-For-Profit Nursing Homes: Does Competition Matter? *Quarterly Review of Economics and Business* (Winter 1988), pp. 50–65; John W. Mayo and Deborah A. McFarland, "Regulation, Market Structure, and Hospital Costs," *Southern Economic Journal* (January 1989), pp. 559–569; and Jack Zwanziger and Glenn A. Melnick, "The Effects of Hospital Competition and the Medicare PPS Program on Hospital Cost Behavior in California," *Journal of Health Economics* (December 1988), pp. 301–320. This last study shows the subtleties that may be involved here. Where price competition prevails, reduced concentration lowers costs (holding quality constant). However, where nonprice competition prevails, reduced concentration lifts costs for differentiation efforts, as illustrated earlier for advertising in the C to B range of Figure 16–2.

- In a comparative study of American and British manufacturing Davies and Caves found X-inefficiencies, as might be measured by low productivity, associated with a lack of competition: "a doubling of a British industry's concentration would depress its relative productivity by 18 per cent."[76] Conversely, exposure to import competition improved productivity, a finding borne out elsewhere as well.[77]

Economywide estimates of monopoly-induced X-inefficiency can only be very rough approximations. It does not seem unreasonable to assume, however, that such waste may amount to as much as 10% of costs where concentration is very high and 5% of costs where concentration is moderate. Compared with our earlier estimates of deadweight loss due to profit-invoked misallocation, these figures are obviously quite large. Conversion to competition would probably reduce X-inefficiency and thereby improve consumer welfare.[78]

SUMMARY

Previous chapters left open the question of market power's impact on *how well* markets work. Now its impact regarding several basic questions raised by scarcity has been disclosed — namely, the questions of what? (allocation efficiency), how? (technical efficiency), and to whom? (distribution equity).

Let's first summarize the empirical evidence before considering its welfare implications.

1. Most statistical studies of profit and concentration find a positive and significant relationship. The positive association has been found for a wide variety of profit measures, concentration indexes, markets, and countries.
2. The positive relationship sometimes displays a "critical" range of concentration over which profit jumps sharply (moving with less magnitude on either side of this range).
3. A significant minority of profit-concentration studies find no relationship or only a weak one raising problems of *significance* and *magnitude*. Some of these are faulty because of poor data, an attenuated variance in concentration, or some other shortcoming.

[76] Stephen Davies and Richard E. Caves, *Britain's Productivity Gap* (Cambridge: Cambridge University Press, 1987), pp. 57–58.

[77] M. Pickford, "A New Test for Manufacturing Industry Efficiency," *International Journal of Industrial Organization*, Vol. 3 (1985), pp. 153–177. On competition and international competitiveness generally, a very interesting source is Michael E. Porter, *The Competitive Advantage of Nations* (New York: The Free Press, 1990).

[78] A good general source is Roger S. Frantz, *X-Efficiency: Theory, Evidence and Applications* (Boston: Kluwer, 1988).

Others are quite valid but show weakness because costs are rising as well as prices along with concentration, obliterating any profit effect (wage and X-inefficiency costs in particular). Likewise, risk is reduced at the expense of profit. Finally, concentration's effect often fades when market share is included as an explanatory variable. This suggests that, of the two forms of market power — single-firm and collusive — the former (measured by market share) quite often, perhaps usually, outweighs the latter (measured by concentration).

4. To the extent there is a positive relationship between profit and concentration, a problem of *interpretation* remains. In particular, critics of the market power hypothesis claim the positive result is due to greater cost efficiency simultaneously causing both higher concentration and profits. There may be a bit of truth to this claim. However, market power is the better explanation on the whole, as revealed for instance in the generally strong positive relationship between *price* and concentration and also by evidence that power derives from market share together with product differentiation, first-mover advantages, and the like. Also, collusive effects often remain detectable in profit data.

5. Profits are positively related to entry barriers and a lack of import competition.

6. Wages are positively related to unionism and to concentration when each is considered separately. Taking account of interactions, the positive effect of concentration is greatest in the presence of unions, and the positive effect of unions is greatest given high concentration. Unions capture a large portion of the monopoly profits associated with high concentration, so the impact of market power on profitability is seriously understated when unionization is ignored (as is the case for most profit-concentration studies).

7. X-inefficiencies sprout in the absence of competition, raising costs in association with concentration, cartelization, barriers to entry, and import protection.

So much for the empirical evidence. What do these findings mean in the context of welfare theory?

In consumer welfare, market power leads to lost consumer surplus. Surplus is lost because higher prices and lower output prevail under concentration than under competition. The higher prices are due to excess profits, excess wages, excess managerial salaries, and X-inefficiency. The destination of the lost consumers' surplus depends largely on the relative effect of each cause. Excess profits go to those controlling ownership shares. Since roughly 2.4% of the populace controls 50% of all business ownership shares, this transfer from consumers to owners tends to warp the distribution of income and wealth. Excess wages and salaries go to workers and managers in unionized-concentrated industries. These transfers may likewise contribute to maldistribution, but to an unknown extent. Exorbitant costs due to X-inefficiency go to no purpose whatever. They are a form of deadweight loss because they represent resources needlessly consumed.

Yet another form of deadweight loss (and of lost consumers' surplus) is attributable to misallocation of resources. Triangles *ABC* and *AED* in Figures 21–1 and 21–4 signify these losses. Unlike the other losses, these are not directly measurable in dollars, but they are no less real.

If one were to hazard a rough guess as to how much all these losses of consumers' surplus amounted to, something in the neighborhood of 7–10% of GNP might be reasonable, at least in times past. Individual contributions might be as follows: excess profits, 1–3%; excess wages and salaries, 2–3%; X-inefficiency 3–4%; and misallocation 0.5–1%. To the extent competition in the economy has recently improved, these numbers might improve.

22

Profits and Policy: Public Utility Regulation

The Supreme Power who conceived gravity, supply and demand, and the double helix must have been absorbed elsewhere when public utility regulation was invented.

—F. M. SCHERER

Public utility regulation is an industrial halfway house. Its residents are sheltered from the cruelties of all-out competition, yet they are not crushed by total government control. Private firms own and operate enterprises, while state and federal governments police structure, conduct, and performance for purposes other than maintaining competition.[1]

Profit level and price structure are the main concerns of utility regulation. Utility regulation also covers such additional matters as accounting procedures, entry, exit, and quality of service. But these we must neglect. Hence our outline:

---

[1] For surveys see Alfred E. Kahn, *The Economics of Regulation*, Vols. I and II (New York: John Wiley, 1970, 1971); Sanford V. Berg and John Tschirhart, *Natural Monopoly Regulation: Principles and Practice* (Cambridge: Cambridge University Press, 1988); and Kenneth Nowotny, David B. Smith, and Harry M. Trebing (eds.), *Public Utility Regulation* (Boston: Kluwer, 1989).

- What industries are regulated?
- Why regulate?
- Who regulates?
- How: Price level regulation?
- How: Price structure regulation?
- Problems and distortions.

I. WHAT INDUSTRIES ARE REGULATED?

Electricity, natural gas, telecommunications, broadcast communications, and railroading are at present the main industries subject to regulation. Together they account for about 4% of national income. In the past, airlines, common carrier trucks, and intercity buses were also regulated, but *de*regulation has now effectively freed them. Indeed, the railroads have been partially deregulated, so our attention will center on what are often called "utilities" — local electric, gas, and telephone services.

Several characteristics of these industries set them apart from most others. First, they are usually considered **vital** industries. To be sure, food and clothing (and books) are equally vital yet unregulated, but communications and energy are necessities not to be sneezed at.

Second, nearly all regulated industries sell **services** rather than commodities. Unlike commodities, services cannot be stored. Their production and consumption coincide inseparably. Most regulated industries must therefore maintain excess capacity to meet peak periods of consumption. In many cases they must also maintain direct connections by wire or pipe with their customers.

Third, most regulated industries are **capital intensive**. The guts of their operations are cables, turbine generators, switches, and steel rails rather than mill hands, raw materials, or merchandise.

II. WHY REGULATE?

The selection of industries to regulate rests with government legislatures. State authority is based on "police power." Federal authority is based on the Constitution's commerce clause, which gives Congress the right "to regulate commerce . . . among the several states." Court interpretations of these powers are now quite liberal. Legislatures may impose regulation for just about any reason that strikes their fancy, subject only to the loose constraint that the industries selected must be "clothed with a public interest." Given such flexibility, the regulatory net is woven from diverse strands of reasoning. Despite the rational diversity, the most commonly cited reasons for regulation can be collected under four categories: (1) natural monopoly, (2) conservation of a publicly owned natural resource, (3) destructive competition, and (4) sharp public indignation against "unfairness."

A. Natural Monopoly

In some situations, economic or technical conditions permit only one efficient supplier, leading to "natural monopoly." The key condition is "subadditivity" of costs, in which case any given level of output can be produced by one firm (the natural monopolist) at less cost than two or more firms.[2] For a single-product firm, this is most easily illustrated by economies of scale. That is, cost per unit of output declines continuously as the scale of operations increases. This is shown in Figure 22–1, where, throughout the range of quantity demanded, long-run average and marginal costs fall for a single firm. Two firms could supply the market's requirements at high price P_2, but only at lofty unit costs. A competitive dual between two such firms could be won handily by the largest rival because greater size brings lower cost, enabling the larger firm to price below its competitor's cost. At price P_1 in Figure 22–1, a sole survivor could meet *all* market demand at a point where the unit cost curve is still falling as a function of output. There is, then, room for only one efficient enterprise.

Among regulated industries, costs decline as scale increases for local water, electric power, gas, telephone, and cable TV. The technology of transmission and the physical fact of direct connection are the main causes of this cost effect. Cables, pipelines, and other conduits have transmission capacities that grow *more* than proportionately to size or material makeup. As a consequence, the least expensive way to transmit electricity, gas, water, or telephone communications is through large lines. Furthermore, local distribution of these services requires direct connection to customers. Competition would therefore entail redundant line duplications, something obviously inefficient and wasteful.

An additional factor contributes to natural monopoly in local telephone service. For one caller to reach another, both must be connected to the same central switch. Almost by definition a central switch must be "central" — that is, monopolistic. With two competing phone companies, there would be *two* central switches. People having only one phone could then call only patrons of the same phone company. Comprehensive interconnection would require either two phones and two lines for everyone or cooperative switching between the central switches of the rival companies.

Although natural monopoly certainly explains much regulation,

---

2 W. J. Baumol, "On the Proper Cost Test for Natural Monopoly in a Multiproduct Industry," *American Economic Review*, Vol. 67 (1977), pp. 808–822.

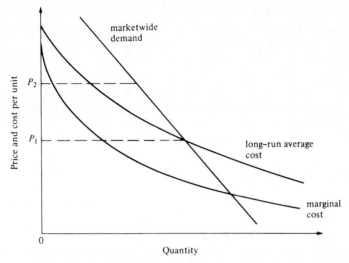

FIGURE 22–1. Decreasing cost industry.

many natural monopolies are *not* regulated and, conversely, many regulated industries are *not* natural monopolies. Among the former, imagine an isolated small town so sparsely populated that demand can support no more than one movie theater. This might qualify as a natural monopoly. But such movie theaters escape regulation apparently because they offer something less than a "vital" service (there being other, perhaps even more enjoyable, things to do on a Saturday night than watching movies). Regarding regulated industries that are not natural monopolies, transportation services have a long history of regulation, but they cannot qualify as natural monopolies. Major air routes can be served efficiently by a flock of airlines. Trucking can be carried on at low cost by very-small-scale operators. And, given the competitive potentials of air, truck, and bus transport, railroads cannot be considered natural monopolies either (even though, a century ago, they generally did fit that description). Thus *de*regulation of transportation should be welcomed.

Similarly, certain *segments* of natural monopoly industries are not naturally monopolistic. Telephone service has certain segments where competition is possible, even desirable. Monopoly is unnatural and unneeded when it comes to manufacturing telephone equipment, now a $20 billion business. The gadgetry ranges from Mickey Mouse phones to complicated PBX terminals, all within the low-cost capabilities of dozens of electronics firms besides AT&T.

B. Resource Conservation

Regulation of radio and television broadcasting is grounded on a different rationale. Economic efficiency requires no more than small-scale local broadcasting. However, the radio spectrum used by broadcasters is a limited resource, with a limited number of bandwidths or channels. If broadcasters were granted free and unrestricted entry, they could very well flood the air waves, interfering with each other and garbling the reception of listeners and viewers. Accordingly, access to the spectrum is limited by licensing. Broadcasters, however, are not subject to price or profit control, only to entry restrictions. Moving farther afield, conservation has also served, rightly or wrongly, to justify past regulation in other areas, such as natural gas, oil, and water.

C. Destructive Competition

Certain characteristics of many regulated industries — their huge capital intensity and potential for excess capacity in particular — expose them to dangers of destructive competition. At least that is what some defenders of regulation contend. Excess capacity is said to induce reckless price cutting. And heavy capital intensity translates into high fixed costs as a proportion of total cost. So once prices start to fall they can plunge deeply before bottoming at average variable cost. The argument concludes, therefore, that such industries will be plagued by periodic price wars financially destructive to producers and disruptive for consumers.

Notice that this argument cannot rationalize regulation in natural monopoly markets, because natural monopolies, once established, face no competition. Notice, too, that the argument is designed to justify *minimum* price regulation, not *maximum* price regulation (as in the case of natural monopolies). Hence, it is an argument that is vociferously applied to justify minimum price regulation in transportation. Yet, as many economists have pointed out, it is precisely in transportation that this line of argument is least valid. Take trucking for instance:

> Capital costs are relatively small compared to variable costs, so that unregulated truckers would not be likely to operate at prices much below cost. Also, the labor and capital resources employed in trucking can easily be shifted to alternative uses. In other industries with low fixed costs, such as retailing, prices seldom fall much below cost, and adjustments for changing market conditions are made quickly and with little disruption.[3]

In short, the argument has limited application.

D. Unfairness

Perhaps the only area where sharp price rivalry might create real problems is railroading. But the main problem is not necessarily bankruptcy. The story begins over a hundred years ago, before trucks and planes.

---

[3] L. W. Weiss and A. D. Strickland, *Regulation: A Case Approach* (New York: McGraw-Hill, 1976), p. 6.

On some routes natural monopolies prevailed (because between any pair of cities railroads experience declining costs up to a point). On these natural monopoly routes, demand was insufficient to support more than one low-cost company. On other routes, such as those between New York and Chicago, traffic volume was big enough to attract competition. Given railroads' steep fixed costs, conditions on these latter routes were right for rambunctious, if not completely ruinous, price rivalry. During the 1870s, for instance, a price war broke out on eastbound grain shipments between Chicago and New York, causing rates to fall from $0.56 to $0.15 per hundred-weight and even lower.[4]

In short, railroading in that era fitted two contrasting models depending on route circumstances—the natural monopoly model or the ruinous competition model. The result was a grossly discriminatory railroad rate structure. Towns without rail competition were charged higher rates than were those blessed with two or more railroads. Indeed, in many instances rates on noncompetitive short hauls exceeded those on competitive long hauls, despite one's common sense expectation that rates should rise with distance since costs rise with distance. Moreover, large shippers were able to extract more favorable rates than small shippers. Folks on the unfavorable side of the tracks found these several discrepancies "monstrous," "evil," and "unfair." Their clamor caused Congress to pass the Interstate Commerce Act in 1887, which established the Interstate Commerce Commission and directed that rates approved by the Commission be "just and reasonable." That is, the act outlawed personal discrimination and prohibited short-haul rates in excess of long-haul rates "under substantially similar circumstances." The importance of "fairness" in motivating this historic first step toward federal regulation may be seen in the fact that Congress made no explicit provision for the ICC to fix maximum overall rate levels until 20 years later with passage of the Hepburn Act of 1906.

In truth, "fairness," or some variant of it, has probably had a hand in motivating most subsequent regulation as well. A principal proponent of this view is Donald Dewey, who contends that citizens' expectations of regulation go well beyond protection from economic exploitation or resource conservation:

> [First] we expect group therapy—a release of tension and frustrations. . . . Fortunately, plenty of angry people in this world would rather testify at a public hearing—preferably before a TV camera—than blow up buildings or beat their kids.

> Second, we expect regulation to protect us from the kind of sharp commercial practice that is generally impossible in competitive industries. . . . The

---

[4] Paul W. MacAvoy, *The Economic Effects of Regulation: The Trunkline Railroad Cartels and the Interstate Commerce Commission Before 1900* (Cambridge, Mass.: MIT Press, 1965).

Penn Central Railroad will never refund a nickel for a breakdown in service unless it is compelled to do so by a Utility Commission.

In short, it may well be that "as citizens we wish the regulatory agency to serve as a forum for group therapy, a better business bureau, a check on bureaucracy, and a brake on economic and social change."[5]

III. WHO REGULATES?

Most regulatory power rests with independent regulatory commissions. They are not legislative, judicial, or administrative. Rather, the duties of these commissions run the gamut of governmental classifications. They make rules and thereby legislate; they hold hearings or adversary proceedings and thereafter adjudicate; they enforce regulatory laws and thereby administer.

Although commission duties are thus typically broad, their scope of jurisdiction is often narrow. One major division of jurisdiction concerns geography. State regulatory commissions govern *intra*state commerce, whereas federal agencies oversee *inter*state commerce. Product or service determines a second division. Many commissions regulate only one type of utility, or a limited class of utilities. As shown in Table 22–1, the Interstate Commerce Commission regulates interstate land transportation (and some waterway carriers), the Federal Energy Regulatory Commission regulates interstate transmission and wholesale price of electricity and rates and routes of natural gas pipelines, and the Federal Communications Commission licenses broadcasters and regulates interstate (long-distance) telephone and telegraph rates and levels of service.

State commissions, as shown in Table 22–1, are often less specialized. With varying scope their main concerns are *local* gas, electric, telephone, water, and transit utilities. State or federal, the U.S. Supreme Court summarized the commission concept when it said that these agencies were "created with the avowed purpose of lodging functions in a body specifically competent to deal with them by reason of information, experience and careful study of the business and economic conditions of the industry affected."[6]

Commission panels usually consist of 3 to 9 members appointed to fixed terms by either the president (for federal posts) or the governor (for state posts, although several states *elect* commissioners). With but few exceptions, the commissioners so selected do not fit the ideal image of objective experts. Some appointments are even humorous. A nominee

---

[5] Donald J. Dewey, "Regulatory Reform?" in *Regulation in Further Perspective*, edited by Shepherd and Gies (Cambridge, Mass.: Ballinger, 1974), pp. 35–37. See also Bruce Owen and Ronald Braeutigam, *The Regulation Game* (Cambridge, Mass.: Ballinger, 1978), pp. 26–29.

[6] *Federal Trade Commission* v. *R. F. Keppel and Bros., Inc.*, 291 U.S. 304, 314 (1934).

TABLE 22-1.   The Main Federal Commissions and Selected State Commissions, Circa 1990

Commission (and Year of Origin)	Number of Members	Number of Staff Members	Jurisdiction
Federal Commissions			
Interstate Commerce Commission (1887)	15	1063	Railroads, some water shipping, and trucking (with powers diminishing)
Federal Energy Regulatory Commission (formerly the Federal Power Commission, 1934)	5	1707	Electric power, some gas, and pipelines
Federal Communications Commission (1934)	15	1975	Telephone, television, radio, telegraph
Selected State Commissions			
California (1912)	5	988	Electric, gas, telephone, railroads, buses, docks, water carriers, and more
Colorado (1913)	3	97	Electric, gas, telephone, telegraph, water, buses, taxis, railroads
Florida (1887)	5	336	Electric, gas, telephone, telegraph, water, sewer, railroads, and more
Indiana (1907)	3	91	Electric, gas, telephone, water, buses, railroads, and more
Massachusetts (1885)	3	122	Electric, gas, telephone, railroads, taxis, water
Pennsylvania (1908)	5	575	Electric, gas, telephone, telegraph, water, sewer, docks, taxis, railroads, and more

for the Federal Communications Commission was asked during his Senate confirmation hearing about his qualifications in communications. "Senator," he replied, "I don't know anything about communications. I came to Washington expecting to be appointed to the Federal Power Commission."[7]

Commissioners are aided by staffs of civil servants comprising mainly accountants, engineers, lawyers, and economists. Many critics of regulation contend that commissions cannot do an adequate job because

---

[7] Louis M. Kohlmeier, Jr., *The Regulators* (New York: Harper & Row, 1969), p. 48.

both staffers and commissioners are underpaid and overworked. The utilities they regulate can well afford personnel. Hence, control of corporate giants with this feeble machinery has been called herding elephants with flyswatters.[8]

Still, commission personnel do not deserve all the blame for regulation's shortcomings. Many legislative mandates under which commissions work are vague or misguided. What is more, the task of regulation is *inherently* difficult. There is no regulatory cookbook with recipes for every occasion, no utility child-care guide. There are a few principles, plus plenty of questions lacking pat answers. It is to these that we now turn. The discussion is divided into two topics: (1) rate level and (2) rate structure. **Rate level** refers to *overall* revenues, costs, and returns. **Rate structure** refers to the *specific prices charged* to specific customers for specific services at specific times.

IV. HOW: RATE-LEVEL REGULATION

A. Objectives

There are any number of objectives that *could* guide rate-level regulation. Among the more obvious possibilities are speedy growth in service, conservation of energy, and optimal allocation of resources in the strict economic sense. For one reason or another, however, *none* of these is the main objective applied in practice. The main objective is to allow the utility sufficient revenues to pay its "full" costs plus a "fair" return on the "fair" value of its capital. Stated differently, *the main objective is to strike a reasonable balance between the interests of consumers* (who should not be gouged by monopoly exploitation) *and the interests of the utility investors and operators* (who should not be cheated by overzealous commissions, or who, in more legalistic language, should not be deprived of their property without "due process of law").

The effort to balance is captured in a simple equation:

$$\text{total revenue} = \text{operating expenses} + \text{current depreciation} + (\text{capital value} \times \text{rate of return}) \qquad (22\text{--}1)$$

Note that, on the right-hand side, operating expenses and current depreciation are both *annual dollar flows*. Capital value is not a dollar flow. It is the asset value of the utility firm at a *given point in time*, also called the **rate base**. However, once this capital value is multiplied by the allowed rate of return (such as 0.10, for 10% per year), the result *is* an annual dollar flow. Thus, the basic problem of rate level regulation is to

---

[8] B. C. Moore, Jr., "AT&T: The Phony Monopoly," in *Monopoly Makers*, edited by M. J. Green (New York: Grossman, 1973), p. 82.

see to it that the annual flow of total revenue covers the annual flow of "full cost," including depreciation, plus a "fair" or "reasonable" return on capital value, no more and no less.

Generally speaking the owners or operators would like to see "more," which means that their interests lie with *high* estimates of the elements on the right-hand side. Consumers, on the other hand, would like to see "less" because their interests are generally served by *low* figures for these elements. It is the job of the commission to balance these conflicting interests — to determine that operating expenses, current depreciation, capital value, and rate of return may be neither too high nor too low, and then to permit a rate level that generates the necessary total revenue. Note that if rates are pressed *too* low, service could suffer and the firm could go bankrupt, injuring everyone involved.

The situation may be seen in Figure 22–2 (which is a total dollar view, not a per unit dollar view as in Figure 22–1). The total payments (or total cost) curve has three components corresponding to the right-hand side of the equation (22–1). Thus, utility payments include a fair or normal profit (which is embodied in rate base x percent return). An *un*regulated, profit-maximizing monopolist would charge an overall price level to yield an output of Q_u, placing the firm at point A on the total revenue curve. Excess profit there would be vertical distance AB. The objective of regulation is to lower price level below the monopolist's profit maximizing price, thereby moving the firm from A to C. At point C, total revenue and total payments, including no more than a fair return, just match. Output is greater at Q_r, and consumers are not exploited. At price levels still lower, output would be still greater but total revenue

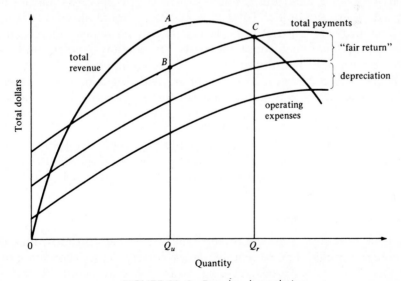

FIGURE 22–2. Rate-level regulation.

would fall to unreasonably low levels, hurting the utility's investors. The process does not exactly simulate competitive results, but it may be helpful to think of it in that way.

Now, to appreciate fully the problems encountered in the regulatory process, each item of rate level decision making needs to be discussed. We begin with operating expenses.

B. Operating Expenses

Operating expenses are to some degree the easiest of all items for a commission to determine. They include such things as fuel costs (for coal, oil, and gas), workers' wages, managers' salaries, materials expense, advertising, and taxes. Together these expenses typically absorb 70–90% of a utility's total operating revenue. They are relatively easy to determine because few such expenses can be padded or faked. Taxes, for example, are beyond the utility's control and therefore unquestioned. Similarly, the costs of fuel are shaped in open markets, and workers' wages are settled by collective bargaining. These, too, are rarely questioned by commissions.

One does not have to go far down the list of expenses, however, before one encounters snarls. How much should be allowed for advertising? Does a monopolist need to advertise at all? What about public relations advertising, which tells us that Giant Electric is doing everything possible to clean up the environment but smokestack scrubbers ought to be scrubbed and that *public* ownership of utilities is sinful? Does the tab for these ads belong to consumers or investors? How much should be allowed for executive salaries, executive secretaries, executive jets, and executive travel? Should the gasoline expenses of corporate Cadillacs be approved when economical Toyotas would do? Should all worker wage rates be approved? Is it not possible that telephone repairpersons could be overpaid? And what about the costs of company lawyers and accountants who represent the utility before the commission? Should consumers pay the company's costs of coping with regulation when these costs support efforts contrary to the consumers' interest? What about donations to charities? Does not "good corporate citizenship" require that community causes be supported?

Answers to these and a stream of similar questions are tricky. Some of these expenses are partly "legitimate," but where does one draw the line? Commissions' answers vary widely, as you might guess.

C. Current Depreciation

Current depreciation is an important item of cost because most utilities have a high capital intensity. For all utilities current depreciation amounts to almost 10% of total sales revenue as against only about 3% for all manufacturing.

No one disputes the necessity of including depreciation as a cost. In one sense, depreciation accounts for the "using up" of capital assets through wear and tear or obsolescence. In another sense, depreciation may be thought of as a payment to capital investors, much as wages, salaries, and materials expenses are payments to other factor suppliers. This means that, of the elements in the summary equation, *both* current depreciation *and* capital value times rate of return go to the investors. As Alfred Kahn explains, "The return to capital . . . has two parts: the return *of* the money capital invested over the estimated economic life of the investment and the return (interest and profit) *on* the portion of the investment that remains outstanding."[9]

Although no one disputes depreciation's inclusion as a cost, its computation is often more controversial than the computation of operating expenses. First, the allowance for depreciation is quite different from operating expenses. Whereas operating expenses entail *actual money outlays*, depreciation does not. It is an *imputed cost*. The portion of total revenues depreciation "permits the company to earn does not, as is the case with normal operating expenses, go out in payments to outside parties — suppliers of raw materials, workers and so on."[10] It goes instead to investors.

Second, since current depreciation is an imputation, there are no hard rules for its reckoning. The actual figure arrived at for any asset in any one year depends on three things: (1) the depreciation base, (2) the asset's estimated life span, and (3) the method of write-off during its life. Each element is judgmental; each is therefore open to dispute.

The depreciation base is the original cost of the asset less any salvage value at life's end. Although original cost is straightforward, salvage value is a matter of estimate. Life span, too, is a matter of estimate. A short life with no assumed salvage value would tend to favor investors over consumers because it would lead to large, early write-offs. Conversely, a long life with high salvage value favors consumers because it leads to small annual write-offs.

As for possible write-off methods, they are too numerous and too complex to summarize here. The major source of difference among them rests with whether the depreciation base is spread *evenly* or *unevenly* over the estimated life span.

D. Capital Value or Rate Base

The most controversial part of regulation concerns capital value times rate of return (or rate base x percent return) because this is the computation that determines profit. The Supreme Court's legal guide to commissions is about as solid as natural gas. Specific estimates or formulas

---

[9] Kahn, *The Economics of Regulation*, Vol. I, p. 32.
[10] Ibid.

are not so important, says the Court. It's the *end result* that counts. The end result must be "just and reasonable." What is "just and reasonable"? Earnings "which enable the company to operate successfully, to maintain its financial integrity, to attract capital, and to compensate its investors for the risks assumed . . . even though they [the earnings] might produce only a meager return."[11]

This gives commissions great leeway in determining both capital value and rate of return. As regards capital value, there is a range of choice concerning (1) accounting devices and (2) what is counted as real investment. Choice offers opportunities for the exercise of value judgment.

Accounting Devices. At least four methods for computing the rate base have been adopted or proposed:

1. *Original cost* values assets at their "actual" or "book" cost.
2. *Reproduction cost* is the estimated cost of buying, building, and installing the same equipment at today's prices.
3. *Replacement cost* is the estimated cost of replacing the present plant and equipment, much of which may be outdated, with the most efficient and reliable technology available, in amounts sufficient to supply the same service.
4. *Mixed method*, or "fair value," which is some combination, or rough averaging, of the items 1 through 3.

Subtractions for *accumulated* depreciation must be made under any of the options, which expands the horizon for judgment still further.

At present, most federal and state commissions apply the original cost approach, followed in popularity by the mixed method. Still, future changes are possible, and the pros and cons of these techniques are endlessly debated. Among the major points at issue are (1) ease of estimation, (2) inflation, and (3) economic efficiency.

It should be obvious that original cost is the easiest of all methods to estimate (a fact that partly explains its great popularity). The replacement cost approach is undoubtedly the most difficult, because it amounts to little more than a playground for opinion. Reproduction cost lies somewhere in between.

Although original cost is most convenient, it is least competent in accounting for changes over time, especially plant and equipment price changes. During periods of inflation, consumers prefer and investors oppose original cost because it yields a *lower* rate base than the other techniques. On the other hand, during periods of deflation (now about as dated as dinosaurs), producers prefer original cost because it yields a *higher* rate base than the other techniques. What is correct? There is no secure answer, but it can be argued that reproduction cost, which does take inflation into account, might be better economically. Why? Because

---

[11] *Federal Power Commission* v. *Hope Natural Gas Co.*, 320 U.S. 591 (1944).

under the "ideal" of pure competition, industry price will move in the long run to a level that just covers costs plus a normal return on a *new* plant. Moreover, during periods of rapid inflation, original cost valuation might sink the rate base so low as to threaten the firm's viability.

Actually, on grounds of allocation efficiency, the replacement cost approach seems most attractive because the *new* plant alluded to should be one *incorporating the latest in new technology*. Although certainly favorable to replacement cost, this argument is undercut by the fact that the main purpose of regulation is *not* allocation efficiency. Commissions make no attempt to see that utility prices always match marginal cost. They only seek a "fair" balance between opposing parties.

Asset Inclusion.   Regardless of accounting technique, there remains the question of what is to be included in the rate base. Buildings, cables, trucks, dams, generators, switches, and the like obviously qualify. But what about the $3 billion nuclear power plant completed only a year ago but now shut down because geologists have just discovered an earthquake fault within one-half mile of it? Who ought to pay for it? If the dead plant is included in the rate base, consumers will howl. If excluded, it would surely thrash investors. How would you decide as a commissioner? (See the appendix to this chapter.) What, further, about *intangible* assets? Would you permit the cost of patents, franchise papers, licenses, and purchase options to enter the rate base? Some commissions do permit them—to some extent.

E. Percent Return

Utility investors own utility bonds, preferred stock, and common stock. Each instrument's rate of return differs because each differs in "priority" of payout, with bonds enjoying top priority and earning the lowest return. Thus, the percent rate of return referred to in the regulatory equation is actually a *weighted average* rate. Reducing the return to its components, most commissions allow the interest actually paid on bonds, the dividends actually paid on preferred stock, and then they add a "fair" return for stockholders' equity.

Equity Returns.   On the whole, equity returns average about 12–14%, which is pretty close to the all-manufacturing average. However, the average masks considerable variety because there is no single scientifically correct rate of return. At best, there is a "zone of reasonableness," within which judgment may roam. What are the limits of this zone? The *bottom* limit would be a rate just high enough to attract continuing investor commitments of capital. The *upper* limit would be considerably more generous but not lavish. Obviously, the zone itself is rather elastic.

Perhaps the best way to appreciate this problem is to imagine yourself as the typical investor whose capital the utility is trying to attract.

What rate of return would the company have to pay (and the commission have to approve) to get you to bite? If you are shrewd, that rate would depend on the following:

1. The rate you could earn if you put your money elsewhere.
2. The risk of losing your investment (here and elsewhere).
3. The extent to which the company's earnings fluctuate, which in turn may depend on its debt/equity ratio, dividend payout policy, general economic condition, and so on.
4. The recent trend in the company's stock price.
5. Your expectations of political changes that may alter regulation.

These would be churning in your head, but the commission cannot read your mind. It therefore has no way of knowing precisely what minimum rate would attract your capital, or that of others. For this reason, commissions must exercise a good bit of judgment.

V. HOW: RATE STRUCTURE REGULATION

The duty of commissions does not stop once overall revenue is set. The question of what *specific* prices or rates to charge remains. According to judicial and legislative instructions, commissions may permit rates that jump around with time, place, type of buyer, and size of transaction. However, the jumps cannot be "unduly discriminatory"; the differences in rates charged various customers or classes of service must be "just and reasonable." In carrying out this vague mandate, commissions have permitted rates to vary with *cost of service* and *value of service*. Each is worth illustrating.

A. Costs and Peak-Load Pricing[12]

For decades we have had to pay more to call long distance during weekday daylight hours than to call during nights and weekends. Likewise, many large buyers of natural gas are charged low prices for "interruptible" service, meaning that they can be cut off if the demand of noninterruptible buyers burgeons. Traditionally, electric power companies have not charged such time-based rates, but now there is a definite trend toward them. In 1977, for instance, Wisconsin Power & Light Company began charging business customers 2.03 cents per kilowatt-hour between 8 A.M. and 10 P.M. and just 1.013 cents per kilowatt-hour at other times. Shortly thereafter rates began to vary with season of the year. By 1989 approximately 50% of all retail electricity sold in Wisconsin was billed

---

[12] This section is based primarily on Weiss and Strickland, *Regulation: A Case Approach*, pp. 18–21.

under time-of-use rates.[13] This is called **peak-load pricing**, because rates are higher to peak users.

The main justification for higher prices during peak periods is that the costs of providing peak service are greater than those of providing off-peak service. One such cost is plant and equipment. Because a utility must have on hand capacity to satisfy total peak demand, capacity costs can be blamed mainly on those who tap into the utility during peak hours. As for off-peak customers, *the plant and equipment are already there for the peak*, so capacity costs of serving them do not apply, although off-peak users do create costs for fuel and other variable inputs. Indeed, even fuel costs per unit tend to vary with time of demand because utilities usually fire up their least efficient, high-cost plants only during peak periods. The differences between plants can be substantial. In 1973, for instance, a major eastern electric company experienced fuel costs of 3.3 mills per kilowatt-hour in its most efficient plant and 9.51 mills per kilowatt-hour in its least efficient plant.[14] (Note that these cost experiences do not contradict the economies of scale mentioned earlier. These are *short-run* cost comparisons, not long-run scalar comparisons).

Figure 22–3 shows peak and off-peak demands set against the short-run marginal cost curve of a hypothetical utility. If a uniform price of P_2 were charged to both peak and off-peak demands, capacity would have to equal $0Q_2$, which is peak quantity demanded at P_2. Off-peak demand would be $0Q_0$ given price P_2. Since $0Q_2$ greatly exceeds $0Q_0$, it is easy to see that peak demand would be responsible for the plant necessary to produce $0Q_2$ (even if off-peak demand were nonexistent). Moreover, a uniform price of P_2 would cause inefficient plant usage, because there would be tremendous excess capacity during off-peak periods. In short, such a uniform price is *too low* for peak demand (producing a state of overbuilding) and *too high* for off-peak demand (causing off-peak under-utilization). Indeed, off-peak demand is to some extent subsidizing peak demand, since the shaded area in Figure 22–3 indicates the amount by which off-peak revenues exceed off-peak costs.

With a more sensible rate structure, peak customers would be charged P_3 and off-peak customers would be charged P_1. At P_3, peak demand would be curtailed to $0Q_3$, eliminating the need for capacity over the Q_3–Q_2 range. (It has been estimated that $13 *billion* of electric utility capital spending would have been avoided over the years 1977–1985 if all U.S. electric companies had been using such peak-load pricing.[15])

As already suggested, a rate structure that fully reflected costs would entail more than charges sufficient to cover whatever capacity

13 J. Robert Malko and Philip R. Swensen, "Pricing and the Electric Utility Industry," in Nowotny, Smith, and Trebing (eds.), *Public Utility Regulation*, p. 65.

14 E. Berlin, C. J. Cicchetti, and W. J. Gillen, *Perspective on Power* (Cambridge, Mass.: Ballinger, 1975), p. 35.

15 *The Wall Street Journal*, August 12, 1977, p. 1.

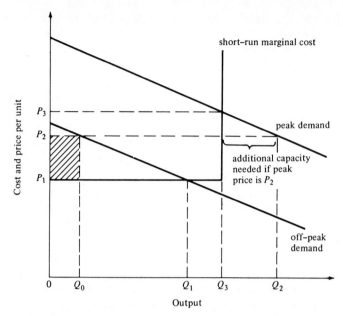

FIGURE 22–3. Peak-load pricing.

various classes of customers were responsible for. Rates would also have to include (1) a charge per unit of service (for example, per kilowatt-hour, or per phone call) to meet the costs that vary with output (fuel especially), (2) a fixed charge for connection, and (3) a fixed charge per month to cover the costs of metering, billing, and the like, costs which do not vary with consumption level or timing.

B. Value-of-Service Pricing

In the main, utility prices are not based strictly on cost of service. Price discrimination of second and third degrees (as defined and explained in Chapter 14) runs rampant. A common feature of such price discrimination is that those customers or classes of service having *in*elastic demands are typically charged more than those having elastic demands. In 1983, for instance, average electric rates to residential customers were about 6.83 cents per kilowatt-hour, whereas those charged to industrial customers were only 4.68 cents per kilowatt-hour.[16] To be sure, supplying a big factory often costs less per unit than supplying a home because many industrial buyers provide their own transformers and other equipment. Still, the main explanation for the higher household rate is found

[16] U.S. Department of Commerce, *Statistics Abstract of the United States 1986* (Washington, D.C.: U.S. Government Printing Office, 1986), p. 570.

in price elasticity of demand. Industrial elasticity appears to be about 1.9, whereas residential elasticity is closer to 1.2.[17] The difference is due to the greater energy options open to industrial buyers. Indeed, many of them generate their own electricity.

Another form of discrimination in electricity is the so-called block rate, that, until recently, confronted virtually every residential consumer in the United States. Under a block-rate schedule, price falls as additional "blocks" of electricity are consumed during the month. The idea is that a high rate could be charged for basic uses like lighting, which lacks energy substitutes, whereas a lower rate could apply to electricity used for cooking and heating, where natural gas might be used instead. Of late, many commissions have abandoned block rates in hopes of encouraging energy conservation.

Telephones further illustrate value-of-service pricing. Business users have traditionally been charged *more* than residential users on the theory that phone service is indispensable to businesses but more or less optional in the home. An even more striking example of AT&T's price discrimination concerns interstate services of various kinds. AT&T's "Seven-Way Cost Study" in the mid-1960s disclosed a pattern of discrimination generated by competition. Profits as a percentage of investment were 9.7% and 13.4% on message toll telephone and WATS services, where the company faced no competition to speak of. In contrast, profits were a piddling 0.3% and 1.4% on TELPAK and private-line telegraph services, where rivals posed a threat.[18] Clearly, Ma Bell's elasticity of demand was higher with competition than without.

Presentation of these examples is not meant to imply that utility price discrimination is always "bad" or "unfair." It may seem unfair because some pay high and some pay low, relative to costs. But there are instances of beneficial price discrimination, "beneficial" in that it can lead to a *lower overall average price* for the company and even allow a *reduction in the high price paid* by those with relatively inelastic demand.

In short, rate structure regulation is complex. Cost-of-service pricing is not the only option. Value-of-service pricing may sometimes be socially valuable.

---

[17] Indeed, the marginal costs of serving industrial buyers are much lower, and price cost margins on industrial sales are consequently higher than on residential sales. See Jon P. Nelson and Mark J. Roberts, "Ramsey Numbers and the Role of Competing Interest Groups in Electric Utility Regulation," *Quarterly Journal of Economics and Business* (Autumn 1989), pp. 21–42.

For a survey of elasticity estimates, see L. D. Taylor, "The Demand for Electricity: A survey," *Bell Journal of Economics* (Spring 1975), pp. 74–110.

[18] Harry M. Trebing and William H. Melody, "An Evaluation of Domestic Communications Pricing Practices and Policies," Staff Paper No. 5, *The Domestic Telecommunications Carrier Industry*, President's Task Force on Communications (1968), p. 217.

VI. PROBLEMS AND DISTORTIONS

As if we have not hung enough problems around regulators' necks, a few more must be mentioned. First, it would be nice if commissions could reward utilities that operate efficiently and progressively and penalize those putting out poorly. This would be "incentive regulation." But no tidy incentive techniques have yet been devised. Measurement of efficiency and progressiveness is imprecise at best. And deviations from whatever measures are adopted may be as much the fault of regulators as managers. Assume, for example, that low profit earnings are taken to signal poor performance. Such a predicament might, in fact, be the result of some commission decision. Until recently the only source of proper incentive has been regulatory "lag." Earnings that rise inordinately from efficiency remain with the firm until regulators act to reduce rate levels, but they act only after a long lag. Conversely, earnings that fall with inefficiency must be borne by the firm until requests for rate increases are answered, which procedure likewise entails some lag. Thus the lag imperfectly and temporarily rewards "goodness" and punishes "badness." Beginning in the 1980s incentive regulation expanded to include specific programs in 20 states. One of the most popular programs allows utilities to keep the fuel cost savings of high-capacity usage.[19]

Second, some regulatory theorists argue that profit regulation contains some particularly unfavorable incentives. Because profit is keyed to the rate base, *there is an incentive to expand the rate base* (to substitute capital for labor) beyond the point that would be optimal in the absence of regulation.[20] Just how serious this so-called "Averch-Johnson effect" actually is no one can say. Empirical tests of the hypothesis have been mixed, half confirming and half refuting it.[21] Even if the effect does exist, it may not be as bad as it might seem. Although in *static* terms the bias favoring capital over other inputs may lift costs undesirably, the *dynamic* result may be *lower* costs through *improved technological progress*, given that most technological change tends to favor capital intensity.[22]

A third problem is what James McKie aptly calls the "tar-baby" ef-

---

[19] Paul R. Joskow and Richard Schmalensee, "Incentive Regulation for Electric Utilities," *Yale Journal on Regulation* (Fall 1986), pp. 1–50.

[20] Harvey Averch and Leland L. Johnson, "Behavior of the Firm under Regulatory Constraint," *American Economic Review* (December 1962), pp. 1052–1069; and Stanislaw H. Wellisz, "Regulation of Natural Gas Pipeline Companies: An Economic Analysis," *Journal of Political Economy* (February 1963), pp. 30–43.

[21] See L. L. Johnson's survey, "The Averch-Johnson Hypothesis after Ten Years," in *Regulation in Further Perspective*, edited by W. G. Shepherd and T. G. Gies (Cambridge, Mass.: Ballinger, 1974), pp. 67–78; plus Charles W. Smithson, "The Degree of Regulation and the Monopoly Firm," *Southern Economic Journal* (January 1978), pp. 568–580; and Robert W. Spann, "Rate of Return Regulation," *Bell Journal of Economics* (Spring 1974), pp. 38–52.

[22] Kahn, *The Economics of Regulation*, Vol. II, pp. 106–107.

fect.[23] Each swipe regulators take at some supposed utility sin seems to ensnare regulators in ever deeper difficulties. The innocent and well-meaning souls who first devised regulation imagined it to be a rather simple matter. What could be easier, they must have asked, than restricting a natural monopolist's profit to some "just" percentage? Yet, as we have already seen, it is not so easy. Taking a punch at profit may mean a bulge in costs, striking at excess cost may hurt quality, and so on. Pretty soon regulators are attempting to cover everything from plant purchases to billing frequencies, and in the process they get covered with tar.

Finally, the main problem with regulation is that, once it gets rolling, it does not stop with appropriate control of natural monopoly or grossly unfair price discrimination. It keeps right on rolling, crushing many opportunities for competition. As Walter Adams once remarked, "Regulation breeds regulation. Competition, even at the margin, is a source of disturbance, annoyance, and embarrassment to the bureaucracy. . . . From the regulator's point of view, therefore, competition must be suppressed wherever it arises."[24]

This is unfortunate. Regulation is a poor substitute for competition (even though it may be a lesser of two evils substitute for unregulated natural monopoly). No one has expressed this sentiment better than Clair Wilcox:

> Regulation, at best, is a pallid substitute for competition. It cannot prescribe quality, force efficiency, or require innovation, because such action would invade the sphere of management. But when it leaves these matters to the discretion of industry, it denies consumers the protection that competition would afford. Regulation cannot set prices below an industry's costs however excessive they may be. Competition does so, and the high-cost company is compelled to discover means whereby its costs can be reduced. Regulation does not enlarge consumption by setting prices at the lowest level consistent with a fair return. Competition has this effect. Regulation fails to encourage performance in the public interest by offering rewards and penalties. Competition offers both.[25]

The proper and improper application of regulation may be seen in the starkly contrasting results of regulation's impact on price that empiricists have uncovered. For electric power and telephone service, regulation seems to have pressed prices *lower* than they would otherwise be, perhaps by as much as 10–20%.[26] But notice, these markets fit the natu-

---

23 James W. McKie, "Regulation and the Free Market: The Problem of Boundaries," *Bell Journal of Economics* (Spring 1970), pp. 6–26.

24 Walter Adams, "Business Exemptions from the Antitrust Laws: Their Extent and Rationale," in *Perspectives on Antitrust Policy*, edited by A. Phillips (Princeton, N.J.: Princeton University Press, 1965), p. 283.

25 Clair Wilcox, *Public Policies Toward Business* (Homewood, Ill.: Richard D. Irwin, 1966), p. 476.

26 William S. Comanor, "Should Natural Monopolies Be Regulated?" *Stanford Law*

ral monopoly model fairly well. In contrast, empirical studies show exactly opposite results in transportation, where natural monopoly does *not* prevail and where in the past competition has suffered the greatest official suppression through entry restriction and minimum price control. Regulation there *raised* prices. Before deregulation, as of the mid-1960s, ICC regulation of railroads, trucks, and water carriers cost the American public perhaps as much as $4–9 *billion* a year in higher rates.[27] Similar conclusions have been reached regarding airline regulation. Over the period 1969–1974, CAB regulation is estimated to have inflated airfares by an average of 22–52%. In annual dollars, that amounted to between $1.4 and $1.8 *billion*.[28] The major causes of these exorbitant rates are various forms of X-inefficiency.

Lest the reader think that these estimates are fabricated from thin air, he or she should recognize that some sectors of transportation escaped tight regulation, and the experience of these fairly competitive sectors guided the estimates. On the ground, agricultural trucking and private trucking have always been beyond the ICC's reach. In the air, travel within California and Texas was not controlled by the CAB. A comparison of *intra*state air fares and interstate regulated air fares in 1975 is shown in Table 22–2. It does not take a pilot's eyes to see that, for routes of similar length and paired-city size, the *intra*state fares were substantially lower.

Deregulation of airlines and trucking during the late 1970s and early 1980 resulted in lower prices than would have prevailed otherwise, mainly because of new entry. Airfares in markets entered by People Express were reduced 40–50%, for example. Prices in short-haul and medium-haul trucking fell 12–14% between 1976 and 1983.[29]

Unfortunately, many of these gains have now been dissipated because lenient antitrust policies during the Reagan administration allowed

Review (February 1970), pp. 510–518; Kahn, *The Economics of Regulation*, Vol. II, pp. 108–111; D. P. Baron and R. A. Taggart, "A Model of Regulation Under Uncertainty and a Test of Regulatory Bias," *Bell Journal of Economics*, Vol. 8 (1977), pp. 151–167; and R. H. Smiley and W. H. Greene, "Determinants of the Effectiveness of Electric Utility Regulation," *Resources and Energy*, Vol. 5 (1983), pp. 65–81.

[27] Thomas G. Moore, "Deregulating Surface Freight Transportation," in *Promoting Competition in Regulated Markets*, edited by A. Phillips (Washington, D.C.: Brookings Institution, 1975), pp. 55–98.

[28] Theodore E. Keeler, "Airline Regulation and Market Performance," *Bell Journal of Economics* (Autumn 1972), pp. 399–424; see also GAO Report CED-77-34, "Lower Airline Costs per Passenger Are Possible in the United States Could Result in Lower Fares" (February 18, 1977).

[29] For details on deregulation, see L. W. Weiss and M. W. Klass (eds.), *Regulatory Reform* (Boston: Little, Brown, 1986); Elizabeth E. Bailey, David R. Graham, and Daniel P. Kaplan, *Deregulating the Airlines* (Cambridge, Mass.: MIT Press, 1985); Alfred E. Kahn, "Deregulating the Vested Interests," in *The Political Economy of Deregulation*, edited by R. G. Noll and B. M. Owen (Washington, D.C.: American Enterprise Institute, 1983), pp. 132–151; and D. F. Greer, *Business, Government, and Society*, 2nd ed. (New York: Macmillan, 1987), pp. 374–382.

TABLE 22–2.   Comparison Between Interstate and Intrastate Airfares, 1975

City Pair	Miles	Fare ($)
Los Angeles–San Francisco	338	18.75
Chicago–Minneapolis	339	38.89
New York–Pittsburgh	335	37.96
Los Angeles–San Diego	109	10.10
Portland–Seattle	129	22.22
Dallas–Houston	239	13.89*
Las Vegas–Los Angeles	236	28.70
Chicago–St. Louis	258	29.63

*This is the night and weekend rate. Daytime weekday rate was $23.15.

Source: *Civil Aeronautics Board Practices and Procedures*, Report of the Subcommittee on Administrative Practice and Procedure, U.S. Senate (1975), p. 41.

mergers and anticompetitive practices. (On airlines, see the Appendix to Chapter 11.) Thus, deregulation is nice insofar as it replaces regulation with competition. However, the early successes of deregulation in transportation encouraged many to call for deregulation of local telephone service, electric power, and other natural monopoly situations. And competition may not work well in these instances, even with antitrust enforcement.[30] To the extent we replace regulated monopoly with unregulated monopoly, we probably lose rather than gain. For example, following liberalization in Britain, the Central Electricity Generating Board was able to manipulate its price *structure* to impose a 10% disadvantage on potential entrants while at the same time raising its price *level*.[31] This behavior clearly fits the "combination" category for dominant firms (cell G in Table 11–1 on page 299), displaying a degree of power that society typically likes to contain.

SUMMARY

Regulation governs major segments of energy and communications, which account for about 4% of GNP. These industries tend to be more capital intensive than others, some experiencing asset/sales ratios of

[30] Harry M. Trebing, "Telecommunications Regulation—The Continuing Dilemma," in Nowotny, Smith, and Trebing (eds.), *Public Utility Regulation*, pp. 93–130; and Paul L. Joskow, "Regulatory Failure, Regulatory Reform, and Structural Change in the Electrical Power Industry," *Brookings Papers on Economic Activity, Microeconomics* 1989 (1989), pp. 125–199.

[31] John Vickers and George Yarrow, *Privatization: An Economic Analysis* (Cambridge, Mass.: MIT Press, 1988), pp. 292–294.

three to one. Moreover, they provide "vital" services, often reaching consumers directly through pipes, wires, and conduits.

Regulation is grounded on several rationales. Natural monopoly justifies regulation of local electricity, water, gas, and telephone service, where economies of scale seem to stretch the full range of demand. Resource conservation vindicates some entry regulation of the airwaves. These and other areas of regulation may also be based on fairness. Another rationale — destructive competition — provides a very weak peg on which to hang regulation, especially in transportation, where it is most frequently invoked.

State and federal commissions with broad powers actually do the regulating. Their procedures are legalistic and their personnel bureaucratic. Among the many criticisms of commissions, the most commonly voiced are incompetence and inadequacy. Although there may be some validity to these charges, it should be acknowledged that the task of regulation is *inherently* difficult.

Profit, or rate level, regulation focuses on the following equation: total revenue = operating expense + current depreciation + (capital value × rate of return). Each element on the right-hand side must be determined to reckon the total revenue needed. The appraisal entails quantities of pure judgment because there are no scientifically established "rights" and "wrongs." There are certain principles, such as the need for a rate of return sufficient to attract capital, but nothing definite. As for objectives, commissions pursue a "balancing act," forever making compromises between the interests of investors and customers. Much the same could be said of rate structure regulation.

Probably the biggest problem with regulation is its potentially anticompetitive effect. To quote a noted economist: "Regulation is like growing old: we would rather not do it, but consider the alternative." Where *un*regulated natural monopoly (or government ownership) is the alternative, this may be correct. Youthful death and unfettered monopoly are both undesirable. But where *competition* is the alternative, it ought to be tried.

APPENDIX: NUCLEAR POWER DUDS: WHO WILL PAY?

"To hear some folks in Little Rock, Ark., you would think that Middle South Utilities Inc. was in league with the devil.

"At a recent public hearing there related to rate increases, a crowd peppered with religious fundamentalists cried 'Amen!' whenever anyone attacked the company's $3.5 billion Grand Gulf 1 nuclear plant. A Baptist preacher clutching a Bible rose and said that the men who built it must have been tainted by bar-hopping and carousing, 'Shout it from the street, shout it from the roof,' the crowd cried, 'we won't pay for their Grand Goof!'"

This report from *The Wall Street Journal* of August 29, 1985 (p. 6) illustrates the intensity of emotions ignited by the single most important issue facing electric utilities during the late 1980s and early 1990s: *Who is going to pay the tremendous costs of nuclear power plants that have been (1) canceled before completion or (2) completed at horrendously high cost and at capacities too large relative to demand to be useful?* Who indeed? Utility customers? Utility investors? Taxpayers generally?

In the case of Grand Gulf the Baptists have not been alone in their anguish. Reynolds Metals, the utility's largest customer, refused to pay its July 1985 electric bill. Regulators reluctantly resisted rate hikes. And the utility put a freeze on hiring, cut executive salaries 10%, delayed building $26 million of electrical substations, omitted dividend payments to its stockholders (the first dividend omission in 36 years), and warned its 48 domestic and 42 foreign banks holding $2.2 billion in construction loans that bankruptcy could be just around the corner.

The aggregate national tallies are amazing. *First*, the cancellations. Between 1978 and 1985, 75 nuclear plants were canceled, including 28 under construction. At least a half-dozen more cancellations are likely before you read this. These duds will cost $35 to $55 billion. *Second*, the excessive costs. Most of those completed during the 1980s—about 60 in number—are hemorrhaging financially from massive cost overruns. The excess costs of these plants (compared to the coal alternative) run in the $45–60 billion range. All told, the total "nuclear power damage bill" will thus be $80–115 billion.[32]

Setting aside the taxpayers, who will end up paying a part of the tab, the key question is how these costs will be distributed between ratepayers on the one hand and utilities and their investors on the other. A basic tool regulators use to tackle this issue is the "prudence test" for including items in the rate base. This compares the cost of the actual investment (say, Grand Gulf 1) and the cost of the alternative that a prudent person would have chosen, including in the rate base only "prudent" amounts. In principle, this test should allow for failures as well as successes. If utilities are granted *no more* than a fair return on *successful* "prudent" investments, they should be granted *no less* than a fair return on *unsuccessful* "prudent" investments. As Alfred E. Kahn explains,

> If [investors] can earn the cost of capital only on the successes and not on
> the failures, it follows that they will earn less than the cost of capital on

---

[32] Charles Komanoff, "Assessing the High Costs of New Nuclear Power Plants," *Public Utilities Fortnightly* (October 11, 1984), pp. 33–38. See also U.S. Department of Energy, *Nuclear Plant Cancellations: Causes, Costs, and Consequences* (Washington, D.C.: U.S. Government Printing Office, April 1983).

all their dollars, taken together. And investors won't play that game once they understand that those are going to be the rules.[33]

Moreover, the only sensible way to apply the "prudence test" is to look at the circumstances prevailing when the *investment commitments were made*, not to look at them through the eyes of hindsight. To quote Kahn again, "Prudency . . . on the basis of hindsight, and only for the *failures*, is to play a regulatory game of heads-the-consumer-wins, tails-the-investor-loses: In effect it expropriates stockholder dollars."[34]

Following the prudence test without hindsight, much of the nuclear damage tab can properly be billed to ratepayers. Many of the problem plants were contracted for during the early 1970s when oil and coal prices were soaring wildly and when the demand for electricity was growing at 7% per year. At 7% growth, a utility must double its productive capacity every ten years, and the lagtime for nuclear plant completion is about ten years. In short, nukes looked good. Hence many if not most plants that are a great pain today looked very promising when first planned, and were therefore "prudent."

On the other hand, utilities and their investors cannot be completely exonerated. Ample evidence points to massive imprudence by way of bad management. Take for example two nuclear plants that are virtually identical in architecture, engineering, reactor supplier, and generating capacity — Marble Hill and Byron. The main difference between the two has been the utilities managing their construction — Public Service of Indiana for Marble Hill versus Commonwealth Edison for Byron. The striking difference in cost . . . $7.0 billion for the former, versus $4.2 billion for the latter (and the former has now been canceled).[35]

Broader comparisons are also possible. In raw dollars per kilowatt of capacity, the cost of plants in the United States have varied widely, from over $5000 (Shoreham in New York) to less than $1000 (McGuire in North Carolina). Once adjustments are made for nonmanagerial factors like inflation, interest rates, and the like, the range from top to bottom is narrowed substantially but it is still immense — $3400 per kilowatt versus $1100 per kilowatt. Further nonmanagerial factors like varying wage rates of construction workers account for much of the remaining difference. In the end though, poor management emerges as the only explanation for hefty chunks of the damage bill, maybe as much as 50% of the costs of some of the most expensive plants.[36]

[33] Alfred E. Kahn, "Who Should Pay for Power-Plant Duds?" *The Wall Street Journal*, August 15, 1985, p. 26.

[34] A. E. Kahn, ibid.

[35] James Cook, "Nuclear Follies," *Forbes*, February 11, 1985, pp. 82–100.

[36] Komanoff, "Assessing the High Costs of New Nuclear Power Plants." A still broader comparison looks to France. The French have built 30 reactors since 1973 at an average cost of about $1000 per kilowatt, less than half the U.S. average of about $2100 per kilowatt.

Let's be more specific. Management "horror stories" abound. As summarized by James Cooke of *Forbes*,

> The ineptitude [has] had no pattern, and virtually anything could go wrong and did. How could an experienced contractor like Bechtel have prepared the Midland plant site so poorly that the diesel generator building began settling excessively? How could Bechtel have installed the reactor backwards at San Onofre? How could Brown & Root have got the reactor supports 45 degrees out of whack at Comanche Peak? How could experienced operators pour defective concrete at Marble Hill and the South Texas project? . . . How could design control have been so lax that PG&E used the wrong drawings in calculating seismic response for the steel in the Diablo Canyon containment building?
>
> The [Nuclear Regulatory Commission] has a partial answer. "In some cases," an NRC study concluded, "no one was managing the project, the project had inertia, but no guidance and direction." . . . [An] Office of Technology Assessment study last spring came to the same conclusion: "Inadequate management has been one of the major causes of construction cost overruns and erratic operation."[37]

Cook's own conclusion is even more blunt. Neither excessive regulation by the NRC nor obstruction by the antinuclear activists have had much of an adverse impact. "The failure of the U.S. nuclear power program ranks as the largest managerial disaster in business history, a disaster on a monumental scale."

Thus when utilities request price increases of up to 50% in order to cover the costs of their nuclear projects, commissions are often reacting reasonably in granting only part of the request. Many utilities and their investors are suffering through these dark days along with ratepayers, and rightly so. Unfortunately, injury to investors today will cause injury to ratepayers tomorrow. Future investors will have to be rewarded for the added risks they will perceive, and ratepayers must eventually pay the higher costs of capital.[38]

[37] Cook, "Nuclear Follies," pp. 91–92.

[38] For more on this issue see A. Lawrence Kolbe and William B. Tye, "The *Duquesne* Opinion: How Much Hope is There for Investors in Regulated Firms?" *Yale Journal on Regulation* (Winter 1991), pp. 113–157 and the comments by Stephen F. Williams and Alan P. Buchmann in the same issue.

23

Technological Change: Theory and Cross-section Evidence

What laws govern the growth of man's mastery over nature?

—JACOB SCHMOOKLER

From the first squawky telephone to the latest jet airliner, technological change has done more than anything else to shape our modern economy and everyday life. Innovation spurs growth, boosts productivity, lifts profits, lengthens lives, generates jobs, and enriches experiences. Nearly half of all this century's gains in real income can be attributed to technological progress. The lion's share of the products we now use and take for granted simply did not exist as little as three generations ago— television, frozen food, zippers, computers, air-conditioning, penicillin, nylon, refrigerators, synthetic detergents, Frisbees, and so on. Among companies, Hewlett-Packard illustrates the importance of technological change more than most. During each year of the late 1980s over 50% of its annual sales of $12 billion came from products developed *within the previous three years.*[1]

[1] *Fortune*, July 2, 1990, p. 73.

During 1989 private firms spent more than $66 billion on R&D. Roughly 60% of this expenditure went for improvement of existing products, 30% for development of new products, and 10% for developing new processes of production. On top of this, private industry conducted the lion's share of government funded R&D, which totaled more than $30 billion in 1989.[2]

In this light, questions concerning industry's performance for progress take on a serious cast. Does high concentration help or hinder technological advance? What sorts and sizes of firms put forth the greatest R&D effort? Are there still active independent inventors of the type of Thomas Edison and the Wright brothers? These queries now occupy our focus. We begin by filling in some background. The remainder of the chapter is then divided into two major portions, one covering the impact of firm size, the other discussing the effect of market structure. It will be seen that bigness comes out looking better than it has in previous chapters, but only to a limited degree.[3]

I. CONCEPTS AND CONDITIONS

A. Definitions

Edison was undoubtedly right when he said that invention is the product of "one percent inspiration and ninety-nine percent perspiration." But for present purposes, **invention** is best defined as *"the first confidence that something should work, and the first rough test that it will, in fact, work."*[4] It requires an *initial concept* and *crude proof*.

Although invention is surely the seed of technical progress, it is only the seed. In monetary weight invention accounts for no more than about 5–15% of the total cost of bringing most new products to market or placing new production processes into service for the first time. By far the greatest amount of time and expense goes into what may be called innovation. **Innovation** *is the first commercial application of an invention*. It entails refinement of the basic idea, testing prototypes, debugging, development, engineering, initial production, and perhaps initial marketing as well.

---

[2] *Business Week*, June 15, 1990, p. 194; June 27, 1977, pp. 62–63; and National Science Board, *Science & Engineering Indicators—1989* (Washington, D.C.: U.S. Government Printing Office, 1989), p. 351.

[3] For surveys, see William L. Baldwin and John T. Scott, *Market Structure and Technological Change* (Chur, Switzerland: Harwood, 1987); F. M. Scherer and David Ross, *Industrial Market Structure and Economic Performance*, 3rd ed. (Boston: Houghton Mifflin, 1990), pp. 613–660; Morton I. Kamien and Nancy L. Schwartz, "Market Structure and Innovation: A Survey," *Journal of Economic Literature* (March 1975), pp. 1–37.

[4] John Jewkes, David Sawers, and Richard Stillerman, *The Sources of Invention*, 2nd ed. (New York: W. W. Norton, 1969), p. 28.

In many cases there is no clear boundary between invention and innovation. Conceptually, however, "Invention is the stage at which the scent is first picked up, development the stage at which the hunt is in full cry."[5] Whereas about 5–15% of a successful new product's cost goes into invention, about 10–20% goes into engineering and design, 40–60% is spent on tooling and manufacturing setup, 5–15% goes into manufacturing start-up, and 10–25% covers initial marketing expenses.[6] A similar pattern is revealed by a breakdown of industrial R&D outlays for 1989 as estimated by the National Science Foundation:

- $2.5 billion, or 4.0%, went toward *basic research*, for the advancement of *general* scientific knowledge.

- $14.0 billion, or 22.4%, went for *applied research*, pursuing what could be called inventions.

- $46.1 billion, or 73.6% went into *development*, that is, innovative activities concerned with translating research findings into commercial products or processes.[7]

Innovation also consumes a tremendous amount of time, further separating the first flash of insight from the marketing debut. John Enos estimated the interval between invention and innovation for 44 major discoveries, finding that, on average, the interval was about 13 years. To mention a few examples: radio was 8 years maturing; jet engine, 14 years; catalytic cracking of petroleum, 9 years; ballpoint pen, 6 years; magnetic recording, 5 years; mechanical cotton picker, 53 years; television, 22 years; and dacron, 12 years.[8] In short, innovation is indispensible; an invention without innovation is like an unsung song.

But advance requires still more, a third stage called **diffusion**. The innovation may flop, or it may spread. Clearly, *the extent and speed of any spread can be very important to overall progress.* Like the earlier stages, diffusion usually takes time and money because it, too, is essentially a learning process. Unlike the earlier stages, however, this learning process is not confined to a single research laboratory or a few firms; it can involve multitudes of producers and users. The digital watch provides a timely example of diffusion. Introduced in 1972 at $2000 apiece, it was at first more a curiosity than a chronometer. But then it caught on. With improvements, climbing sales, longer production runs, and cost reductions, prices fell from $2000 to $10 in just 5 years ($10 being the bottom

---

5 Ibid.

6 U.S. Department of Commerce, *Technological Innovation: Its Environment and Management* (Washington, D.C.: U.S. Government Printing Office, 1967), p. 9.

7 *Science & Engineering Indicators 1989*, pp. 266–270.

8 John L. Enos, "Invention and Innovation in the Petroleum Refining Industry," reprinted in *Economic Concentration Hearings*, Part 3, U.S. Senate 98th Cong., 1st Sess., Subcommittee on Antitrust and Monopoly (1965), pp. 1486–1491.

of the line, of course). Now more than half of all watches sold are digital.[9]

It may be concluded that a full assessment of progressive performance must take into account *invention, innovation,* and *diffusion.* Each is different. Yet each is crucial to progress. And it will be shown that, to some degree, certain firm sizes and certain market structures perform better at one stage than others. These distinctions should therefore be put in warm storage.

B. Measurement

One more preliminary comment needs mention. Good performance in these several respects cannot be measured in absolute terms. Given that IBM spends $5201 million on R&D and Amdahl spends $277 million, as they did in 1989, one cannot conclude therefrom that IBM is necessarily the more progressive of the two. *Relative to sales,* Amdahl spent 13.2% as against IBM's 8.3%. *Relative to profits* Amdahl spent 109% to IBM's 78%. The implication should be obvious. Accordingly, subsequent analysis places heavy reliance on a varied assortment of *relative* measures.

Unfortunately, the problem cuts even deeper than can be controlled by converting all statistics to percentage or per unit values. Let private R&D spending as a percentage of sales be 10.1% for drugs and 0.8% for textiles, as shown in Table 23–1. One is tempted to deduce from this marked disparity that performance in drugs is better than in textiles. But such a supposition might be wrong. Although relative outlays are plainly higher for drugs, the *opportunity* for technical progress is also much greater for drugs than for textiles. One reason is that drug products tend to occupy earlier stages of their *life cycle* as compared to textiles.

Given a greater opportunity, the profitability of R&D will be greater over a larger range of expenditure. It is only natural to expect, then, that industries and firms with richer opportunities will outspend those with relatively impoverished prospects. Much of the interindustry variation on outlays observed in Table 23–1 can probably be pinned on just such differences. At the top of the list we find semiconductors, computers, drugs, aerospace, instruments, motor vehicles, electronics, and chemicals. All enjoy dazzling opportunities and spend accordingly. These industries alone account for over 80% of all industrial R&D. Toward the bottom of the list are food, textiles, apparel, and paper. Centuries of attention paid to their design and production apparently curtails pres-

---

[9] *Business Week,* October 27, 1975, pp. 78–92; January 26, 1976, pp. 27–28; May 2, 1977, pp. 78–80. Between 1852 and 1897 the price of aluminum fell from $545.00 to $0.36 a pound, electrolitic reduction being the key innovation. See George David Smith, *From Monopoly to Competition* (Cambridge: Cambridge University Press, 1988), p. 34.

TABLE 23–1. Selected Data for R&D Performing Companies:
By Industry, 1989

Industry	Company R&D Funds as a Percentage of Sales (%)	Company R&D Funds ($ millions)
Drugs	10.1%	$5,143.6
Semiconductors	9.3	2,155.1
Computers	9.0	11,736.5
Instruments	5.8	1,431.8
Telecommunications	4.7	3,304.0
Aerospace	4.1	3,936.7
Electrical, electronics	3.9	2,906.1
Chemicals	3.8	4,752.9
Cars and trucks	3.6	9,512.2
Machinery	2.6	1,191.3
Tires, rubber	2.4	355.2
Office equipment	2.2	267.7
Building materials	1.9	463.8
Paper	1.0	432.3
Textiles, apparel	0.8	49.8
Food, beverage	0.7	459.5

Source: *Business Week*, June 15, 1990, pp. 196–217.

ent-day leeway for change. Hence progressiveness ought to be measured *relative to the potential for progress.*

It is of course difficult to know exactly where potentials of this sort lie. Indeed, it was once thought that meaningful economic research in this area was impossible, that ignorance of technological opportunities was fatal to the undertaking.[10] Luckily, this is not so. Ways around the problem have been devised. These should therefore be noted.

First, and most obviously, federal contributions to R&D have to be excluded when calculating private industry performance. Otherwise, those few industries benefiting from federal largess—aircraft, electronics, and communications, in particular—would have an unfair edge. The data in Table 23–1 thus exclude federal funds.

Second, much can be learned by comparing the progressiveness of individual firms *within a single industry.* All such firms presumably face the *same* opportunities, whatever they may be. Hence we shall review more evidence concerning individual firms here than anywhere else in the book. This evidence is not only intriguing, it is also pertinent; if an industry's small firms outdo their bigger brethren, it might pay to slice

---

[10] Joe Bain, *Industrial Organization* (New York: John Wiley, 1968), p. 460.

the big ones smaller. Then again, the evidence might suggest the opposite conclusion.

Finally, *inter*industry comparisons of progressiveness are possible if potentials are accounted for in some fashion. The techniques tried thus far include use of "dummy" variables in regression analysis and international comparisons. The latter are easiest to explain. French steel and American steel industries presumably face the same opportunities, but one may be more highly concentrated than the other, in which case any differences in progressiveness between them might be due to this structural difference.

Within the confines of these various techniques, it will be assumed that more progressiveness means better performance. This, too, has its problems. Sensitive readers need no prodding to realize that "more" is not necessarily "better." Newness can be unsettling and even dangerous. Faster cars and deadlier pesticides might mark progress in terms of "more," but they might also raise costs of safety and pollution. This particular objection to progressiveness certainly has its merits. But we shall assume that "more" R&D, "more" patents, "more" innovations, and "more" rapid diffusion are indeed for the better.

II. FIRM SIZE AND PROGRESSIVENESS

A. Theory

Confident that big firms were more progressive than small, J. K. Galbraith wrote some time ago that "a benign Providence . . . has made the modern industry of a few large firms an excellent instrument for inducing technical change."[11] He was not alone in his praise of bigness. Others, like Joseph Schumpeter, have expressed the same sentiment. They rest their case on a chain of arguments.

1. *Absolute size:* It is alleged that big firms can better afford R&D outlays. They have bigger bank balances and richer cash flows than smaller firms. Given the immense expense of R&D projects, small firms simply cannot compete.
2. *Economies of scale:* Invention and innovation often require costly specialized equipment—wind tunnels, test tracks, electron microscopes, and so on. Researchers themselves are growing ever more specialized, necessitating teamwork. These R&D inputs can be used more efficiently by large scale enterprises, or so it is argued.
3. *Risk:* Every project is a gamble. Large size enables numerous projects, so the hits can offset the misses. Risk thus diminishes with added size.

[11] John Kenneth Galbraith, *American Capitalism* (Boston: Houghton Mifflin, 1956), p. 86.

4. *Time horizon:* It is contended that a larger firm can wait longer for a payoff than a smaller firm. This argument presumably gives larger firms longer time horizons, and innovation is time consuming.
5. *Diversification:* R&D often yield unexpected outcomes. Search for a synthetic fiber may turn up a new paint. Since bigger firms tend to be more diversified than smaller firms, the giants can better exploit these happenstances.

Though plausible, these arguments are not unassailable. Those who question the view that bigness is better quarrel with these theoretical assertions. It can be argued that, although many projects are indeed costly and require large absolute size, many are not. Some run into the millions, some into the thousands. The range leaves ample room for smaller firms, and, on average, the cost of a typical project is not gargantuan. By one estimate the typical project of the late 1980s had a total cost of $1 million to $2 million.[12] Small firms like Oshkosh Truck could afford several such projects per year.

As for economies of scale, a small firm may be able to overcome a handicap by hiring the services of a large independent R&D outfit, whose sole activity is research and whose costs are spread over its many contract customers. The fact that most contracted R&D is done for large firms does not negate this possibility. Moreover, it can be argued that since R&D is a *creative* activity, the bureaucratic tangles that bigness brings may be stifling rather than liberating, inefficient rather than efficient. Ralph Hardy, who headed a research division of Du Pont before leaving to join a small biotechnology firm in 1984, says

> . . . there's an intensity in a small company that you don't see at a large corporation like [Du Pont]. In a small company, most employees are participants, and there's nothing like that to bring out the best in an individual. . . . I can do more in a day at Biotechnica than I could in a month at Du Pont.[13]

Risk, too, may be questioned as a force favoring bigness. To be sure, the bigger firm may be able to back more projects and thereby assure itself success in some of them, just as "the richer gambler who backs more horses in the race is, other things being equal, more likely to pick the winner."[14] However, it may be doubted whether the returns from this strategy are *more than proportionate* to the outlay. If they are not, then great size gives no particular advantage.

Moreover, it may be questioned whether the risk in funding only a few projects intimidates the smaller firms. Do race tracks draw only the wealthy who can wager on a number of horses each time round? Don't

---

12 Scherer and Ross, *Industrial Market Structure and Economic Performance*, p. 619.
13 *The Washington Post, National Weekly Edition*, January 18–24, 1988, p. 20.
14 Jewkes, Sawers, and Stillerman, *The Sources of Innovation*, p. 130.

bet on it. There are countless little guys who *really* gamble; there are countless small firms accepting great risks. Conversely, there are many large firms whose bureaucrats seem to shun almost everything short of a sure thing. Approval of projects in big firms typically requires clearance of several managerial layers, something that heightens the chances that uncertain undertakings will be vetoed by "an abominable noman."[15] IBM repeatedly rejected opportunities to develop and produce the Xerox machine, saying it was too risky. But it was not too risky for Haloid, the half-pint company that actually undertook the task and later changed its name to Xerox. IBM management also ordered IBM researchers to drop development of disk memories, one of the most significant of all computer inventions. Although IBM later claimed credit for these devices, it could do so only because several unruly IBM researchers ignored orders, endangered their jobs, secretly persisted, and eventually succeeded.[16]

Several studies by Edwin Mansfield indicate that the risks of R&D may not be as awesome as commonly supposed.[17] Mansfield quantifies the probabilities of success at three stages that roughly correspond to invention, innovation, and diffusion but go by different labels. He finds considerable variation, but the average probability of successful "technical completion" was 57%. Of those projects passing "technical completion," 65% were "commercialized." And of those "commercialized," 74% returned a profit. In other words, the probability of prizewinning was better than 50:50 at the purely technical level. These good odds seem "to be due to the fact that the bulk of R&D projects are aimed at fairly modest advances in the state of the art." Eventual profitability is much more precarious, however. Of all projects in Mansfield's sample entering the front end of the R&D pipeline, only about 27% emerge profitably at the rear end (a figure attained by multiplying the several probabilities, $0.57 \times 0.65 \times 0.74 = 0.27$). Still, 27% is not dreadfully risky. The odds do not imply a game of utterly foolish gambles. It may therefore be a game that small firms can play without suffering nightmares.

The remaining arguments favoring large size — time horizon and diversification — are equally vulnerable to counterargument. But the debate will now be dropped. Resolution cannot be reached without recourse to the facts. So let's now turn to the facts as they relate to invention, innovation, and diffusion (keeping in mind that the statistics often blur these stages). Truth on both sides will be revealed.

[15] C. Northcote Parkinson's expression, cited by F. M. Scherer, *Industrial Market Structure and Economic Performance* (Chicago: Rand McNally, 1970), p. 354.

[16] *Economic Concentration Hearings*, p. 1217.

[17] Edwin Mansfield, J. Rapoport, A. Romeo, E. Villani, S. Wagner, and F. Husic, *The Production and Application of New Industrial Technology* (New York: W. W. Norton, 1977), pp. 21–43.

B. Firm Size and Invention: The Evidence

The facts concerning invention are best kept in three separate compartments: (1) inputs, (2) outputs, and (3) outputs/inputs, or efficiency. Inputs of R&D money and personnel obviously reflect *effort*, but they may indicate nothing about *results achieved*. The most common and convenient measure of results, or R&D output, is patents. In lieu of patents, which fail to discriminate between marvelous and mundane discoveries, some students of the subject have tried to measure output by selecting only "significant" inventions then tracing their sources. Finally, systematic comparison of outputs and inputs yields a measure of efficiency, such as patents *per dollar* of R&D investment. Such a measure is needed to test the presence of scalar economies.

1. Inputs. At first glance, statistics reflecting effort overwhelmingly favor the big firms as being most progressive. R&D expenditures are tightly concentrated. In 1982, for instance, U.S. manufacturing firms with 10,000 or more employees accounted for 45% of all manufacturing employment. At the same time they made 81.3% of all privately financed expenditures on R&D performed by manufacturing companies.[18] One of the main reasons R&D effort is so dramatically concentrated is that virtually all large firms undertake some R&D, whereas most small firms have no formal R&D program whatsoever. Over 90% of all firms with more than 5000 employees engage in some R&D, but below this, as firm size drops, the proportion of firms engaging in R&D sinks. The result: 800 companies account for over 80% of all private R&D spending.[19] Thus there is some element of truth to the claim that bigness is better.

These aggregate statistics, however, exaggerate the prominence of the largest enterprises. They take no account of differing technical opportunities across industries, and they make no distinction between what could be considered large middle-sized firms and the genuine giants among those who do have R&D programs. The most pertinent questions is this: *Within* a given industry or a cluster of industries of given technological opportunity, is the effort of the largest firms greater, *relative to their size*, than the effort of medium-sized firms? The question is diagrammed in Figure 23–1. The vertical axis is R&D outlay per dollar of sales or some other measure of *relative* effort. The horizontal axis is firm size. The solid line indicates what we already know, namely, the effort of really small firms *is* relatively small. The dashed lines indicate the possibilities among the medium and large sizes. If relative effort

---

[18] Scherer and Ross, *Industrial Market Structure and Economic Performance*, p. 654.
[19] *Business Week*, June 22, 1987, p. 158; and National Science Foundation, *Research and Development in Industry: 1987* (Washington, D.C.: NSF, 1989), p. 17.

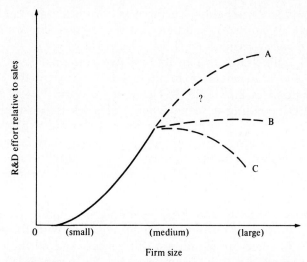

FIGURE 23–1. Effort and firm size within a given industry.

always rose with size, pattern A would prevail. If medium and large firms put forth the *same* relative effort, pattern B would be observed. Finally, pattern C would hold if relative effort dwindled beyond the middle range.

There have been more than a dozen statistical studies of this question.[20] They vary in number of industries and firms included, time periods, and measures of size and effort. Although the results vary a little, the preponderance of evidence indicates that among firms with

[20] J. S. Worely, "Industrial Research and the New Competition," *Journal of Political Economy* (April 1961), pp. 181–186; D. Hamberg, "Size of Firm, Oligopoly and Research: The Evidence," *Canadian Journal of Economics and Political Science* (February 1964), pp. 62–75; Edwin Mansfield, *Industrial Research and Technological Innovation* (New York: W. W. Norton, 1968), pp. 38–40; William S. Comanor, "Market Structure, Product Differentiation, and Industrial Research," *Quarterly Journal of Economics* (November 1967), pp. 639–657; F. M. Scherer, Testimony, *Economic Concentration Hearings*, pp. 1194–1196; H. G. Grabowski, "The Determinants of Industrial Research and Development: A Study of the Chemical, Drug, and Petroleum Industries," *Journal of Political Economy* (March 1968), pp. 292–306; Ronald E. Shrieves, "Firm Size and Innovation: Further Evidence," *Industrial Organization Review*, Vol. 4, no. 1 (1976), pp. 26–33; John E. Tilton, "Firm Size and Innovative Activity in the Semiconductor Industry," mimeo (April 1972); Douglas W. Webbink, *The Semiconductor Industry* (Washington, D.C., Federal Trade Commission Economic Report, 1977), pp. 103–108; Peter D. Loeb and Vincent Lin, "Research and Development in the Pharmaceutical Industry," *Journal of Industrial Economics* (September 1977), pp. 45–51; W. F. Mueller, J. Culbertson, and B. Peckham, *Market Structure and Technological Performance in the Food-Manufacturing Industries* (Madison: Research Division, College of Agricultural and Life Sciences, University of Wisconsin, 1982); Albert N. Link, Terry G. Seaks, and Sabrina R. Woodbery, "Firm Size and R&D Spending: Testing for Functional Form," *Southern Economic Journal* (April 1988), pp. 1027–1031; and Wesley M. Cohen, Richard C. Levin, and David C. Mowery, "Firm Size and R&D Intensity: A Re-examination," *Journal of Industrial Economics* (June 1987), pp. 543–565.

R&D efforts, added size neither encourages nor discourages greater R&D effort (pattern B, Figure 23–1). In general *business unit size has no effect on R&D intensity among business units that have R&D programs.*

Table 23–2 illustrates this in its first two columns. F. M. Scherer's findings for 196 industries are summarized in terms of the three possibilities identified in Figure 23–1. The vast majority, 71.4%, fit case B, in which R&D spending as a percentage of sales is constant over the medium to large range of firm sizes. Of the remaining two cases, A has an edge over C in these results, suggesting bigness may be slightly better. But other recent studies confirm the neutrality of size once the medium threshold is crossed.[21] Hence bigness is better only up to a point.

2. Outputs. Patents and R&D spending are highly correlated, so observations concerning outputs generally conform with those concerning inputs. Still, there are significant differences, and all the differences tend to favor smallness. Take patent statistics for instance. Whereas 90% of all private R&D funds can be credited to about 900 firms, they cannot claim the same percentage of patents. Approximately 80% of all patents issued nowadays go to corporations, both big and small, while 19% go to *individuals.*[22]

Moreover, *within* the corporate sector itself, patents are nowhere near as highly concentrated as R&D dollars. Detailed data from the mid-1970s on 443 of the largest manufacturing corporations reveal their shares to be:

- Share of industrial R&D expenditure: 73%
- Share of industrial corporate patents: 61%

The same data, when put into the format of Table 23–2, disclose that with respect to patents, only about 11% of the industries follow the A pattern of Figure 23–1 in which bigness is better (down from 20% regarding R&D expenditure). Just over 15% favor medium size over large. And the vast majority of industries, 73.4%, display neutrality. Thus the B and C patterns unfavorable to large firms are even more prevalent for *outputs* than they are for *inputs.*

A defender of large corporations might at this point like to explain the discrepancy in output and input by claiming that the *quality* of large firm inventions is superior to that of small-firm or individual inventions. But the claim would collapse for lack of evidence. One index of quality

---

[21] Link, Seaks, and Woodbery, "Firm Size and R&D Spending"; and Cohen, Levin, and Mowery, "Firm Size and R&D Intensity." It must be noted, however, that big firms perform better when spending on *basic* research. E. Mansfield, "Composition of R&D Expenditures," *Review of Economics and Statistics* (November 1981), pp. 610–614; and Albert N. Link, *Research and Development Activity in U.S. Manufacturing* (New York: Praeger, 1981).

[22] U.S. Department of Commerce, *Statistical Abstract 1986*, p. 539.

TABLE 23–2. The Relationship Between Line of Business
Size and Two Measures of Technology Performance:
R&D Spending and Patents, 1974

| | Number and Percentage of Sampled Industries According to the Categories of Figure 23–1 | | | |
| | R&D Spending | | Patents | |
Category of Performance	Number of Industries	% of Total	Number of Industries	% of Total
Case A: Improved performance with added size	40	20.4%	14	11.3%
Case B: No effect from size	140	71.4	91	73.4
Case C: Diminished performance with added size	16	8.2	19	15.3
Totals	196	100.0%	124	100.0%

Source: F. M. Scherer, "Technical Change and the Modern Corporation," in Betty Bock et al. (eds.), *The Impact of the Modern Corporation* (New York: Columbia University Press, 1984), pp. 290–291.

is commercial utilization, and several studies show that a greater percentage of small-firm patented inventions are used commercially than large-firm patented inventions.[23] Moreover, as Scherer notes, "Interview studies also reveal that large corporations with an active staff of patent attorneys are less discriminating in their choice of inventions on which patent protection is sought."[24]

As for the inventions of individuals, the evidence is almost astounding. John Jewkes, David Sawers, and Richard Stillerman carefully compiled case histories for 70 momentous twentieth-century inventions and found that only 24 of them, or one-third, were the work of corporate research laboratories. In contrast, 38, or more than half, "can be ranked as individual invention in the sense that much of the pioneering work was carried through by men who were working on their own behalf without the backing of research institutions and usually with limited resources."[25] Among these individual discoveries are: air-conditioning; jet engine; Kodachrome; penicillin; "Polaroid" Land camera; power steer-

[23] Jacob Schmookler, *Invention and Economic Growth* (Cambridge, Mass.: Harvard University Press, 1966), pp. 48–51.
[24] Scherer *op. cit.* (1970), p. 358.
[25] Jewkes, Sawers, and Stillerman, *The Sources of Invention*, p. 73.

ing; automatic transmissions; safety razor; cyclotron; xerography; titanium; helicopter; electron microscope; gyro-compass; and cellophane.

Corroborating these results, one study found that of 27 major inventions made during the decade of 1946–1955, only 7 (26%) came from large industrial laboratories. The remainder came from independent inventors, small firms, and universities.[26] A separate study of seven major inventions for the refining and cracking of petroleum, found that all seven were made by independent inventors.[27] However instructive (and inspirational) these statistics might be, it nevertheless seems to be true that, *over time*, the *relative* importance of individual inventors seems to be shrinking. Whereas today 20% of all patents go to individuals, at the turn of the century individuals garnered 80%.[28]

3. Output/Input. When the input and output records of the largest firms are compared, it appears that their inventive output is much the weaker. For this, there are two main explanations. First, the inputs are probably more imperfectly measured than the outputs, and the imperfections shift as a function of firm size. In particular, data on R&D spending tend to understate the inventive effort of small firms and individuals. Such efforts tend to be more casual, less formal, and therefore less fully reported than the efforts of large firms.[29] Conversely, R&D spending data may somewhat overstate the inventive efforts of larger firms because most of the larger firms' money goes into *innovation* rather than invention. And in the area of innovation, many large firms make up for their embarrassing record regarding invention. Thus, for example, virtually all the inventions credited to *individuals* by Jewkes, Sawers, and Stillerman were not innovated by individuals but rather by industrial firms, many of which are immense.[30] Not too much should be made of this qualification, however, because "development" and "innovation" do produce patents, the main measure of invention.

The second explanation for the discrepancy shows bigness in a less praiseworthy light. That is, output/input tends to fall directly with increased size, everything else being equal, because of *diseconomies of scale in invention*. Telling statistics demonstrating these diseconomies were gathered by Jacob Schmookler. They may be seen in Table 23–3, which reports the number of patents pending per million dollars of R&D outlay for firms formally engaged in R&D, broken down by size classes. In short, the data are patent output ÷ million dollars R&D input. Reading

[26] Daniel Hamberg, "Invention in the Industrial Research Laboratory," *Journal of Political Economy* (April 1963), p. 96–98.

[27] Enos, "Invention and Innovation in the Petroleum Refining Industry," pp. 1481–1486.

[28] Schmookler, *Invention and Economic Growth*, p. 26.

[29] Alfred Kleinknecht "Measuring R&D in Small Firms: How Much Are We Missing?" *Journal of Industrial Economics* (December 1987), pp. 253–256.

[30] Richard R. Nelson, *Economic Concentration Hearings*, p. 1145.

TABLE 23–3. Number of Patents Pending per Million Dollars Spent on R&D, 1953

	Size of Firm		
Industry	Fewer than 1000 Employees	1000 to 4999 Employees	5000 or More Employees
Machinery	117.3	70.4	41.3
Chemicals	89.3	50.0	42.4
Electric equipment	63.7	79.4	39.1
Petroleum	100.0	119.0	64.1
Instruments	63.3	69.4	26.7
All other industries	64.9	140.8	35.9
Average all industries	78.1	74.6	39.1

Source: Derived from Jacob Schmookler, *Economic Concentration, Hearings,* Part 3, U.S. Senate Subcommittee on Antitrust and Monopoly, 89th Cong., 1st Sess. (1965), p. 1,258.

across the rows, you will spy a fairly consistent pattern. Patent productivity is always *lowest in the largest size class.* In four of the industry groups it is highest among medium-sized firms. And in two industries — machinery and chemicals — the *smallest* firms display the greatest patent productivity. The smallest firms, in fact, are rarely far below the medium firms, and the smallest typically twice as efficient as the largest. Using different data drawn from the petroleum, chemical, and steel industries, plus a different analytical technique, Mansfield came up with similar results. He concluded that, "contrary to popular belief, the inventive output per dollar of R&D expenditure in most of these cases seems to be lower in the largest firms than in large and medium-sized firms."[31]

Stated differently, costs per patent rise with size. The obvious next question is why? There is of course no answer universally propounded by all observers, but most seem to agree with the answer derived by Arnold Cooper, whose comparative study of large and small research organizations is widely cited:

Large firms, he found, seem to become enmeshed in bureaucracy and red tape, resulting in a less hospitable atmosphere for creative contributions by operating personnel. Superior technical personnel tend to be attracted to

[31] Mansfield, *Industrial Research and Technological Innovation,* p. 42. See also Tilton, "Firm Size and Innovative Activity in the Semiconductor Industry." A major exception is drugs: J. M. Vernon and Peter Gusen, "Technical Change and Firm Size: The Pharmaceutical Industry," *Review of Economics and Statistics* (August 1974), pp. 294–302. Scherer's line of business study of patenting is less favorable to smallness than these, but his data included fewer small firms, as the FTC sample he used centered on large firms. See F. M. Scherer, "The Propensity to Patent," *International Journal of Industrial Organization* (March 1983), pp. 107–128.

smaller companies where greater latitude may be afforded them. The larger the firm, the more difficult it may be to recognize the problems needing solution. Finally there is evidence of greater cost consciousness in smaller firms.[32]

Because big firms are often frustrated when trying to hire creative personnel, they sometimes try to compensate by *acquiring* the small *firms* they work for, but the result is frequently the same:

Xerox . . . saw the founders of two of its key data processing acquisitions of the 1970s—Diablo Systems and Shugart Associates—walk out to start companies that became major competitors. "There is a natural temptation to go in and overlay your reporting procedures, your own benefit plans, sometimes even your own management people," says Wayland R. Hickes, a Xerox vice-president. "You create frustration, and to an extent you stifle creativity."[33]

It seems then that "nothing is more characteristic of the individual inventor than this disposition to fold his tent and quietly steal away to other territory when large-scale organized research comes into his field."[34]

To sum up, inventive inputs, outputs, and output/input ratios all seem to be positively associated with size only among very small and medium-sized firms. Beyond that, no additional gains from size are evident. If anything, losses are thereafter more likely than gains. There is, moreover, still a place for the individual inventor.

C. Firm Size and Innovation: The Evidence

A rather forceful case can be made that *innovation* is affected by size much as invention is. Observe first that the bulk of R&D money goes to "development," and that many if not most corporate patents are offspring of "development" instead of "research." So the preceding section's message necessarily overflows to cover much present ground.

Second, "hare and tortoise" stories abound, wherein an unlikely little firm outraces the unsuspecting, all-powerful large firm, whose overconfidence or lackadaisical attitude instills sloth:

- It was not the Big Three who innovated small cars in the United States after World War II, but rather Kaiser, Willys, American Motors, and Studebaker. The Big Three resisted, fearing dilution of their large-car sales.[35]

[32] Kamien and Schwartz, "Market Structure and Innovation," p. 10.

[33] *Business Week*, April 18, 1983, p. 88. See also "Can Semiconductors Survive Big Business?" *Business Week*, December 3, 1979, pp. 66–85; and *The Wall Street Journal*, May 14, 1984, p. 27, which tells the story of the No. 1 robot maker in the United States after its acquisition by Westinghouse.

[34] Jewkes, Sawers, and Stillerman, *The Sources of Invention*, p. 99.

[35] Lawrence J. White, "The American Automobile Industry and the Small Car, 1945–70," *Journal of Industrial Economics* (April 1972), pp. 179–192.

- When inventors of the digital watch offered it to the major old-line watch companies for development, they ran into a brick wall. Innovation thus fell to electronics companies like Time Computer, Fairchild, and Texas Instruments.[36]

- Stephen Wozniak tried to persuade his bosses at Hewlett-Packard Company to back his efforts to build a personal computer. He "couldn't get anybody to listen," so in 1977 he founded Apple Computer.[37]

- The fastest-growing field in computers during the late 1980s was workstations, the speedy cousins of personal computers. Two upstarts, Sun Microsystems and Apollo, deserve most of the innovative credit, leaving IBM, Unisys, and other computer giants to play catch-up.[38]

- Federal Express, a newcomer, founded the field of air-express delivery, zipping past regular delivery stalwarts like UPS, who are still huffing and puffing to recover.[39]

- Everest & Jennings did not greatly improve the wheelchair that gave it 50 years of industry dominance until the early 1980s, when small upstarts like Motion Designs developed revolutionary wheelchairs that were half the weight of the old ones yet equally collapsible.[40]

- Infant firms like Genentech founded biotechnology in the late 1970s. Much later, in 1987, *Fortune* entitled an article, "The Big Boys are Joining the Biotech Party," to herald the belated efforts of Eli Lilly and its big brethren.[41]

The foot-dragging behavior of leading firms is so common that theorists have dubbed it "the fast-second strategy." Briefly, the idea is that, for a large firm, *innovation* is often costlier, riskier, and less profitable than *imitation*. A large firm can lie back, let others gamble, then respond quickly with a "fast second" if anything started by their smaller rivals catches fire. Being large to begin with minimizes any eventual market share losses, as explained by William Baldwin and Gerald Childs: "The dominant firm is likely to be favored as an imitator because of such factors as its ability to distribute a new product far more widely and in

---

36 *Business Week*, October 27, 1975, pp. 78–92.

37 *Business Week*, December 6, 1982, p. 75.

38 *Fortune*, October 10, 1988, pp. 108–114; and *Business Week*, July 24, 1989, pp. 70–74. This is typical of IBM, by the way. See, for example, Kenneth Flamm, *Creating the Computer* (Washington, D.C.: Brookings Institution, 1988) and Gerald W. Brock, *The U.S. Computer Industry: A Study of Market Power* (Cambridge, Mass.: Ballinger, 1975).

39 *Fortune*, January 18, 1988, pp. 56–64.

40 *Forbes*, September 24, 1984, pp. 196–198. The innovations allow much greater mobility for the handicapped.

41 *Fortune*, July 6, 1987, pp. 58–64. See also *Business Week*, January 23, 1984, pp. 84–94; and Steve Olson, *Biotechnology* (Washington, D.C.: National Academy Press, 1986), pp. 84–90.

a shorter period of time than a smaller innovator, its current reputation among a large number of customers, ability to engage in more extensive advertising than its rivals and, conceivably, because its leading position in current markets is attributable to greater efficiency and the general ability to produce better products at lower costs than any of its rivals."[42] In short, "A firm with a dominating position, conscious of its power to pounce if its position should suddenly be put in jeopardy, may be so confident of being able to deal with incipient competition as to become sluggish."[43]

For fairly obvious reasons, the strategy would pay off best (1) where the innovations in question are easily copied, both technically and legally, and (2) where the leading firm faces an inelastic demand and the innovations in question are "durable" or "economy" models, representing substantial price cuts. (Thus the stainless steel blade was not Gillette's baby.)

On the other hand, there are several reasons to doubt that the last section's conclusions on invention carry over to innovation. The evidence concerning R&D and patented inventions, although instructive, is only loosely applicable to innovation. Given the significant differences between invention and innovation, bigness may be better for innovation. Moreover, casual empiricism concerning wheelchairs and compact cars lacks resolve, even when it is backed up by plausible theories. Counterexamples and counterarguments are available to defenders of giant enterprises. RCA's color television, Du Pont's nylon, AT&T's transistor, GM's diesel locomotive, and IBM's "Selectric" typewriter are just a few instances of large-firm innovation involving vision, risk, and voluminous cost.

What is needed, then, is some *systematic* analysis of this question. Edwin Mansfield and his associates pioneered in this area, conducting detailed studies of major innovations in the steel, petroleum, coal, drug, and chemical industries from about 1910 to 1971. Their approach was, first, to obtain information on *what* innovations had been made, *which* were the most important, and *who* was most responsible for the pioneering. This information was obtained by canvassing knowledgeable experts

[42] William L. Baldwin and Gerald L. Childs, "The Fast Second and Rivalry in Research and Development," *Southern Economic Journal* (July 1969), p. 24.

[43] Jewkes, Sawers, and Stillerman, *The Sources of Invention*, p. 166. To illustrate, Royal Crown is the most innovative firm in the soft drink industry. Its credits include the first decaffeinated cola, the first use of cans, the first with 16–ounce returnable bottles, the first to introduce diet cola, and the first cola company to carry ginger ale and other flavors in its line. "At each stage, the industry pooh-poohs what we consider a breakthrough, then follows our lead," says RC's vice president. Yet the followers end up with most of the spoils. *The Wall Street Journal*, May 24, 1982, p. 21; *Forbes*, August 16, 1982, pp. 50–51. For other such stories see *The Wall Street Journal*, September 13, 1982, pp. 1, 16; *Business Week*, July 21, 1986, pp. 96–97; *Business Week*, December 8, 1986, pp. 42; *Forbes*, January 25, 1988, pp. 46–47; and Kenneth Flamm, *Creating the Computer* (Washington, D.C.: Brookings Institution, 1988).

on these industries—engineers, scientists, trade associations, and so on. All told, 325 major innovations were included. Next, economic data on each industry were assembled, such as firm size and market concentration. Finally, the innovation information and economic data were compared.[44]

Their results may be summarized by referring again to Figure 23–1. This is because they estimated the distribution of performance across all innovating firms in each industry they studied to determine which size of firm was *the* best for innovation. In referring back to Figure 23–1, we can mentally relabel the vertical axis to read "Number of innovations per sales dollar" and note that an 0A pattern would once again indicate added size to be always disproportionately favorable to progress. In fact, of Mansfield's five industries, only chemicals followed an 0A pattern for major innovations, mainly because the largest firm, Du Pont, was the most intense innovator of all chemical producers. The other four industries followed 0C patterns, wherein the biggest firms were not the best. The best (or peak) in coal was ranked fourth; in petroleum, sixth; in drugs, twelfth; and in steel, the peak was estimated to be "among very small firms."

A much larger sample of 247 industries and 4476 innovations has recently been analyzed by Acs and Audretsch.[45] The innovations occurred during 1982, as reported in over 100 technology, engineering, and trade journals. Once these innovations were credited to firms, those firms were identified as either "large" or "small" depending on whether they had more or fewer than 500 employees (a definition that comes from the U.S. Small Business Administration). *The results were remarkably favorable to small firms, as their share of innovations greatly exceeded their share of employment in all but a few of the industries accounting for most of the innovations.*

Table 23–4 illustrates this by reporting the small firms' share of employment and innovations in the 20 four-digit industries having the highest number of innovations. The ratio of innovation share to employment share is given in the last column. In 17 of the 20 industries the small firms' share of innovations exceeded their share of employment, yielding a ratio greater than one. Their average employment share was 32.1% in Table 23–4, while their innovations averaged 44.7% of the industry totals.

Going beyond Table 23–4 to include all cases, "large firms in manufacturing introduced 2,608 innovations in 1982, and small firms contri-

---

[44] Mansfield, *Industrial Research and Technological Innovation*; E. Mansfield, J. Rapoport, J. Schnee, S. Wagner, and M. Hamburger, *Research and Innovation in the Modern Corporation* (New York: W.W. Norton, 1971), Mansfield, Rapoport, Romeo, Villani, Wagner, and Husic, *The Production and Application of New Industrial Technology*.

[45] Zoltan J. Acs and David B. Audretsch, "Innovation in Large and Small Firms: An Empirical Analysis," *American Economic Review* (September 1988), pp. 678–690.

TABLE 23–4.   Small Firm* Shares of Employment and Innovations
in the 20 Most Innovative Four-Digit Industries, 1982

Industry (Total Number of Innovations)	Share of Employment	Share of Innovations	Ratio I/E
Electronic computing equipment (395)	5.7%	69.0%	12.1
Process control instruments (165)	38.0	57.8	1.5
Radio and TV equipment (157)	17.2	46.4	2.7
Pharmaceutical preparations (133)	4.9	9.8	2.0
Electronic components (128)	52.8	57.5	1.1
Engineering and science institutes (126)	47.7	65.9	1.4
Semiconductors (122)	14.8	25.2	1.6
Plastics products (107)	75.1	78.9	1.1
Photographic equipment (88)	5.2	10.2	2.0
Office machinery (77)	86.9	13.0	0.1
Instruments (77)	32.5	62.7	1.9
Surgical appliances and supplies (67)	21.9	19.4	0.9
General industrial machinery (67)	50.6	19.4	0.4
Surgical instruments (66)	21.9	54.6	2.5
Special industry machinery (64)	26.9	32.8	1.2
Industrial controls (61)	36.6	75.4	2.1
Toilet preparations (59)	15.9	30.5	1.9
Valves and pipe fittings (54)	29.3	62.3	2.1
Electric housewares (53)	5.5	11.3	2.1
Measuring and contrtol devices (52)	53.6	93.7	1.7

*"Small firm" is one with fewer than 500 employees.

Source: Zoltan J. Acs and David B. Audretsch, "Innovation in Large and Small Firms: An Empirical Analysis," *American Economic Review* (September 1988), pp. 678–690.

buted slightly fewer, 1,923," while at the same time "small-firm employment was only about half as great as large-firm employment." Acs and Audretsch therefore concluded that "the average innovation rate for small firms was about 43% higher than that for large firms."[46] (Shortly before these results were published in 1987, a British study disclosed that "firms with fewer than 1000 UK employees accounted for only 3.3 percent of the R&D in 1975, but for 34.9 percent of the identified significant innovations between 1970 and 1979."[47])

[46] Zoltan J. Acs and David B. Audretsch, "Innovation, Market Structure, and Firm Size," *Review of Economics and Statistics* (November 1987), pp. 567–574. Small firms tend to have especially good performance in industries which are highly innovative, unconcentrated, and depend heavily on skilled labor.
[47] K. Paritt, M. Robson, and I. Townsend, "The Size Distribution of Innovating Firms in the UK: 1947–1983," *Journal of Industrial Economics* (March 1987), pp. 297–316.

It would thus appear that our previous conclusion concerning invention applies here as well. Huge size offers no advantage and may even be disadvantageous. Eloquent testimony to this conclusion is found in the fact that many large corporations deliberately try to create conditions of smallness to improve their performance. IBM, 3M, and Hewlett-Packard are among those who have turned to small "teams."[48] Business consultant Thomas Peters calls these "Skunkworks":

> The finding stands out more and more as evidence rolls in: when a practical innovation occurs, a skunkwork, usually with a nucleus of six to 25 [people], is at the heart of it.[49]

D. Firm Size and Diffusion

Diffusion typically traces a path similar to a "logistic" curve, as it is called. Three such S-shaped curves are captured in Figure 23–2, where zero represents the date of innovation. As time passes (on the horizontal axis), the percentage of firms adopting the innovation rises slowly at first, picks up steam over the middle stretch, and then tapers off as the stragglers finally convert. Curves I and II show cases of complete conversion by all members of the industry. Of the two, curve I depicts the more rapid diffusion. Curve III illustrates a case where the innovation is very slow to spread and is never fully adopted by all. Nuclear power illustrates partial adoption, as it seems highly unlikely that nuclear reactors (as we know them today) will ever be universally accepted.

Whether an innovation spreads quickly or slowly, completely or partially, depends on many factors.[50] Market growth, capital cost magnitude, risk, patent protection, and the technical competency of management are among them. Most important, however, is the potential profitability of the innovation. If it promises remarkable cost savings or skyrocketing sales, converts will not timidly hesitate. Dim profit prospects have the opposite effect. Both ups and downs are illustrated by the textile industry. High-speed shuttleless looms were innovated in the 1950s, but U.S. textile manufacturers delayed extensive adoption until the 1970s when rising labor costs made the new looms significantly more profitable than the older, relatively labor-intensive looms. In 1973, an old-style loom cost $8,000 as against $35,000 for a new shuttleless loom. Conversion at that time was nevertheless "the only way to go," accord-

---

[48] *The Wall Street Journal*, August 19, 1983, pp. 1, 7; *Fortune*, October 15, 1984, pp. 66–84; *The Economist*, July 22, 1989, pp. 78–79; *The Wall Street Journal*, April 22, 1988, p. 25; *Business Week*, April 10, 1989, pp. 58–62; and *Fortune*, July 2, 1990, pp. 72–77.

[49] Thomas J. Peters, "The Mythology of Innovation, or a Skunkworks Tale," *The Stanford Magazine* (Summer 1983), pp. 13–21.

[50] Bela Gold, "Technological Diffusion in Industry," *Journal of Industrial Economics* (March 1981), pp. 247–269.

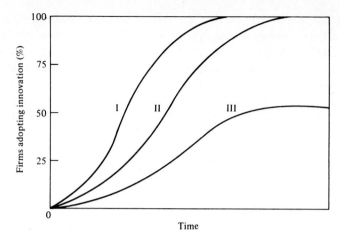

FIGURE 23–2. Three patterns of diffusion.

ing to one textile executive, because the new looms could "get 70% more output with 15% less manpower."[51]

Firm size also has a bearing, and its influence has been measured two ways. The first is merely a matter of positioning. Which firms are the *quickest to begin* using an innovation? Mansfield's studies of diffusion in the coal, brewing, steel, and railroad industries led him to conclude that larger firms were quicker to adopt innovations. He estimated that a 10% increase in firm size would, on the average, reduce delay time 4%.[52] Other results indicating a favorable influence of firm size have been found for the diffusion of numerically controlled machine tools in a number of industries,[53] and diffusion in grocery retailing[54] (optical scanners), banking (ATMs),[55] and the British textile industry.[56]

Although these results seem to conflict with those concerning invention and innovation, they do not. Several qualifications attend them. For one thing, as a matter of sheer statistical probability, one would expect big firms to be quicker, on the average, than small firms. But it does not

[51] *Business Week*, October 27, 1973, p. 124.

[52] Mansfield, *Industrial Research and Technological Innovation*, pp. 155–172.

[53] Anthony A. Romeo, "Interindustry and Interfirm Differences in the Rate of Diffusion of an Innovation," *Review of Economics and Statistics* (August 1975), pp. 311–319; and Steven Globerman, "Technical Diffusion in the Canadian Tool and Die Industry," *Review of Economics and Statistics* (November 1975), pp. 428–434.

[54] Sharon G. Levin, Stanford L. Levin, and John B. Meisel, "Intermarket Differences in the Early Diffusion of an Innovation," *Southern Economic Journal* (January 1985), pp. 672–680.

[55] Timothy H. Hannan and John M. McDowell, "The Determinants of Technology Adoption," *Rand Journal of Economics* (Autumn 1984), pp. 328–335.

[56] J. S. Metcalfe, "Diffusion of Innovation in the Lancashire Textile Industry," *Manchester School* (June 1970), pp. 145–159.

appear that they are *disproportionately* quicker. Mansfield explains the difference nicely: "To illustrate this, consider an industry with two firms, one large (80 percent of the market), one small (20 percent of the market). If the large firm does its share of the innovating (no more, no less), it will be first in 80 percent of the cases—and it will be quicker on the average than the small firm."[57] There is, indeed, some evidence of diminishing returns to size.[58]

For another thing, one would expect the effect of firm size to emerge only or mainly where the costs of introduction are particularly high or risky because the big firms should be at their best in such instances. In fact, a study of numerous innovations in chemicals turned up just such differential effects. Firm size had a favorable impact only for high-cost innovations.

Finally, there are many cases where firm size appears to have had *no* effect or an *adverse* effect on the speed of adoption, even where high costs are involved. Examples of these innovations and their industries include "special presses" in Canadian paper,[59] nonflammable dry cleaning in British dry cleaning,[60] basic oxygen process in U.S. steel,[61] and Sulzer shuttleless looms in U.S. textiles.[62]

There is thus some sketchy evidence favorable to firm size regarding firm-by-firm diffusion. However, the evidence regarding *intra*firm diffusion, the second measure of diffusion, is definitely stacked on the side of small firms. That is to say, small firms may be somewhat slower to take up an innovation once it is introduced, but, once they do pick it up, they adopt it *throughout their operations* more quickly than large firms. Thus, although small firms may be "late starters," they also tend to "catch up" with *internal* rates of diffusion exceeding those of large firms. The phenomenon has been observed in railroading, paper manufacturing, chemicals, and in ten industries using numerical machine tools.[63] The main explanations for small-firm speed here seem to be that (1) their

[57] Mansfield, *Industrial Research and Technological Innovation*, pp. 171–172.

[58] Anita M. Benvignati, "Interfirm Adoption of Capital-Goods Innovations," *Review of Economics and Statistics* (May 1982), pp. 330–335.

[59] Steven Globerman, "New Technology Adoption in the Canadian Paper Industry," *Industrial Organization Review*, Vol. 4, no. 1 (1976), pp. 5–12.

[60] R. W. Shaw and C. J. Sutton, *Industry and Competition* (London: Macmillan, 1976), pp. 108–119.

[61] Joel Dirlam and Walter Adams, "Big Steel, Invention, and Innovation," *Quarterly Journal of Economics* (May 1966), pp. 167–189; James B. Sumrall, Jr., "Diffusion of the Basic Oxygen Furnace in the U.S. Steel Industry," *Journal of Industrial Economics* (June 1982), pp. 421–437.

[62] *Business Week*, October 27, 1973, p. 124. See also Jewkes, Sawers, and Stillerman, *The Sources of Invention*, pp. 303–304.

[63] Romeo, "Interindustry and Interfirm Differences"; Globerman "New Technology Adoption in the Canadian Paper Industry"; and Mansfield, *Industrial Research and Technological Innovation*, Chapter 9; Mansfield, et al., *The Production and Application of New Industrial Technology*, p. 118 (referring to a study by Peter Simon).

nonbureaucratic nature enables quicker, more comprehensive decision making and (2) the later they start, the more certain they are of the innovation's good value, having the benefit of positive experiences among their adopting predecessors.

To summarize, there is some evidence that large firms adopt innovations earlier than small firms, all else being equal. But the big ones may not be disproportinately faster. Indeed, other evidence indicates no differential at all. Moreover, where the small-fry have been slow to pick up a new ball, they run with it faster toward complete internal conversion.

E. Firm Diversification and Progress

The diversification aspect of the topic has been explored very little. Theoretically, firm diversification is often said to have a favorable impact on invention and innovation.[64] Yet empirical tests have neither confirmed nor refuted this hypothesis. Some studies, especially those concerning *basic* research, find a positive effect of diversification on R&D input and output. Others find a negative impact. Still others find nothing. A definite answer thus awaits further study.[65]

F. Firm Size: An Overview

Overall, medium-sized firms emerge as the most willing and able to spur advance. A little bit of bigness may be good; too much often seems bad. Still, a *range* of sizes may be best for an industry, just as they are for a basketball team. Invention, innovation, and diffusion each demand talents and resources. Projects vary widely in size and scope. "All things considered," Scherer aptly concludes, "the most favorable industrial environment for rapid technological progress would appear to be a firm size distribution which includes a preponderance of companies with sales below $500 million, pressed on one side by a horde of small technology-oriented enterprises bubbling over with bright new ideas and on the other by a few larger corporations with the capacity to undertake exceptionally ambitious developments."[66]

---

[64] Richard R. Nelson, "The Simple Economics of Basic Research," *Journal of Political Economy* (June 1959), p. 320.

[65] For a survey see Kamien and Schwartz, "Market Structure and Innovation," pp. 26–27. For new evidence, see Mueller, et al., *Market Structure and Technological Performance*, (1982); Scherer, "Technological Change and the Modern Corporation," mimeo (1982); Albert N. Link and James E. Long, "The Simple Economics of Basic Scientific Research," *Journal of Industrial Economics* (September 1981), pp. 105–109; and John T. Scott and George Pascoe, "Purposive Diversification of R&D in Manufacturing," *Journal of Industrial Economics* (December 1987), pp. 193–205.

[66] Scherer, *Industrial Market Structure and Economic Performance*, (1980), p. 442.

III. MARKET STRUCTURE AND PROGRESS

A. Theory

Theories on the impact of market structure on progress differ from those on firm size by giving greater consideration to *rivalry*, or the lack thereof. Early theorists, like Galbraith, argued that high concentration and high barriers to entry would foster progressiveness. They reasoned that the *lack* of rivalry implied by these conditions would (1) boost profits, thereby supplying abundant monetary wherewithal to engage in risky R&D, and (2) protect inventors and innovators from imitators, poachers, and like-minded creatures who would "steal" the pioneers' ideas, thereby discouraging the initiation of progressive efforts by jeopardizing the chance of just rewards.

Of course these arguments are no more overpowering than those defending large firm size. We have already seen that much, if not most, R&D is neither as risky nor as expensive as one might think. Counterargument concerning bloodsucking imitators and interlopers is even easier. The whole idea behind patents is to protect technical frontiersmen from just such discouraging fates. Patents are an even more efficient protection than indiscriminate approval of monopoly because patents grant *temporary* monopoly control *after* the birth of an invention rather than *permanent* power *before*.

More recent and more complicated theories cast added doubt on the notion that progressiveness is necessarily positively associated with monopoly power. Unfortunately, these theories defy compact discussion because they bend and branch with each varying assumption about the ease of imitation, cost contours, technological opportunity, risk, price elasticity of demand, and time horizon.[67] This gives the present writer latitude to express his own preferences. The theories of greatest appeal to me postulate a nonlinear, inverted "U" relationship between concentration and innovative effort, as in Figure 23–3, (much like the relationship between concentration and advertising shown earlier on page 482). A simple explanation of this expectation might go something like this:

Two elements are imperative to vigorous progressiveness — ability and incentive. **Ability** includes some modicum of financial treasure that can be sunk into long-term risky projects, and some freedom from the pressures that arise from daily uncertainty about survival. We naturally

---

[67] Examples include Douglas Needham, "Market Structure and Firms' R&D Behavior," *Journal of Industrial Economics* (June 1975), pp. 241–255; Raymond Jackson, "Market Structure and the Rewards for Patented Inventions," *Antitrust Bulletin* (Fall 1972), pp. 911–926; and K. J. Arrow, "Economic Welfare and the Allocation of Resources for Invention," in *The Rate and Direction of Inventive Activity* (Princeton, N.J.: Princeton University Press, 1962). In general, see Baldwin and Scott, *Market Structure and Technological Change*, pp. 4–63.

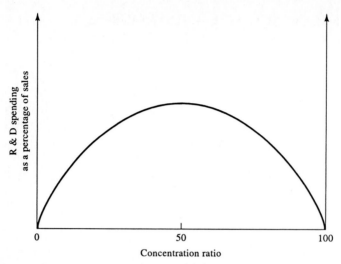

FIGURE 23–3. Inverted U theory of the relationship between R&D spending and concentration.

could not expect a firm whose vitality was flickering to take on extra burdens that a secure firm might assume without strain. Quite obviously, monopolies are usually strong enough to shoulder the added load, for they enjoy both wealth and security. It is indeed these attributes that are emphasized by those who believe that monopolies are ideal for spearheading technical advance.

On the other hand, **incentive** includes prospects of profit and loss. The larger the prospective profit from some endeavor, the greater the incentive to undertake it. Conversely, the larger the prospective loss from stagnation, the greater the incentive to get moving. For various reasons, competition probably heightens both incentives. The greater the competition, the greater the industry's output and the greater the expansion opportunities for any one firm that gets a jump on the others. Likewise, the greater the profit prospects will be for any technical breakthrough. As for considerations on the loss side, the greater the competition, the greater the chances are that stagnant firms will be outdistanced by their rivals. Competition thus propels movement with fear.

All told, it appears that monopolies probably have a great deal of ability but very little incentive, whereas purely competitive firms probably have little ability but ample incentive. Neither structural extreme is therefore particularly conducive to progress. However, the elements blend in intermediate structures, where market power is sufficient to secure ability but not so strong as to eradicate the incentives brought by rivalry. With both ability and incentive present, intermediate ranges of oligopoly may be expected to display the least lassitude.

Elaborations on this theme could generate additional arguments for the same conclusion. For example, more than half of all private R&D effort is aimed at "product improvement," which of course is one form of product differentiation, a form that extends to producer goods as well as consumer goods. The vigor of such product-improvement differentiation could well be most spirited in some middle range of concentration, just as advertising is, and for many of the same reasons. As concentration rises from low to moderate levels, price competition becomes less and less attractive while *nonprice* competition, including competition on the technology front, becomes more and more attractive. However, *further* increases in concentration, above oligopolistic levels, are not likely to continue intensification of R&D aimed in the nonprice direction. Approach toward monopoly tends to subdue rivalry of all forms, especially if under oligopoly that rivalry is excessive from the marketwide, profit-maximizing point of view.[68]

Complicating matters a bit is the possibility that causation may not run just one way, from structure to performance. Particularly rapid technical change, where it is attributable mainly to an independent march of science, could *cause* high concentration. Firms that fail to keep step with the march will fall to the wayside, dying from self-destructive mistakes — such as delays that are never overcome or costly trips down blind alleys. These possibilities appear to be the explanation for rising concentration in aircraft manufacturing,[69] and they could apply to other industries. Patents constitute another mechanism that encourages concentration. Historically, they have contributed to concentration in such fields as electric lamps, aluminum, synthetic fibers, and telephone equipment. On this empirical note, we now leave theory behind.

The evidence of structure's impact is reviewed below in three categories — R&D effort, innovative output, and diffusion. In no case is the evidence crystal clear. In each case the results for concentration have been mixed — showing positive, negative, and neutral associations with technological progress. This frustrates summation. Perhaps interindustry differences in technical opportunity cannot be sufficiently accounted for. Perhaps the available measures of technical vigor are less reliable in the interindustry context. Whatever the reason, the present picture is murky. ("Our test tubes are dirty," Richard Miller would say.) The one generality possible is that *factors other than market structure seem to be much more important to interindustry variances in technological change* — factors such as technological opportunity, stage of the product life cycle, and industry growth rate.[70]

---

[68] More sophisticated theories to roughly the same effect may be found in Scherer and Ross, *Industrial Market Structure and Economic Performance* (1990), pp. 630–644; Kamien and Schwartz, "Market Structure and Innovation," pp. 30–31.

[69] Almarin Phillips, *Technology and Market Structure* (Lexington, Mass.: Lexington Books, 1971).

[70] Zvi Griliches (ed.), *R&D, Patents, and Productivity* (Chicago: University of Chicago

B. Market Structure and R&D Effort: The Evidence

As regards R&D effort, there are about two dozen statistical studies exploring the relationship between concentration or barriers to entry and R&D intensity. Most studies measure intensity by R&D expenditure relative to sales, but a few use counts of scientific personnel relative to total employment or patents relative to sales. Unfortunately, the results lack consistency. Several studies find a positive relationship between concentration and R&D intensity.[71] A few disclose a negative association.[72] Many detect no significant relationship whatever or wobble between positive and negative relationships.[73]

The evidence is such a jumble that patterns seem to defy detection. But the present author sees two. First, a number of studies offer some support for the inverted U hypothesis developed earlier. Second, to the extent the inverted U hypothesis may be doubted, it appears that concentration is positively associated with innovative efforts under "low-tech" conditions and negatively related under "high-tech" conditions. Let's consider each pattern in turn.

First, the Nonlinear Hypothesis. A number of statistical studies tentatively reveal a *positive* relationship between concentration and R&D intensity over a low to medium range of concentration, plus a *negative* relationship over a medium to high range of concentration.[74] I say "ten-

Press, 1984); and Richard C. Levin, Wesley M. Cohen, and David C. Mowery, "R&D Appropriability, Opportunity, and Market Structure," *American Economic Review* (May 1985), pp. 20–24.

71 D. Hamberg "Size of Firm, Oligopoly and Research" (1964); F. M. Scherer, "Market Structure and the Employment of Scientists and Engineers," *American Economic Review* (June 1967), pp. 524–531; Blake Imel, Michael R. Behr, and Peter G. Helmberger, *Market Structure and Performance* (Lexington, Mass.: Lexington Books, 1972), pp. 65–75; and F. M. Scherer, "Concentration, R&D, and Productivity Change," mimeo, (1980).

72 Robert W. Wilson, "The Effect of Technological Environment and Product Rivalry on R&D Effort and Licensing of Inventions," *Review of Economics and Statistics* (May 1977), pp. 171–178; and R. E. Caves, *Britain's Economic Prospects* (Washington, D.C.: Brookings Institution, 1968).

73 F. M. Scherer, "Firm Size and Patented Inventions," *American Economic Review* (December 1965), pp. 116–121; Richard E. Caves and Masu Uekusa, *Industrial Organization in Japan* (Washington, D.C.: Brookings Institution, 1976), p. 128; Comanor "Market Structure, Product Differentiation, and Industrial Research"; Stephen Farber, "Buyer Market Structure and R&D Effort," *Review of Economics and Statistics* (August 1981), pp. 336–345; and Albert N. Link, "An Analysis of the Composition of R&D Spending," *Southern Economic Journal* (October 1982), pp. 342–349.

74 F. M. Scherer, "Market Structure and the Employment of Scientists and Engineers," *American Economic Review* (June 1967), pp. 524–531; T. M. Kelly, "The Influences of Firm Size and Market Structure on the Research Efforts of Large Multiproduct Firms," Ph.D. dissertation, Oklahoma State University, 1970 (as summarized in Kamien and Schwartz, "Market Structure and Innovation"); S. Globerman, "Market Structure and R&D in Canadian Manufacturing Industries," *Quarterly Review of Economics and Business* (Summer 1973), pp. 59–67 (assuming the high-technology industries are highly concentrated, as in Scherer); William J. Adams, "Firm Size and Research Activity: France and the United States," *Quarterly Journal of Economics* (August 1970), pp. 386–409; Ronald E. Shrieves,

tatively" because in some of these studies the effect of concentration is obscured once the authors attempt to account for technical opportunity. This is most dramatically demonstrated in the studies by Scott, Levin, Cohen, and Mowery, who find robust inverted U relationships between concentration and R&D spending when these are the only variables included in their regression analysis (with maximum R&D intensity occurring when the four-firm concentration ratio is 54–64).[75] Yet once they add industry dummies or variables for "science base," this relationship disappears. This is why we must consider the high-tech, low-tech pattern shortly.

Setting this problem aside momentarily, there are several grounds for accepting the nonlinear results as more than merely tentative. Scherer's study of this issue is among the best, and he concluded that "technological vigor appears to increase with concentration mainly at relatively low levels of concentration." In the higher ranges, he felt that "additional market power is probably not conducive to more vigorous technological efforts and may be downright stultifying."[76] Furthermore, William Adams' study produces a nonlinear relation, and he controls for technical opportunity fairly well. He compared R&D intensity and concentration *industry-by-industry* between the United States and France.[77] For 5 of the 14 industries so studied, he found R&D intensity to be higher in the country where concentration was higher. One such industry is textiles: the R&D outlay/sales ratio for textiles was 2.4 in France and 0.5 in the United States, whereas concentration was 30 in France and 19 in the United States. In *all* such cases the concentration comparison was over a low range of concentration. The concentration ratios in these comparisons averaged 19 on the low side of the Atlantic and 31 on the high side. Conversely, seven of the industries compared revealed an opposite tendency, and they were generally more concentrated. That is to say, there were seven instances in which the country with the *higher* concentration had the *lower* R&D intensity, and, for these, topside con-

---

"Market Structure and Innovation: A New Perspective," *Journal of Industrial Economics* (June 1978), pp. 329–347; John D. Culbertson and Willard F. Mueller, "The Influence of Market Structure on Technological Performance in the Food-Manufacturing Industries," *Review of Industrial Organization* Vol. 2, no. 1 (1985), pp. 40–54; and Christos Papachristodoulou, *Inventions, Innovations and Economic Growth in Sweden: An Appraisal of the Schumpeterian Theory* (Stockholm, 1988) as reviewed in *The Economic Journal* (December 1988), pp. 1232–1233.

[75] John T. Scott, "Firm Versus Industry Variability in R&D Intensity," in *R&D, Patents and Productivity,* edited by Zvi Griliches (Chicago: University of Chicago Press, 1984), pp. 233–248; and Levin, Cohen, and Mowrey, "R&D Appropriability, Opportunity, and Market Structure," *American Economic Review* (May 1985), pp. 20–24.

[76] Scherer, "Market Structure and the Employment of Scientists and Engineers" (1967).

[77] William J. Adams "Firm Size and Research Activity"; another study with fairly good control because of its limited product range is that by Culbertson and Mueller, "The Influence of Market Structure on Technological Performance."

centration averaged 54. Combining the averages of these two sets, R&D rose when concentration rose over a low range, but R&D *fell* as concentration rose over the high range.

A study of Canadian manufacturing likewise contains a positive relationship between concentration and R&D intensity where concentration is in a low range and a negative relationship where concentration covers a high range — the inverted U. However, this holds only because a division of industries into "low- and high-technology" subsamples yielded two subsamples with average concentration of "low" and "high" levels. Thus, instead of revealing the inverted U with concentration, this study could be disclosing the second possible pattern we wish to consider.[78]

Second, the Low-Tech/High-Tech Division. The Canadian study was among the first of a number of studies revealing a *positive* association between R&D intensity and concentration under conditions that could be characterized as "low tech," while at the same time disclosing a *negative* (or zero) association under conditions that could be considered "high tech."[79] There is enough consistency across these studies to warrant speculation that, on the one hand, high concentration (though not necessarily monopoly) might be boosting R&D when it would otherwise be low and yet, on the other hand, be stifling R&D when it would otherwise be high.

R. Angelmar provides a plausible explanation for what might be going on here.[80] There are two cases:

- *Low Tech:* R&D investment will tend to be unrewarding under conditions of (1) high cost R&D, (2) high uncertainly of its success, and (3) speedy imitation by rivals when it is successful. When R&D goes unrewarded, it will be discouraged, and technological change will likely be slow. High concentration might *help* here because it could supply excess profit to cover the high costs and uncertainty while also reducing the number of rivals who might be speedy imitators. Hence, under these "low-tech" conditions, R&D and concentration could be positively related.

- *High Tech:* R&D investment will tend to be profitable under conditions of (1) low-cost R&D, (2) low uncertainty of its success, and (3)

---

[78] Steve Globerman, "Market Structure and R&D in Canadian Manufacturing Industries," (1973), pp. 59–67.

[79] John Lunn and Stephen Martin, "Market Structure, Firm Structure, and Research and Development," *Quarterly Review of Economics and Business* (Spring 1986), pp. 31–44; Henry W. Chappell, Jr., Jane T. Pietrowski, and Ronald P. Wilder, "R&D, Firm Size, and Concentration," *Quarterly Journal of Business and Economics* (Spring 1986), pp. 32–49; and John Lunn, "An Empirical Analysis of Firm Process and Product Patenting," *Applied Economics* (June 1987), pp 743–751.

[80] Reinhard Angelmar, "Market Structure and Research Intensity in High-Technological-Opportunity Industries," *Journal of Industrial Economics* (September 1985), pp. 69–79.

slow imitation by rivals when it is successful. Here R&D is richly rewarded, so it is encouraged and technological change will likely be brisk. High concentration would *not help* under these circumstances. In fact, high concentration could lead to reduced R&D spending if it smothered incentive. Evidence shows a zero or negative impact from concentration in high-tech situations, so this explanation could be on target.

In summary, there appears to be a positive-negative concentration effect hinging on low-tech/high-tech underlying conditions. There also appears to be some support for the inverted U, which means a positive-negative split hinging on a low versus a high range of concentration. There could of course be a mix of both patterns. It is worth stressing that, in any case, the influence of concentration on R&D outlay seems very weak in comparison to other factors — technological opportunity in particular.[81]

C. Market Structure and Innovative Output: The Evidence

Measurement and data problems make interindustry studies of innovative output extremely difficult. About all that can be said with certainty is that few gains in progressiveness would be obtained by transforming all our industries into near monopolies or tightly-knit oligopolies.

This conclusion is suggested, first, by studies analyzing interindustry variations in innovations. The Acs and Audretsch sample of 4476 innovations spread across 247 four-digit industries for the year 1982 proves to be especially persuasive here. Holding other factors constant, higher concentration is *negatively* associated with innovation activity to a significant degree.[82] (Among other variables, innovation was positively associated with R&D expenditures, industry size, and skilled employment. It was negatively associated with unionization.) Recalling that small firms are especially innovative in these data, it is interesting that Acs and Audretsch also find a *negative* association between market concentration and two measures of small-firm innovative activity — (1) the *number* of small-firm innovations per industry and (2) the *share* of total industry innovations accounted for by small firms. Overall, Acs and Au-

---

[81] Scherer and Ross reach a similar conclusion, *Industrial Market Structure and Economic Performance*, pp. 645–648. The notion that R&D intensity is most feverish in the intermediate values of market structure is buttressed by William Comanor's conclusion regarding barriers to entry: "Where technical barriers either effectively foreclose the entry of new firms or where they are quite low, research spending tends to be limited. Where barriers are moderate, however, and where prospects for some entry exist, research spending is greater." See Comanor, "Market Structure, Product Differentiation, and Industrial Research," p. 657.

[82] Zoltan J. Acs and David B. Audretsch, "Innovation in Large and Small Firms: An Empirical Analysis," *American Economic Review* (September 1988), p. 686.

dretsch conclude that their results are "unequivocal — industry innovation tends to decrease as the level of concentration rises."[83]

Productivity growth is another measure of "output" in this context. A *positive* and statistically significant relationship between productivity growth and seller concentration has been found for U.S. manufacturing industries over various time periods dating back to 1919.[84] This is inconsistent with the innovation results just given. However, the positive correlation with concentration disappears when industry spending on R&D as a percentage of sales enters the analysis.[85] Thus the best evidence indicates a neutral effect for concentration in productivity growth. (It might, though, under some circumstances, be negative. In electric utilities duopolies perform better than monopolies in productivity growth.[86])

Finally, we should acknowledge that the payoff to improved productivity is lower product prices. Figure 23–4 illustrates this for computer equipment over the period 1967–1983. Product as well as process innovation contributed to the downward trend in IBM disk and processor prices. Notice also the contrasting upward price trend for telecommunications electronic switching systems (ESS). Although the technological opportunities in switching systems and computers were similar over the period of Figure 23–4, it is clear that IBM is much more progressive than AT&T. Kenneth Flamm, who studied computers and telecommunications in depth, argues that "an absence of competition" in telecommunications was a major contributor to this difference.[87] Given the important contributions of new entrants to technological change in computers, the "competition" referred to here could mean relatively low barriers to entry as well as relatively low concentration.[88]

[83] Ibid., p. 688. This is consistent with Paul Geroski's conclusion regarding a sample of 1203 U.K. innovations over the period 1970–1979. See Scherer and Ross, *Industrial Market Structure and Economic Performance*, pp. 648–649.

[84] D. F. Greer and S. A. Rhoades, "Concentration and Productivity Changes in the Long and Short Run," *Southern Economic Journal* (October 1976), pp. 1031–1044; and Louis Amato and J. Michael Ryan, "Market Structure and Dynamic Performance in U.S. Manufacturing," *Southern Economic Journal* (April 1981), pp. 1105–1110.

[85] F. M. Scherer, "Concentration, R&D, and Productivity Change," *Southern Economic Journal* (July 1983), pp. 221–225; and Catherine Sveikauskas and Leo Sveikauskas, "Industry Characteristics and Productivity Growth," *Southern Economic Journal* (January 1982), pp. 769–774.

[86] Rodney Stevenson, "X-Inefficiency and Interfirm Rivalry: Evidence from the Electric Utility Industry," *Land Economics* (February 1982), pp. 52–65. See also Karin Wagner, "Competition and Productivity," *Journal of Industrial Economics* (September 1980), pp. 32–33.

[87] Kenneth Flamm, "Technological Advance and Costs: Computers Versus Communications," in *Changing the Rules: Technological Change, International Competition, and Regulation in Communications*, edited by Robert W. Crandall and Kenneth Flamm (Washington, D.C.: Brookings Institution, 1989), pp. 13–61.

[88] A comparison of computers, semiconductors, and photographic equipment would further support this suggestion: Nancy S. Dorfman, *Innovation and Market Structure* (Cambridge: Mass.: Ballinger, 1987); James W. Brock, "Structural Monopoly, Technological Performance, and Predatory Innovation," *American Business Law Journal* (Fall 1983), pp. 291–306; *Business Week*, June 10, 1985, pp. 92–94; and *Business Week*, February 24, 1986; pp. 37–38.

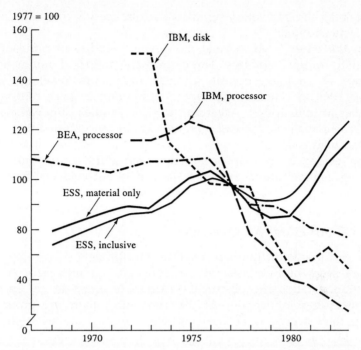

FIGURE 23–4. Linked indexes of prices for computers and telecommunications switches, 1967–1983. Source: Kenneth Flamm, "Technological Advance and Costs: Computers Versus Communications," in *Changing the Rules*, edited by R. W. Crandall and K. Flamm (Washington, D.C.: Brookings Institution, 1989), p. 35.

D. Market Structure and Diffusion: The Evidence

Hampered by data difficulties, early tests of structure's impact on diffusion were no more than makeshift. These tests nevertheless suggested that competition was stimulating and monopoly power encumbering. Thus, early analysis of diffusion in the coal, steel, brewing, and railroad industries led to a qualified conclusion: "We have too few industries to test accurately the hypothesis often advanced that the rate of imitation is faster in more competitive industries, but the differences seem to be generally in that direction."[89] Anthony Romeo corroborated this suggestion in a study of the diffusion of numerically controlled machine tools across different user industries (e.g., farm machinery manufacturing and aircraft engines). He found that the *less* concentrated among these indus-

[89] Mansfield, *Industrial Research and Technological Innovation*, p. 154. See also John E. Tilton, *International Diffusion of Technology: The Case of Semiconductors* (Washington, D.C.: Brookings Institution, 1971), p. 166.

tries adopted the innovation significantly *more* quickly than did the more highly concentrated.[90]

On the other hand, several more recent studies of diffusion have completely contrary findings. These cover the spread of automatic teller machines in banking, optical scanners in grocery retailing, energy-efficient kilns in cement, and laptop computers in sales forces across a number of industries.[91] According to these studies, innovations, once they become available, spread more quickly in concentrated than unconcentrated markets.

The evidence on market structure and diffusion is thus mixed, thwarting generalization. Still, the slant of recent evidence favors concentration.

E. Market Structure: An Overview

Except for these latest findings on diffusion, the data concerning market structure seem fairly consistent with the data on firm size. Towering concentration ratios and obstructive barriers to entry do not encourage R&D effort and innovation. At the same time, there are grounds for arguing that structures of the opposite extreme — atomistic structures with fluid firm turnover — might be less than ideal, especially for R&D effort. Intermediate structures, leaning toward the competitive side of the continuum, seem best. The one exception might be diffusion.

SUMMARY

Our progress through this chapter took three steps. First, by way of background, it was explained that technological progress itself entails three steps — invention, innovation, and diffusion. Invention is the first realization and crude proof that something will work. Innovation is the first commercial application of the invention. And diffusion is the spread of its adoption. Each step demands somewhat different talents and resources. A surprising amount of invention can still be carried out in basements and garages, although the relative importance of truly independent inventors is waning. Innovation requires refinement, testing,

---

[90] Romeo "Interindustry and Interfirm Differences"; and A. A. Romeo, "The Rate of Imitation of a Capital-Embodied Process Innovation," *Economica* (February 1977), pp. 63–69.

[91] Timothy H. Hannan and John M. McDowell, "The Determinants of Technology Adoption: The Case of the Banking Firm," *Rand Journal of Economics* (Autumn 1984), pp. 328–335; Sharon G. Levin, Stanford L. Levin, and John B. Meisel, "Intermarket Differences in the Early Diffusion of an Innovation," *Southern Economic Journal* (January 1985), pp. 672–680; David I. Rosenbaum, "The Impact of Market Structure on Technological Adoption in the Portland Cement Industry," *Quarterly Review of Economics and Business* (Autumn 1989), pp. 102–110; and H. Gatignon and T.S. Robertson, "Technology Diffusion: An Empirical Test of Competitive Effects," *Journal of Marketing* (January 1989), pp. 35–49.

sometimes further invention, and initial production, all of which can be costly. Diffusion involves some risk acceptance on the part of buyers. Since progress in these three categories is partly determined by technological opportunities, as dictated by divergent growth rates in different branches of science, the impact of market conditions is both limited and difficult to measure. Nevertheless, measurement is not impossible because firms within a given industry face similar opportunities and interindustry comparisons can be devised.

Early theorizing on the relation between progress and *firm size* stressed the virtues of bigness. But two decades of subsequent study have shown that emphasis to be misplaced. In the aggregate, R&D effort is concentrated in the hands of the top 800 firms, but inventive output is not commensurate with the input of these firms. Within specific industries there is no evidence indicating that R&D intensity, relative to firm size, typically increases beyond medium-sized firms in many industries. Moreover, within most industries, inventive output does not match measured input, apparently because diseconomies of scale occur beyond moderate size levels.

The record regarding innovation and firm size is much the same. The largest firms cannot claim credit for a disproportionate share of the innovations. Firms of less than ponderous proportions are the best. The largest firms in some industries lead in diffusion. But their showing in that respect is tarnished by several qualifications, the most important of which is the more rapid *internal* diffusion displayed by small firms.

The influence of market structure is still somewhat uncertain because test results conflict. Nevertheless, several faint outlines seem discernible. First, it is perhaps most plausible to suppose that neither monopoly nor pure competition (nor the nearby neighboring structures of either) are very good for vigorous advance. Incentive and ability blend in the middle ranges of structure, as evidence on R&D effort sometimes bears out. Second, concentration might be favorable to R&D efforts under circumstances where it can slow imitative poaching or defray costly and risky research endeavors—as signaled by "low-tech" conditions. Conversely, high concentration appears neutral or negative in "high-tech" situations.

The data concerning market structure and innovation go against high concentration and lofty entry barriers rather decisively. On the other hand, concentration fares better with diffusion in a field of mixed results.

24

Technological Change: Public Policy

The patent system added the fuel of interest to the fire of genius.

— ABE LINCOLN

The list of 17 innovations was unimpressive—a stain remover, a construction material, and a sewing thread were highlights. Yet the list produced amazing results when assessed by Edwin Mansfield and his associates. They sought to estimate the private and social rates of return generated by run-of-the-mill innovations. The *private* rate of return is the *innovator's* reward, or profit before tax. The *social* rate of return is the *users'* prize, namely, the cost savings or added consumers' surplus that users of innovations gain.

The difference between private and social reward can best be illustrated with an extreme case not included on Mansfield's list: Dr. Jonas Salk donated his discovery of polio vaccine to the public, declining patent monopoly and with it a staggering fortune, thereby minimizing his return. But the public's return was stupendous, amounting to untold millions, perhaps billions, of dollars in reduced medical bills, a more productive populace, and relieved suffering. Although none of the 17 innovations on Mansfield's list could match the polio vaccine, and although none were charitably donated to the public, the median social rate of return for the group was a bountiful 56% as compared to the

688

median private rate of 25%.[1] That is a gap of 2 to 1! For one reason or another—imitators' poaching, "satisficing" rather than profit maximizing prices, and so on—the innovators did not capture all the benefits society received. They shook the tree while others ran off with most of the apples.

Of course we would not want to arrange the world so that every discoverer appropriated the full value of his discovery. Such is not needed to motivate trailblazers, given the alternative inducements of fame and psychic pleasure. Such is not even desirable, given the crazy implications full reward would have for income and wealth distribution. (Imagine the consequences to us and the heirs of Columbus if he could have claimed America as his private property.) Nevertheless, the gap between private and social gain does suggest that reliance on private markets, plain and simple, may lead individuals and enterprises to invest *too little* in research, development, and innovation as compared to a socially optimal investment. Thus, we do not rely on private markets alone. Government intervenes to encourage invention and innovation. Two government policies having this purpose—patents and R&D funding—are the focus of this chapter.

Our discussion of patents answers such questions as: What is a patent? What can be patented? Why have patents? What are the benefits and costs of patents? Our discussion of government funding of research and development covers two basic questions: What amounts of money are involved? Why is such funding needed?

We conclude with a review of other policies that promote progress.

1. THE PATENT SYSTEM: NATURE AND SCOPE

A. Background

A patent is a **monopoly right** to make and sell some product, or use some process, that is governmentally granted for a limited number of years as a reward for invention. The character and duration of this right differs from country to country. U.S. law grants "for the term of seventeen years [from the patent's date] . . . the right to exclude others from making, using, or selling the invention throughout the United States."[2] The right is a form of private property that can be bought and sold, traded, given away, and leased or licensed for the use of others (who pay a "royalty" for the privilege). The invention covered can even go unused if the owner wishes. Moreover, although only individuals can be

---

[1] E. Mansfield, J. Rapoport, A. Romeo, E. Villani, S. Wagner, and F. Husic, *The Production and Application of New Industrial Technology* (New York: W. W. Norton, 1977), pp. 144–166.

[2] U.S.C. Section 154 (1970).

awarded patents, corporate employees typically "assign" their patents to their employers, and independent inventors often sell or license their patents to others for commercial application.

Regardless of ultimate ownership, roughly half of all patents go unused because the inventions they cover are too far ahead of their time, too costly to develop relative to the potential profit, or too unsettling to the ultimate owner's old way of doing things. Many go unused because close substitutes for the invention are available. Thus, the monopoly granted may be only a measly one.

Indeed, more than 4 million patents have been issued since inception of the system. Of late, the annual flow tops 70,000. If these figures are not big enough to suggest to you that many if not most patented inventions are rather pedestrian, consider the following: an electric fork that winds spaghetti, an alarm clock that hits you on the head, and a diaper for parakeets. (Emerson once said, "Build a better mousetrap and the world will beat a path to your door." People still believe that. About 3,300 mousetrap patents have been granted since 1838, when the first one was issued).[3]

Fortunately, enforcement of any patent is left up to the patent holder. Accused infringers must be hauled into court by patentees. The original Bell telephone patents, for instance, were enforced with more than 600 infringement suits initiated by Bell interests. What is more, the patent office does not have final say as to what constitutes a valid patent. The federal courts have final say. So, once in court, an infringer almost always defends himself against a patentee's attack by claiming the patent is invalid. This defense is by no means futile because court judges generally hold more stringent standards of patentability than the patent office. Approximately 20% of all patents coming under court review are declared invalid and unenforceable. The chief cause for rejection is a lack of "inventiveness".[4] The remaining reasons for invalidation can be understood only after an explanation of what can and cannot be patented.

B. Patentability

According to statute law, "Whoever invents or discovers any new and useful process, machine, manufacture, or composition of matter, or any new and useful improvement thereof, may obtain a patent therefor." Embedded in the language are four criteria for patentability: (1) inventiveness, (2) novelty, (3) utility, and (4) subject matter.

To cross the threshold of **inventiveness** the discovery must be "nonobvious" at the time "to a person having ordinary skill in the art."

---

[3] Penny Ward Moser, "Dreams, Schemes, and 3,300 Better Mousetraps," *Discover* (December 1985), p. 72.

[4] Stacy V. Jones, *The Patent Office* (New York: Praeger, 1971), pp. 43–44.

There must, in other words, be some creativity. Just how much creativity is required and how much creativity went into any claimed invention are often difficult to judge. The uncertainties in the "nonobvious" standard are, in fact, almost vague and various enough to call for discriminating "creativity" on the part of patent examiners. To restate the problem more concretely, do you think the following should qualify? Putting a rubber erasure on the end of a pencil? Making doorknobs of clay rather than metal or wood? Devising a motorized golf bag cart? All three were in fact awarded patents, but when tested in court, two were found wanting. Given the nature of the problem, it is hard to disagree with Judge Learned Hand, who once grumbled that the test of invention was little more than a vague and fugitive "phantom."[5]

As for **novelty**, the invention must not be previously known or used. This standard is fairly straightforward, but it takes patent examiners a long time to review past patents and published scientific papers in search of duplication. Of all standards, **utility** is certainly the least demanding. As the extravagant examples given earlier and Figure 24–1 illustrate, many approved inventions are empty of all but the most fantastic applications.

Because patentable **subject matter** is limited to mechanical, electrical, or chemical processes and compositions, much is excluded. Discovery of fundamental laws of nature, such as $E = mc^2$, may not be patented, however brilliant or useful their discovery may be. The same holds for mathematical formulas, managerial strategies, teaching methods, and the like. Products of nature are likewise unpatentable, although this rule has exceptions.

In 1980, the Supreme Court made headlines by deciding that man-made living organisms could be patented. The organism at issue was a

The Twidd

FIGURE 24–1. The Twidd, a device that facilitates thumb twiddling, won patent number 4,227,342 in 1979. The patent states: "To those twiddlers who lack sufficient coordination, not only is the repose and peace of mind which thumb twiddling normally brings not available, but the inability to carry out the twiddling successfully, including inadvertent bumping of the thumbs . . . causes additional frustration." Source: *The Wall Street Journal,* January 19, 1983, p. 25.

[5] *Harries* v. *Air King Prods. Co.,* 183 F.2d 158, 162 (2d Cir. 1950).

new bacterium capable of "eating" crude oil, making it useful in cleaning up oil spills. But the decision had broad implications because it opened the door for patents on all kinds of newly created creatures. In 1988 a patent was granted for a genetically engineered mouse (to be used in tests of carcinogenic substances). Genetically altered cattle, swine, and chickens are now in the works. These developments have sparked controversy because to some people they gave birth to a Brave New World. One overwrought group claimed that such patenting "lays the groundwork for corporations to own the processes of life in the centuries to come."[6]

C. Obtaining a Patent

The rules and regulations of patentability give appearances of an imposing thicket, blocking all but a privileged few. But of the more than 100,000 patent applications filed annually, 65% or so gain patent office approval. Applicants are aided not only by lenient standards of invention and utility but also by an army of clever, well-heeled patent attorneys. Indeed, these attorneys are often more crucial to obtaining a patent than an invention is.[7]

The point is driven home by citing patent 549,160, which a patent attorney obtained for himself in 1895, and which covered what later proved to be the wonder machine of our modern age—the automobile. According to legend, George Selden stole ideas from genuine auto engineers and bluffed his way far enough along to see his auto patent earn $5.8 million in royalties and gain the approval of a U.S. District Court. The only person willing and able to challenge the validity of Selden's patent was Henry Ford, who eventually won his case in Circuit Court.[8]

II. TWO CASE STUDIES

At its best, the patent system stimulates progress, rewards deserving inventors and innovators, and arouses competition. At its worst, it fosters opposite tendencies. Each extreme may be vividly depicted by a case history.

---

6 *The Wall Street Journal*, June 17, 1980, p. 3; December 31, 1980 pp. 1, 8; April 13, 1988, p. 32.

7 Specific evidence is provided by F. M. Scherer, "Firm Size, Market Structure, Opportunity, and the Output of Patented Inventions," *American Economic Review* (December 1965), p. 1111, note 20. See also Corwin D. Edwards, *Maintaining Competition* (New York: McGraw-Hill, 1964), p. 218.

8 Jones, *The Patent Office*, pp. 77–79; Irene Till, "The Legal Monopoly," in *The Monopoly Makers*, edited by M. J. Green (New York: Grossman, 1973), pp. 293–294.

A. United States Gypsum and Wallboard[9]

There is nothing especially clever about wallboard, looking at it with today's familiarity. It is plaster sandwiched between two sheets of paper. At the turn of the century, all wallboard was produced with open edges that exposed the plaster filler. Exposure caused the edges to chip and crumble when bumped in transit. The obvious remedy for this problem—paper covering for the edges as well as the body of the wallboard—was hit upon in 1912 and won for its discoverer, one Utzman, patent 1,034,746. This patent covered the process of closing the edges of wallboard by folding the bottom cover sheet over the edge and then affixing the top cover sheet.

Realizing its great value, United States Gypsum Corporation (called U.S. Gypsum), the leading wallboard producer of the day, acquired the Utzman patent and then used it as a springboard to four decades of industry dominance. On the face of it, the odds against U.S. Gypsum's conquest were rather large, for it was based on a brittle springboard. Aside from the fact that the Utzman patent lasted only 17 years, competitors could easily "invent around" it by closing wallboard edges in other, equally obvious ways. The top cover sheet could fold toward the bottom, the two cover sheets could *both* fold to overlap the edge, the two cover sheets could be imbedded in the center of the plaster edge, a separate sheet could cap the edge, and so on. U.S. Gypsum, however, was able to control the competition these options offered its smaller rivals by tenaciously suing for infringement at every fold. After thus "softening" up its competitors, U.S. Gypsum bought their renegade patents.

In exchange for the cooperation of its rivals, U. S. Gypsum licensed them to use its accumulated patents through agreements that fixed the prices all parties charged for their wallboard. While building these arrangements, U.S. Gypsum seems to have avoided court and favored nontrial settlements as often as possible, perhaps out of fear that its patents would be found invalid if ever truly tested. In other words, competitors were sufficiently strong and U.S. Gypsum's patents were sufficiently weak that the company could not monopolize the trade. At best, it attained a 57% market share. Even so, U.S. Gypsum was resourceful enough to construct a network of license agreements that effectively cartelized the industry. "According to the plans we have," an optimistic executive said at one point, "we figure that there is a possibility of us holding the price steady on wallboard for the next fourteen or fifteen years which means much to the industry."[10] How much it meant is measured by the fact than in 1928, U.S. Gypsum reportedly earned a

---

[9] This section is based primarily on *United States* v. *United States Gypsum Co.* 333 U.S. 366 (1974); and Clair Wilcox, *Competition and Monopoly in American Industry.* Monograph No. 21 of the Temporary National Economic Committee, U.S. Congress (1940), pp. 161–163.

[10] *United States* v. *United States Gypsum,* 374.

profit of $11.09 per 1000 square feet of wallboard over the manufacturing cost of $10.50.

Subsequent patents on wallboard became the basis of subsequent cartelization. But the cartel's life was cut short by action of the Antitrust Division of the Department of Justice. Attacked for violating the Sherman Act, the cartel was dissolved after the Supreme Court decided in 1947 that "regardless of motive, the Sherman Act bars patent exploitation of the kind that was here attempted."[11]

B. Chester Carlson and Xerox[12]

Born to the wife of an itinerant barber and raised in poverty, Chester Carlson invented xerography. Various family tragedies compelled Carlson to work unceasingly from age 12 to support his family and his education. His dire boyhood circumstances induced dreams of escape. In his own words,

> At this stage in my life, I was entranced by the accounts I read of the work and successes of independent inventors and of the rewards they were able to secure through the patents on their inventions. I, too, might do this, I thought; and this contemplation gave stimulus and direction to my life.

After working his way through to a physics degree at the California Institute of Technology, Carlson accepted a research position at Bell Telephone Laboratories in 1930, a position made temporary by the Great Depression. Though plagued by financial difficulties during the depression, he found a job in the patent department of another company. His tasks there impressed upon him the need for quick, inexpensive copies of drawings and documents. Thus it was that in 1935 Carlson began a spare-time search for a copy machine. Although he was working full time and attending law school at night (in hopes of becoming a patent attorney!), his research and experimentation were extensive, leading eventually to his key idea of combining electrostatics and photoconductive materials. The first successful demonstration of Carlson's ideas took place in a room behind a beauty parlor in Astoria, Long Island, on October 22, 1938. He used a crude device to copy the message "10–22–38 Astoria."

---

11 Ibid., p. 393.

12 This section is based on J. Jewkes, D. Sawers, and R. Stillerman, *The Sources of Invention* (New York: W. W. Norton, 1969), pp. 321–323; D. V. DeSimone, Testimony, *Economic Concentration*, Part 3, U.S. Senate Subcommittee on Antitrust and Monopoly, (1965), pp. 1108–1111; E. A. Blackstone, "The Copying-Machine Industry: Innovations, Patents, and Pricing," *Antitrust Law & Economics Review* (Fall 1972), pp. 105–122; and F. M. Scherer, *The Economic Effects of Compulsory Patent Licensing* (New York: New York University Graduate School of Business Admininstration, 1977), p. 9.

Four patents awarded to Carlson between 1940 and 1944 covered his basic concepts. During the same years he tried to find a firm that would develop his invention for commercial use, but he encountered a stream of rejections, including those of 20 large firms—IBM, Remington Rand, and Eastman Kodak among them. The project was finally picked up for experimentation by Battelle Memorial Institute, a nonprofit research outfit, which thereby gained partial rights to any future earnings on the patents. Battelle devised a number of major patentable improvements, including use of a selenium plate, which allowed copies to be made on ordinary as opposed to chemically coated paper. But Battelle did not have the resources to manufacture and market the machine.

Quest for a commercial innovator led to another round of rejections from big companies, whereupon, in 1946, the task was undertaken by Haloid Company, a small firm earning an annual net income of only $101,000. Motivated by partial rights to potential earnings and led by a bright, enthusiastic fellow named Joseph Wilson, Haloid pushed the project to fruition. Among the landmarks on the long road that followed were (1) the first marketing of an industrial-use copier in 1950; (2) a change of company name from Haloid to Xerox; (3) first profit earnings in 1953; (4) development by 1957 of a prototype office copier, the cost of which nearly bankrupted the company; and (5) commercial introduction of the famous 914 console copier in 1959, more than 20 years after Carlson began his initial experiments.

All told, over $20 million was spent on the development of xerography before 1959. It is doubtful whether such a large financial commitment would ever have been made by the people who made it without patent protection. Besides Carlson's first four patents, the project generated well over 100 improvement patents for various machine designs, selenium drums, paper feeding devices, copy counters, powder dispensers, and so on. The significance of patents to Xerox is summarized by Joseph Wilson:

> We have become an almost classic case for those who believe the [patent] system was designed to permit small, weak companies to become healthy. During the early years of xerography we were investing almost as much in research as we were realizing in profit. Unless the first faltering efforts had been protected from imitators, the business itself probably would have foundered, thus obliterating opportunities for jobs for thousands throughout the world.[13]

(Carlson, Battelle and Wilson were each eventually rewarded with eight-digit earnings.)

---

13 DeSimone, Testimony p. 1111.

III. WHY PATENTS?

The Xerox story implies several justifications for the patent system that now ought to be openly stated. At bottom, support rests on three legs: "natural law" property, "exchange for secrets," and "incentives."

A. Natural Law

The natural law thesis asserts that inventors have a natural property right to their own idea. "It would be a gross immorality in the law," John Stuart Mill argued, "to set everybody free to use a person's work without his consent and without giving him an equivalent."[14] Although this view appeals to our sense of fairness, it is not without its practical problems. For one thing, it implicitly assumes that invention is the work of a single, identifiable mind, or at most a few minds. But today invention is usually the product of a faceless corporate team, and any resulting patent rights rest with the corporation, not with the deserving inventors, individual or otherwise. Of course corporations may fund the research and thereby accept the risks, so the property argument could be extended to corporate research on grounds of "just" compensation.

This extension does not square with the fact that corporations doing research for the U. S. Department of Defense get exclusive patent rights on their defense work without bearing any financial risk. The property rationale is further undermined by the fact that patents protect only a few classes of ideas. If one is seriously concerned about the fair treatment of thinkers, why forsake those who push back the frontiers of knowledge in areas excluded from patent eligibility—such as pure science, mathematics, economics, and business administration? Is the inventor of parakeet diapers more deserving than the inventor of double-entry bookkeeping?

B. Exchange for Secrets

Patent law requires that inventors disclose their invention to the public. Without patent protection it is a pretty safe bet that inventors would try to rely on secrecy more than they now do to protect their ideas from theft. Thus the exchange-for-secrets rationale "presumes a bargain between inventor and society, the former surrendering the possession of secret knowledge in exchange for the protection of a temporary exclusivity in its industrial use."[15] Widespread public knowledge is assumed to

---

[14] Cited by Floyd L. Vaughan, *The United States Patent System* (Norman: University of Oklahoma Press, 1956), p. 27.

[15] Fritz Machlup, *An Economic Review of the Patent System*, Study No. 15, U. S. Senate, Subcommittee on Patents, Trademarks, and Copyrights, 85th Cong., 2nd Sess. (1958), p. 21.

be more beneficial than secret knowledge because openness fertilizes technological advance. One discovery may trigger dozens of others among many inventors. And, although the initial discovery cannot be used freely for 17 years, secrecy might prevent full diffusion of its application for an even longer duration.

Just how well society comes out in the bargain is impossible to say. The benefits of openness and the costs of temporary monopoly defy accurate estimation, especially the former. About all that can be said with confidence is that abolition of the patent system would cause the burial of *some* knowledge currently revealed in patent applications.[16]

C. Incentive

The justification most solidly illustrated by the story of Xerox, and the justification most supportive of the patent system, is that it provides incentive to invent and innovate. This rationale rests on two propositions: first, that more invention and innovation than would occur in the absence of some special inducement are desirable, and second, that giving out patents is the best method of providing such special inducement. In other words, discoveries would surely occur without patents, but it is believed that their unearthing will be appreciably hastened, or that more of them will be obtained, if the vast profit potential exclusive patents provide is used to lure inventors and innovators into action.

There can be no doubt that many inventions and innovations depend on patents for their existence or early arrival. Stories of people like Chester Carlson tell us that garrets and garages shelter thousands of inventors so inspired. As for innovation, which is the commercial application of an invention rather than the invention itself, evidence shows patents providing further incentive. A good test of this incentive would compare the commercial development of inventions *with* and *without* patent protection. The inventions that emerge from government-funded research and development yield data for such a test because those doing the research sometimes get exclusive patent rights and sometimes not. (When not, the patent is publicly available to anyone.) These data show that commercial development of inventions (i.e., innovation) is two or three times more common *with* exclusive patent protection than without.[17] Results like these prompted a change in policy in 1980. Amendments to patent law now allow universities and small businesses to patent all technology developed with federal funds.

Still, the incentive thesis needs qualification at two levels. First, social

16 C. T. Taylor and Z. A. Silberston, *The Economic Impact of the Patent System* (Cambridge: Cambridge University Press, 1973), p. 352.

17 U.S. House of Representatives, Subcommittee on Domestic and International Scientific Planning and Analysis, *Background Materials on Government Patent Policies*, Vol. II, 94th Cong., 2nd Sess. (1976), p. 97.

benefits of cost savings and added consumer surplus may be rightly credited to the patent system for fathering "patent-dependent" inventions and innovations, but patent protection of these discoveries also creates social costs. These costs are the usual ones associated with monopoly — such as higher prices than otherwise. When these costs are deducted from the social benefits provided by these patent-dependent discoveries, the *net result* is considerably smaller than that suggested by brash talk of the gross benefits. This qualification of the incentive thesis is nevertheless not very serious because theory can demonstrate that the social benefits of these patent-dependent discoveries nearly always exceed those social costs to yield a positive net social benefit.[18] (See appendix to this chapter.)

The second and higher-level qualification is critical, however. We may comfortably assume that patent-dependent inventions and innovations are always, on balance, beneficial. But we *cannot* jump from there to conclude that the *patent system itself* is, on balance, always beneficial. Inability to make this leap weakens the incentive thesis. Thus a more thorough discussion of the patent system's costs and benefits is needed.

IV. BENEFITS AND COSTS OF PATENTS

If the net social benefits of patent-dependent discoveries and developments were all that counted, the value of patent systems could not be questioned. However, patents, are extended to *all* inventions that meet the legal qualifications, including inventions that are *not* dependent on the patent system for their existence. Whatever social benefits may be claimed for these *non*patent-dependent inventions, they cannot be attributed to the patent system for the simple reason that their existence does not hinge on patent protection. Patent protection for these nondependent inventions does create social costs, however, costs of the monopoly kind. So in such cases there will *always be net social costs* from patents. Given that (1) patent dependency always yields net social benefits and (2) *non*patent dependency of patented inventions always yields net social costs, economists have devised the following criterion for judging the value of the patent system. As stated by F. M. Scherer, one "must weigh the *net* benefits associated with inventions which would not have been available without patent protection against the *net* social losses associated with patented inventions that would be introduced even if no patent rights were offered."[19]

---

[18] For a review, see Scherer, *The Economic Effects of Compulsory Patent Licensing*, pp. 25–34.

[19] F. M. Scherer, *Industrial Market Structure and Economic Performance* (Chicago: Rand McNally, 1970), p. 384.

Unfortunately, balance scales capable of this weighing have not yet been invented (patentable or otherwise). Some have even said the task is and always will be impossible because there is no sure way of telling whether a given invention is, or is not, patent dependent. Still, the major considerations that would guide educated guesswork on the issue have been sketched, and they include the following.

A. Tallies of Patent Dependency

Rough approximations have occasionally been made about the number of patent-dependent versus nonpatent-dependent inventions on the assumption that, if the former number falls considerably short of the latter, the net benefits of the former are also likely to fall short of the net costs of the latter. For example, these two figures have been crudely estimated by classifying discoveries of individual inventors (and perhaps those of small firms too) in the patent-dependent group and relegating those of corporations (or *large* corporations) into the nonpatent-dependent group. Questionnaire surveys of patentees rather consistently reveal that, in general, individual inventors rely heavily on patent protection to sustain their efforts, whereas most corporations claim that patents are neither the chief goal nor principal determinant of their innovative efforts.[20]

By this broad measure it would appear that *non*patent-dependent inventions easily outnumber patent-dependent inventions by a ratio somewhere in the neighborhood of 3 or 4 to 1. However, the very rough nature of this approximation is underscored by substantial differences of patent dependency across industries. Edwin Mansfield asked the R&D directors of 100 U. S. corporations what proportion of their 1981–1983 inventions could be considered patent dependent—that is, would not have been developed but for the protection patents gave them. Table 24–1 reports his findings. Of the 12 industry groups, 4 appear to count very little on patents, their executives replying with a zero rate of patent dependency. In fact, the only industries reporting notably large proportions were pharmaceuticals, chemicals, and petroleum.

Patent dependency has also been examined by study of situations in which patents have not been available. Neither Switzerland nor the Netherlands had patent systems during the latter half of the nineteenth century and the first decade of this century. Yet the absence of patents failed to petrify industry in either.[21]

If, on the whole, patents are no more forceful in stimulating invention and innovation than is indicated by these items of evidence, obviously there must be other sources of incentive, other factors propelling

[20] For a survey of the surveys, see Scherer, *The Economic Effects of Compulsory Patent Licensing*, pp. 50–56.

[21] Eric Schiff, *Industrialization Without Patents* (Princeton, N. J.: Princeton University Press, 1971).

TABLE 24–1.   The Estimated Percentage of Patent-Dependent
Inventions in 12 Industry Groups, 1981–1983

Industry Group	Percentage of Inventions Whose Existence Depends on Patent Protection
Pharmaceuticals	60%
Other chemicals	38
Petroleum	25
Machinery	17
Fabricated metal products	12
Electrical equipment	11
Primary metals	1
Instruments	1
Office equipment	0
Motor vehicles	0
Rubber products	0
Textiles	0

Source: Edwin Mansfield, "Patents and Innovation: An Empirical Study," *Management Science* (February 1986), p. 175.

progress. In the first place, to the extent *secrecy* can be maintained, it provides protection in lieu of patent protection. Second, many companies engage in progressive activities to remain *competitive* or gain competitive leadership. Introduction of new products or product improvements is a form of product differentiation, much like advertising. Natural lags, including temporary secrecy and retooling requirements, prevent immediate imitation of these efforts, gaining prestige and customer loyalty for the innovators. Third, even where imitation is not substantially delayed, innovative investments are not always or even usually flushed down the drain by the price competition of imitators. High concentration, stiff barriers to entry, first mover advantages, and similar sources of *market power other than patents* furnish a basis for post-imitation price discipline in many industries. Finally, even when R&D does not on average pay its own way, it may nevertheless persist. Like gamblers, inventors and innovators often have distorted visions. They tend to see the Chester Carlsons more clearly than the Feckless Floyd failures. They *overrate their chances* of winning the spectacular treasures, and, as a consequence, they often subsidize their R&D efforts from unrelated earnings.

Table 24–2 contains interesting data reflecting on this issue. A team of economists at Yale University surveyed 650 high-level R&D managers representing 130 different lines of business to get their judgments about the effectiveness of different methods of protecting their innovations. Their judgments were expressed on a scale of 1 (not effective at all) to

TABLE 24-2. Effectiveness of Alternative Means of Protecting the Competitive Advantages of New or Improved Processes and Products (1 = not effective, 7 = very effective)

Method of Appropriation	Overall Average Responses	
	Processes	Products
Patents to prevent duplication	3.52	4.33
Patents to secure royalties	3.31	3.75
Secrecy	4.31	3.57
Lead time	5.11	5.41
Moving quickly down the learning curve	5.02	5.09
Sales or service efforts	4.55	5.59

Source: R. C. Levin, A. K. Klevorick, R. R. Nelson, and S. G. Winter, "Appropriating the Returns for Industrial Research and Development, "*Brookings Papers on Economic Activity*, No. 3 (1987), p. 794.

7 (very effective for protection). The averages of the responses for the six alternative methods shown in Table 24–2 turn out to be rather remarkable. Respondents rated patents the least effective means of protecting process innovations, scoring them lower than secrecy, lead time (first mover advantages), learning and experience (another form of first mover advantage), and marketing hustle. Patents were ranked a little better for product innovations, but they still trailed all other methods except secrecy. Breaking down the responses by individual industry yielded results consistent with those of Table 24–1. Those in the pharmaceutical and chemical industries judged patents to be the most important method of protecting the potential profits appropriated from their innovations.

Note that most of these nonpatent protections probably apply most strongly to medium-sized or large firms. Secrecy cannot be maintained by a small individual inventor who must go around displaying his or her ideas in hopes of finding a firm that will commercialize them. A small company cannot gain much of a jump on its rivals if its brand name is less entrenched and its distribution channels are shallower than those of its larger rivals. A small company likewise tends to be less diversified than its larger foes, so it may have fewer opportunities to subsidize its R&D during periods of financial drought. Perhaps these considerations explain why individual inventors and small firms profess greater reliance on the patent system, and claim a keener interest in its perpetuation, than big firms. (This does not necessarily mean that the patent system is, on balance, procompetitive. The story of U.S. Gypsum should dispel hasty conclusions of that kind.)

To summarize, various empirical tallies of patent dependency indicate that the system provides life support for only a minority of inventions and innovations, a minority whose origins are of usually humble size. This minority wins credit for the system. But since patents are also showered indiscriminately on the nonpatent-dependent majority of inventions, it would appear from tally-type evidence that the net costs of the majority exceed the net benefits of the minority, and the system should therefore be reformed or abolished. However, we must hold off the executioners, at least momentarily.

B. The Economic Significance of Patent-Dependent Inventions

Although the weight of numbers suggests the patent system is economically unfit, that measure may be misleading. It has been estimated that relatively few patented inventions account for most of the economic value of all patented inventions. According to the numbers of Pakes and Simpson, more than half of the value of all patents accrues to between 5% and 10% of the patents.[22] What if the relatively few inventions that are patent dependent include the relatively few inventions that are truly revolutionary, whereas, at the same time, the relatively numerous nonpatent-dependent inventions include only simple improvements or inanities? It has been argued that, to some extent, there is a direct relationship between the economic significance of inventions and their patent dependency. F. M. Scherer speaks for this view:

> It is conceivable that without a patent system some of the most spectacular technical contributions—those which effect a genuine revolution in production or consumption patterns—might be lost or (more plausibly) seriously delayed. . . . Such innovations may lie off the beaten paths of industrial technology, where no firm or group of firms has a natural advantage, and the innovator may be forced to develop completely new marketing channels and production facilities to exploit them. They may entail greater technological and market uncertainties, higher development costs, and longer inception-to-commercialization lags than the vast bulk of all industrial innovation. Entrepreneurs may be willing to accept their challenge only under highly favorable circumstances—notably, when it is anticipated that if success is achieved, it can be exploited to the fullest through the exercise of exclusive patent rights.
>
> That such cases exist is virtually certain. Black and white television and the development of Chester Carlson's xerographic concepts are probable examples.[23]

Undoubtedly it is this possibility, coupled with notions of "natural law" property, that persuades politicians to keep the patent system intact. At a bare minimum, such crude *qualitative* accounting raises serious

---

[22] Ariel Pakes and Margaret Simpson, "Patent Renewal Data," *Brookings Papers on Economic Activity* (Microeconomics, 1989) pp. 331–401.

[23] Scherer, *Industrial Market Structure and Economic Performance*, p. 388.

doubts about the accuracy of negative conclusions derived from simple *quantitative* tallies.

C. The Social Cost of Nondependent Inventions

But the qualifications cannot end there, not in fairness to those critical of patents, anyway. Just as the net benefits of dependent cases need qualification, so too the net costs of granting patents in nondependent cases need amplification—an exercise that tips the balance back in the negative direction, especially where revolutionary innovations of this nondependent stripe are concerned.

First, granting monopoly rights over knowledge that is not dependent on patents artificially restricts use of that knowledge below what is socially optimal. The marginal cost of using technical knowledge is zero in the sense that knowledge can be used over and over and over again, by one person or many, without even the slightest danger of exhaustion through wear and tear. No one is compelled to get less of it when anyone else gets more. Ideally, therefore, technology should be *freely* available to all potential users because the "pure" marginal cost of its dissemination and application is zero. But the grant of monopoly leads to exclusions, either directly or by the extraction of a royalty price that exceeds zero.[24]

A second social cost, one stemming from that just mentioned, is a blocking effect. Potential inventors who might like to use a patented invention to further their research in different or related fields may be blocked from doing so, in which case the patent would not be fostering progress but rather inhibiting it.

Third, if a patent is extended to a firm with a pre-existing monopoly position, then suppression of the patented invention is possible under certain circumstances.[25]

(These first three points were dramatically illustrated in May 1989 when some of the nation's top computer scientists took to the streets to picket against the prospect that basic computer software would become patented. They claimed that patenting would stifle creativity because it would raise costs of litigation, restrict the use of new ideas, and so on. Their picket signs said, "Innovation Not Litigation" and "No Writs for Bits."[26])

Fourth, patents give rise to monopoly powers and restrictive practices that go well beyond those inherent in patents themselves.

---

[24] Wassily Leontief, "On Assignment of Patent Rights on Inventions Made Under Government Research Contracts," *Harvard Law Review* (January 1964), pp. 492–497.

[25] For a review of suppression cases, see Vaughan, *The United States Patent System*, pp. 227–260.

[26] *San Jose Mercury News.* May 25, 1989, p. F1. See also *The Wall Street Journal*, March 14, 1989, p. B1.

It is at this last point that patent policy collides with antitrust policy. Pure and simple patent monopoly escapes antitrust attack for obvious reasons. But, as seen earlier in the story of U. S. Gypsum, patents may be cleverly accumulated and manipulated to construct fortresses of monopoly power or networks of price-fixing agreements. The line between proper use and malevolent abuse of patent rights is difficult to draw, but the antitrust authorities and federal courts have over time made the attempt. As a result, the following practices, among others, have been declared illegal:

Restrictive Licensing. If a number of patent licensees are restricted to charging prices specified by the patent holder, or if a number of licensees collude to allocate markets using patent licenses to formalize their agreement, violation is likely, as in the *Gypsum* case.[27]

Cross-licensing. Two or more patent holders may exchange rights of access to each other's patents, something which is often desirable in light of the fact that several firms may contribute to the technology of a single item, such as a TV set. However, patent "pools" that exclude others, or fix prices, or otherwise restrain trade are illegal.[28]

Acquisition of Patents. Monopoly power built on the acquisition of many patents (as opposed to relying on one's own inventiveness) may be attacked under Section 7 of the Clayton Act.[29]

Tying. Tying the sale of an unpatented product (like salt) to a patented product (a salt-dispensing machine used in food processing) is virtually per se illegal.[30]

In brief, antitrust policy permits patent holders to earn their "legitimate" reward for invention, a reward that may be monopolistically plump. But patent rights cannot be stretched beyond "legitimate" rights. Tight interpretation of legitimacy has held down the social costs of the patent system, but not to the point of quieting cries for reform.

V. PROPOSALS FOR REFORM

A. Proposals to Weaken the System

Ideology and evidence lead few folks to advocate complete abolition of the U.S. patent system. The natural law property thesis rests on strongly held value judgments unrelated to economic benefits and costs. There is

---

[27] *United States* v. *United States Gypsum Co.* 333 U.S. 364 (1948); *United States* v. *Masonite Corp.*, 316 U.S. 265 (1942); *Newburgh Moire Co.* v. *Superiors Moire Co.*, 237 F.2d 283 (3d Cir. 1956).

[28] *United States* v. *Line Material Co.*, 333 U.S. 287 (1948); *United States* v. *Singer Manufacturing Co.*, 374 U.S. 174 (1963).

[29] *United States* v. *Lever Bros. Co.*, 216 F.Supp. 887 (S.D.N.Y. 1963); *Kobe, Inc.* v. *Dempsey Pump Co.*, 198 F.2d 416 (10th Cir. 1952).

[30] *International Salt Co.* v. *United States* 332 U.S. 392 (1947).

also enough incentive provided by the system to produce some social benefits. Whether these benefits exceed the social costs is, as we have seen, uncertain, but the benefits are large enough that abolition of the system might give appearances of throwing the baby out with the bath water. Hence critics who want the system weakened usually advocate reform, not abolition.

One of the most obvious improvements that could be made in the system is the elimination of improvident patent grants. The test of inventiveness could be tightened substantially.

A number of other proposed changes would lessen the monopoly power of patents. These include such things as shorter patent life and compulsory licensing. Reducing patent life below 17 years would reduce monopoly's duration. Compulsory licensing would simply require patent holders to license their patents to all who wanted to use them at a "reasonable" royalty fee. This would reduce monopoly power because it would end the exclusiveness that patents presently bestow. Empirical studies of compulsory licensing indicate that it would also substantially deflate the system's incentives, but by less than abolition would.

B. Changes That Strengthen the System

As the U.S. economy grew sluggish in the late 1970s, our technological superiority was called increasingly into question. This spurred proposals to *strengthen* the patent system rather than weaken it. The result was a new patent law in December 1980. The law gives small businesses and universities exclusive patent rights to products invented with federal research funding.

Another provision of the new law reduced the likelihood that courts would declare patents invalid. Unlike before, the Patent Office can now recheck on the validity of a challenged patent. The results of the recheck, if favorable to the patent, solidify its validity. Moreover, all appeals in U.S. patent-infringement suits now go to the Court of Appeals for the Federal Circuit, a court of last resort for patent cases. This new court is upholding patents 80% of the time versus the 30% under the previous system.

(Getting caught for patent infringement can be costly. In early 1986, Kodak's instant-photography cameras and film were judged to be in violation of Polaroid's patents. Kodak had to cease production and grant refunds on all instant cameras already sold — moves that cost it an estimated $800 million. In addition, Kodak will have to pay damages to Polaroid, which could amount to some $1 billion.[31])

Finally, recent legislation strengthens drug-related patents. The

---

31 *Fortune*, March 3, 1986, pp. 34–39; and *The Wall Street Journal*, May 17, 1988, p. 33 and October 17, 1989, p. B10.

change, in effect, lengthens the life of patents covering products that must receive Food and Drug Administration approval prior to marketing. The problem addressed was the lengthy time it takes the Food and Drug Administration to approve new products—ten years in many cases. Thus new product "X" might be patented shortly after invention in 1980, but not sold until after 1990. With the patent expiring in 1997, there would be only seven years of legal monopoly in the market instead of the 17 accorded products not needing premarket clearance. The intent of the new legislation, then, is to extend patent life by the amount of time the product is under premarket regulatory review.[32]

All in all, these several changes indicate the prevailing mood of recent years. Rather than tear down the patent system, there has been a substantial movement to build it up, to grant more protection to inventors.[33]

VI. FEDERAL FUNDING OF R&D

A. Trends

The federal government has seated itself at the dining table of technology, supped gluttonously, and has begun picking up the tab. Back in 1940 federal expenditures on R&D amounted to no more than $74.1 million, which was 0.8% of the total federal budget and barely 0.07% of GNP. A further mark of that era is the fact that federal spending on *agricultural* R&D exceeded *defense* R&D spending. World War II, the cold war, the space race, and the war in Vietnam conspired to change all that. By the mid-1960s federal R&D spending had soared to exceed $14 *billion*, which relative to total federal spending of all kinds topped 12%, and compared to GNP exceeded 2%. Defense R&D spending exploded to 41 times the size of agriculture outlays.[34]

The contribution this jump in federal R&D funding made to overall R&D may be seen in Figure 24–2, which shows total outlays in constant (1982) dollars over the period 1955 to 1989. Between 1955 and 1965, federal funding tripled in real terms. Private expenditures, though also growing in real terms, slipped as a percentage of the total to 35% in 1965.

Between 1965 and 1980 federal real outlays remained fairly constant except for a slight drop in 1975. Then during the 1980s federal expenditures skyrocketed, mainly because of a jump in spending for defense R&D. Defense R&D nearly doubled during the Reagan administration,

---

32 *Business Week*, February 16, 1981, p. 29.

33 *Business Week*, May 22, 1989, pp. 78–89; and *Fortune*, June 23, 1986, pp. 57–63.

34 National Science Foundation, *Federal Funds for Research, Development, and Other Scientific Activities* (NSF 77–301, 1977), p. 4; and Edwin Mansfield, *The Economics of Technical Change* (New York: W. W. Norton, 1968), p. 163.

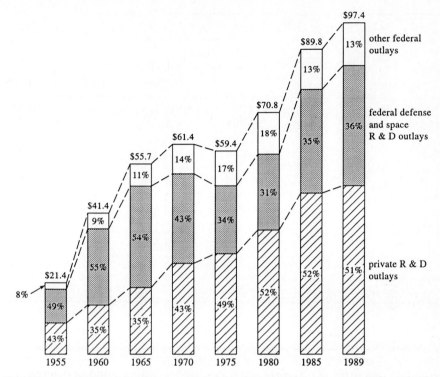

FIGURE 24—2. Trend in private and federal R&D outlays, constant dollars (1982). Source: U.S. Department of Commerce, *Statistical Abstract of the United States, 1981* (Washington, D.C.: U.S. Government Printing Office, 1981), p. 598; National Science Board, *Science and Engineering Indicators, 1989* (Washington, D.C.: NSB, 1989).

rising from $16.5 billion in 1980 to $30.0 billion in 1988 (in 1982 constant dollars). Private R&D spending likewise rose during the 1980s, so the combination of increases in defense and private R&D during the 1980s make that decade stand out in Figure 24–2. By 1989 total spending was $97.4 billion in 1982 dollars (or nearly $125 billion in current dollars), with about equal shares being spent by government and industry. Figure 24–2 also shows that defense and space were big beneficiaries of the spurt in federal outlays over 1955–1965. Defense and space, especially space, then experienced a real and relative decline in support between 1965 and 1975.

More recent and more detailed trends in the composition of federal expenditures are depicted in Table 24–3. The most notable change is again the enormous increase for defense, going from $13.7 billion in 1979 to $40.6 billion in 1989.

As a percentage of the federal total, defense jumps from 48.9% to 65.6% during the same years. Among the items moving in the opposite

TABLE 24–3. Federal R&D Funding by Function: 1979 and 1989

Function	Amount (millions of dollars)		As a % of Total	
	1979	1989	1979	1989
National defense	$13,791	$40,574	48.9%	65.6%
Health	3,401	7,724	12.1	12.5
Energy	3,461	2,427	12.3	3.9
Space	3,136	4,589	11.1	7.4
General science	1,119	2,379	4.0	3.8
Natural resources	1,010	1,208	3.6	2.0
Transportation	798	1,019	2.8	1.6
Agriculture	552	910	2.0	1.5
Other	941	993	3.3	1.6
Total	$28,208	$61,823	100.0%	100.0%

Source: U. S. Department of Commerce, *Statistical Abstract of the United States, 1986* (Washington, D.C.: U.S. Government Printing Office, 1986), p.579: National Science Board, *Science and Engineering Indicators, 1989* (Washington, D.C.: NSB, 1989), p. 285.

direction, energy deserves special mention. It slid in absolute dollars and in percentage share over the Reagan era. (Yet its slide put it back to where it was in 1973.) Natural resources, transportation, and agriculture all fell in percentage share although they experienced current dollar increases.

B. The Reasons for Federal Funding

Why has the government opened its purse so widely to these pursuits? Why has the distribution of money moved around so much? What guides Washington in these matters? There are no really solid answers because noneconomic value judgments play a crucial role in the decision making. Which will reduce the threat of death more—a billion dollars spent for a new military weapon or for a cure for cancer? Which will do more to relieve the energy crisis by the year 2000—a billion dollars spent on nuclear or on solar power? No one knows for sure; speculation reigns amid the inherent uncertainties. Hence, value judgments are inescapable, and these shift under the press of political, social, international, and technical developments.

Still, there are a few broad economic foundations for this effort.[35] To begin with, most federal R&D is allocated to areas where the federal government stands as the sole or chief consumer of the ultimate prod-

[35] For details see Mansfield, *The Economics of Technical Change*, pp. 186–187; *Priorities and Efficiency in Federal Research and Development*, A Compendium of Papers, Subcommittee on Priorities and Economy in Government of the Joint Economic Committee, U.S. Congress, 94th Cong., 2nd Sess. (1976); John E. Tilton, *U.S. Energy R & D Policy* (Washington,

uct. National defense and space are the most obvious instances. Because the federal government has prime responsibility for provision of these "public goods" (a responsibility recognized by even the most miserly conservatives), it is strongly felt that the government should also take responsibility for technological advance in these areas, the advances themselves being "public goods."

Other R&D programs are grounded on the belief that private incentives are lacking. That is, the social benefits of advancement greatly exceed the benefits that can be privately captured, or if they can be captured, such would be undesirable. Research in basic science, health, environmental protection, and crime prevention probably fit this justification.

Still other programs can be defended as offsets to market imperfections of somewhat different sorts. Single R&D projects in such areas as nuclear power and urban mass transportation couple costs of billions of dollars with risks of ominous magnitudes, so much so that even our largest and most courageous private companies are scared to undertake them without government support. The necessity for government R&D funding in agriculture, housing, construction, and coal is often defended because these industries tend to be populated with firms too small and too scattered to shoulder the burdens of even medium-sized R&D projects.

Two interesting economic findings in this connection are the following. First, the payoffs to federal sponsorship of nondefense projects are sometimes immense. For example, the rate of return to federal investment in softwood plywood research has been estimated to be in the range of 200% to 700%.[36] Second, federal funding does not seem to cause private funding to fall below what it would be otherwise. Rather, there is complementarity here. By one estimate of the average impact, every $1.00 of government contract R&D performed in industry induced about $0.27 of private R&D expenditure.[37]

VII. MISCELLANEOUS POLICIES

The government's influence on technological progress reaches well beyond patents and R & D funding. Indeed, the government's influence may be negative as well as positive. Regulations concerning consumer safety and health, or worker safety and health, may occasionally have adverse impacts. For example, changes in regulations governing new

D.C.: Resources for the Future, 1974); and Paul Horwitz, "Direct Government Funding of Research and Development," in *Technological Innovation for a Dynamic Economy*, edited by C. T. Hill and J. M. Utterback (New York: Pergamon Press, 1979), pp. 255–291.

[36] Barry J. Seldon, "A Nonresidual Estimation of Welfare Gains from Research," *Southern Economic Journal* (July 1987), pp. 64–80.

[37] David M. Levy and Nestor E. Terleckyj, "Effects of Government R&D on Private R&D Investment and Productivity," *Bell Journal of Economics,* (Autumn 1983), pp. 551–561.

drug introductions during early 1960s apparently contributed to a dramatic decline in the number of subsequent drug innovations.[38] Accentuating the positive, we shall briefly mention three possibilities: (1) competition, (2) procurement, and (3) taxes.[39]

1. Competition. As suggested by the analysis of the previous chapter, competition spurs technological change, so government would do well to pursue policies that maintain competition. Such policies include, most obviously, antitrust. The antitrust need not be of the traditional type, but it can make a big contribution.[40] In a similar vein, we should not smother the competition that foreign firms can provide through imports. We should, in other words, avoid protective tariffs and quotas. Were it not for imports, the auto industry, for one, would be a lot less progressive than it is today.

2. Procurement. Although parakeet diapers might be contrived without much of a prospective market to promote the effort, heavy commitments of resources to most innovations would disappear without visions of buyers at the ready. The government can serve as a buyer, indeed a very big buyer. Hence government procurement policy has been successfully used in the past to stimulate innovation. Semiconductor technology, among others, received a tremendous boost from this quarter:

> the importance of the government's role as a high-volume purchaser of quality goods at premium prices cannot be exaggerated. The presence of government demand reduced the risks of investment in new technology, and the government's willingness to purchase large volumes at premium prices permitted the accumulation of production experience necessary for the realization of dynamic economies and the penetration of the commercial markets.[41]

3. Taxes. Because small, new, high-technology firms (such as those in California's "Silicon Valley") are especially good sources of innovation, tax policies that encourage the formation of such companies would stimulate innovation. In particular, start-up companies need "venture" capital to get off the ground—that is, money from venturesome investors willing to take big risks in sprouting companies. Taxes influence the expected return on such "venture" investment, thereby also influencing its availability. As if to illustrate this point, venture capital has bur-

---

[38] H. G. Grabowski and J. M. Vernon, "Consumer Protection Regulation in Ethical Drugs," *American Economic Review* (February 1977), pp. 359–364; and H. G. Grabowski, *Drug Regulation and Innovation* (Washington, D.C.: American Enterprise Institute, 1976.)

[39] For a more complete survey see J. Herbert Hollomon, "Policies and Programs of Governments Directed Toward Industrial Innovation," in Hill and Utterback (eds.), *Technological Innovation for a Dynamic Economy*, pp. 292–317.

[40] Burton H. Klein, "The Slowdown in Productivity Advances: A Dynamic Explanation," in Ibid., pp. 66–117.

[41] Richard C. Levin, "The Semiconductor Industry," in *Government and Technical Progress*, edited by R. R. Nelson (New York: Pergamon Press, 1982), p. 94.

geoned since 1978: "Spurring this shower of investment are tax law changes starting in 1978 that cut the maximum capital gains tax bite to 20% from nearly 50% for individuals. The corporate rate was eased to around 28% from about 30%."[42] Changes in tax treatment of losses (carried forward) and tax treatment of R&D expenditures could also serve as stimulants to start-ups.[43]

SUMMARY

The U.S. government's promotion of technical progress dates from the days of the Founding Fathers. Patents originate in the Constitution, which authorizes legislation to "promote the progress of science and useful arts, by securing for limited times to authors and inventors the exclusive right to their respective writings and discoveries." Under present law, patents last 17 years and cover discoveries that pass fairly lenient standards of inventiveness, novelty, and utility. Admissible subject matter is essentially limited to mechanical and chemical products or processes, thereby excluding fundamental laws of nature and other worthwhile discoveries.

At its best, the patent system stimulates progress, rewards deserving inventors and innovators, and arouses competition by nourishing small firms. The history of Xerox illustrates these beneficent effects. On the other hand, deserving and getting do not always coincide under the system, with the result that patents protect discoveries that would be available anyway. Moreover, patents often provide hooks on which to hang restrictive practices, and they occasionally even stifle technical progress. Many of these blemishes in the system were underscored by the story of wallboard.

The main justifications for the patent system are "natural law" property, "exchange for secrets," and "incentives." Each has appeal; each has problems. As the law presently stands, too much is arbitrarily excluded to make the natural law argument natural, and society gets in on too few of the secrets it bargains for. That patent incentives pull some discoveries from the nether world cannot be doubted, but this effect is easily exaggerated.

Ideally, a benefit-cost analysis would compare the net benefits of patent-dependent inventions with the net costs of extending patents to nonpatent-dependent inventions. Unfortunately, data deficiencies permit no more than speculation on this score. What little evidence is available indicates that net benefits have the best chance of exceeding net costs on those patents that are extended to individual inventors and small

---

42 *Business Week*, April 18, 1983, p. 79.
43 Hollomon, "Policies and Programs of Governments," p. 305.

firms. Chemicals and pharmaceuticals might also enjoy favorable balances. These findings have led reformists to call for changes in the system.

Federal funding of R&D has grown from little more than a teen-ager's weekly allowance to amounts in excess of $60 billion. In recent years defense and space R&D have been emphasized at the expense of civilian R&D, but the thaw in the cold war will probably reverse this in the 1990s. Noneconomic value judgments play a particularly prominent role in this policy area.

Other policies promoting progress focus on competition, procure-ment, and taxes.

APPENDIX:
THE ECONOMIC BENEFITS OF COST-REDUCING INVENTIONS

In cases where patents bring forth new *products*, the net social benefits are easy to imagine because new products yield new consumer surpluses even when priced at monopoly levels. Less intuitively plausi-ble are the net benefits associated with *production process* innovations, where no new product is involved and where the monopoly control granted by the patent can convert a purely competitive industry into a monopoly. Figures 24–3 (a) and (b) illustrate the two possibilities in this regard.

If, as in Figure 24–3 (a), production costs per unit drop substantially from C_1 under pure competition to C_2 under monopoly, then buyers will gain an immediate benefit from the invention—namely, a price reduc-tion from P_1 to P_2, which increases quantity from Q_1 to Q_2. Under pure competition, price equals marginal cost, as P_1 equals C_1 in Figure 24–3 (where marginal cost is assumed constant and therefore also equal to average cost). When cost falls from C_1 to C_2 because of the invention, price will not fall as much because patent monopoly prevails as well as cost C_2, and the monopolist's price, P_2, will be above C_2. Still, the price reduction increases consumers' surplus from AEP_1 to ABP_2.

Aside from the price reduction, society also gains by the fact that, after the invention, fewer resources are used to produce Q_1, a savings represented by the area JP_1EH. Although most of these savings are pock-eted by the monopolist in the form of excess profits, they are neverthe-less genuine and the monopolist is, after all, a member of society, not a Martian. Once the patent expires the industry could return to a purely competitive structure (assuming favorable conditions), at which time price will drop to C_2 and all gains then pass to buyers (consumers).

The cost reduction in panel (b) of Figure 24–3 is smaller, C_1 to C_3. Indeed, it is small enough to suggest that, with conversion to monopoly, price could actually rise from P_1 to P_3, given that marginal revenue MR equals marginal cost C_3 at quantity Q_3, which is less than Q_1. However,

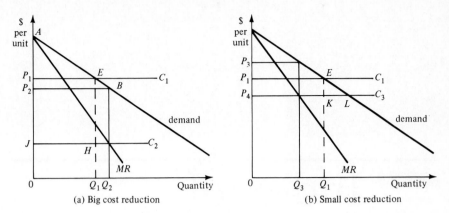

FIGURE 24—3. The Economic Effects of Patent-Dependent Cost-Reducing Inventions.

the monopolist's price cannot rise above P_1 because the pure competitors can sell at P_1, and they would be encouraged to do so at any price above P_1. Thus in this case price is likely to remain at P_1, implying no immediate gain for buyers. All the immediate social gains take the form of reduced resource use in the production of Q_1, a reduction represented by area P_1EKP_4. These savings go to the monopolist (still a member of society). If pure competition returns after expiration of the patent, buyers then reap the benefits when price falls to P_4 from P_1. The gain in consumer surplus then equals P_4P_1EL, because triangle ELK is added to the cost savings of P_1EKP_4 just mentioned. Thus in this case, too, a patent dependent invention yields net social benefits even though the patent creates a 17-year monopoly.[44]

[44] For further discussion, see Dan Usher, "The Welfare Economics of Invention," *Economican* (August 1964), pp. 279–287; William D. Nordhaus, *Invention, Growth and Welfare* (Cambridge, Mass.: MIT Press, 1969); and F. M. Scherer, *Industrial Market Structure and Economic Performance*, 2nd ed. (Chicago: Rand McNally, 1980), pp. 442–444.

Index of Authors

▬ Index of Major Companies

726

Index of Industries

728

Index of Legal Cases

■ Subject Index